FEMINIST CONSTITUTIONALISM

Constitutionalism affirms the idea that democracy may not lead to the violation of human rights or the oppression of minorities. This book aims to explore the relationship between constitutional law and feminism. The contributors offer a spectrum of approaches and the analysis is set across a wide range of topics, including both familiar ones like reproductive rights and marital status and emerging issues such as new approaches to household labor and participation of women in constitutional discussions online. The book is divided into six parts: I) feminism as a challenge to constitutional theory; II) feminism and judging; III) feminism, democracy, and political participation; IV) the constitutionalism of reproductive rights; V) women's rights, multiculturalism, and diversity; and VI) women between secularism and religion. As a collection, the book seeks to examine, challenge, and indeed redefine the very idea of constitutionalism from a feminist perspective.

Beverley Baines is a Professor of Law, Gender Studies, and Policy Studies at Queen's University. Since 2005, she has served as head of the Department of Gender Studies. Since coediting *The Gender of Constitutional Jurisprudence* with Ruth Rubio-Marín in 2004, she has authored papers on sex equality jurisprudence under the Canadian Charter of Rights and Freedoms; the implications of long-term-care homes legislation for women; feminism and contextualism in the jurisprudence of former Supreme Court of Canada Justice Bertha Wilson; and the Charter conflicts posed for feminist sex equality proponents by religious freedom claimants in the contexts of polygamy (in Canada), faith-based family arbitrations (in Ontario), and multicultural accommodation (in Quebec).

Daphne Barak-Erez is a Professor of Law and Dean at the Faculty of Law of Tel-Aviv University, where she also holds the Stewart and Judy Colton Chair of Law and Security. She specializes in administrative law, constitutional law, comparative law, and gender law. She was awarded several prizes, including the Rector's Prize for Excellence in Teaching (twice), the Zeltner Prize, the Heshin Prize, the Woman of the City Award (by the City of Tel-Aviv), and the Women in Law Award (by the Israeli Bar Association). She is the author or editor of several books, most recently the author of *Outlawed Pigs* (2007) and the coeditor of *Exploring Social Rights* (2007), and she has more than one hundred published articles and book chapters.

Tsvi Kahana is an Associate Professor of Law at Queen's University. He is the coeditor (with Richard W. Bauman) of *The Least Examined Branch – The Role of Legislatures in the Constitutional State* (2006). He works in the areas of constitutional law, constitutional theory, and comparative constitutionalism. He is a former Executive Director of the Centre for Constitutional Studies at the University of Alberta.

Feminist Constitutionalism

GLOBAL PERSPECTIVES

Edited by

BEVERLEY BAINES
Queen's University, Ontario

DAPHNE BARAK-EREZ
Faculty of Law, Tel-Aviv University

TSVI KAHANA
Queen's University, Ontario

Foreword by

CATHARINE A. MACKINNON
University of Michigan & Harvard Law School

CAMBRIDGE
UNIVERSITY PRESS

CAMBRIDGE
UNIVERSITY PRESS

University Printing House, Cambridge CB2 8BS, United Kingdom

One Liberty Plaza, 20th Floor, New York, NY 10006, USA

477 Williamstown Road, Port Melbourne, VIC 3207, Australia

314-321, 3rd Floor, Plot 3, Splendor Forum, Jasola District Centre, New Delhi - 110025, India

103 Penang Road, #05-06/07, Visioncrest Commercial, Singapore 238467

Cambridge University Press is part of the University of Cambridge.

It furthers the University's mission by disseminating knowledge in the pursuit of
education, learning and research at the highest international levels of excellence.

www.cambridge.org
Information on this title: www.cambridge.org/9780521137799

© Cambridge University Press 2012

First published 2012

A catalogue record for this publication is available from the British Library

Library of Congress Cataloging in Publication data
Feminist constitutionalism : global perspectives / [edited by] Beverley Baines,
Daphne Barak-Erez, Tsvi Kahana.
    p.   cm.
Includes bibliographical references and index.
ISBN 978-0-521-76157-4 (hardback) – ISBN 978-0-521-13779-9 (paperback)
1. Women's rights.   2. Constitutional law.   3. Feminist jurisprudence.
I. Baines, Beverley, 1941–   II. Barak-Erez, Daphne.   III. Kahana, Tsvi, 1967–
K3243.F456   2011
342.08'78 – dc23   2011020197

ISBN 978-0-521-76157-4 Hardback
ISBN 978-0-521-13779-9 Paperback

Contents

Foreword

If feminism is what some of its purported academic adherents have made it over the last two decades or so, many of us have long been part of some other movement. The present volume goes far in reclaiming its promise as, in the words of Dean Daphne Barak-Erez, "a new interpretive perspective on human knowledge, including in the legal sphere,"[1] as well as a tool for intervening in legal practice.

Women have not, in general, written or agreed to constitutions. Powerful men have written them a long time ago as if women did not exist, after wars in the waging and peacemaking of which women often did not actively participate, by foreign experts who assumed that liberalism was enough for women, by the accretion of practices in which women have had more or less say. More recently, women have had some voice in constitutive processes, but nowhere near half of the clout. With exceptions, dominant men have largely interpreted constitutions, and have overwhelmingly confined debates they deem authoritative on them, to terms they set.

Constitutions are artifacts of a particular male legal intervention, defining nations and establishing states as they ground their governance. The idea is to write down the terms to which the men involved agree to hold one another. As such, they are the particular focus of certain legal actors, most specifically white upper-class liberal men in the Anglo-Saxon tradition, although others have taken them up. In these systems – not usually squarely criticized as colonialist since freedom fighters have embraced the form even as they have often altered the content – law is a real vehicle of social power. The constitution typically occupies the apex of its power pyramid, hence their intense interest in it and their lack of interest in questioning it *as* a form.

The skilled assistance of Lisa Cardyn with the footnotes is gratefully acknowledged. The support of The Diane Middlebrook and Carl Djerassi Visiting Professorship at the University of Cambridge Centre for Gender Studies provided time to write this Foreword. © Catharine A. MacKinnon 2011, 2012.

[1] Chapter 4, this volume.

A feminist constitutionalism would be animated by alternate principles. It would face male supremacy strategically but squarely. It would require a substantive equality of women both as an overarching theme in the document and as an underlying reality in the social order, in active engagement with a society recognized as unequal based on sex and gender, necessarily in interaction with all salient inequalities. Remaining sensitive to context, it would not be sidetracked by essentialist questions as to whether women are the same as or different from men or cultural relativist questions as to whether each culture's particular form of female subordination should be respected simply because it is culturally specific. It would not assume that a private sphere defined around home and family or any other jurisdictional locality is a place of sex equality exempt from public rules. Respect and dignity for women would be accorded in appropriate ways across the social order that would be accepted and enforced in each setting, without favoritist exemption or other corruption or backing off on necessary changes. Whether the issue is the form of government or sexual access, forms of force – from socialization to threats to physical aggression – would not be rationalized as consensual where no effective freedom to dissent or power to affect the shape of options or outcomes exists. Collective power of some social groups over others would be challenged as what it is rather than rationalized as differing moral values or normative choices.[2] A feminist constitutionalism would ask whether the state and the law, its quintessential tool, are socially hegemonically male in ways that, at the least, call for investigation of the container as well as the content.

Should a feminist constitutionalism exist, or even a dialogue on constitutionalism that took feminist insights seriously, the present volume would certainly be part of it.[3] As things are, a number of the chapters here productively examine conventional constitutional subjects.[4] Taken as a whole, and particularly strongly in certain

---

[2] In terms of states, rather than constitutions, these four dimensions are discussed in detail in CATHARINE A. MACKINNON, TOWARD A FEMINIST THEORY OF THE STATE (1989), and applied to international law in Catharine A. MacKinnon, *Women's Status, Men's States, in* ARE WOMEN HUMAN? 1 (2006).

[3] Useful forerunners include THE GENDER OF CONSTITUTIONAL JURISPRUDENCE (Baines and Rubio-Marín 2004), and CONSTITUTING EQUALITY: GENDER EQUALITY AND COMPARATIVE CONSTITUTIONAL LAW (Williams 2009), as well as Kathleen M. Sullivan's insightful article, *Constitutionalizing Women's Equality,* 90 CAL. L. REV. 735 (2002).

[4] *See especially* Jennifer Nedelsky, *The Gendered Division of Household Labor: An Issue of Constitutional Rights, in* FEMINIST CONSTITUTIONALISM, *supra* note 1, at 15; Tsvi Kahana & Rachel Stephenson, *The Promise of Democratic Constitutionalism: Women, Constitutional Dialogue, and the Internet, in id.* at 240 (arguing that legislative approaches are preferable for women to judicial ones). Further strong examples include the structural analysis of gender provided by Kerri A. Froc, *Will "Watertight Compartments" Sink Women's Charter Rights? The Need for a New Theoretical Approach to Women's Multiple Rights Claims under the Canadian Charter of Rights and Freedoms, in id.* at 132; the examination of horizontal and vertical constitutions by Elizabeth Katz, *Women's Involvement in International Constitution-Making, in id.* at 204; and the inquiry into the use of the tutela by Carolina Vergel Tovar, *Between Constitutional Jurisdiction and Women's Rights Organizations: Women, War, and the Space of Justice in Colombia, in id.* at 223. Mary Ann Case innovatively combines an argument that gay marriage is supported by constitutional sex equality principles with a critique of marriage in *Feminist Fundamentalism and the Constitutionalization of Marriage, in id.* at 48.

sections,[5] these contributions go further to suggest that constitutionalism, although significant, as such may not be the most illuminating framework for interrogating the role of law in the lives of women, including their status and treatment under male-dominant institutions. Although the legal form "constitution" is inspired by liberalism and democracy, which are, for the most part, taken for granted in this volume, they are importantly interrogated by Blanca Rodríguez-Ruiz and Ruth Rubio-Marín, who argue that constitutionalism's inherited model of democracy rests on an ideology of social-sexual contract that structurally restricts women's full citizenship.[6]

Throughout, by the scope of materials found necessary to engage, as well as the range of subjects taken up,[7] these papers – although no one says so – find constitutionalism too narrow and formalistic a container for addressing the problems feminism identifies. Directives, criminal law, religious law, and customary law are easily as portentous, they notice de facto, often more potent. International law, it might be added, has proven more nimble and visionary.[8] Social reality is authoritatively ordered, conflict acceptably resolved, the means of force legitimately monopolized by legal arrangements that – so far as women's status is concerned including relationships with men, are far from confined to constitutions or even usually accountable to them. Custom, habit, norms, roles, and other dominant regularities powerfully constitute the law for women, that is, the real rules to which they are held. The chapters of this book accordingly range productively over multiple nonconstitutional systems with the constitutional ones, interrogating gendered rules, contextualized by gendered social realities, sometimes at an explicit interface with constitutions and sometimes not.[9]

If constitutionalism is too restrictive a cabin for the legal issues raised by taking the substance of sex inequality seriously, the chapters in this collection further indicate that feminism has become something to be done more than a flag to be flown. Fortunate, as feminism as a flag can become a way to confine work by gender, saluted so that it can be ignored, a means to cede the rest of the world to everyone who is not labeled, so they can continue doing what they imagine is everything else, unchallenged and unchanged. The evasion of feminist content is reminiscent of Tolstoy's observation:

> I know that most men – not only those considered clever, but even those who are very clever, and capable of understanding most difficult scientific, mathematical,

---

5 *See, e.g.*, Chuma Himonga, *Constitutional Rights of Women under Customary Law in Southern Africa: Dominant Interventions and "Old Pathways," in id.* at 317; Jewel Amoah, *Watch GRACE Grow: South African Customary Law and Constitutional Law in the Equality Garden, in id.* at 357.

6 Blanca Rodríguez-Ruiz & Ruth Rubio-Marín, *On Parity, Independence and Women's Democracy, in id.* at 188.

7 Strangely, there is no sustained discussion of sexual abuse.

8 See MacKinnon, *Women's Status, Men's States, supra* note 2.

9 The refreshing analysis of abortion by Rachel Rebouché, *Challenges for Contemporary Reproductive Rights Advocacy: The South African Example, in* FEMINIST CONSTITUTIONALISM, *supra* note 1, at 298, strongly suggests that constitutionalism is the wrong question.

or philosophic problems – can very seldom discern even the simplest and most obvious truth if it be such as to oblige them to admit the falsity of conclusions they have formed, perhaps with much difficulty – conclusions of which they are proud, which they have taught to others, and on which they have built their lives.[10]

That feminism as a philosophy as well as by its focal topics should have become a form of scholarly marginalization by gender is, of course, ironic. Its entire impetus has been to end the confinement of people and work to and by sex and gender, in the process transforming the legal project from one that promotes male dominance to one that promotes equality of the sexes, freeing women as well as legal scholarship. Yet in the legal academy, feminist analysis is not yet considered an expertise; it remains regarded as autobiographical and ideological: that stuff about women, a statement about the speaker rather than the spoken-about, a narrow solipsistic fixation rather than an approach to comprehending reality that increases accuracy by identifying a bias in prior approaches that makes them incapable of meeting even their own standards. Instead, it has become at best an academic niche to be occupied, if minimally; a little square of turf to be tilled by perhaps one person per faculty, likely a visitor; an eddy at the edge of the mainstream; a brand to be cultivated and competed over; a private faith like a religion, internally sustaining but unbecoming and unscholarly and stigmatic to expose or acknowledge, far less explicitly to pursue as the backbone or compass of an intellectual agenda.

Tokenism is the practical organizing principle of this ghettoizing reduction. One is a feminist legal scholar, not a legal scholar with particular information and focus and perspectives to offer. Meantime Marxists and conservatives and most of all liberal legal scholars of all stripes are simply legal scholars – defined by their subject matter or expertise or angle of vision, however male-valenced, however little relevance to women it has, their insights contended with for their content rather than as a this-kind-of-point from a scholar who is a one-note one-of-those. Confining feminism to a separate sphere, even if more room than it had before, becomes another way of maintaining male dominance as a discourse of power, as if it is neutral and tolerant.

Which is not to say there should be no feminist books. This book calmly challenges these limits, unsettles this complacency by exceeding its own envelope, putting more solid ground under women's feet as it expands law's horizons.

Catharine A. MacKinnon
August 4, 2011

---

[10] LEO TOLSTOY, WHAT IS ART? 124 (Aylmer Maude trans., 1899).

Contributors

Jewel Amoah is a PhD candidate at the University of Cape Town, South Africa. Her research focuses on equality rights in both constitutional and customary law contexts.

Mary Anne Case is Arnold I. Shure Professor of Law and the Director of the Feminist Theory Project of the Center for the Study of Gender and Sexuality at the University of Chicago. She researches constitutional law and regulation of family, sex, and gender.

Rosalind Dixon is an Assistant Professor at the University of Chicago Law School, and Senior Visiting Fellow at UNSW Faculty of Law. Her research focuses on constitutional law, comparative constitutional law and design, international human rights, and law and gender.

Hilal Elver is a research professor at the Global and International Studies Program at the University of California, Santa Barbara. Her research and teaching focus on international environmental law and human rights law.

Pascale Fournier is Vice-Dean of Research and Associate Professor of Law at the University of Ottawa. Her research focuses on comparative family law, constitutional law and freedom of religion, and the relationship between multiculturalism, laïcité, and gender equality.

Kerri A. Froc is a PhD candidate at Queen's University and an Adjunct Professor at Carleton University. Her research interests include constitutional hermeneutics and feminist legal theory.

Suzanne B. Goldberg is Herbert and Doris Wechsler Clinical Professor of Law and Director of the Center for Gender and Sexuality Law at Columbia Law School. Her research focuses on barriers to equality in theory and practice.

Jennifer S. Hendricks is an Associate Professor at the University of Tennessee College of Law. Her research areas include constitutional family law and federalism.

Chuma Himonga is a Professor of Law and holder of the National Research Foundation Chair in Customary Law at the University of Cape Town. Her research areas are customary law, family and succession law, and women's and children's rights in Southern Africa.

Nicole Huberfeld is the Gallion and Baker Professor of Law at the University of Kentucky. Her research focuses on the relationship between constitutional law and health-care law.

Puja Kapai is an Assistant Professor of Law and Deputy Director of the Centre for Comparative and Public Law in the Faculty of Law at the University of Hong Kong. Her areas of research are minority rights, equality and non-discrimination, constitutional theory, citizenship studies, and domestic violence.

Elizabeth Katz is an Associate with Covington & Burling LLP. She specializes in appellate litigation and Supreme Court practice as well as white collar defense and investigations.

Kelley Loper is an Assistant Professor, the Director of the Master of Laws in Human Rights program, and a Deputy Director of the Centre for Comparative and Public Law in the Faculty of Law at the University of Hong Kong. Her research interests include equality rights and the protection of refugees in Asia.

Eileen McDonagh is a Professor in the Department of Political Science at Northeastern University.

Paula A. Monopoli is a Professor of Law at the University of Maryland School of Law. Her research interests include inheritance law and gender and constitutional design.

Vrinda Narain is an Assistant Professor and Chair of Women's Studies in the Faculty of Law and the Institute for Gender, Sexuality, and Feminist Studies at McGill University. She is a Research Associate at the International Institute for Studies in Race, Reconciliation and Social Justice at the University of the Free State, South Africa. Her research focuses on constitutional law and feminist legal theory.

Jennifer Nedelsky is a Professor of Law and Political Science at the University of Toronto. Her primary research area is legal and political theory.

Martha C. Nussbaum is Ernst Freund Distinguished Service Professor of Law and Ethics at the University of Chicago, appointed in Law, Philosophy, and Divinity. Her work focuses on moral and political philosophy.

Rachel Rebouché is an Assistant Professor of Law at the University of Florida Levin College of Law. Her research areas are family law, health policy, and comparative law.

Heather Roberts is a Lecturer at the ANU College of Law at The Australian National University. Her research focuses on constitutional law, legal biography, and the swearing-in ceremonies of Australian judges.

Blanca Rodríguez-Ruiz is an Associate Professor of Constitutional Law at the University of Seville, Spain. Her work analyzes fundamental rights, the modern family, and democratic citizenship from a gender perspective.

Ruth Rubio-Marín is a Professor of Constitutional and Public Comparative Law at the European University Institute, Florence, Italy. Her research focuses on constitutional law, citizenship, migration, cultural rights, and transitional justice.

Rachel Stephenson is an associate at a litigation firm in Toronto, Ontario.

Carolina Vergel Tovar is a PhD candidate at Université de Paris X Nanterre / EHESS and a Fellow at Universidad Externado de Colombia. Her research examines activist and institutional uses of law with regard to women victims of armed conflict in Colombia.

Susan Williams is the Walter W. Foskett Professor and Director of the Center for Constitutional Democracy at Indiana University Maurer School of Law. Her research focuses on constitutional design and feminist theory. She advises constitutional reformers in several countries, including Burma, Cuba, and South Sudan.

Introduction

The Idea and Practice of Feminist Constitutionalism

Beverley Baines, Daphne Barak-Erez, and Tsvi Kahana

What is feminist constitutionalism? Basically, it is the project of rethinking constitutional law in a manner that addresses and reflects feminist thought and experience.
We use this term in contrast with the "constitutional law and" approach – constitutional law and gender or constitutional law and feminist theory – because we aspire
to explore the *relationship between* constitutional law and feminism by *examining,
challenging, and redefining the very idea* of constitutionalism from a feminist perspective. Feminist constitutionalism demands that we not only revisit classical topics
from new perspectives but, more importantly, pose new questions, introduce new
topics, and take responsibility for changing the focus of constitutional discussion and
debate. We embrace the questions raised by studies of gender or feminism "and"
constitutional law even as we urge scholars to move beyond them.

We acknowledge the importance of constitutional law for feminist analysis. Constitutional law is foundational to most of the world's legal systems. It shapes fundamental assumptions regarding citizenship, rights, and responsibilities. Feminists
who critique law must understand that legal systems cannot really be transformed
without addressing their constitutional foundations. Historically, the second-class
status of women in law derived from constitutional structures and assumptions. For
instance, in the Anglo-American countries – Great Britain, the United States of
America, and Canada – women were denied the right to vote in the nineteenth
and early twentieth centuries in part because constitutional norms were phrased in
masculine terminology (e.g., "men," "he") or given a gendered interpretation (e.g.,
"persons" as referring to "men").

It is timely for constitutionalists – scholars, jurists, lawyers – to attend to the
contributions that feminism offers to the traditional domains of constitutionalism.
Basically, constitutionalism engages with the institutions of government, the rights
of individuals and groups, and the formulation of limitations on institutional power.
It was traditionally associated with formalized rules often expressed in written texts,

but has developed through the years to include constitutional conventions and traditions.[1] Feminist constitutionalism engages with all these aspects of discipline, exposing their hidden assumptions and challenging their claims to gender neutrality. Let us briefly enumerate the central themes derived from this endeavor.

Equality Jurisprudence – A basic tenet of feminism is engagement with different understandings of the right to equality. For women, as well as for other disadvantaged groups, the first struggles for equality were focused on claiming formal equality while objecting to reliance on stereotypes. Despite many victories, these struggles remain relevant today, especially when addressed from a global perspective. Moreover, it is clear that formal equality forms only one aspect of the multifaceted aspiration to achieve gender equality. Feminist challenges to laws that rely on biological differences between the sexes,[2] to the hidden biases of supposedly neutral investigations of equality,[3] and to the discriminatory nature of subordination and sexual harassment[4] should be integral to constitutionalism's endeavors.

Center and Periphery in Constitutional Law – Feminism calls on constitutional discourse to attend to issues that shape the reality of life for women. These issues will reshape the way in which we traditionally define constitutional law. More specifically, constitutional law should address reproductive rights, social rights, the regulation of group rights of minorities (that endorse discriminatory community practices), and more – not as "side issues" but rather as central issues deserving equal respect and attention with the "big questions" of national security and separation of powers. The scope of thinking on "national security," to continue this point, might be broadened to include not only borders and armed forces, but also security at home and in the streets, a security that mandates protection from physical abuse, knives, sexual offenses, and emotional, medical, and nutritional want, and not only from guns, bombs, or missiles.

Revisiting Constitutional Assumptions and Categories – Feminism invites scholars of constitutional law to be critical of the assumptions that underlie their theories. One such assumption is the traditional distinction between the public and private realms so inherent to liberal constitutionalism. Indeed, the critique of the public–private distinction is a long-standing theme of feminist writings.[5] However, it is important to address it in a manner that transcends reforms of ordinary legal rules and policies (e.g., opposing the traditional unwillingness to deal with domestic violence). To be effective, we must address this criticism at the constitutional

---

[1] *See, e.g.,* Ernest A. Young, *Constitutive and Entrenchment Functions of Constitutions: A Research Agenda,* 10 U. PA. J. CONST. L. 399 (2007–2008).

[2] *See, e.g.,* Sylvia Law, *Rethinking Sex and the Constitution,* 132 U. PA. L. REV. 955 (1984).

[3] *See also* Martha L. Minow, *Foreword: The Supreme Court, 1986 Term – Justice Engendered,* 110 HARV. L. REV. 10 (1987).

[4] CATHARINE A. MACKINNON, THE SEXUAL HARASSMENT OF WORKING WOMEN: A CASE OF SEX DISCRIMINATION (1979).

[5] Frances E. Olsen, *The Family and the Market,* 96 HARV. L. REV. 1497 (1983); Ruth Gavison, *Feminism and the Public/Private Distinction,* 45 STAN. L. REV. 1 (1992).

level because it is constitutional law that shapes the understanding of the public and private and elaborates the principles that apply to this distinction.[6] The way the public–private distinction applies in other spheres is the product of constitutional foundations. Another assumption that feminist critique exposes is the hierarchy attached to protection of first-generation rights such as "liberty"[7] and "speech."[8]

Rights and Institutions – Promoted by feminist theories, feminist constitutionalism must embrace the two fundamental dimensions of constitutional law – institutions and rights. In contrast to the temptation to associate gender issues in constitutional law with specific rights-promoting struggles, it is vital to understand that a comprehensive discussion of constitutional law should also embrace institutions. In this context, for example, we must study electoral laws while focusing on parity and representation. More broadly, we must critically assess the role that judicial review of legislation had and might have in promoting the rights of women. Without this institutional feature (judicial review) certain path-breaking precedents (such as *Roe v. Wade*)[9] could not have been possible.[10]

Global and Comparative Law – Feminist constitutionalism poses a global challenge to legal scholarship. Shaping it should be based on the experience of women in different countries. This accumulated experience helps in uncovering endemic or grave problems and persistent challenges. This is not to say the problems and challenges are similar everywhere. However, the broader perspective helps in uncovering themes that the local focus often blurs. The use of comparative law can also shed light on differences between countries with old and new constitutions and thus on the role of constitution-making for gender justice. In general, old constitutions (such as the U.S. Constitution), in a manner that reflects their time, do not tend to mention gender equality expressly, whereas new constitutions (such as Canada's 1982 Constitution Act, which included the Charter of Rights and Freedoms, and the 1996 South African Constitution) have done that and thus give robust support to equality arguments at the national level. Feminism has the potential to contribute to the study of comparative constitutional law, which so far has not focused enough on gender issues (aside from the interesting example of abortion rights, which often

---

[6] *See, e.g.*, Catharine A. MacKinnon, *Privacy v. Equality: Beyond Roe v. Wade* (1983), in FEMINISM UNMODIFIED (1987).

[7] The constitutional understanding of liberty tends to focus on formal freedoms and disregard social subordinations that limit the autonomy of women in their actual lives.

[8] According to Catharine MacKinnon, pornography should not be regarded as speech. *See* CATHARINE A. MACKINNON, ONLY WORDS (1993). Her challenge to the conventional understanding of "speech" should be acknowledged as important even by those who ultimately do not accept it.

[9] *Roe v. Wade*, 410 U.S. 113 (1973).

[10] At the same time, feminist constitutionalism critically enquires into the way such doctrines are developed. Although the protection of women's choice in *Roe v. Wade*, for example, has been a positive and important development in its outcome, it raised concerns due to its reliance on the right to privacy, a right that also has problematic implications for women, as we mentioned earlier.

calls for a comparison between U.S. case law and the decisions of the German Constitutional Court).[11]

Integrating Diversity Theories – Feminism has the potential to bring into the constitutional arena the richness of feminist thought about diversity. Feminist constitutionalism would insist that research and adjudication be antiracist, anti-homophobic, anticlassist, anti-ageist, and reflective of claims for ableism as well as for respect of ethnic, cultural, and religious views that are consistent with gender equality. The discourse of feminist constitutionalism about diversity is not monolithic. Feminists do not pretend to know all there is to know about diversity, but rather they proclaim their openness to instruction from the writings and practical expertise of the full range of diversity theorists. Thus feminism aspires not only to understand diversity theories and to critique them from the perspective of gender, but also to hold constitutionalism accountable if it fails to take the same steps.

* * *

This book presents a snapshot of the current state and potential contributions of feminist constitutionalism. The contributors offer a spectrum of approaches and topics that delineates the scope of this field and its richness. Following this Introduction and a preface by Catharine MacKinnon, the book is divided into six parts: Feminism as a Challenge to Constitutional Theory; Feminism and Judging; Feminism, Democracy, and Political Participation; The Constitutionalism of Reproductive Rights; Women's Rights, Multiculturalism, and Diversity; and Women between Secularism and Religion. We offer here a brief description of the contributions in each part.

Part I, which illustrates the potential contribution of feminist theorizing to feminist constitutionalism, opens with Jennifer Nedelsky's *Gendered Division of Household Labor: An Issue of Consitutional Rights*. Nedelsky focuses on the division of household labor and its impact on shaping core values in society. This division excludes women from the political domain, thus depriving this domain of the knowledge and experience of women and ultimately detracting from good social policy making. It also deprives women of access to various rights, such as access to education, health care, and employment. Nedelsky complements her argument by considering the road to transforming the current division of labor. She believes this task can be done only by redefining core values; moreover, it should not be left to state-based institutions alone but rather should evoke open public discourse in various arenas, including classrooms, corporate retreats, international organizations, and more.

The second chapter, *Feminist Fundamentalism and the Constitutionalization of Marriage* by Mary Anne Case, focuses on the institution of marriage and its historic contribution to the subordination of women. Case addresses this criticism in the

---

[11] This case study opens Vicki Jackson and Mark Tushnet's casebook of comparative constitutional law. *See* VICKI C. JACKSON AND MARK TUSHNET, COMPARATIVE CONSTITUTIONAL LAW (2nd ed., 2003).

context of the new debates regarding the recognition of same-sex marriage. As long as the institution of marriage is closed and protected only for heterosexual couples, the chances for reforms that will transcend nonegalitarian traits are low. Accordingly, Case argues that allowing same-sex couples to marry would help to distance the concept of marriage from its patriarchal past. Such a reform would have benefits, not only for gay and lesbian couples, but for all who value liberty and equality on the basis of sex.

Rosalind Dixon and Martha Nussabum's chapter, *Abortion, Dignity, and a Capabilities Approach*, offers a new perspective on the regulation of the controversial area of reproductive freedom. The chapter adopts as its starting point the concept of the right to human dignity, as interpreted according to the capabilities approach. As a result, it aims at drawing a ceiling as well as a floor on the basic rights of access to abortion, and then deals with the concretization of these rights with regard to the public funding of abortion and health care.

Part II of the book addresses some of the contributions feminism holds for the study of the judiciary and judicial decision making. In *Her-meneutics: Feminism and Interpretation*, Daphne Barak-Erez evaluates the potential contribution of feminist interpretation to the practice of constitutional law. Traditionally, stereotypes and discriminatory practices have left their mark on constitutional and legal traditions and interpretations. Barak-Erez argues that feminism has a role to play in rectifying these influences, and that feminist interpretation has the potential to be an effective tool in achieving gradual legal change. She reviews several understandings of feminist interpretation, as shaped by the different streams of thought in legal feminism, and ultimately promotes an approach based on presenting the "woman question" – which calls for avoiding interpretive choices that have disproportionate effects on women.

The next chapter, *Intuition and Feminist Constitutionalism*, by Suzanne Goldberg, examines the role that intuition and intangible rationales play in judicial decision making in the context of gender and sexuality. The chapter demonstrates that judges' reliance on these intangible rationales is problematic. Such reliance enables judges to make decisions in a way that masks their personal biases and to engage in stereotyping. At the same time, Goldberg acknowledges that there is some merit to the use of intuition. Ignoring intuition could lead to skewed results and to an overemphasis on empirical research, which can also be subject to manipulation. Ultimately, she suggests that judges need to make better use of data that work against their intuition and to offer extensive explanations when their rulings break from empirical evidence.

Another view on feminism and judging comes from the study of women on the bench. *Women Judges, "Maiden Speeches," and the High Court of Australia* by Heather Roberts exemplifies this area of study. This chapter utilizes the speeches made at the swearing-in ceremonies of women judges in the High Court of Australia as a prism to explore perceptions regarding the participation of women in the Australian legal community in general and in the Australian judiciary in particular. It points to differences between those who mentioned their identity as women jurists and those who refrained from doing so, and shows how these speeches reflect a continuing pressure faced by women judges to distance themselves from the perception of their "otherness" on the bench.

Kerri Froc examines judicial decisions dealing with a "cluster" of rights violations in *Will "Watertight Compartments" Sink Women's Charter Rights? The Need for a New Theoretical Approach to Women's Multiple Rights Claims under the Canadian Charter of Rights and Freedoms.* Froc studies cases involving arguments about gender discrimination coupled with a violation of another civil liberty. She not only argues that in such cases judges should recognize the more severe, complex, and intractable suffering, but also criticizes the "watertight compartments" approach to rights wherein judges analyze each of the rights violations separately. Froc advocates an integrated approach, contending that an experience of subordination implicating more than one right is not simply a collection of rights violations, but rather may result in a rights violation that is unique.

In her chapter on *Constitutional Adjudication and Substantive Gender Equality in Hong Kong*, Kelley Loper offers a case study of judging equality claims. Loper points to the shortcomings of equality jurisprudence in Hong Kong, which acknowledges the right to equality while making it difficult to challenge laws influenced by traditional patriarchal cultural practices and socioeconomic policies. With regard to policies that impact migrant and immigrant women, for example, the judgments generally fail to consider their gender dimensions and focus instead on distinctions based on residence status and immigration categories. These judgments reveal the potential and limits of Hong Kong's equality jurisprudence for achieving substantive gender equality.

Part III of the book focuses on women's political participation and questions of institutional design related to it. In *The Gendered State and Women's Political Leadership: Explaining the American Puzzle*, Eileen McDonagh and Paula A. Monopoli study the large gap between the percentage of women in the population and their representation in the U.S. House of Representatives. McDonagh and Monopoli employ a policy feedback model, explaining that the gendered character of the state's political institutions and public policies teaches the public who should be considered suitable as officeholders in the public sphere of governance. More specifically, they point to the masculine bias inherent in the founding documents of the American state and its constitutional formulation. Their study argues that these teach voters to associate the state with masculine traits such as war and autonomous behavior patterns. Against this backdrop, McDonagh and Monopoli examine a range of public policies and illustrate the masculine specificity of those associated with the United States in contrast to the hybrid character of public policies that typify most comparable democracies.

The next chapter, *On Parity, Interdependence, and Women's Democracy*, by Blanca Rodríguez-Ruiz and Ruth Rubio-Marín analyzes the constitutional implications of legal measures directed at imposing gender parity and gender electoral quotas. Rodríguez-Ruiz and Rubio-Marín examine a variety of possible perspectives, including the more traditional rights perspective. They argue for a different perspective – that of citizenship in a representative democracy. Their analysis refers to case studies from several countries, including France, Italy, Switzerland, Colombia and, most recently, Spain. Eventually, Rodríguez-Ruiz and Rubio-Marín propose a new model for dealing with the parity challenge – the distinct parity democracy model.

In *Women's Involvement in International Constitution-Making*, Elizabeth Katz studies women's participation from the perspective of women's involvement in the constitutional-drafting process. Katz presents four case studies – Afghanistan, Colombia, Kenya, and Nicaragua – that serve as the basis for analyzing the important elements for ensuring effective participation. In general, she concludes that women's participation in the constitutional-drafting process has made a difference. In addition, she demonstrates that even where their wishes may not have been fully incorporated into the constitutional text, women's participation in the constitutional-drafting process paves the way for future discussions and improvements.

The theme of women's mobilization for action recurs in Carolina Vergel Tovar's *Between Constitutional Jurisdiction and Women's Rights Organizations: Women, War, and the Space of Justice in Colombia*. Tovar focuses on a path-breaking decision of the Colombian Constitutional Court on the protection of internally displaced women. This decision declared that the overwhelming majority of victims of displacement have been women and ordered the government to create special programs to assist them. Tovar situates this decision in the context of the political mobilization of women.

The third part concludes with *The Promise of Democratic Constitutionalism: Women, Constitutional Dialogue, and the Internet* by Tsvi Kahana and Rachel Stephenson. Kahana and Stephenson adopt an approach known as democratic constitutionalism, which generally advocates for replacing judicial supremacy by various forms of popular participation, in comparison with the more traditional approaches of judicial-supremacy constitutionalism and legislative supremacy constitutionalism. Their objective is to evaluate the impact of this approach on women. They argue that democratic constitutionalism provides important opportunities for the direct participation of women in the project of constitutional interpretation. It does so by focusing on the special possibilities offered by the various uses of the internet owing to its faceless, fluid, and textual nature.

Part IV turns to the gender-specific rights controversies surrounding reproductive rights (also seen in the contribution of Dixon and Nussbaum in Part I), opening with Jennifer S. Hendricks' discussion of *Pregnancy, Equality, and U.S. Constitutional Law*. Hendricks embraces pregnancy as the model for the parental relationship – because of the way it combines a biological tie and a caretaking relationship.

Hendricks shows that this model has guided the jurisprudence of the U.S. Supreme Court in the way it dealt with the parental claims of unwed fathers. She examines the effect of understanding pregnancy as a parental relationship on the analysis of abortion law. While acknowledging that it also has the potential to undermine the right to abortion, Hendricks argues that denying the relational component of pregnancy distances abortion discourse from women's reproductive experiences, and undermines women's legal claims in other contexts.

Abortion law in the United States is also the subject of Nicole Huberfeld's chapter titled *Federal Spending and Compulsory Maternity*, dedicated to the funding aspects of this body of law. Huberfeld focuses on decisions that allow the states as well as the federal government to burden the privacy right to obtain abortion by withholding funds in public health-care programs, particularly Medicaid. She criticizes this case law and points to the disconnect it creates between the acknowledgment of women's reproductive rights and the actual denial of the same rights in the Spending Clause jurisprudence.

In *Challenges for Contemporary Reproductive Rights Advocacy: The South African Example*, Rachel Rebouché examines the distinction between reproductive rights and their realization. Rebouché starts by describing the regulation of abortion during apartheid and moves on to understand the processes that enabled the incorporation of reproductive rights in the new South African Constitution. In fact, South Africa is the only country to recognize a constitutional right to reproductive freedom. Against this background she discusses current law, which was largely influenced by the experience of the U.S. reproductive rights activism, without taking full account of the unique domestic conditions. More specifically, the analysis focuses on the treatment of parental involvement in minors' abortion decisions as an example of the unintended consequences of the advocacy strategy that led to the law. Rebouché concludes by suggesting considerations that contemporary reproductive rights reform projects might incorporate in pursuit of an approach that would be more responsive to the actual needs of women making decisions about abortion.

Part V discusses current tensions around women's rights in a world of multiculturalism and diversity. It opens with *Constitutional Rights of Women in Customary Law in Southern Africa: Dominant Interventions and "Old Pathways,"* by Chuma Himonga. This chapter calls for revisiting the idea of using custom, tradition, and culture to protect women's rights. The analysis starts by describing and critiquing the prevailing methods of implementing the rights of women in Southern Africa in areas such as customary marriage, polygamy, and succession rights. Humonga highlights the limitations of these interventions, which justify the considering of alternative approaches. She proposes an approach based on engagement with customary law within a dialogic human rights analytical framework. Her model would emphasize the aspects of customary law that protect women, use its language, and take into account the importance of family in the customary decision-making process.

In *Minority Women: A Struggle for Equal Protection against Domestic Violence*, Puja Kapai focuses her culturally sensitive analysis on the challenge of fighting domestic violence in a way that will be accessible to women of ethnic minority and immigrant communities. Kapai seeks to critically examine the basic assumptions inherent in preventive and interventionist measures against domestic violence. She highlights factors such as cultural values of obedience and self-sacrifice, language barriers, financial dependence, immigration status, spatial isolation, and racial discrimination. Kapai advocates taking a varied and systemic approach that will be responsive to the realities of ethnic and immigrant women.

Watch GRACE Grow: African Customary Law and Constitutional Law in the Equality Garden by Jewel Amoah offers an intersectional analysis of equality claims, using the acronym GRACE to represent an African girl child whose Gender, Race, Age, and Culture intersect to impact on her experience of Equality. Amoah's premise is that the different aspects of GRACE's identity change her experience as well as the way she is perceived in her environment. Her experience occurs at the point at which the elements of her identity intersect. The discussion embraces legal pluralism, and argues that the development of customary law in accordance with equality principles in general, and gender equality in the constitution in particular, is vital for the prospects of GRACE to achieve and enjoy equality.

In her chapter *Critical Multiculturalism*, Vrinda Narain addresses the accommodation of group difference within the framework of multiculturalism. Narain's perspective is critical and she insists that policies respecting this difference will promote gender equality. Her study focuses on the experience of Muslim women situated at the intersection of a religious community and a secular state, making them a compelling category of analysis. Muslim women experience discrimination along multiple axes – as women, as Muslims, and as Muslim women. Their situation illustrates the paradox of multicultural vulnerability where the commitment to protecting minority rights may result in the subordination of women. Against this background, Narain aspires to craft an understanding of multicultural citizenship that allows for the possibility of difference without exclusion.

Susan Williams continues to develop the theme of moderating between minority culture and women's rights in *Democratic Theory, Feminist Theory, and Constitutionalism: The Challenge of Multiculturalism*. Williams presents the two extreme choices faced by women in this context – departure from their cultural norms using "freedom of exit" and departure from the dominant culture's rules. She exposes the shortcomings of this choice, proposing as an alternative a dialogic model of democracy. The dialogue proposed is not only a dialogue between the minority and the larger community, but also an internal dialogue within the minority community. Williams is aware of the dangers attached to this proposal, which may lead to hierarchy and oppression if not implemented correctly. Therefore, for the purpose of promoting internal dialogue in the minority community, she proposes to provide the community with recognition and resources, and to make accommodation contingent on the adoption of practices that encourage dialogue. Williams argues that employing her approach would yield long-term benefits for women by assuring their voices are heard and incorporated in the reshaping of equality rights.

Finally, Part VI continues the analysis of gender rights in circumstances of multiculturalism with a special focus on cultural claims that are situated in religion. *Secular Constitutionalism and Muslim Women's Rights: The Turkish Headscarf Controversy and Its Impact on the European Court of Human Rights* by Hilal Elver draws on the debate about the acceptability of Muslim women wearing a headscarf or *hijab.* Elver explores the Turkish headscarf controversy that led the country into political turmoil, and demonstrates the complex implications of this controversy on domestic and transnational legal order. The Turkish headscarf controversy is one of the earliest and most deeply complex cases of this sort – both because of the gap between the constitutional secularism of the country and the prevalent Muslim sentiment in the population at large and because of the Turkish reliance on secularism to prohibit headscarves, which became a model legal argument for European courts. More specifically, Elver evaluates the pivotal role of the decisions of the European Court of Human Rights that upheld national bans on headscarf use. Her analysis focuses on the role of judges as interpreters of human rights principles and constitutional order in domestic and international courts.

In *On God, Promises, and Money: Islamic Divorce at the Crossroads of Gender and the Law,* Pascale Fournier explores the legal implications of the custom of *Mahr* in divorce. Fournier reviews the interpretations of *Mahr* in Western courts (in Canada, the United States, France, and Germany), comparing them to the ways in which *Mahr* is conceived in its place of origin, represented by Egypt, Tunisia, and Malaysia, three countries that have incorporated Islamic law into their national legal frameworks. She describes the conflicting faces of *Mahr* – a bonus or a penalty – and explains the different legal implications that they convey. Fournier demonstrates how Islamic law travels with a multiplicity of voices, and shows how this complex hybridity is mediated in Western legal adjudication.

The last chapter, *Polygamy and Feminist Constitutionalism,* by Beverley Baines discusses another controversy in the intersection of religion and equality claims – polygamy. It highlights the dilemma posed by polygamy when it is evaluated from the dual perspective of both feminism and constitutionalism – because most feminists believe polygamy is harmful to women, whereas constitutionalists often advocate limiting the powers of liberal states, and therefore may seek decriminalization. In other words, polygamy provides a test case for the inclusivity of the concept of feminist constitutionalism. Baines proposes to deal with this conflict, not by formulas that compel a direct clash of values, which result in a zero-sum game and therefore are doomed to fail, but rather by listening to the voices of the women who live in polygamous relationships. This method is presented as a paradigm for feminist constitutionalists to explore for the promotion of women's constitutional citizenship.

* * *

The contributors to this book explore and take up the challenges of feminist constitutionalism, presenting it as a rich practice dedicated not only to studying present constitutional injustices and feminist reforms, but also to developing a theoretical arena for evaluating constitutional arguments and experimentalism. They demonstrate the relevance of applying a multiplicity of feminist voices to the traditional terrain of constitutional law. Their contributions include assessing both the feminist impact on constitutional law and the feminist evaluation of current constitutional controversies and proposed reforms. Constitutional reform does not always take the form of constitutional amendment; it may manifest itself also in the appearance of new modes of feminist constitutional argumentation and decision making.

This collection grew from a conference held at Queen's University, in Kingston, Ontario, in the winter of 2009. We would like to thank the many participants in the conference whose presentations and discussions were the building blocks of this project. The conference was generously supported by the Law Foundation of Ontario, as well as the Faculty of Law, the Office of Research Services, and the Principal's Office at Queen's University. Erin Durant's administrative assistance was crucial in preparing and running the conference, and Joanna Si was instrumental in assisting us in the editorial process. They both worked significantly more than what they had committed to, and we would like to thank them for their hard work, relentless dedication, and good judgment. We also thank Hila Shamir and Yofi Tirosh for reading and commenting on this introduction.

We look forward to the development of the academic discourse around feminist constitutionalism.

PART I

Feminism as a Challenge to Constitutional Theory

The Gendered Division of Household Labor

An Issue of Constitutional Rights

Jennifer Nedelsky

In my view, one of the major projects of contemporary constitutionalism is finding ways of holding democratic decision making accountable to core values.[1] The standard way of doing so is to constitutionalize rights and establish some kind of judicial review, which authorizes courts to overturn governmental action that violates those rights. But this rhetorical and institutional form of using rights as standards of legitimacy has many widely recognized limitations. Most of those limitations have to do with the lack of democratic legitimacy – which goes beyond the basic problem of courts overturning the decisions of elected legislatures.

Here I present feminist constitutionalism as part of my broader project of seeing constitutionalism as a dialogue of democratic accountability.[2] I will argue that feminist constitutionalism invites us to 1) reimagine the scope of practices and institutions that should be held accountable to core values, 2) reimagine the forms of deliberation about those values and their practical meaning, and 3) reimagine multiple forms of accountability – so that judicial review becomes only one highly specific and democratically limited mechanism. The project of rights implementation becomes less state focused, as does the process of deliberation and accountability – while recognizing that there always remains the question of how existing law structures relations in ways that perpetuate inequality. This just is no longer the sole focus.

In this chapter, I use issues of gender as a focus for reflecting on alternative ways of deliberating on the meaning of core values and the ways they are fostered or undermined by structures of relations. This involves seeing the links among legal rights, core values, and the human relationships that are structured by rights and that, at the same time, affect the practical availability of rights. In particular, I link

---

[1] *See* Jennifer Nedelsky, *Reconceiving Rights and Constitutionalism*, 7 J. Hum. Rts. 139 (2008). I also develop this argument in Law's Relations: A Relational Theory of Self, Autonomy and Law (2011).

[2] *Id.*

I would like to thank Sarah Drummond and Michelle Dean for excellent research assistance.

issues of rights to the long-standing feminist concerns with the gendered division of
household labor.

Calling attention to the significance of the gendered division of household labor
was one of the earliest contributions of what is often called "second-wave" American
feminism. This issue was hotly contested then, and often dismissed by ostensible
male allies on the left as not a serious issue.[3] By the phrase household labor, I mean
to include the vital labor of care for young children and sick or frail members of
the household, acquiring and preparing food, and all the work of maintaining a
household from washing clothes and dishes to sweeping and tidying. This work can
be done in a perfunctory way meeting bare material needs, and it can be done in a
way that includes emotional nurture and the creation of beauty in a home. Despite
the articulate account by feminists in the 1970s of why a fair distribution of this labor
was necessary for gender equality, North American society has made only a small
amount of progress on this front.[4] And the (now mostly tacit) disdain for this topic as
a serious matter of justice also remains. The distribution of household labor is still
largely absent from discussions of human rights.

It is time to take this issue seriously. I argue that the structure of domestic relationships through which this labor is organized is crucial for the enjoyment of rights.
These relationships, therefore, and their impact on the distribution of labor – and
thus on rights – should not be dismissed as either trivial or private. In making this
argument I am reversing the focus on my previous work. Previously, I argued that
we should see legal rights as structuring relationships – of duty, care, responsibility,
and power.[5] Here I argue that a just structure of household relationships is crucial
for the enjoyment of rights.

I trace some of the links between gendered division of labor in the household
(generally not thought of as a rights issue) with more obvious rights issues such
as access to education, health care, and employment. Perhaps less obvious is the
crucial link to leisure, to the ability to exercise a right to play.[6] In short, women
cannot fully enjoy (largely uncontested) rights unless (highly contested) relations
of household labor are changed. By shifting the direction of the rights–relationship
link, I also shift the focus away from law and formal legal structures. I address the
question of what kinds of forums for collective deliberation about household labor
we can imagine. By thinking about this concrete – but intractably far-reaching and
pervasive – problem, we can start to see how feminist constitutionalism invites us to

[3] Pat Mainardi, *The Politics of Housework, in* SISTERHOOD IS POWERFUL: AN ANTHOLOGY OF WRITINGS FROM THE WOMEN'S LIBERATION MOVEMENT 501 (Robin Morgan ed., 1970).

[4] COLIN LINDSAY, ARE WOMEN SPENDING MORE TIME ON UNPAID DOMESTIC WORK THAN MEN IN CANADA? (2008) Statistics Canada Catalogue no. 89–630-X, www.statcan.gc.ca/pub/89–630-x/2008001/article/10705-eng.pdf. This report concludes that, although the gender gap in unpaid housework is closing, women still spend about two hours more than men, per day, on unpaid housework including childcare, cooking, and shopping.

[5] *See supra*, note 1.

[6] MARTHA NUSSBAUM, WOMEN AND HUMAN DEVELOPMENT: THE CAPABILITIES APPROACH 80 (2000).

reimagine the scope of practices and institutions that should be held accountable to core values, and to reimagine the forms of deliberation that could accomplish such accountability.

Before turning to my approach to constitutionalism, let me offer a note about context. I am taking up the problem of division of labor in households containing both men and women. A widespread form of these relations is heterosexual couples who raise children, sometimes in extended families, sometimes in nuclear families. I am not presuming heterosexual couples as the optimal arrangement. And I think it is an interesting question the extent to which same-sex relationships end up following the heterosexual model of one partner having primary responsibility for bringing in income and the other for childcare and household work and management. This issue reminds us of the wider meaning of gender norms, not just their assignment to different biological sexes.

Similarly, I think an important piece of the project I outline here is the facilitation of multiple family forms to help break patterns of gendered division of labor as well as to meet other needs. But I do not develop that argument here.

My focus here is on household labor, but there is also important, and often gendered, caretaking that happens outside the immediate household. Care for elderly parents is an example that is receiving increased attention. Many of the general points I make here about the implications of assuming primary responsibility for care work and for making the workplace compatible with caretaking responsibilities extend to this wider issue.

Finally, I do not claim to offer enough evidence here to *prove* the links I point to among household labor, respect, and rights, but I think there is enough to make the claim that we should seriously examine these links and what it would take to transform them.

I. RELATIONAL RIGHTS AND DIALOGUE OF DEMOCRATIC ACCOUNTABILITY

Let me briefly situate my argument in the context of my previous work on a relational approach to rights and to constitutionalism as a dialogue of democratic accountability. First, I treat "rights" as a rhetorical and institutional means for implementing core values. I prefer this language to simply defining all core values as rights. (Usually when people do this they mean to claim that the values are *moral* rights.) The distinction between rights and values allows one, among other things, to emphasize that it is a certain kind of choice to describe a value as a legal right and to construct institutions for implementing that right.

Next, my relational approach to rights makes two basic claims: 1) Questions of rights are best analyzed in terms of how they structure relations, and 2) what rights actually do (rather than should do) is structure relations, which, in turn, promote or undermine core values such as autonomy, security, or equality. Rights structure relations such as those of power, trust, responsibility, and care. This is as true of rights in domains like property and contract as it is of the more obvious areas like family law. I focus on the ways certain kinds of relationships are necessary for core values such as equality – and thus for many of the basic values institutionalized as rights.

In my previous work on constitutionalism, I argued that rights should not be understood as "trumps" (in the famous American phrase of Ronald Dworkin), but as means of holding governments accountable to core values through a dialogue of democratic accountability. I emphasized the importance not only of institutional dialogue (say between courts and legislatures), but also of public deliberation about the meaning of core values. Here I carry this argument further.

As I noted at the outset, using judicial review as the primary means of holding public decision makers accountable to core values raises serious problems of democratic legitimacy. But these problems arise not just from the widely discussed issue of whether judges are democratically accountable. The deeper problem is the lack of public comprehension and capacity for deliberation. When core values are construed as rights that are seen as legal instruments to be defined and implemented by judges, then only lawyers and judges are seen as fully competent to understand, assess, and debate them. Members of society generally are excluded from these vital conversations.

The amount of actual dialogue that takes place, either between institutions such as the judiciary and the legislature or more generally as a matter of public deliberation, varies in different constitutional systems – but existing systems are almost always weak on the matter of public deliberation.

In earlier work I argued for the need to be much more creative about the kinds of governmental institutions that could generate real, democratic dialogue as part of the process of accountability.[7] *This is essential because the core objective of protecting rights necessarily includes defining those rights.* This is a point often neglected in rights discourse. The focus is often simply on the protection of rights – as though their meaning were not contested. The process of definition must be democratically defensible. Entrusting it exclusively, or even primarily, to the courts cannot be adequate. Indeed, entrusting it to government institutions alone cannot be adequate. Increased deliberation about the meaning of rights within and among legislators and those who administer the law (such as social assistance provisions) would be an important improvement,[8] but it would not be an adequate substitute for deliberation at the popular level.

---

[7] *See supra* note 1.
[8] *See, e.g.,* Nova Scotia (Workers' Compensation Board) v. Martin; Nova Scotia (Workers' Compensation Board) v. Laseur, [2003] 2 S.C.R. 504, 2003 SCC 54, holding that if administrative tribunals are authorized to decide questions of law, they must have the authority to consider the relevance of the Canadian Charter of Rights and Freedoms unless their enabling statute explicitly states otherwise.

I want to move beyond state institutions to think much more broadly about new forms of deliberation about core values and accountability to them. We will see that to ensure basic rights, such as equality, we need deeply transformative dialogue about gendered division of labor. We need to rethink our values so that we can hold many layers of norms, practices, institutions, and laws accountable to those values. The core idea of constitutionalism must be expanded for its basic objective to be achieved.

II. (UNCONTESTED) RIGHTS AND (HIGHLY CONTESTED) DIVISION OF HOUSEHOLD LABOR

My claim, as I noted at the outset, is that women cannot fully enjoy rights that almost no one denies are rights without changing relations of household labor – which almost no one thinks are rights issues. I begin by sketching some of the links between acknowledged rights and structures of household labor.

When it is widely accepted that women should bear primary or exclusive responsibility for childcare and for the basic maintenance activities of food, clothing, and home care, they are accorded a second-class status that directly affects their enjoyment of rights. Despite the fact that this work is essential to sustaining the life, development, and comforts of both individuals and the community, this "women's work" is almost universally accorded lower status than the work men do.[9] There are, of course, variations in the details of the work assigned to women both across and within cultures, but the lower status is virtually universal. This is true whether the work takes the form of unpaid labor within families or the poor wages "the market" offers for "domestic labor" such as care for children or the elderly or housecleaning.[10] It is often difficult to tell whether the work is undervalued because women do it, or

---

[9] Women continue to earn about 70 percent of men's earning for the same work; and women's labor is also concentrated in lower-paying sectors. *See* Statistics Canada, WOMEN IN CANADA: A GENDER-BASED REPORT (5th ed. 2006) Catalogue no. 89–503-XPE, *available at* www.statcan.gc.ca/pub/89–503-x/ 89–503-x2005001-eng.pdf. This study notes the average income of Canadian women at 71 percent of men in 2003 for full-time, full-year work. *Id.* at 139. In 2004, 67 percent of all employed women were working in teaching, nursing, and related health occupations, clerical or other administrative positions, and sales and service occupations. This is compared with just 30 percent of employed men. *Id.* at 113.

[10] In North America, the wages are low whether the work is performed within a household by paid caregivers such as nannies or within institutions such as daycare centers or nursing homes. *See* Statistics Canada, *Services Indicators, 4th Quarter 2001*, at 29 (2001) Catalogue no. 63–016-XIB, *available at* www.statcan.gc.ca/pub/63–016-x/63–016-x2001004-eng.pdf. This report shows that the average annual income of daycare workers in Canada was slightly more than $20,000 in 2000; well short of the average of $34,000 in the economy at large. Some provincial employment standards legislation excludes domestic and live-in care workers from minimum-wage provisions. Human Resources and Skills Development Canada publishes working requirements for those working as live in caregivers under the Live-In Caregiver Program. Prevailing wages are published, and are between $8 and $10 per hour; for a full year of 40-hour weeks, this totals $18,720 at $9 per hour.

women are assigned to do it because it is undervalued. Either way, the lower status of the work and the women are intertwined.

Once it is accepted that women are of lower status and their contributions are of lower value, it is only a short step to practices that give them less access to education, health care, and sometimes even basic nutrition.[11] This is, of course, particularly so in poor countries where resources are very scarce. If a family will have a hard time providing education for its children, the more important children (the ones who can earn more, who will become "breadwinners," and the ones who will not leave upon marriage to perform their work elsewhere) should take priority. The fact that women across the world have less access to widely recognized rights such as education, health care, and nutrition is now well documented.[12] Without claiming that the gendered division of household labor is the *sole* cause of these rights deprivations, I think the link deserves closer examination.

In poor countries the consequences of rights deprivation are more acute, but the link between rights deprivation and gendered division of labor exists in wealthy countries as well. Of course, the idea that household labor is women's work is linked to ideas about the kinds of work outside the home that are appropriate for women. However, all over the world women are both working outside the home and sustaining a vastly disproportionate burden of household labor. In North America I think there has actually been more movement on the de-gendering of work in the paid labor force than in the division of household labor.

I focus here on outlining the links between rights deprivation and gendered division of household labor in North America. This is the context I know best, and I think it is the context in which people are least likely to have thought of the link to rights deprivation. It is in general easier for people to recognize how "others" violate the rights of their women. This is the context I use to think about how to effect transformation in the modes of deliberation about core values.

I begin by briefly noting the ways in which the gender disparities of health, education, and employment that are widely recognized in developing countries are also present in North America. The direct link between these disparities and women's responsibilities for household labor is clearest with respect to employment. However, my broad point is that the denigration of women and the denigration of

See also Human Resources and Skills Development Canada (HRSDC), *Regional Wages, Working Conditions, and Advertisement Requirements for the Live-In Caregiver Program ("LCP"),* available *at* www.rhdcc-hrsdc.gc.ca/eng/workplaceskills/foreign_workers/advertReq/wageadreq.shtml. An informal review of websites that provide information to prospective nannies or families looking to hire nannies indicates that the average pay for nannies is $350 per week; this is consistent with the $8–10 salary range indicated by HRSDC. Of note is that daycare workers in Quebec are unionized, and in 2006 negotiated a pay raise to $16.90 per hour. This pay rate is much higher than the numbers cited by the Statistics Canada report indicates; it may be that there is variation among provinces, depending in large part on whether workers are unionized.

[11] Nussbaum, *supra* note 6, at 3, 113.
[12] *Id.*

the labor they perform are tied together, and that they contribute to women being treated as "second-class citizens" in many ways. Those links with respect to health (including nutrition) are easy to see in the context of developing countries. Here, as I said, my point is to show that similar disparities exist in North America.

Increasingly, studies show gender disparities in the quality of health care.[13] For example, these disparities take the form of the kind of respect doctors pay to women, and thus to the crucial willingness to actually listen to them[14] and provide accurate diagnosis and appropriate treatment. We have only recently begun to see shifts in the long-standing pattern of important research being conducted on men only and then applied to women.[15] People with low incomes experience a disparity in quality and access to health care (even in publicly funded systems like Canada's), and this will disproportionately affect women because they are poorer.

In Canada, and I think most wealthy Western countries, women have increasingly equal access to education. But studies suggest that men and boys have much more "air time" in class discussions. Their teachers, both male and female, pay more attention to them than to their female peers.[16] These imbalances persist, with gender disparity evidenced in graduate school classrooms as well.[17]

Even success in education does not translate to equal access in employment. Consider the professions in which access is generally noted as an area of success for white, middle-class women.[18] For example, women now routinely graduate at the top of their law school class and are hired by good firms. But the failure of large law firms to create a family-friendly (or even family-tolerant) work structure, as well as the lack of professional support for women in small firms or sole practices,

[13] Joseph P. Ornato, *Gender Delay in Emergency Medical Services: Does it Really Exist?*, 2 CIRCULATION: CARDIOVASCULAR QUALITY AND OUTCOMES 4 (2009); Thomas Concannon et al., *Elapsed Time in Emergency Medical Services for Patients with Cardiac Complaints: Are Some Patients at Greater Risk for Delay?*, 2 CIRCULATION: CARDIOVASCULAR QUALITY AND OUTCOMES 9 (2009).

[14] Bernadine P. Healy, *Listening to America's Women*, 4 JOURNAL OF WOMEN'S HEALTH 539 (1995).

[15] Regina Vidaver et al., *Women Subjects in NIH-Funded Clinical Research Literature: Lack of Progress in Both Representation and Analysis by Sex*, 9 JOURNAL OF WOMEN'S HEALTH & GENDER BASED MEDICINE 495 (2009). Particularly striking are sex differences in certain drug-metabolizing enzymes, resulting in sometimes dangerous side effects being disproportionately experienced by women receiving the drugs, which have been tested exclusively or primarily on men.

[16] Robyn Beaman, Kevin Wheldall, & Coral Kemp, *Differential Teacher Attention to Boys and Girls in the Classroom*, 58 EDUCATIONAL REV. 339 (2006); Jane French & Peter French, *Gender Imbalances in the Primary Classroom: An Interactional Account*, 26 EDUCATIONAL RESEARCH 127 (1984).

[17] Myra Sadker & David Sadker, *Sexism in the Classroom: From Grade School to Graduate School*, 67 THE PHI DELTA KAPPAN 512 (1986); Mary Frank Fox, Women in Scientific Fields: Doctoral Education and Academic Careers, Workshop on Women's Advancement, American Political Science Association (March 2004), *available at* www.apsanet.org/imgtest/maryfrankfox.pdf.

[18] Of course, a full picture of the inequalities women face would involve an analysis of gender disparities across all spheres of employment. My point here is that even those women who overcome barriers in education continue to face barriers in the professions – and that we have evidence that those barriers are related to gendered division of household labor.

disproportionately drives out young women.[19] The situation is slowly improving in
the academic context, but there is still a long way to go. In many of Canada's top law
schools, fewer than 40 percent of the faculty is women, despite the fact that women
have made up more than 50 percent of their graduating classes for nearly a decade.[20]
The American Political Science Association's Committee on the Status of Women
in the Profession (CSWP) notes that:

> A variety of reports of the CSWP and of others have directed attention to women's dif-
> ferential success within the academy. Although the numbers of women in academia
> have been growing, the status of women in the academy has not improved as
> dramatically: women remain disproportionately clustered in the lower ranks of
> the academic ladder, underrepresented at research institutions, overrepresented in
> community colleges, and disadvantaged in terms of salary. This pattern holds true
> in our profession [Political Science] as well. And, although there has been improve-
> ment in the last 10 years, significant gaps remain. See, for example, Stetson et al.

---

[19] *See, e.g.*, LAW SOCIETY OF UPPER CANADA, EXECUTIVE SUMMARY – RETENTION OF WOMEN IN PRIVATE
PRACTICE WORKING GROUP (May 22, 2008), *available at* www.lsuc.on.ca/media/convmay08_retention_
of_women_executive_summary.pdf.

   1. Women have been entering the legal profession and private practice in record numbers for at least
     two decades. However, they have been leaving private practice in droves largely because the legal
     profession has not effectively adapted to this reality.
   2. Women's realities, which often include childbirth and taking on a significant share of the family
     responsibilities, impact on the choices they make in their professional lives.

It is interesting that they saw fit to add, "While neither the Law Society nor the profession generally
should, nor can, determine the roles women play in their own family relationships, the failure of the
profession to adapt to what is not a neutral reality will inevitably affect the quality and competence of
the legal services available to the public."

"More than 45 law firms across Ontario have pledged their support to the Law Society's new
precedent-setting Justicia Project designed to retain and advance women lawyers in private practice.
The three-year pilot project is the first of its kind in Canada, and includes representatives from medium
and large firms committed to identifying and adopting principles and best practices that promote the
retention and advancement of women.

Each of the participating Ontario firms has signed written commitments to achieve ambitious
goals in four core areas: tracking gender demographics, flexible work arrangements, networking and
business development mentoring and leadership skills development for women."

See Law Society of Upper Canada, *List of Law Firms Participating in the Justicia Project*,
available at www.lsuc.on.ca/about/b/equity/retentionofwomen/list-of-law-firms-participating-in-the-
justicia-think-tank/; LAW SOCIETY OF UPPER CANADA, EXECUTIVE SUMMARY, *id.*

[20] Fiona Kay & Joan Brockman, *Barriers to Gender Equality in the Canadian Legal Establishment*, 8
FEMINIST LEGAL STUD. 169 (2000); AMERICAN ASSOCIATION OF LAW SCHOOLS (AALS), 2007–2008
AALS STATISTICAL REPORT ON LAW FACULTY, www.aals.org/statistics/2008dlt/gender.html. The AALS
report indicates that, in 2007–2008, just shy of 37 percent of law faculty were women. Though
there is no formal statistic for Canadian law schools, an informal review of five top Canadian law
schools (University of Toronto, University of British Columbia, University of Alberta, Osgoode Hall
Law School, and McGill University) indicates that the percentage of women faculty members is
similar at about 38 percent; CATALYST, WOMEN IN LAW: MAKING THE CASE 7 (2001), *available at*
www.catalyst.org/file/165/women_in_law_making_the_case.pdf. This report surveyed the entrants to
five of the top ten U.S. law schools in 2001, the year that it was expected that women outpaced men
in entry to law school in the United States.

1990; Guy 1992; van Assendelft et al. 2001; and Committee on the Status of Women in the Profession 2001. APSA recently received funding from NSF to explore what can be done to advance the progress of women within the discipline. A one-day workshop, held at APSA in March, 2004, reviewed data on the status of women in a variety of social science disciplines, as well as in political science, and indicated that *"familial" responsibilities are among the significant barriers to women's equal participation within the academy.* (emphasis added)[21]

Women are also significantly underrepresented in top management jobs and significantly overrepresented in low-status, care-type jobs such as secretarial work and nursing.[22] In addition, the wage differential remains at around 70 percent.[23]

The CSWP report includes a quote that offers a more general point that makes the link between responsibilities for care work and household labor and the disadvantages for anyone (still predominantly women) who assumes those responsibilities:

> The ideal worker is someone who enters a profession immediately upon receiving the relevant credential, works his or her way up the career ladder by putting in long hours without interruptions beyond short vacations, and continues in this fashion until retirement age. The ideal worker can contribute financially to the family, but cannot make substantial time commitments to children or other family members without endangering his or her career. Pay and promotion systems, rules around working time, and the beliefs of those from previous generations who have succeeded as ideal workers and currently manage our organizations, are all built upon the presumption that only ideal workers should be hired, retained, and rewarded.[24]

Equality of access to employment is, of course, widely recognized as a right. The fact that no deliberate discrimination is required to make caregiving and domestic

[21] Martha Ackelsberg et al., *Remembering the 'Life' in Academic Life: Finding a Balance between Work and Personal Responsibilities in the Academy: Report of the Committee on the Status of Women to the Profession*, 2004, 37 PS-POLITICAL SCIENCE AND POLITICS 879 (2004) citing Maresi Nerad, The Advancement of Women Ph.Ds. in Political Science: Defining the Problem, Paper presented to NSF-APSA Workshop on Women's Advancement in Political Science, Washington, D.C. (2004); Mary Ann Mason & Marc Goulden, Marriage and Baby Blues: Redefining Gender Equity. Paper delivered at the "Mommies" and "Daddies" on the "Fast Track": Success of Parents in Demanding Professions conference, University of Pennsylvania (2003); Susan Kolker Finkel & Steven G. Olswang, *Child Rearing as a Career Impediment to Women Assistant Professors*, 19 REV. OF HIGHER EDUCATION 123 (1996); Mary Ann Mason & Marc Goulden, *Do Babies Matter: The Effect of Family Formation on the Life-Long Careers of Academic Men and Women*, 88 ACADEME 21 (2002); Diane S. Young & Ednita Wright, *Mothers Making Tenure*, 37 JOURNAL OF SOCIAL WORK EDUCATION 555 (2001).

[22] 2009 Catalyst Census: *Financial Post* 500 Women Board Directors. This report indicates that women represent 14 percent of corporate directorships in companies listed in the *Financial Post* 500 as published by the *National Post Business Magazine. See also*, Ronald Burke, *Women on Corporate Boards of Directors: A Needed Resource*, 16 JOURNAL OF BUSINESS ETHICS 909 (1997).

[23] *See supra* note 8.

[24] Ackelsberg, *supra* note 21, at 880; citing Robert Drago et al., *Final Report to the Alfred P. Sloan Foundation for the Faculty and Families Project* 3–4 (The Pennsylvania State University, Work-Family Working Paper #01–02 March 14, 2001), *available at* http://lser.la.psu.edu/workfam/FFExecutiveSummary.pdf.

responsibilities a barrier to the enjoyment of that right, makes it no less a rights violation. As the quote above concludes, the effective discrimination happens because "care-giving activities signal that the faculty member is not an ideal worker and therefore a substandard academic,"[25] or I would add, employee more generally.

Another link between rights deprivation and care work is the worldwide phenomenon of comparatively wealthy societies using women from poorer countries to do domestic labor. These women are usually far from home and often vulnerable to rights abuses.[26] In their excellent collection, *Global Woman: Nannies, Maids, and Sex Workers in the New Economy*, Ehrenreich and Hochschild comment that the ancient gendered pattern of women providing domestic work, childcare, and sexual services to men is now being played out in a North–South division of labor, where women of the global south provide these services to the global north.[27] The denigration of both the labor and the women remains constant.

The heart of the link between enjoyment of rights and the gendered division of labor is the same in both rich and poor countries: lack of respect and attribution of importance to women's work. There is a set of assumptions about women that both sustains and is sustained by the gendered division of labor. Childcare and household maintenance are seen as things anyone can do. This work is seen as low skilled, which is, the economists tell us, why it is low paid (when paid at all). The idea that care of young children is low-skilled work continues despite widespread recognition that the early years of child development are the most important. Housecleaning, although low status and low paid, is better paid than childcare. The disjuncture between status and wage rates on the one hand, and ideas about child development on the other is further evidence for the mutually reinforcing disparagement of women and care work. Women overwhelmingly are the ones who do this work (whether paid or unpaid), reinforcing the idea that they are suited to it.[28] Often there is some kind of biological argument lurking in the background – women are naturally nurturers. In any case, they are willing to do the work – reinforcing the ideas that they are suited to it and that they cannot get anything better.

The fact that women perform the majority of unpaid caregiving labor when it comes to both children and aging parents means that they resist, refuse, or are seen to fail at work that denies sustained accommodation for these obligations.[29] Notions of their lesser status and competence are then reinforced.

---

[25] *Id.* at 4.
[26] *See, e.g.*, Allison Weir, *The Global Universal Caregiver: Imagining Women's Liberation in the New Millennium*, 12 CONSTELLATIONS 308 (2005).
[27] Barbara Ehrenreich & Arlie Hochschild, eds, GLOBAL WOMAN: NANNIES, MAIDS, AND SEX WORKERS IN THE NEW ECONOMY (Metropolitan Books 2003).
[28] NANCY FOLBRE, WHO PAYS FOR THE KIDS?: GENDER AND CONSTRAINT 92–93 (Routledge 1994).
[29] *See, e.g.*, Kay & Brockman, *supra* note 20, which discusses the attrition of female lawyers from private law practice. For a comprehensive exploration of Canadian women's unpaid care work, see CARING FOR/CARING ABOUT: WOMEN, HOME CARE, AND UNPAID CAREGIVING (Karen Grant et al., eds., Garamond Press 2004).

Women who are seen as having limited competence, and limited visibility in the positions of power that command respect, do not receive respect. Those who are not accorded the respect due to "the full citizen," the unencumbered economic actor, the competent adult bearer of rights, often find that they are not accorded full rights either.

I suggest that we can see links among rights, respect, economic success, and the gendered division of household labor. Another way of stating these links is that it is very hard to imagine women having equal access to and success in all forms of employment without a radical restructuring of the work environment to accommodate the demands of care work. In my view, imagining that even optimally available and funded daycare can solve this problem vastly underestimates its scope.

Perhaps the most obvious reason daycare alone cannot solve the problem is the widely recognized, but still unaddressed, problem of the double shift, which, again, exists worldwide.[30] In North America, women who do paid work all day still have a huge amount of work to do after they pick up their children from daycare.[31] This is part of the often slighted, but crucial, disadvantage women suffer in access to leisure and to play.[32]

One of Martha Nussbaum's most important contributions in her argument for a basic list of universal human capabilities is the inclusion of play: "being able to laugh, to play, to enjoy recreational activities."[33] Although she does not spend much time discussing why and how play is important, she is right to give it that status and priority. Play and leisure are crucial not only to the enjoyment of life, but to the capacity for creativity and autonomy as well. It is difficult to imagine what one really wants to do with one's life, let alone implement such visions, without the space for reflection and the regular experience of the creativity of play. Women's huge relative deprivation of leisure time and play is one of the least recognized (by those who talk about human rights) consequences of the current distribution of household labor – and yet its harm is serious.

---

[30] ARLIE HOCHSCHILD, THE TIME BIND: WHEN WORK BECOMES HOME AND HOME BECOMES WORK, 2nd ed. (Henry Holt and Company 2001); FOLBRE, *supra* note 28.

[31] Nancy Fraser makes the point that any attempted solution to the current distribution of care work will have to address the problem of "free riding": "*Contra* conservatives, the real free riders in the current system are not poor solo mothers who shirk employment. Instead they are men of all classes who shirk care work and domestic labor, as well as corporations who free ride on the labor of working people, both underpaid and unpaid." Nancy Fraser, *After the Family Wage: Gender Equity and the Welfare State*, 22 POLITICAL THEORY 591 (1994) (reprinted in JUSTICE INTERRUPTUS: CRITICAL REFLECTIONS ON THE "POSTSOCIALIST" CONDITION 62 (Routledge 1997) [hereinafter Fraser, JUSTICE INTERRUPTUS]).

[32] Nussbaum, *supra* note 6, at 80. *See also*, Janet Fast et al., *The time of our lives . . .*, in CANADIAN SOCIAL TRENDS 22 (2001). Statistics Canada Catalogue No. 11–0008, www.statcan.gc.ca/pub/11–008-x/2001003/article/6007-∗eng.pdf; Janet Fast & Judith Frederick, *The Time of Our Lives: Juggling Work and Leisure over the Life Cycle*, Research Paper. No. 4, at 21 (1998) Statistics Canada Catalogue no. 89–584-MIE, www.statcan.gc.ca/pub/89–584-m/89–584-m2003004-eng.pdf.

[33] Nussbaum, *supra* note 6, at 80. I have various objections to her argument, but this stands as an important contribution.

The chronic exhaustion women face around the world and the lack of access to leisure time and play ought to be seen as rights violations. Nothing but a fundamental restructuring of the gendered division of household labor can redress this problem. And if men were to assume equal responsibility for this labor so that virtually all adults engage in routine caretaking and maintenance work, we would see even more clearly the need to restructure the workplace.

III. RESTRUCTURING THE WORKPLACE

The need to restructure the workplace is an important part of the institutional changes necessary to redress the core problems of the inequality that results from gendered division of labor. Of course, there is more than one possible solution. Nancy Fraser in her classic essay "After the Family Wage: A Postindustrial Thought Experiment" argues that there are currently two main approaches to how to advance women's equality in relation to labor – both unpaid household labor and paid participation in the workforce:

> I call the first the Universal Breadwinner model. It is the vision implicit in current political practice of most U.S. feminists and liberals. It aims to foster gender equity by promoting women's employment; the centerpiece of this model is state provision of employment-enabling services such as day care. The second possible answer I call the Caregiver Parity model. It is the vision implicit in the current political practice of most Western European feminists and social democrats. It aims to promote gender equality chiefly by supporting informal care work; the centerpiece of this model is state provision of caregiver allowances.[34]

In her essay she argues that these models need to be assessed in terms of seven distinct normative principles: the antipoverty principle, the anti-exploitation principle, the income equality principle (between men and women), the leisure-time equality principle, the equality of respect principle, the anti-marginalization principle, and the anti-androcentrism principle.[35] She offers pictures of highly idealized forms of these two models, for example, a Universal Breadwinner model where daycare and elder care were actually available, and sex discrimination and sexual harassment in the workplace were prevented. She then persuasively argues that even with such idealized models, neither the Universal Breadwinner nor the Caregiver Parity model could actually do a good job of meeting the seven principles. (The two models, of course, have different strengths and weaknesses.)

She concludes that not only are optimal versions of either model highly unlikely to be realized in the near future, but neither is even an adequate ideal. We need something better, an even more utopian aspiration:

[34] Fraser, JUSTICE INTERRUPTUS, *supra* note 31, at 43.
[35] Fraser, JUSTICE INTERRUPTUS, *supra* note 31 at 45–49.

The key to achieving gender equity in a postindustrial welfare state, then, is to make women's current life-patterns the norm for everyone. Women today often combine breadwinning and caregiving, albeit with great difficulty and strain. A postindustrial welfare state must ensure that men do the same, while redesigning institutions so as to eliminate the difficulty and strain. We might call this vision *Universal Caregiver*.[36]

I agree completely. Although my project here is not to try to envision what it would take to implement a Universal Caregiver model, I note that a good first step would be to move toward widespread availability of well compensated part-time work with the kinds of (prorated) benefits associated with full-time employment. Any system that would see both men and women enjoying the benefits of both paid employment and the rewards of caretaking will require a norm of part-time paid work.

Trying to maintain the existing structure of both paid work and household labor while large numbers of women are in the paid workforce has caused huge strains in families.[37] Arlie Hochschild offers a depressing and persuasive picture of people at all levels of employment from assembly line to CEO spending longer hours at work. Part of her account for this phenomenon is that being at home has become so stressful that both parents avoid it by increasing work hours. Children who see little of their parents are stressed and their demands encourage parents to exacerbate the situation by seeing even less of them. I do not know the extent to which her particular account speaks to the strain felt by families throughout North America, but I think it captures an important part of the failure of our current arrangements.

A model of work that had presumed a wife at home and a family wage (although, of course, this was never the case for some classes of workers) has incorporated large numbers of women into the workforce without serious modifications to the structure of work. This is true of the professions as well as factories. This seems to be one of many examples where no one thought through the kinds of privileges that were built into the original system. People seem to have thought (and continue to think) that women's equality could be accomplished simply by extending to them the opportunities of men (never fully of course), without seeing that those opportunities relied on the unpaid labor of women. They still rely on that unpaid labor, but now women are supposed to also be able to take up paid employment responsibilities. The result has been both the burden of the double shift and the practical inequality of access to equal opportunity of employment.[38]

Sadly, it seems that it is mostly those on "the right" who comment on the cost to children and family life of a system that draws women into the paid workforce without changing the structure of work. The collective failure to address the problem fuels "family values" talk and the failure to make a case for more than "daycare"

[36] *Id.* at 61.
[37] HOCHSCHILD, *supra*, note 30.
[38] See discussion in Part II.

casts feminist policy as inadequate.[39] Meanwhile, children, women, men, and aging parents suffer.

So far, the discussion on figuring out what to do about the existing situation has been fairly limited in its scope – both few academics and few policy makers taking it up – and in its content. One important exception is Eva Kittay's *Love's Labor*, which is increasingly being noticed in the academic world.[40] She makes the crucial argument that a just distribution of care work is essential for justice and equality. No theory of justice that does not address it directly can be adequate. An important part of her argument is that those who do the care work require care and support. If it is not forthcoming, then exploitation and coercion will be characteristics of the social structure.

Kittay does not, however, directly address the structure of work or the question of whether the norm should be that all workers are also care workers[41] with responsibility for household labor. For reasons that Nancy Fraser points to, it seems unlikely that care work and household labor will ever be accorded high esteem and compensation (as Kittay's system would require) as long as some distinct subset of people engage in it. Of course, following Fraser's principles the solution to existing problems cannot be organized around the exploitation of other women to make the Universal Breadwinner model work. Unfortunately, this is the path followed for well-off professional women around the world. And central as gender has been to the problem, equally unacceptable are other solutions of hierarchy and exclusion, such as a de-gendered, class-based system that leaves the denigration of the work in place, but assigns different "others" to do it. Similar rights consequences would follow.

---

[39] ELIZABETH FOX-GENOVESE, FEMINISM IS NOT THE STORY OF MY LIFE: HOW TODAY'S FEMINIST ELITE HAS LOST TOUCH WITH THE REAL CONCERNS OF WOMEN (1996); Elaine Tyler Max, *"Family Values": The Uses and Abuses of American Family History*, 97 REVUE FRANCAISE D'ETUDES AMERICAINES 7 (2005); JUDITH STACEY, IN THE NAME OF THE FAMILY: RETHINKING FAMILY VALUES IN THE POSTMODERN AGE (Beacon Press 1996); DAVID POPENOE, WAR OVER THE FAMILY (Transaction Publishers 2005). On the "family values" debate, the conservative group Eagle Forum published the article *Careers, Choices, Costs, and Biases*, among others, criticizing feminist work promoting daycare and childcare alternatives financed by the state. Eagle Forum, *Careers, Choices, Costs, and Biases* (July 2002), *available at* www.eagleforum.org/psr/2002/july02/psrjuly02.shtml.

Similarly in Canada, REAL Women of Canada posits itself as an alternative women's movement, and has a position paper on childcare that proposes tax reform to ensure women can stay home and raise their children. The paper also denounces any right to universal daycare. REAL Women of Canada, Statement on Childcare, www.realwomenca.com/page/statechildcare.html (last visited May 12, 2010).

[40] *See* MARTHA C. NUSSBAUM, FRONTIERS OF JUSTICE: DISABILITY, NATIONALITY, SPECIES MEMBERSHIP (THE TANNER LECTURES ON HUMAN VALUES) (2006) and ALASDAIR MACINTYRE, DEPENDENT RATIONAL ANIMALS: WHY HUMAN BEINGS NEED THE VIRTUES (THE PAUL CARUS LECTURES) (Open Court Publishing Company 1999).

[41] Kittay has a very distinctive and limited definition of care work: care for those who cannot care for themselves. This definition is important for the structure of her argument, but (like many others) I am addressing a much wider range of work under the term care work.

My main point so far has been to claim that the "private" and trivialized arrangements of household labor and childcare are inseparable from the project of achieving rights for women, and the solution to the problem must bear in mind the rights of all. Once we see the link to rights, we should turn to the question of the core values rights are to implement. This in turn brings me to my central point: how to foster the kind of collective deliberation about core values that could begin to address these questions. But first, I want to briefly note two related points.

First, I do not want to simply focus on women's disadvantage, despite its centrality in my argument. Inequality and even rights violations do not alone prove that women's lot is always worse than men's. It seems possible to me that as between many women and men in the developed world, the life women lead in their intense engagement with children and home, is, all in all, better than that of men whose lives revolve around paid work – whether the grind of the assembly line, the "cubicle," or the very different grind of the corporate lawyer or executive. I say this despite the "double shift" of crushingly long days for women in heterosexual relations and the anxiety about money, childcare, and time for social life of women who are single parents; and despite the significant limitations of opportunity that women face in their choice of work and advancement. Men who are cut off from intimate relations with their children suffer a deep loss (whether they are conscious of it or not). Often, this involves a more general loss of capacity for intimacy and connection with their feelings.

Of course, there will be exceptions to this assessment of loss and disadvantage. Women sometimes face desperate choices about leaving abusive relationships, sometimes involving giving children "into care" when they cannot afford to care for them on their own.[42] Similarly, women are far too often subject to intimate partner violence without effective recourse.[43] I do not suggest that these harms might be outweighed by the loss uninvolved dads experience. However, one should also remember that our current gender norms (which undergird the division of household labor) also put males at risk of violence in ways not faced by women. One can see examples of this ranging from schoolyard violence to life expectancies of young African-American males in American ghettos.

The harms of the existing system are complex. It is important to articulate the many forms of disadvantage that flow to women because they are overwhelmingly the ones who do the care work and other household labor. It seems to me also important to acknowledge that the existing system has very significant costs to men too. In addition to being honest about the difficulty of measuring costs, this acknowledgment is the

---

[42] Aysan Sev'er, *A Feminist Analysis of Flight of Abused Women, Plight of Canadian Shelters: Another Road to Homelessness*, 11 JOURNAL OF SOCIAL DISTRESS AND THE HOMELESS 307, 320 (2002).

[43] Statistics Canada, *Family Violence in Canada: A Statistical Profile*, at 4 (Released on Oct. 15, 2009) Catalogue no. 85–224-XWE. This report concludes that in 2007, nearly 40,200 incidents of spousal violence were reported to police, representing about 12 percent of violent crime reported to police in Canada.

basis for a compelling argument that this is not simply a zero-sum game: women can gain a fairer shot at the benefits of life if men take up more of its burdens. Part of the project here is to rethink what counts as a benefit and a burden, so that one can convincingly argue (as most feminists want to) that a better arrangement can truly be better for all – including men who are currently in positions of privilege.

My second point is that it is crucially important to note the public consequences of the gendered division of labor that go beyond the issue of rights and equality. *When the gendered division of labor means that women are responsible for care work and men are responsible for making policy, men will not have the knowledge and experience necessary to make good policy.* They will be too ignorant of crucial dimensions of human life to be entrusted with policy making.[44] Even if one were willing to discount women's loss of rights, the public costs of such a division of labor are too high. This is not an essentialist argument about women's nurturing nature and how it would improve politics. It is an argument about the knowledge and experience of caretaking necessary for the judgments involved in good public policy.

If one wants to restructure the gendered hierarchy of power in decision making – whether in politics, health-care research, or corporate management – we will have to transform the gendered patterns of childrearing and household care (which of course also model practices for our children).

Otherwise we will continue to exclude women from positions of power where policy is made: both the many women who find the lack of accommodation to care responsibilities unacceptable and women who are effectively steered from this path by assumptions about their abilities – assumptions sustained by the gendered division of labor. At the same time, we will continue to draw into crucial positions of policy making men who are ignorant about the most basic requirements of sustaining individual and collective well-being.

IV. DELIBERATION ABOUT TRANSFORMING CORE VALUES

Part of the point of constitutionalism as a dialogue of democratic accountability is that the protection of core values necessarily involves the *definition* of core values. They cannot be protected unless we know what they are and how they are defined. Who will do that defining? Surely it cannot just be left to the courts. The dialogue of democratic accountability is thus not just a matter of the best institutional means of determining when governments violate rights. It equally means finding democratically defensible (thus highly inclusive) means of defining – that is contesting, debating, deliberating about – the meaning of core values like equality. These core values must be stable enough, deeply held enough to be able to do the work of

---

[44] Or, one might add, being a judge or participating in the construction of law as a lawyer, or teaching or writing political theory.

holding decision making accountable to them. They must also be open to popular collective deliberation.

When I think about the core values to which I want to hold democratic decision making accountable – the values that should shape the basic structures of relations in society – I think it helps to begin in an expansive mode: what are our aspirations for equality, for a full life, for optimal childrearing? Which of these aspirations should have the normative status of guiding as well as setting limits to public policy backed by the power of the state?

In the context of promoting equality through the transformation of gendered division of labor, I think it is clear that Supreme Courts (or constitutional courts) are not the best place for this deliberation to happen.[45] Indeed, none of the state-based institutions are adequate: neither legislatures nor courts are sufficiently inclusive or flexible to carry out the kinds of conversations I think are necessary to collectively rethink these long-standing, deeply engrained patterns. And many of the solutions cannot be state generated (although as I will note we always have to ask in what ways law shapes practices as well as preferences).

There are many reasons why feminist constitutionalism must help with imagining new forums for deliberation about core values. I will note three important reasons here. The first is what can be called a right to participate in norm creation. This is a core issue one can find echoed around the world. When women are governed by norms – whether based in religion, family practices, workplace structures, or laws – they must have a right to participate in the shaping and transformation of those norms. For some, like Madhavi Sunder, this right becomes the foundational right against which all others, even freedom of religion, must be measured.[46] I see the right to participate in norm creation for all members of society as a central part of constitutionalism as a dialogue of democratic accountability.

In the case of division of household labor, there must be forums for men and women to deliberate both together and apart. The issue, as well as the need for alternative forums, is, of course, shaped by the fact that the relations most centrally involved are highly personal. Not surprisingly, therefore, both the solutions and the modes of deliberation that can lead to them are not conventionally legal – although this does not mean that law plays no role.

The second reason new forums are necessary is that gendered division of household labor is connected to core dimensions of gender identity, thus arousing unconscious passion, fear, anxiety, and anger. Any effort to challenge or change core

---

45 Although it is interesting when they do consider it, as in the *Hugo* case in South Africa. *President of the Republic of South Africa and Another v. Hugo* (CCT11/96) [1997] ZACC 4; 1997 (6) BCLR 708; 1997 (4) SA 1 (18 April 1997). In this case, a male prisoner challenged the constitutionality of a law that permitted all mothers with minor children under the age of twelve to be considered for special remission of their sentence. A majority of the court upheld the law on the basis that it was not unfairly discriminatory.
46 *See* Madvahi Sunder, *Piercing the Veil*, 112 YALE L. J. 1399 (2003).

dimensions of gender identity risks bringing up such feelings. Asking men to take up and women to relinquish control over childcare and other household labor can involve feelings of humiliation, inadequacy, and insecurity. Of course, other issues of equality, like racism or even greater economic equality, can also exacerbate an already highly charged issue. But I think the inevitability of stirring up powerful emotions around gender identity makes particularly acute the need for non-state-centered dialogue and thus imagination about adequate forums.

The third related reason is that changes in the relationships through which household labor is allocated cannot be accomplished without changes in *desire*. Justice arguments alone will not be sufficient – although they will certainly be necessary to motivate change. My argument above about the impact on rights of gendered division of labor is a justice argument. This kind of argument has the advantage that it can use familiar terms like equality, a core value, which can take the form of a constitutional right. I think it is essential that such justice arguments are made in part because the invocation of rights can serve as a background claim or motivation, but justice arguments are not sufficient. Unless men learn to *want* to engage in care work, particularly the care of young children, no restructuring can work. Similarly, women must want to share their responsibility for childcare with men whom they may now see as not fully competent to take up that responsibility. The institutional changes that I will note next are unlikely to be implemented, and will fail even if they are, unless people's desires change.[47]

There is a fundamental problem here: it is hard to change belief and desire without institutional change. And without a change in desire, there is insufficient motivation for institutional change. That is why it is necessary to move on multiple fronts simultaneously.

So what do we need to deliberate about? Here I will suggest first institutions, and then desire.

A. *Institutional Change*

First, it is important to have collective forums in which to think about the institutional changes that could encourage a shift in gendered division of labor, which would provide the kinds of experience that could encourage a shift in desire.

I begin by briefly noting some of the institutional changes that could move things in the right direction. One of the obvious places to look is to the structure of maternity/paternity leave. There are different levels of problems and potential here. At the most basic level there is the question of whether there are legally mandated and publicly funded leaves at least around childbirth, so that women can have good

---

[47] Both men and women will also need to change their affect around the non-childcare dimensions of household labor. Physical caretaking labor has been so demeaned in our culture, that how little of it one does oneself has become a primary indicator of status.

jobs and bear children without undue strain and without putting their jobs at risk. This is vital, but, of course, on its own does nothing to shift the organization of care work. At every stage of analysis, one must distinguish between policies that mitigate the strain and disadvantage that women currently suffer, on the one hand, and policies aimed at transforming the gendered division of labor on the other.

It is sometimes difficult to insist on this transformational agenda when there is still so much lacking in terms of accommodating women's needs – given that they *are* doing the care work. So, for example, in my earlier references to the project being undertaken by a committee of the Law Society of Upper Canada, they saw fit to comment that "[w]hile neither the Law Society nor the profession generally should, nor can, determine the roles women play in their own family relationships, the failure of the profession to adapt to what is not a neutral reality will inevitably affect the quality and competence of the legal services available to the public."[48] My argument here is that it is time for many more forums to take up exactly the question of "the roles women play in their own family relationships."

The next level, then, is to ask whether parental leaves are at least formally equally available to both men and women. Are there financial incentives for women to take them rather than men? For example, in systems like Canada's where maternity-leave benefits are paid (through Employment Insurance) at rates well below those most professionals earn, do employers offer "top ups" to these rates for both men and women? Do employers have family-friendly policies (such as parental leave) on the books, but do nothing to dispel men's sense that taking them would damage their careers?[49] Again, it is important to ask whether all employees, both men and women, think it will hurt their careers to take advantage of policies on the books[50] *and* whether there are gender differences in who actually uses the policies.[51]

---

[48] Law Society of Upper Canada, *supra* note 19.

[49] Hochschild, *supra* note 30.

[50] Of course, not only men perceive taking advantage of leave policies as a risk to their career. As the Catalyst, Beyond a Reasonable Doubt: Creating Opportunities for Better Balance (2005), *available at* www.catalyst.org/file/18/2005%20canadian%20flex%20in%20law%202.pdf shows, four out of five women perceive using family-friendly flexible work arrangements as detrimental to their careers. I offer two additional anecdotes from law graduate students. One who worked for a big law firm asked a male lawyer who had just had a baby with his wife if he would consider taking parental leave; he laughed and said one colleague asked once, and the firm actually said "no" – even though there is a statutory right to take such leaves in the employment standards legislation of every province. A different student told me a partner in the firm she was working for, upon learning she had children, told her he would not have hired her if he had known that.

[51] Countries that offer "parental" leaves to both parents, allowing the parents to decide who should take the leave, implicitly create incentives for women to take more time away from work than men. This results from the benefit schemes providing a percentage of the parent's average salary as a benefit, and because women generally earn less than men, it is economically advantageous for mothers rather than fathers to take advantage of the parental leave. This is true in Canada, where the Employment Insurance Act provides a "parental leave" of thirty-five weeks, which is shared between parents. Quebec's Parental Insurance Plan, on the other hand, offers five weeks of nontransferable benefits to fathers. Sweden and Iceland both offer a paternity leave to be used

In addition to ensuring that there are not disincentives for men to take paternity leave, one could try to construct positive incentives that would actually give men additional benefits for taking the leave. For example, if men take part of the leave, they could be afforded extra time off so that the total paid leave is longer.[52]

We need also to think more creatively about how both men and women can enjoy demanding jobs and time with young children. Full-time leave may be the best response in the first months after a child is born (especially given the demands of recovering from childbirth, nursing, and connection to the child's siblings.) But the intense demands of children under two routinely make enjoying home life and optimal functioning at work extremely difficult under the current arrangements. The 2004–2008 collective agreement for the University of Montreal provided for a reduction in teaching load while there was a child under two in the home.[53] Short of a full shift to a part-time work norm (to which I will return), this seems like an ideal response to the realities of care for young children. Under current arrangements, many women want to return to work (and need to for financial reasons because maternity benefits rarely fully cover a professional salary),

by fathers immediately after the birth of a child, and then a paternity quota, a number of days to be used by fathers within a given period from the time of birth. Uptake rates among men for benefits that are nontransferable are significantly higher than those which are offered as "family benefits" and can be shared between parents. See Katherine Marshall, *Fathers' Use of Paid Parental Leave*, in PERSPECTIVES ON LABOUR AND INCOME (2008) Statistics Canada Catalogue no. 75-001-x, *available at* www.statcan.gc.ca/pub/75-001-x/2008106/pdf/10639-eng.pdf; Peter Moss & Margaret O'Brien eds., *International Review of Leave Policies and Related Research 2006*, in EMPLOYMENT RELATIONS RESEARCH SERIES NO. 57, 43, Online Department of Trade and Industry, London, United Kingdom, www.berr.gov.uk/files/file31948.pdf.

[52] For example, countries such as Sweden and Denmark have experimented with what is sometimes referred to as "daddy days" or "father's quotas" where parental leave includes, within it, not only some days that can be *shared* between parents as they wish, but also the establishment of clear and *nontransferable* days set aside *just* for the mother (mommy days) and *just* for the father (daddy days) (so daddy days/father's quota differ from "paternity leave" because the latter is often used just to refer to *any* days that father uses generally – which could include the portion of parental leave that is open to being shared between parents). *See* ANITA HAATAJA, FATHERS' USE OF PATERNITY AND PARENTAL LEAVE IN THE NORDIC COUNTRIES (The Social Insurance Institution, Research Department, Finland 2009), *available at* http://helda.helsinki.fi/bitstream/handle/10250/8370/FathersLeaves_Nordic.pdf?sequence=1; Linda Haas & C. Philip Hwang, *The Impact of Taking Parental Leave on Fathers' Participation in Childcare and Relationships with Children: Lessons from Sweden*, 11 COMMUNITY, WORK, & FAM. 85 (2008); KATHY O'HARA, COMPARATIVE FAMILY POLICY: EIGHT COUNTRIES' STORIES (Redouf Publishing Co. 1999).

[53] "When back from her maternity leave, the professor, upon request, benefits, with full treatment, from an annual reduction equivalent to one three-credit course out of her teaching assignments, up until the child reaches two years old. The professor must come to a direct understanding with the dean in regard to the modalities of application of her teaching schedule arrangement."

Convention Collective Intervenue entre l'Université de Montréal et le Syndicat Général des Professeurs et Professeures de l'Université de Montréal 2004–2008 AS 6.05.

Au retour du congé de maternité, la professeure, à sa demande, bénéficie avec plein traitement, d'un allègement annuel équivalent à un (1) cours de trois (3) crédits de sa tâche d'enseignement et d'un aménagement de son horaire d'enseignement, jusqu'à ce que l'enfant ait atteint l'âge de deux (2) ans. Elle s'entend avec son directeur sur les modalités d'application de l'aménagement de son horaire d'enseignement.

but would be extremely grateful for a recognition that during this time they have extraordinary demands on their time. Without a reduction in teaching load, those demands will come out of research time with lasting consequences for the assessment of their academic "productivity." Of course, for purposes of restructuring the gendered division of labor, it would be important for men also to receive such reductions, or to share them in the case of both partners working at the university.

Laws or norms requiring large-scale employers or office buildings to provide space for daycare would be another contribution. This would especially be the case if children were as frequently in the daycare at the father's place of employment. One could imagine in a transformed world that the quality of the space would be an important benefit of the job for recruitment purposes. Part of the advantage of such an arrangement would be that it would become the norm to have children around workplaces. That would undercut the idea that children are somehow part of peoples' private lives, entirely separate from the public world of work and policy. It would allow people to take coffee breaks and lunches with their children. (This leaves open the question of who would run and pay for these daycares.)

High-quality childcare is expensive, whether counted in terms of the unpaid labor of parents or family members (who could be spending the time in paid labor) or paid care (despite the extremely low wages paid to workers). North American society seems unwilling to pay that cost. As one small example, the University of Toronto is reducing rather than increasing its support for childcare. The Law Faculty is in the planning process of building a big new building. This is obviously the moment to plan for on-site childcare. But the University has said it will not support that project, and to date the Faculty has not organized a serious demand that it change its mind. There is, of course, a general commitment to women's equality and to children's well-being, but such commitments do not translate into this important practical move. I see this as typical of the current priority accorded to both.

Yet good care arrangements for children are essential to the well-being of everyone in society.[54] A serious commitment to quality care for children is also part of the transformation that is necessary to accomplish a fundamental change in the gendered division of labor. Unless changes are made in the structure of work and the availability of high-quality, flexible institutional childcare, I think it will be impossible to persuade men to take on the existing burdens of the "double shift" – even if the demands of that double shift are cut in half by being shared. The norms of professions foster an ever-increasing workload that is hard to sustain even without family commitments. In tight economic times, everyone is worried about enough paid work. If current work structures and current institutional childcare remain the

---

[54] There are deep moral harms to all those living in a society where the vulnerable, whether children, the poor, the mentally ill, or the elderly, are not well cared for. *See* JENNIFER NEDELSKY, LAW'S RELATIONS: A RELATIONAL THEORY OF SELF, AUTONOMY, AND LAW (Oxford University Press, 2011). Of course, harm to children also brings more tangible costs in term of the kinds of adults they turn out to be.

same, I see it as close to an impossible task to persuade men to add to an already highly stressed life by taking on what will rightly (at least in part) be seen as additional burdens. Justice arguments about women's stress, exhaustion, reduced opportunity, and large-scale societal consequences of inequality will not be enough.

There are both short-term and long-term challenges here, and my intention is not to map out either a strategy or a model of optimal arrangements. All I am trying to do here is to insist upon the urgency of vastly more collective deliberation about these issues, and in aid of that to give some sense of what some of the options and aspirations might be.

As I have indicated, one of the areas that seems urgently in need of rethinking is the structure of work. It seems to me likely that an optimal model would include norms of part-time work.[55] I picture many parents of young children choosing to work twenty to twenty-five hours a week, and to take advantage of some form of paid childcare (say two to four hours a day) on a regular basis. Flexible childcare centers would give children a chance to socialize and be cared for by people with specialized knowledge of early childhood education. It would give parents flexibility in orchestrating their part-time hours of work, and some time each day that was neither paid work nor active childcare.

In the short term, people should be talking about how their workplaces could start to develop patterns of part-time work with good benefits and the same quality of work as found in full-time positions. Both universities and law firms are exceptionally well suited to flexible, part-time work. Yet almost no headway has been made in this area. On the contrary, part-time positions, when available, are seen as second-class positions.[56] At the University of Toronto, like most universities, it is normally not possible to be hired part-time for a tenure-track job.[57] (It is sometimes possible to negotiate a part-time position after one has tenure.)

Another piece of this puzzle is likely to be shifting more and more benefits such as health care and retirement away from an employment base. That would increase employers' incentives to allow part-time work.

A further project would be improvement in ensuring that women receive equal pay for work of equal value. One of the incentives for having women make all career

---

[55] One might expect some variance with respect to the age of the worker. There might be periods of peoples' lives when they have relatively few care-taking obligations and full-time work might be attractive. And there may be variations by field, such that, say mathematicians and physicists – both men and women, of course – might want to work more intensively in the early stages of their careers. Although if competition were not the driving force (given norms of part-time work), I doubt we know whether intensity requires full-time work.

[56] *See, e.g.,* Catalyst, *supra* note 22. This report offers recommendations on how to make law firms more flexible for women. Another report by the same group finds that most women perceive flexible job arrangements as detrimental to their careers, CATALYST, BEYOND A REASONABLE DOUBT: LAWYERS STATE THEIR CASE ON JOB FLEXIBILITY (Catalyst 2006), *available at* www.catalyst.org/file/19/beyondreasdoubtjobflexibility.pdf.

[57] I do know of one notable exception. But only a counteroffer from a highly prestigious American university gave her the bargaining power to negotiate a part-time tenured position.

accommodation is the disparity in the money men and women make. This is also why it is important for employers to provide "top ups" for paternity leave, so that the economic calculus does not always suggest that women should take all of the parental leave.

With all such institutional changes there are a variety of ways of implementing them. People can advocate for voluntary compliance, both governments and advocacy groups can facilitate this by disseminating information about "best practices," and of course, there can be legislative requirements such as those of nondiscrimination and mandatory maternity leave.

Of course, any sustained exploration of institutional change should include an analysis of the efficacy of policies that different countries have used to try to shift the patterns of gendered division of household labor.[58]

B. *Gifts Not Burdens: Transforming Desire*

It is important for many different forums to be discussing the kinds of institutional changes I have suggested here. But, as I have noted, none of these institutional changes can work without a change in attitude, belief, and *desire*. Men need to *want* to take care of their kids. They need to feel the bonding with young children that only hands-on, physical care brings – so that breaking that bond is a physical pain. They need to learn the pleasure of creating a sense of home. Under decent conditions, *these are gifts not burdens. But how do men learn to want them?* (I do return to the question of women's corresponding shift in desire to share responsibility.)

As I have already noted, this problem is acute because we do not now have decent conditions in our structures of work. The prevailing versions of the Universal Breadwinner model do not yield enough leisure to allow these gifts not to become burdens. When home life becomes more and more stressed, kids are unhappy, and

---

[58] See note 52. In addition to parental leave transferability policies aimed at fathers, for example, several countries, including Greece, Sweden, Finland, and Norway, have mandated comparatively high amounts of wage replacements to fathers who take parental leave. *See, e.g.,* Rebecca Ray et al., *Who Cares? Assessing Generosity and Gender Equality in Parental Leave Policy Designs in 21 Countries,* 20 JOURNAL OF EUROPEAN SOCIAL POLICY 206–207 (2010). Furthermore, a right to negotiate a flexible work arrangement, either for a particular reduction of hours set by statute or a mere contractual right to renegotiate the terms of one's employment entirely, for purposes of childcare even *after* the parental leave period has been extended to men as well as women in several countries, including the U.K., Sweden, Norway, Austria, and Portugal. See Ariane Hegeswich, *Flexible Working Policies: A Comparative Review* (Equality and Human Rights Commission (U.K.), Institute for Women's Policy Research, 2009) at 6–8, *available at* www.equalityhumanrights.com/uploaded_files/research/16_flexibleworking.pdf. Few other policies typically cited for this end, such as state-subsidized childcare, however, seem deliberately aimed at encouraging fathers to participate in childrearing. As one scholar has observed, the European policies are increasingly viewed as encouraging "employment," i.e., women's entry into the workforce, rather than gender equality per se. *See* JANE LEWIS, WORK/FAMILY BALANCE, GENDER AND POLICY 12–13 (2009).

it becomes harder and harder to derive pleasure from caring for them.[59] With both parents working, both childcare and home care are often a burden.

But many, probably most, women have learned how to gain pleasure as well as exhaustion from caring for their children and their home. I put it in those terms because I believe that that pleasure (of childcare in particular) is something one can learn. I offer as an anecdote about such learning my own experience with nursing. I found that there was a constant temptation to read or watch TV while nursing. But I learned that if I resisted that temptation and tuned into the experience, it was profoundly pleasurable and satisfying. The pleasure was not just natural or instinctual. It was available, but required a learning and a discipline. Another anecdote was part of my early sense that men had not realized they needed to engage in similar learning. A colleague with a toddler explained that he had learned the joys of books on tape while caring for his child. There was, he said, quite a lot of dead time during the babysitting hours. I was shocked, but silent. I thought he needed to learn the pleasures of attentive interaction instead of ways of coping with the tedium of babysitting.

This was, perhaps, a lost "teachable moment." It is part of a general absence of discussion about norms around childcare. The question of transforming desire is a huge one, and I have only glimmers of ideas about how to educate men about the pleasures of childcare. But I do think that at least two things are necessary. The first is a renewed focus by feminists on the issue of gendered division of household labor, and a focus that includes the pleasures from which so many men are excluded as well as the burdens imposed on women. As I will note in the next section, this means many different forums in which these issues are discussed. Some of these discussions need to be specifically about the rewards and pleasures of childcare and what nurtures and sustains them. In optimal forums, talking about these things will foster the articulation of relevant insights and the ability to share them with men. The second is finding as many ways as possible to give men the practical experience that can, with help, develop an appetite for these pleasures. This involves advocating for institutional change as well as encouraging men – at both the personal and institutional level – to take the opportunities that exist and then helping them learn from them.

Of course, as I noted earlier, women need their own transformation of desire. For many women learning to be comfortable with relinquishing control over the care of their children would be a significant challenge. I think there is some reason to hope that some of the processes of shifting men's desire and increasing their competence would also increase women's willingness to genuinely share childrearing responsibilities with their partners.

My suggestion here is that even if we do not know all of what it would take to transform desire, if we acknowledge that this is a necessary part of the project, then

---

[59] Hochschild, *supra* note 30.

it, too, will become part of the collective deliberation about core values. I would note that the idea of getting people to feel differently about things, to want things they do not now want, may (for some) have a mind control or brainwashing (or just advertising) ring to it. But the idea that affect must be educated is at least as old as Aristotle. For him, one must learn not just to know the good, but to love it.[60]

Finally, while I have focused on childcare in my previous discussion, it is important to note other aspects of household labor. Here I want to advocate for collective deliberation about organizing and allocating this labor in a way that aspires to something more than a better division of labor in the existing desperate efforts to get food on the table and dishes and clothes washed. North American eating habits are widely recognized to be unhealthy (both nutritionally and socially in terms of dinner in front of the TV).[61] Fast food and frozen dinners are the recourse of families who are constantly on the run, trying to manage impossible demands of work and home. The picture of "homemaking," like the very term itself, seems to come from a prefeminist era. The idea that people should try to create a home of beauty, peace, and joy seems like an aspiration suitable only to the middle-class "wife and homemaker" of the 1950s. (And of course, it was part of the early arguments of the second-wave feminists that the mythical homemaker of the 1950s did not live a life of peace, beauty, or joy.)[62] But in thinking about the restructuring of work and the kind of home life that would be conducive to the enjoyment of basic values, we need to think beyond the existing frame of barely coping. And, of course, part of the project is to de-gender the work of "homemaking." This, too, is likely to be an area in which men need to learn a different set of pleasures and women a willingness to relinquish control.

Upping the aspirations for what home life could be would also have implications for the kind of support that social assistance should provide. Many women trying to raise children on their own face even more intractable (although not unrelated) problems than gendered division of household labor.

Finally, I expect that good deliberation about optimal institutional change will reveal very significant differences in people's preferences. Under the current arrangements in academic life – with great flexibility of time, if little real accommodation – women who are serious about their work and their family commitments make very different choices about how much time to spend at the university and what kind of

---

[60] *See* Jennifer Nedelsky, *Embodied Diversity and the Challenges to Law*, 42 McGill L. J. 91 (1997).

[61] The social consensus on this point is reflected in Michelle Obama's "Let's Move" campaign, which among other initiatives, focuses on teaching better eating habits to American children in order to combat childhood obesity. *See, e.g.,* Solving the Problem of Childhood Obesity Within a Generation (White House Task Force on Childhood Obesity, 2010). There is much debate about the precise environmental determinants of healthy eating habits, even among nutritional scientists. See, e.g., Johannes Brug et al., *Environmental Determinants of Healthy Eating: In Need of Theory and Evidence*, 67 Proceedings of the Nutrition Society 307 (2008).

[62] The most famous version of this argument was made in Betty Friedan, The Feminine Mystique (1963).

childcare arrangements to use. It is important to recognize that a single model is not likely to suit everyone. In trying to reimagine work and family structures, it is important to consult people's preferences. But, of course, it does not make sense to simply rely on existing preferences. That has been the heart of my point here. Right now, women are so much more likely than men to know that they want more time with their kids.

C. *Dangers of the Transformative Project*

Before turning to the next section, I want to close by noting four kinds of dangers that I think lurk in the kind of project I am proposing. First is one I have already mentioned: there will be a constant temptation to skew efforts toward accommodating women who currently bear the burden of care work rather than focusing on shifting gender norms of who does this care work. Accommodation is important, but for the purposes of the kind of collective deliberation I am advocating I think keeping the focus on transformation is crucial. When it gets to the point of choosing which institutional change to push for, there may be times when there is a tension between accommodation and transformation. As a general rule of thumb, I would opt for transformation. It is ultimately essential to values not just of justice but of a decent society, good foundations for children's development, and a healthy, more balanced life for everyone.

The second danger is that in the absence of changes in men's desire, efforts at transformation may backfire. For example, I have increasingly heard anecdotal evidence that in the academic world men take advantage of the now gender-neutral parental leave to hire a nanny and use the time off from teaching to get ahead on their research agenda.[63] The report from the committee for the American Political Science Association mentions this problem, suggesting that it is widespread. While the anecdotes spread, to my knowledge there has been no public conversation about this problem at the University of Toronto. This is just the kind of thing that seems awkward to talk about, but should be part of the diverse forums of conversation about core values and their implementation.

Third, it is important to recognize that while individual couples manage to shift the gendered division of labor, they cannot redress the wider problem of the structure of work. Brooke Ackerly's remarks attest to this beautifully:

> The habits of my daily life and discourse enact patriarchal norms. For example my husband takes our daughters to do our grocery shopping Saturday mornings so that I can work. Though the gender roles are reversed (the man doing the caregiving, the

---

[63] Presumably some women do this, too. Indeed I heard a distressing story that a junior colleague was advised by a senior male colleague that this is exactly what she should do after the birth of her second child. He was concerned that her publication record was not what it should be and this seemed a way for her to move it forward. He told her of a successful female colleague who had done this.

woman working), the roles of child care and shopping are linked in a traditionally gendered way. Similarly, when a friend comments that her family has a similar inversion of traditional gender roles – she with a primary breadwinning income, her husband with a job that lets him be the primary caregiver – she is reifying a conventional way of understanding of income-earning work and caregiving work. Certainly, we wouldn't say that by our daily practices we were violating the human rights of a woman on the phone with a domestic violence shelter trying to decide if she should leave her husband, go to a shelter, and begin a long process of education and training that might lead her to be able to earn a family-sustaining wage. But neither does our working within these roles (reversed as they may be) help us as a society to consider why we organize work and care such that "work" requires seventeen-hour days and weekends and "care" means going shopping. Why aren't I at the park with my children while my husband shops? Why are there kinds of work ("breadwinning" jobs) that require someone else to care for children, shop for groceries, or the worker's double shift to do these things? If work and care were differently organized – with the hours required for success more closely matched with the number of hours that it is reasonable for a child to be in institutionalized care – the woman on the phone with the domestic violence hotline would be facing a different decision. Even if the abusive patterns in which abusers discourage their spouses from furthering their education or from having jobs that enable their economic independence remained the same, the context of her decision would be different if work and care were not as opposed as they are in the US economy.[64]

One might say this is the opposite of the second danger. There, institutional change was thwarted by absence of change of desire. Here there is the hoped-for desire, but it is limited by the absence of institutional change. Both things are necessary, both will be mutually supporting or undermining, and both need to be tackled simultaneously, even though each seems to require the other.

The last danger to attend to is that in thinking about any new structures, one must always be aware of the difficult challenge of avoiding rewarding those (male or female) who consistently give paid work preference over family. Obviously existing norms will make employers think that it is in their interest to do so.

V. FORUMS FOR DELIBERATION

I turn now to the issue of new forums for deliberating about these issues, forums that are likely to promote open inquiry and creative solutions.[65] Remember that I began with the idea that legal rights are means of structuring the relations that allow values such as equality to be experienced in people's lives. And that I argued that neither rights nor values can be protected without defining them, which bring us to

[64] BROOKE ACKERLY, UNIVERSAL HUMAN RIGHTS IN A WORLD OF DIFFERENCE 15–16 (Cambridge University Press 2008) (footnotes omitted).
[65] *See* MONA HARRINGTON, CARE AND EQUALITY: INVENTING A NEW FAMILY POLITICS 176–188 (Routledge, 2000) for a related discussion.

the question of who does the defining and how. Although I want to hold the link between rights and values before you, I think we need to step away from courts and legal language in thinking about the best forums for deliberating about the values at stake in the gendered division of household labor. Here I think we need to turn directly to the relationships at stake, and not always turn to the way the state promotes them.

A. *Requirements for the Forums*

The question then becomes, What kinds of forums can respond to the issue of desire (as well as shame, humiliation, identity)? Where can men and women talk about the joys, responsibilities, and demands of caretaking? Where can they talk about the justice issues, the implications for rights, and the gifts that men miss out on, the gifts that all too quickly become burdens under unfavorable institutional arrangements? What are good forums for talking about the way almost everyone becomes implicated in injustice (from using underpaid childcare workers often far from home to tacitly reinforcing patriarchal norms) in our childcare arrangements? Where can we begin to publicly acknowledge the ways that injustice weighs on us and our children?[66] In sum, how and where can we talk about the ways that we in the post-industrial world have collectively arrived at a situation where our children often do not get the care and attention they need and want, where women are exhausted and anxious, where men exclude themselves from some of the best parts of human life, and where we routinely rely on unjust relationships to patch together a way of coping?

As I noted earlier, there also need to be forums in which to talk about how the skills of care are learned, not genetic or even the automatic consequences of motherhood. For example, how does one learn to enjoy, to be fully engaged by very young children, not just babysit? There are skills like learning to direct your attention to the child, to avoid rather than seek out distractions of radio or television.

Optimal forms of deliberation will allow people to see the intersection of justice, personal relations, core values, and deep satisfaction in life. There is reason to be optimistic that the very process of such conversations can help people to see that both preferences and perceptions of interest can shift.

Optimal forums will also take an expansive view of the role of caretaking in life. I assume there will be those who do not want to bear children. But many of them would still value intimate connections with children. Part of what needs to be discussed is creative new arrangements so that you don't have to "have" a child to have an intimate relationship with one. One might make a similar argument

---

[66] For a discussion of the low wages for both in-home caregivers and institutional care providers, *see supra* note 9. *See also* Jennifer Nedelsky, *Dilemmas of Passion, Privilege, and Isolation, in* MOTHER TROUBLES: RETHINKING CONTEMPORARY MATERNAL DILEMMAS 304 (Julia Hanigsberg & Sara Ruddick eds., Beacon Press 1999).

about relations with the elderly. Deliberation on caretaking should at least be open to the claim that the presumption of all forms of policy (of course, in particular the structure of the workplace) should presume that everyone will have caregiving and homemaking responsibilities for large parts of their life. Caregiving could be to lovers, friends, parents, relatives, and neighbors as well as children.

B. *Where Can We Find or Create These New Forums of Public Deliberation?*

Here I am just going to give some brief suggestions. My main point is that the conversations should be happening everywhere. The current absence seems to me to be an odd (and depressing) endurance of the public–private distinction that feminists have so thoroughly critiqued in theory and yet collaborated with in practice. It is as though our old hostile "allies" of the 1960s and 1970s have won out in tacitly persuading us that these matters are trivial and private. They are far too rarely incorporated in our teaching and our scholarship. They are far too rarely raised at faculty meetings. Rumors of abuse of parental leave by male colleagues are whispered about in the hallways, but not brought forward for public conversation. The lack of daycare at universities is bemoaned, but daycare is not demanded.

Part of the problem is that given the demands of contemporary work life together with the fact that women still bear the primary responsibility for household labor, women have little time or energy to take on additional battles for transformation of their workplaces. Perhaps the same is true for their home life.

A further contributing factor to be overcome is what I believe is a hesitation, at least among the female academics I know, to reveal how hard they find coping with these problems is. We learn to project confidence, to present ourselves as competent and successful. Talking about how fragile our coping mechanisms seem to be, or our distress over participating in systems of global injustice in the nannies we hire, or even our unhappiness about the distribution of labor in our personal relationships does not seem to promote the right image. Good deliberation about alternatives will require openness about existing difficulties. My purpose is to call for that openness.

To be more concrete, one of the places I think this should happen is in classrooms. There are thousands of university courses about justice. How many of them take up the gendered division of labor and its consequences? Feminists should make sure that their courses do. I made it the organizing theme of a course on "Can There Be Universal Human Rights," with participants from the law faculties of University of Toronto, Ateneo University in the Philippines, the Centre of Human Rights in South Africa, and Vanderbilt University in Tennessee in the United States. I think it facilitated a more open exchange about differing views of human rights than in previous versions of the course. Of course, classroom discussions of global justice and immigration often include the dilemmas of live-in caregiver programs and other forms of female migration for care purposes.[67] But how many of them situate the problem in the context of the overarching issue of gendered division of labor, which defines both the demand and the supply? How would the situation change in the face of the kinds of changes I have proposed here? Most of the discussions I have seen take the need for the labor in the receiving countries as a given. If the gendered division of labor (and the structure of work) were itself a central focus, might not different solutions arise for both sending and receiving countries?

The general point here is to bring these issues into the classroom as legitimate parts of studies of justice and policy. Classrooms (I think this would work at high school and grade school levels as well) would then become one of the forums in which people could talk about the core values at stake. Parent organizations could bring in suggestions and materials for teachers. Indeed, they could make it a topic of conversation in their own meetings.

Workshops, lunches, and retreats should be organized at corporations, perhaps beginning with those who have family-friendly policies on the books. Perhaps the Justicia project of the Law Society of Upper Canada can serve as a model of a starting point. Part of their "pitch" was that it is very costly for law firms to recruit and train highly talented young women and then lose them because they cannot tolerate the work regime's hostility to family (or more generally balanced) life. While, as I noted, their focus is accommodation to the needs of women rather than transformation of the gendered nature of household labor, they do bring up these issues. As long as one is alert to the distinction between accommodation and transformation, one can start to raise the issue of the costs of structures of work that are incompatible with active engagement with family life.

Places of spiritual connection, churches, synagogues, mosques, temples, sacred circles, are other forums that should be encouraged to take up the issue. In my view it is easy to see that a human structure of work and a fair organization of caregiving and household work are crucial to a just and spiritually fulfilling life. Politicians at every level who might be sympathetic should be asked to organize "town halls" to talk about these issues. At the international level, Oxfam Canada organized an "asset audit" in Ethiopia that helped communities recognize the range of contributions of members of their communities, including women's unpaid labor.[68]

---

[67] Citizenship and Immigration Canada, *Working Temporarily in Canada: The Live-In Caregiver Program, available at* www.cic.gc.ca/english/work/caregiver/index.asp; for debate about the Live-In Caregiver Program *see, e.g.,* Tami Friesen, *The Live-in Caregiver Program: Inequality under Canada's Immigration System,* 22 JURISFEMME 8 (2003); Patricia Daenzer, *An Affair between Nations: International Relations and the Movement of Household Service Workers, in* NOT ONE OF THE FAMILY: DOMESTIC WORKERS IN CANADA 81 (Abigail Bakan & Daiva Stasiulis eds., University of Toronto Press 1997); Abigail Bakan & Daiva Stasiulis, *Foreign Domestic Worker Policy in Canada and the Social Boundaries of Modern Citizenship, in* Bakan & Stasiulis eds., *id.* at 3.

[68] In a report I received in hard copy (and no longer have) from Oxfam Canada, this asset audit highlighted the way in which it brought women's contributions to light. This was consistent with Oxfam Canada's important decision to give priority to women in their fight against poverty. However,

In short, as I said, these conversations should be going on everywhere. And, as I argue in my last section, they should be seen as integral to a thriving constitutionalism.

I see my argument here as a call – backed by the language of rights and constitutionalism, but really more foundational than that – to take seriously the adage of the 1970s: the personal is political.[69] Both men and women should stop being shy or embarrassed about raising this issue in every public forum available to them.

VI. WHY ALL THIS IS A MATTER OF CONSTITUTIONALISM

The first, and most important, part of the answer is the point I have already made: for a flourishing form of constitutionalism the values invoked in legal arguments must be deeply embedded in the society whose institutions are held accountable to those values. The kind of deliberation I am calling for here is one of the best ways of ensuring this and, at the same time ensuring that the precise content of those values is arrived at through broad-based public deliberation rather than the reflection of legal elites alone. When one sees rights as implementing core values, both the meaning of the values and the rights should, in a society committed to democracy as well as rights, be widely understood and discussed.

The second answer is that the core values articulated and implemented through legal forms of constitutionalism should guide the structures of relations at every level

you will see in the quote from their website that women's contribution now appears in the context of "even grandmothers":

> Instead of focusing on a community's weaknesses, Oxfam, in close collaboration with the Coady International Institute and three local Ethiopian nongovernmental organizations (NGOs), is helping communities identify and build on their assets and capacities – what they know, what they do, the resources they can tap.
>
> The process starts with a detailed mapping of the community and its environment engaging the whole community in drawing up an inventory of its assets. They list everything from their labor to the stones that line the seasonal streambed, their livestock, their water source, even the grandmother who teaches young girls to sew.

Ethiopia: The Road to Self Reliance – ABCD, OXFAM CANADA (May 17, 2010), www.oxfam.ca/what-we-do/where-we-work/horn-of-africa/ethiopia-the-road-to-self-reliance-abcd/?searchterm=asset.
  See also the serious reflection on these issues in Caroline Sweetman, *Feminist Economics*, in FROM POVERTY TO POWER: HOW ACTIVE CITIZENS AND EFFECTIVE STATES CAN CHANGE THE WORLD (Oxfam International 2008), *available* at www.oxfam.org.uk/resources/downloads/FP2P/FP2P_Feminist_Economics_BP_ENGLISH.pdf.
[69] I think part of the problem at that time was that white, middle-class feminists made the mistake of thinking "my personal is the political." But I think there is reason to be optimistic – feminists have learned better by now. Rooting one's activism in personal experience is a good thing as long as one is alert to issues of privilege. In my own view, as I noted earlier, one of the worst things about current arrangements for relatively privileged women is that we become complicit in injustice when we make our childcare arrangements. The sort of conversations I have in mind would help make that obvious.

of society. Part of the reason for this (in addition to the first reason) is that the issue of the gendered division of household labor reveals that if there is an important set of relations (such as that governing division of labor between intimate partners) that is inconsistent with core values, those values will be undermined.

This understanding of the function and articulation of core values means that all the institutions responsible for the kinds of conversations and policies I suggested earlier should begin to think of themselves as accountable to the core values of constitutionalism. This does not mean, of course, that employers, churches, or families would be subject to Charter challenges (in the Canadian context). In many contexts they would not even be subject to complaints under human rights legislation – although I think people should use the previous arguments to think expansively about the meaning of family status as a prohibited ground of discrimination.

For optimal forms of constitutionalism – feminist constitutionalism – accountability to core values needs to be understood not just in formal legal terms, but in terms of norms of collective self-reflection as well as norms that guide policy.

It is important for schools, corporations, universities, and even places of worship to reflect on the links between their own norms and values and the basic norm of equality. They need then, in turn, to think about the relation between equality and gendered division of household labor that I have pointed to here. For example, the question of on-site childcare would, then, sound not in the language of convenience, support, or even accommodation, but of rights and equality.[70] The failure to take it seriously would be a failure with respect to equality.

At the level of personal relationship, at the risk of encouraging unhelpful self-righteousness, I think it is important to make these same links. Personal practices of gendered division of household labor enact and sustain injustice. Personal "preference" must be reflected on in this context.

One might then ask, Is there no private realm that is immune from the intrusion of collective values? My answer is that there is no domain that should be immune to normative reflection and the potential for normative challenge. I am not envisioning neighborhood Maoist self-criticism sessions, but I am envisioning deep norms of collective and individual reflection about how the structures of people's lives reflect or diverge from their own deepest values. What I do not envision is consensus on the answers.

---

[70] Of course, there might be counterarguments about the best policies governing the location of childcare facilities. One might argue, for example, that parents should have options between locations at the workplace and neighborhood locations near their homes. Perhaps every public school should be equipped with space for flexible childcare, so that everyone (in urban environments) would have such a facility in walking distance from their home. What matters is that the debate is grounded in reflection on what optimal childcare would look like from the perspective of the interests of both children and parents – in the context of rights and equality.

CONCLUSION

In sum, there should be multiple forms of challenging institutions, employment practices, and norms to be consistent with deep values like equality. Some challenges will be informal, some will make institutional demands, some will call for new legislation and regulation, and some will ask for judicial review. An ethos of feminist constitutionalism will involve all of these levels.

The deeper meaning of constitutionalism as accountability to core values reminds us of the importance of multiple, widely accessible locations for deliberation about values and their implementation. More conventional notions of constitutional values remain engaged, for we are reminded that (uncontested) rights can only be realized through public contestation and deliberation about conventionally private and trivial patterns of relationship. Retaining a link to the language of rights is important: the claim for the necessity of restructuring the gendered division of labor if women's *rights* are to be given meaningful effect provides a legitimacy to bring these issues to the forefront of public attention.

Feminist constitutionalism brings together rights, values, and participation in norm creation to give a sense of urgency about finding ways to reflect on what our core values really are and to hold ourselves and our institutions to account.

2

Feminist Fundamentalism and the Constitutionalization of Marriage

Mary Anne Case

For several years now, I have sought to vindicate what I call feminist fundamentalism, which I define as an uncompromising commitment to the equality of the sexes as intense and at least as worthy of respect as, for example, a religiously or culturally based commitment to female subordination or fixed sex roles.[1] As I have argued, both individuals and nation-states can have feminist fundamentalist commitments that, like the religious commitments to which they can fruitfully be analogized, may differ somewhat in content as well as in character. Although all feminists repudiate female subordination, for example, some may seek equality in separate spheres, whereas others insist instead that "fixed notions concerning the roles and abilities of males and females"[2] are anathema.[3] Although, in the late twentieth century, feminist fundamentalist commitments of the latter kind were central to the constitutionalization of the law of marriage in the United States and elsewhere, more recent disputes at the intersection of constitutional and family law in Western constitutional democracies have foregrounded other concerns, including sexual orientation nondiscrimination, religious liberty, and respect for cultural diversity.

In this chapter, I analyze what a feminist fundamentalist perspective might bring to one of these ongoing disputes, the question of whether same-sex couples have a constitutional right to marry. Taking the bulk of my examples from state

---

[1] See, e.g., Mary Anne Case, *Feminist Fundamentalism and Constitutional Citizenship*, in Dimensions of Women's Equal Citizenship 107 (Joanna Grossman & Linda McClain eds., 2009); Mary Anne Case, *Feminist Fundamentalism on the Frontier between Government and Family Responsibility for Children*, 2009 Utah L. Rev. 381; and Mary Anne Case, *What Feminists Have to Lose in Same-Sex Marriage Litigation*, 57 UCLA L. Rev. 1199 (2010) (containing an expanded version of the argument of this chapter).

[2] *Miss. Univ. for Women v. Hogan*, 458 U.S. 718, 725 (1982).

[3] The repudiation of such stereotyped notions as a basis for law has become the orthodox view of constitutional sex equality guarantees under the U.S. Constitution since the 1970s. See Mary Anne Case, *'The Very Stereotype the Law Condemns': Constitutional Sex Discrimination Law as a Quest for Perfect Proxies*, 85 Cornell L. Rev. 1447 (2000) [hereinafter Case, *The Very Stereotype*].

constitutional cases in the United States, I shall argue that the growing trend toward rejection of a constitutional prohibition on sex discrimination as one basis for invalidating restrictions on same-sex marriage has broader adverse consequences for the sexual liberty and equality of all individuals, particularly but not exclusively for heterosexual women from a feminist perspective.

As I explain – in part because an explicitly feminist perspective has been underrepresented and undervalued in the same-sex marriage debates – heterosexual feminist couples, including but not limited to those who resist marriage from a feminist perspective, are among the losers in recent U.S. state constitutional decisions concerning same-sex couples. They lose whether they live in a state such as New York, whose legislature authorized same-sex marriage only after its high court held it to be constitutionally permissible for marriage to be reserved for heterosexuals so as to inculcate traditional sex roles;[4] or a state like California, whose pre-Proposition 8[5] state supreme court decision opening marriage to all went out of its way to reject the claim that sex discrimination was at issue in the state's prior exclusion of same-sex couples;[6] even, perhaps especially, if they live in states that have vindicated the claims of gay and lesbian couples for recognition of their relationships under another name, but have allowed marriage to be (p)reserved – or at least the name of "marriage" to be (p)reserved – for heterosexual couples "'because of,' not merely 'in spite of,'"[7] its traditions. The traditions of marriage, including its legal traditions, are anything but free of "fixed notions concerning the roles and abilities of males and females," and also anything but free of female subordination.

This is not to say that civil marriage today need be a prisoner of its restrictive and subordinating traditions. Only that because of its traditions, explicitly continuing to limit marriage to male–female couples, the law so imprisons it and the couples who enter it.[8] To grant civil marriage licenses to couples regardless of their sex would be

---

4 *Hernandez v. Robles*, 7 N.Y.3d 338, 349 (2006).

5 Proposition 8 is the ballot designation for the state constitutional amendment, passed by referendum of California voters in November 2008, adding to the California Constitution the provision "Only marriage between a man and a woman is valid or recognized in California." The passage of Proposition 8 overturned that portion of the California Supreme Court's earlier ruling opening marriage in California to same-sex couples.

6 *In re* Marriage Cases, 43 Cal. 4th 757, 837 (2008). Even if it had wanted to make clear that heightened scrutiny for sexual orientation, rather than sex discrimination or substantive due process, was the basis for its decision in the Marriage Cases, the California Supreme Court majority could have done as the Iowa or the Connecticut Supreme Court did, and simply declined to reach the sex discrimination claim, instead of gratuitously rejecting it.

7 *But cf.* Mass. v. Feeney, 442 U.S. 256, 279 (1979) (requiring discriminatory intent as well as disparate impact for claims of violation of equal protection on grounds of sex).

8 As I have been arguing since 1993, but for the lingering cloud of repressive history hanging over marriage, it would be clear that marriage today provides far more license, and has the potential to be far more flexible, liberatory, and egalitarian than most available alternatives, such as most existing domestic partnership schemes or ascriptive schemes; see Mary Anne Case, *Couples and Coupling in the Public Sphere: A Comment on the Legal History of Litigating for Lesbian and Gay Rights*, 79 VA. L. REV. 1643 (1993); Mary Anne Case, *Marriage Licenses*, 89 MINN. L. REV. 1758 (2005).

to eliminate the last vestige of sex stereotyping from the law of marriage. As feminist theorists have insisted for decades,[9] this would have benefits, not only for gay and lesbian couples, but for all who value liberty and equality on the basis of sex. It would help complete a process of evolution away from sex-role differentiated, in-egalitarian marriage law that began with nineteenth-century efforts to ameliorate the effects of coverture and continued in legislative reform and constitutional adjudication in the United States through the last third of the twentieth century.

HOW SEX EQUALITY JURISPRUDENCE TRANSFORMED MARRIAGE UNDER U.S. LAW

Ruth Bader Ginsburg, now a Justice of the U.S. Supreme Court, was, while a litigator for the American Civil Liberties Union (ACLU) Women's Rights Project, influential in the development of the U.S. constitutional law of equal protection on grounds of sex. Many of her path-breaking cases were brought on behalf of married couples, which enabled her to demonstrate that the law's reliance on sex-role stereotyping and presumptions of female subordination in marriage hurt both men and women.[10] Consider, for example, *Frontiero et Vir v. Richardson*,[11] in which Justices of the Supreme Court first articulated the now orthodox view that laws based on sex stereotypes are constitutionally impermissible. The case's very caption is the first indicator that sex stereotypes will be shattered: *Frontiero et Vir* (Frontiero and[her]Man) is a twist on the more conventional addition of *et ux* (and wife) after a plaintiff's name. The caption indicates that instead of the stereotypical wage-earning husband with a dependent wife, this case was brought by a wage-earning wife, one in the unstereotypical job of lieutenant in the United States Air Force, seeking benefits including housing and medical insurance for her husband.

In *Frontiero*, the Justices acknowledged the central historical role the law of marriage had played in the subordination of women. Taking their language almost verbatim from Ginsburg's briefs, they observed that:

> throughout much of the 19th century the position of women in our society was, in many respects, comparable to that of blacks under the pre–Civil War slave codes. Neither slaves nor women could hold office, serve on juries, or bring suit in their own names, and married women traditionally were denied the legal capacity to hold or convey property or to serve as legal guardians of their own children.[12]

---

[9] *See, e.g.,* Sylvia Law, *Homosexuality and the Social Meaning of Gender*, 1988 Wisc. L. Rev. 187.

[10] She may have been influenced by her own marriage to Martin Ginsburg, by all accounts a true partnership, in which they jointly decided on a career in law, broke with stereotypes in their division of household tasks (he did the cooking, for example), and cooperated on the early *Moritz* case, at the intersection of his specialty and hers – tax law and sex discrimination. *See, e.g.,* Fred Strebeigh, Equal: Women Reshape American Law 12–13, 24–25 (2009).

[11] *Frontiero et Vir v. Richardson*, 411 U.S. 677 (1973).

[12] *Id.* at 684–85. *Compare, e.g.,* Brief for Appellant at *28, Reed v. Reed, 404 U.S. 71 (1971) (No. 70–4), 1970 U.S. Briefs 4; 1970 U.S. S. Ct. Briefs LEXIS 5.

Indeed, in nineteenth-century America, as in Ancient Rome, slavery, like marriage, was one of the domestic relations; and the law of marriage, like that of slavery, was premised not only on role differentiation, but on hierarchy: wives were subordinate to husbands as slaves were to masters. On the widely influential view of marriage set forth in *Blackstone's Commentaries*,[13] a marriage license could be seen to function in ways loosely analogous to a modern dog license, as something like a certificate of ownership of the wife; entitling the husband to her property, her body and its products, including the labor she engaged in for wages and the labor that produced offspring; obliging him to provide for her care and feeding; giving him a cause of action against those who injured her or his interest in her; making him responsible for her actions and giving him the right to control her. She did not have the same rights over and duties to him, although she was obliged to provide him domestic services and sexual access, and to share his residence. Just as dog licenses require that the animal wear a collar and tag with its owner's name, so, as late as the 1970s, many U.S. states required by law that a wife take her husband's name; she also customarily always wore a wedding ring. A husband did not ordinarily take his wife's name, or indicate his marital status in his name or title in any way; nor, in much of U.S. society for long periods of history, did husbands tend to wear wedding rings. This asymmetry of roles, duties, and privileges in the law of marriage, although on the decline since at least the passage of the first Married Women's Property Acts in the mid-nineteenth century, remained very much a part of the legal landscape at the time of *Frontiero*.[14]

It was also central to the early, now thoroughly discredited U.S. constitutional law of sex discrimination, even when the issues in a case were on their face far removed from marriage. Thus, infamously, Justice Bradley, concurring in the denial of a right to practice law to women generally, focused on petitioner Myra Bradwell's status as a married woman:

The constitution of the family organization, which is founded in the divine ordinance, as well as in the nature of things, indicates the domestic sphere as that which properly belongs to the domain and functions of womanhood. The harmony, not to say identity, of interests and views which belong, or should belong, to the family institution is repugnant to the idea of a woman adopting a distinct and independent career from that of her husband. So firmly fixed was this sentiment in the founders of the common law that it became a maxim of that system of jurisprudence that a woman had no legal existence separate from her husband, who was regarded as her head and representative in the social state; and, notwithstanding some recent modifications of this civil status, many of the special rules of law flowing from and

[13] WILLIAM BLACKSTONE, *Of Husband and Wife, in* COMMENTARIES ON THE LAW OF ENGLAND 333 (Wayne Morrison ed., Cavendish Publishing Ltd. 2001).
[14] *See* Mary Anne Case, *Marriage Licenses*, 89 MINN. L. REV. 1758, 1767–68 (2005). For an analysis of similarities in attitudes toward pets, slaves, and wives, see Mary Anne Case, *Pets or Meat*, 80 CHI.-KENT L. REV. 1129, 1132 (2005).

dependent upon this cardinal principle still exist in full force in most States. One
of these is, that a married woman is incapable, without her husband's consent,
of making contracts which shall be binding on her or him. This very incapacity
was one circumstance which the Supreme Court of Illinois deemed important in
rendering a married woman incompetent fully to perform the duties and trusts that
belong to the office of an attorney.

It is true that many women are unmarried and not affected by any of the duties,
complications, and incapacities arising out of the married state, but these are
exceptions to the general rule. The paramount destiny and mission of woman are
to fulfil the noble and benign offices of wife and mother. This is the law of the
Creator. And the rules of civil society must be adapted to the general constitution
of things, and cannot be based upon exceptional cases.[15]

In *Frontiero*, husband and wife had a shared fate and a common interest, so as to
make it difficult to disentangle whose rights were at issue. Similarly, in another of
Ginsburg's Supreme Court victories as an advocate, *Weinberger v. Wiesenfeld*, to
deny survivor's benefits to widower Wiesenfeld would have discriminated against
both his deceased wife as wage earner and him as surviving caregiver to their child.[16]
The net effect of such cases was to dismantle, as a matter of constitutional law, legally
(r)e(i)nforced sex-role differentiation in marriage. Couples were still free to have a
role-differentiated marriage, but no longer could the law require or even assume
that breadwinners were male and homemakers female.

Shortly after deciding *Wiesenfeld*, the U.S. Supreme Court extended its prohibition of legal reinforcement of sex-role stereotypes to a case involving, not spouses,
but children being prepared for their adult roles. In the *Stanton* case, it held that, for
the following reason, it would be unconstitutional for the state to require a divorced
father to support his son until age twenty-one, but his daughter only until age eighteen: "No longer is the female destined solely for the home and the rearing of the
family, and only the male for the marketplace and the world of ideas. . . . [B]ringing
her education to an end earlier coincides with the role-typing society has long
imposed."[17]

While *Stanton* focused on preparing women as well as men for a role in the
marketplace, *Hibbs*, written by Chief Justice Rehnquist as if he were channeling his
colleague Justice Ginsburg, put the prophylactic power of Section 5 of the Fourteenth Amendment behind the Family and Medical Leave Act, which facilitated a
role for men as well as women in the care work of the home.[18]

Years earlier, Rehnquist had opposed the Equal Rights Amendment (ERA) on
the grounds that its supporters evinced "overtones of dislike and distaste for the
traditional difference between men and women in the family unit, and in some cases

[15] *Bradwell v. State*, 83 U.S. 130, 141–42 (1873).
[16] *Weinberger v. Wiesenfeld*, 420 U.S. 636 (1975).
[17] *Stanton v. Stanton*, 421 U.S. 7, 14–15 (1975).
[18] *Nevada Dept. of Human Resources v. Hibbs*, 538 U.S. 721 (2003).

very probably a complete rejection of the woman's traditionally different role in this regard."[19] Other opponents of the ERA, such as Paul Freund, had expressed fear that it would lead perforce to invalidation of "laws outlawing wedlock between members of the same sex."[20] Although the ERA never did pass, in the end Rehnquist himself put the capstone on a constitutional jurisprudence that nevertheless amounted to a virtually "complete rejection" of laws reinforcing "the traditional difference between men and women in the family unit." As of the date of *Hibbs*, bans on same-sex marriage were virtually all that was left in the law of "the traditional difference between men and women in the family unit." Unfortunately, as the remainder of this chapter will discuss, the fight to eliminate such bans has led to as much retrogression as progress in the fight to eliminate from the law in the United States "fixed notions concerning the roles and abilities of males and females."

SEX DISCRIMINATION CLAIMS AND SAME-SEX MARRIAGE IN THE 1970S

The first same-sex couple whose quest for a marriage license reached the U.S. Supreme Court, Jack Baker and Michael McConnell, did include in their case a claim of sex discrimination, together with a multiplicity of other claims. However, Baker and McConnell's legal challenge to the sex distinctions in marriage laws began in 1970, before the U.S. Supreme Court had held *any* sex-respecting rule to be constitutionally problematic, and their appeal was dismissed by the U.S. Supreme Court "for want of a substantial federal question" in 1972, before the now well-established doctrinal structure governing claims of denial of equal protection on grounds of sex was put in place.[21] Rather than being able to strengthen their claim by invoking a line of other successful constitutional challenges to sex discrimination in the law of marriage, therefore, Baker and McConnell could only draw an analogy to *Loving v. Virginia*,[22] the then recently decided case striking down bans on interracial marriage. However, the Minnesota Supreme Court held that "in commonsense and in a constitutional sense, there is a clear distinction between a marital restriction based merely upon race and one based upon the fundamental difference in sex."[23] According to the Minnesota Supreme Court,

> The institution of marriage as a union of man and woman, uniquely involving the procreation and rearing of children within a family, is as old as the book of Genesis.... This historic institution manifestly is more deeply founded than

[19] William Hubbs Rehnquist, *Rehnquist: ERA Would Threaten Family Unit*, LEGAL TIMES, Sept. 15, 1986, at 4.

[20] 118 CONG. REC. 9096–97 (1972) (testimony of Professor Paul Freud against the ERA).

[21] The first U.S. Supreme Court case invalidating any sex discrimination in the law was *Reed v. Reed*, 404 U.S. 71 (1971). There is now a well-established doctrinal structure governing claims of denial of equal protection on grounds of sex; *see* Case, *The Very Stereotype*, *supra* note 3.

[22] *Loving v. Virginia*, 388 U.S. 1 (1967).

[23] *Baker v. Nelson*, 191 N.W.2d 185, 187 (Minn. 1971), appeal dismissed, 409 U.S. 810 (1972).

the asserted contemporary concept of marriage and societal interests for which
petitioners contend. The due process clause of the Fourteenth Amendment is not
a charter for restructuring it by judicial legislation.[24]

In their jurisdictional statement to the U.S. Supreme Court, Baker and McConnell
note that "they were asked orally at the time of application which was to be the
bride and which was to be the groom ... [although] the forms for application for
a marriage license did not inquire as to the sex of the applicants"[25] and although
they "were not questioned as to which physical sex classification they belonged."[26]
The clerk did ask, however, "Where is the female in this marriage?"[27] and a reporter
waiting outside the county clerk's office insisted on knowing "'Who's going to be
the wife.' ... 'We don't play those kind of roles' came the reply."[28] It is important to
remember that in 1970, the reporter's question could be far more than a facetious
putdown or an inquiry into potential effeminacy. Which one would be the wife
had serious legal consequences at a time when legally enforced sex-role differentiation in marriage was firmly entrenched in law and not yet seen as constitutionally
problematic.[29]

   After all, the wife was the one to whose household services the husband was
entitled, such that her loss, not necessarily his, gave rise to a claim for loss of
consortium by the survivor; the process by which state courts and legislatures made
consortium claims reciprocal was still underway in 1970.[30] The wife was the one
presumed to be dependent, and who as a result could be eligible and make her
husband eligible for benefits; not until *Frontiero* in 1973 did the U.S. Supreme
Court begin to dismantle on constitutional grounds the asymmetry in law between
what a wife was entitled to on account of her husband and what a husband was
entitled to on account of his wife.[31] The wife was the one the husband was obligated
to support during marriage and who could be entitled to alimony on divorce; not
until *Orr v. Orr* in 1979 did the Supreme Court insist that husbands be eligible for
alimony equally with wives.[32] The wife was also the one whose share of jointly owned
property could be disposed of by her husband as "head and master" of the marital
community without her knowledge or consent; not until *Kirchberg v. Feenstra*[33] in

---

[24] *Id.*

[25] Jurisdictional Statement at 4, *Baker v. Nelson*, 409 U.S. 810 (1972) (No. 71–1027).

[26] Alternative Writ of Mandamus, Hennepin County District Court, Jurisdictional Statement at 11a,
    Baker, 409 U.S 810 (No. 71–1027).

[27] Kay Tobin & Randy Wicker, The Gay Crusaders 145 (1972).

[28] *Id.*

[29] Not all the legal consequences described later were part of Minnesota law in 1970, however.

[30] Minnesota wives had been accorded claims for loss of consortium by 1969, but, as late as 1977, a
    Minnesota treatise noted that this remained one of the "legal remedies unavailable [to wives] in most
    States." Ellen Dresselhuis, The Legal Status of Homemakers in Minnesota 6 (1977).

[31] *See Frontiero v. Richardson*, 411 U.S. 677, 688–91 (1973).

[32] *Orr v. Orr*, 440 U.S. 268 (1979).

[33] 450 U.S. 455, 459–60 (1981).

1981 did the U.S. Supreme Court hold that state statutes giving the husband such exclusive control violated the Equal Protection Clause.

In recommending Baker be denied a marriage license, the County Attorney stressed that "if one were to permit the marriage of two male persons, it would result in a complete confusion as to the rights and duties of husband and wife, man and woman, in the numerous other sections of our law which govern the rights and duties of married persons . . . [and] result in an undermining and destruction of the entire legal concept of our family structure in all areas of law."[34] As of 1970, these claims might well have had merit. In the interim, virtually all the laws that speak in a legally differentiated way in terms of husband and wife, except those governing entry into civil marriage, have been "undermin[ed] and destroy[ed]" by the U.S. Supreme Court's decisions holding such differentiation an unconstitutional deprivation of equal protection on grounds of sex. In ways not foreseen by the Minnesota Supreme Court as it decided *Baker*, the Fourteenth Amendment was indeed "a charter for restructuring" the "historic institution" of marriage so as to guarantee to men and women the equal protection of the laws.

THE SECOND WAVE OF SAME-SEX MARRIAGE LITIGATION IN THE UNITED STATES

When same-sex marriage litigation resumed two decades after *Baker*, state rather than federal constitutional claims were raised.[35] In 1993, the Hawaii Supreme Court held that denying same-sex couples entry into marriage was discrimination on the basis of sex that, under the Hawaii Constitution, could only be upheld if narrowly tailored to serve a compelling state interest.[36] The only purportedly compelling justification offered on remand was based on stereotypes and was, as such, rejected by the lower court.[37] Specifically, the state offered evidence on remand only with respect to its interest in promoting the well-being of children. In rejecting any "causal link between allowing same-sex marriage and adverse effects upon the optimal development of children,"[38] the trial court relied on evidence from Hawaii's own expert witnesses that there were gay and lesbian parents who provided good homes for children; heterosexual, married, biological parents who did not; as well as, more broadly, a diversity in functioning family structure. In other words, being a male–female couple was an imperfect proxy for being good parents.

---

[34] Appellee's Motion to Dismiss Appeal and Brief, *supra* note 24, at 12–13.

[35] A case decided shortly after *Baker, Singer v. Hara*, 522 P.2d 1187 (Wash. Ct. App. 1974) also disposed of same-sex marriage claims on state constitutional grounds, holding, after considering evidence of voter intent, that Washington's then recently approved state constitutional Equal Rights Amendment did not extend the right to marry to same-sex couples.

[36] *Baehr v. Lewin*, 852 P.2d 44, 63–64 (Haw. 1993).

[37] I use stereotype here in the sense of an archaic normative template for a given sex, as well as an imperfect descriptive proxy.

[38] *Baehr v. Miike*, No. 91–1294, 1996 WL 694235 at *18 (Haw. Cir. Ct., Dec. 3, 1996).

The Hawaii case was the first and last case to date in which a plurality of the judges on the highest court of any U.S. state accepted the claim that denial of marriage to same-sex couples constituted discrimination on the basis of sex. Because a state constitutional amendment authorizing the legislature to deny marriage to same-sex couples mooted the Hawaii case before a final resolution, there is not even a definitive high court holding in place that no compelling governmental interest justifies the sex discrimination inherent in the denial of marriage to same-sex couples. Some subsequent state high court majority opinions that have addressed the question of same-sex marriage have avoided deciding the sex discrimination question entirely. Among them are those of the Massachusetts Supreme Judicial Court and the Iowa and Connecticut Supreme Courts, all three of which ruled on other grounds that same-sex couples had a right to marry under their respective state constitutions.[39] However, only when a court rules in favor of marriage on other grounds can it easily avoid the sex discrimination question. To rule against marriage for same-sex couples requires a court to dispose of all of the arguments raised in their favor, including sex discrimination. In addition, because laws found to discriminate on the basis of sex are entitled to heightened scrutiny under a state as well as the federal constitution, it is particularly difficult, as the trial on remand in Hawaii demonstrated, for those laws to survive such scrutiny, whether by proof that they are not based on impermissible stereotypes or by proof that they are tailored well enough to a sufficiently important governmental interest. Perhaps for this reason, every state high court that has ruled adversely on marriage for same-sex couples – whether by denying them any state constitutional right to relationship recognition whatsoever, as the New York Court of Appeals did, or by holding that their constitutional claims can be satisfied by providing for them under state law another relationship status that is not called marriage, as the Vermont Supreme Court did – has held that granting marriage licenses only to male–female couples simply does not discriminate on the basis of sex.

The Vermont Supreme Court's analysis is typical:

> [W]e do not doubt that a statute that discriminated on the basis of sex would bear a heavy burden. . . . The difficulty here is that the marriage laws are facially neutral; they do not single out men or women as a class for disparate treatment, but rather prohibit men and women equally from marrying a person of the same sex. . . . "[I]in order to trigger equal protection analysis at all . . . a [litigant] must show that he was treated differently as a member of one class from treatment of members of another class similarly situated." . . . Here, there is no discrete class subject to differential treatment solely on the basis of sex; each sex is equally prohibited from precisely the same conduct.[40]

---

[39] *Goodridge v. Dep't. of Pub. Health*, 44 Mass. 309 (2003); *Varnum v. Brien*, 763 N.W.2d 862 (Iowa 2009); *Kerrigan v. Comm'r. of Pub. Health*, 957 A.2d 407 (Ct. 2008).

[40] *Baker v. Vermont*, 170 Vt. 194, 215 n. 13 (1999) (citations omitted).

As Justice Denise Johnson, the only member of the Vermont Supreme Court to see sex discrimination in the denial of marriage to same-sex couples, and, not coincidentally, the only justice on the court to opine that prompt access to marriage rather than legislative approval of the separate institution of civil unions was the appropriate remedy, correctly responded,

> Under the State's analysis, a statute that required courts to give custody of male children to fathers and female children to mothers would not be sex discrimination. Although such a law would not treat men and women differently, I believe it would discriminate on the basis of sex.[41]

A holding such as that of the Vermont Supreme Court majority, gratuitously echoed by the California Supreme Court majority in its apparent eagerness to reach and answer in the affirmative the question of whether denial of marriage licenses to same-sex couples is discrimination on the basis of sexual orientation and as such is entitled to heightened scrutiny under the California Constitution, is a repudiation, not only of the entire body of U.S. Supreme Court sex discrimination law of the last forty years, but of more general fundamental principles of U.S. equal protection law established for more than a century.

The individual, rather than the group, has long been the touchstone for discrimination claims under U.S. law. Even in the days when the U.S. Supreme Court tolerated segregation of blacks and whites, it insisted that

> the essence of the constitutional right is that it is a personal one . . . It is the individual who is entitled to the equal protection of the laws, and if he is denied . . . a facility or convenience . . . which under substantially the same circumstances is furnished to another, . . . he may properly complain that his constitutional privilege has been invaded.[42]

The anti-stereotyping sex discrimination jurisprudence first developed in statutory cases under Title VII and then extended into the constitutional realm by cases such as those brought by Ginsburg for the ACLU, a jurisprudence that has been criticized for focusing on the exceptional individual rather than the more typical member of a group, is often derided as "formal equality." Yet the doctrine of equal application courts such as the Vermont and California Supreme Courts now used to reject a sex discrimination challenge is no less formal – what differentiates it is a focus on the formal equality of groups rather than the formal equality of individuals.

In highlighting the harm to individuals, Justice Johnson also vindicates the rights of one of the few bisexuals to be discussed explicitly in same-sex marriage litigation, the hypothetical Ms. C, for whom the choice between a male and a female suitor is

---

[41] *Id.* at 254 (concurring and dissenting opinion).
[42] *McCabe v. Atchison, Topeka, & Santa Fe Railway Co.*, 235 U.S. 15, 161–62 (1914) (rejecting argument that limited demand by blacks justified providing sleeping cars only for whites).

seen as open rather than foreclosed by an immutable sexual orientation toward one
and not the other sex:

> [C]onsider the following example. Dr. A and Dr. B both want to marry Ms. C, an
> X-ray technician. Dr. A may do so because Dr. A is a man. Dr. B may not because
> Dr. B is a woman. Dr. A and Dr. B are people of opposite sexes who are similarly
> situated in the sense that they both want to marry a person of their choice. The
> statute disqualifies Dr. B from marriage solely on the basis of her sex and treats her
> differently from Dr. A, a man. This is sex discrimination.[43]

To characterize the discrimination in the marriage laws as sexual orientation discrimination and not as sex discrimination foregrounds anti-subordination concerns,
something most scholars of equal protection other than myself have been urging
for a long time. On their face, bans on same-sex marriage do not discriminate on
the basis of sexual orientation – no state has ever sought to prohibit a gay man
from marrying a lesbian, although the bans on same-sex marriage clearly have an
overwhelming disparate impact on those with a gay or lesbian orientation. Denying
that such bans also discriminate on the basis of sex, however, has serious costs for the
equality of the sexes and the liberty of all. There are two main ways of formulating
the principle behind the constitutional norm against the denial of equal protection
on grounds of sex. The first is that women should not be subordinated by the law or,
more broadly, by men. The second is that sex should be irrelevant to an individual's
treatment by the law, and, more broadly, to his or her life chances. On the latter
view, "fixed notions concerning the roles and abilities of males and females" are
problematic even when embodied in law that does not in any articulable way subordinate women to men.[44] I have long argued that, however important the former, or
anti-subordination view, may be, the latter, anti-differentiation or anti-stereotyping
view, is an independently important guarantee of equal liberty. Among its many
advantages is that it obviates the necessity of forcing individuals into well-defined
rigid groups to whose standards they must conform – gay or straight, male or female,
masculine of feminine – as a precondition for vindicating their rights.[45]

Thus, the rejection of the constitutional sex discrimination claim in same-sex
marriage cases disturbs me for many of the same reasons that I am disturbed by
the Ninth Circuit's recent rejection of Darlene Jespersen's statutory claim of sex
discrimination against her employer, Harrah's Casino.[46] Harrah's had imposed separate grooming standards on its male and female employees – requiring women and
prohibiting men from wearing makeup, and requiring women and prohibiting men

---

[43] *Baker,* 170 Vt. at 253.
[44] See Case, *The Very Stereotype, supra* note 3, at 1473.
[45] *See, e.g.,* Mary Anne Case, *Unpacking Package Deals: Separate Spheres Are Not the Answer,* 75 U.
DENVER L. REV. 1305 (1999).
[46] *Jespersen v. Harrah's Operating Co., Inc.,* 444 F.3d 1104, 1108 (9th Cir. 2006).

to wear their hair long and "teased, curled, or styled."[47] As the majority that ruled against her summarized it,

> Jespersen described the personal indignity she felt as a result of attempting to comply with the makeup policy. Jespersen testified that when she wore the makeup she "felt very degraded and very demeaned." In addition, Jespersen testified that "it prohibited [her] from doing [her] job" because "[i]t affected [her] self-dignity . . . [and] took away [her] credibility as an individual and as a person.[48]

Had Jespersen been willing to claim that she was a transsexual, she might, under recent case law, have prevailed.[49] But, as an individual seeking to diverge from the norms set for her group, she lost. A majority of the Ninth Circuit *en banc* disrespected Jespersen's commitments, describing her as idiosyncratic and Harrah's rules as neither rooted in sex stereotypes nor posing an undue burden on women. Just as I am disheartened and disturbed to see the Jespersen case abandon the statutory prohibition on sex stereotyping in employment I thought had been firmly established by the U.S. Supreme Court in *Price Waterhouse v. Hopkins*,[50] so I am disheartened and disturbed to see so many state courts in same-sex marriage cases abandon the constitutional prohibitions on sex stereotyping I thought had been firmly established by the line of cases Ruth Bader Ginsburg began as a litigator and then reaffirmed as a Justice in her majority opinion in *U.S. v. Virginia*, the Virginia Military Institute (VMI) case. Ginsburg's opinion in this case, like her litigation strategy for the ACLU, vindicated the individual who diverged from group norms. It was Chief Justice Rehnquist, writing only for himself in a concurring opinion, who held out the possibility that some sort of rough equality between groups might suffice to meet the demands of equal protection. According to Rehnquist,

> It is not the "exclusion of women" [from VMI] that violates the Equal Protection Clause, but the maintenance of an all-men school without providing any – much less a comparable – institution for women. . . . An adequate remedy in my opinion might be a demonstration by Virginia that its interest in educating men in a single-sex environment is matched by its interest in educating women in a single-sex institution. To demonstrate such, the Commonwealth does not need to create two institutions with the same number of faculty Ph.D.s, similar SAT scores, or comparable athletic fields . . . Nor would it necessarily require that the women's institution offer the same curriculum as the men's; one could be strong in computer

---

47 *Id.* at 1107.
48 *Id.* at 1108.
49 *Compare Schroer v. Billington*, 577 F. Supp. 2d 293 (DDC 2008) (distinguishing Jespersen from the case of an MTF transsexual).
50 *Price Waterhouse v. Hopkins*, 490 U.S. 228, 251 (1989) (holding it to be impermissible sex discrimination to demand of a female candidate for an accounting partnership that she "'walk more femininely, talk more femininely, dress more femininely, wear make-up, have her hair styled, . . . wear jewelry,' and go to 'charm school.'"). *See* Mary Anne Case, *Disaggregating Gender from Sex and Sexual Orientation: The Effeminate Man in the Law and Feminist Jurisprudence*, 105 YALE L. J. 1 (1995).

science, the other could be strong in liberal arts. It would be a sufficient remedy, I think, if the two institutions offered the same quality of education and were of the same overall caliber.[51]

Not only would Rehnquist's solution deny liberty, but, as Justice Souter noted at oral argument in the VMI case, because we do not stand "on the world's first morning" with respect to sex distinctions, but rather at the close of millennia of subordination, continued separation of the sexes along the remedial lines suggested by Chief Justice Rehnquist cannot be free of a subordinating taint.[52]

A similar problem arises when states attempt to set up "separate but equal" institutions for same-sex couples while reserving marriage for male–female couples. This was the solution accepted by the Vermont Supreme Court, which allowed the state legislature to create a new status denominated civil union, with "all the same benefits, protections, and responsibilities under [state] law . . . as are granted to spouses in a marriage,"[53] but limited in access to same-sex couples.

Such a bifurcated regime sends a message of subordination to both gays and lesbians on the one hand and heterosexual women on the other while reaffirming patriarchy. Withholding from same-sex couples the opportunity to marry devalues their unions both symbolically and practically, while restricting marriage to male–female couples and male–female couples to marriage forces women who wish to unite themselves to men under state law to do so in an institution whose all too recent legal history is one of subordinating wives both practically and symbolically, an institution reserved for them alone because of and not in spite of its "traditional" (i.e., patriarchal) significance. Although civil union may have gone a long way toward constitutionalizing the equality of gay men and lesbians in the states that offer it to them, so long as it is reserved to same-sex couples it is, in my view, a step backward for constitutionalizing the equality of straight women.[54]

Note that if a state had opened either marriage to same-sex couples or civil union to male–female couples, I myself, unlike some other feminist fundamentalists, would not be complaining about an affront to women's equality. For if marriage were opened to all couples, it could continue its development away from its patriarchal past rather than be preserved in the tradition of that past. And if civil unions were open to all couples, as it now is in Illinois, women who wished to receive state recognition of their union with a man, together with the associated bundle of legal benefits, could do so without being forced into a form of union that traditionally has subordinated them.

[51] *United States v. Virginia*, 518 U.S. 515, 565 (1996) (Rehnquist, C. J., concurring).
[52] See Case, *The Very Stereotype, supra* note 3, at 1476.
[53] VT. STAT. ANN. tit. 15, § 1204(a) (2002). As of 2009, Vermont opened civil marriage to all couples, but it never opened civil unions to any male–female couples, and bifurcated regimes in which no same-sex couples may marry remain in a number of other states.
[54] As of 2011, Illinois became the first U.S. state to offer civil unions to male–female couples as well as to same-sex couples.

In some ways marriage is like the abaya in *McSally v. Rumsfeld*. Martha McSally, a female U.S. Air Force fighter pilot, challenged regulations requiring female U.S. military personnel to be accompanied by a male companion and to wear an abaya on any trips off base in Saudi Arabia. McSally claimed that these regulations violated her constitutional rights, *inter alia*, "by forcing her to communicate the false and coerced message that she adheres to the belief that women are subservient to men, by according her different treatment and status based solely upon her gender, and by undermining her authority as an officer."[55] Among other similarities, marriage and the abaya both historically involve the "covering" of women in circumstances where men are not similarly covered: an abaya physically through its cumbersome enveloping folds; marriage legally, through the encumbrance of coverture, which subsumed a wife's identity in her husband's. Some women who voluntarily enter the one or put on the other do so without feeling or intending to "communicate . . . a belief that women are subservient to men."[56] Others by such acts embrace and announce their adherence to such a belief, as is their personal right. However, a government committed to constitutionalizing women's equality in the way that U.S. law now demands should not condition important privileges, including membership in the armed forces or in a legally recognized union, on a woman's willingness to accept trappings whose social meaning she reasonably associates with a message of subordination she (and this nation) rejects.

There have been heterosexual feminist fundamentalist marriage resisters, male and female, in the United States for centuries, but they have never gotten much respect from the law. In recent years, challenges to benefits extended by employers and units of government only to those unmarried couples whose members were of the same sex have been met with the judicial response that because heterosexual couples can legally marry, they suffer no impermissible discrimination.[57] No weight at all is given to their fundamentalist objections to civil marriage. Indeed, the affront to heterosexuals who resist marriage from a feminist perspective may be all the greater in states such as New Jersey, which opens up its civil union status, as California does its domestic partnership, to only those heterosexual couples one of whose members is older than age sixty-two. Unlike heterosexual marriage resisters, senior citizens who opt for civil union or registered domestic partnership over marriage tend to do so to preserve the benefits they have already accrued from a prior traditional marriage – for example, they are widows who do not wish to lose Social Security and pension benefits accrued through a deceased husband by remarrying.

I have tried to suggest a variety of ways in which even those state courts who have granted some rights to same-sex couples in recent years have set back the cause of liberty and equality on grounds of sex. Worst of all, one state court that denied all

55 Pl.'s Compl., *McSally v. Rumsfeld*, No. 1,01CVO2481 (D.D.C. 2001).
56 *Id.*
57 *See, e.g., Irizarry v. Bd. of Educ.*, 251 F.3d 604 (7th Cir. 2001).

relief to same-sex couples recently approached the question of same-sex marriage in a majority opinion more closely resembling that of Bradley in *Bradwell* than that of Rehnquist in *Hibbs*, or even Rehnquist in *U.S. v. Virginia*, thus threatening all settled understandings of constitutional sex equality. The New York Court of Appeals, in an opinion by Judge Robert Smith, held that the following constituted a sufficient basis for not extending civil marriage to same-sex couples:

> The Legislature could rationally believe that it is better, other things being equal, for children to grow up with both a mother and a father. Intuition and experience suggest that a child benefits from having before his or her eyes, every day, living models of what both a man and a woman are like.[58]

As a feminist theorist and a constitutional law scholar, I find this rationale deeply disturbing. Far from being an acceptable rational basis for excluding same-sex couples from marriage, it does not even set forth a permissible governmental interest. It is directly contrary to the federal constitutional prohibition on embodying in law any "fixed notions concerning the roles and abilities of males and females." Smith could only have been assuming the Legislature wished to encourage more nudity in the home, because any other assumptions about "living models of what both a man and a woman are like" would run afoul of federal constitutional prohibitions on basing legal distinctions on sex stereotypes.

Although he rules against them, Smith seems far from hostile to gay people. He goes out of his way to acknowledge, not only the careful and thoughtful way in which they become parents, but also "that there has been serious injustice in the treatment of homosexuals" and to speak favorably of New York legislative responses such as the Sexual Orientation Non-Discrimination Act of 2002.[59] But if, for Smith, homosexuals are, like African Americans, victims of a long history of unjust prejudice, women seem to remain like children and imbeciles, in special need of the protection of the laws. He seems much more interested in preserving sex-role differentiation than in putting gays down.

Smith insists that "the traditional definition of marriage is not merely a by-product of historical injustice. Its history is of a different kind."[60] In my view he can only reach this conclusion by focusing exclusively on the injustice of exclusion on gay and lesbian couples and ignoring any historical injustice to heterosexual women. Justice Johnson's concurring and dissenting opinion in the Vermont same-sex marriage case, by tracing aspects of the history of the legal regulation of marriage Smith ignores, makes clear why "[v]iewing the discrimination [in the marriage laws] as sex-based . . . is important."[61] As she correctly observes, the discrimination is "a vestige of sex-role stereotyping that applies to both men and women" in "that, historically,

[58] *Hernandez v. Robles*, 7 N.Y.3d 338, 359 (2006).
[59] *Id.* at 361.
[60] *Id.*
[61] *Baker v. Vermont*, 170 Vt. 194, 254 (1999) (Johnson, J., concurring and dissenting).

the marriage laws imposed sex-based roles for the partners to a marriage – male provider and female dependent – that bore no relation to their inherent abilities to contribute to society."[62] Worse, the intent and effect of the common law of marriage was to subordinate a woman completely to her husband, wiping out her own independent legal existence. Only with the passage in the nineteenth century of laws such as Vermont's Rights of Married Women Act did state legislatures begin "to set a married woman free 'from the thralldom of the common law.'"[63] As Justice Johnson notes,[64] it took until 1973 for the Supreme Court of Vermont to declare:

> Having rejected the archaic principle that husband and wife are "one person," it must necessarily follow that a married woman is a "person" under the Constitution of Vermont, and is entitled to all the rights guaranteed to a person.[65]

Acknowledging that a history of denying the full personhood of married women and that a continued commitment to traditional fixed sex roles outside the bedroom, not just aversion to homosexuality,[66] can undergird opposition to legal recognition of same-sex marriages does not weaken the constitutional case in favor of same-sex marriage, it strengthens it, given the strength of our existing well-established constitutional prohibitions against embodying fixed sex roles in law.

---

[62] *Id.* at 257.

[63] *Id.* (citation omitted).

[64] *Id.*

[65] *Richard v. Richard*, 131 Vt. 98, 106 (1973).

[66] *Cf.* Michel Foucault, *Sexual Choice, Sexual Act: An Interview*, 58 SALMAGUNDI 21 (Fall 1982 – Winter 1983) ("I think that what most bothers those who are not gay about gayness is the gay life-style, not sex acts themselves. . . . It is the prospect that gays will create as yet unforeseen kinds of relationships that many people cannot tolerate").

3

Abortion, Dignity, and a Capabilities Approach

Rosalind Dixon and Martha C. Nussbaum

In the United States, as Reva Siegel has recently noted, the right to abortion has increasingly been linked by pivotal justices to the idea of individual human dignity.[1] This connection between ideas about human dignity and rights of access to abortion also finds support in a broader comparative context.[2]

For example, in Canada, in her concurring judgment in *R v. Morgentaler*,[3] Justice Wilson suggested that "respect for human dignity" was central to the issue of access to abortion because "the right to make fundamental personal decisions without interference from the state" was a key aspect of human dignity, as one of the central values on which the Canadian *Charter of Rights and Freedoms* 1982 was founded.[4] In Germany, in the *Abortion I* Case,[5] the German Federal Constitutional Court (GFCC) held that "pregnancy belongs to the sphere of intimacy of the woman, the protection of which is guaranteed by the Basic Law"; and further

1 Reva Siegel, *Dignity and the Politics of Protection: Abortion Restrictions Under Casey/Carhart*, 117 YALE L. J. 1694 (2008). *See, e.g., Planned Parenthood v. Casey*, 505 U.S. 833 (1992) (affirming the central holding in *Roe v. Wade*, 410 U.S. 113 (1973) that women enjoy a constitutionally protected right to terminate a pregnancy prior to viability, and in doing so, holding that prior decisions recognized that the Constitution protects "personal decisions relating to marriage, procreation, contraception, family relationships, child rearing, and education" and that "these matters, involving the most intimate and personal choices a person may make in a lifetime [are] choices central to personal dignity and autonomy"). For other usages of dignity, both explicit and implicit, in U.S. Constitutional jurisprudence at a Supreme Court, and also at the state level, see Vicki C. Jackson, *Constitutional Dialogue and Human Dignity: States and Transnational Constitutional Discourse*, 65 MONT. L. REV. 16 (2004).
2 *Cf.* Reva Siegel, *Dignity and the Abortion Debate*. The Seminario en Latinoamérica de Teoría Constitucional y Política [the Seminar in Latin America on Constitutional and Political Theory] [hereinafter SELA], June 2009, Asunción, Paraguay (on file with authors).
3 [1988] 1 S.C.R. 30.
4 *Id.* at 166.
5 39 BVERFGE I, 1975 (Ger.).

Our thanks to Mary Anne Case, Vicki Jackson, and Reva Siegel for helpful comments on earlier drafts of the chapter; and to Emily Tancer and Amy Benford for excellent research assistance.

that this sphere of intimacy, and the right of self-determination it implied, were "values to be viewed in their relationship to human dignity."[6] In the *Abortion II* Case,[7] the GFCC was even more explicit in recognizing that access to abortion was supported, or indeed probably even required, by "the human dignity of the pregnant woman, her . . . right to life and physical integrity, and her right of personality."[8] In Brazil, in 1999, in the case of a pregnancy involving an anencephalic fetus, the Supreme Court of Brazil placed similar reliance on the idea of human dignity – and the capacity of "gestating pain, anguish, and frustration" in the context of such a pregnancy to cause "violence to human dignity" – as the prime basis for invalidating a prohibition on access to abortion in such circumstances.[9] More recently, in Colombia in 2006, in holding that the Colombian Constitution protects certain minimal rights of access to abortion, the Colombian Constitutional Court cited a concern for human dignity as a basis for striking down the criminalization of abortion in three sets of circumstances: where a pregnancy is the result of rape; involves a nonviable fetus; or threatens a woman's life or health.[10] In other countries, such as Australia, the idea of human dignity has also been relied on to support recognition of related reproductive rights claims, such as the freedom from involuntary sterilization.[11]

Likewise at an international level, in recent years, the United Nations Human Rights Committee has held that a concern for human dignity implies limits on states' freedom to restrict access to legal abortion services. Article 7 of the International Covenant on Civil and Political Rights prohibits state conduct that is "cruel and inhuman," and this, according to the Committee, prohibits states party from any action that infringes "the *dignity* and the physical and mental integrity of the individual."[12] The Committee has further held that where carrying a fetus to term

---

[6] As discussed later, this was also the axis according to which the Court suggested fetal interests should be viewed. See notes 23–24 *infra*.

[7] 88 BVerfGE 203, 1993 (Ger.).

[8] See translation of *Abortion II* provided by Donald P. Kommers, *in* The Constitutional Jurisprudence of the Federal Republic of Germany 350 (2d ed., 1997).

[9] Arguição de Descumprimento de Preceito Fundamental – DF 54/2004 (Translation by Amy Benford, on file with authors). *See also* Debora Diniz, *Selective Abortion in Brazil: The Anencephaly Case*, 7 Developing World Bioethics 1471 (2007).

[10] Colombian Constitutional Court, Decision C-355/2006.

[11] In Australia, for example, the High Court of Australia held that the right to bodily security was underpinned by the idea of human dignity, or that "each person has a unique dignity which the law respects and which it will protect," and that respect for human dignity requires "that the whole personality be respected: the right to physical integrity is a condition of human dignity but the gravity of any invasion of physical integrity depends on its effect not only on the body but also upon the mind and on self-perception." *Department of Health v. JWB* ("Marion's Case"), (1992) 175 C.L.R. 218.

[12] *See* Office of the High Commissioner for Human Rights, CCPR General Comment No. 20 (1992), www.unhchr.ch/tbs/doc.nsf/0/6924291970754969c12563ed004c8ae5?Opendocument.

would involve significant physical or psychological harm to a woman, restricting access to legal abortion services would directly violate the guarantee of individual dignity and integrity in Article 7.[13]

At the same time, the idea of dignity as a constitutional value that supports a right of access to abortion also remains undertheorized in comparative constitutional scholarship. This is particularly so when it comes to the relationship between human dignity and women's physical and psychological health or integrity. There is a deep body of theoretical writing dating back (in the Western tradition[14]) at least to the ancient Greek and Roman Stoics, and prominently exemplified in the writings of Immanuel Kant, which supports the idea that respect for human dignity involves seeing a human being as an end and not merely a means. This respect involves a reciprocal willingness, on the part of individuals, to treat others as subjects and not merely as objects, and thus entails the protection of areas of freedom around people so that they can determine their own destiny in areas of central concern.[15] There have also been numerous attempts, both judicial and scholarly, to connect this idea of dignity to the specific abortion context.

By contrast, with the exception of previous work by one of us in this area, there have been few attempts at a theoretic level to connect the idea of human dignity to claims by individuals to a certain threshold level of material, physical, and psychological well-being – that is, dignity as entailing a baseline of affirmative material support[16] – and to date this work has not sought to focus specifically on the issue of abortion. Without such a theoretical account of dignity and its potential relationship to rights to abortion, it is, moreover, extremely difficult to justify much of the existing reliance on the idea of human dignity in countries such as Germany, Brazil, Colombia, and Australia, and also internationally. This is because in all of these contexts a core part of the concern of relevant decision makers has been with the connection between human dignity and physical and psychological health, rather than simply human dignity and individual liberty or decisional autonomy.

In this chapter, we therefore offer the beginnings of a more complete theoretic account of the link between ideas about human dignity and constitutional abortion rights. We do so by drawing on the capabilities-based approach developed by one of

---

[13] See *Llantoy Huamán v. Peru*, Communication No. 1153/2003, U.N. Doc. CCPR/C/85/D/1153/2003 (2005).

[14] For related ideas in Asian traditions, see generally AMARTYA SEN, HUMAN RIGHTS AND ASIAN VALUES (1997).

[15] Siegel refers to this as "dignity as liberty," but, as we shall argue, this locution is misleading: dignity *entails* liberty, but is not equivalent to liberty. *See generally* Siegel, *supra* note 1.

[16] For this distinction between dignity in the Kantian sense, and dignity in the baseline sense, see Rosalind Dixon, *Creating Dialogue about Socioeconomic Rights: Strong Form versus Weak Form Judicial Review Revisited*, 5 ICON 391, 400–401 (2007).

us elsewhere;[17] and by explaining for the first time in detail the logical implications of such an approach for the constitutional regulation of abortion.

The chapter proceeds in three parts. Part I provides a basic explanation and outline of the capabilities approach, and the capabilities most directly relevant to the abortion context. Part II considers the implications of a capabilities approach and a concern for human dignity for the treatment of fetal life, and the degree to which such considerations may provide support for some form of ceiling, as well as a floor, on basic rights of access to abortion. Part III considers the potential practical payoff for reproductive rights advocates, in the context of issues such as the public funding of abortion and health-based arguments for access to abortion, of being able to connect the idea of dignity in an abortion context to a capabilities approach.

I. THE CAPABILITIES APPROACH AND WOMEN'S ACCESS TO ABORTION

The Capabilities Approach (CA), a theoretical approach to quality-of-life assessment and to theorizing about basic social justice, emerged as an alternative, in the global development context, to theories that focus on economic growth as the main indicator of a nation's or region's quality of life. Departing from this narrow economic focus – which fails even to ask about the distribution of social wealth – the CA holds that the key question to ask, when comparing societies and assessing them for their decency or justice is, "What is each person able to do and to be?" In other words, like the Kantian approach mentioned earlier, it treats *each person as an end*, asking not just about the total or average achievements of a nation, but about the opportunity set available to each person. It is focused on choice or freedom, holding that the crucial thing societies should be promoting for their people is a set of opportunities, or substantial freedoms, which people then may or may not exercise in action. It thus commits itself to respect for people's powers of self-definition. The approach is resolutely pluralist about value: it holds that the capability achievements that are central for people are different in quality, not just in quantity, that they cannot without distortion be reduced to a single numerical scale, and that a crucial part of understanding and producing them is an understanding of the specific nature of each. It ascribes an urgent task to government and public policy, namely, the improvement of quality of life for all people, as defined by their capabilities.

---

[17] *See generally* MARTHA C. NUSSBAUM, WOMEN AND HUMAN DEVELOPMENT: THE CAPABILITIES APPROACH (2000); MARTHA C. NUSSBAUM, FRONTIERS OF JUSTICE: DISABILITY, NATIONALITY, SPECIES MEMBERSHIP (2006) [hereinafter FRONTIERS]; Martha C. Nussbaum, *Capabilities as Fundamental Entitlements: Sen and Social Justice*, 9 FEM. ECON. 33 (2003); Martha C. Nussbaum, *Constitutions and Capabilities: Supreme Court Foreword: "Perception" Against Lofty Formalism*, 121 HARV. L. REV. 4 (2007) [hereinafter *Constitutions and Capabilities*]. The relationship between Nussbaum's version of the approach and that of Amartya Sen is discussed in Nussbaum, *Capabilities as Fundamental Entitlements, supra,* and the entire related group of theories is discussed in MARTHA C. NUSSBAUM, CREATING CAPABILITIES: THE HUMAN DEVELOPMENT APPROACH (2011).

So much is common to various users of the CA. In Nussbaum's specific version, these ideas are used as building blocks of a minimal theory of social justice, in combination with an idea of human dignity.[18] The idea is that a minimally just society is one that secures to all citizens a threshold level of a list of key entitlements, on the grounds that such entitlements are requisite of a life worthy of human dignity (there is also an account of the entitlements of other animal species, and here reference is made to the dignity appropriate to the species in question). The notion of dignity is an intuitive notion that is by no means utterly clear.[19] If it is used in isolation, as if it is utterly self-evident, it can be used capriciously and inconsistently. Thus it would be a mistake to use it if it were an intuitive self-evident and solid foundation for a theory that would then be built upon it. The CA does not do this: dignity is one element of the theory, but all of its notions are seen as interconnected, deriving illumination and clarity from one another. But the basic idea is that some living conditions deliver to people a life that is worthy of the human dignity that they possess, and others do not. In the latter circumstance, they retain dignity, but it is like a promissory note whose claims have not been met. As Martin Luther King, Jr. said of the promises inherent in national ideals: dignity can be like "a check that has come back marked 'insufficient funds.'"[20]

Although the idea of dignity is a vague idea that needs to be given content by placing it in a network of related notions, it does make a difference. A focus on dignity is quite different, for example, from a focus on satisfaction. Think about debates concerning education for people with severe cognitive disabilities. It certainly seems possible that satisfaction, for many such people, could be produced without educational development. The arguments that opened the public schools to such people used, at crucial junctures, the notion of dignity: we do not treat a child with Down syndrome in a manner commensurate with that child's dignity if we fail to develop the child's powers of mind through suitable education. In a wide range of areas, moreover, a focus on dignity will dictate policy choices that protect and support agency, rather than choices that infantilize people and treat them as passive recipients of benefit.

So far, the CA looks like a close relative of the Kantian notions mentioned earlier, and this is not altogether wrong. On the other hand, the CA conceives of the human being as inherently animal and a member of the natural world. Dignity is something in and of this world, not something belonging to a noumenal realm of freedom impervious to worldly accidents. This emphasis leads the CA to take issue with Kantian ideas in two ways. First, whereas Kant conceives of our human dignity as residing entirely in rationality, the CA understands the basis of human dignity far

---

[18] See references *supra* note 17.

[19] *See* Martha C. Nussbaum, *Human Dignity and Political Entitlements, in* Human Dignity and Bioethics: Essays Commissioned by the President's Council on Bioethics 351 (Adam Schulman & Martha C. Nussbaum eds., 2008).

[20] Martin Luther King, "I Have A Dream," Washington D.C., August 28, 1963.

more inclusively: human dignity inheres in sentience, emotion, affection, physical health, and appetite, as well as in rationality. Thus it can see human beings with severe cognitive disabilities as full equals in human dignity, and damages to any of these elements as assaults on human dignity.[21] It also recognizes that dignity is not the private possession of the human species alone: each animal species possesses a type of dignity. (In the human case, this dignity inheres in the entire organized set of its characteristic capacities, whatever they are in each case, and not in any putative set of "higher powers."[22]) Second, whereas Kant imagines dignity as like a diamond, impervious to the blows and shocks of natural accident, the CA imagines dignity as vulnerable, capable of suffering assaults from the world of nature. When such assaults occur, dignity is not removed, but is profoundly harmed (just as we would say that rape does not remove a woman's dignity, but does profoundly harm or violate it). From the perspective of the CA, then, deprivations of opportunities for health or emotional well-being are just as pertinent to the concept of human dignity as deprivations of liberty of choice.

Another way in which the CA differs from Kantian approaches is in its sensitivity to social context. Although at a high level of generality, entitlements are recommended as norms for all nations, the nation itself is assigned the task of specifying each of these entitlements more concretely. Often different nations will define these entitlements in line with each nation's specific histories and circumstances. For example, a free speech right that suits Germany well (allowing a complete ban on anti-Semitic speech) would be too restrictive in the different social climate of the United States: in this case, both countries are correct, although they define entitlements differently. In other cases, we may feel that a nation's tradition has been used as a mere excuse to avoid the claims of human dignity in a given area: thus, the U.S. failure (until very recently) to guarantee even minimal health care could be seen as growing out of a distinctive tradition, but it is not for that reason right. The only way to adjudicate these difficult cases is by requiring each nation to show that its traditions give humanly good reasons, reasons consistent with equal human dignity, for defining an entitlement differently.[23]

The primary claim of the CA is that each and every person is entitled to a minimum threshold level of ten "Central Capabilities" or opportunities, and that the job of securing these belongs to the state in which they live (in some cases with the assistance of global redistribution).[24] What does this approach imply for abortion rights? The CA does not follow Kant in grounding dignity in rationality alone; it recognizes a variety of ways in which laws restricting abortion may burden or violate

---

[21] Thus not people in a permanent vegetative condition, or anencephalic infants, but all children born of human parents, and who possess some minimum level of sentience and striving.

[22] NUSSBAUM, FRONTIERS, *supra* note 17, at 346–52.

[23] *Id.* at 78–80.

[24] For the list, see Appendix *infra*. On global redistribution, see NUSSBAUM, FRONTIERS, *supra* note 17, at ch. 5.

the dignity of women: by restriction of liberty and choice, but also by damage or risks to health, bodily integrity, emotional well-being, employment options, and affiliations. All of these are similar threats to human dignity, because human dignity is understood as involving the "animal" side of human nature as well as the side that chooses. Indeed, the two "sides" are understood as thoroughly interwoven: giving someone a life worthy of human dignity requires not just giving some food, but giving choices regarding nutrition; not just health, but choices regarding health. Only then can these "animal" functions be performed in a way worthy of human dignity. The policy direction of this theoretical conception is thus clear: laws should not simply shield women from a variety of burdens; it should create full-fledged capabilities, or opportunities for choice, in each area.

II. THE CAPABILITIES APPROACH AND FETAL LIFE

The idea of human dignity has not only been invoked by those supporting a women's right to legal access to abortion. It has also been used in various contexts by opponents of abortion, and indeed also by various constitutional courts, as supporting arguments in favor of the protection of fetal life. In Germany in the *Abortion I* case, for example, the GFCC recognized that the fetus enjoyed constitutional protection under the Basic Law's guarantee of the right to life.[25] It also held that this right should be understood through the prism of its "relationship to human dignity [as] the center of the value system of the constitution."[26] Likewise in the United States, in *Gonzales v. Carhart* (*Carhart II*),[27] in the context of Congress' attempts to ban certain procedures used to conduct late-term abortions (intact dilation and extraction or "D&X"), the Supreme Court suggested that by "proscrib[ing] a method of abortion in which a fetus is killed just inches before completion of the birth process," the congressional statute in question "expresse[d] respect for the dignity of human life."[28]

Under the CA itself, it is plausible to make similar arguments about the standing of the fetus. The CA sees human beings with severe cognitive disabilities as full equals in human dignity. It also recognizes that dignity is not the private possession of the human species: each animal species possesses a type of dignity. Although the fetus does not possess a great deal in the way of agency, it does appear to have a stronger claim to agency than a person in a permanent vegetative condition (not a bearer of dignity, according to the CA), because it is at least potentially sentient and an agent. So it would seem inconsistent if the CA refused all moral status to the fetus. Indeed, the CA does recognize that the fetus possesses a type of human dignity – although its dependent and merely potential status means that its type of dignity is distinctive, and not directly commensurable with that of independent human beings.

[25] See translation of *Abortion I*, in KOMMERS, *supra* note 8, at 338.
[26] *Id.* at 339.
[27] 550 U.S. 124 (2007).
[28] *Id.* at 156–57.

The CA, then, both grants the fetus a type of (potential) human dignity and (in its focus on agency and striving) explains why that status is distinct from that of post-birth human beings.

Because of this, in some subset of constitutional contexts (i.e., those that in general draw a close connection, in constitutional terms, between shared national values and a duty on the part of the state to advance those values), the CA may, to some degree, also support, rather than undermine, the validity of the state imposing some form of ceiling on legal access to abortion. However, even if this is so, recognizing the fetus as having potential standing under the CA does not undermine the case the CA makes for recognizing some form of constitutional, or quasi-constitutional, minimum *floor* on access to abortion of the kind provided by a majority of countries worldwide.[29]

Among more than 100 countries worldwide, there is a clear "overlapping consensus"[30] in favor of permitting access to abortion where a woman's health as well as life is at stake; and also broad (if somewhat lesser) recognition of a legal right of access to abortion where a pregnancy is the result of sexual violence or continuing a pregnancy that would otherwise impose a particularly serious psychological or economic burden on a woman.[31] The CA also provides a variety of reasons to support recognizing legal access to abortion in each of these circumstances.

Prior to viability, the fetus's continued existence as a being entitled to human dignity is entirely contingent on the provision of affirmative support by a woman.[32] In these circumstances, a fetus cannot be said to have a "right to life" unless, from a normative perspective, a woman is also under a corresponding duty to provide such affirmative support.[33] In a liberal society that prizes individual autonomy, there will

---

[29] On the potential for such protections to take different constitutional form, or indeed quasi- or sub-constitutional, form, according to the context, see *id.*; Reva Siegel, *Sex Equality Arguments for Reproductive Rights: Their Critical Basis and Evolving Constitutional Expression*, 56 EMORY L. J. 815 (2007).

[30] On the idea of and significance of an overlapping consensus of this kind from a normative perspective, compare JOHN RAWLS, POLITICAL LIBERALISM 212–20 (1993).

[31] *See* SUSHEELA SINGH ET AL., ABORTION WORLDWIDE: A DECADE OF UNEVEN PROGRESS 50 (Guttmacher Institute 2009). For a broader survey of global abortion laws, see for example UNITED NATIONS, ABORTION POLITICS: A GLOBAL REVIEW (2002), *available at* www.un.org/esa/population/publications/abortion/; Rosalind Dixon & Eric A. Posner, *The Limits of Constitutional Convergence* (Working Paper, 2010); Siegel, *supra* note 29.

[32] After viability, there is perhaps greater scope for disagreement among reasonable persons as to how the balance ought to be struck between the constitutional rights or interests of the fetus, and those of the woman, because for some, the importance of human life as a constitutional value will mean that the claims of the fetus should take priority except in cases where the life of a woman is at stake. However, for those who see human dignity as the "center of the value system of the constitution" (compare *Abortion I*, translated in KOMMERS, *supra* note 8, at 339), there will still be an argument that in some cases a physical or mental health exception should be allowed – because, for example, continuing a pregnancy prevents a woman from obtaining treatment (such as chemotherapy) that is critical for her own health, risks triggering a serious latent illness, or requires a woman to give birth to a child she knows will die shortly after birth, and is subject to other severe forms of impairment: compare for example *Llantoy Huamán v. Peru*, Communication No. 1153/2003, U.N. Doc. CCPR/C/85/D/1153/2003 (2005).

[33] *Cf.* Wesley Hohfeld, *Some Fundamental Legal Conceptions as Applied in Judicial Reasoning*, 23 YALE L. J. 16 (1913); Judith Jarvis Thomson, *A Defense of Abortion*, 1 PHIL. & PUB. AFF., 47, 56 (1971).

also be few circumstances in which it is legitimate – from the standpoint of notions of equal justice – to impose such a duty.[34]

Such a duty certainly could not reasonably be said to arise where a woman's own life was in danger if she continues a pregnancy to term, given her right, as a normative matter, to engage in at least certain limited forms of self-defense.[35] A similar self-defense argument can be made in cases where the woman risks severe bodily injury. If a pregnancy seriously threatens to undermine a woman's physical or psychological health because of the danger associated with the pregnancy itself, or the trauma associated with giving birth to a child who is the result of sexual violence or subject to severe impairments, in most instances it would also be unreasonable in a liberal society that generally prizes individual human dignity over notions of communal obligation to impose such a duty, even if the fetus itself has a claim to be treated with dignity.[36]

As Part I notes, one of the key contributions of the CA in this area is to make clear how and why health is central to a woman's *own* dignity.[37] It makes clear how it is that any demand a woman makes to access an abortion on therapeutic grounds is based on claims with the same *type* of normative force as those made on behalf of the fetus, and therefore why it would be unreasonable for the state to seek systematically to prefer one of these claims over another, by (for example) broadly criminalizing access to abortion.[38] (Where claims are of the same rather than a different type, it is far easier to weigh competing claims against one another, and therefore, where the state prefers a particular claim to another, we infer from this that what is involved is a form of disrespect toward particular persons, rather than simply disagreement about the merits of particular claims.) Once we add recognition of the potential

---

[34] *See* Jarvis Thomson, *supra* note 33 at 51–53.

[35] *See id.* at 60–64. As Cass Sunstein notes, any notion that the act of a woman in refusing such support is in fact active killing, rather than a more passive refusal to provide affirmative support, rests on deeply gendered, stereotypical assumptions about women's presumptive or baseline role in society, see Cass R. Sunstein, *Neutrality in Constitutional Law (with Special References to Pornography, Abortion, and Surrogacy)*, 92 COLUM. L. REV. 1, 35 (1992).

[36] Compare Jarvis Thomson, *supra* note 33 at 58–60, 64 (making similar arguments, though not ones based on the same language of capabilities); Paul Freund, *Storms over the Supreme Court*, 69 A. B. A. J. 1474 (1983). Jarvis Thomson raises the possibility that, in some circumstances, where a woman could be shown affirmatively to have assumed the risk of pregnancy – with full knowledge of its potential risks and consequences – a different position might apply. Like Jarvis Thomson, however, we believe that in practice such cases would tend to be relatively rare, and that in any event, such considerations would only justify constraints on women's access to abortion in limited circumstances, where, for example, the costs to her in terms of dignity of continuing a pregnancy were relatively insignificant.

[37] *See* Part I *supra*.

[38] One argument that is sometimes made to the contrary is that a woman's claim in this context is of lesser standing because she voluntarily assumed the risk of pregnancy. At most, however, such an argument could only legitimately be deemed to apply in very narrow circumstances – where a woman had truly voluntary, unprotected sexual intercourse with full knowledge of the potential risks of pregnancy that entailed: compare Jarvis Thomson, *supra* note 33, at 58–59; Sunstein, *supra* note 35, at 41.

and dependent status of the fetus pre-viability, the *degree* of normative force in the woman's claim also seems stronger.

A similar analysis also applies, under the CA, in circumstances where a woman claims that if she were denied access to an abortion, she would lose all meaningful chance to determine the shape of her future.[39] Not only would a woman in such circumstances lose the opportunity to exercise a central human capability – that is, her capacity for practical reason – the possibility that pregnancy could occur even from fully protected sex could also serve to discourage women more generally from forming the kind of intimate relationship, or seeking the kind of sexual pleasure, that is integral for a life worthy of full human dignity. Again, the woman in this context also invokes the same *type* of normative claim that is made on behalf of the fetus, but the asymmetry between a potential and an actual being suggests that, pre-viability, the woman's claim should in general prevail.

Consistent with this understanding, in comparative constitutional jurisprudence there is broad recognition, even among most constitutional courts that explicitly recognize the fetus as having constitutional standing, that clear limits exist as to when the state may *reasonably* require a woman to continue a pregnancy to term.[40] The GFCC, for example, has held that, even though the fetus possesses human dignity from the moment of conception, and the state is affirmatively obliged under Article 2 of the Basic Law to protect fetal life, a woman's right to freedom and dignity prevents one from insisting that a woman continue a pregnancy that would involve "unreasonable demands."[41] In France, in the face of statutory principles that enshrine a "principle of respect for all human beings from the inception of life,"[42] the *Conseil Constitutionel* has likewise held the Voluntary Interruption of Pregnancy Act is consistent with both statutory and constitutional principles, given that the act both limits the circumstances in which abortion is available (to cases in which there are therapeutic grounds for an abortion or "reasons of distress," and is designed to respect the "freedom of persons" (i.e., the woman)).[43]

For those who advocate moral standing for the fetus, under the CA or otherwise, it is also important to recognize what this entails for the practice of sex-selective abortion common in many parts of the world, particularly the nations of East and South

---

[39] In many countries, this is recognized by the provision for access to abortion after a process of counseling and deliberation, and in others, by provision for access to abortion in cases of "social emergency." *See, e.g., Abortion II, supra* note 8.

[40] One exception is Poland; *see Family Planning Act Amendment*, K. 26/96 (1997).

[41] *See* KOMMERS, *supra* note 8, at 353. *See also* Mary Anne Case, *Perfectionism and Fundamentalism in the Application of the German Abortion Laws, in* CONSTITUTING EQUALITY: GENDER EQUALITY AND COMPARATIVE CONSTITUTIONAL LAW (Susan Williams ed., 2009).

[42] *See* VOLUNTARY INTERRUPTION OF PREGNANCY ACT, Conseil constitutionnel [CC] [Constitutional Court] decision No. 74-54 DC, 1975 (Fr.).

[43] *Id.*

Asia.[44] Sex-selective abortions affect human capabilities in two different ways: instrumental and intrinsic. Instrumentally, such abortions serve to perpetuate denigrating stereotypes of the worth of female life; and also, in many cases, to reinforce gender-based hierarchies in social and economic life. Intrinsically, sex-selective abortions are a type of discrimination that expresses the unequal worth of female life: the fetus, which has some standing, is harmed because it is female. Here we see the value in allowing the fetus to have moral standing: not any and every claim of the parents, but only a claim securely grounded in protection of the woman's central capabilities, will clearly trump the claim of the fetus. "I must protect my health" has one kind of force; "I don't want to pay a dowry" or "I am longing for sons," quite another.

III. REPRODUCTIVE RIGHTS ADVOCACY AND
THE CAPABILITIES APPROACH

Theories shape practical debates, for better or worse. For many years, the equation of economic growth with improvement in quality of life skewed the emphasis of public policy.[45] Similarly, Kantian and other theories that equated human dignity with rationality contributed to the marginalization of people with severe cognitive disabilities. Getting the theories out into the open and articulating them with clarity is important, so that we can challenge what we find defective once we see it plainly. When a defective theory exercises wide influence on public policy, articulating a countertheory is usually the best way of clearing the way for a more adequate set of policies. In one sense, the CA does not say anything that nontheoretical people themselves could not say, if given the chance. It does, however, provide an explicit critique of what is defective in dominant theoretical approaches, at the same time spelling out a richer set of goals with clarity. In the abortion area as well, it has distinct advantages over other theoretical paradigms, not only as Part I argued, in its ability to explain the connection between human dignity in the baseline sense and rights of access to abortion, but also in its capacity to shed light on existing state practices regarding public funding for abortion and on the deficiencies of "women protective" anti-abortion arguments.[46]

---

[44] For data *see* JEAN DRÈZE & AMARTYA SEN, INDIA: DEVELOPMENT AND PARTICIPATION 257–62 (2002). Natality ratios (the biologically common ratio being 95 girls born to 100 boys (95/100)) suggest a high rate of sex-selective abortion not only in poorer nations with low levels of female education and economic participation (such as India, with 92.7/100), but also in Singapore (92/100), Taiwan (92/100), South Korea (88/100), and China (86/100). Wide regional differences exist within India, corresponding to cultural differences.

[45] *See* JOSEPH E. STIGLITZ ET AL., REPORT BY THE COMMISSION ON THE MEASUREMENT OF ECONOMIC PERFORMANCE AND SOCIAL PROGRESS (2009), *available at webcache.googleusercontent .com/search?q=cache*:http://www.stiglitz-sen-fitoussi.fr/documents/rapport_anglais.pdf.

[46] *See* Siegel, *supra* note 1; Reva B. Siegel, *The New Politics of Abortion: An Equality Analysis of Woman-Protective Abortion Restrictions*, 2007 U. ILL. L. REV. 991 [hereinafter Siegel, *The New Politics of Abortion*].

The CA, as Part I notes, helps show why, as a normative matter, rights of access to abortion should be understood in terms that refer to both barriers against state interference and affirmative duties on the part of the state to provide support. A life with human dignity requires protection of all the Central Capabilities up to a minimum threshold level; but all are conceived as opportunities for choice, and thus none has been secured unless the person has the opportunity to exercise choice in matters of actual functioning.

The CA also helps show the close connection between autonomy and health-based reasons for allowing access to abortion, in a way that can help highlight the deep normative inconsistency in allowing a woman access abortion on health grounds, while at the same time denying her capacity for rational decision making about her health. Under the CA, practical reason is not merely one capability on the list: it also suffuses and shapes all the others, making their pursuit truly worthy of human dignity. By providing a theoretical vocabulary in which these interrelationships are articulated, the CA thus gives advocates and policy makers a way of articulating these claims that is richer and more precise than that promised by Kantian or narrowly economic approaches.

In the United States in particular, given the nature of ongoing controversies surrounding access to abortion, both of these theoretical insights are likely to be especially valuable. Access to abortion for poor women remains a major issue in many U.S. states in the wake of the 1977 Hyde Amendment, restricting access to abortion under federal Medicaid programs in all but the most extreme circumstances,[47] which the Supreme Court in *Harris v. McRae* upheld as constitutional.[48] There have also been increasing challenges in the United States in recent years to legal rights of access to therapeutic abortions, or certain abortion procedures designed to protect women's health, based on women-protective anti-abortion arguments.[49] Following *Carhart II* in which the Supreme Court dismissed a facial challenge to the Partial-Birth Abortion Ban Act of 2003,[50] it is illegal in

---

[47] Many recent proposals to expand health care coverage for uninsured Americans also specifically exclude the possibility of indirect government funding for abortion services. *See, e.g.,* Heather D. Boonstra, *The Heart of the Matter: Public Funding of Abortion for Poor Women in the United States,* 10 GUTTMACHER POL'Y REV. 12 (2007).

[48] *See Harris v. McRae,* 448 U.S. 297, 317–18 (1980) (holding, in the context of provisions of the Hyde Amendment preventing use of Medicaid funds for all abortions – including medically necessary abortions – the Court held that "[a]lthough the liberty protected by the Due Process Clause affords protection against government interference with freedom of choice in the context of certain personal decisions, it does not confer an entitlement to such funds as may be necessary to realize all the advantages of that freedom"). *See also Maher v. Roe,* 432 U.S. 464, 475 (1977) (holding in the context of state-based limitations on public funding for nonmedically necessary abortions that "[t]he indigency that may make it difficult – and in some cases, perhaps, impossible – for some women to have abortions is neither created nor in any way affected by" state law and therefore such laws were "not [an impingement] upon the fundamental right recognized in *Roe*").

[49] Siegel, *The New Politics of Abortion, supra* note 46; Siegel, *supra* note 1.

[50] 18 U. S. C. §1531 (2000 ed., Supp. IV)

almost all cases in the United States for medical practitioners to use D&X procedures to perform a late-term abortion. In eight states, there is also legislation that
(at least prima facie) prohibits the use of all abortion procedures (including non-
intact D&E) postviability, unless they are necessary to save the life of a woman,
or justified on very limited health grounds.[51] In the earlier stages of pregnancy,
at least until recently, there have also been concerted attempts to limit access to
RU486 or medical abortion as another medically beneficial abortion option for many
women.[52]

In other countries, however, there are also similar ongoing controversies surrounding access to abortion services. While most countries other than the United States
allow legal access to abortion, they also provide at least some form of public funding
for abortion. In many countries there continues to be important gaps in the adequacy
and universality of such funding.[53]

As to women-protective, anti-abortion arguments, there has also been a rise in
the prevalence of such arguments outside the United States in recent years. Such
arguments have been voiced in the context of the Parliamentary Assembly of the
Council of Europe deliberations[54] and also the United Nations Committee on the

---

[51] *See* Guttmacher Institute, *State Policies in Brief: State Policies on Late Term Abortions* (June 1, 2010), *available at* www.guttmacher.org/statecenter/spibs/spib_PLTA.pdf (listing ten states that impose such procedural restrictions, and eight states that impose relevant substantive limitations).

[52] *See* Siegel, *The New Politics of Abortion, supra* note 46; Siegel, *Dignity and the Abortion Debate, supra* note 2; Siegel, *Dignity and the Politics of Protection, supra* note 1. *See also, e.g.,* arguments in a "citizen's petition" by W. David Hager, member of the FDA Advisory Committee for Repro- ductive Health Drugs, that mifepristone "endangers the lives and health of women." *See* American Association of Pro Life Obstetricians and Gynecologists, *Petition Filed with FDA Regarding Seri- ously Flawed Mifeprex (RU-486) Approval Process,* Aug. 20, 2002 (cited in NARAL, *The Safety of Legal Abortion and the Hazards of Illegal Abortion, available at* www.prochoiceamerica.org/issues/ abortion/medical-abortion/mifepristone-abortion-politics.html, which continues a reliance on such arguments).

[53] In some cases, this is because of an unwillingness on the part of public, as well as private, hospitals to pro- vide abortion services: *see, e.g.,* Press Release, Center for Reproductive Rights, Center Praises Momen- tous Decision in Abortion case in Columbia (Oct. 27, 2009), *available at* http://reproductiverights .org/en/press-room/center-praises-momentous-decision-in-abortion-case-in-colombia (discussing the Constitutional Court's ruling that institutions had to ensure that they had qualified medical staff on hand to perform abortions, a decree that was later suspended by the Council of State. *See* Neda Vanovac, *State Council Suspends Abortion Decree,* COLOMB. REP. (Oct 22, 2009), *available at* http:// colombiareports.com/colombia-news/news/6522-state-council-suspends-abortion-decree.html); in others it is because of budgetary shortfalls: *see, e.g., Women 'Forced to Pay for Private Abortions',* BBC NEWS, Dec. 7, 1999, http://news.bbc.co.uk/2/hi/health/553204.stm (discussing the situation in the United Kingdom in the early 1990s). In yet others, threats to the public funding of abortion arise because of political opposition to access to at least certain forms of abortion: *see, e.g.,* Don MacPherson, *Morgantaler wins NB Challenge for Funding Abortions,* EDMONTON SUN, May 21, 2009, www.edmontonsun.com/news/canada/2009/05/21/9530486.html (describing challenges in New Brunswick, Canada to funding for medically necessary abortions); *Barnett calls for action on late-term abortions,* ABC NEWS, Dec. 22, 2008, www.abc.net.au/news/stories/2008/12/22/2452586.htm?site=news (describing political challenges to the public funding of late-term abortions in Australia).

[54] See discussion in Siegel, *Dignity and the Abortion Debate, supra* note 2 at *5.

Elimination of Discrimination Against Women hearings.[55] More recently, such arguments have also been made in domestic courts such as the High Court of New Zealand, in the context of a challenge to the administration and supervision of various exceptions to the general prohibition on abortion under section 183 of the Crimes Act.[56]

In almost all these contexts, and particularly in the United States, there is also some existing at least quasi-constitutional commitment to recognizing the importance of human dignity, either in a Kantian or baseline sense, in the context of rights of access to abortion, that provides a natural starting point for reproductive rights advocates in seeking to make arguments based on a CA.[57]

Across a wide variety of contexts, therefore, the CA has the potential to make a difference to existing rights of access to abortion on the ground. This is particularly so if it is used by reproductive rights advocates so as to complement or supplement, rather than wholly replace, existing constitutional discourses – such as those based on gender equality.

The CA draws a close connection between human dignity and human equality. The dignity of all human beings (who possess a minimum of agency and sentience) is held to be fundamentally equal.[58] The deep equality of human beings does not necessarily mean that they are only treated justly if they are treated alike: it remains

---

55 See *"Abortion Bad For Women," Protests United Nations Women's Representative*, LIFESITENEWS, July 21, 2005, www.lifesitenews.com/ldn/2005/jul/05072102.html (citing arguments by Hungarian member of the Committee Krisztina Morvai, that "One thing that is invisible and lost in the debate is that abortion is bad for women.... No woman actually wants to have an abortion. We have this illusion that women have free choices. But abortion is a terribly damaging thing psychologically, spiritually, and physically").

56 See *Right to Life New Zealand Inc. v. Abortion Supervisory Committee* [2008] 2 NZLR 825, ¶ 152 (noting that "there is expert evidence that abortions can have adverse psychological side-effects, although the existence and extent of such problems is controversial" but declining to deal with the issue). For ongoing controversy surrounding the administration of the act, see also *Right to Life v. Abortion Supervisory Committee* (Unreported High Court judgment No 2 of Miller, J., July 20, 1999).

57 In the United States, there is a particularly strong constitutional grounding for both dignity as liberty and dignity as equality as applied to the abortion context: *see, e.g., Roe v. Wade*, 410 U.S. 113 (1973); *McRae*, 448 U.S. at 316 (noting that "it could be argued that the freedom of a woman to decide whether to terminate her pregnancy for health reasons does, in fact, lie at the core of the constitutional liberty identified in *Wade*"); *Casey*, 505 U.S. at 846 (affirming "the right of the woman to choose to have an abortion before viability and to obtain it without undue interference from the State" and the right of women, postviability, to access medically necessary abortions). However, in many other countries that have recently experienced debates over access to public funding for abortion, or the rise of women-protective, anti-abortion arguments, there is also some form of quasi-constitutional commitment to recognizing the importance of either dignity as liberty, or dignity in the baseline sense, that provides a starting place for making such arguments in the political sphere: *see, e.g., Right to Life* [2008] 2 NZLR 825, ¶ 77 (holding in the context of statutory provisions allowing abortion in circumstances where "the continuance of the pregnancy would result in serious danger (not being danger normally attendant upon childbirth) to the life, or to the physical or mental health, of a woman or girl" that "from the perspective of a woman who wants an abortion, pregnancy and childbirth impose burdens of a profound and private nature, affecting her physical autonomy, her health, her relationships, and her socioeconomic status."

58 See NUSSBAUM, FRONTIERS OF JUSTICE, *supra* note 19 at ch. 5.

to be seen, in each area, what sort of treatment sufficiently acknowledges the fact of human equality. In some areas – voting, religious liberty – it will readily be agreed that the recognition of human equality requires equal treatment: giving some people more votes than others would be offensive to their equal human dignity. In areas like education, it remains controversial whether respect for human equality requires giving *equal* educational provisions.[59] Yet in areas such as housing, it may seem that respect for human equality requires only a threshold of adequacy: adequate, but not similar housing for all. But one thing that is clearly unacceptable is to give a disadvantage or burden to a group within the population that is already marginalized or disadvantaged on other grounds; this insight, which lies behind modern Equal Protection Clause review, is also articulated by the CA.[60] This insight will show us why the CA supports a common form of argument for abortion rights based on women's equality.

In many countries, as a matter of existing constitutional practice, there is also an extremely close link between, on the one hand, constitutional commitments to human dignity, and on the other, constitutional guarantees of equality. Indeed, in countries such as Canada, Germany, and South Africa, perhaps the most important determinant of whether a constitutional guarantee of equality is violated is in fact whether a measure adversely affects individual dignity – in the sense of an individual's sense of self-worth or enjoyment of respect from others.[61] In the United States, there are also arguable emerging traces of such an understanding in the jurisprudence of Justice Kennedy.[62] In the specific context of abortion, as Canadian Justice Wilson noted in *Morgentaler*, there is also a particularly close connection between the struggle for human dignity and gender equality, given that for many women the struggle for reproductive rights advocates is parallel to previous struggles by men to "assert their common humanity and dignity against an overbearing state apparatus," such that "the right to reproduce or not to reproduce . . . is properly perceived as an integral part of modern woman's struggle to assert *her* dignity and worth as a human being."[63]

At a more theoretic level, Kenneth Karst, Ruth Bader Ginsburg, Cass Sunstein, and Reva Siegel, among others, have further made powerful equality-based arguments in favor of recognizing a constitutional right of access to abortion.[64] Sunstein

[59] *See id.* (arguing that it does).
[60] *See* Nussbaum, *Constitutions and Capabilities, supra* note 17.
[61] In Canada, *see, e.g., Law v. Canada,* [1999] 1 S. C. R. 497; in South Africa, *see, e.g., President of the Republic of South Africa and Another v. Hugo* [1997] ZACC 4; *Harksen v. President of South Africa and Others* [2000] ZACC 29; *City Council of Pretoria v. Walker* [1998] ZACC 1; *Khosa v. The Minister of Social Development* [2003] CCT 13/03.
[62] Siegel, *supra* note 1 (noting the idea of dignity as equality in various U.S. Supreme Court opinions).
[63] *See R. v. Morgentaler,* [1988] 1 S.C.R. 30 at 172 (emphasis in original).
[64] *See generally* Kenneth L. Karst, *Supreme Court Foreword: Equal Citizenship Under the Fourteenth Amendment,* 91 HARV. L. REV. 1 (1977); Sunstein, *supra* note 5; Ruth Bader Ginsburg, *Some Thoughts*

argues that imposing a burden of life support on women, given that they are already a "suspect class" for Equal Protection purposes, is unconstitutional, even if we should grant for the sake of argument that the fetus is a full person – in much the way that a law requiring all and only African Americans to make kidney donations would be unconstitutional.[65] Karst's argument rests, instead, on a notion of equal citizenship, taken to mean equality of legal and social status.[66] The choice to become a parent, he argues, is, among other things, a choice of a social role or status. For the state to deny such a choice is for society to deny the person's equal worth.[67] Ginsburg makes similar arguments. Siegel argues that restrictions on abortion not only express invidious stereotypes about women's role, but also create a caste-like hierarchy by increasing women's dependence on men and impairing women's access to sexual pleasure.[68]

All such arguments, however, gain in clarity when they are expressed in connection with an idea of human capabilities. We always need to say in what respect people are equal or unequal, and assessing capability equality and inequality is particularly pertinent to Equal Protection analysis.[69] Compared to an abstract equality-based approach to reproductive rights advocacy, an approach that seeks to ground the relevant equalities in the idea of human capabilities is, in our view, likely to offer a more robust basis for defending abortion rights in many countries – at least over the long term.

Equality arguments are important because they may persuade people who are convinced that the fetus has a moral status fully equal to that of a born person. They are, however, historically contingent: they depend on a finding that a given classification is "suspect" for Equal Protection purposes, and this, in turn, depends on finding that the class suffers from (at least) a history of discrimination. If women were ever fully equal in a given society, however, they – like all the other people in that society – would still need protections for choice across the entire list of the capabilities, and such guarantees are not supplied by the reliance on equality alone.[70] Laws forbidding marriages between white and black could be struck down on Equal Protection grounds, as they were. Laws prohibiting the marriages of Episcopalians and Presbyterians, should they exist, would be profoundly offensive to the idea of

on *Equality and Autonomy in Relation to Roe v. Wade*, 63 N. C. L. Rev. 375 (1985); Siegel, *supra* note 1; Siegel, *supra* note 6.

[65] See Cass R. Sunstein, The Partial Constitution (1993). *See also* Sunstein, *supra* note 35.

[66] Karst, *supra* note 64.

[67] *Id.* at 32.

[68] See Siegel, *supra* note 1; Siegel, *supra* note 29.

[69] See Nussbaum, *Constitutions and Capabilities*, *supra* note 17 on a range of equal protection cases, especially those of Justice Ginsburg in *U.S. v. Virginia*, 518 U.S. 515 (1996).

[70] *Cf.* Vicki C. Jackson, Constitutional Engagement in a Transnational Era 210–22 (2009) (exploring the distinction between equality and liberty as basis for recognizing rights of access to abortion); Siegel, *supra* note 1 (distinguishing notions of "dignity as liberty" and "dignity as equality").

minimal social justice, even though they would not involve an equality component. The CA reminds us that the protection of human dignity requires the protection of spheres of choice and bodily and mental health in all contexts, not just a situation in which interference is equal for all. In that sense, it not only builds on, but also enriches, the current global constitutional jurisprudence connecting legal rights of access to abortion to the idea of respect for human dignity.

APPENDIX

The Central Human Capabilities

1. **Life.** Being able to live to the end of a human life of normal length; not dying prematurely, or before one's life is so reduced as to be not worth living.
2. **Bodily Health.** Being able to have good health, including reproductive health; to be adequately nourished; to have adequate shelter.
3. **Bodily Integrity.** Being able to move freely from place to place; to be secure against violent assault, including sexual assault and domestic violence; having opportunities for sexual satisfaction and for choice in matters of reproduction.
4. **Senses, Imagination, and Thought.** Being able to use the senses, to imagine, think, and reason – and to do these things in a 'truly human' way, a way informed and cultivated by an adequate education, including, but by no means limited to, literacy and basic mathematical and scientific training. Being able to use imagination and thought in connection with experiencing and producing works and events of one's own choice, religious, literary, musical, and so forth. Being able to use one's mind in ways protected by guarantees of freedom of expression with respect to both political and artistic speech, and freedom of religious exercise. Being able to have pleasurable experiences and to avoid nonbeneficial pain.
5. **Emotions.** Being able to have attachments to things and people outside ourselves; to love those who love and care for us, to grieve at their absence; in general, to love, to grieve, to experience longing, gratitude, and justified anger. Not having one's emotional development blighted by fear and anxiety. (Supporting this capability means supporting forms of human association that can be shown to be crucial in their development.)
6. **Practical Reason.** Being able to form a conception of the good and to engage in critical reflection about the planning of one's life. (This entails protection for the liberty of conscience and religious observance.)
7. **Affiliation.**
    A. Being able to live with and toward others, to recognize and show concern for other human beings, to engage in various forms of social interaction; to be able to imagine the situation of another. (Protecting this capability means

protecting institutions that constitute and nourish such forms of affiliation, and also protecting the freedom of assembly and political speech.)

    B. Having the social bases of self-respect and nonhumiliation; being able to be treated as a dignified being whose worth is equal to that of others. This entails provisions of nondiscrimination on the basis of race, sex, sexual orientation, ethnicity, caste, religion, national origin.

8. **Other Species.** Being able to live with concern for and in relation to animals, plants, and the world of nature.

9. **Play.** Being able to laugh, to play, to enjoy recreational activities.

10. **Control over One's Environment.**

    A. **Political.** Being able to participate effectively in political choices that govern one's life; having the right of political participation, protections of free speech and association.

    B. **Material.** Being able to hold property (both land and movable goods), and having property rights on an equal basis with others; having the right to seek employment on an equal basis with others; having the freedom from unwarranted search and seizure. In work, being able to work as a human being, exercising practical reason and entering into meaningful relationships of mutual recognition with other workers.

PART II

Feminism and Judging

4

Her-meneutics

Feminism and Interpretation

Daphne Barak-Erez

Does feminism have anything to do with interpretation? The answer is yes. Because stereotypes and discriminatory approaches have left their mark on constitutional and legal traditions, it is only logical to assume that feminism should play a role in counteracting these influences. Feminist interpretation can be a very effective tool in the service of gradual legal change. In fact, the connection between feminism and interpretation can be presented even more ambitiously: feminism should also be understood as offering a new interpretive perspective on human knowledge, including in the legal sphere.

Classical examples of the influence of stereotypes and discrimination on interpretation come from cases in which seemingly neutral documents were interpreted as not applying to women because of cultural biases. One illuminating example comes from the United States in the late nineteenth century, when the Equal Protection Clause in the Constitution was found not to apply to women when they brought equality demands to the Supreme Court – Mira Bradwell was denied access to the Illinois Bar[1] and around the same time women were not recognized as entitled to vote (although the U.S. Constitution used neutral terms in drafting the right to vote, which presumably applied to all "persons").[2] The real shift in the case law did not emerge until as late as the 1970s.[3]

The potential contribution of egalitarian interpretation to the transformation of existing legal norms can be exemplified by the story of the Daughters of Tzlofhad in the Biblical Book of Numbers. The daughters claimed they should have had a right to inherit from their father, despite the rule of male inheritance, because their father

---

[1] *Bradwell v. Illinois*, 83 U.S. 130 (1873).
[2] *Minor v. Happersett*, 88 U.S. 162 (1875). *See also* Adam Winkler, *A Revolution Too Soon: Woman Suffragists and the "Living Constitution,"* 76 N.Y.U. L. REV. 1456 (2001).
[3] Starting with *Reed v. Reed*, 404 U.S. 71 (1971).
I would like to thank Tsvi Kahana, Yofi Tirosh, Tsvi Triger, and Dina Zilber for their comments and Yonatan Nadav and Heather Webb for their research assistance.

had died without a male heir. The text notes that their claim was accepted, and
the Biblical rule was changed accordingly for such cases.[4] The story illuminates the
potential of constitutional reform through interpretation, as well as its limitations.
In the Daughters of Tzlofhad case, the feminist challenge led to a more egalitarian
rule, but the basic gender structure of inheritance rights remained in place.

This chapter discusses the potential contribution of feminist-oriented interpretation to constitutional law in the following stages: Part I presents the potential of
different directions of feminist-oriented interpretation, based on the different theoretical foci of the main streams of thought in feminist legal theory. Part II develops
the analysis by addressing the potential for not only different foci offered by different
schools of legal feminism but also of clashes between different feminist approaches
to the same case. Lastly, Part III tries to offer a shared common denominator for
feminist interpretation, based on the aspiration to avoid interpretation that disproportionately burdens women.

I. THE MANY FACES OF FEMINIST INTERPRETATION

Because "feminism" does not refer to a single theory, it is important to stress at
the outset that a feminist approach to interpretation may lead in various directions
depending on which feminist theory is used.

a. *Liberal Feminism and Interpretation*

Liberal feminism, which focuses mainly on equal opportunities and denies stereotypical distinctions between men and women, can inspire several interpretive tools,
all in the service of formal equal opportunities. First, it insists on reading gender-
neutral texts as generally applying to both men and women (in contrast to the
historical precedents mentioned earlier, where neutral drafting was injected with
discriminatory interpretations).[5] Second, it aspires to give narrow meanings to provisions that do contain distinctions between men and women.[6] The Israeli Supreme
Court, which has only limited capacity to judicially review discriminatory legislation
(because of a constitutional tradition of parliamentary sovereignty that had undergone a partial change only in the 1990s),[7] used these strategies in several instances.
It ruled that the Military Service Law provisions that distinguish the service duties

---

[4] *Book of Numbers* 27:1–11.
[5] *See Bradwell*, 83 U.S. 130 and *Happersett*, 88 U.S. 162.
[6] For these interpretive techniques, see also Daphne Barak-Erez, *Can Equality Survive Exceptions?*, 107
    MICH. L. REV. FIRST IMPRESSIONS 134, 236 (2009).
[7] Basic Law: Human Dignity and Liberty, originally enacted in 1992, was interpreted by the Israeli
    Supreme Court as authorizing judicial review of legislation. However, this power is subject to an
    express limitation found in the Basic Law, which protects legislation enacted prior to its enactment
    from such review.

of men in the Israeli Defense Forces (IDF) from those of women[8] did not justify a sweeping refusal to consider women candidates for the military pilots' course.[9] Similarly, the Israeli Supreme Court was unwilling to endorse distinctions between men and women for nominations to state positions in the area of religious services in legislative contexts that did not dictate such distinctions expressly (although Israeli legislation recognizes distinctions of this sort in the context of nominations for rabbinical positions).[10] In a completely different area of law, the Israeli Supreme Court interpreted discriminatory provisions on the taxation of married women[11] as creating rebuttable presumptions that can be pushed aside when women litigants prove their independent economic status.[12]

The liberal feminist approach has a particularly important role when the law recognizes the power of decision makers to revisit and reform traditional rules. An example can be found in the South African case of *Shilubana*,[13] which discussed the possibility of reinterpreting customary law in a manner that recognizes the rights of women to inherit positions of tribal chiefs. The court answered this question in the affirmative, holding that customary law, as recognized by the Constitution,[14] could be interpreted in a way that promotes gender equality.[15]

---

[8] According to the Israeli Defense Service Law, 1986 (SH 1170), women serve only two years, in contrast to the three years of mandatory service of men, and there are special exemptions that apply to them – pregnant women, married women, and mothers are exempted from service, as well as women who declare that they reject service for religious or conscientious reasons.

[9] HCJ 4541/94 *Miller v. Minister of Defense* 49(4) IsrSC 94 [1995]. The petitioner, a woman who was not accepted to the IDF's pilots' course, did not question the statutory arrangements applying to women's service. The Supreme Court declined to justify the military policy in this matter, despite the different regulation of service duties for men and women.

[10] HCJ 153/87 *Shakdiel v. The Minister of Religious Affairs* 42(2) IsrSC 221 [1988]; HCJ 953/87 *Poraz v. The Mayor of Tel-Aviv-Yafo* 42(2) IsrSC 309 [1988].

[11] According to Israeli income tax legislation, the income of married women whose work is "connected" to their husbands' income (due to partnership, etc.) is considered "dependent" on their husbands' income. In this case, the income of the woman is added to her husband's income, subjecting it to a higher level of taxation than it would be had it been taxed independently (according to Income Tax Ordinance [New Version], 1961, sections 64B-66).

[12] See CA 900/01 *Kales v. The Income Tax Assessor of Tel-Aviv 4* 57(3) IsrSC 750 [2003]. The court ruled that the purpose of every statutory provision is to fulfill the basic rights and values of the legal system, one of which is the right of equality, and that interpreting the presumption in a way that prevents the separate calculation of the couple serves as a negative incentive for women to work and thus contributes to their exclusion of the work circle. A similar approach of objecting to nonrebuttable presumptions is found in CA 3185/03 *Flam v. The Officer of the Land Increment* 59(1) IsrSC 123 [2004].

[13] *Shilubana v. Nwamitwa* 2008 (9) BCLR 914 (CC) (S. Afr.).

[14] Section 211 of the South African Constitution states that "the institution, status and role of traditional leadership, according to customary law, are recognised, subject to the Constitution" (sub-section 1); that "[a] traditional authority that observes a system of customary law may function subject to any applicable legislation and customs, which includes amendments to, or repeal of, that legislation or those customs" (sub-section 2); and that "[t]he courts must apply customary law when that law is applicable, subject to the Constitution and any legislation that specifically deals with customary law" (sub-section 3).

[15] The South African Constitutional Court explained that the traditional authorities had the power to develop customary law in accordance with the constitutional right to equality.

b. *Cultural Feminism and Interpretation*

The perspective of cultural feminism stresses the "different voice" of women, focusing on their adherence to an ethic of care.[16] Accordingly, it may serve as a source of inspiration for interpretive tools that inject into current law the willingness to recognize positive duties toward disempowered peoples. A major example of the potential inherent in this approach to reform law through interpretation touches on the reluctance of constitutional traditions to recognize social rights, which impose affirmative duties on the state to provide for basic welfare. Interpretation may play an important role against the background of many vague constitutional texts in this area.

In India, for example, Section 21 of the Constitution (which protects life and liberty) was interpreted as also protecting social rights, such as the right to shelter.[17] This interpretation was not presented as inspired by feminist values, but it may still serve as an example of the willingness to inject an ethic of care into existing constitutional texts.

Other jurisdictions are more reserved about going in this direction. In Canada, for example, the Supreme Court left open the question of recognizing the constitutional status of social rights in its famous decision of *Gosselin v. Quebec (A.G.)*.[18] In this case, the appellant was a welfare recipient who brought a challenge against the provincial social assistance scheme that set the base amount of welfare payable to persons younger than thirty at about one-third of the amount payable to those older than thirty. The Supreme Court of Canada found that the legislation did not violate the appellant's right to life, liberty, and security under Section 7 of the Canadian Charter of Rights and Freedoms, 1982. However, the court explicitly stated that Section 7 might be read one day as imposing "positive obligations" on the state: "It would be a mistake to regard s. 7 as frozen, or its content as having been exhaustively defined in previous cases."[19] Therefore, while the appellant was unsuccessful in proving discrimination on the facts of this case, the court left open the question of whether social rights might one day be recognized under the Charter.[20]

Another example comes from Israel, where the Supreme Court was willing to take only a modest step forward in this area in the case of *Commitment to Peace & Social Justice Assoc. v. Minister of Finance*.[21] This petition sought to challenge

---

[16] *See* CAROL GILLIGAN, IN A DIFFERENT VOICE (1982).

[17] *See* Jayna Kothari, *Social Rights in India – Developments of the Last Decade*, in EXPLORING SOCIAL RIGHTS: BETWEEN THEORY AND PRACTICE 171 (Daphne Barak-Erez & Aeyal M. Gross eds., 2007).

[18] 2002 SCC 84, [2002] 4 S.C.R. 429.

[19] *Id.* ¶ 82. Justice Abella, in her dissenting opinion, held that Section 7 imposes a positive obligation on the state to provide the basic means of subsistence for its citizens.

[20] For an additional analysis of this decision, see POVERTY: RIGHTS, SOCIAL CITIZENSHIP, AND LEGAL ACTIVISM (Margot Young et al., eds., 2008).

[21] HCJ 888,366/03 *Commitment to Peace & Social Justice Assoc. v. Minister of Finance* (unpublished) [2005].

the constitutionality of significant reductions in the level of state income support, which had led to an average reduction in excess of 30 percent in the level of support, in addition to the revocation of other benefits and subsidies. The petition rested on the argument that these changes had violated the social component of the constitutional right to dignity. The Israeli Supreme Court dismissed the petition (in a majority opinion). The leading majority opinion, written by Chief Justice Aharon Barak, stated that the constitutional right to human dignity also encompasses a positive right to a minimum level of living, but no more than that. The judgment accepted the argument of the state that the right to human dignity is engaged only in cases of material deficiency that prevents a person from subsisting.[22] Thus, the court was willing to inject an ethic of care to the constitutional text, but only in a very restrained and hesitant manner.[23]

In addition to its potential contribution to concrete interpretive choices, cultural feminism may also have an important contribution to the drafting of constitutional texts. Cultural feminism celebrates the feminine voice that objects to binary normative decisions. Accordingly, it may inspire complex and contextualized drafting choices with regard to new constitutional texts.[24]

c. *Radical Feminism and Interpretation*

Radical feminism focuses on the liberation of women from their social subordination to men and from their subjection to violence. It endorses interpretive choices that lead to more effective resistance to such subordination and violence. Major examples of interpretation inspired by radical feminism are drawn from the work of Catharine MacKinnon. Viewing sexual harassment as a form of discrimination[25] and pornography as an action rather than speech[26] are in fact two important interpretative choices in the service of resisting subordination.

---

[22] *Id.* ¶¶ 14–16. The minority opinion of Justice Levi was willing to go beyond this standard and interpret the right to human dignity as including a right to adequate conditions of living, as opposed to the minimum approach advocated by Chief Justice Barak.

[23] *See* Daphne Barak-Erez & Aeyal M. Gross, *Social Citizenship: The Neglected Aspect of Israeli Constitutional Law, in* EXPLORING SOCIAL RIGHTS: BETWEEN THEORY AND PRACTICE 243 (Daphne Barak-Erez & Aeyal M. Gross eds., 2007).

[24] For another argument against legislative integrity, because it suffocates the "moral fragmentation" necessary for societal pluralism, *see* Andrei Marmor, *Should We Value Legislative Integrity?, in* THE LEAST EXAMINED BRANCH: THE ROLE OF LEGISLATURES IN THE CONSTITUTIONAL STATE 125, 132–33 (Richard W. Bauman & Tsvi Kahana eds., 2006).

[25] MacKinnon's classic work in this area is CATHARINE A. MACKINNON, SEXUAL HARASSMENT OF WORKING WOMEN: A CASE OF SEX DISCRIMINATION (1979). This theory was accepted by the U.S. Supreme Court in *Meritor Saving v. Vinson*, 477 U.S. 57 (1986).

[26] CATHARINE A. MACKINNON, ONLY WORDS (1993). MacKinnon's view on this matter was rejected in the United States, *American Booksellers v. Hudnut* 771 F.2d 323 (1985), but was accepted in Canada, *R v. Butler*, [1992] 1 S.C.R. 452. The *Butler* case, *id*, is discussed further later in the chapter.

More examples can be drawn from the case law on rape, specifically where "consent" has been interpreted to exclude situations with silent victims or victims who were coerced to agree to sex under the threat of authority, as was the case in the Israeli Supreme Court's *Kibbutz Shomrat* decision.[27] The court interpreted the concept of consent with reference to the reality of social coercion, and accordingly dismissed the contention that a girl who was gang-raped by teenagers known to her actually "consented" by not actively resisting her attackers.[28]

d. *Diversity in Feminism and Interpretation*

The broadening of feminist jurisprudence to include voices of women from different backgrounds, going beyond the model of the "middle-class, educated white" feminist,[29] is also relevant for legal interpretation. These voices are important, for example, to the operation of affirmative action programs aimed at securing adequate representation of women in government service or legislatures. Awareness of the diversity of women could inform an interpretive choice that sees adequate representation as taking into account other group affiliations of the women candidates, such as their ethnic origin.[30]

II. CONFLICTING FEMINIST INTERPRETATIONS

The interpretive approaches offered thus far may add valuable perspectives to the interpretive arena. At the same time, they carry the potential of intensifying the conflicts between feminists because they import into the interpretive arena the bitter controversies between the various feminist schools of thought. More concretely, when the methods described so far are applied in the circumstances of the same case, they may lead in different directions.

---

[27] See Crim A. 5612/92 *The State of Israel v. Be'eri* 48(1) IsrSC 302 [1993]. The decision is known as the *Kibbutz Shomrat* case, after the kibbutz in which this group rape occurred.
[28] In the circumstances of the case, a fourteen-year-old girl was raped by a group of seventeen-year-old boys. Despite a verbal refusal in the beginning, the girl's behavior was mostly passive. The judgment of the Israeli Supreme Court laid down several important rules on consent. Most importantly, it stated that consent may not be inferred from lack of resistance.
[29] See, e.g., Kimberlé Crenshaw, *Demarginalizing the Intersection of Race and Sex: A Black Feminist Critique of Antidiscrimination Doctrine, Feminist Theory, and Antiracist Politics*, 1989 U. CHI. LEGAL F. 139; PATRICIA J. WILLIAMS, THE ALCHEMY OF RACE AND RIGHTS: A DIARY OF A LAW PROFESSOR (1991).
[30] The goal of securing adequate representation of women coming from various backgrounds is not always found expressly in legislation despite the fact that affirmative action to historically disadvantaged groups has been acknowledged in various constitutional contexts. See, e.g., *Grutter v. Bollinger*, 539 U.S. 306 (2003); *R. v. Kapp*, 2008 SCC 41, [2008] 2 S.C.R. 483 (Can.). An example of a statutory provision that expressly mentions the goal of diversity in the context of representative appointments of women is found in section 6C1 of the Israeli Women's Equal Rights Law, 1951 (on the issue of representation in public committees).

Examples of such clashes are found in three interesting cases decided by the Israeli Supreme Court – the *Nachmani* affair,[31] which dealt with surrogacy litigation; the *Milo* decision,[32] involving a conscientious objection to military service; and the *Shin* decision,[33] which dealt with limitations on pornography. The three cases present tensions between rival feminist views – between the firm liberal views of the court in decisions authored by women justices and the challenges brought by women litigants whose views can be characterized as more closely related to other forms of feminism (cultural feminism in the first two, and radical feminism in the third).

The *Nachmani* affair concerned the fate of the frozen pre-embryos of Ruti Nachmani and her estranged husband Danny Nachmani. Ruti had a hysterectomy, and therefore could not bear a child. She and her husband decided to attempt *in vitro* fertilization, a process involving the implantation of a fertilized ovum, using a surrogate mother. Later, the relationship between the couple ran into difficulties, and Danny wanted to stop the process. He also became a father within the framework of a new family unit. Ruti still wanted to become a mother and asked to use the pre-embryos for a surrogacy procedure, noting the fact that she probably could not become a mother by other means because of her age and health, and that she had already suffered considerable pain in the course of the fertility treatments.

The majority of the justices of the Israeli Supreme Court accepted Danny's argument for the following reasons: according to the principle of human dignity, one should not compel a person to be a parent; due to the principle of equality, a man has the right to decide to stop the surrogacy process, just as a woman has the right to decide to stop her pregnancy at will. This decision was authored by the only female judge on the panel, Justice Tova Shtrasberg-Cohen, who was supported by three other justices, against the minority view of Justice Tal.

The minority opinion was based on a preference for parenthood, as well as on estoppel. According to Justice Tal, the court faced two difficult options, either "compelled parenthood" or barrenness. He held that the former was the lesser of the two evils. Whereas compelled parenthood imposes uncomfortable emotional burdens and other obligations on the father, compelled sterility deprives the woman of the basic fundamental right to become a mother. Moreover, the woman in this case went through a hard, invasive process based on the man's consent. The process of fertilization deprived the woman of other options, such as fertilization by sperm donation, and her situation was radically changed because of the father's consent.

Justice Shtrasberg-Cohen for the majority seemed to have written the judgment from the perspective of traditional liberal feminism. She refused to be inspired by the traditional stereotype of motherhood. In addition, she gave priority to the negative

---

[31] CA 5587/93 *Nachmani v. Nachmani* 49(1) IsrSC 485 [1995] [hereinafter *Nachmani* 1] and CFH 2401/95 *Nachmani v. Nachmani* 50(4) IsrSC 661 [1996] [hereinafter *Nachmani* 2].

[32] HCJ 2383/04 *Milo v. Minister of Defense* 59(1) IsrSC 166 [2004].

[33] HCJ 5432/03 *Shin – For Equal Representation of Women v. the Council of Cable and Satellite Broadcasting* 58(3) IsrSC 65 [2004].

right (the protection against compelled parenthood) over the positive right (the right to become a parent) entailing potential burdens. However, a different feminist view could have led to a different interpretive approach to the balancing stage. From an ethic-of-care perspective, the possibility of living a life of barrenness is more threatening than the possibility of incurring unwanted burdens of parenthood. This analysis is not aimed at deciding the case differently. Rather, it aspires to stress that the *Nachmani* affair was not about *whether* to choose a feminist view; in fact, it posed to the question *which* feminist view to prioritize.[34]

The *Milo* decision is another interesting example taken from the case law of the Israeli Supreme Court. In this case, Laura Milo, a female high school graduate, asked to be exempted from army service altogether for reasons of conscience "given her opposition to the IDF policy in the territories."[35] She based her request on the statutory provision regulating women's exemption from military service "for reasons of conscience or for reasons connected with her family's religious way of life."[36] The exemptions committee refused to allow Laura Milo's request, which was based on her critique of the army's policy in Israel's occupied territories. The committee regarded the request as motivated by a political rather than a conscientious reason. This decision was consistent with the army's policy concerning men who refuse to serve. Men are exempted from service only when they object to military service in general on pacifist grounds (and not when their objection is related to the government's policy concerning specific battle areas or aims of combat).

The legal controversy that evolved from the petition had to address the fact that the Defense Service Law does not include a general provision on exemptions for reasons of conscience and, ostensibly, does not acknowledge exemptions for these reasons where men are concerned. In contrast, Section 39 of the Defense Service Law includes an explicit provision allowing the exemption of a woman from service "for reasons of conscience," as well as for "reasons connected with her family's religious way of life." The question in the *Milo* case was how this provision should be interpreted. Does the exemption in Section 39, granted only to women, apply only to pacifist conscientious objectors (following the general policy with regard to men) or to other conscientious objectors as well? Moreover, did the law intend to grant women an exemption for reasons of conscience separate and independent from the exemption granted to them for religious reasons?

The Supreme Court rejected Laura Milo's petition, adopting a restrictive inter- pretation of Section 39. This decision too was authored by the only woman on the

---

[34] Eventually, *Nachmani 1* was changed, but with no direct reference to the reasoning of the original decision. In *Nachmani 2*, many of the (new) majority Justices were guided by considerations of "justice," assuming that the case touched on a legal lacunae. For more discussion of this affair, with an emphasis on the normative choices of the court in its original balancing between the right to become a parent and the right not to become a parent, see Daphne Barak-Erez & Ron Shapira, *The Delusion of Symmetric Rights*, 19 OXFORD J. LEGAL STUD. 297 (1998).

[35] *Id.* at 170.

[36] Defense Service Law, § 39.

panel, Justice Procaccia, with Justices Matza and Levi concurring. The court's decision stated that Section 39 grants women an exemption from service only when the reason for their refusal is related to a communal or religious tradition. According to Justice Procaccia, "an exemption for 'reasons of conscience' in the special context of this provision is closely related to reasons of religious, traditional, or ethnic–custom conviction, which prevent a woman from serving in any defense service as such."[37] She then explained that "the statutory exemption for reasons of conscience granted to women was meant to protect the status of women in traditional communities where members find army service incompatible with the protection of the women's honor and chastity, and may even contradict explicit injunctions in the religious commandments incumbent on them."[38] This interpretation attached the "reasons of conscience" in Section 39 to the "reasons of her family's religious way of life" and erased the option of an independent exemption for nonreligious reasons of conscience under Section 39. According to the decision, the exemption of women for reasons of conscience, insofar as it exists, can be found in the general provision of Section 36, which allows for exemption from service for "other reasons," and is therefore identical in scope to the exemption given to men. According to the court, despite the special provisions for women under the Defense Service Law, the army's current policy, negating the recognition of "selective" nonpacifist conscientious objection related to the army's policies or mode of action, extends to women as well.

Like the *Nachmani* affair, the *Milo* decision presents a clash of feminist views. The opinion of the court represents the standard liberal feminism approach.[39] The petitioner, however, seems to be closer to cultural feminism in her resistance to militarism and her willingness to base her arguments on legal provisions that distinguish between men and women (although her arguments did not take a stand in this matter expressly).[40]

The third example is taken from the *Shin* case, which dealt with the decision of the Council of Cable and Satellite TV Broadcasting to permit the broadcasting

---

[37] *Milo*, 59(1) IsrSC 166 [2004].

[38] *Id.*

[39] Justice Proccacia was firm in her support of equal treatment of men and women, even to the extent of not addressing the fact that the specific statute at hand endorsed distinctions between men and women with regard to the required length of their service as well as to exemptions from service – granted to married women, mothers, etc. (and not to men). Therefore, the *Milo* decision did not lead to genuinely egalitarian service schemes for men and women. The failure to acknowledge an exemption for women for reasons of so-called selective conscience led to equality between men and women objectors, but did not change the overall picture of women's military service and its perception as "something different."

[40] Laura Milo's case was not argued as a feminist case. She did not make any statements implying that her being a woman was in any way relevant to her petition. However, the full public meaning of her struggle is determined not only by her declarations but rather by the wider context of her actions. This context requires to consider the petitioner's request to ground her exemption in a statutory provision specific to women, her choice to undergo a legal struggle (as opposed to taking advantage of the relatively lenient policy applying to women who seek not to serve) and the fact that her struggle was a harbinger of other young women's declarations of refusal to serve.

of the Playboy channel on cable and satellite. The relevant statute prohibited "a depiction of a person or any part of a person as a sex object" as well as "a depiction of sexual intercourse that involves violence, abuse, humiliation, degradation, or exploitation."[41] Hence, legally speaking, the question was whether the Council's decision reflected these statutory criteria.

The petitioners, who were inspired by radical feminism, argued that the purpose of the legislation was to prevent any broadcasting that depicts women as sexual objects, and that the Playboy channel fell within the scope of this definition. They resisted distinctions between different forms of pornography and erotica, and objected to the view that displays of women as tradable objects should enjoy the protection of freedom of speech. The Israeli Supreme Court dismissed the petition in a decision that was heavily inspired by traditional liberal thinking (liberal feminism included). The main opinion of the court was authored by Justice Dorner, who is perceived as a feminist judge (and even had a significant role in authoring the majority opinion in the *Miller* decision on women military pilots). Justice Dorner stressed that pornography should enjoy freedom of speech protections. According to her, "pornographic and erotic expression . . . is part of human creativity in modern times, furthers public debate and influences the positions of those who participate therein."[42] She admitted that according to balancing theory, freedom of speech should be balanced against other rights, and in this case specifically against the right to human dignity, which also protects the dignity of women. She even mentioned the controversy concerning pornography among feminists – between the liberal approach and the radical one. Yet, eventually, she was willing to assume that the Playboy channel did not infringe the dignity of women. In addition, considering the fact that pornography is legal and available in many other media besides cable and satellite broadcasting, Justice Dorner explained that the additional harm to women's dignity caused by the channel could not be regarded "particularly serious."[43] Justice Dorner stressed in her opinion the concern that giving the statutory prohibition broad interpretation might lead to regression to the old days of dangerous, nondemocratic censorship. In sum, Justice Dorner's judgment, which was supported by the other ten Justices on the panel (with reservations regarding the availability of freedom of speech protections for pornography in only two of the other opinions), exemplifies once again the potential clash between two conflicting feminist interpretations.[44]

---

[41] Section 6Y(2) of the Communications (Telecommunications and Broadcasting) Law, 1982.

[42] *Shin*, 58(3) IsrSC 65, 81 [2004].

[43] *Id.*, at 85.

[44] In contrast, the Supreme Court of Canada has found laws restricting the sale and possession of obscene material justifiable, although they limit freedom of expression and therefore infringe Section 2(b) of the Canadian Charter of Rights and Freedoms. In *Butler*, [1992] 1 S.C.R. 452, the accused owned a shop that sold and rented "hard core" pornographic videotapes and related merchandise. He argued that a law prohibiting the distribution of obscene material infringed his Section 2(b) rights. The court agreed, but held that the prohibition was a justified limitation because such material, which depicts sex in a degrading or dehumanizing manner, is harmful to society and in particular to women. The

III. ASKING "THE WOMAN QUESTION" AND FEMINIST INTERPRETATION: FROM THEORY TO CONTEXT

Rather than deciding between the previously discussed feminist views, which are all important for informing the interpretive discourse, I would like to concentrate on another overarching interpretive principle: giving preference to interpretive choices that are less inclined to disproportionately disadvantage women, by asking "the woman question." "The woman question" was proposed as a legal method by Katherine Bartlett, who argued that feminist jurisprudence in general should expose the impact of legal rules and principles on women.[45] For her, the question was a method for the study and critique of law. I argue that it is possible to apply this method for the purpose of legal interpretation to avoid interpretive choices that disproportionately burden women and to prefer, where possible, interpretive alternatives that promote the just allocation of social burdens (and thus eventually improve also the situation of men, who are burdened by other social stereotypes and expectations).

Asking the woman question may help us earn a fresh start in the debates on constitutional interpretation in the area of abortion rights. The abortion controversy is truly an interpretive debate, as older constitutional texts do not regulate it expressly. It was debated as such in both the U.S. Supreme Court[46] and the German Constitutional Court.[47] The two courts interpreted different documents and reached different decisions: the U.S. Court acknowledged a right to abortion in the first stages of pregnancy, but was open to placing limitations on it in later stages, whereas the German Court did not recognize such a right but was willing to accept the choice not to criminalize abortion. Asking the woman question enables us to go beyond these differences, acknowledge them as legitimate, and at the same time argue that, at any rate, a constitutional interpretation that enables a sweeping ban

---

court followed the same line of argumentation in *Little Sisters Book and Art Emporium v. Canada* (Minister of Justice), 2000 SCC 69, [2000] 2 S.C.R. 1120. In that case, the appellant bookstore sold gay and lesbian pornographic material in addition to more general-interest inventory. It imported a large part of its total inventory from the United States, and Customs inspectors detained some of the material on the basis that it was "obscene." The court again held that the legislation prohibiting the importation of obscene material infringed the right to freedom of expression guaranteed under Section 2(b) but that it was justified under Section 1. This decision was subject to criticism because of its potential to marginalize sexual minorities. *See* Brenda Cossman, *Disciplining the Unruly: Sexual Outlaws, Little Sisters and the Legacy of Butler*, 36 U.B.C. L. REV. 77 (2003); Aleardo Zanghellini, *Is Little Sisters Just Butler's Little Sister?*, 37 U.B.C. L. REV. 407 (2004); Christopher N. Kendall, *Gay Male Pornography and Sexual Violence: A Sex Equality Perspective on Gay Male Rape and Partner Abuse*, 49 McGILL L. J. 877 (2004).

[45] Katharine T. Bartlett, *Feminist Legal Methods*, 103 HARV. L. REV. 829, 837–49 (1990). Bartlett's approach was inspired by earlier writings, especially Heather Wishik, *To Question Everything: The Inquiries of Feminist Jurisprudence*, 1 BERKELEY WOMEN'S L. J. 64 (1985) and SIMONE DE BEAUVOIR: LE DEUXIÈME SEXE (1949).

[46] *Roe v. Wade*, 410 U.S. 113 (1973); *Planned Parenthood v. Casey*, 505 U.S. 833 (1992).

[47] *See* Gerald L. Neuman, *Casey in the Mirror: Abortion, Abuse and the Right to Protection in the United States and Germany*, 43 AM. J. COMP. L. 273 (1995).

on abortion should be rejected because of the disproportionate burden it puts on women.

Asking the woman question also opens additional possibilities for thinking about the status of social rights in the constitutional regime. Denying constitutional status to social rights has a disproportionate effect on women, who are in general poorer (alongside other disadvantaged groups) and carry the burden of caring for their dependent relatives.[48] Accordingly, an interpretive choice that promotes the protection of social rights within vague constitutional texts is a feminist one because of its positive impact on women's life conditions. In this sense, supporting social rights is not only a matter of an "ethic of care" (as argued before),[49] but also a material interest of women as a group.[50]

Acknowledging the disproportionate effect of a legal rule on women is not always enough. It is important not only to trace this effect, but also to deny the legitimacy of this result. Even when the disproportionate burden is acknowledged, it is sometimes approved as justified.[51]

Another context in which the disproportionate burden on women may have an impact on interpretive choices concerns the legal prohibitions on domestic violence. Domestic violence disproportionately harms women and children. Therefore, interpretive choices that promote the enforcement of such prohibitions should be considered feminist in the sense that they decrease this disproportionately incurred social harm.[52]

More generally, an interpretive method that focuses on identifying norms that impose disproportionate burdens has many advantages. First, as argued before, it has a lesser tendency to expose conflicts among feminist theorists (although it cannot eliminate them altogether). Second, asking the woman question is a contextualized

---

[48] On the "feminization of poverty," *see* Diane Pearce, *The Feminization of Poverty: Women, Work, and Welfare*, 11 URBAN AND SOCIAL CHANGE REV. 28 (1978); Emily M. Northrop, *The Feminization of Poverty: The Demographic Factor and the Composition of Economic Growth*, 24 J. ECON. ISSUES 145 (1990); DAILY STRUGGLES: THE DEEPENING RADICALIZATION AND FEMINIZATION OF POVERTY IN CANADA (Maria A Wallis & Siu-ming Kwok eds., 2008); Robyn I. Stone, *The Feminization of Poverty Among the Elderly, in* THE OTHER WITHIN US: FEMINIST EXPLORATIONS OF WOMEN AND AGING (Marily Pearsall ed., 1997); SHIRLEY A. LORD, SOCIAL WELFARE AND THE FEMINIZATION OF POVERTY (1993); CATHERINE KINGFISHER, WESTERN WELFARE IN DECLINE: GLOBALIZATION AND WOMEN'S POVERTY (2002); JOHANNA BRENNER, WOMEN AND THE POLITICS OF CLASS (2006); VALERIE POLAKOV, LIVES ON THE EDGE: SINGLE MOTHERS AND THEIR CHILDREN IN THE OTHER AMERICA (1994).

[49] See text accompanying fns. 17–23, *supra*.

[50] *See also* Daphne Barak-Erez, *Social Rights as Women's Rights, in* EXPLORING SOCIAL RIGHTS: BETWEEN THEORY AND PRACTICE 397 (Daphne Barak-Erez & Aeyal M. Gross eds., 2007).

[51] For example, in *Newfoundland (Treasury Board) v. Newfoundland and Labrador Association of Public and Private Employees*, [2004] 3 S.C.R. 381, 2004 SCC 66 the Supreme Court of Canada acknowledged that eliminating pay equity adjustments in order to satisfy government budgets constituted discriminatory treatment under Section 15(1) of the Charter, but nevertheless held that the action was justified under Section 1 of the Charter.

[52] *See also* Sheilah L. Martin, *Some Constitutional Considerations on Sexual Violence Against Women*, 32 ALTA. L. REV. 535 (1994).

approach that avoids general assumptions regarding "women" as a legal and social category, and in this respect answers postmodernist feminism concerns.[53] Third, it takes into consideration additional burdens that are carried by women who come from disadvantaged backgrounds.[54] In addition, it avoids the need to develop a comprehensive theory but rather concentrates on practice and facts, in the tradition of feminist thinking.[55]

CONCLUSION

This chapter has argued that interpretation should be an important focus of legal feminism, and even more so in the sphere of constitutional law, which shapes the foundations of every legal system. It has shown the potential inherent in different feminist approaches to offer different interpretive perspectives and has then exposed the clashes that may arise when different feminist-oriented interpretations are applied. Eventually, the analysis aspired to emphasize the unique contribution of feminism to constitutional interpretation by focusing on the "woman question," which aims at avoiding interpretations that place a disproportionate burden on women.

---

[53] For the post feminist critique on feminism, see JUDITH BUTLER, GENDER TROUBLE: FEMINISM AND THE SUBVERSION OF IDENTITY (1999); Patricia A. Caine, *Feminism and the Limits of Equality*, 24 GA. L. REV. 803, 839 (1990).

[54] *See supra* note 29.

[55] Bartlett herself calls it "feminist practical reasoning." *See* Bartlett, *supra* note 45, at 849.

5

Intuition and Feminist Constitutionalism

Suzanne B. Goldberg

In any constitutional system, we must ask, as a foundational inquiry, when and why a government may distinguish between groups of constituents for purposes of allocating benefits or imposing penalties. For feminists and others with a stake in challenging inequalities, the rationales that a society deems acceptable for justifying these classifications are centrally important. Heightened scrutiny jurisprudence for sex-based and other distinctions may help capture some of the rationales that rest on stereotypes and outmoded biases. However, at the end of the day, whatever level of scrutiny is applied, the critical question at any level of review is whether, according to the decision maker, the government has adequately justified the distinction it has drawn.[1]

For most official classifications, the rationales for differentiating among people are obvious and unremarkable, and the laws at issue provoke no challenges. Age-based rules that require only some people (youth) to attend school are a classic example. Similar are rules that restrict the issuance of drivers' licenses to individuals without significantly impaired vision. In these instances, the government's line-drawing is linked to a demonstrable characteristic of the people who are burdened by the measure at issue.[2]

---

[1] Of course, the relationship between the rigor of review and quality of acceptable justifications can be an interactive one. Under the tiered approach to equal protection analysis applied by federal courts in the United States, for example, certain justifications that might be sufficient at the lowest level rational-basis review will be deemed inadequate when heightened scrutiny is applied. *See, e.g., Cook v. Babbitt*, 819 F. Supp. 1, 21 n.19 (D.C. Cir. 1993) (finding that, where the "only rational basis for a gender-based exclusion policy would be... administrative convenience," it is an "open question" "whether this rational basis could survive heightened scrutiny") (citations omitted).

[2] We see this as well in the rationales proffered for other sorts of restrictions on rights. The government justifies restriction of rights of enemy combatants, for example, by pointing to national security concerns. *See Hamdi v. Rumsfeld*, 542 U.S. 507 (2004). Likewise, schools have argued that students' free speech rights must be restricted to prevent the undermining of educational institutions' objectives. *See Morse v. Frederick*, 551 U.S. 393 (2007).

In this vein, early gender and sexuality litigation was aimed at showing courts that discriminatory classifications rested on unfounded stereotypes about the competency of the group members in question rather than on a factually demonstrable defining characteristic of the burdened group.[3] So, for example, in the U.S. Supreme Court's earliest ruling to reject a sex-based classification, the Court invalidated a law favoring husbands over wives as estate administrators, finding that women had shown themselves to be as capable as men at the task.[4] Likewise, many courts that once treated mothers and heterosexual parents as more capable of supporting healthy child development than fathers, or gay or lesbian parents, now take the default position that sex and sexual orientation are neutral factors, absent evidence to the contrary.[5]

Although many so-called facts about social groups have later been shown to embody bias or stereotypes,[6] a regime that requires demonstrable facts before the state can discriminate creates the possibility, at least, for empirical contestation of the proffered characterization of group members.[7] So, for example, a decision resting

---

[3] For example, early decisions upholding interracial marriage bans often resorted to pseudo-scientific conclusions that the children of interracial couples would be genetically inferior. *See, e.g., Jackson v. State*, 72 So.2d 114, 115 (Ala. Ct. App. 1954) (upholding Alabama's anti-miscegenation statute based on the "well authenticated fact that if the [issue] of a black man and a white woman, and a white man and a black woman, intermarry, they cannot possibly have any progeny"); *Naim v. Naim*, 87 S.E.2d 749, 756 (Va. 1955) (asserting that interracial marriage would produce a "mongrel breed of citizens"); *Perez v. Lippold*, 198 P.2d 17, 26 (Cal. 1948) (striking down California's ban on interracial marriages and criticizing the underlying beliefs "that such minorities are inferior in health, intelligence, and culture, and that this inferiority proves the need of the barriers of race prejudice"). *See also* Keith E. Sealing, *Blood Will Tell: Scientific Racism and the Legal Prohibitions Against Miscegenation*, 5 MICH. J. RACE & L. 559 (2000) (discussing the development of and justifications for anti-miscegenation laws in the United States).

[4] *Reed v. Reed*, 404 U.S. 71, 77 (1971).

[5] Michael S. Wald, *Adults' Sexual Orientation and State Determinations Regarding Placement of Children*, 40 FAM. L. Q. 381, 422 (2006) ("Most courts now apply what is commonly called the *nexus* test: a parent's sexual orientation will be deemed relevant only if there is evidence that the parent's sexual orientation is having, or is likely to have, a negative impact on the child."); Laura T. Kessler, *Transgressive Caregiving*, 33 FLA. ST. U. L. REV. 1, 30–31 (2005) (observing that "the majority of states no longer take into account the sexual orientation of a parent in custody disputes" and characterizing the "nexus test" as "mak[ing] the sexual orientation of a parent irrelevant unless there is evidence that it will negatively impact the best interests of the child"). *See also S.E.G. v. R.A.G.*, 735 S.W.2d 164, 166 (Mo. App. 1987) (ruling that in order to deny parental rights, "[t]here must be a nexus between harm to the child and the parent's homosexuality"); *S.N.E. v. R.L.B.*, 699 P.2d 875, 879 (Alaska 1985) (declining to consider the homosexuality of a parent where "there is no suggestion that [the parent's sexual orientation] has or is likely to affect the child adversely"); *M.P. v. S.P.*, 404 A.2d 1256, 1263 (N.J. Super. Ct. 1979) (declining to consider the homosexuality of a mother where "[n]othing suggests that her homosexual preference in itself presents any threat of harm to her daughters").

[6] Many arguably "demonstrable" facts themselves embody bias or stereotypes, and the American case law is full of instances in which courts have relied on "facts" about a social group to sustain what was later understood to be an invidious distinction. *See* Suzanne B. Goldberg, *Constitutional Tipping Points: Civil Rights, Social Change, and Fact-Based Adjudication*, 106 COLUM. L. REV. 1955 (2006); Suzanne B. Goldberg, *On Making Anti-Essentialist and Social Constructionist Arguments in Court*, 81 OR. L. REV. 629 (2002) (hereinafter *Anti-Essentialist Arguments in Court*).

[7] Of course, facts, as well as norms, are inevitably theory-soaked and socially constructed; by distinguishing between the two, I do not mean to suggest that they are easily separable. *See, e.g.,* Katherine M.

on the "fact" that fathers or gay people have less ability to parent well than mothers or heterosexuals is subject to data-based contestation. Again, this is not to suggest that courts will be persuaded by data that runs counter to their impressions. Indeed, empirical research also shows that people often hold to their views about social groups even in the face of contrary data.[8] However, for purposes here, the point is that a regime that insists on demonstrable facts before the state can discriminate offers those burdened at least some opportunity to contest the basis for the burdens imposed on them.

In this sense, intangible rationales present a special challenge for anyone concerned with eradicating traditional or long-standing barriers to equality, and these kinds of rationales – in particular, intuition, morality, and "common sense" – are this chapter's focus. When a decision maker relies on any of these to sustain government regulation, factual contestation is beside the point, as the rationale is avowedly nonempirical. For example, when the U.S. Supreme Court held in 1986 that an electorate's "presumed moral disapproval" was sufficient, standing alone, to sustain a state law that criminalized the private sexual intimacy of consenting adults,[9] the move was, in essence, a conversation-ender, at least for purposes of litigation. So long as something as noncontestable as moral disapproval could suffice as a basis for limiting equal treatment, advocates could offer little to overcome the rationale.[10]

For feminists, the judicial embrace of "intuition" and other intangible rationales ought to give particular pause, as such terms can – and often do – function as

---

Franke, *The Central Mistake of Sex Discrimination Law: The Disaggregation of Sex from Gender* 144 U. PA. L. REV. 1, 98–99 (1995) (making this point with respect to treatment of sex as fact and gender as norm); Goldberg, *Anti-Essentialist Arguments in Court, supra* note 6, at 650–53 (discussing occasional recognition by courts of socially constructed nature of facts).

[8] *See, e.g.,* Dan M. Kahan, *Commentary: The Theory of Value Dilemma: A Critique of the Economic Analysis of Criminal Law,* 1 OHIO ST. J. CRIM. L. 643, 649 (2004) (citing studies showing that individuals who are confronted with empirical assertions that counter their views tend to reinforce their prior views by turning to those whom they trust and whom share their values rather than shifting their views in light of the new evidence) (citations omitted).

[9] *Bowers v. Hardwick,* 478 U.S. 186 (1986). Writing in concurrence, Justice Burger emphasized the claim that "[c]ondemnation of [sexual relations between same-sex couples] is firmly rooted in Judeo–Christian moral and ethical standards" to support the conclusion that the Constitution afforded no right to private, consensual sexual intimacy between same-sex partners. *Id.* at 196 (Burger, C. J., concurring).

[10] In fact, gay and lesbian rights advocates in many cases after *Bowers v. Hardwick* sought to reframe the morals justification as a factual claim. They made showings, in their own briefs and through amicus briefs from religious and other organizations, that moral views about homosexuality were, in fact, diverse and not nearly as monolithic as the Supreme Court had suggested. The Supreme Court ultimately agreed when it invalidated sodomy laws in *Lawrence v. Texas,* 539 U.S. 558 (2003). In *Lawrence,* the Court also ruled the *Bowers* Court's references to historical condemnation of homosexuality to be erroneous, finding that "there is no longstanding history in this country of laws directed at homosexual conduct as a distinct matter.... Thus, the historical grounds relied upon in Bowers are more complex than the majority opinion and the concurring opinion by Chief Justice Burger there indicated. They are not without doubt and, at the very least, are overstated." *Lawrence, id.* at 559.

stand-ins for stereotypes and biases. This is particularly the case when it comes to regulation of gender and sexuality, I argue. After all, these are topics about which few people, lawyers and nonlawyers alike, lack strong opinions and intuitions – yet those strong views typically derive more from personal experience and upbringing than from social science analysis or rigorous evaluation of relevant empirical data. We can see this, for example, in the vigorous claims by commentators who would limit access to abortion because of negative mental health consequences for pregnant women[11] or restrict gay people from parenting because of purported harms to child development or the social fabric more generally[12] even when there is little or no data to support those positions. We see this, as well, where courts acknowledge that they lack data to support a gender- or sexuality-based regulation yet nonetheless sustain the regulation because it is consistent with their intuition or common sense.

The remainder of this chapter develops the claim that intangible rationales present cause for concern when constitutional adjudicators rely explicitly on them to sustain sexuality- and gender-based restrictions. I first outline the two ways in which these intuitions can operate to the detriment of careful analysis and offer several illustrations of judicial reliance on intangible rationales in gender- and sexuality-related cases. I then flag several specific concerns raised by judicial reliance on these rationales, including general problems associated with the reliability of intuitions and specific issues related to the way that intangible rationales skew constitutional analysis. At the same time, I acknowledge the inevitable, and arguably appropriate, role that intuition and other noncontestable modes of reasoning play in shaping governmental decisions about which restrictions to impose. Still, I argue that concerns about their skewing the constitutional analysis press in favor of limiting courts' reliance on them as compared to rationales based on demonstrable evidence. Specifically, I suggest that analytic frameworks that require courts to expose and defend the intuitions they rely on could potentially prompt reflection and cabin judicial inclinations to mask bias or hostility with neutral-sounding justifications.

---

[11] *See, e.g.,* DAVID C. REARDON, MAKING ABORTION RARE: A HEALING STRATEGY FOR A DIVIDED NATION (1996).

    See also Reva B. Siegel, *The Right's Reasons: Constitutional Conflict and the Spread of the Woman-Protective Antiabortion Argument,* 57 DUKE L. J. 1641 (2008) (analyzing the field of woman-protective arguments against abortion); Reva B. Siegel, *Dignity and the Politics of Protection: Abortion Restrictions Under Casey/Carhart,* 117 YALE L. J. 1694 (2008) (identifying the woman-protective arguments in the *Casey* and *Carhart* decisions).

[12] *See, e.g.,* Lynn D. Wardle, *The Potential Impact of Homosexual Parenting on Children,* 1997 U. ILL. L. REV. 833, 833–34 (arguing that, contrary to the findings of some studies, there are "significant potential effects of gay childrearing on children, including increased development of homosexual orientation in children, emotional and cognitive disadvantages caused by the absence of opposite-sex parents, and economic security"); Lynn D. Wardle, *Considering the Impact on Children and Society of "Lesbigay" Parenting,* 23 QUINNIPIAC L. REV. 541, 543 (2004) ("Logically, it is not unreasonable to expect that lesbigay parenting will not prove to be as beneficial for children or for society as parenting by a mother and father who are married to each other. But we do not know for sure.").

INTANGIBLE RATIONALES AS COVERS FOR CONSCIOUS BIAS
AND UNCONSCIOUS STEREOTYPING

From a jurisprudential standpoint, the problem for constitutional analysis posed
by judicial embrace of intangible rationales arises in two distinct but ultimately
interrelated ways. First, in some instances, courts might invoke intuition deliberately to use its patina of legitimacy as cover for either contestable or impermissible
outcome-oriented, ideologically motivated aims. A judge who believes mothers are
better than fathers at instilling values in their children, for example, might not find
an empirical fact to support that view when considering a challenge to a citizenship law's preference for mothers of foreign-born children over fathers. However,
by deferring to the legislature's intuition or common sense regarding women's relatively greater ability to imbue citizenship values in their children, the same judge
could escape the evidentiary deficit and avoid disclosure of his or her personal
views while sustaining the law's classification.[13] Similarly, a judge who believes
that abortion negatively affects society and should never occur, or that gay parents negatively affect their children's development, might also invoke presumptions
about the lawmakers' intuitions when there are no credible facts to sustain those
positions.[14]

Second, in other instances, a judge who has no particular ideological motivation
might reiterate the received wisdom that mothers are more likely than fathers to
bond with and transfer citizenship values to their children. Or he or she might
simply assume that having an abortion is more detrimental to a woman's mental
health than giving birth or that children do "better" with a mother and a father than
with two mothers or two fathers. In these instances, as earlier, a judge's intuition or

---

[13] *See Nguyen v. INS*, 533 U.S. 53 (2001). In this case, at issue was the constitutionality of a U.S.
immigration law provision that made it easier for U.S. citizen mothers than fathers to extend U.S.
citizenship to their foreign-born children. The majority declared, *inter alia*, that the opportunity for
mother–child bonding "inheres in the very event of birth." *Id.* at 65. Although the Court did not invoke
the sorts of intangible rationales I am focused on here, the case remains an interesting one for the
dissent's challenge to the way in which the majority imbued the "event of birth" with a significance
that it then used to justify the sex-based classification at issue. Justice O'Connor wrote for the four
dissenters:

> [T]he idea that a mother's presence at birth supplies adequate assurance of an opportunity to
> develop a relationship while a father's presence at birth does not would appear to rest only on
> an overbroad sex-based generalization. A mother may not have an opportunity for a relationship
> if the child is removed from his or her mother on account of alleged abuse or neglect, or if the
> child and mother are separated by tragedy, such as disaster or war, of the sort apparently present
> in this case. There is no reason, other than stereotype, to say that fathers who are present at birth
> lack an opportunity for a relationship on similar terms. The "[p]hysical differences between
> men and women," therefore do not justify [the statute's] discrimination.

Id. at 86–87 (citation omitted).

[14] *See Gonzales v. Carhart*, 550 U.S. 124 (2007); *Lofton v. Sec'y of Dep't of Children & Family Servs.*
(*Lofton I*), 358 F.3d 804 (11th Cir. 2004).

unsubstantiated assumptions can result in uncritical affirmation of flawed classifications, even if, as here, ideology is not driving the turn to intuition.

In both of these contexts, a framework that allows courts to embrace noncontestable rationales as justifications for government action has the potential to facilitate implementation of both deliberate and unconscious stereotypes and biases. In other words, when intangible, nondemonstrable rationales can suffice as justifications for restrictions on rights, decision makers have few incentives to back away from implementing their biases.[15] Likewise, the analytic framework does not prompt those without a particular outcome-orientation to expose and defend the intuitive bases for their decisions.

THE INTANGIBLE RATIONALES AT WORK

Before turning to the particular ways in which these rationales skew the analysis, a few examples are in order to illustrate the work these intangible rationales perform in adjudication of rights claims. Consider, first, the U.S. Supreme Court's recent decision to sustain the federal "Partial-Birth Abortion Ban Act of 2003."[16] The measure imposes criminal penalties on physicians who carry out specified procedures while performing a second- or third-trimester abortion. Setting the stage for its determination that the government's interest in protecting women sufficed to justify the restriction, the Court first asserted, without citation, that "[r]espect for human life finds an ultimate expression in the bond of love the mother has for her child."[17] After observing that "[w]hether to have an abortion requires a difficult and painful moral decision," the Court then concluded – based on its own sense of things – that women need special protection from the state to make this decision. Specifically, the Court wrote that "[w]hile we find no reliable data to measure the phenomenon, it seems unexceptionable to conclude some women come to regret their choice to abort the infant life they once created and sustained." In other words, the Court

---

[15] It is well settled that governments – including judges as well as legislatures – may not impose or sustain burdens because of hostility toward the targeted group. *See Romer v. Evans*, 517 U.S. 620, 635 (1996) ("Even laws enacted for broad and ambitious purposes often can be explained by reference to legitimate public policies which justify the incidental disadvantages they impose on certain persons."); *U.S. Dept. of Agriculture v. Moreno*, 413 U.S. 528, 534 (1973) ("[I]f the constitutional conception of 'equal protection of the laws' means anything, it must at the very least mean that a bare . . . desire to harm a politically unpopular group cannot constitute a *legitimate* governmental interest."). Yet persuading a reviewing court that another judge relied deliberately on intuition to mask an impermissible purpose is an exceedingly difficult task for a variety of reasons, including both institutional commitments to collegiality within the judiciary and the difficulty of proving something (hostile motivation) that cannot be seen. For more on the latter point, see generally Suzanne B. Goldberg, *Discrimination by Comparison*, 120 Yale L. J. 728 (2011). I have found no reported majority opinion from an appellate court suggesting that hostility, rather than a more benign error, led a court to accept a rationale that was ultimately rejected on appeal.

[16] *Gonzalez v. Carhart*, 550 U.S. 124 (2007).

[17] *Id.* at 159. Reva Siegel has written extensively about the judicial and public discourse regarding this "woman-protective" argument. *See* Siegel, *supra* note 11.

acknowledged that it lacked empirical support yet forged on to hold that "[t]he State has an interest in ensuring so grave a choice is well informed."[18]

We also see this judicial willingness to opt for intuition rather than data in the context of marriage cases where courts have considered whether states can restrict marriage to different-sex couples as a means of favoring heterosexual parents over gay and lesbian parents. In New York, for example, the State's highest court relied explicitly on intuition regarding childrearing to sustain the state's exclusion of same-sex couples from marriage.[19] More specifically, the court found that "[t]he Legislature could rationally believe that it is better, other things being equal, for children to grow up with both a mother and a father."[20] However, the basis for deeming the belief rational was not research. Instead, the court wrote, "[i]ntuition and experience suggest that a child benefits from having before his or her eyes, every day, living models of what both a man and a woman are like."[21] With intuition as the foundation for its conclusion, the court then reiterated that actual evidence to the contrary of those intuitions and experiences was not relevant:

> Plaintiffs seem to assume that they have demonstrated the irrationality of the view that opposite-sex marriages offer advantages to children by showing there is no scientific evidence to support it. Even assuming no such evidence exists, this reasoning is flawed. In the absence of conclusive scientific evidence, the Legislature could rationally proceed on the commonsense premise that children will do best with a mother and father in the home.[22]

Given that "conclusive" scientific evidence is rarely available on any point, any rationale that is consistent with the court's intuitions could potentially be deemed constitutionally adequate.[23]

Other state judges addressing the marriage question similarly have gauged the reasonableness of a legislature's continued exclusion of same-sex couples from marriage not by social science evidence but instead by whether the impulses underlying the exclusions could be justified by intuition. A plurality of the Washington Supreme Court, for example, sustained the state's ban on same-sex couples' marrying in part

---

[18] *Gonzalez*, 550 U.S. 124 at 159 (emphasis added).
[19] *Hernandez v. Robles*, 855 N.E.2d 1, 7 (N.Y. 2006).
[20] *Id.*
[21] *Id.*
[22] *Id.* at 8.
[23] Arguably if the standard of review were less lenient than the one applied by the court in this case, more might have been required to survive constitutional review. The court characterized its inquiry as aimed to determine whether "this long-accepted restriction [on access to marriage] is a wholly irrational one, based solely on ignorance and prejudice against homosexuals." *Id.* at 8. It then observed that, until recently, marriage between same-sex couples was virtually unimaginable. With this framing, it should be no surprise that the court's intuition (or the court's view of the legislature's intuition) was consistent with that tradition; indeed, the court wrote, in what was arguably a projection of its own concerns about its views, that it "should not lightly conclude that everyone who held this belief was irrational, ignorant or bigoted." *Id.*

based on its (unsubstantiated) view that "children *tend to thrive*" in a "traditional" nuclear family.[24] Likewise, one of the justices of the Massachusetts Supreme Judicial Court, dissenting from that court's recognition of marriage rights, found that the state legislature could have rationally concluded that "married opposite-sex parents" are "the optimal social structure in which to bear children." Same-sex couples, he wrote, "present[] an alternative structure for child rearing that has not yet proved itself."[25] Yet the opinion gives little sense that "proof" of any sort could actually overcome the view, permissible according to this justice, that gay and lesbian parents are simply suboptimal.

This same view was strongly articulated by a federal appeals court that sustained Florida's ban on adoption of children by gay and lesbian adults.[26] In its opinion, the court embraced two of the state's intuition-driven justifications. First, the court accepted that Florida could restrict adoption to heterosexuals because "the marital family structure is more stable than other household arrangements."[27] And second, the court accepted the state's claim "that children benefit from the presence of both a father and mother in the home."[28] Yet the court relied on no evidence to support these fact-like claims. Nor could it have: there are no credible studies to support the proposition that married mothers and fathers have more stable relationships than partnered mothers and mothers or fathers and fathers; instead, the studies showing the relative stability of marital relationships when children are in the home encompass only heterosexual couples.[29] Likewise, there are no peer-review studies indicating that children raised by heterosexual couples are better off on child development measures than children raised by same-sex couples; to the contrary, the overwhelming consensus of experts in the field is that sexual orientation is irrelevant

---

[24] *Andersen v. King County*, 138 P.3d 963, 983 (Wash. 2006) (plurality opinion) (emphasis added).

[25] *Goodridge v. Dep't of Pub. Health*, 798 N.E.2d 941, 999–1000 (Mass. 2003) (Cordy, J., dissenting). In a related fashion, a Kansas appellate court found that the state's legislature "could have reasonably determined that" an age-of-consent statute that imposed greater punishment on same-sex than different-sex couples could help "prevent the gradual deterioration of the sexual morality approved by a majority of Kansas." In hypothesizing in this way, there was surely no evidence that could overcome (or support) the court's reasonableness determination observation. *See State v. Limon*, 83 P.3d 229, 236 (Kan. Ct. App. 2004), *rev'd*, 122 P.3d 22 (Kan. 2005).

[26] *Lofton I*, 358 F.3d 804 (11th Cir. 2004). In a recent challenge, a Florida appeals court sustained a trial court ruling striking down the ban. *See Fla. Dept. of Children and Families v. Adoption of X.X.G. and N.R.G.*, 35 FLA. L. WEEKLY D2107 (Fla. Dist. Ct. App. 2010) (opinion not yet released for permanent publication).

[27] *Lofton I*, 358 F.3d at 819.

[28] *Id.*

[29] *See, e.g.*, Gregory M. Herek, *Legal Recognition of Same-Sex Relationships in the United States: A Social Science Perspective*, 61 AM. PSYCHOL. 607 (2006), draft *available at* http://psychology.ucdavis.edu/ rainbow/html/AP_06_pre.PDF; *see also* Brief of the Am. Psychol. Ass'n et al. as Amici Curiae in Support of Plaintiffs-Appellees, Conaway v. Deane, 903 A.2d 416 (Md. 2006) (No. 44) (mem.), *available at* www. aclu.org/lgbt/relationships/27253lgl20061019.html; L. A. Kurdek, *Are Gay and Lesbian Cohabiting Couples Really Different from Heterosexual Married Couples?*, 66 J. MARRIAGE & FAM. 880 (2004).

to parenting ability and to healthy outcomes for children.[30] The court had little difficulty sidestepping this consensus, however, declaring that it is not "irrational for the legislature to proceed with deliberate caution before placing adoptive children in an alternative, but unproven, family structure that has not yet been conclusively demonstrated to be equivalent to the marital family structure that has established a proven track record spanning centuries."[31] In other words, no matter how much evidence the law's challengers might muster, the legislature could reasonably find, according to the court, that it would never be conclusive enough, unless perhaps several more centuries pass.

Even more interesting for purposes here is the court's reasoning behind its embrace of the state's mother-father preference as a sufficient basis for imposing a categorical exclusion on gay adults (and no others in the state) from adopting. After finding no evidence bearing on the question, the court stated simply, "We find this premise to be one of those 'unprovable assumptions' that nevertheless can provide a legitimate basis for legislative action."[32] Its source for this confidence in the state's unprovable assumption? None other than the long track record of married heterosexuals raising children together,[33] suggesting, again, that longevity itself functioned as a justification for the continued exclusion.

> Although social theorists from Plato to Simone de Beauvoir have proposed alternative child-rearing arrangements, none has proven as enduring as the marital family structure, nor has the accumulated wisdom of several millennia of human experience discovered a superior model. *See, e.g.,* Plato, *The Republic*, Bk. V, 459d–461e; Simone de Beauvoir, *The Second Sex* (H. M. Parshley trans., Vintage Books 1989) (1949).[34]

While citing Plato and de Beauvoir as creators of failed models, the court apparently found its own conclusion about the state's reasonableness in preferring heterosexuals

---

[30] *See* E. C. PERRIN, SEXUAL ORIENTATION IN CHILD AND ADOLESCENT HEALTH 110–30 (2002) (reviewing studies and finding no material disparities in mental health and social adjustment between children of gay and nongay parents); Melanie A. Gold et al., *Children of Gay or Lesbian Parents*, 15 PEDIATRICS IN REV. 354, 357 (1994) ("There are no data to suggest that children who have gay or lesbian parents are different in any aspects of psychological, social, and sexual development from children in heterosexual families."); *see also* Brief for Am. Psychol. Ass'n et al. as Amici Curiae Supporting Plaintiffs-Respondents at 36, *Hernandez v. Robles*, 855 N.E.2d 1 (N.Y. 2006) (No. 86), 2006 WL 1930166; Brief for Child Rights Orgs. as Amicus Curiae Supporting Respondents at 11, *Andersen v. King County*, 138 P.3d 963 (Wash. 2006) (No. 75934–1), 2006 Wash. LEXIS 598.

[31] *Lofton I*, 358 F.3d at 826.

[32] *Id.* at 819–20.

[33] Of course, even this assertion sidesteps entirely the substantial data showing that for most of this history, the male spouse had little to do with childrearing other than providing financial support and setting household disciplinary rules. *Cf.* SUSAN MOLLER OKIN, JUSTICE, GENDER, AND THE FAMILY 149 (1989) ("It is no secret that in almost all families women do far more housework and child care than men do.").

[34] *Lofton I*, 358 F.3d at 820.

to gay people as parents to be sufficiently self-evident not to warrant any citation at all.

In short, while the question in all of these cases concerns whether the state has a sufficient justification for its restriction on individual rights, data related to the justification(s) becomes largely irrelevant. Instead, the filter through which the state's assertions are evaluated in the sexuality and gender areas, at least in some instances as illustrated by the examples just discussed, is whether the state's rationales are consistent with the court's intuition about what the legislature reasonably might have intuited itself. If they are, the court deems them constitutionally adequate.

If an unprovable assumption is all that a state needs to restrict rights related to gender and sexuality, and if the court's willingness to question the legislature's intuitions serves as the only check on misuses of these assumptions in service of intentional or implicit bias, we have reasons to be concerned. It is to these reasons that the next section turns.

INTUITION AND UNPROVABLE ASSUMPTIONS AS RIGHTS-LIMITING RATIONALES: THE CENTRAL CONCERNS

There are any number of reasons why feminists, in particular, might be concerned about courts allowing legislatures to act on their intuitions and unprovable assumptions when regulating gender and sexuality. Among the most obvious of these, as highlighted earlier, is the increased authority given to naturalized assumptions, stereotypes, and conscious biases that are rife in these areas. The more attenuated government action becomes from data-based or demonstrable justifications, the more likely it is that these biases and stereotypes will be elevated from the public debate to a position of heightened permanency and influence within the constitutional fabric. Simply put, the rationales that are accepted for government action – including intuitions about abortion's negative effect on women and the relative desirability of heterosexuals as parents – directly shape the meaning of a state's foundational equality guarantees. Allowing intuition and assumptions to function as rationales raises the risk that these guarantees will be diminished.

Yet beyond this concern, two additional points related to the judicial embrace of intangible rationales, and of intuitions in particular, are troubling as well. The first has to do with the fallibility of intuitions. The second concerns the skewing effect that intuitions, unprovable assumptions, and other similar intangible rationales have on constitutional adjudication.

With respect to the limitations of intuitions as a basis for evaluating the legitimacy of a state's rights-limiting rationale, Judge Richard Posner's observations are particularly helpful. As a general matter, Posner embraces the role of intuition in decision making, explaining that intuition "frequently encapsulates highly relevant experience" and "produces tacit knowledge that may be a more accurate and speedier alternative in particular circumstances to analytical reasoning, even though, being tacit, it is inarticulate."[35] Yet he acknowledges that intuition, as an analytic filter, is limited by the experiences of the person doing the intuiting. "We must not...suppose intuition a sure guide to sound decision making," he adds. "An intuitive decision may ignore critical factors that lie outside the range of the person's experience that informs his intuition...."[36] Others who have reviewed the empirical literature on the relative virtues of probabilistic reasoning and intuitive reasoning confirm that intuition is often unreliable because it derives mainly from the necessarily limited life experiences of the individual in question.[37]

In addition to their experience-based limitations, intuitions are also a weak filter for constitutional review of rationales for limiting rights because they are particularly susceptible to biases, often without the awareness of the decision maker himself or herself. As some scholars have observed, "Intuition is...the likely pathway by which undesirable influences, like the race, gender, or attractiveness of the parties, affect the legal system."[38]

Related to this point, we can see that a state's invocation of an unprovable assumption as the basis for its limiting the rights of particular constituents can produce a skewed constitutional analysis. In equality cases, for example, the central question is not whether the state's justification for limiting rights is legitimate in the abstract, but instead whether there is a sufficient reason for distinguishing between those who are granted the right or benefit in question and those who are not. So, for example, in the Florida adoption case, the question is not whether, as a general matter, married heterosexuals are good parents. Instead, it is whether the state has a legitimate reason for singling out gay adults and rendering them categorically ineligible to adopt while allowing all other adults residing in the state to have their adoption applications considered on a case-by-case basis. Thus, the fact-like claim embraced by the court – that children "benefit" from the presence of a mother and father in the home – is

---

[35] Richard A. Posner, *The Role of the Judge in the Twenty-First Century*, 86 B. U. L. REV. 1049, 1064 (2006) [hereinafter Poser, *Role of the Judge*] (footnotes and citations omitted); *see also* RICHARD POSNER, HOW JUDGES THINK (2008).

[36] Posner, *Role of the Judge*, *supra* note 35, at 1064.

[37] *See, e.g.*, Jonathan J. Koehler & Daniel N. Shaviro, *Veridical Verdicts: Increasing Verdict Accuracy Through the Use of Overtly Probabilistic Evidence and Methods*, 75 CORNELL L. REV. 246, 271–72 (1990) (highlighting literature from fields outside law that "suggests the superiority of probabilistic methods" of reasoning). C. C. Guthrie and his coauthors identify similar challenges and perils associated with reliance on intuition in medicine. Citing a widely read medical writer's observation that "'[c]ogent medical judgments meld first impressions – gestalt – with deliberate analysis,'" they argue that the same balance between intuition and more rigorous forms of analysis should carry over to law. "Like cogent medical judgments, cogent legal judgments call for deliberation. Justice depends on it," they write. C. C. Guthrie, J. J. Rachlinski, & A. J. Wistrich, *Blinking on the Bench: How Judges Decide Cases*, 93 CORNELL L. REV. 1, 43 (2007). Cass Sunstein has made similar observations with respect to judicial reliance on heuristics more generally, which he describes as "quite valuable" in general, but also as leading, in some cases, "'to severe and systematic errors.'" Cass R. Sunstein, *Hazardous Heuristics*, 70 U. CHI. L. REV. 751 (2003) (citation omitted).

[38] Guthrie et al., *supra* note 37, at 31.

not responsive to the equal protection inquiry, given that children "benefit" from many things that are not treated as linchpins for special adoption rules.

Further, as we know, because the state lacked demonstrable evidence to support its categorical rejection of gay prospective adoptive parents, unprovable assumptions filled the gap as a justification for the sexual orientation-based line-drawing at issue. The constitutional problem with this move is that the unprovable assumption, as used in this case, restates the classification instead of explaining it. Reduced to its essence, the rationale is that heterosexual parents are preferable to gay or lesbian parents because we (the state) assume they are.

Although this reasoning appears to be circular – the state can differentiate because the state assumes that groups A (heterosexuals) and B (lesbians and gay men) are different in some relevant way – many courts, including those discussed earlier, treat the unprovable assumption as a justification. Specifically, they find that the assumption's intangible nature and its ultimate nonfalsifiability convert the description of the state's preference for heterosexuals into a stand-alone justification for the state's preference. In this way, the embrace of the intangible rationale enables the court to elide the baseline constitutional requirement that state-imposed inequalities be explained by something more than reference to the state's desire to differentiate. As the U.S. Supreme Court wrote when it invalided a state constitutional amendment that blocked the state and local government from protecting gay people against discrimination, "[b]y requiring that the classifcation bear a rational relationship to an independent and legitimate legislative end, we ensure that classifications are not drawn for the purpose of disadvantaging the group burdened by the law."[39]

Indeed, in the Florida case, a dissenting judge reinforced this point by showing the ill fit between the state's assumptions and the classification it had drawn. As she explained, "[t]he adoption statute accords everyone other than homosexuals the benefit of an individualized consideration that is directed toward the best interests of the child." Pointing to the state's lack of a categorical bar for "[c]hild abusers, terrorists, drug dealers, rapists, and murderers," she highlighted how the unprovable assumption that had been offered could not overcome the "pure[] form of irrationality" reflected in the categorical ban on adoption by gays and lesbians.[40]

We see this skewed analysis in the marriage cases as well. The Massachusetts high court, for example, when invalidating the state's exclusion of same-sex couples from marriage, highlighted the flaw in the dissenters' claim that the state's ban was justified to ensure "optimal" homes for children headed by heterosexual parents. Instead of engaging with the dissenters' unprovable assumption that heterosexual parents could provide better homes than their gay counterparts, the majority showed that the very assertions regarding optimality were off point with respect to the equal

---

[39] *Romer v. Evans*, 517 U.S. 620, 633 (1996). The Court further stated that, "[e]qual protection of the laws is not achieved through indiscriminate imposition of inequalities." *Id.* (citations omitted).

[40] *Lofton v. Sec'y of Dep't of Children & Family Servs. (Lofton II)*, 377 F.3d 1275, 1301 (11th Cir. 2004) (Barkett, J., dissenting from the denial of review en banc).

protection inquiry. The question in the case was not whether heterosexuals are desirable parents or whether children deserved good homes but, again, whether the state had a sufficient reason for excluding gay people from marriage. In that regard, the court noted that the state had "offered no evidence that forbidding marriage to people of the same sex will increase the number of couples choosing to enter into opposite-sex marriages in order to have and raise children."[41] Furthermore, the court found that the exclusion would harm children of same-sex parents by not allowing them to "enjoy[] the immeasurable advantages" that would flow from their parents being able to marry. As a result, the court concluded that "[r]estricting marriage to opposite-sex couples . . . cannot plausibly further" the state's interest in ensuring optimal homes for children.[42]

In short, intuitions and other intangible justifications present particular risks in constitutional adjudication in part because, as a general matter, they are often unreliable and potentially biased. In addition, to the extent courts defer to the legitimacy of the unprovable assumption or intuition, they often fail to ask, as the constitutional jurisprudence requires, whether that sense of things actually provides an explanation for the rights-limitation at issue. Instead, as we have seen, these rationales often merely restate or otherwise express the state's inclination to limit rights but gain traction by cloaking that inclination in the form of an assumption or intuition, which the reviewing court then erroneously treats as a substantial and independent explanation for the state's action.

THE INEVITABLE (AND DESIRABLE?) ROLE OF INTUITION AND OTHER INTANGIBLE JUSTIFICATIONS

Notwithstanding the potential for intuition and other intangible rationales to stand in for conscious and unconscious bias and stereotypes, I do not claim here that we should eradicate their role in decision making. Indeed, an effort to do so would fly in the face of all we know about the integral role of intuition in judicial reasoning as well as cognitive decision making.

As one group of authors has observed, "[e]liminating all intuition from judicial decision making is both impossible and undesirable because it is an essential part of how the human brain functions."[43] And another: "In general, there is no plausible form of adjudicative absolutism that can consistently escape the need for intuitionism at some crucial point."[44]

[41] *Goodridge v. Dep't of Pub. Health*, 798 N.E.2d 941, 963 (Mass. 2003). The court found, as well, that excluding same-sex couples from marriage would not "make children of opposite-sex marriages more secure." *Id.* at 634.
[42] *Id.* at 962.
[43] Guthrie et al., *supra* note 37, at 5.
[44] R. G. Wright, *The Role of Intuition in Judicial Decisionmaking*, 42 HOUS. L. REV. 1381, 1406 (2006); *see also id.* at 1384 (arguing that "intuition is invariably central – whether overtly so or not – to the process of arriving at a judicial outcome by any standard recognized means").

Indeed, one might argue that even if it were possible to substantially or entirely restrict the effect of judicial intuition on decision making, the cost would outweigh whatever gains might be had.[45] Particularly in areas where intuitions run so strong, to preclude their influence on decision making could itself skew the analysis. If we were to insist that all justifications be empirically demonstrable, courts might move, detrimentally, to disregard the limitations of extant empirical research. In the gender and sexuality law area, these might include not only questions related to parenting as are addressed in the adoption and marriage cases, but also other important issues related to gender identity and human sexuality, as in the abortion regulation and parenting contexts more generally.

Moreover, as noted earlier, empirically based rationales are no panacea for purposes of eliminating the conscious and subconscious biases that are of concern here. As is well known, methodological choices shape the results that empirical research produces and data can be manipulated to serve ideological ends. Most importantly, perhaps, the presence of data does not necessarily lead to greater deliberation or analysis where an adjudicator's inclinations run contrary to the empirically based research results.[46]

NEXT STEPS – DISCIPLINED INTUITION?

We have, thus, a serious tension. There are real risks in the areas of gender and sexuality posed by states proffering intangible rationales for limiting rights and by courts endorsing as constitutionally sufficient whatever state-proffered rationales fit with their own intuitions about right and wrong. At the same time, states' turns to these rationales and courts' filtering of them through their own intuitions are, as just discussed, both inevitable and in some ways desirable.

My brief proposal here is that two aspects of the judiciary's interaction with intangible rationales deserve particular attention because of their potential to support flawed constitutional analysis. The first is the inadequate reasoning in many of the decisions that rely on improvable assumptions, intuitions, and other intangible rationales to sustain burdens on individual rights. Second is the *de minimis* way in which courts tend to engage with significant, credible data that run contrary to their conclusions.

Returning to the first, my suggestion is that more be done to show the way in which intangible rationales can evade serious review. The idea is that heightened

---

45 Similar questions arise in debates regarding judicial candor. *See generally* Scott Altman, *Beyond Candor*, 89 MICH. L. REV. 296 (1990) (maintaining that judges who are misguided may reach better decisions than judges who clearly understand their decision making so that an insistence on candor would be ill-advised); Gail Heriot, *Way Beyond Candor*, 89 MICH. L. REV. 1945 (1991) (critiquing Altman's claims).

46 *See generally* Suzanne B. Goldberg, *Constitutional Tipping Points*, *supra* note 6 (showing the ways in which judicial responses to changed views of social groups lag behind changed understandings of facts related to those groups); Kahan, *supra* note 8.

exposure of the circularity or self-serving nature of rights-limiting justifications such as unprovable assumptions and intuitions may increase the motivation for legitimacy-sensitive legislatures and courts to find demonstrable, accessible reasons for their actions. One might operationalize this aim by showing, at greater length and with greater context specificity than is possible here, that courts often use intangible rationales not to safeguard constitutional rights but instead to mask outcome-oriented aims. More moderately, efforts could avoid impugning judicial motives but still put a stark focus on the risks for the integrity of constitutional analysis posed by judicial acceptance of those rationales, as set out earlier.

On the second point, which concerns courts' frequent failure to engage seriously with data that conflict with their intuitions, doctrinal change would surely be difficult to achieve. Although it might be desirable for courts to offer extended explanations when they accept legislative actions that run contrary to strong demonstrable evidence, that demand would trigger concerns about the judiciary's overreaching into the legislature's role. Legislatures are, after all, sometimes better suited to sift through and weigh competing strands of evidence by virtue of their institutional resources and capacity. Moreover, even a doctrinal shift that demands greater exposition of judicial reasoning would not be likely to limit the work of outcome-oriented judges.

Yet doctrinal change may well be worth pushing despite these limitations. Without some meaningful constraint on the power of intangible rationales to justify rights restrictions, our constitutional framework retains the potential for unthinking or deliberate enforcement of long-entrenched yet unsupported biases about sexuality and gender and, indeed, many more issues. Even a limited shift – in decision-making norms, if not doctrine – has the potential to move much of the judicial conversation about these issues onto more accessible terrain. That shift, in turn, would not only enhance constitutional review as a general matter but also open new possibilities, consistent with the aims of feminism, for challenging the opportunity-limiting effects of gender- and sexuality-related stereotypes and biases.

6

Women Judges, "Maiden Speeches," and the High Court of Australia

Heather Roberts

[T]he way one tells one's story is a way of positioning one's gender identity vis-à-vis an audience taking part in the process . . . as an ongoing process of articulating sameness and difference.[1]

On February 3, 2009, a historic event occurred in the Australian legal community. Of the seven judges of the High Court of Australia, three are now women: Justices Susan Crennan, Susan Kiefel, and Virginia Bell.[2] Never before has Australia's constitutional and ultimate court of appeal achieved near equality in the gender composition of its bench.[3] In 1987, when Mary Gaudron was appointed as the first woman to the court, this achievement may have seemed a far-off dream.

Since the Australian High Court was established in 1903, ceremonies have been held to mark the swearing-in of a new Justice. This chapter utilizes the speeches made at the swearing-in ceremonies of Gaudron, Crennan, Kiefel, and Bell as a prism to explore the representation of women judges in the Australian legal community, and in particular, the Australian High Court.[4]

These ceremonies are a rich resource by virtue of the two kinds of speeches made on these occasions. First, leaders of the Australian legal community make speeches welcoming the new High Court judge to the bench. In a legal system where federal

---

[1] Silvia Gherardi, *Gendered Organizational Cultures: Narratives of Women Travellers in a Male World*, 3 GENDER, WORK & ORGANIZATION, 187, 187–88 (1996). For further discussion of this quotation in relation to legal work cultures, *see* Rosemary Hunter, *Talking Up Equality: Women Barristers and the Denial of Discrimination*, 10 FEMINIST LEGAL STUD. 113, 116 (2002).

[2] Hereinafter, Justices Mary Gaudron, Susan Crennan, Susan Kiefel, and Virginia Bell are referred to in the text as "Gaudron," "Crennan," "Kiefel," and "Bell."

[3] In addition, a Full Court of the Australian High Court, comprising three justices, may now be constituted exclusively by women judges. The historic first hearing by Crennan, Kiefel, and Bell was noted in the press. *See, e.g.*, Michael Pelly, *Finally it's Ladies Day at High Court as Crennan Takes Her Seat*, THE AUSTRALIAN (SYDNEY), Apr. 3, 2009.

[4] Transcripts of the swearing-in ceremonies of High Court Justices held after 1995 are available electronically: www.austlii.edu.au/au/other/HCATrans/. Where available, citations are to this electronic resource. Copies of all transcripts cited in this chapter are on file with the author.

judges are chosen behind closed doors, the welcome speeches have performed a
key role in introducing the new judges to the public, and attesting to their skills
as lawyer and judge.[5] Importantly, the litany of a new judge's accomplishments on
these occasions contextualizes the concept of "merit" in a High Court appointment.[6]
Furthermore, the speech by the Commonwealth Attorney-General has provided a
measure of public justification of his[7] decision to appoint a particular judge. This
chapter explores how the welcome speakers have grappled with the novelty of the
feminine in the stories about the four female High Court judges. I argue that gender
too often dominated this narrative, to a discriminatory and feminizing effect. In this
regard, however, Bell's ceremony may signal a new direction in the Australian legal
community's attitude toward female judges.

The second element of the swearing-in ceremony is the judge's response to the
welcome speeches. As his or her inaugural speech as a member of the High Court,
this speech is the judicial equivalent of the "maiden speech" by members of parliament. The judge's speech is delivered in a setting rich with contradiction: a
statement from the bench, yet of no judicial force; liberated in content and style
from the boundaries of a legal dispute and yet constrained by the weight of convention regarding the "appropriate" remarks for an incoming judge; and, a statement of
individual identity, values, and principles made from the "identity-less" judge of the
common law tradition. For present purposes, the critical feature of the inaugural
speeches of Australia's four female High Court judges is how they tell their stories
and the place of gender in that narrative.[8] I argue that these speeches reflect a *continuing* pressure faced by women judges to distance themselves from the perception of
their "otherness" on the bench.[9] This pressure manifested first in Gaudron's speech,

---

[5] On the process of appointing Australian High Court Justices, see Simon Evans, *Appointment of
Justices, in* THE OXFORD COMPANION TO THE HIGH COURT OF AUSTRALIA 19 (Tony Blackshield et al.
eds., 2001) at 19. In 2008, the federal government amended the appointments process and selected
a panel of advisors, from outside the government, to provide recommendations for federal judicial
appointments. For an outline of this additional process, *see, e.g.,* Michael Pelly, *Gerard Brennan's
Tips on the Best for Bench,* THE AUSTRALIAN (Sydney), Aug. 8, 2008.

[6] On the gendered concept of "merit" in the context of Australian judges, *see* Margaret Thornton,
"*Otherness" on the Bench: How Merit is Gendered,* 29 SYDNEY L. REV. 391 (2007) [hereinafter Thornton,
"Otherness"].

[7] At the time of writing, no woman has held the position of Commonwealth Attorney-General.

[8] On the role of stories in producing legal cultures, and particularly stories about women judges and the
concomitant cultural pressure to silence their voices as women, *see* Erika Rackley, *Judicial Diversity,
The Woman Judge, and Fairy Tale Endings,* 27 LEGAL STUD. 74 (2007) [hereinafter Rackley, *Judicial
Diversity*]. The swearing-in speeches of High Court judges also hold insights beyond questions of
gender and the legal profession, such as signals of the new judge's judicial approach and constitu-
tional vision. *See, e.g.,* Heather J. Roberts, Fundamental Constitutional Truths: The Constitutional
Jurisprudence of Justice Deane, 1982–1995 (2007) (unpublished Ph.D. dissertation, The Australian
National University).

[9] I am not suggesting that women judges *should* acknowledge their identity as women in their swearing-in
speeches and that the absence of such statements *must* therefore be interpreted as a silence responding
to the pressure to conform to the "benchmark male" judge. However, where a woman judge has
elsewhere indicated the place of gender in her identity, *silence* in her swearing-in speech raises

when she tempered her bold acknowledgment of her identity as the first woman to join the High Court with affirmations of her *sameness* with her brother judges. Significantly, twenty years later, Bell's swearing-in speech continued to display both a self-conscious silencing of her feminine voice and statements affirming her distance from outsiders on the bench.

JUSTICE MARY GAUDRON

The court's ceremonial sitting on February 6, 1987, was significant for a number of reasons. Three judges were sworn in on this day: Sir Anthony Mason, as Chief Justice, and John Toohey and Mary Gaudron, as Justices. Not since the Court was created in 1903 had three Justices been sworn in at the same ceremony. None of the preceding Justices or Chief Justices of the Australian High Court had been women.

The transcript records that the court was crowded with dignitaries. In attendance were fifteen former and currently serving Australian judges, eight Solicitors-General, eleven presidents of representative legal associations, and a further thirty-nine Queen's Counsel.[10] As was often the case in her career as "first woman" to achieve many heights in the Australian legal profession, Gaudron was also the *sole* woman whose presence was officially recorded in the transcript. Mary Gaudron's status as the "first woman" at the pinnacle of the Australian legal fraternity in 1987 was a theme underpinning her swearing-in ceremony.

Welcome Speeches: "First Woman"

Three speakers welcomed Gaudron to the bench, and each emphasized Gaudron's "outstanding" qualifications for high judicial office.[11] The first speaker was the Commonwealth Attorney-General Lionel Bowen. Although the appointment of the first female High Court judge was a political achievement for the Hawke Labor government, Bowen's speech was not overtly political in nature. Without a single feminine

---

an important question regarding the reasons for that silence. These omissions become particularly conspicuous and significant given that High Court swearing-in ceremonies are key symbolic events for both the Court and a judge's career. On the "otherness" of women judges from the "benchmark" male of the court, see Margaret Thornton, Dissonance and Distrust: Women in the Legal Profession 2 (1996) and Thornton, *"Otherness," supra* note 6, at 391.

[10] Transcript of Proceedings, *Swearing-in Ceremony, Gaudron, J.* (High Court of Australia, Justice Mary Gaudron, Feb. 6, 1987), 2–7 [hereinafter *Swearing-in Gaudron, J.*]. Justice Gaudron's speech has also been reprinted as Justice Mary Gaudron, *Speech at the Swearing in of the Honourable Justice Gaudron* (1987) 68 ALR xxxiii–xxxviii [hereinafter Gaudron, *Speech*].

[11] *Swearing-in Gaudron, J., supra* note 10, at 25 (Bowen), 26 (Gyles), 27 (Williams). There had, however, been some criticism of Gaudron's appointment. *See, e.g.*, the unnamed author claiming "a melancholy catalogue of sins of omission and commission as well as the better claims of others" were ignored in Gaudron's appointment, quoted in Fergus Shiel, *A Different Kind of Justice*, The Age (Melbourne), Dec. 9, 2002, www.theage.com.au/articles/2002/12/08/1038950270361.html.

pronoun, the speech contained little differentiating Gaudron from the (male) judges also sworn in on this occasion.

However, Gaudron's role as "first woman" entered the Attorney's speech by implicit comparisons. For instance, opening his speech by reflecting on the government's "great pleasure in being associated with your appointment," Bowen reiterated

> The pleasure which is felt by the Government in being associated with *this* appointment is shared by a great many, including many who are non-lawyers. The High Court is the apex of Australia's legal system. It is an institution of great, if not fully understood, significance. I trust it will always remain so and *that there will never be any artificial or irrelevant barrier placed to the appointment of Australian lawyers of great excellence to this Court.*[12]

The Attorney's speech did not explain why Gaudron's appointment generated this particular national pride. His catalog of Gaudron's career undoubtedly evinced her intellect and work ethic. He noted her first-class honours degree and University medal and her practice at the New South Wales bar. Also acknowledged was her service as Deputy President of the Conciliation and Arbitration Commission and later as New South Wales Solicitor-General. As described by the Attorney, this career chronology did not differ significantly from that of the two (male) judges sworn in a few short moments earlier. Only Gaudron's gender, unacknowledged and yet in plain sight, could explain the *particular* joy felt at *this* appointment.

The Attorney's unarticulated emphasis on Gaudron's gender is a fascinating insight into the perception of trailblazing women lawyers in Australia in the 1980s. For the Attorney, Gaudron's appointment to the High Court was a testament to the *absence* of sex discrimination in the Australian legal system.[13] This perspective may explain why his speech did not list Gaudron's "firsts" as a woman lawyer; such a list would have invited questions regarding (previous) "barriers" to women's advancement in the profession. However, given that Gaudron was the *sole* woman whose presence at the ceremony was recorded in the transcript, the Attorney must have literally closed his eyes to the evidence of a gender-based "barrier" at this time.

In contrast to the Attorney, the final speaker, Daryl Williams, then President of the Law Council of Australia, acknowledged Gaudron's trailblazing role as a woman in the law. Williams reflected on her "most notable career" and "predilection for pioneering" and was alone in noting that Gaudron had been the *youngest* person appointed as Deputy President of the Conciliation and Arbitration Commission and

---

[12] *Swearing-in Gaudron, J., supra* note 10, at 25 (Bowen) (emphasis added).
[13] *Compare* Deborah L. Rhode, *The "No-Problem" Problem: Feminist Challenges and Cultural Change,* 100 Yale L. J. 1731 (1991).

Solicitor-General for New South Wales.[14] The absence of these career highlights from earlier speeches was striking as these achievements could have been noted without emphasizing Gaudron's status as "first woman."[15]

Then, in an extraordinary passage, Williams reflected on the consequences of Gaudron's appointment for the homogeneity of the High Court bench:

> You are the first Justice of the High Court whose children have not addressed you as "Father." You are, according to my research, the first Justice of the High Court in its more than 80-year-long history who has not had a wife. In this respect, Your Honour has bravely paved the way for the regular appointment to the Court of bachelors.[16]

Although adopting an ironical stance, by referring to Gaudron as "paving the way for bachelors," Williams expropriated her experience as a woman and subsumed it into that of the "benchmark" male.[17] Thus, rather than welcoming Gaudron to the court, the overall effect of Williams' speech was to marginalize her experience as a female judge. It was against this background, speaking immediately after Williams, that Gaudron delivered her inaugural speech.

In Her Own Words

Mary Gaudron's speech displayed a complex understanding of her role as a female judge of the Australian High Court: succinctly acknowledging her identity as its first woman while simultaneously downplaying the difference that identity would make in her performance of the judicial role.[18] Her Honour chose to begin and conclude her remarks by affirming her shared identity with the court's six male members. She commenced,

> *Because I believe that too often we emphasize difference at the expense of common cause,* I would wish that the day had arrived when the appointment of a woman to this Court was unremarkable.[19]

---

[14] Justice Gaudron was also one of the youngest High Court appointments (age forty-four). The High Court's legendary judge, Sir Owen Dixon, was appointed at the age of forty-two.

[15] The second speaker, Roger Gyles, then President of the Australian Bar Association, had eschewed a catalog of Gaudron's career achievements as "first woman" on the basis that "it would be unduly sexist of me *to* list them." *Swearing-in Gaudron, J., supra* note 10, at 26 (Gyles) (emphasis added).

[16] *Id.* at 27 (Williams). On narratives describing the effect of women on the homogeneity of the bench, see Rackley, *Judicial Diversity, supra* note 8, at 76.

[17] Thornton, *supra* note 9, at 2.

[18] On the language of difference in debates surrounding women judges since Carol Gilligan's work, IN A DIFFERENT VOICE – PSYCHOLOGICAL THEORY AND WOMEN'S DEVELOPMENT (1982), see Erika Rackley, *Detailing Judicial Difference,* 17 FEMINIST LEGAL STUD. 11, 13–16 (2009). Gaudron's inaugural speech is discussed in PAMELA BURTON, FROM MOREE TO MABO: THE MARY GAUDRON STORY 258–260 (2010).

[19] *Swearing-in Gaudron, J., supra* note 10, at 28; Gaudron, *Speech, supra* note 10, at xxxvii (Gaudron, J.) (emphasis added).

Then concluding,

> I shall do my very best to discharge my judicial duties... and *in so doing I hope to be and, to be perceived to be, simply one of seven* doing their collective best to uphold the law and the institutions of the law.[20]

In this way, Gaudron seemed to desire the very kind of recognition given to her by the Attorney, as a judge *the same as* her male colleagues. Perhaps for this reason Gaudron's speech remained exclusively in the "public" sphere and was silent on the obvious differences in her private identity: wife (not husband) and mother (not father).[21]

These aspects of Gaudron's swearing-in speech appear to locate her voice within the recurring experiences of first Australian women lawyers identified by Professor Margaret Thornton in her groundbreaking work *Dissonance and Distrust*.[22] Thornton observed that first women were unwilling to identify as women lawyers, as this acknowledged a difference in experience or perspective and so challenged the legal community's dominant "malestream" discourse. This discourse also encouraged silence among women regarding burdens or barriers faced in their journey as "others" in the practice of law.[23]

In speeches given after her swearing in, Gaudron would discuss the pressures placed on women lawyers to become "honorary men."[24] For instance, in 1989, Gaudron observed,

> There is a danger that women professionals who proclaim their differentness, even by separate association within their professional groups, will thereby be seen to be less serious, less professionally motivated than their male counterparts. Worse still, they may be seen as having an axe to grind, lacking professionalism and objectivity. To that extent they are vulnerable, and particularly if, as I have suggested, assertions of separateness engender male resentment.[25]

---

[20] *Swearing-in Gaudron, J., supra* note 10, at 29; Gaudron, *Speech, supra* note 10, at xxxviii (emphasis added).

[21] Compare Crennan's statements of gratitude to her husband, children, and grandchildren. Transcript of Proceedings, *Swearing-in Ceremony, Crennan, J.* (High Court of Australia, Justice Susan Crennan, Nov. 8, 2005), www.austlii.edu.au/au/cases/cth/HCATrans/2005/895.html [hereinafter *Swearing-in Crennan, J.*].

[22] Thornton, *supra* note 9, at 67–70. For reflections on the experience of "first women lawyers" in other jurisdictions, see Mary Jane Mossman, *The First Women Lawyers* (2006).

[23] Thornton, *supra* note 9, at 67–70.

[24] Jennifer Batrouney, *The Contribution that the Hon Mary Gaudron QC has Made to Women and the Law*, 15 PUB. L. REV. 339, 341 (2004), (citing Justice Mary Gaudron, The Professional Woman – Her Separate Identity, Remarks at the Women Lawyers Association of Western Australia (Oct. 26, 1989) [hereinafter Gaudron, The Professional Woman]). On the concept of women lawyers as "honorary men" see further Rosemary Hunter, *Women Barristers and Gender Difference, in* WOMEN IN THE WORLD'S LEGAL PROFESSIONS 103, 120 (Ulrike Schultz & Gisela Shaw eds., 2003) [hereinafter Hunter, *Women Barristers and Gender Difference*].

[25] Gaudron, The Professional Woman, *supra* note 24.

A decade later, in a prominent speech to launch the association "Australian Women Lawyers," Gaudron acknowledged that she had shared the belief of many women of her generation that "once the doors were open, women could prove that they were every bit as good, and certainly no different from their male counterparts."[26] These views may explain the emphasis in Gaudron's swearing-in speech on her common identity, her sameness, with her brother judges.

However, it is significant that in her swearing-in speech Gaudron also identified her unique responsibilities as the "first woman" appointed to the court. In this critical passage, Gaudron spoke forcefully of her identity as a woman lawyer:

> Whilst I am the first woman to be appointed to this Court, my appointment is the result of the courage, determination, and professionalism of women who made their mark in the profession in days when the value of women's contribution had to be established.
>
> Of the many women lawyers who were instrumental in advancing the status of women within the legal profession, Dame Roma Mitchell's contribution merits particular acknowledgement. I am particularly honoured by her presence here [in Court at the swearing-in ceremony]. My constitutional duty is to all Australians but I hope that consistent with and by reason of the discharge of that responsibility, I shall be able to contribute as effectively to the status of women lawyers as has Dame Roma.[27]

It is true that compared to Gaudron's earlier (and later) speeches, these remarks appear self-consciously circumspect. For instance, in 1973 at the Women's Electoral Lobby Conference, Gaudron urged that for sex discrimination to become "impracticable in terms of reality . . . it will be necessary for women to organize as women."[28] Similar sentiments were absent in her swearing-in speech.

However, like the woman herself, Gaudron's swearing-in speech was groundbreaking. Previously, women had appeared in swearing-in ceremonies as the (frequently unnamed) "wife" thanked for her love and sacrifice to the career of the new (male) judge. In contrast, Gaudron's tribute was to the trailblazing women *in law*, and so both by her actions, by physically assuming her place on the bench, and by her words, Gaudron affirmed a woman's place at the highest levels of the Australian legal system. Thus, whatever pressures Gaudron encountered to become an "honorary man" on her path to the High Court, in framing her identity as a new judge in 1987 she chose to voice her commitment to serving the needs of women lawyers.

---

[26] Justice Mary Gaudron, Opening Speech to launch Australian Women Lawyers, Remarks at the Launch of Australian Women Lawyers (Sep. 19, 1997), *available at* www.highcourt.gov.au/speeches/ gaudronj/gaudronj_wlasp.htm. For further discussion of this speech, see Batrouney, supra note 24, at 340–41.

[27] *Swearing-in Gaudron, J., supra* note 10, at 28 (Gaudron, J.); Gaudron, *Speech, supra* note 10, at 37–38. Dame Roma Mitchell was Australia's "first woman": Queen's Counsel; Judge; and Governor of a State. *See*, further, DAME ROMA: GLIMPSES OF A GLORIOUS LIFE (Susan Magarey ed., 2002).

[28] Mary Gaudron, Women and the Law and Women in the Law, Remarks at the Women's Electoral Lobby Conference, Canberra (Jan. 1973) at 3 (Copy on file with author).

Conclusion

Although Gaudron quarantined her "private" life in her swearing-in speech, and so distanced herself from her identity as a wife and mother, she has been alone among the High Court's women judges in identifying herself as a woman lawyer on this occasion. Assuming for herself the mantle of mentor, Gaudron's speech implicitly acknowledged the challenges faced by women in the profession. At the same time, her emphasis on her shared identity with her "brother judges" reflected the pressure placed on women lawyers to downplay their difference from the "benchmark" male of the law.

Through its interwoven threads, Gaudron's swearing-in speech evokes the complex experiences of a "first woman" judge. However, the complexity of Gaudron's understanding of the interaction between her identity as a woman and as a judge stood in stark contrast to the place of gender in the speeches welcoming her to the bench. In different ways, each of the (male) speakers ignored, marginalized, or expropriated women's experiences in the law. As will be seen, the speeches welcoming Crennan to the Court illustrated different paths to the same effect.

JUSTICE SUSAN CRENNAN

Australia waited almost twenty years before a second woman was appointed to the High Court. When Susan Crennan was sworn in on November 8, 2005, she, like Gaudron before her, joined an all-male bench.[29] However, in contrast to Gaudron's ceremony, Crennan was not recorded in the transcript as the sole woman in attendance. For the first time at an Australian High Court swearing-in ceremony, two serving women judges were seated as dignitaries on the bench, both Chief Justices of their own courts.[30] In addition, Crennan was not the only woman to speak at her swearing in.[31] This presence of women in court illustrated the measurable (albeit still disproportionately small) increase in the representation of women at the highest levels of the Australian legal system since 1987.[32] For example, at the time of Crennan's appointment to the High Court, approximately 9 percent of Federal Court judges were women, while female barristers accounted for 16 percent of the independent bar in Victoria, Crennan's home state.[33]

---

[29] Gaudron retired from the court on January 31, 2003. Her replacement was Justice (John) Dyson Heydon.

[30] Chief Justice of the Family Court, Diana Bryant, and Chief Justice of the Supreme Court of Victoria, Marilyn Warren.

[31] Crennan had spoken on April 21, 1995, at the swearing-in ceremonies of Sir Gerard Brennan (Chief Justice) and William Gummow (Justice).

[32] The Transcript of Proceedings records the following women at the ceremony: 9 out of 55 judges and magistrates (16%); 1 of 5 Solicitors-General (20%); 9 of 74 barristers and Queen's Counsel (12%): *Swearing-in Crennan, J.*, *supra* note 21.

[33] See, e.g., Rosemary Hunter, *Women in the Legal Profession: The Australian Profile*, in WOMEN IN THE WORLD'S LEGAL PROFESSIONS 87, 89–101 (Ulrike Schultz & Gisela Shaw eds., 2003).

The difference in gender representation between the swearing-in ceremonies of Gaudron and Crennan was not limited to the comparative numbers of women in positions of prominence on these occasions. While Gaudron's gender was largely a silent theme of the welcome speeches, Crennan's identity as a woman, and particularly a grandmother, was the overt and overarching theme of her swearing-in ceremony.[34]

Welcome Speeches: "Grandmother Judge"

Feminist lawyers may respond in a variety of ways to the representation of Crennan in the welcome speeches. It is true that the first three speakers, including the Attorney-General Philip Ruddock, devoted a significant portion of their remarks to her legal achievements as well as her gender. For instance, then President of the Australian Bar Association Glenn Martin catalogued a range of "very significant" matters dealt with during her term as president of that organization.[35] However, the degree that family was emphasized during Crennan's swearing in was unprecedented in the High Court's history. For example, the Attorney emphasized in his chronicle of Crennan's career that "[d]espite the demands of your legal career you and your husband, Michael, have raised three children."[36] Although Gaudron had also completed her studies with a young family (Gaudron's first child was born the same year she completed her law degree), it was in Crennan's ceremony that her role as lawyer/judge *and* wife/mother/grandmother was emphasized.

One interpretation of the welcome speeches is as a victory for the feminist critique of the public–private distinction. Until Crennan's ceremony, welcome speakers had kept a positivist's distance from the private. In contrast, the welcome speeches to Crennan implicitly acknowledged that to inform the public about the new appointee, it was necessary to go beyond a catalog of the judge's career highlights to acknowledge her broader life experience.

However, different questions are raised if, rather than illustrating an attitudinal shift in the legal community's understanding of judges, the heightened attention to Crennan's "private" life was deemed relevant by the speakers *because* of her gender. On the one hand, the portrayal of Crennan as judge and mother/grandmother exposed the different experiences of women lawyers and so challenged the assumption that the life of the "benchmark man" was the only valid experience for a judge. This representation of Crennan might be regarded as challenging the public–private

---

34 Thornton concluded that Crennan's "grandmother" status was similarly a significant theme in media commentary on her appointment: Thornton, *"Otherness," supra* note 6, at 397.

35 *Swearing-in Crennan, J., supra* note 21 (Martin).

36 *Swearing-in Crennan, J., supra* note 21 (Ruddock). That Crennan's husband was a successful lawyer may explain why he featured in her welcome in a way that judges' wives seldom have. On marriage within the legal community and women lawyers' social ease, see Thornton, *supra* note 9, at 141; Hunter, *Women Barristers and Gender Difference, supra* note 24, at 108.

distinction, and recognizing that "the personal aspects *of a woman's* life necessarily intersect with the professional."[37] On the other hand, the emphasis on Crennan's family, and role as grandmother, arguably perpetuated the "otherness" of women judges on the bench. Writing in response to the media's representation of Crennan, which like the welcome ceremonies had (over)emphasized Crennan's identity as a grandmother, Thornton observed,

> The connotations of this grandmotherly image are that of a woman of mature years who is safe and unthreatening because her "manned" state is likely to mitigate the dangerousness of the feminine in an unrestrained position of authority.[38]

Ironically, it was Kate McMillan's speech, President of the Victorian Bar Association and the only woman speaking to welcome Crennan, which went furthest to perpetuate this discriminatory "grandmotherly image" of Crennan. McMillan related a story of Crennan's response to receiving "toddler's whack":

> With your Honour's well-earned reputation for patience, you dealt with the issue fittingly by continuing on with your story, remaining unruffled and unperturbed.[39]

In an era when unrepresented litigants demand increased portions of a judge's time, it may be conceded that patience should be praised as a judicial attribute. However, this was not the context of McMillan's words. Instead McMillan explained the relevance of the anecdote as eliciting "further proof of *your quality as a grandmother.*" In this way, McMillan's fervent praise of Crennan's grandmotherly qualities diverted attention from the purpose of the speech – to evince "proof" of her skills *as a judge* – and infused the ceremony with a feminized image of Crennan.

In Her Own Words

Just as her husband and offspring featured in the welcome speeches to Crennan, her Honour acknowledged their support at the outset of her speech. With these remarks, in contrast to Gaudron, Crennan allowed a glimpse into her "private" life and placed her gender literally at the forefront of her inaugural speech.

Despite this opening, the balance of her remarks did not suggest that Crennan embraced an identity as a *"woman* judge." For example, in contrast to Gaudron's swearing-in speech, Crennan did not speak to the role of women in the legal profession more generally. Nor did she identify any women mentors in her career,

---

37 Carol Sanger, *Curriculum Vitae (Feminae): Biography and Early American Women Lawyers*, 46 STAN. L. REV. 1245, 1274 (1994) (emphasis added).

38 Thornton, *"Otherness," supra* note 6, at 397.

39 *Swearing-in Crennan, J., supra* note 21 (McMillan). McMillan also recounted Crennan's granddaughter's response to the news of the appointment: "If Nana's going to be working in Canberra, what is happening about our Sundays?"

reserving her expressions of gratitude exclusively for prominent men in the legal profession.[40]

It is possible that the disproportionate emphasis on her gender in the media at the announcement of her appointment to the court influenced the way Crennan framed her identity in her swearing-in speech. A year following her swearing in, at her first sitting in South Australia as a High Court judge, Crennan had praised the heroine of the local bar, Dame Roma Mitchell, as a trailblazing woman in the Australian legal profession and *"an enduring model for women judges."*[41] This statement reflected both a sensitivity to the importance of such examples for women lawyers in contemporary Australia and Crennan's openness to her own identity as a "women lawyer," not simply as a "judge." However, Crennan's swearing-in speech contained no such statements, and distanced her identity as a judge from her gender.

In part, Crennan's emphasizing of her identity as a lawyer, not a woman lawyer, may have reflected the dominant ethos of the legal community in which she had formerly practiced. In her study of women's status at the independent bar in Victoria, published in 2002, Professor Rosemary Hunter analyzed the results of in-depth interviews with leading members of the Victorian Bar, and observed that for the majority of the women interviewed,[42]

> [T]he denial of femininity, in the face of obvious feminine embodiment, is something that must be achieved – performed – at least partly through talking. By talking up equality, and talking down their gender, senior women barristers represented versions both of themselves and of the Bar that were designed for public consumption, within the simmering debates over the Bar's claims to be an equal opportunity institution.[43]

Drawn from interviews of Crennan's contemporaries at the bar, Hunter's conclusions speak to the environment within which Crennan built her career and assumed representative and leadership positions. By identifying herself as a lawyer – and "not a feminist"[44] – in high-profile speeches made for "public consumption," like her

---

[40] See also Crennan's swearing-in speech as a Federal Court judge: Transcript of Proceedings, *Swearing-in Ceremony, Crennan, J.* (Federal Court of Australia, Justice Susan Crennan, Feb. 3, 2004). It is possible that in recounting her story, including by naming male lawyers as mentors in her speeches, Crennan chose to focus "on instances of affirmative assistance," in order to "inspire others to emulate egalitarian behaviour." *See* Constance Backhouse, *Bertha Wilson and the Politics of Feminism, in* REFLECTIONS ON THE LEGACY OF JUSTICE BERTHA WILSON 33, 35 (Jamie Cameron ed., 2009).

[41] Transcript of Proceedings, *Special Sitting to Welcome Crennan, J. to Adelaide* (High Court of Australia, Justice Susan Crennan, Aug. 7, 2006), *available at* www.austlii.edu.au/au/cases/cth/HCATrans/2006/429.html (emphasis added).

[42] Hunter, *Talking Up Equality, supra* note 1.

[43] *Id.* at 128.

[44] For a number of these suggestions, see references listed in Thornton, *"Otherness," supra* note 6, at 395–97. This identity is likely to have been an important criterion in Crennan's appointment to the court by the conservative Howard government.

swearing-in speeches, Crennan thus distanced herself from the controversy of gender and the law.

Conclusion

Although Gaudron and Crennan shared the title of "first women" to achieve many heights in the Australian legal system, their gender pervaded their swearing-in ceremonies in different ways. For Crennan, familial relations were central to the speeches welcoming her to the court. As never before, nor since, these speeches spoke of Crennan as a woman first, then a judge. Although Crennan acknowledged her identity as a wife and mother in her speech, she self-identified as "the same as" her brother judges. Similar themes infused the swearing-in speech of Crennan's soon-to-be sister on the bench, Susan Kiefel.

JUSTICE SUSAN KIEFEL

Susan Kiefel was sworn in on September 3, 2007.[45] A striking feature of Kiefel's swearing-in ceremony was how little it revealed of her personality and judicial philosophy. Although not overtly dominating the welcome speeches, Kiefel's gender appears to have influenced the ceremony indirectly, in the speakers' responses to questions of "merit."

Welcome Speeches: "Meritorious Judge"

Four (male) speakers welcomed Kiefel to the High Court bench, including Attorney-General Ruddock.[46] Two aspects of the Attorney's welcome to Kiefel distinguished his remarks, in style and substance, from his welcome to Crennan two years earlier. The first difference was the absence of explicit reference to Kiefel's gender. In this speech, Ruddock did not utilize the female pronoun, nor did any aspect of the biographical sketch acknowledge that Kiefel was a woman.[47] In fact, in none of the speeches was Kiefel's gender more than of briefest comment. The second difference lay in the degree of detail the Attorney provided regarding Kiefel's career highlights

---

[45] It did not escape the media's attention that "two Susans" now graced the court. *See, e.g.*, Phillip Hudson, "Ruddock Names New High Court Judge," *Sydney Morning Herald*, Aug. 13, 2007, www.smh.com.au/news/national/ruddock-names-new-high-court-judge/2007/08/13/1186857421228 .html.

[46] The Transcript of Proceedings records the following women at Kiefel's ceremony: 11 of 32 judges and magistrates (34%); 1 of 8 Solicitors-General (12%); 2 of 32 barristers and Queen's Counsel (6%).

[47] *Contra* Fraser's speech related that at Cambridge, Kiefel was "introduced to the sport of rowing and to your coach and now husband Michael Albrecht." See Transcript of Proceedings, *Swearing-in Ceremony, Kiefel, J.* (High Court of Australia, Hugh Fraser, Sept. 3, 2007), www.austlii.edu.au/au/cases/cth/HCATrans/2007/493.html [hereinafter *Swearing-in Kiefel, J.*]. Like Crennan's husband, Albrecht was himself a prominent lawyer.

and extralegal pursuits. In contrast to the extensive catalog of Crennan's legal, and sporting, accomplishments, the Attorney's portrait of Kiefel appeared notably nondescript.

The style of the welcome speeches to Kiefel may have been influenced by the media's response to the announcement of her appointment. As the Howard Government had filled two successive High Court vacancies with women, questions were asked whether Kiefel's elevation was designed to ensure greater gender equity on the bench. In response, in a fierce statement the Attorney denied that anything other than "merit" had influenced Kiefel's appointment:

> She will make an outstanding judge, it is a factual matter that there are five male judges now [and] there will be two female judges. *They* are both people who were appointed on their *merits* ... Any suggestion that [Kiefel's] appointment was to secure two female appointments would be quite wrong. The way she came to qualify as a barrister initially ... is a very significant achievement.[48]

On the same day, but in a different context, the Attorney shed light on his understanding of "merit":

> Judicial appointments in Australia are made on merit. It has become fashionable for intellectuals and other elites to ask, well what does merit mean? How boringly postmodern. Merit means legal excellence and independence.[49]

This context may explain the Attorney's choice not to refer to Kiefel's gender in his speech. However, having felt the need to defend the "merit" of Kiefel's appointment, why was his catalog of Kiefel's career highlights seemingly lackluster, and missing the flourish and detail that accompanied his welcome to Crennan?[50] It cannot be said that Kiefel's career lacked those lofty legal accomplishments that had inspired the Attorney's earlier hyperbole. For example, as Ruddock observed, Kiefel had left school early to engage in administrative work, but took silk at age thirty-three. In fact, Kiefel was the *youngest* person in Queensland – male or female – to have taken silk, an achievement evincing both an enviable legal career and recognition among her peers as an exceptional lawyer.[51]

---

[48] Patricia Karvelas & Nicola Berkovic, "Kiefel will Make High Court History," *The Australian* (Sydney), Aug. 14, 2007, www.theaustralian.news.com.au/story/0,25197,22240944-601,00.html (Attorney-General Ruddock) (emphasis added). That the Attorney stated "both" were appointed on "merit" reinforces that "merit" is only an issue in respect of female candidates for judicial office. *See generally*, Thornton, *"Otherness," supra* note 6.

[49] Philip Ruddock, "Ruddock: Bringing Judgment to Account," *The Australian* (Sydney), Aug. 14, 2007, http://blogs.theaustralian.news.com.au/yoursay/index.php/theaustralian/comments/ruddock_bringing_judgment_to_account.

[50] Strikingly, the second speaker, Tim Bugg, devoted even less of his speech to Kiefel, reflecting instead on questions of "judicial activism." *Swearing-in Kiefel, J., supra* note 47 (Bugg).

[51] Compare the high praise given to this aspect of Kiefel's career at a later ceremonial sitting of the court. Transcript of Proceedings, *Special Sitting to Welcome Justice Kiefel to Sydney* (High Court of Australia, Michael Slattery, Oct. 5, 2007), www.austlii.edu.au/au/cases/cth/HCATrans/2007/603.html.

Similarly, it emerged from other speeches that Kiefel had participated in sport at various stages in her career. For instance, Hugh Fraser, President of the Bar Association of Queensland, referred at Kiefel's swearing-in ceremony to her participation in rowing at Cambridge University. Others alluded to Kiefel's enthusiastic participation in bar association cricket competitions, activity that could have been framed by the Attorney to demonstrate her twin attributes of collegiality and competitiveness. These aspects of Kiefel's life would have added color and context to the Attorney's introduction of the new judge. Without such allusions, his speech conveyed the portrait of a determined lawyer, of imprecisely defined "merit" and hence failed to foreclose the suggestion that gender may indeed have played a part in Kiefel's appointment.

In Her Own Words

Like Crennan, Kiefel did not identify herself as a "woman lawyer" in her High Court swearing-in speech. Kiefel's catalog of thanks to colleagues and mentors (a list representing the majority of her speech) did not include a single woman.[52] This absence in Kiefel's swearing-in speech was particularly significant given that she had reflected on the topic of women lawyers in her earlier swearing-in speech as a Supreme Court Justice. On this earlier occasion, Kiefel drew attention to gender equity issues:

> I have for the most part enjoyed my time at the Bar. It has both puzzled and saddened me to observe that the rate of women law graduates coming to the Bar has not grown. I could not pretend to them that their day-to-day practice is likely to be as readily facilitated as some, but I hasten to add not all, men. Society has yet to deal with the more deeply entrenched and subtle institutionalized discrimination, but women will find that the Bar and the judiciary will treat them simply as a professional person and on merit. I encourage them to consider the benefits of the career which offers extraordinary variety and richness of experience.[53]

It is true that this passage does not demonstrate a particularly strong feminist consciousness. Instead, Kiefel implicitly denied that discrimination had been a feature in her career or that of women lawyers of her acquaintance.[54]

However, what should we make of the absence of similar reflections by Kiefel in her later speech of 2007? Had her time on the bench changed her perception of the

---

[52] Kiefel did, however, thank her (female) personal assistant and her female family members: *Swearing-in Kiefel, J., supra* note 47 (Kiefel, J.).

[53] Transcript of Proceedings, *In the Matter of the Swearing-in of the Honourable Justice SM Kiefel as a Judge of the Supreme Court of Queensland* (Supreme Court of Queensland, Justice Susan Mary Kiefel, June 16, 1993) at 13.

[54] As in Crennan's silence regarding the assistance of women mentors, it is possible that Kiefel chose to emphasize examples of "affirmative assistance" by male lawyers. *See* Backhouse, *supra* note 40.

opportunities for women in the law? Or had speculation regarding the importance of her gender in her appointment to the court influenced this silence in Kiefel's later speech? Or was this silence attributable to the change in her new environment, the High Court of Australia?

Conclusion

Susan Kiefel's swearing-in ceremony appears both to maintain and break the patterns in the treatment of gender in the swearing-in speeches of Australian High Court judges. Kiefel chose to locate herself within the malestream Australian legal community and to excise from her remarks an identity as a "woman judge" she had acknowledged in an earlier swearing-in speech. In 2007, Kiefel had thus self-consciously silenced her feminine voice. However, the welcome speeches made to Kiefel marked a significant shift in the representation of the gender of the incoming Justice. Absent from this ceremony were the marginalizing and feminizing stories of women judges that had characterized the welcomes to Gaudron and Crennan. What remains unclear, however, is the extent to which the generalized discussion of Kiefel's "merit," by the Attorney in particular, reflected a deeper ambivalence regarding the role of her gender in her appointment to the court.

JUSTICE VIRGINIA BELL

The latest appointment to the Australian High Court was Virginia Bell, sworn in on February 3, 2009. For feminist lawyers, the media's coverage of this appointment was again a mixed blessing.

For instance, featured in this coverage was the statement that Bell "had never married."[55] This was the closest much of the mainstream media came to identifying Bell as a lesbian judge.[56] On the one hand, the media's silence regarding her sexuality may have reflected a respect for Bell's private persona; on the other, it may have manifested a deeper aversion to recognizing the "otherness" of a lesbian judge on the High Court.[57] For whatever reason, this statement, and the prominent reporting

---

[55] Her marital status was not integrated into a discussion of "private" aspects of her life. Rather, for example "[The Attorney-General] said Justice Bell, *who has never married*, was one of 40 people nominated for the position." Michael Pelly & Nicola Berkovic, "Virginia Bell Rings in New Era for High Court," *The Australian*, Dec. 16, 2008, www.theaustralian.news.com.au/story/0,25197,24806008–601,00.html (emphasis added).

[56] *Contra* Berkovic's reference to the fact that Bell in her swearing-in speech "did not mention her female barrister partner in her speech." Nicola Berkovic, "Family Pride as Revel Makes it to the Top," *The Australian* (Sydney), Feb. 4, 2009, www.theaustralian.com.au/news/family-pride-as-rebel-makes-it-to-top/story-e6frg6o6-1111118749090.

[57] Thornton has argued that if a woman judge is "already consigned to 'otherness' . . . the lesbian [judge] is beyond the pale because she is not 'manned' and is unlikely to be." Thornton, *supra* note 9, at 221.

of Bell's theatrical interests (a flamboyant "barrel-*girl*"[58]), reinforced Bell's distance from the overwhelming pattern of straight-laced married-male, or more recently, married-female, High Court judges.

Difference also pervaded the media's account of Bell's "unconventional" legal career. Bell was a lawyer at a community legal center and public defender rather than the conventional commercial/public law practice of her contemporaries on the bench. This emphasis on Bell's "difference" allowed the press to manufacture a dramatic climax in its reporting of her swearing-in ceremony. Would she bring a bold, "different" perspective to the bench? A "new social consciousness"? According to the media, Bell "dashed the hopes" of many, delivering a "cautious" inaugural speech.[59] However, for present purposes the more important surprise was the place of gender in the ceremony.

Welcome Speeches: "Outstanding Judge"

The praise of Bell as a lawyer and judge was the most generous to date for a woman High Court Justice, and rivaled the warmest welcomes to her brothers on the court.[60] In his first welcome speech to a High Court Justice, Attorney-General Robert McClelland oozed enthusiasm for Bell's character and "totality" of her legal experience. Identifying the diversity of career, he praised her fire and combativeness (traditionally expected from zealous counsel) alongside her "social conscience" and inclusiveness.[61] Although noting Bell's warmth, openness, and compassion, McClelland's portrait did not feminize Bell as had Attorney Ruddock's portrayal of Crennan. Instead, McClelland's speech presented a heartfelt welcome to an inevitable appointee to the High Court.

The three speakers that followed the Attorney echoed his warm welcome. In striking contrast to the previous welcomes to women judges, these speakers self-consciously reflected on the slow movement toward equality in gender representation in the Australian legal profession. For instance, John Corcoran, President of the Law Council of Australia, observed,

[58] *See, e.g.,* Yuko Narushima, "On a Roll: From Barrel Girl to High Court Judge," *Sydney Morning Herald,* Dec. 16, 2008, www.smh.com.au/news/national/on-a-roll-from-barrel-girl-to-high-court-judge/2008/12/15/1229189534072.html.

[59] David Marr, "Justice Bell's Swearing in Brings Up a High Court Trio," *Sydney Morning Herald,* Feb. 4, 2009, www.smh.com.au/news/national/justice-bells-swearing-in-brings-up-a-high-court-trio/2009/02/03/1233423223161.html.

[60] An increased presence of women was recorded at Bell's ceremony: 12 of 34 judges and magistrates (35%); 1 of 7 Solicitors-General (14%); 5 of 31 barristers and Queen's Counsel (16%). *See* Transcript of Proceedings, *Swearing-in Ceremony, Bell, J.* (High Court of Australia, Justice Virginia Bell, Feb. 3, 2009), www.austlii.edu.au/au/other/HCATrans/2009/4.html [hereinafter *Swearing-in Bell, J.*].

[61] McClelland also emphasized Bell's "dedication"; "incisive cross-examinations"; "strong sense of public duty"; and "deep interest in, and respect for, people from all walks of life." *Id.* (McClelland).

[I]t is certainly a different "judicial world" today than when your Honour commenced practising as a solicitor, when, in New South Wales, there were no female judges on that State's District or Supreme Courts.[62]

As the previous discussion has shown, recognition of the challenges facing Australian women in law at a High Court swearing-in ceremony was unprecedented. Did the court's new gender balance mean that systemic questions about law and gender could be asked in safety? Or did the content of these speeches reflect individual rather than systemic change: *these* speakers considered this an appropriate topic in connection with *this* judge. For whatever reason, these prominent members of the Australian legal community considered 2009 an appropriate moment to lift the silence on this topic at a High Court swearing-in ceremony.

In Her Own Words

In 2007 at her swearing in as a Justice of the New South Wales Supreme Court, Bell had paid tribute to the "first women" judges, acknowledging their struggles and their support for younger women in the profession.[63] In March 2009, at her welcome to Sydney as a High Court Justice, Bell confirmed her willingness to speak as a "woman judge"; reflecting on the "changing face" of the profession and the increase in women judicial officers during her career.[64] As Bell had spoken about women and the law on these ceremonial occasions, her *silence* in her High Court swearing-in speech on this topic may be interpreted as a conscious omission from this particular speech.

A number of factors, including her identity as a female judge, may have influenced how Bell told her story on this occasion. For instance, Bell may have quarantined references to her gender to reduce speculation regarding the possible influence of her lesbian identity on her judicial role. In addition, Bell used her swearing-in speech to distance herself from her predecessor on the Court, Michael Kirby. Given Kirby's larger-than-life persona, it was perhaps necessary for his successor to reject the implication that they would "fill his shoes" on the court. For Bell, a lesbian judge succeeding the court's controversial "out"(sider) judge, this pressure may have been greater, even without Kirby's own intervention. However, in a remarkable statement during his highly publicized swearing-out speech, Kirby suggested that

---

[62] *Id.* (Corcoran), and *see*, further, the remarks of Anna Katzmann SC, President of the New South Wales Bar Association.

[63] Transcript of Proceedings, *Swearing-in Ceremony, Bell, J.* (New South Wales Supreme Court, Justice Virginia Bell, Mar. 25, 1999), *available at* www.lawlink.nsw.gov.au/lawlink/supreme_court/ll_sc.nsf/pages/SCO_speech_bell_250399. Parts of this speech were cited in Michael Pelly, "Court Gets a Go-Getter," *The Australian* (Sydney), Dec. 16, 2008, www.theaustralian.news.com.au/story/0,25197,24804981-28737,00.html.

[64] Transcript of Proceedings, *Special Sitting to Welcome Justice Bell to Sydney* (High Court of Australia, Justice Virginia Bell, Mar. 13, 2009), www.austlii.edu.au/au/other/HCATrans/2009/46.html.

Bell's experience as a public defender would ensure that *his* legacy as protector of the "little people" in Australia would continue. Indeed, Kirby "warned" Bell that his "ghost" would "haunt [the chamber and] will come down and whisper in her ear" should she ever forget that duty.[65]

In these circumstances, how polite then was Bell's own statement the following day. Observing that unlike Kirby (and the Chief Justice, Robert French) she was unable to deliver speeches while jetlagged from long flights, Bell said

> This may not be the only respect in which I do not, as some people have suggested I should, fill the shoes of the Honourable Michael Kirby. No one person could do that.[66]

Earlier in her speech, she had also reminded court observers to resist labeling judges, stating that titles of "conservative or progressive or indeed dangerous radical" were inappropriate as ignoring "the discipline of judgment writing."[67] Taken as a whole Bell's speech was thus a carefully constructed narrative reinforcing her shared identity with her fellow judges, and distancing herself from the perception that she was an "other" on the court.

Conclusion

Virginia Bell's swearing-in ceremony illustrates a positive step in the representation of women judges in the High Court. The welcome speeches wholeheartedly endorsed her qualifications as a judge, and her gender was neither marginalized nor feminized. However, Bell's inaugural speech attests to the continuing pressure faced by judges to distance themselves from the perception of "otherness" on the bench.

CONCLUSION

This chapter has shown that, for feminist lawyers, the patterns regarding the role of gender in the swearing-in ceremonies of women judges of the Australian High Court are a mixed blessing. The legal community's welcome to the new judges described the skills, attributes, and experiences of three of the four women judges in a way that markedly differed from their brother judges. In Gaudron and Crennan's ceremonies in particular, their gender was the pivot around which the speakers crafted their largely discriminatory remarks. Fortunately, Bell's welcome suggests that the Australian legal community has moved beyond feminized depictions of women High Court judges.

---

[65] Nicola Berkovic & Michael Pelly, "Departing Kirby's Plea to Successor," *The Australian* (Sydney), Feb. 3, 2009, www.theaustralian.news.com.au/story/0,25197,25000224–5013404,00.html (citing Justice Michael Kirby).

[66] *Swearing-in Bell, J. supra* note 59 (Bell, J.).

[67] *Id.*

The inaugural speeches of these four women tell a more complex story. Only Gaudron, the High Court's first woman judge, embraced her identity as a woman lawyer in her swearing-in speech. At the same time, she also underlined her sameness with the court's male judges. More dramatically, the omissions from the speeches of Kiefel and Bell – particularly contrasted against their other ceremonial speeches – suggest that these women silenced their feminine voice in the speech marking their elevation to Australia's highest court. Although women now represent three of the seven High Court judges, these inaugural speeches tell the story of a continuing perception of the "otherness" of women judges in the Australian legal system.

7

Will "Watertight Compartments" Sink Women's Charter Rights? The Need for a New Theoretical Approach to Women's Multiple Rights Claims under the Canadian Charter of Rights and Freedoms

Kerri A. Froc

In principle, the Supreme Court of Canada has stated that rights under the Canadian Charter of Rights and Freedoms[1] represent a nonhierarchical "complex of interacting values" that must be interpreted in light of one another.[2] Further, equality in particular has been singled out as a right whose interpretive influence traverses the confines of Section 15; it "applies to and supports all other rights guaranteed by the Charter."[3] One would assume therefore that the more severe, complex, and intractable the oppression suffered – the kind that often manifests in a "cluster" of rights violations – the more likely it is that it will receive judicial recognition. However, the poor track record of women's multiple rights claims at the Supreme Court, claims that arise through a combination of an equality rights violation under Section 15 of the Charter[4] coupled with another civil liberty violation, belies this assumption. Even in the rare multiple rights case that could be considered a "win" for women, it resulted from a truncated analysis that would not assist in preventing future subordination beyond the narrow parameters of the case.[5]

[1] Canadian Charter of Rights and Freedoms, Part I of the Constitution Act, 1982, being Schedule B to the Canada Act 1982 (U.K.), 1982, c.11 [Hereinafter *Charter*].

[2] *R. v. Lyon*, [1988] 37 C.C.C. (3d) 1, 20 (S.C.C.). *See also R. v. Mills*, [1999] 3 S.C.R. 668, ¶ 21 (citing *Dagenais v. Canadian Broadcasting Corp.*, [1994] 3 S.C.R. 835); *Trinity Western University v. British Columbia College of Teachers*, [2001] 1 S.C.R. 772, ¶ 39; *Chamberlain v. Surrey School District No. 36*, [2002] 4 S.C.R. 710; and *Health Services and Support – Facilities Subsector Bargaining Assn. v. British Columbia*, [2007] 2 S.C.R. 391, ¶ 80 (citing *Dubois v. The Queen*, [1985] 2 S.C.R. 350, 365).

[3] *Andrews v. Law Society of British Columbia*, [1989] 1 S.C.R. 143, 185.

[4] Section 15(1) states, "Every individual is equal before and under the law and has the right to the equal protection and equal benefit of the law without discrimination, and in particular, without discrimination based on race, national or ethnic origin, colour, religion, sex, age or mental or physical disability."

[5] *See, e.g., R. v. Morgentaler*, [1988] 1 S.C.R. 30. The enduring problems with abortion funding resulting from the court's decision to strike down the Criminal Code abortion provisions purely on the basis of Section 7, and refusing to address Section 15, is discussed, for example, in Diana Majury, *The Charter, Equality Rights and Women: Equivocation and Celebration*, 40 OSGOODE HALL L. J. 297 (2002); Beverley Baines, *Abortion Judicial Activism and Constitutional Crossroads*, 53 U. N. B. L. J. 157

The reason for such a fundamental contradiction between philosophy and outcome, I believe, lies in the "watertight compartments" approach to rights. By this, I mean that the courts have constructed rights in multiple rights claims as abstract, discrete, and oppositional, much the same way as it has employed grounds in analyzing discrimination claims, making them resistant to an intersectional analysis.[6] Intersectionality theory demonstrates that discrimination law has required women of color to separate out and compartmentalize the aspects of their experience that relate to racism and those that relate to sexism. Because discrimination law has required them to show either that they experience sexism like white women or racism like racialized men, their experiences of subordination are considered "too aberrant" to be recognized.[7]

Similarly, in multiple rights cases, the focus of the court is on separating elements of a claimant's experience into one (dominantly defined) right or another, rather than viewing it as claimants do – as a singular experience of rights violation that arises from complex circumstances of subordination. Where the claim is based upon discrimination and another rights violation, elements of the claimant's experience that the dominant group ascribes to gender are put into the "discrimination" category under Section 15, whereas other elements of her experience considered comparable to those of the dominant social group are put into the other rights category. Where her experiences are considered too "aberrant" to those of the dominant, Section 15 completely overwhelms the constitutional analysis and there is nothing left to be considered under the other right – it is exclusively "a Section 15 case." On the other hand, where women's experience can be subsumed into that of the dominant, elements of social identity that depart from the "norm" are repressed within these non-Section 15 rights. Claimants have to show that they are "like" the traditional white, male civil rights bearer. Yet in doing so, claimants accept, rather than challenge, the underlying racialized, gendered, classed, heteronormative status quo. Thus, rights violations are viewed as conflicting phenomenon. Either one differs from the dominant (and makes an equality claim) or one does not (and makes a civil rights claim). It is exceedingly difficult for multiple rights claimants to walk this

---

(2004); Sanda Rodgers, *Abortion Denied: Bearing the Limits of Law, in* JUST MEDICARE: WHAT'S IN, WHAT'S OUT, HOW WE DECIDE 107, 121 (Colleen M. Flood ed., 2006); and Martha Jackman, *Health Care and Equality: Is there a Cure?* 15 HEALTH L. J. 87 at 107–109 (2007).

[6] See Kimberlé Crenshaw, *Demarginalizing the Intersection of Race and Sex: A Black Feminist Critique of Antidiscrimination Doctrine, Feminist Theory, and Antiracist Politics,* U. CHI. LEGAL F. 139 (1989); *Mapping the Margins: Intersectionality, Identity, Politics, and Violence Against Women of Colour,* 43 STAN. L. REV. 1241 (1991) [hereinafter Crenshaw, *Mapping the Margins*]; *Race, Gender, and Sexual Harassment,* 65 S. CAL. L. REV. 1467 (1992); *Beyond Racism and Misogyny: Black Feminism and 2 Live Crew, in* WORDS THAT WOUND: CRITICAL RACE THEORY, ASSAULTIVE SPEECH, AND THE FIRST AMENDMENT 111 (Mari Matsuda et al. eds., 1993).

[7] In the words of Crenshaw, "Under this view, Black women are protected *only to the extent that their experiences coincide with those of either of these two groups.*" Crenshaw, *Mapping the Margins, supra* note 6, at 143 (emphasis added).

tightrope and show the court that their experience of inequality is unique to them as women but that their other civil rights violation is analogous to that experienced by the dominant. Often, this results in a court concluding that there has been no rights violation (thereby punishing a claimant who is perceived as "wanting to have it both ways"). Thus, women continue to languish on the horns of the "sameness/difference" dilemma.

Whether the "watertight compartments" approach is applied to rights or grounds, it stems from the same fundamental misunderstanding of subordination as unidimensional and monocausal, rather than composed of intertwined and mutually reinforcing systems of oppression, whose effects are obscured by their synergistic operation. And just as intersectionality theory insisted upon a recognition of the unique oppression experienced by those whose identity is multiply subordinated along the axes of race and sex, my contention is that subordination that implicates multiple rights requires different conceptual tools that recognize its unique nature and that it is more than the sum of its parts. Next, I examine the Canadian Supreme Court case of *Gosselin v. Quebec (Attorney General)*,[8] a constitutional challenge to a provincial "workfare" program as a violation of equality and a Section 7 violation of personal security,[9] to illuminate how the court adopted a "watertight compartments" approach to rights in the case, resulting in a distortion of Louise Gosselin's experience of oppression.[10]

GOSSELIN − DISEMBODIED EQUALITY

Many Canadian theorists have criticized the *Gosselin* decision as representing the *sine qua non* of the decontextualized, classical liberal approach to equality rights.

---

[8] [2002] 4 S.C.R. 429.

[9] *Charter*, Section 7 states, "Everyone has the right to life, liberty, and security of the person and the right not to be deprived thereof except in accordance with the principles of fundamental justice."

[10] The other Supreme Court cases involving women's multiple rights claims are: *R. v. Morgentaler*, [1988] 1 S.C.R. 30; *Native Women's Association of Canada v. Canada*, [1994] 3 S.C.R. 627 (finding constitutional the government's decision to fund only "male dominated" indigenous groups in constitutional consultations); *Rodriguez v. British Columbia* (Attorney General), [1993] 3 S.C.R. 519 (Criminal Code proscribing assisted suicide consistent with Section 7; the court found it "preferable" not to make a finding on Section 15 because any violation would be justified under Section 1); *Little Sisters Book and Art Emporium v. Canada* (Minister of Justice), [2000] 2 S.C.R. 1120 (disproportional targeting of lesbian erotica for review and confiscation was contrary to Section 15 but legislation providing discretion to customs officials was consistent with Sections 2(b) and 15); and *Health Services and Support-Facilities Subsector Bargaining Assn., Health Services and Support-Facilities Subsector Bargaining Assn. v. British Columbia*, [2007] 2 S.C.R. 391 (legislation interfering with collective bargaining violated Section 2(d), but the court simply upheld lower courts' finding that discrimination against health care and social services sector did not discriminate against women, despite the fact that they consist of female-dominated professions). In my view, the analyses in these cases demonstrate similar tendencies to those in *Gosselin*, [2002] 4 S.C.R. 429.

This approach exaggerates the significance of individual choice and "benign" governmental intent to encourage self-sufficiency, and was perpetuated by the Supreme Court of Canada's decision in *Law v. Canada*.[11] Of late, the Supreme Court has seemingly retreated from rigid adherence to the *Law* approach in Section 15 cases.[12] Yet, it is unlikely that we have seen the last of a *Gosselin*-type analysis. I maintain that the analytic separation of *Charter* Section 15 and Section 7 played a significant role in the outcome in *Gosselin*, and will continue to plague multiple rights cases if not addressed.[13]

Gosselin demonstrates the dangers in a multiple rights case of assessing an equality claim without adequately integrating security of the person issues. Such an approach enables the law to deny that it does damage to real bodies and psyches when it removes poor people's access to the necessities of life. Consistent with Austin Sarat and Thomas R. Kearns' theory, the law "seems intent on (and is largely successful at) threatening violence while denying or making invisible the violence it inflicts" on bodies subject to the law, applying not only in cases of "incarceration or execution . . . [but also with respect to] the suffering imposed say, on a welfare mother when her benefits are reduced. . . . "[14] They maintain that the "conditions for successful

---

[11] *Law v. Canada*, [1999] 1 S.C.R. 497. Representative of the *Gosselin* critiques are Diana Majury, *Women are Themselves to Blame: Choice as a Justification for Unequal Treatment*, in MAKING EQUALITY RIGHTS REAL: SECURING SUBSTANTIVE EQUALITY UNDER THE CHARTER, 209, 228 (Faraday, Denike, & Stephenson eds., 2006); Gwen Brodsky, *Autonomy with a Vengeance*, 15 CAN. J. WOMEN & L. 194 (2003); Sonia Lawrence, *Harsh, Perhaps Even Misguided: Developments in Law, 2002*, 20 S.C.L.R. (2D) 93 (2003).

[12] Following *Law*, the court required claimants to prove discrimination by demonstrating an infringement of human dignity, using four contextual factors: (a) Preexisting disadvantage, stereotyping, prejudice, or vulnerability experienced by the individual or group at issue; (b) the correspondence, or lack thereof, between the ground or grounds on which the claim is based and the actual need, capacity, or circumstances of the claimant or others; (c) the ameliorative purpose or effects of the impugned law on a more disadvantaged person or group in society; and (d) the nature and scope of the interest affected by the impugned law (*Law*, [1999] 1 S.C.R. 497, ¶ 88). In *R. v. Kapp*, [2008] 2 S.C.R. 483, the court admitted that "several problems" resulted from the calcification of "human dignity" and the contextual factors into a *"legal test"* (*Kapp*, ¶ 21). It therefore refocused the equality analysis on the broader "perpetuation of disadvantage or stereotyping" test for discrimination in *Andrews v. Law Society of British Columbia*, [1989] 1 S.C.R. 143. Subsequent Section 15 decisions (*Ermineskin Band and Nation v. Canada*, [2009] 1 S.C.R. 222; *A.C. v. Manitoba (Director of Child and Family Services)*, [2009] 2 S.C.R. 181; *Alberta v. Hutterian Brethren of Wilson Colony*, [2009] 2 S.C.R. 567) repeated the latter test and do not mention the four contextual factor in *Law* whatsoever. However, the most recent equality decision, *Withler v. Canada (Attorney)*, 2011 SCC 12, cites with apparent approval the trial judge's analysis of the *Law* contextual factors. Without an express statement from the court that it is overruling the *Law* approach, it is difficult to say whether the current case law represents a true departure.

[13] Canadian scholars have talked about the possibilities of equality and the right to life, liberty, and security of the person interacting in the context of poverty, but relying primarily on international conventions: *see, e.g.*, Gwen Brodsky & Shelagh Day, *Beyond the Social and Economic Rights Debate: Substantive Equality Speaks to Poverty*, 14 CAN. J. WOMEN & L. 186 (2002).

[14] Austin Sarat & Thomas R. Kearns, *A Journey Through Forgetting: Toward Jurisprudence of Violence*, in THE FATE OF LAW 209, 209–10 (Austin Sarat & Thomas R. Kearns eds., 1991).

'interpretive violence'"[15] include those where the court is able to position itself as a "mere conduit of constitutional messages. . . . Interpretation and the interpretive act are made invisible by the simple device of refusing to acknowledge any alternative readings."[16] It is further intensified where law's interpretive violence is treated as "exclusively cultural and symbolic, rather than the physical and the bodily," that is, directed exclusively toward decontextualized, philosophical concepts like dignity or autonomy and not toward *real people*.[17] By maintaining a rule-laden "cold separation between law's words and law's deeds,"[18] its violence is obscured, and when it appears, it is visible only as a necessary evil that is done to prevent the greater damage caused by the "cravings and drives of 'human nature.'"[19] Whether this is in the form of capital punishment to keep "the community" safe from criminality,[20] or the denial of welfare to keep the poor from their slothful inclination toward dependency,[21] this justification for law's violence is the same.

Louise Gosselin was a young woman who lived in extreme poverty, in the midst of an economic downturn in Quebec during the 1980s that saw a drastic increase in unemployment among young adults.[22] She was subject to regulations under Quebec's Act Respecting Income Security[23] that drastically reduced monthly welfare amounts paid to those under thirty to $170. The $466 received by those over thirty was deemed by the legislature to be the amount necessary for an adult's basic needs,[24]

[15] *Id.* at 211.
[16] *Id.* at 214.
[17] *Id.* at 221. See also their reference *id.* at 259 that "The question becomes not why there is so much violence or pain or how law might be transformed through the recognition of its lethal character, but, rather, why people put up with a life *in which human dignity is denied in the details of everyday life.* Law is thought to colonize souls so that it can leave bodies intact" (emphasis added). This passage recalls the court's preoccupation with human dignity, separated from bodily integrity, in the *Gosselin* Section 15 analysis.
[18] *Id.* at 211.
[19] *Id.* at 224.
[20] Hegel, for example, regarded criminality as arising from the state of natural will: Angeliki Kontou, *Hegel on Crime, Evil, and Punishment: Reconciliation Between the 'Individual' and the 'Social'*, in EVIL, LAW, AND THE STATE: ISSUES IN STATE POWER & VIOLENCE 63 (Istar Gozaydin & Jody Lynée Madeira eds., 2006).
[21] The "constitutive violence" against the poor produces the "illegitimate homeless body" from which the "self-regulating bourgeois subject" can separate himself and thereby convince himself of his mastery over his own body: Sherene Razack, *Introduction: When Space Becomes Race*, in RACE, SPACE, AND THE LAW: UNMAPPING A WHITE SETTLER SOCIETY 1, 10–11 (Sherene Razack ed., 2002). These constituted illegitimate bodies of the poor were historically segregated and "trained not to be idle . . . not for the purpose of punishment but for moral regulation." *Id.* (quoting Foucault, *Madness and Civilization*, in THE FOUCAULT READER 124, 131 (Paul Rabinow ed., 1984)). Thus, poor regulation creates a vicious circle whereby it produces "illegitimate" poor bodies and obscures this constitutive process by instead implicating the moral failings of the poor, which consequently justifies regulation.
[22] *Gosselin*, [2002] 4 S.C.R. 429, ¶ 6 (McLachlin, C. J. C.).
[23] S.Q. 1988, c.51. The relevant regulations were sections 23 and 29(a), *Regulation Respecting Social Aid*, R.R.Q., c. A-16, r.1.
[24] *Gosselin*, [2002] 4 S.C.R. 429, ¶ 251 (Bastarache, J., dissenting).

and could be achieved by those under thirty only *if*: a "workfare" program for educational upgrading or on-the-job training was available to them, they were able to become registered for a program, and that particular program provided a gross-up to the full amount.[25] Gosselin was able to participate in some of these programs[26] and was periodically employed despite considerable mental health problems and addictions.[27] However, for most of her life as a young adult, she was in receipt of welfare and subject to the lower rate, which rendered her incapable of obtaining food or shelter, much less other necessaries of life. Ironically, living in such straitened conditions also negatively affected her ability to look for and obtain employment.[28] As a result of the reductions, many young women, including Louise Gosselin, were forced to exchange sexual services in return for a place to stay or for food. Gosselin also experienced an attempted rape from a man from whom she was obtaining food, and sexual harassment by male boarders while she was staying in male-dominated boarding houses.[29] Gosselin commenced a class action on behalf of all Quebec welfare recipients under thirty, and claimed that the welfare regulations violated their Section 7 rights and discriminated on the basis of age, contrary to Section 15 of the Charter.[30]

---

[25] These factors did not align very often: *Gosselin, id.* ¶¶ 245–48 (Bastarache, J.) and ¶ 393 (Arbour, J., dissenting). As these justices note, there were only 30,000 places for 75,000 potential under-thirty registrants, there were restrictive eligibility criteria, and there were times when no program was available for registration. As a result, only 11.2 percent of those under thirty were able to increase their benefits in this fashion. *Id.* ¶ 130 (L'Heureux-Dubé, J., dissenting) and ¶ 371 (Arbour, J., dissenting).

[26] This was acknowledged by McLachlin, C. J. C., *id.* ¶ 8, although the Chief Justice attributes her failure to maintain her registration in them to her "personal problems and personality traits."

[27] Her difficulties with the training programs and employment due to her depression, anxiety, and physical health problems are outlined *id.* ¶¶ 164–67 (Bastarache, J., dissenting). She did receive the full rate from time to time while she was registered in the programs or qualified for a medical exemption.

[28] Factum of the Intervener, National Association of Women and the Law, *in Gosselin, id.* ¶¶ 4, 11, *available at* www.nawl.ca/ns/en/documents/Pub_Brief_Gosselin01_en.doc.

[29] *Id.* ¶¶ 7–9.

[30] It is possible that the claim was based on age alone (and not in combination with sex) because this was seen as "low hanging fruit" given that the distinction was explicit. *Andrews v. Law Society of British Columbia*, [1989] 1 S.C.R. 143, ¶ 37 (McIntyre, J.) suggested that explicit distinctions on enumerated grounds would rarely be found nondiscriminatory. Further, attempting to prove adverse effects discrimination on the basis of sex under Charter Section 15 or under the Quebec Charter's ground of social condition would have been a risky proposition. Sheila McIntyre has documented the increasing impossibility of proving adverse effect discrimination. Sheila McIntyre, *Deference and Dominance: Equality without Substance, in* DIMINISHING RETURNS: INEQUALITY AND THE CANADIAN CHARTER OF RIGHTS AND FREEDOMS 95 (Sheila McIntyre & Sandra Rodgers eds., 2006). The last significant adverse effects sex discrimination claim accepted by the court was not in relation to the Charter, but human rights legislation, and concerned adverse effects based on women's biological, not social, difference: *British Columbia (Public Service Employee Relations Commission) v. BCGSEU*, [1999] 3 S.C.R. 3.

The majority decision, written by C. J. C. McLachlin and two of the four dissenting decisions,[31] accepted Section 15 (particularly the protection against "age discrimination") as the operative right. In denying Gosselin's Section 15 claim, the majority implicitly relied on a conceptualization of equality as a "special right" reserved for "discrete and insular minorities,"[32] who are deemed by the dominant as having been stigmatized *unfairly* by the state. As economic disparity (particularly women's)[33] is treated as a natural source of differential treatment, it receded into the background of the case.[34] To the extent that Gosselin's poverty was considered at all, it was as a signifier of "individual choice and merit."[35] As a result, the majority constructed Gosselin as a liberal, autonomous subject whose self was a bundle of choices and will, rather than as an embodied self existing in particular historic and social relations.[36] Without the grounding in the material that the Section 7

---

[31] Bastarache and LeBel, J. J. both found that Section 7 did not apply in the circumstances, while Arbour, J. (L'Heureux-Dubé, J. concurring on this point) found a Section 7 violation.

[32] I borrow this concept from Charles Lawrence III, who advances the argument that equality and traditional civil rights are read hierarchically in dominant culture – the latter are included in the "regular" rights of "everyone" and equality is a "special right" for "a minority of different people." Charles Lawrence III, *If He Hollers Let Him Go: Regulating Racist Speech on Campus*, 1990 DUKE L. J. 431, 474.

[33] This disparity is naturalized as part of what it means to be a woman rather than reflecting patterns of subordination: "[W]omen's poverty and consequent financial dependence on men (whether in marriage, welfare, the workplace or prostitution)... effectively constitutes their social status *as women*, as members of their gender." CATHERINE MACKINNON, TOWARDS A FEMINIST THEORY OF THE STATE 228 (1989). *See also Falkiner v. Ontario* (Ministry of Community and Social Services) (2002), 212 D.L.R. (4th) 633, 159 O.A.C. 135, 59 O.R. (3d) 481 (C.A.), in which the Ontario Court of Appeal confronts the stereotypical assumption of women's financial dependence on men.

[34] Courts have consistently refused to accept socioeconomic status as an "analogous" ground under Section 15 (explicit grounds not being exclusive under the wording of the right). *See, e.g., Masse v. Ontario* (Ministry of Community and Social Services) (1996), 134 D.L.R. (4th) 20, 35 C.R.R. (2d) 44 (Ont. Div. Ct.), leave to appeal to C.A. denied, [1996] O.J. No. 1526, leave to appeal to S.C.C. denied [1996] S.C.C.A. No. 373; *Dunmore v. Ontario* (Attorney General) (1997), 37 O.R. (3d) 287, 155 D.L.R. (4th) 193 (Gen. Div.), aff'd (1999), 182 D.L.R. (4th) 471, 49 C.C.E.L. (2d) 29 (C.A.), appeal allowed but not on this issue, *Dunmore v. Ontario* (Attorney General), [2001] 3 S.C.R. 1016; *R. v. Banks*, [2005] O.J. No. 98 (Ont. S.C.J.), aff'd, 2007 ONCA 19, leave to appeal denied, [2007] S.C.C.A. No. 139. *See also Guzman v. Canada* (Minister of Citizenship and Immigration), [2006] FCJ No. 1443 (T.D.) (QL), and *Bailey v. Canada*, [2005] FCJ No. 81 (T.D.) (QL) (receipt of social assistance and (low) income level, respectively).

[35] This is how poverty/socioeconomic status is regarded "within a capitalist liberal ideology." Nitya Iyer, *Categorical Denials: Equality Rights and the Shaping of Social Identity*, 19 QUEEN'S L. J. 179, 189 (1993).

[36] This disembodied liberal self is inherently masculine: "[T]he power and privilege of the masculine relies precisely on being disembodied, on lacking the contingency of the body in the pursuit of a perspective which is transcendent, objective, and universal... the 'individual' of the modern liberal state is simultaneously disembodied as it is construed *from* a male body." Sara Ahmed, *Deconstruction and Law's Other: Towards a Feminist Theory of Embodied Legal Rights*, 4 SOCIAL & LEGAL STUD. 55, 56 (1995).

guarantee of "security of the person" represents,[37] Louise Gosselin's sexed,[38] exploited, and starving body disappears in the Section 15 determination, and with it, law's complicity in the violence done to her body.

In the majority decision, McLachlin framed her approach to Section 15 as an unavoidable imperative driven by evidentiary rules, rationality, and the requirements of the *Law* test, thereby enabling her to obscure the exercise of choice in anchoring the entire analysis in the purported legislative purpose of promoting self-sufficiency:[39] it simply "makes sense to consider what the legislator intended in determining whether the scheme denies human dignity."[40] With the preeminence given to legislative purpose before the discrimination analysis even began in earnest, the stage was set for the four contextual factors from *Law*[41] to be transformed from the material to "the cultural and the symbolic" when the court applied the test.

Time and again, while the contextual factors from *Law* on their face direct courts to consider material conditions of "preexisting disadvantage" and actual circumstances,[42] the majority in *Gosselin* veered into ruminations on the lack of evidence of "unfair" stereotyping of young people[43] and the sage intention of the legislature to provide them with education and skills. Consequently, under the first

---

[37] Although not restricted to physical integrity, the court has been consistent that in order to constitute a violation of security of the person under Section 7, the state action must have a "serious and profound effect on a person's psychological integrity." *New Brunswick (Minister of Health and Community Services) v. G.(J.)*, [1999] 3 S.C.R. 46, ¶ 60. Implicit in this statement is a requirement that the psychological impairment must have a material basis. *See also* Bruce Judah, The Meaning and Possible Scope of 'Psychological Integrity,' *in* S.7 JURISPRUDENCE, 8 (April 2001) (unpublished paper presented at the Canadian Bar Association's Conference, "The Canadian Charter of Rights and Freedoms: Twenty Years Later").

[38] In referring to her body as "sexed," I am speaking about how her body is marked as female not just through bodily signifiers but "the discussion and language that interpret the body and the social arrangements surrounding it." ZILLAH R. EISENSTEIN, THE FEMALE BODY AND THE LAW 85 (1988).

[39] *See* Brodsky, *Autonomy with a Vengeance, supra* note 11, at 207–10 regarding this flaw in the court's analysis, which places a heavy burden on the claimant to show the lack of rationality of the legislative purpose within Section 15, and a minimal requirement on governments to justify their approach to the problem.

[40] *Gosselin v. Quebec (Attorney General)*, [2002] 4 S.C.R. 429, ¶¶ 19, 26.
    McLachlin, C. J.C. went on to remark that "[a]s a matter of common sense, if a law is designed to promote the claimant's long-term autonomy and self-sufficiency, a reasonable person in the claimant's position would be less likely to view it as an assault on her inherent human dignity," *id.* ¶ 27. The application of the *Law* test commences after these statements, under the subheading, "Applying the Test."

[41] Again, this is phrased as an imperative, "we must consider the four factors set out in *Law*," *id.* ¶ 29. *R v. Kapp*, [2008] 2 S.C.R. 483 and subsequent case law put the lie to the contention that recourse to the four contextual factors in *Law* is self-evident or necessary. For instance, in *Ermineskin*, the court instead discusses more generally "the larger social, political, and legal context," *Ermineskin, id.* ¶ 193 (citing *R. v. Turpin*, [1989] 1 S.C.R. 1296, 1331).

[42] *Law v. Canada*, [1999] 1 S.C.R. 497, ¶ 70, referring to a claimant's "actual needs" and "actual situation."

[43] *Gosselin v. Quebec (Attorney General)*, [2002] 4 S.C.R.429, ¶ 33: "There is no reason to believe that individuals between ages 18 and 30 in Quebec are or were particularly susceptible to negative

factor, preexisting disadvantage, the court made no inquiry into the claimant's lived conditions of oppression.[44] As well, McLachlin seized on the fact that the only ground of discrimination claimed was "age." This allowed her analysis to become even more abstract, excluding any consideration of how Gosselin's experience as a young person was also influenced by poverty, patriarchy, and subordination based on mental disability.[45] By constructing an essentialized class of privileged youth, the Chief Justice was thus able to conclude that "young adults as a class simply do not seem especially vulnerable or undervalued.... If anything, people under 30 appear to be advantaged over older people in finding employment."[46]

When the claimant attempted to problematize this essentialist picture of young people by bringing into account the historic disadvantage of welfare recipients to which these *particular* young people were subject, the majority prevented her from doing so. Because this socioeconomic subordination affected under-thirty welfare recipients, and the group of thirty-and-over welfare recipients to which they were being compared, the majority found that it could not be considered at all in the discrimination analysis.[47] This curious "weigh scale" approach to comparators, where subordination on both sides means it can be disregarded, resulted in the majority refusing to consider stereotypes particular to young welfare recipients as lazy and predisposed to welfare dependence,[48] or the particular vulnerability of poor women on welfare to violations of their personal security through male coercion and violence.[49]

Under *Law*'s second contextual factor, correspondence between the distinction and the claimant's actual characteristics and circumstances, the majority turned, yet again, to government purpose and used evidentiary rules to foreclose any attempt by the claimant to challenge the alleged "fit" of the statute in light of its material

preconceptions. No evidence was adduced to this effect, and I am unable to take judicial notice of such a counterintuitive proposition."

[44] The emphasis on government intent and stereotype "serve to shift the focus of the analysis from the effect on the claimant to the actions of the government." Lawrence, *supra* note 11, at 103. The most recent distillation of the test for discrimination post-*Kapp* is "does the distinction create a disadvantage by perpetuating prejudice or stereotyping." Unfortunately, this formulation seems only to further entrench the primacy of these concepts.

[45] The court described Ms. Gosselin's experience with mental illness in terms of her "psychological problems and drug and alcohol addiction." *Gosselin*, [2002] 4 S.C.R. 429, ¶ 1.

[46] *Id.* ¶¶ 33, 34. It is interesting to note here how youth is not "embodied" but defined exclusively in terms of enhanced ability to exert will.

[47] *Id.* ¶ 35 ("Ms. Gosselin attempts to shift the focus from age to welfare, arguing that *all* welfare recipients suffer from stereotyping and vulnerability. However, this argument does not assist her claim... because the 30-and-over group that Ms. Gosselin asks us to use as a basis of comparison also consists entirely of welfare recipients.").

[48] See the evidence cited by Lebel, J., *id.* ¶ 407, regarding the falsity of this stereotype.

[49] *See* HOLLY JOHNSTON, MEASURING VIOLENCE AGAINST WOMEN. STATISTICAL TRENDS 2006 36, 36 & 40 (2006) for statistics verifying this risk. *See also* J. E. Mosher, *Managing the Disentitlement of Women: Glorified Markets, the Idealized Family, and the Undeserving Other, in* RESTRUCTURING CARING LABOUR: DISCOURSE, STATE PRACTICE, AND EVERYDAY LIFE 30, 33–34 (S. M. Neysmith ed., 2000).

effects. McLachlin found that, in light of the dismal state of the Quebec economy at the relevant time, providing young people with education and skills training rather than "simply handing over a bigger welfare cheque" reflected "practical wisdom."[50] Because the legislation was intended to encourage self-sufficiency, it was dignity-affirming. In order to come to this conclusion, however, the Chief Justice elided the distinction between the educational and training programs themselves, which were not under challenge, and the coercion exerted by the government in reducing benefits to those under thirty who were not registered in a program. The embedded assumption that coercion was necessary to force young adults to "benefit" from these programs is thus unchallengeable as discriminatory in and of itself. Here, the law's violence in coercing young recipients by denying the necessaries of life is acknowledged, obliquely, as "short-term pain."[51] Nevertheless, as Kearns and Sarat might have predicted, this "pain" is quickly justified as a necessary evil so that young welfare recipients do not allow the baser elements of their human nature to overtake them: lack of industry, indolence, and resulting welfare dependency, which "can contribute to a vicious circle of inability to find work, despair, and increasingly dismal prospects."[52]

The dissonance between the stark reality of welfare recipients struggling to survive on the reduced benefit of $170 a month and the abstract (bordering on philosophic) iterations of the majority about the laudable government purpose makes the violence of interpretation visible, for an instant. Perhaps this is why the majority, for several paragraphs, attempted to distance the court from the material implications of its decision, citing first judicial deference to the legislature as imperative.[53] It then individualized the effects of tying young people's receipt of the full benefit to participation in inaccessible programs because of a lack of evidence of any systemic, adverse effect. Instead, the Chief Justice called these difficulties the result of "personal problems."[54] When reflecting on the involvement of the welfare system itself, the Chief Justice uses the nomenclature of "accident," noting that while some "fell through the cracks of the system," and failed to have their needs met,

---

[50] *Gosselin*, [2002] 4 S.C.R. 429, ¶¶ 42, 43.

[51] *Id.* ¶ 53. This is the only time that the majority judgment acknowledges the violence of the legislation.

[52] *Gosselin*, *id.* ¶ 43. This portion of the judgment reverberates with echoes of the "Protestant work ethic" arising from Calvinist religious philosophy. This philosophy espoused work as essential to saving humanity from their innate sinful, heedless natures, Paul Bernstein, *The Work Ethic: Economics, Not Religion*, 31:3 BUSINESS HORIZONS 8, 10 (1988). Interestingly, Bernstein points out that this philosophy arose in the 1500s at the very time there was an increase in European population, high inflation, and a high rate of unemployment. He argues that cities were not able to perceive these systemic, economic problems and instead misconstrued the growing numbers of the poor as resulting from human sin, called by one contemporary writer, "that loathsome monster, idleness," Bernstein, *id.* Bolstered by religious edict, governments responded through increasingly punitive measures; "[i]n short, the prevailing values of the time strongly supported the view that forced labor would discourage those who would stray 'from the path of righteous living,'" Bernstein, *id.*

[53] *Gosselin*, [2002] 4 S.C.R. 429, ¶ 44.

[54] *Id.* ¶¶ 47–48.

this "does not permit us to conclude that the program failed to correspond to the claimant's characteristics and circumstances."[55] Because the program was based on "real needs," and because the majority denied that it confined a particular group to "extreme poverty" (given the theoretical possibility of always participating in workfare programs),[56] there was no violation of human dignity.

The next two contextual factors were dealt with in an abbreviated fashion, functioning to again reassert the primacy of legislative intent over lived experience. Under the third factor, ameliorative purpose or effect of the impugned legislation, the majority admitted that while the provision in question was not ameliorative (and therefore this contextual factor was "neutral"), it was appropriate to consider the overall ameliorative purpose of the legislation of reducing welfare dependency for those under thirty. Regarding the last contextual factor, "the nature and scope of the interests affected by the impugned law," the majority again shifted the focus from the impact of the legislation on bodily and psychological integrity to legalistic terminology, finding no "significant adverse impact"[57] but rather only "greater financial anxiety in the short term."[58] Thus, in a world imagined to be unaffected by social power, the methods used by the Quebec government are reconceptualized as an "incentive" rather than a use of force that causes suffering[59] and, particularly for women, further vulnerability to violence and exploitation. The court's preoccupation with legislative purpose entrenches this worldview into judicial pronouncement: the violence obscured by the legislators through euphemisms like "self-sufficiency," "training," and "education" becomes invisible.[60]

Although the separation of Section 15 from Section 7 causes a Section 15 analysis that is preoccupied with stereotype and a disembodied, abstract notion of "dignity," it in turn keeps Section 7 firmly attached to its traditional civil libertarian moorings. In *Gosselin*, this analytic separation has the effect of removing from consideration how substantive access to the Section 7 right by subordinated persons might require material deprivations to be interpreted in their social context. Despite the court's

[55] *Id.* ¶ 54.
[56] *Id.* ¶ 52.
[57] *Id.* ¶ 64.
[58] *Id.*
[59] For a discussion on the use of "metaphysical ideas and expressions" to obscure the fact that "the function of the courts is to determine the use of force," see Sarat & Kearns, *supra* note 14, at 218 (citing KARL OLIVECRONA, LAW AS FACT (1939)). They later point out that this, in itself, is a further insult (or, as Canadian constitutionalists might phrase it, injury to dignity) as "their pain recedes further and further from the centre of the law." Sarat & Kearns, *id.* at 246.
[60] Mona Oikawa discussed similar phenomenon in relation to the language used by Canadian legislators to describe the incarceration and displacement of Japanese–Canadians in internment camps – "relocation," "resettlement," and "repatriation." She noted that "the euphemistic language distanced the government and its administrators from the effects of their actions and left a semantic legacy with which we continue to struggle," even to the extent that it affected the ability of survivors to remember the violence. Mona Oikawa, *Cartographies of Violence: Women, Memory and the Subject(s) of the 'Internment,'* in Razack ed., *supra*, note 21, 71 at 88–89.

remaking Louise Gosselin into a liberal subject within Section 15, such a construction cannot be sustained within the Section 7 analysis. Her claim is perceived as too aberrant compared to the traditional civil liberty claims made by liberal subjects to merit in-depth consideration under Section 7. She is defined exclusively by her need for "a particular level of social assistance,"[61] anathema to the (neo)liberal subject.[62] By separating out the social context that Section 15 provides, the Section 7 analysis constructs her needs, her dependency on the state, the physical violations she has already experienced as simply personal traits. She is constituted therefore as a "defective" liberal self, not a civil rights holder.

The crux of the majority's rejection of Gosselin's Section 7 claim lies in their characterization of it as seeking to impose a "positive obligation" on government to provide an adequate level of benefits, rather than a traditional "negative rights" claim against state intrusions upon bodily integrity. Gosselin's Section 7 claim was read as the former because it was inherently gendered, despite all the court's efforts to eradicate this vestige of bodily particularity. Not only are the actual bodies of the poor disproportionately female,[63] women's bodies are socially constructed as "naturally" in need of assistance.[64] In law particularly, "representations of the [female] body continue to hint at passivity and dependency."[65] In turn, this feminine dependence is viewed as an object of disgust.[66] This disgust manifests in the *Gosselin* majority's multiple derogatory references to dependency,[67] which is literally viewed as a fate worse than death. The palpable need and dependency of Gosselin made analogies between her and the liberal male subject difficult, if not impossible. Bodily need, which arises "naturally" in women (rather than through state action), is thus viewed by the law as alien to the claims of the traditional, self-sufficient civil rights bearer.

---

[61] *Gosselin*, [2002] 4 S.C.R. 429, ¶ 75.

[62] Mosher describes him as a capitalist who "maximize[s] his private, rational self-interest as a buyer and seller in market exchanges. As a responsible citizen, he provides for himself and his family, and he has reduced expectations of social provision." Janet Mosher, *Welfare Reform and the Re-Making of the Model Citizen, in* POVERTY: RIGHTS, SOCIAL CITIZENSHIP, AND LEGAL ACTIVISM 119, 123 (Margot Young et al. eds., 2007).

[63] STATISTICS CANADA, WOMEN IN CANADA 2005 144 (2005). *See also* Brodsky & Day, *supra* note 13, at 191.

[64] Thérèse Murphy, *Feminism on Flesh, in* VIII: 1 LAW AND CRITIQUE 37, 49 (1997).

[65] *Id.* at 51.

[66] Nussbaum argues that women's bodies (and "feminized" racial/homosexual male bodies) have been used to inscribe the superior status of white, heterosexual men, by assigning to the former the "dirt of the body," bodily needs and dependency, in essence, mortality. MARTHA NUSSBAUM, HIDING FROM HUMANITY: DISGUST, SHAME, AND THE LAW 107–15 (2004). It is the feminine association with "need and receptivity," "the force of animal nature, striving to preserve itself" that repulses masculinity, NUSSBAUM, *id.* at 109, 112.

[67] *See* the references in *Gosselin*, [2002] 4 S.C.R. 429, where welfare dependence is referred to as "not socially desirable," *id.* ¶ 7, in terms of "chronic pattern" and "risk," *id.* ¶ 60, and as having "pernicious side effects," *id.* ¶ 65. This is coupled with the disdain displayed toward Louise Gosselin herself as the most visible signifier of dependency. She is defined by the majority in terms of her addictions, her problems, and her inability to remain employed; *see* Majury, *supra* note 11, at 228 (commentary on the majority's depiction of Gosselin).

Consequently, the satisfaction of "natural" need is constructed as requiring the court to impose nonjusticiable positive obligations under Section 7.

Could the problems in the case have been solved simply by a Section 15 analysis that was more sensitive to context and social power? Obviously, it does not require an integrated Section 15/Section 7 analysis to broaden Section 15's focus from the promotion of stereotype, and/or impaired societal or self-perception (self-worth or dignity). That Section 15 encompasses more is something that the judges in *Gosselin* recognized,[68] including the Chief Justice herself (in principle).[69] What I am contending is that in circumstances where the law jeopardizes life and health, by separating and arranging Section 15 and Section 7 hierarchically so that Section 15 is the "foreground" right, the equality analysis overemphasizes social construction, stereotype, and legislative purpose, and diminishes the significance of material deprivations.[70] This effect is because a separate Section 15 analysis proceeds on the basis that the claimant does not suffer from the kind of severe deprivations that engage Section 7. In the words of Martha Jackman, claims under other rights, *"presuppose a person who has moved beyond the basic struggle for existence."*[71]

An integrated approach to rights would challenge this "presupposition" within Section 15 (and other rights) of the claimant's assured survival, and is supported by J. L'Heureux-Dubé's equality analysis in *Gosselin*. In her dissenting decision, she downplayed the role of stereotype, finding that it was "not determinative."[72] Instead, she found that where there was a severe enough harm to a claimant's "fundamental

---

[68] *Gosselin*, [2002] 4 S.C.R. 429, ¶ 128 (L'Heureux-Dubé, J., dissenting). Bastarache, J. in dissent also gave particular importance to the contextual factor of the severity of the provision's effect.

[69] McLachlin, C. J. C. stated, "I do not suggest that stereotypical thinking must always be present for a finding that s.15 is breached." *Id.* ¶ 70. The more recent Supreme Court Section 15 jurisprudence does, however, risk a heightened emphasis on stereotype, as it directs courts now to consider only "perpetuation of disadvantage or stereotyping" rather than the four contextual factors. *See R. v. Kapp*, [2008] 2 S.C.R. 483 and the other cases discussed at footnote 12.

[70] Robert Leckey identifies the same problem with the majority's *Gosselin* analysis in *Embodied Dignity*, 5:1 O.U.C.L.J. 63 (2005). However, he attributes the lack of attention to material deprivations to the erasure of physical integrity as a component of essential human dignity within the Court's equality analysis. While he acknowledges the objections to dignity as the touchstone for equality, he ultimately relies upon it in advocating for an understanding that "'dignity' is not a purely mental capacity or attribute that judges assume can be enjoyed irrespective of the effect of government action upon individuals' bodies" (at 81–82). Given the serious misgivings of feminists that human dignity as a construct does not permit an interrogation of systemic inequalities (*see, e.g.*, Martha Jackman, "Sommes-nous dignes? L'egalité et l'arrêt Gosselin," 17:1 C.J.W.L. 161 (2005)), the insertion of physical integrity into dignity does not appear to be an adequate solution. This is particularly the case where the body under analysis is not specifically identified as enculturated, as will be discussed later. Further, the problem does not seem to originate in "dignity" per se. Despite the fact that the Court has now retreated from the notion that a violation of human dignity is a discrete element of the discrimination test, the problem with ignoring bodily integrity within s.15 remains in multiple rights cases (see A.C. v. *Manitoba (Director of Child and Family Services)*, [2009] 2 S.C.R. 181).

[71] Martha Jackman, *The Protection of Welfare Rights Under the Charter*, 20 OTTAWA L. REV. 257, 326 (1988) (emphasis added).

[72] *Gosselin*, [2002] 4 S.C.R. 429, ¶ 117.

interest" (i.e., "severe threats to their physical or psychological integrity") this was sufficient to conclude that a legislative distinction on the basis of an enumerated or analogous ground is discriminatory.[73] Her focus on the claimant's whole being rather than abstracted notions of stereotype and dignity has been referred to as the "knit[ting] together" of equality and security of the person.[74]

This approach would be further assisted by the concept of the "lived body," first described by Toril Moi and further elaborated upon by Iris Marion Young.[75] Young used this concept to escape the conceptual bind of the gender/sex dichotomy experienced by feminist theorists in attempting to describe women's oppression. She remarked that utilization of "gender" as a conceptual term has resulted in theory that is too estranged from the materiality of the body, and that the use of "sex" tends to result in women's oppression being described in ways that are overdetermined by biology and lacking social context. This has obvious similarities to the conceptual bind experienced in Section 15/Section 7 claims. Young described the lived body as follows:

> The lived body is a unified idea of a physical body acting and experiencing in a specific sociocultural context; it is a body-in-situation ... [It] refuses the distinction between nature and culture.... The body as lived is always enculturated.... Contexts of discourse and interaction position persons in systems of evaluation and expectations that often implicate their embodied beings; the person experiences herself as looked at in certain ways, described in her physical being in certain ways, she experiences the bodily reactions of others to her, and she reacts to them.[76]

In other words, the lived body is concerned with the significance of the body and bodily sensations "in the constitution of subjectivity."[77]

Through the concept of the lived body, a Section 7 and Section 15 analysis would examine the reactions of Gosselin to her body, and how others would react to her body in the midst of her frantic scramble for shelter and food. In such conditions, Gosselin's starved and exploited body cannot be considered by others as inviolate, given her increased vulnerability to male violence and sexual assault. Against the backdrop of the extremely limited opportunities for youth employment in the Quebec economy, women's economic inequality, the disparity of treatment compared with older welfare recipients, and her health obstacles to remaining in workfare programs, she herself is likely to experience the intense bodily sensations of hunger and exposure as an interference with her bodily integrity and as a practice of

---

[73] *Id.* ¶¶ 134–35.
[74] Gwen Brodsky & Shelagh Day, *Women's Poverty is an Equality Violation, in* Faraday, Denike, & Stephenson eds., *supra* note 11, 319 at 328.
[75] Iris Marion Young, *Lived Body vs. Gender: Reflections on Social Structure and Subjectivity, in* On Female Body Experience: "Throwing Like a Girl" and Other Essays 12 (2005).
[76] *Id.* at 16–17.
[77] Diana Fuss, Essentially Speaking: Feminism, Nature, and Difference 52 (Routledge 1989).

subordination, rather than as a dignity-enhancing expression of her own autonomy, as the majority argued.

As well, the lived body would also have something to say about whether such a violation was consistent with the principles of fundamental justice, a requirement under Section 7. One element of fundamental justice is that laws must not be arbitrary; there must be a "real connection" between the legislative goal and the limitation of the Section 7 interest, with the test being more stringent where life itself is put at risk.[78] Considering that Gosselin's suffering was related to a government's unproven social experiment to prevent or eradicate perceived dependency, that this experiment was based on a discriminatory belief that dependency is worse than the "cure" of abject poverty and starvation, and the stereotype that an extreme measure like this "cure" was necessary for those "sturdy beggars" under thirty who would not get jobs,[79] the drastic reduction in benefits cannot accord with fundamental justice.[80] Although the majority asserted that a certain degree of arbitrariness in an age-based cutoff is inevitable and does not detract from its legitimacy,[81] the observations of what happens to people who have "fallen through the cracks" would proscribe such a margin of error. Within the concept of "fundamental justice," the concept of the lived body heightens the contrast within the welfare regime between "a bureaucratic pathology and an excessively narrow preoccupation with rules" and "shared humanity and a shared aversion to human suffering" expressed through the basic tenets of our legal system.[82]

A focus on the lived body within Section 15 would also recognize that there cannot be autonomy without a healthy body capable of executing intention. A primary aspect of the analysis would be to consider the impact on the body of living in circumstances of inequality, particularly those circumstances that limit women's choices to preserve their bodily integrity or to resist state coercion. In this light, state intervention to provide adequate food and shelter facilitates autonomy and the ability to exercise rights.[83] Lastly, a focus on the lived body would discourage obsession with legislative intent, requiring instead a focus on the embodied

---

[78] *Chaoulli v. Quebec* (Attorney General), [2005] 1 S.C.R. 791, ¶¶ 129–30.

[79] *See* Natasha Kim & Tina Piper, *Gosselin v. Quebec: Back to the Poorhouse*, 48(4) McGILL L. J. 749, ¶ 26 (2003); and Brodsky & Day, *supra* note 73, at 325 regarding these stereotypes.

[80] Here, I rely on Wilson, J.'s statement in *R. v. Morgentaler*, [1988] 1 S.C.R. 30, that a violation of another right would not accord with fundamental justice under Section 7. It appeared there that Wilson, J. was not maintaining that a claimant need prove a separate Charter violation to rely upon this principle, but rather that the purpose of this other right is violated in tandem with the violation of security of the person. Here, the gendered assumptions embedded in the treatment of "dependency" would meet this requirement.

[81] *Gosselin v. Quebec* (Attorney General), [2002] 4 S.C.R. 429, ¶ 57 (in relation to the Section 15 analysis).

[82] *See* Austin Sarat, . . . *The Law is All Over: Power, Resistance, and the Legal Consciousness of the Welfare Poor*, 2 YALE J. L. & HUM. 343 (1990), discussing how welfare recipients attempt to confront the web of rules that seek to deny them the basic necessities of life by appealing to the latter principles.

[83] Martha Jackman, *What's Wrong With Social and Economic Rights?*, 11 N.J.C.L. 235, 243 (2000).

claimant within her social context. The concept means taking the body as it is experienced by the claimant herself and the community, as a *whole*, when assessing rights.

CONCLUSION

As *Gosselin* suggests, the strategy of women making multiple rights claims does not necessarily heighten their chances of success under the present Charter analysis. The "watertight compartments" approach to rights has meant that the context of social relations, critical to Section 15, is not permitted to inform the traditional liberal constructs of civil rights, and that noncomparative concepts of subordination within civil rights have not been allowed to reinvigorate Section 15. I have suggested that a concept like "lived body," which integrates Section 7 into Section 15 (and vice versa), permits us to consider how to animate the theory of rights integration. Fundamental to this notion is the understanding that an experience of subordination implicating more than one right is not simply a collection of rights violations, but may result in a rights violation that is unique and requires unique conceptual tools for it to be recognized and redressed.

The Supreme Court jurisprudence of J. L'Heureux-Dubé and J. Wilson provides a glimmer of hope for an integrated analysis. Wilson demonstrated in *R. v. Morgentaler* that traditional civil rights are able to incorporate a gendered perspective, that women's decisions whether to carry a child to term is a matter of liberty.[84] L'Heureux-Dubé, in advocating for an approach to Section 15 that integrated Section 7 in *Gosselin*, relied upon her earlier dissenting judgment in *Egan v. Canada*[85] where she decried "an analysis that is distanced and desensitized from real people's real experiences."[86] She advocated instead starting from the impact of a legislative distinction on a vulnerable group. In considering the severity of this impact, she directly addressed the importance of looking to non-Section 15 rights. She remarked that to understand the discriminatory nature of a distinction a court must consider the "constitutional dimensions" of its impact, namely, whether it "somehow restricts access to a fundamental social institution, or affects a basic aspect of full membership in Canadian society...."[87]

There are signals that the court may be willing to take up these Justices' challenge of interpreting the Charter so that courts recognize rights violations as they are experienced in real life. The current court signaled in *Kapp* its acknowledgment that the form of Section 15 analysis has sometimes been permitted to triumph over substance. Perhaps it was not a coincidence that it signaled the need for a new

---

[84] *R. v. Morgentaler*, [1988] 1 S.C.R. 30.
[85] *Egan v. Canada*, [1995] 2 S.C.R. 513.
[86] *Id.* at 552.
[87] *Id.* at 556.

approach in the same decision that introduced some new risks for equality-seeking groups. Thus, it is now more important than ever that the court reflect on whether the current analytic structure of the Charter truly serves the purpose of preventing the "evil of oppression."[88]

[88] This phrase is used by the Supreme Court in *Andrews v. Law Society of British Columbia*, [1989] 1 S.C.R. 143, 180–81.

8

Constitutional Adjudication and Substantive Gender Equality in Hong Kong

Kelley Loper

This chapter considers the constitutional right to equality and nondiscrimination as it has developed in Hong Kong and the extent to which it promotes substantive gender equality.[1] Hong Kong provides an interesting comparative study for an examination of feminist constitutionalism given its unique status as a special administrative region (SAR) within China, the world's most populous and arguably most quickly developing nation. Hong Kong's constitutional document, the Basic Law, grants the territory a high degree of autonomy, and its common law system and judicial independence have generally survived since the transfer to Chinese sovereignty in 1997.[2] With some exceptions, human rights are well protected and Hong Kong's role as a financial center has bolstered its influence. In the field of equality law, Hong Kong's increasingly robust judicial interpretation of a constitutional right to equality coupled with its growing body of antidiscrimination legislation highlight its potential to set an example within Asia.[3] This experience also contributes to a better understanding of the potential – and the limits – of international human rights law for furthering gender equality at the domestic level.[4]

---

[1] Substantive equality seeks to tackle structural discrimination, marginalization, and actual disadvantage based on group membership and is generally contrasted with a formal, equal treatment principle – treating like cases alike. SANDRA FREDMAN, THE FUTURE OF EQUALITY IN BRITAIN (2002).

[2] Zhonghua Renmin Gongheguo Xianggang Tebie Xingzhengqu Jibenfa [*The Basic Law of the Hong Kong Special Administrative Region of the People's Republic of China*], XIANGGANG JIBENFA arts. 2, 8, 18, & 85 [hereinafter *Hong Kong Basic Law*].

[3] Lau argues that one landmark Hong Kong case on sexual orientation discrimination, *Leung T. C. William Roy v. Secretary of Justice (Leung)*, [2006] 4 H.K.L.R.D. 211, warrants attention from scholars, advocates, and lawmakers around the world. *See* Holning Lau, *Sexual Orientation and Gender Identity: American Law in Light of East Asian Developments*, 31 HARV. J. L. & GEN. 67 (2008).

[4] The Hong Kong case can also be understood within a broader critique of the shortcomings of the right to equality in international law and its ability to achieve feminist objectives. Seminal works contributing to this debate include, for example, Hilary Charlesworth, Christine Chinkin, & Shelley Wright, *Feminist Approaches to International Law*, 85 AM. J. INT'L L. 613 (1991); Christine Chinkin, Shelley Wright, & Hilary Charlesworth, *Feminist Approaches to International Law: Reflections from*

This chapter examines several Hong Kong judgments that interpret the right to
equality expressed in Article 25 of the Basic Law and relevant provisions of the Bill
of Rights, which essentially duplicates the 1966 International Covenant on Civil and
Political Rights (ICCPR). The courts have also relied on legislation that prohibits
direct and indirect discrimination in both the public and private sectors on the
grounds of sex, marital status, pregnancy, and family status.

An analysis of this jurisprudence sheds light on the conceptualization of the
equality principle and the theoretical underpinnings of a right to equality in Hong
Kong. Although much of the courts' reasoning has been firmly grounded in a formal
notion of equality, some decisions have exhibited substantive elements, recognizing
the existence of indirect and systemic discrimination and the legitimacy of special
measures. This chapter examines the interplay between the tentative progression
toward a model of substantive equality and the obstacles to its realization. Hong
Kong courts' general willingness to refer to international human rights instruments
and comparative constitutional jurisprudence has influenced these developments
and pushed the courts toward accepting a richer equality framework.[5] This process is
likely to continue in light of the U.N. human rights treaty bodies' further elaboration
of the substantive nature of the equality principle in recent years.

At the same time, however, the evolution of Hong Kong equality law has been
limited by a political culture influenced by a laissez-faire, capitalist ideology and
the reality of conservative business interests that have viewed equality as potentially
inimical to economic efficiency and growth.[6] In some of the cases considered in this
chapter, the judiciary has not fully comprehended the reach of the relevant domestic and international standards, and the available legal tools to promote equality
remain underutilized. At the same time, the government has attempted to reduce

---

Another Century, in INTERNATIONAL LAW: MODERN FEMINIST APPROACHES 17 (Doris Buss & Ambreena
Manji eds., Hart Publishing 2005); Rachael Lorna Johnstone, *Feminist Influences on the United
Nations Human Rights Treaty Bodies*, 28 HUM. RTS. Q. 148 (2006); and HUMAN RIGHTS OF WOMEN:
NATIONAL AND INTERNATIONAL PERSPECTIVES (Rebecca J. Cook ed., University of Pennsylvania Press
1994).

[5] *The Queen v. Sin Yau-ming*, [1992] 1 H.K.C.L.R. 127. The court held that "[i]n interpreting the Hong
Kong Bill of Rights, the Court can be guided by decisions of supra-national tribunals such as the
European Court of Human Rights, the European Rights Commission, comments and decisions of
United Nations Human Rights Committee, but greater assistance can be derived from decisions
of domestic courts in jurisdictions, such as the United States of America and Canada, which have
constitutionally entrenched Bills of Rights."

[6] Petersen notes that when antidiscrimination statutes were first introduced in the mid-1990s in Hong
Kong, "[m]any in the business community view[ed] the legislation, as well as the associated Codes
of Practice on Employment, as an unhealthy departure from Hong Kong's laissez-faire economic
policies." See Carole J. Petersen, *Investigation and Conciliation of Employment Discrimination Claims
in the Context of Hong Kong*, 5 EMPL. RTS. & EMPLOY. POL'Y J. 627 (2001) and Carole J. Petersen,
Engendering a Legal System: The Unique Challenge of Postcolonial Hong Kong, in GENDER AND
CHANGE IN HONG KONG: GLOBALIZATION, POSTCOLONIALISM, AND CHINESE PATRIARCHY 23, 23 (Eliza
W. Y. Lee ed., UBC Press 2003).

the judiciary's influence by introducing numerous exceptions in new antidiscrimination legislation that could allow unjustifiable discrimination.[7] It has also sought to weaken the Equal Opportunities Commission, which has broad investigative powers and is charged with overseeing the four antidiscrimination statutes.[8] The overall reaction of the executive authorities to the challenge of equality has been a rejection of a more robust concept and the implications that this could have for policy change.

Section I provides background on the sources of a legal right to equality in Hong Kong, including a discussion of the constitutional provisions, the relevance of international human rights law, and the antidiscrimination statutes. Section II analyzes how the courts have interpreted a constitutional right to equality generally, including the development of a justification test for differential treatment and a definition of discrimination that includes indirect discrimination. It also explores the judiciary's understanding of the nature of special measures. Section III examines several cases that deal with gender-related issues. Some demonstrate the lingering influence of traditional patriarchal cultural practices and some challenge government policies that disproportionately and negatively affect migrant and immigrant women. The judgments, however, generally fail to consider the gender dimensions inherent in these claims and focus instead on distinctions based on residence status and immigration categories. The courts are also more willing to accept government justifications for discrimination in the substance and application of socioeconomic policies. As a result, the equality analysis is overly constrained by arguments attempting to justify limitations on social welfare and health benefits for nonresidents.[9] The chapter concludes with some thoughts about the potential and limits of Hong Kong's equality jurisprudence for achieving substantive gender equality.

---

7 The Race Discrimination Ordinance that was enacted in July 2008 provides less protection from discrimination than the earlier ordinances. *See* Carole J. Petersen, Hong Kong's Race Discrimination Bill: A Critique and Comparison with the Sex Discrimination and Disability Discrimination Ordinances, Submission to the Hong Kong Legislative Council's Bills Committee to Study the Race Discrimination Bill, LC Paper No. CB(2)2232/06–07(01), June 2007, *available at* www.legco.gov.hk/yr06–07/english/bc/bc52/papers/bc52cb2–2232-1-e.pdf and Kelley Loper, *One Step Forward, Two Steps Back? The Dilemma of Hong Kong's Draft Race Discrimination Legislation*, 38 Hong Kong L. J. 15 (2008). The UN Committee on the Elimination of Racial Discrimination has expressed concern that the RDO may not fully implement Hong Kong's international obligations. *See* Committee on the Elimination of Racial Discrimination (CERD), *Concluding Observations: China*, ¶¶ 27–28, U.N. Doc. CERD/C/CHN/CO/10–13 (Aug. 28, 2009).

8 *See* Carole J. Petersen, A *Clash of Values? Barriers to Equality in Hong Kong's Education System*, 2004 Hawaii International Conference on Education 2004 Conference Proceedings (January 3–6, 2005), 24–27 and Puja Kapai, *The Hong Kong Equal Opportunities Commission: Calling for a New Avatar*, 39 Hong Kong L. J. 339 (2009).

9 In Hong Kong the concept of permanent residency is, to some degree, analogous to citizenship because Hong Kong's autonomous powers include responsibility for its own immigration policy and control over its borders with the rest of China (generally referred to in Hong Kong as "mainland China").

I. THE LEGAL FRAMEWORK

Hong Kong's constitutional document, the Basic Law, was promulgated in 1990 by the National People's Congress and has governed Hong Kong since the territory's return to Chinese sovereignty in 1997. Article 25 does not elaborate specific grounds and does not explicitly mention sex or gender but simply provides that all Hong Kong residents shall be equal before the law.[10] Despite its formal articulation, Hong Kong courts have interpreted this provision broadly in light of Article 39 of the Basic Law, which provides that "[t]he provisions of the International Covenant on Civil and Political Rights (ICCPR), the International Covenant on Economic, Social, and Cultural Rights (ICESCR), and international labour conventions as applied to Hong Kong shall remain in force and shall be implemented through the laws of the Hong Kong Special Administrative Region." Essentially, Article 39 implements these international treaties into Hong Kong law and the courts have generally read Article 25 alongside similar provisions in the Bill of Rights Ordinance – an ordinary law that contains a "Bill of Rights" in Part II that largely duplicates the ICCPR and has thus attained constitutional status.[11] The courts have been willing to rely on the interpretive materials produced by the Human Rights Committee, the U.N. human rights treaty body that monitors implementation of the ICCPR by state parties, when interpreting Article 25.

The provisions in the ICCPR that are particularly relevant include Articles 2(1), 3, and 26 (replicated in Articles 1 and 22 of the Hong Kong Bill of Rights). Article 2(1) requires that states parties respect and ensure the rights recognized in the Covenant "without distinction of any kind, such as race, colour, sex, language, religion, political or other opinion, national or social origin, property, birth or other status." Article 3 reinforces Article 2(1) and emphasizes the importance of gender

---

[10] Article 41 of the Basic Law extends this protection to persons in Hong Kong other than Hong Kong residents, *Hong Kong Basic Law* art. 41.

[11] Despite the position of the ICESCR alongside the ICCPR in Article 39 of the Basic Law, there is no equivalent to the Bill of Rights for economic and social rights and the courts have referred to the ICESCR as "promotional in nature," and an "aspirational Covenant," which does not create "absolute obligations." *See Mok Chi Hung & Another v. Director of Immigration*, [2001] 2 H.K.L.R.D. 125, [2001] H.K.E.C. 8 and *Chan To Foon & Others v. The Director of Immigration and the Secretary for Security*, [2001] H.K.C.U. 1. In its Concluding Observations on Hong Kong's periodic report in 2001, however, the Committee on Economic, Social, and Cultural Rights commented that it "greatly regrets that some judgments of the High Court in [Hong Kong] express the opinion that the Covenant is 'promotional' . . . or 'aspirational'. . . . in nature. As the Committee has confirmed on numerous occasions, such opinions are based on a mistaken understanding of the legal obligations arising from the Covenant." *See* Committee on Economic, Social and Cultural Rights (CESCR), *Concluding Observations: (Hong Kong) China*, ¶ 16, U.N. Doc. E/C.12/1/Add.58 (May 21, 2001). On the other hand, the CFA acknowledged that the ICESCR could be useful when interpreting Hong Kong laws that deal with economic and social issues, such as housing. *See Ho Choi Wan v. Hong Kong Housing Authority*, [2005] 4 H.K.L.R.D. 706, [2005] H.K.E.C. 1894, ¶¶ 64–67. The Court of First Instance referred favorably to a General Comment issued by the Committee on Economic, Social, and Cultural Rights in *Catholic Diocese of Hong Kong v. Secretary for Justice*, [2007] 4 H.K.L.R.D. 483, ¶¶ 245–46.

equality.[12] The Human Rights Committee has observed in a General Comment that "[w]hile Article 2 limits the scope of the rights to be protected against discrimination to those provided for in the Covenant, Article 26 does not specify such limitations."[13] Article 26 is, therefore, an autonomous right that generally guarantees equality before the law, equal protection of the law without discrimination, and equal and effective protection against discrimination on any of the enumerated grounds.[14] In the same General Comment, the Committee indicates that equality should be understood in its substantive sense. For example, it defines discrimination as a distinction that has the "purpose or *effect*" of nullifying human rights and freedoms implying the inclusion of *de facto* or indirect discrimination.[15] It also adds that "the principle of equality sometimes requires States parties to take affirmative action in order to diminish or eliminate conditions which cause or help to perpetuate discrimination prohibited by the Covenant."[16]

Other U.N. human rights treaty bodies have also elaborated a substantive equality principle in their General Comments. The Committee on Economic, Social, and Cultural Rights states that the rights in the Covenant must be enjoyed on a basis of equality, "a concept that carries substantive meaning."[17] It adds that

> substantive equality for men and women will not be achieved simply through the enactment of laws or the adoption of policies that are, prima facie, gender-neutral. . . . States parties should take into account that such laws, policies and practice can fail to address or even perpetuate inequality between men and women because they do not take account of existing economic, social and cultural inequalities, particularly those experienced by women.[18]

In another General Comment published in July 2009, the Committee recognizes that

> [m]erely addressing formal discrimination will not ensure substantive equality as envisaged and defined by article 2, paragraph 2 [of the ICESCR]. . . . Eliminating discrimination in practice requires paying sufficient attention to groups of individuals which suffer historical or persistent prejudice instead of merely comparing the formal treatment of individuals in similar situations. States parties must therefore immediately adopt the necessary measures to prevent, diminish and eliminate

---

[12] Art. 3 provides that "[t]he States Parties to the present Covenant undertake to ensure the equal right of men and women to the enjoyment of all civil and political rights set forth in the present Covenant." Arts. 2(2) and 3 of the ICESCR duplicate arts. 2(1) and 3 of the ICCPR.

[13] Human Rights Committee, *General Comment No. 18: Nondiscrimination*, ¶12, U.N. Doc. CCPR/C/21/Rev 1/Add 1 (1989).

[14] *Id.*

[15] *Id.* ¶ 7 (emphasis added).

[16] *Id.* ¶ 10.

[17] CESCR, *General Comment No. 16: The Equal Right of Men and Women to the Enjoyment of All Economic, Social, and Cultural Rights (Art. 3 of the Covenant)*, ¶ 6, U.N. Doc. E/C.12/2005/4 (Aug. 11, 2005).

[18] *Id.*

the conditions and attitudes which cause or perpetuate substantive or de facto discrimination.[19]

The Committee on the Elimination of Discrimination against Women and the Committee on the Elimination of Racial Discrimination have also interpreted the right to nondiscrimination with reference to a substantive equality principle.[20]

The treaty bodies' substantive approach to equality, coupled with the Hong Kong courts' willingness to refer to these documents as authoritative interpretations of international standards, creates potential for these standards to further influence the development of a substantive equality principle in the Hong Kong context.

In addition to a constitutional right to equality derived from Articles 25 and 39 of the Basic Law, Articles 1 and 22 of the Bill of Rights, and international human rights instruments, Hong Kong's legislature (the Legislative Council) has also enacted four antidiscrimination laws.[21] The Sex Discrimination Ordinance (SDO), based on the U.K. Sex Discrimination Act (1975) as well as Australian antidiscrimination legislation, was the first of these and prohibits direct and indirect discrimination in both the public and private sectors on the grounds of sex, marital status, and pregnancy.[22] It also explicitly prohibits harassment, which includes hostile environment harassment in a range of settings, including employment and education.[23]

II. THE JUSTIFICATION TEST AND SPECIAL MEASURES

The judgments discussed in this section begin to clarify several aspects of the content of the right to equality in Hong Kong constitutional law and reveal the judiciary's halting move toward a substantive interpretation of a right to equality. Although the courts have not explicitly referred to substantive equality, they have nonetheless elaborated a definition of discrimination that includes indirect, *de facto* discrimination[24] and have recognized that intent to discriminate is not necessarily a relevant consideration. They have also developed a test for justifiable distinctions that could support a requirement of special measures or affirmative action in certain circumstances.

---

[19] CESCR, *General Comment No. 20: Nondiscrimination in Economic, Social, and Cultural Rights (Art. 2, para. 2, of the International Covenant on Economic, Social, and Cultural Rights)*, ¶ 8, U.N. Doc. E/C.12/GC/20 (July 2, 2009).

[20] *See, e.g.,* the Committee on the Elimination of Discrimination against Women, *General Recommendation No. 25: Temporary Special Measures*, U.N. Doc. A/59/38 (2004); and CERD, *General Recommendation No. 32: The Meaning and Scope of Special Measures in the International Convention on the Elimination of Racial Discrimination*, Aug. 2009, U.N. Doc. CERD/C/GC/32 (Sept. 24, 2009).

[21] Ordinary statutes are referred to as "ordinances" in Hong Kong.

[22] Other antidiscrimination statutes in Hong Kong include a Family Status Discrimination Ordinance, (1997) Cap. 527 [hereinafter FSDO], which prohibits discrimination against those with responsibility for the care of an immediate family member; a Disability Discrimination Ordinance, (1996) Cap. 487 [hereinafter DDO]; and a Race Discrimination Ordinance, (2008) Cap. 602 [hereinafter RDO].

[23] Sex Discrimination Ordinance, (1995) Cap. 480, § 2(5).

[24] *Leung*, [2006] 4 H.K.L.R.D. 211.

Hong Kong courts have favorably cited the Human Rights Committee's observation that "not every differentiation of treatment will constitute discrimination if the criteria for such differentiation are reasonable and objective and if the aim is to achieve a purpose which is legitimate under the Covenant."[25] The Court of Appeal (CA) relied on this principle when interpreting the equality provisions in the Bill of Rights in 1992 and developed a three-part test for determining when differential treatment could be justified.[26] The court first recognized that "[c]learly, there is no requirement of literal equality in the sense of unrelentingly identical treatment always. For such rigidity would subvert rather than promote true even-handedness. So that, in certain circumstances, a departure from literal equality would be a legitimate course and, indeed, the only legitimate course."[27] At the same time, however, "the starting point is identical treatment. And any departure therefrom must be justified."[28] The court then held that to justify such a departure, "it must be shown: one, that sensible and fair-minded people would recognize a genuine need for some difference of treatment; two, that the difference embodied in the particular departure selected to meet that need is itself rational; and, three, that such departure is proportionate to such need"[29] (the Man Wai Keung test).

This test does not necessarily signal the court's embrace of a substantive equality principle because it could simply be used to justify invidious discrimination in order to balance competing interests or allow for a margin of appreciation when developing economic and social policies.[30] It does, however, represent a move away from a purely formal analysis and could be applied to uphold special measures aimed at achieving substantive equality for marginalized groups. As noted in Section I, the Human Rights Committee has pointed out that affirmative action may sometimes be necessary and "as long as such action is needed to correct discrimination in fact, it is a case of legitimate differentiation under the Covenant."[31]

The Court of Final Appeal (CFA) elaborated on and refined the Man Wai Keung test in the case of *Secretary for Justice v. Yau Yuk Lung (Yau)*,[32] a judicial review application that challenged a provision in the Hong Kong Crimes

---

[25] Human Rights Committee, *supra* note 13, ¶ 13.
[26] *R v. Man Wai Keung* (No. 2), [1992] 2 H.K.C.L.R. 207. The Bill of Rights Ordinance came into force in 1991. Although the Basic Law had not yet come into force in 1992, the pre-1997 equality jurisprudence under the Bill of Rights is still relevant because the judiciary has conflated article 25 of the Basic Law with the equality provisions of the Bill of Rights and the ICCPR since 1997 in light of Article 39 of the Basic Law (see Section I, earlier). Subsequent judgments have reaffirmed and modified this test. *See, e.g., So Wai Lun v. HKSAR,* [2006] 9 H.K.C.F.A.R. 530 and *Secretary for Justice v. Yau Yuk Lung,* [2007] 3 H.K.L.R.D. 903.
[27] *Man Wai Keung,* [1992] 2 H.K.C.L.R. at 217.
[28] *Id.* at 217.
[29] *Id.*
[30] *See* the discussion in Section III later in the chapter.
[31] Human Rights Committee, *supra* note 13.
[32] *Yau Yuk Lung,* [2007] 3 H.K.L.R.D. 903.

Ordinance.[33] The CFA decided that the provision discriminated against homosexual men, that sexual orientation is a ground that falls within the category of "other status" in Articles 2(1) and 26 of the ICCPR, and that the provision was therefore unconstitutional. The court emphasized that it would scrutinize with intensity attempted justifications of differential treatment based on grounds such as race, sex, or sexual orientation.[34]

Chief Justice Li began by generally accepting the primacy of a formal equal treatment principle, which mandates that "like cases should be treated alike" and "unlike cases should not be treated alike."[35] Then, like Bokhary in *Man Wai Keung*, he acknowledged that "the guarantee of equality before the law does not invariably require exact equality. Differences in legal treatment may be justified for good reason."[36] His three-part justifiability test includes the following elements: 1) the difference in treatment must pursue a legitimate aim – which involves establishing a genuine need for such a difference; 2) "the difference in treatment must be rationally connected to the legitimate aim"; and 3) it "must be no more than is necessary to accomplish the legitimate aim"[37] (the Yau test).

As Li elaborates on this test, he departs somewhat from an earlier CA judgment that also dealt with a discriminatory provision in the Crimes Ordinance.[38] In that case, the CA held that determining whether a piece of legislation is unconstitutional involves two stages: first, the court will decide whether a right protected by the Basic Law or the Bill of Rights (such as the right to equality) has been infringed. If the answer is yes, then the court will consider whether the infringement can be justified. In *Yau*, Li recalls this view that in requiring differential treatment to be justified, "the difference in treatment in question is an *infringement of the constitutional right to equality* but that the infringement may be constitutionally justified."[39] He rejects this characterization of the justification test, however, as inappropriate in the equality context: "Where the difference in treatment satisfies the justification test, the correct

---

[33] Crimes Ordinance (1971) Cap. 200, § 118F(1) provides that "a man who commits buggery with another man otherwise than in private shall be guilty of an offence." There is no equivalent provision related to heterosexual "buggery" or intercourse.

[34] *Yau Yuk Lung*, [2007] 3 H.K.L.R.D 903, ¶ 21.

[35] *Id.* ¶ 19.

[36] *Id.* ¶ 20.

[37] *Id.* ¶ 20.

[38] *Leung T. C. William Roy v. Secretary of Justice*, [2006] 4 H.K.L.R.D. 211. The challenged provision created an offense for a man to commit "buggery" with another man under the age of twenty-one. Although it was also an offense for a man to commit "buggery" with a girl under the age of twenty-one – and therefore the provision applied equally in the formal sense – the court held that the provision amounted to "disguised discrimination" on the basis of sexual orientation because the age of consent for heterosexual sex was sixteen. Crimes Ordinance (1971) Cap. 200, §§ 118C, 118D.

[39] *Yau Yuk Lung*, [2007] 3 H.K.L.R.D. 903, ¶ 22. (Li, C.J.) (citing *Leung*, [2006] 4 H.K.L.R.D. at 234) (emphasis added).

approach is to regard the difference in treatment as not constituting discrimination and not infringing the constitutional right to equality."[40]

This distinction between the CA's and Li's tests is important because it signals a conceptual shift toward a substantive equality framework and an apparent understanding of its implications. The Yau test, although based on the Man Wai Keung test, arguably provides a stronger basis for the development of a substantive equality principle. Differential treatment is not always discriminatory and the *nature* of the differential treatment is critical to distinguishing between invidious and benign distinctions. To apprehend this nature, the courts must consider the impact of the policy, law, or practice that is at issue, a process that necessitates a contextual analysis of actual disadvantage and marginalization based on a substantive equality principle.

Sadurski makes a similar argument when critiquing a judgment handed down by the Australian High Court in 1985.[41] That case involved a claim that special land rights that had been granted to an indigenous community were discriminatory because they involved a distinction based on race. The court accepted this formal understanding of discrimination, but held that the land rights provisions constituted an *exception* to the nondiscrimination principle because they could be characterized as "special measures." Sadurski critiqued the court's reasoning as overly formal:

> By considering the 'special measures' as an exception to a general prohibition of racial discrimination rather than . . . a proper inference from the principle of non-discrimination, the Court has assumed that racial distinctions are per se discriminatory and invalid, even if they are aimed at the improvement of the situation of traditionally disadvantaged groups . . . the test of discrimination must not abstract from the invidiousness of its aims and/or effects, and, hence, that a substantive moral theory of justice is a necessary element of reasoning about discrimination.[42]

Although Li does not expound a substantive moral theory of justice in *Yau*, his analysis of the justification test opens the door for further development of a substantive equality principle by the Hong Kong courts.

This is reinforced by Bokhary's concurring opinion in *Yau* because he explicitly articulates the applicability of the justification test to support affirmative action. He acknowledges that "there may be cases in which the complaint is of discrimination

---

[40] *Yau Yuk Lung*, [2007] 3 H.K.L.R.D. 903, ¶ 22. Although Li, C. J. rejects the CA's formal two-stage test of constitutionality in equality cases, the *Leung* case contributes to the development of substantive equality in other ways. Significantly, the CA recognized that the constitutional right to equality includes a prohibition against indirect discrimination – or "disguised" discrimination in the words of the court. This interpretation corresponds with the human rights treaty bodies' General Comments indicating that States' understanding of discrimination must include indirect discrimination (or discrimination in *effect*, as discussed earlier). See *Leung*, [2006] 4 H.K.L.R.D at 237.

[41] *Gerhardy v. Brown* (1985) 159 C.L.R. 70.

[42] Wojciech Sadurski, *Gerhardy v Brown v. the Concept of Discrimination: Reflections on the Landmark Case that Wasn't*, 11 SYDNEY L. REV. 6, 7 (1986–1988).

in the form of a failure to accord different treatment in circumstances calling for it or in which affirmative action is involved. Such cases may raise other considerations as to what is called for by equality before the law."[43] He clarifies that "[t]hat is what I had in mind when I said in Man Wai Keung's case that in certain circumstances a departure from literal equality would be a legitimate course and, indeed, the only legitimate course."[44] He favorably refers to the Permanent Court of International Justice's advisory opinion in Minority Schools in Albania, which emphasizes that "equality in fact may involve the necessity of different treatment in order to attain a result which establishes an equilibrium between different situations."[45] He then cites Rosalyn Higgins, who wrote in 2002 that it is "not fanciful . . . to see in [the linkage between special needs and equality in the Minority Schools advisory opinion] both the precursor of more contemporary notions of affirmative action and the response to suggestions that special protections themselves constitute a form of discrimination."[46]

The *Yau* judgment moves toward a substantive equality principle to a greater extent than earlier Hong Kong jurisprudence because it recognizes the unique nature of the justification test when adjudicating a constitutional right to equality. In other words, the Yau test does not simply involve a formal application of the equal treatment principle that would render any distinction made on a prohibited ground "discriminatory" – even if it could be justified at a later stage of analysis. Instead, passing the justification test means the distinction was not discriminatory in the first place. Formal distinctions are not necessarily invidious and a substantive, contextual approach is needed. Courts are now free to consider whether distinctions are designed to redress historical or *de facto* discrimination against a marginalized group and would therefore not be deemed discriminatory.

The nature of special measures was an issue in an earlier case that considered whether certain aspects of a centrally administered system for allocating secondary school places (the secondary school place allocation [SSPA] system) discriminated on the basis of sex. This case was groundbreaking because it was one of the first successful challenges to a government policy based on both a constitutional right to equality and an antidiscrimination statute. It also recognized that the SDO implemented Hong Kong's obligations under CEDAW and therefore "the words of that Ordinance should be construed, if they are reasonably capable of bearing such a meaning, as intended to carry out Hong Kong's obligations under CEDAW and not to be inconsistent with those obligations."[47]

---

[43] *Yau Yuk Lung*, [2007] 3 H.K.L.R.D. 903, ¶ 49.

[44] *Id.* ¶ 49.

[45] *Id.* ¶ 49.

[46] *Yau Yuk Lung*, [2007] 3 H.K.L.R.D. 903, ¶ 49 (Bokhary, J.) (citing Rosalyn Higgins, *The International Court of Justice and Human Rights, in* HUMAN RIGHTS PROTECTION: METHODS AND EFFECTIVENESS 166 (Frances Butler ed., 2002)).

[47] *Equal Opportunities Commission v. Director of Education*, [2001] 2 H.K.L.R.D. 690, 731.

In the late 1990s, an investigation conducted by the Hong Kong Equal Opportunities Commission found that the SSPA system discriminated on the basis of sex. In essence, the way the system operated, an individual boy who achieved the same test score as an individual girl had a greater chance of securing a place at the school of his choice.[48] The government justified this policy by arguing that the system was a special measure designed to achieve the advancement of boys because they believed that boys were "late bloomers" and, overall, girls tended to score higher on tests at the age of eleven or twelve when they were applying for secondary school places.[49] The court dismissed this argument – partly because of lack of evidence that boys were in fact "late bloomers." However, it also relied on the requirement in CEDAW that special measures must be "temporary" in nature.[50] The court held that because the system had operated for more than twenty years it was a "settled regime," clearly not "temporary," and therefore not justifiable.[51] It also reasoned that the rights of the individual could not be undermined by broad assumptions or generalizations.

Although this case was instrumental in dismantling a directly discriminatory policy, the reasoning of the court was highly individualized and ultimately demonstrated a conceptual bias toward formal equality. The court sidestepped a contextual analysis and missed an opportunity to interpret special measures with reference to a substantive equality model. The court could have reflected on the actual relative advantage or disadvantage of the group for which the measures were designed.[52] Girls and women in Hong Kong certainly still face serious obstacles to opportunities in the workplace and in many areas of life.[53]

Three years after the SSPA judgment, the Committee on the Elimination of Discrimination against Women issued a General Recommendation elaborating on the substantive nature of the special measures provision in CEDAW.[54] It clarified

---

[48] *Id.* at 700. Although the SSPA system mainly negatively affected girls, in some cases it also discriminated against individual boys.

[49] *Id.* at 703, 726.

[50] *Id.* at 731–32 and United Nations Convention on the Elimination of All Forms of Discrimination against Women (CEDAW) art. 4, Dec. 18, 1979, 1249 U.N.T.S. 13.

[51] *Equal Opportunities Commission*, [2001] 2 H.K.L.R.D. at 732. The court also relied on CEDAW to reject assumptions and stereotypes about boys' and girls' inherent learning abilities.

[52] Andrew Byrnes, *The Committee on the Elimination of Discrimination against Women*, in THE UNITED NATIONS AND HUMAN RIGHTS: A CRITICAL ANALYSIS (Philip Alston ed., Oxford Clarendon Press 2d ed. 1999).

[53] *See generally* MAINSTREAMING GENDER IN HONG KONG SOCIETY (Fanny M. Cheung & Eleanor Holroyd eds., Chinese University Press 2009).

[54] Committee on the Elimination of Discrimination against Women, *General Recommendation No. 25: Temporary Special Measures*, U.N. Doc. A/59/38 (2004). Earlier feminist critiques of CEDAW discussed the limitations of the Convention for achieving substantive equality outcomes. In particular, the "temporary" nature of special measures could undermine the potential of such measures "in light of women's entrenched disadvantage and the long-term nature of the project of dismantling gender hierarchies through affirmative action." *See* Diane Otto, *Disconcerting Masculinities*, in INTERNATIONAL LAW: MODERN FEMINIST APPROACHES, 117–118 (D. Buss & A. Manji eds., Hart Publishing 2005).

that special measures must be understood in light of the object and purpose of the Convention, which the committee interprets as achieving substantive equality for women. The Committee also stated that

> the Convention goes beyond the concept of discrimination used in many national and international legal standards and norms. While such standards and norms prohibit discrimination on the grounds of sex and protect both men and women from treatment based on arbitrary, unfair and/or unjustifiable distinctions, the Convention focuses on discrimination against women, emphasizing that women have suffered, and continue to suffer from various forms of discrimination because they are women.[55]

Because this General Recommendation was published after the court's decision in the SSPA case, it could not of course have informed the court's analysis of the special measures provision. Going forward, however, the U.N. treaty bodies' increasingly explicit substantive interpretation of a right to equality could be especially influential in a jurisdiction like Hong Kong, given the courts' willingness to rely on CEDAW and other international standards when interpreting domestic human rights obligations.[56]

III. LIMITATIONS

Despite the developments discussed in Section II and the potential influence of international human rights standards, other cases reveal a less robust approach. Whereas the application of a formal equality principle has sometimes been adequate to tackle gender discrimination – such as the entrenched discrimination in the SSPA system – the courts have failed to recognize the impact of a number of other policies on gender equality. This deficiency is especially evident in claims involving the rights of indigenous villagers, migrant domestic workers, and new immigrants from mainland China.

Article 40 of the Basic Law provides that "the lawful traditional rights and interests of the indigenous inhabitants of the 'New Territories' shall be protected by the Hong Kong Special Administrative Region."[57] This provision constitutionally entrenches the British colonial practice that preserved – and arguably strengthened – Chinese

---

[55] Committee on the Elimination of Discrimination against Women, *supra* note 54, ¶ 5.

[56] *See* Carole J. Petersen, *Embracing Universal Standards? The Role of International Human Rights Treaties in Hong Kong's Constitutional Jurisprudence*, in INTERPRETING HONG KONG'S BASIC LAW : THE STRUGGLE FOR COHERENCE, 33–53 (Hualing Fu, Lison Harris, & Simon N. M. Young eds., Palgrave MacMillan 2007); Anthony Mason, *The Place of Comparative Law in Developing the Jurisprudence on the Rule of Law and Human Rights in Hong Kong*, 37 HONG KONG L. J. 299 (2007); and Johannes M. M. Chan, *Hong Kong's Bill of Rights: Its Reception of and Contribution to International and Comparative Jurisprudence*, 47 INT'L COMP. L. Q. 306 (1998).

[57] In 1898, the British acquired the "New Territories," a substantial area of land north of Hong Kong Island and Kowloon, and allowed the continuation of traditional laws and customs among the Chinese inhabitants. The current "indigenous inhabitants" are descendants of those who were residents of

laws and customs in Chinese villages in the New Territories. The New Territories Ordinance[58] provides that the courts shall recognize and enforce Chinese custom and customary rights in proceedings relating to land in the New Territories. In 1994, the Legislative Council – after a bitter debate between women's rights advocates and those representing the interests of male indigenous villagers – passed the New Territories Land (Exemption) Ordinance that repealed provisions on land succession rights that had discriminated against women.[59] In a 2003 case involving the succession rights of two daughters to their deceased father's land, however, the CA decided that Chinese customary succession law still applied.[60] In that case, a male nephew of the deceased claimed that he had a right to inherit the land as the closest male relative. Although the court eventually dismissed the man's claim, it did not refer to the constitutional right to equality at all. Instead, the court considered whether the male relative could be posthumously adopted by the deceased man, therefore allowing him to inherit the land as a male heir. The court held that even if he could be adopted in such a manner, he would not be entitled to succeed to the estate because he had already inherited his own father's estate and there was a general prohibition in customary law that an adopted son could not inherit in more than one of his families.[61]

In another case, the CFA referred to the SDO when ruling that the method of electing village representatives in an indigenous village in the New Territories of Hong Kong discriminated on the basis of sex. Ironically, in this case, it was a male nonindigenous villager who challenged the validity of the electoral arrangements in his village. Although married to an indigenous villager, he was unable to vote, unlike the female nonindigenous spouses of male indigenous villagers. The judgment did not refer to the equality provisions in the Basic Law but relied entirely on section 35 of the SDO that provides that the government shall not approve the results of a rural election where that person or body (or any of its members) has been elected or otherwise chosen by a procedure in which men and women have not been able to participate on equal terms.

Another land-related policy that clearly discriminates against indigenous women has yet to face a constitutional challenge. The "small house policy," which is listed as an exception in the SDO,[62] entitles any male descendant of an indigenous villager over the age of eighteen to construct a three-story dwelling on a 700-square-foot plot

---

villages established in Hong Kong in 1898. *See* SIU KEUNG CHEUNG, GENDER AND COMMUNITY UNDER BRITISH COLONIALISM: EMOTION, STRUGGLE, AND POLITICS IN A CHINESE VILLAGE (Routledge 2006).

[58] New Territories Ordinance, Cap. 97.

[59] Quinton Chan, *Bill Aims to Make Women Heirs to New Territory Village Land*, SOUTH CHINA MORNING POST, Mar. 6, 1994.

[60] *Liu Ying Lan v. Liu Tung Yiu & Another*, [2003] 3 H.K.L.R.D. 249. The decision was based on transitional provisions in the 1994 law that essentially exempted the land in question from the reforms.

[61] *Id.*

[62] SDO, sched. 5, pt. 2.

of land within the boundaries of his village.[63] This policy has been criticized as discriminatory as well as unsustainable and the government has failed to complete a promised review of the system.[64]

Migrant domestic workers and new immigrants from mainland China have faced even greater obstacles when challenging discriminatory government policies. In these cases, the courts have avoided considering gender entirely, although women make up the large majority of both of these groups.[65] The Committee on the Elimination of Discrimination against Women has observed that

> [a]lthough both men and women migrate, migration is not a gender-neutral phenomenon.... To understand the specific ways in which women are impacted, female migration should be studied from the perspective of gender inequality, traditional female roles, a gendered labour market, the universal prevalence of gender-based violence and the worldwide feminization of poverty and labour migration. The integration of a gender perspective is, therefore, essential to the analysis of the position of female migrants and the development of policies to counter discrimination exploitation and abuse.[66]

Although the Hong Kong government reported to the Committee in 2004 that it was committed to gender mainstreaming in the policy-making process, the following cases raise questions about its implementation in practice because they all involve policies that arguably indirectly discriminate against women.[67]

In the case of *Raza*, five foreign domestic workers (FDWs) challenged the government's decision in 2003 to impose a levy on the employers of FDWs, while reducing the minimum wage of those workers by the same amount.[68] The applicants argued that it constituted an indirect and discriminatory tax on the FDWs themselves because it did not apply to many other categories of imported labor.

---

[63] *See* Hong Kong SAR Government, Lands Department, *How to Apply for a Small House Grant*, *available at* www.landsd.gov.hk/en/legco/house.htm.

[64] Christine Loh Kung-wai, *Small House Fiasco*, SOUTH CHINA MORNING POST, Sept. 13, 2007.

[65] According to the *Hong Kong Government's Report to the UN Committee on the Elimination of Racial Discrimination*, ¶ 76, U.N. Doc. CERD/C/HKG/13 (July 28, 2008), "[a]s of 31 December 2006, some 232,781 people – mostly women – were working in Hong Kong as foreign domestic helpers." The majority were from the Philippines, Indonesia, and Thailand. Immigrants from other parts of China outside of Hong Kong are generally referred to in Hong Kong as "mainland immigrants" or "new arrivals from the mainland." Hong Kong allows a quota of 150 "one-way permit holders" per day to enter Hong Kong from mainland China for the purpose of settlement and family reunion and many of these immigrants are the spouses of Hong Kong resident men. In 2008, approximately 70 percent of new mainland immigrants who were one-way permit holders were women or girls. In the first quarter of 2009, 73 percent of all one-way permit holders and 85 percent of those above the age of 25 were female. *See* Home Affairs Department and Immigration Department, *Statistics on New Arrivals from the Mainland*, 7 (First Quarter of 2009).

[66] Committee on the Elimination of Discrimination against Women, *General Recommendation 26*, ¶ 6, U.N. Doc. CEDAW/C/2009/WP.1/R (Dec. 8, 2008).

[67] *Report by China to the Committee on the Elimination of Discrimination against Women*, U.N. Doc. CEDAW/C/CHN/S-6/Add.I.

[68] *Raza & Others v. Chief Executive in-Council and Others*, [2005] 3 H.K.L.R.D. 561.

When evaluating the claim, the court took a formal, equal treatment approach and considered whether the policy involved differential treatment between "lower-skilled and higher-skilled workers."[69] It did not evaluate, however, whether the policy amounted to indirect gender discrimination or national origin discrimination although most of the migrant workers affected were women originating from certain Southeast Asian countries. The judge then applied the Man Wai Keung justification test (discussed in Section II) and decided that because the issues concerned socio-economic matters "a wider margin of appreciation must be given to the Legislature and the policy-makers than would be given in respect of matters concerning rights that are fundamental."[70]

The case of *Kong Yunming v. The Director of Social Welfare*[71] raises similar concerns and also demonstrates the shortcomings of the courts' failure to identify gender discrimination. The applicants challenged the constitutionality of a seven-year residency requirement for receiving social welfare benefits (Comprehensive Social Security Assistance or CSSA). The case involved a woman from the mainland who was married to a Hong Kong permanent resident. After waiting for a period of time, she received a one-way permit and immigrated to Hong Kong. Her husband died the day after she arrived and although she was left destitute, her application for social welfare was denied on the ground that she had not lived in Hong Kong for seven years. She argued that the policy violated both her right to social welfare (Article 36 of the Basic Law) as well as her right to equality (Article 25) and that she had been discriminated against on the basis of her residency status.[72]

In its analysis of the equality guarantee, the court cited the case of *R (Carson) v. Secretary of State for Work and Pensions* in which Lord Hoffman made a distinction between two different categories of prohibited grounds:[73] the first includes race, caste, noble birth, membership in a political party, and gender; while the second includes ability, education, wealth, and occupation.[74] Lord Hoffman suggested that it would be difficult to justify differential treatment on a ground in the first category but that justification in the second category would "usually depend upon consideration of the general public interest."[75] The Hong Kong court reasoned that "length of residence" fell within the second category of grounds and therefore held that "as regards whether the policy was no more than necessary to accomplish the legitimate aim, it must be firmly remembered that one is here concerned with a discretionary area of judgment enjoyed by the government in relation to social and economic

---

[69] *Id.* at 593.

[70] *Id.* at 595.

[71] *Kong Yunming v. The Director of Social Welfare*, [2009] 4 H.K.L.R.D. 382.

[72] In Hong Kong, permanent residency – which is roughly equivalent to "citizenship" (*supra* note 9) – may be obtained after seven years of continuous stay in the territory.

[73] *Kong Yunming*, [2009] 4 H.K.L.R.D. 382, ¶¶ 74–75 (citing *R (Carson) v. Secretary of State for Work and Pensions*, [2006] 1 A.C. 173, ¶¶ 14–17).

[74] *Id.* ¶ 74 (citing *Secretary of State for Work and Pensions*, [2006] 1 A.C. 173, ¶ 15).

[75] *Id.* ¶ 75 (citing *Secretary of State for Work and Pensions*, [2006] 1 A.C. 173, ¶ 16).

matters."[76] As in *Raza*, the court failed to consider the possible existence of indirect gender discrimination – most new immigrants to Hong Kong are on one-way permits from the mainland, and most new mainland immigrants on one-way permits are women. As a result, the court was quick to accept the government's justifications for the policy.

The applicant in *Fok Chun Wa v. Hospital Authority*[77] was also a woman from the mainland married to a Hong Kong permanent resident but was still waiting for a one-way permit from the Chinese authorities to settle in Hong Kong. She gave birth in a Hong Kong hospital while visiting her husband on a two-way permit and was classified as a noneligible person (NEP) for the purposes of receiving subsidized medical care in a public hospital. NEPs were charged significantly higher fees for obstetric services than permanent and nonpermanent Hong Kong residents (Eligible Persons or EPs). The spouses of Hong Kong residents who were not themselves Hong Kong identity card holders had qualified as EPs in the past but were reclassified as NEPs in 2003. In this case, the applicant was charged the NEP rate for obstetric services but argued that this amounted to discrimination because the spouses of Hong Kong residents were not in a similar position as individuals who fell within other categories of NEPs with no family ties to Hong Kong. The court once again failed to consider the impact of the policy on women (most NEPs accessing obstetric services in public hospitals are the mainland wives of Hong Kong residents)[78] and categorized the issues as matters concerning "broad social policy."[79]

In these cases, the courts have avoided a more rigorous analysis based on a substantive principle of equality and nondiscrimination that would require a consideration of the context and the actual disadvantage of the groups affected (migrant and immigrant women). The cases also demonstrate the courts' formal approach to equality and deference to policy makers when the issues involve what they broadly term "social policy."

CONCLUSION

The Hong Kong experience illustrates one of the central problems of equality: that while the equality principle – when understood in its most substantive sense – has the power to transform relations within society and effectively address disadvantage, difficulties often arise at the level of implementation. Legal formulations may not fully reflect or support a substantive concept of equality and a conservative judiciary may rely on formal interpretations of equality guarantees that fail to address

---

[76] *Id.* ¶ 127.

[77] *Fok Chun Wa v. Hospital Authority*, [2008] H.K.E.C. 2161; *Fok Chun Wa Suing by his Next Friend Fok Siu Wing & Anor v. The Hospital Authority & Anor* [2010] H.K.C.U. 1027.

[78] The judgment notes that in 2004, 75 percent of the babies born of NEP women were fathered by Hong Kong permanent residents. *Id.* ¶ 33.

[79] *Id.* ¶¶ 75–78.

the actual disadvantage women face in society. This is particularly evident in the Hong Kong courts' failure to take gender into account in cases involving migrant workers, new immigrants, and economic and social policies. Despite the courts' formal, noncontextual, and deferential interpretation in these cases, other developments demonstrate some movement toward a more substantive equality guarantee. These include a justification test that could be used to support special measures for marginalized groups and the courts' reliance on international human rights standards, including CEDAW and the ICCPR. The human rights treaty bodies' interpretation of a right to nondiscrimination has evolved and now clearly endorses substantive equality providing the theoretical basis for fashioning more effective legal tools.

PART III

Feminism, Democracy, and Political Participation

9

The Gendered State and Women's Political Leadership

Explaining the American Puzzle

Eileen McDonagh and Paula A. Monopoli

INTRODUCTION

The United States has presented a puzzle to those trying to understand women's political representation. Political representation is a basic component of every democratic political system. Democracy refers to the participation of people in their own government, that is, the rule of the people. In a representative democracy such as the United States, the two most important components of political rule are the right to vote and the right to hold office. One of the major principles in a democratic political system is that a democratic body such as Congress should reflect the characteristics of the population. If the population is 51 percent women then something close to 51 percent women should be in representative institutions.[1] However, as of 2008, women constitute only 16.8 percent of the House of Representatives. This means that women are underrepresented in the House by 34.1 percent. The extreme gap between the population percentage of women and their representation in the House makes women the most underrepresented subordinate group in American society, more so than that of African Americans, Hispanics, or Asians, as illustrated in Figure 9.1.

The low political representation of women in Congress also ranks the United States an abysmal eighty-fourth in the world, trailing behind comparable Western democracies such as Sweden, 47 percent, Finland, 41.5 percent, the Netherlands, 39.3 percent, Denmark, 38 percent, Spain, 36.3 percent, Belgium, 35.3 percent, Germany, 31.6 percent, and Switzerland, 28.5 percent, but also trailing behind

---

[1] There is a significant body of literature that explores "descriptive representation," but for purposes of this chapter, we assume that gender does matter in representation. *See, e.g.*, Jane Mansbridge, *Should Blacks Represent Blacks and Women Represent Women? A Contingent 'Yes'*, 61 J. POL. 628 (1999).

The authors would like to thank Susan G. McCarty and Amy Wasserman for their research assistance with this chapter.

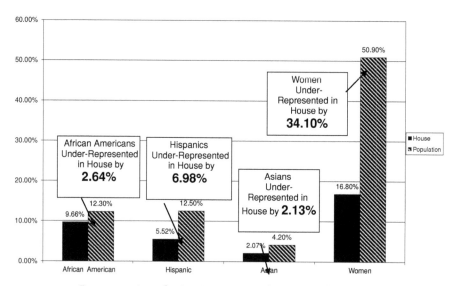

FIGURE 9.1. Representation of minority groups in the House of Representatives, 2008.

many less wealthy and less economically privileged countries such as Ecuador, 25 percent, Seychelles, 23.5 percent, Tunisia, 22.8 percent, and Eritrea, 22 percent.[2]

When we turn to the executive branch, since the mid-twentieth century, eighty-five countries have elected a woman to be their executive leader as prime minister, deputy prime minister, president, or vice president.[3] Regrettably, the United States is not among those nations. Rather, it remains a country that has not yet even nominated a woman to be the presidential candidate of a major political party. Thus, when it comes to women's political representation, the United States is a dramatic laggard[4] – a wealthy, industrial, Western democracy in which women are radically underrepresented compared to other subordinate groups in the United States and cross-nationally to other countries. The question is, Why?

One significant explanation for the laggard status of the American state is the power of political structures. Many other democracies have multiple parties, systems of proportional representation, and a parliamentary legislature, all of which have been shown to improve women's electoral chances when running for national political

[2] For a full list of the countries and the percentage of women who serve in the legislature in 2008, see Eileen McDonagh, *It Takes a State: A Policy Feedback Model of Women's Political Representation*, 8 PERPSP. ON POL. 69 (2010).

[3] For a full list of the countries and the women who served in executive leadership positions, see EILEEN McDONAGH, THE MOTHERLESS STATE: WOMEN'S POLITICAL LEADERSHIP AND AMERICAN DEMOCRACY 112–18 (2009).

[4] *Id.* at 3.

office.[5] The United States, however, has none of these features. New research confirms that political structures do contribute to the explanation of why the United States is so far behind most comparable democracies when it comes to women's political representation. However, it also points to another set of institutional traits, namely the way a democratic state's adoption of public policies generates a *political context* that teaches people the meaning of gender in relation to the state.[6]

We argue that the gendered character of the state's political institutions and public policies teaches the public who is suitable as officeholders in the public sphere of governance. Even in democracies, the state in its most basic formulation reflects traits that voters associate with men. However, most democracies other than the United States balance their political institutions by adopting public policies that also represent traits voters associate with women. Such democracies have a hybrid political context embodying characteristics that voters associate with both men and women. In a hybrid state, voters learn that both women's sameness with men and women's difference from men correspond to the public sphere of political governance. As a result, voters' view of women as suitable political leaders improves, as does electoral support for women running for political office.

This research adds to our understanding of women's political representation by investigating the policy feedback effects of gendered political institutions and public policies. Political attitudes and policy preferences, as mediated by political parties, interest groups, and social movements, contribute to the adoption of institutional configurations and public policies in the first place. However, a growing body of research establishes that once institutions and policies are in place, they have feedback effects on the public's view of society and the state, including who is suitable as a political leader.[7] The policy feedback model has been applied to a wide range of issue areas, but it has only recently been applied to a study of women's political representation.[8] Doing so adds new insights to an understanding of how the historical and contemporary characteristics of the American state depress women's access to political leadership roles. Although the political institutions and public policies of most comparable democracies represent traits attributed to both men and women, the United States has failed to establish such a hybrid political context.

The framework of our analysis is as follows. First, we establish that voters associate masculine traits with war and autonomous behavior patterns, in contrast to relational traits associated with women derived from social and biological maternal attributes.

[5] R. Darcy et al., Women, Elections, and Representation (2nd ed. 1994); Passages to Power: Legislative Recruitment in Advanced Democracies (Pippa Norris ed., 1997); Richard E. Matland, *Women's Representation in National Legislatures: Developed and Developing Countries*, 23 Legislative Stud. Q. 109–25 (1998).

[6] McDonagh, *supra* note 3.

[7] McDonagh, *supra* note 3. For analysis of the policy feedback model, see Andrea Louise Campbell, How Policies Make Citizens: Senior Political Activism and the American Welfare State (2003).

[8] McDonagh, *supra* note 2; McDonagh, *supra* note 3.

Second, we examine the masculine bias inherent in the founding documents of the American state and its constitutional formulation as contrasted with the more hybrid political contexts of most comparable democracies that include relational and cooperative-based traits. Third, we examine a range of public policies to illustrate the masculine specificity of those associated with the American state in contrast to the hybrid character of public policies that typify most comparable democracies. In so doing, we discuss the policy feedback effects on women's political representation that emanate from masculine versus hybrid political contexts.

I. GENDERED POLITICAL INSTITUTIONS

A. *Defining Masculine*

In the Western world that defines the American heritage, aggression and the use of physical force are traditionally associated with men, not women.[9] The very definition of the modern state, therefore, represents traits associated with men.[10] We see that precept in the definition of the state offered by Max Weber. The state is the institution in a human community that has a monopoly on the legitimate use of physical force – including deadly force – within a given territory.[11] Or, as Leon Trotsky stated at Brest-Litovsk, "Every state is founded on force."[12] Weber's definition of the state as the sole institution exercising physical force legitimately focuses attention on the armed forces, state bureaucracy, the courts, and the domestic police force as the key components of the state. Thus, Weber defines the state in terms of the legitimacy of the *means* it uses to define and execute public policies rather than the *content* of those policies themselves. As he establishes in *Politics as a Vocation*, the policy goals of states, such as providing for people's welfare, can also be found in a wide range of associations, including the family, voluntary associations, and religious organizations. What distinguishes the state from other institutions, therefore, is not welfare provision or policies constituting an ethic of care, but rather the *legitimacy of*

---

[9] There are a few historically verified examples of women serving effectively as warriors, such as the 5,000 women in the Dahomey Kingdom armed forces in the eighteenth and nineteenth centuries. This "Amazon Corps" was renowned for its ferocious and courageous battle expertise, and also for their cruelty. *See* Joshua S. Goldstein, War and Gender: How Gender Shapes the War System and Vice Versa 59–127 (2001).

[10] This association is exemplified by the age-old "castle doctrine," that "old adage that a man's house is his castle." *See* Jeannie Suk, *The True Woman: Scenes from the Law of Self-Defense*, 31 Harv. J. L. & Gender 237, 238–40 (2008) (referring to the principle that men have a right to use deadly force in self-defense of their person and property, which generally extends to the right to use deadly force to defend their families, including their wife and children). Transferring the masculine precept of the castle doctrine to the police power of the state renders the gendered character of the state as male, with citizens expecting that "men" will protect the country as leaders of the state.

[11] Max Weber, *Politics as a Vocation*, in From Max Weber: Essays in Sociology 77, 77–78 (H. H. Gerth & C. Wright Mills eds. & trans., 1946).

[12] *Id.* at 78 (quoting Trotsky).

its monopoly on the use of force to implement public policies. Without that premise, a state cannot be called a state, because without that feature, a political system would be in a state of anarchy.

B. *Defining Maternal*

When it comes to traits associated with women that have institutional and public policy counterparts in the state, the comparison term is not "feminine," but rather "maternal." Maternal refers to the way voters associate women with social and biological reproductive labor capacities. *Social* maternalism refers to the way voters view women as more oriented toward care work, that is, meeting the dependency needs of people once they are born. These include the dependency needs of infants, children, the ill, the elderly, and family members. Although presumably men as well as women can engage in care work, it remains the case that women continue to do more care work than men, both within the home and in the service sector of the market. This is true of even the most industrialized democracies, such as Sweden.[13] Care work, by definition, is relational.

Women are associated with care work as the caregivers, not only as the recipients of care work. In their 1993 study, Deborah Alexander and Kristi Andersen found that 98 percent of the voters they surveyed attribute issue positions based solely on a candidate's gender. When respondents were asked which gender would handle a given issue more competently in office, women outpaced the men in maternal interests such as daycare (82.7 percent women, 1 percent men) and health care (44.9 percent women, 3.1 percent men). Contrast this to how men clearly had the advantage in what is commonly thought of as a masculine interest, military spending (53.1 percent men, 16.3 percent women).[14]

Voters also associate women with *biological* maternalism, which refers to the generation of a new human being. There are two components to women's biological maternalism: (1) a female sex classification, where to be female refers to the group containing the individuals with the capacity to be pregnant and to give birth; and (2) women who have actually given birth, and, thus, who are biological mothers. Biologically, to be pregnant is to be defined in relation to a potential, new human being and in terms of a relationship with someone or something other than oneself. Although both men and women contribute to the generation of a new human being, individuals from the group "women" rather than "men" must make the additional contributions of being pregnant and giving birth. This continues the association of women, more closely than men, with the generation of a new human being.

---

[13] NANCY BURNS ET AL., THE PRIVATE ROOTS OF PUBLIC ACTION: GENDER, EQUALITY, AND POLITICAL PARTICIPATION (2001).

[14] Deborah Alexander & Kristi Andersen, *Gender as a Factor in the Attribution of Leadership Traits*, 46 POL. RES. Q. 527, 535 (1993).

C. *Gendering the State*

Gendering the American state as male begins ideologically and institutionally with the very founding of the American state on the basis of a bloody war, the American Revolution. In the words that grant authority to the citizens in the Declaration of Independence, Americans are exhorted to believe that they not only have the right, but the duty to alter their system of government – by force:

> But when a long train of abuses and usurpations, pursuing invariably the same Object evinces a design to reduce them under absolute Despotism, it is their right, it is their duty, to throw off such Government, and to provide new Guards for their future security.[15]

In fact, the Declaration alludes to war and to the pledging of the signers' lives, an allusion to deriving the legitimacy of their leadership to their willingness to engage as warriors. Thus, the very nature of claims to leadership and the concept of the American state itself derive from a masculine archetype.

1. Monarchies and Maternalism

Needless to say, monarchies are an antiquated form of government with tenets orthogonal to those based on an electoral principle of political rule. One must be a member of the dynastic family to be eligible to be the political executive of the state – the sovereign. Once chosen as sovereign, there are no mechanisms whereby the people have the political authority to remove the executive from office. In addition, the sovereign is not accountable to the people for his or her political decision making. That monarchies must give way to other forms of political rule as part of the larger, macro processes making up democratization is self-evident.

What is not self-evident, however, is that a political system must use violence, political force, bloodshed, and war to make a democratic transition from monarchical to electoral political rule. Violent revolution is the hallmark of the American state and of its sister republic, France. However, even a cursory look at democracies comparable in industrialization and wealth to the United States and France powerfully illustrates how those two countries are the exception, not the rule. As is evident from Table 9.1, of the twenty-one democracies comparable to the United States in wealth, industrial, and European heritage, more than half have retained their monarchies *to this day* rather than destroying them by means of a violent revolution. In 2008, the average percentage of women elected to the legislatures of these countries is 28.3 percent.

In lieu of a violent revolution, some countries like Austria and Germany simply allowed their monarchies to fade away. Others like Greece and Italy peacefully dissolved their monarchical heritage by means of referenda that voted them out

---

[15] THE DECLARATION OF INDEPENDENCE para. 2 (U.S. 1776).

TABLE 9.1. *Contemporary democracies, 2009*

	Historical status of monarchy	Military spending; per capita GDP	Death penalty: date prohibited	Constitution: welfare provision	Health spending: % government contribution, 2001	Gender quotas	Has had women as exec. leader	Percent women elected legislature, 2009
Australia	Retain	2.4	No, 1984	Yes	67.9	Yes	No	26.8
Austria	Fade Away	0.9	No, 1950	Yes	69.3	No	Yes	27.9
Belgium	Retain	1.3	No, 1996	Yes	71.7	Yes	No	38.0
Canada	Retain	1.1	No, 1976	Yes	70.8	Yes	Yes	22.1
Denmark	Retain	1.5	No, 1933	Yes	82.4	Yes	No	38.0
Finland	No Indigenous	2	No, 1949	Yes	75.6	No	Yes	41.5
France	Revolutionary Destruction	2.6	No, 1981	No	76	No	Yes	18.2
Germany	Fade Away	1.5	No, 1949	Yes	74.9	No	Yes	32.8
Iceland	No Indigenous	0	No, 1928	Yes	82.9	No	Yes	42.9
Ireland	No Indigenous	0.9	No, 1990	Yes	76.0	No	Yes	13.3
Italy	Fade Away	1.8	No, 1947	Yes	75.3	No	No	21.3
Luxembourg	Retain	0.9	No, 1979	Yes	89.9	Yes	No	20.0
Netherlands	Retain	1.6	No, 1870	Yes	63.3	Yes	No	41.3
New Zealand	Retain	1	No, 1961	No	76.8	Yes	Yes	33.6
Norway	Retain	1.9	No, 1905	Yes	85.5	Yes	Yes	36.1
Portugal	Revolutionary Destruction	2.3	No, 1867	Yes	69.0	No	Yes	28.3
Spain	Retain	1.2	No, 1978	Yes	71.4	Yes	No	36.3
Sweden	Retain Monarchy	1.5	No, 1921	Yes	85.2	Yes	Yes	47.0
Switzerland	No Indigenous Monarchy	1	No, 1942	No	57.1	No	Yes	28.5
United Kingdom	Retain Monarchy	2.4	No, 1973	Yes	82.2	Yes	Yes	19.5
United States	Revolutionary Destruction	4.06	Yes, –	No	44.4	No	No	16.8

of existence. In 2008, for countries following a peaceful exit strategy from their monarchical heritage, the average percent for women elected to their national legislatures was 27.3 percent.

The historical heritage of some countries never included an indigenous monarchy in the first place. They did not have in place a dynastic family representing their ethnic, religious, or linguistic heritage. Rather, as was the case for Finland, Iceland, Ireland, and Switzerland, they were subject to alien, foreign monarchical rule. Political efforts or wars for national independence in this political framework avoid de-legitimizing monarchies as a form of government, because the "problem" or political goal is not to extinguish monarchies as much as it is to extinguish a political imposition by a country with an alien ethnic, religious, and/or linguistic heritage. Switzerland never had its own dynastic monarchy, but rather was ruled by the Holy Roman Empire. In 1291, three cantons broke away to form a confederation that eventually grew to become modern Switzerland, thereby avoiding a bloody revolution.

In 2008, countries that fall into the category of never destroying an indigenous monarchy because they never had one elected an average of 31.6 percent women to their national legislatures. The remaining three countries that did employ revolutionary exit strategies in relation to an indigenous monarchy in 2008 elected the lowest percentage of women to their legislatures, only an average of 21.1 percent.

Hence, the American revolutionary heritage, while not exceptional, is not the rule. Monarchy as an institution fuses family with the state, thereby associating maternalism with the state. The United States' valorization of militarism and war combined with its destruction of monarchy has resulted in an unusually extreme degree of masculine traits. This is in contrast to the overwhelming majority of democracies comparable to the United States that bypassed such a violent heritage when making the transition from monarchical to democratic political rule.

2. The Structure of the Executive

In her article *The Fractured Soul of the Dayton Peace Agreement: A Legal Analysis*, Fionnuala Ni Aolain describes the powerful psychological influence that constitutions may have on the citizens of a state:

> Installing a constitution is a signal to society that the rules on political and social behavior are being regulated and will bear scrutiny. The absorption of that basic creed by a state's citizenry may have a crucial sociological impact on their perception of the state and their status within it.[16]

---

[16] Fionnuala Ni Aolain, *The Fractured Soul of the Dayton Peace Agreement: A Legal Analysis*, 19 MICH. J. INT'L L. 957, 980 (1998). Aolain suggests "[f]or this view in the context of the framing of the United States Constitution, see generally M. FARRAND, FRAMING OF THE CONSTITUTION OF THE UNITED STATES (1913)." *Id.* at n.75.

Thus, language and structure of founding documents can have an effect on how citizens view who is part of the body politic, who is not, and who is qualified to lead. In the debates surrounding the design of our Constitution, the nature of the executive and its relation to the legislative branch was a major source of contention. For example,

> In *Federalist No. 70*, Alexander Hamilton lauded energy in the executive as essential to protecting the young nation from internal and external threat. To Hamilton, the energetic executive was characterized by the agentic attributes of decision, dispatch, and action. These attributes, however, are not gender neutral.[17]

For Hamilton, the traits embodied in an effective executive were identified as masculine. That same belief resonates with today's voters.[18] As conceived in the Constitution, the executive has particularly male attributes, echoing the indivisible nature of a father's power and authority within the private sphere of the family as extrapolated to the state. For example, the president is given almost complete power to act unilaterally in the realm of foreign policy (analogous to the father being the sole repository of power when it comes to representing the family in the public sphere), while the president must share power with the legislative branch when it comes to domestic policy (akin the father's deference to the mother within the private sphere of the family).

The ancient claim that rulers derived their right to rule from their willingness to act in battle to protect those they seek to govern is also echoed in the Constitution, which connects the role of president to the role of Commander-in-Chief. Separating the functions of political ruler from those of the military was presumably a powerful reaction away from the framework of the British monarchy in which both functions were situated in the monarch. However, in their efforts to separate these functions, the framers not only granted the president authority as a result of an election that represented the will of the people – but by vesting the president with the Commander-in-Chief power, they also retained the connection between the legitimacy of the president's claim to govern with the ancient claim of rulers' willingness to fight in battle for those they ruled. Citizens associate all men with this attribute even though individual men may not choose to exercise it – akin to how people often associate all women with biological maternalism even though some women choose not to become mothers. Subsequently, voters are unlikely to connect women with the role of Commander-in-Chief.[19] Connecting the executive branch

---

[17] Paula A. Monopoli, *Gender and Constitutional Design*, 115 YALE L. J. 2643, 2643 (2006) (citations omitted).

[18] *Id.* at 2646–47 (citing Jennifer L. Lawless, *Women, War, and Winning Elections: Gender Stereotyping in the Post-September 11th Era*, 57 POL. RES. Q. 479, 482 (2004)).

[19] When John Kerry made his military service an essential credential for the presidency, some argued that he did damage to the possibility of a woman president. In fact, women are still excluded by military regulation from certain combat positions, reinforcing the idea that a woman cannot fulfill the role of Commander-in-Chief. *See* Martha McSally, *Women in Combat: Is the Current Policy Obsolete?*,

of government with aggression and physical courage – both particularly masculine attributes – associates the nature of the political leader in the United States with masculine norms and men, not with women and maternalism.

When we turn to democracies comparable to the United States, we find presidential systems that are much less marked by a unitary executive. Rather the executive branch of government is characterized by fragmentation, often including a split between a head of state and a head of government, as well as a greater connection with the legislative branch of government in the form of parliamentary association, if not control, of the executive branch. The legislative branch of government generally reflects ongoing relationships of service between elected officeholders and their constituents. Even with mediating features such as political parties, legislators are given the task of "representing" the policy interests of those who elect them to office. The relative frequency of legislative elections and the myriad of issues on which legislators are called upon to register their positions via explicit votes make it easy for their constituents and others to keep track of policy congruence between legislators and their constituents. In this respect, the legislative branch of government, with its focus on constituency service and the translation of constituency opinions into government decrees, is a more relational, coalition-building, interactive, and less hierarchical branch of government than the executive branch. Thus, the traits typifying the legislative branch correspond more with traits associated by voters with women's relational skills and propensities than with men's.

Tempering the masculine traits associated with the executive branch by the maternal traits associated with the legislative branch produces a hybrid set of government institutions that link both men and women to the public sphere of the state. Executive organization that connects executive authority to the legislative branch of government tempers the gendering of the executive as solely male in character. Most comparable democracies have an executive branch that is organized on the basis of its connection with Parliament. In addition, they fragment executive authority by distinctive designations of head of state versus head of government. This is unlike the United States' presidential system that concentrates executive authority by fusing the head of state with head of government.

When we turn to the democracies comparable to the United States in terms of their industrialization and wealth, we find that diffusion and fragmentation of the executive branch is the rule, not the exception. As noted earlier, more than half of these democracies have retained their monarchies. As a result, more than half can be designated as constitutional democracies that split the executive branch into a head of state, represented by the monarch, and a head of government, represented by a prime minister. In addition, with the exception of Switzerland and the United

14 Duke J. Gender L. & Pol'y 1011, 1014 (2007) (describing the still-in-force 1994 Department of Defense "ground combat exclusion policy" and the "collocation policy" restricting certain positions to male service members).

States, all other democracies in this group separate the offices of head of state and head of government. In most cases, the president is elected by popular vote and then appoints the prime minister, sometimes pending the approval of the legislative branch. In the case of Switzerland, there is no designated person who is head of state or head of the government, but rather the Federal Council serves to represent both offices. The United States exhibits the most concentration of authority in the executive branch because the head of state and head of government are fused into the office of the presidency with the attendant powers noted earlier. The result is an executive branch that is gendered as male without counterbalancing attributions that associate the traits voters attribute to women as constituent characteristics of the state.

3. The Scope of Executive Power

The system of checks and balances laid out in the U.S. Constitution is peculiarly masculine, with clashing branches in structured conflict with each other because of the manner by which each branch is constrained and held in check by the other branches. However, it is the executive branch that stands out as particularly emblematic of male traits. The more expansive the executive, the more masculine or agentic it becomes in the eyes of citizens. The framers' original vision of what constituted an effective executive revolves around executive activism, an issue that continues to engage scholars and political commentary to this very day. In *Federalist No. 70*, Alexander Hamilton described traditionally male attributes such as decisiveness, dispatch, and unilateral action as positive attributes in the executive. It is clear why the voters associate executive political leadership with men rather than with women, given the fundamental way the contemporary modern state in general and the executive branch in particular represent male traits, even in a democracy.[20]

a. Executive Activism and the Unitary Executive

The rise of executive activism in the United States illustrates the appeal of agentic or masculine behavior by executives at the local, state, and national levels. For example, growing attention has been directed to the "theory of the unitary executive," which "is a brief for the president to act as exclusive manager of all matters that fall within the purview of the instrumentalities of the executive branch."[21] As political scientist

---

[20] GENDER POWER, LEADERSHIP, AND GOVERNANCE (Georgia Duerst-Lahti & Rita Mae Kelly eds., 1996). For a definition of agentic traits see Alice H. Eagly & Steven J. Karau, "Role Congruity Theory of Prejudice Toward Female Leaders," 109 Psychol. Rev. 573 (2002). Eagly and Karau note that "...agentic characteristics, which are ascribed more strongly to men, describe primarily an assertive, controlling, and confident tendency – for example, aggressive, ambitious, dominant, forceful, independent, self-sufficient, self-confident, and prone to act as a leader." Id. At 474.

[21] Stephen Skowronek, *The Conservative Insurgency and Presidential Power: A Developmental Perspective on the Unitary Executive*, 122 HARV. L. REV. 2070, 2075 (2009).

Stephen Skowronek notes, the idea is to establish "an integrated and hierarchical administration – a unified executive branch – in which all officers performing executive business are subordinate to the president, accountable to his interpretations of their charge, and removable at his discretion."[22]

This idea can be traced back to the very founding of the American state when efforts were made to consolidate political power in the executive branch in general and in the office of the president in particular. As he notes, "[d]uring the Washington Administration, Alexander Hamilton ventured that when the framers of the Constitution vested 'the Executive Power' in the President, they were drawing on a well-established model of what those powers encompassed. It followed that the clauses of Article II should be read expansively in light of what the 'general theory and practice' of other nations at the time considered the executive's 'natural' domain, and that presidential powers are limited only narrowly by the qualifications stipulated in the rest of the document."[23]

Efforts to reinforce the power of the presidency continued with Jefferson, who "sought to extricate presidential strength from the constitutional text and anchor it instead in externalized expressions of public opinion. . . . For Jefferson, extraordinary assertions of presidential power could be justified as a collective act of popular will, a mandate from the people, a populist intervention."[24]

Skowronek also views the Jacksonian presidency as one focused on the goal of presidential power in which Jackson "set about mobilizing majorities on the electoral battlefield."[25] This trend continued with the Progressive Era, as exemplified by Theodore Roosevelt's stewardship theory of the presidency and his "larger conception of the presidency as a 'bully pulpit' for mobilizing the public."[26] Views of a unitary, powerful, autonomous executive in charge of an executive branch reinforce associations of the state with characteristics voters associate with men rather than with women.

b. Executive Activism and the Media

The media frequently associate executive activism with male traits. Consider, for example, the assertion that: "[Martin] O'Malley is a political stud."[27] Martin O'Malley, the young, charismatic Maryland governor, fits squarely within the widely held gender schema that holds that men are "assumed [by men and women] to be more assertive, ambitious, dominant, forceful, independent, self-sufficient, and

[22] *Id.* at 2077.
[23] *Id.* at 2078.
[24] *Id.* at 2080.
[25] *Id.* at 2081.
[26] *Id.* at 2084.
[27] See Matt Labash, *The Next Kennedy: Part 2*, DAILY STANDARD, July 27, 2002, *available at* www.weeklystandard.com/Content/Public/Articles/000/000/001/510andeo.asp (quoting former Governor Robert Ehrlich's spokesman Paul Shurick).

prone to act as leaders."[28] Gender schemas produce conscious or unconscious gender bias in selecting a candidate for or evaluating an incumbent favorably as a leader.[29] The current research also demonstrates that women who behave in a masculine way are viewed unfavorably and women who behave in a maternal way are viewed as not capable of assuming this supposed male role.[30] Women who wield or seek to wield power are perceived by the public in a very different way than men.[31]

Recent American executive activists, including George Bush, Martin O'Malley, Gavin Newsom, and Eliot Spitzer, have operated outside what some have argued are the appropriate power boundaries of mayors, attorney generals, governors, and presidents. Garnering extensive media coverage is now integral to electoral success for both state and national office.[32] The media often describes these executives in traditionally male archetypal terms, as warriors or cowboys.[33] This feedback mechanism reinforces the party and public's image of a successful executive as male. The media – always a powerful *de facto* institution of government in modern democracies – has become an even more significant political institution, pumping messages about the government and its policies into American homes twenty-four hours a day

[28] Marianne LaFrance, *The Schemas and Schemes in Sex Discrimination*, 65 BROOK. L. REV. 1063, 1067 (1999) (citing T. Eckes, *Explorations in Gender Cognition: Content and Structure of Female and Male Subtypes*, 12 SOC. COGNITION 37 (1994)).

[29] *See* VIRGINIA VALIAN, WHY SO SLOW: THE ADVANCEMENT OF WOMEN (1998).

> [I]mplicit, or nonconscious, hypotheses . . . [or] *gender schemas*, affect our expectations of men and women, our evaluations of their work, and their performance as professionals. . . . Their most important consequence for professional life is that men are consistently overrated, while women are underrated.

> *Id.* at 2.

[30] *See id.* at 134:

> [L]eaders are likely to be judged in terms of the fit between their sex and the conception of the job. If the job is characterized as masculine, men will be considered more effective leaders, but if the job is characterized as feminine, women will be perceived as better leaders.

> *Id.* at 134 (citing A. H. Eagly et al., *Gender and the Effectiveness of Leaders: A Meta-analysis*, 117 PERSONALITY & SOC. PSYCHOL. 125 (1995)).

[31] *See* KARIN KLENKE, WOMEN AND LEADERSHIP: A CONTEXTUAL PERSPECTIVE 154 (1996). She continues,

> [I]t has been shown that power is positively related to evaluations of leader effectiveness. . . . For example, subordinates may respond . . . to differences in power presumably held by male and female leaders. Therefore, power perspectives of gender and leadership may provide an important key to understanding why followers react differently to female and male leaders when exposed to similar leader behaviors.

> *Id.* (citing J. Trempe et al., *Subordinate Satisfaction with Male and Female Managers: Role of Perceived Supervisory Influence*, 70 J. APPLIED PSYCHOL. 44 (1985)).

[32] *See* Chris Nolan, *A Star is Born*, POLITICS FROM LEFT TO RIGHT, Feb. 17, 2004, www.chrisnolan. com/archives/000295.html ("This is the stuff that makes political careers: good timing, smart politics and . . . properly orchestrated grandstanding and intelligent media manipulation.").

[33] Some commentators argue that the public has always "responded well to macho behavior" on the part of politicians. *See* Alexander DeConde, *The History of Macho Presidents*, HIST. NEWS NETWORK, Sept. 16, 2002, *available at* http://hnn.us/articles/970.html.

on cable news channels. It is a powerful mechanism in terms of teaching citizens who is a suitable public leader.[34]

Thus, the design of the U.S. Constitution itself and the media have a feedback effect on who citizens view as an appropriate political leader. The idea embedded in the original design is that an expansive and agentic executive is the model that yields an energetic and effective executive. However, the norm in comparable democracies is a less agentic and more communal model that includes attributes such as consultation. Similarly, when we turn to a consideration of public policies, we see that in contrast to the American state, most comparable democracies have adopted public policies representing not only traits associated with men, but also traits associated with women.

III. GENDERED PUBLIC POLICIES

All democracies, if they are to be classified as such, at a minimum must guarantee that the government will treat all individuals the same "in spite of" their ascriptive group differences, such as their class, race, or sex, in the areas of civil and political rights. The civil rights to be married, to engage in business transactions, for example, and the political rights to vote and to run for office must be open to everyone in spite of their race, class, or sex. To the extent that the government adopts public policies that treat men and women the same, voters learn that women's sameness with men signifies women's inclusion in the public sphere along with men.

Even in democracies affirming women's sameness with men, however, voters continue to attribute a maternal group difference to women running for public office. For this reason, it becomes important for the state to adopt public policies that represent that maternal group difference. Voters then learn that women's sameness with men *and* women's maternal group difference from men *both* signify a location in the public sphere of the state.

A. *Individualism*

When we examine how public policies represent masculine traits, military spending and use of the death penalty are obvious choices. All democracies must adopt public policies that guarantee civil liberties and political rights on the basis of a principle of individual equality. However, there is a great deal of variation when we consider military spending and the affirmation of capital punishment as a permissible form of state action. In terms of military expenditures per capita, the United States not only spends more than other comparable democracies, but almost twice as

---

[34] See KLENKE, *supra* note 31, at 133. The importance of the media in constructing the social reality of leadership and shaping our perceptions and attitudes toward women leaders has been widely recognized by social scientists and media analysts. The media do not simply provide facts and information, but serve as socializing agents by giving meaning to events.

much: 4.06 percent of Gross Domestic Product (GDP) compared to the next highest spender, France, which spends 2.6 percent of its GDP on the military, as reported in Table 9.1.

In terms of the death penalty, the United States is radically more "masculine" than any other comparable democracy by virtue of the fact that it is the only one that permits the use of capital punishment. Other comparable democracies prohibit the use of capital punishment, and many established this prohibition decades, if not centuries, ago, such as Portugal (1867), the Netherlands (1870), Norway (1905), Sweden (1921), Iceland (1928), Denmark (1933), Switzerland (1942), Italy (1947), Finland (1949), Austria (1950), New Zealand (1961), United Kingdom (1973), Canada (1976), Spain (1978), and Luxembourg (1979). The United States, therefore, affirms masculine policies in the form of military expenditures and use of the death penalty in a much more extreme way than is characteristic of most comparable democracies.

B. *Maternalism*

We can define at least three public policies that represent maternalism: welfare provision, gender quotas, and hereditary monarchies.

1. Welfare Provision

State welfare provision refers to government assistance in meeting the dependency needs of people for food, housing, education, and health care. As researchers note, we can think of care work in terms of delivery systems that encompass the home, charitable organizations, the market, and the state. Initially, the site of care work is the home. It is here that infants, children, the elderly, the disabled, and others in need of care find their dependency requirements addressed, most often by women in their roles as wives, mothers, daughters, sisters, and so on. In more advanced industrial countries, market employment often becomes the mechanism for purchasing care work to meet dependency needs as a necessary supplement to the home and the state itself must step in as a delivery system that provides welfare for those in need.

2. Gender Quotas

When it comes to identifying public policies that represent a female sex classification as a definition of biological maternalism, we need look no further than gender quotas. Such quotas are public policies that give women an advantage when it comes to being elected to national legislatures solely because of their sex classification as female. Gender quotas as public policy assign to women's biological maternal group difference from men a political meaning that signifies a location within the state rather than outside the state. The study of gender quotas is becoming a subfield in its own right.[35] Included in the new scholarship is the symbolic impact of gender quotas.[36] This project draws upon that perspective, arguing that the adoption of gender quotas by a country entails adopting a gendered symbol that associates women's biological maternalistic difference from men with the state itself.

3. Hereditary Monarchies

In terms of biological maternalism, when a woman gives birth to a child, by definition, she generates a family. The mother and child dyad itself is a minimalist family, and in addition, by definition it requires a biological father. Both the biological mother and father by necessity had biological mothers and fathers, and so forth. Thus, there is no way to bear a child, without simultaneously extending family–kinship networks. The question becomes, What public policy represents biological motherhood in terms of the way biological maternalism generates the family? We contend that the answer is *hereditary monarchies*.

Hereditary monarchies fuse the family with the state. In so doing, hereditary monarchies represent women's biological motherhood as the vehicle by which the dynastic family, a foundation of the state, is created. When women of the dynastic family give birth, they are doing political work. Without their biological maternalism, there would be no dynastic family and no possibility of a hereditary monarchy in the first place. Hereditary monarchies are a form of government that gives a political character to women's biological maternalism. In hereditary monarchies, women's biological maternalism is not only the foundation of the home, society, or human life more generally conceived, but also the foundation of the state itself.

It is true, of course, that hereditary monarchies generally have been patriarchal in giving preference to men as sovereigns. However, that preference did not historically exclude women. To the contrary, more than 3,500 women over time have been sovereigns. Even in highly patriarchal hereditary systems, such as the Roman Empire, women nevertheless ruled as regents (akin to vice presidents) when a male sovereign was under age, disabled, absent, or otherwise incapacitated. Hence, preference for male sovereigns did not exclude women's access to political rule.

4. The Impact of Maternalism

In terms of the adoption of welfare provision, we can look to two indices: (1) the presence of constitutional guarantees that it is the affirmative duty of the state

[35] Drude Dahlerup, *Using Quotas to Increase Women's Political Representation, in* GENDER QUOTAS IN A COMPARATIVE PERSPECTIVE (ECPR Research Session Report, Sept. 2002); Mona Lena Krook, *Reforming Representation: The Diffusion of Candidate Gender Quotas Worldwide*, 2 POL. & GENDER 303 (2006).
[36] Pär Zetterberg, *Do Gender Quotas Foster Women's Political Engagement?*, POL. RES. Q. ONLINEFIRST (2008), http://prq.sagepub.com/cgi/content/abstract/1065912908322411v1.

to provide for welfare needs; and (2) levels of social spending, measured by the percentage of the funds contributed by the government to health care. Most comparable democracies do endorse welfare in terms of a constitutional affirmation of the state's responsibility for welfare provision. The United States is one of the few that does not, along with France, New Zealand, and Switzerland. Even countries that do not provide constitutional guarantees for welfare provision nevertheless fund welfare considerably more than the United States. The United States has the lowest percentage contributed by the government for health care and the federal government provides less than half the funds spent, 44.4 percent, as reported in Table 9.1. Even in France, where there is no constitutional guarantee for welfare provision, the government contributes 76 percent of the costs of health care. Most comparable democracies contribute considerably more than 50 percent. Thus, unlike the United States, most modify the way the state represents masculine traits by also adopting public policies that represent maternal traits in the form of constitutional guarantees and/or funding for welfare needs, such as health care.

In terms of gender quotas as public policies that represent biological maternalism, more than half the comparable democracies have adopted some form of gender quota. The United States, however, has not.[37] Hence, while many other democracies teach the public that females have a location in the public sphere of political governance, voters in the United States learn no such lesson from the state's public policies.

We can see the contrasts between the unadulterated masculinity of the American state in contrast to the way other democracies combine masculine and maternal traits in their political institutions and public policies by considering an example that comes from no further away than Canada. Not only is Canada a neighbor, but it is also similar to the United States in a variety of ways. Both countries are democracies that perform individualism by guaranteeing equal individual rights. Demographically, both countries are wealthy industrialized democracies with high literacy rates, large

---

[37] It is ironic that United States played such an important role in imposing parity quotas in the Iraqi Constitution since the idea of such requirements would arguably offend strongly held views against such quotas by many American voters. *See* Darren Rosenblum, *Parity/Disparity: Electoral Gender Inequality on the Tightrope of Liberal Constitutional Traditions*, 39 U.C. DAVIS L. REV. 1119, 1123–24 & 1124 n.17 (2006). As used in this chapter, the term "gender quotas" means a legislative quota more than 15 percent in lower or upper house or a voluntary political party quota of 30 percent or more in at least two parties or a voluntary political party quota of 40 percent or more in at least one party and the political party is represented in the legislature in 1999 and 2003. Data for gender quotas are from the Global Database of Quotas for Women, Institute for Democracy and Electoral Assistance (IDEA), Stockholm University and from Mona Lena Krook & Diana O'Brien, The Politics of Group Representation: Quotas for Women and Minorities Worldwide (unpublished manuscript) (presented at the Annual Meeting of the Midwest Political Sci. Ass'n (Apr. 12–15, 2007)), *available at* http://krook. wustl.edu/doc/Krook%20and%20OBrien%20MPSA%202007%204.doc. All women political parties are not included in this measure. South Africa is included in this measure. France is not included in this measure because its legislated principle of gender quotas, *parité*, is premised on the universality of human beings, not their sex difference, JOAN WALLACH SCOTT, PARITÉ!: SEXUAL EQUALITY AND THE CRISIS OF FRENCH UNIVERSALISM (2005).

percentages of women high school and college graduates, and significant numbers of women professionals. The similarities end, however, with maternalism, which Canada performs, but the United States does not. Canada performs all three modes of maternalism by means of gender quotas, welfare provision, and a hereditary monarchy. The New Democratic Party and the Liberal Party of Canada, two of the four main political parties, institute gender quotas. The state recognizes its affirmative duty to provide welfare, as expressed in the Canadian Constitution and carried out by substantial public funding. Additionally, Queen Elizabeth II is the hereditary monarchical head of state.

In these respects, Canada is more like Sweden than the United States. Canada also has a higher percentage of women in its legislature than does the United States and has elected a woman as Prime Minister, Kim Campbell, making it a country more like Germany and Norway than like its English-speaking neighbor. The Nordic countries are not unusual when it comes to the performance of maternalism and individualism. It is the norm. This norm correlates with women's access to executive and legislative political representation. The United States is the odd nation out as one of the few wealthy, urban democracies that represents exclusively masculine traits in its public policies rather than a hybrid combination of masculine and maternal traits.[38]

CONCLUSION

The solution to the puzzle as to why the United States is such an outlier when it comes to electing women to political office, vis-à-vis comparable democracies, is threefold. First, beginning with its very founding, it associates the state with the violent destruction of the ideological and institutional legitimacy of a maternally defined form of government, an indigenous hereditary monarchy. Second, the United States is marked by the adoption of an expansive executive model that valorizes masculine attributes. It has a constitution that links the presidency with the Commander-in-Chief function. This combination teaches voters that women are not suited to the presidency and in fact cannot carry out many of the functions, given public policy. Third, while most democracies similar to America have adopted one, if not more, public policies representing maternal traits, the United States has adopted none. The United States is in that sense a "motherless," lopsided country, which guarantees only that the government will treat people the same in spite of

---

[38] The United States, of course, does provide some welfare provision by means of policies such as Social Security, Medicare, and Medicaid. However, the scope and level of funding of the latter two fail to measure up to the health care provisions of most comparable democracies, and Social Security is tied to employment patterns, thereby making it an insurance policy more than one designed to meet the dependency needs of targeted populations. Most analysts concur that, with the exception of the Progressive Era decades in the early twentieth century, the United States notably lacks the welfare policies characterizing most comparable democracies.

their ascriptive group differences, such as race, class, or sex, without the orthogonal complement that the state will also guarantee to groups positive rights representing maternal traits. Thus, both how the state is constructed and what it does combine to produce an exclusively masculine political context. Such an environment teaches citizens that the maternal attributes associated with women signify *only* a location in the private sphere of the home, and not in the home *and* the public sphere of the state. The result is a laggard American state when it comes to the status of women's political leadership.

10

On Parity, Interdependence, and Women's Democracy

Blanca Rodríguez-Ruiz and Ruth Rubio-Marín

Women's low presence in political representative bodies has become a common concern in present-day democracies.[1] It raises doubts as to how effectively democracies are capable of implementing women's political rights on an equal footing with men's and arouses concerns about women's substantive equality with men more generally. Furthermore, women's low presence in political representative bodies raises questions as to women's status as citizens, and consequently as to the state of health of citizenship in democratic systems. At the same time, however, legal measures designed to increase women's presence in representative bodies are problematic both from the perspective of rights and equality and from the perspective of citizenship in representative democracies. Some of these measures, and those that we will focus on, consist of legally sanctioned representation quotas for women or of legally sanctioned gender parity in representative bodies.[2] Both raise a variety of constitutional issues. These issues can be confronted as issues of constitutional rights or as issues of citizenship and democratic representation. Most often, constitutional reasoning regarding legally sanctioned quotas or parity in political representation has centered on a debate focusing on the right to equality, about whether the political sphere allows for substantive equality and, if so, what implications this has. Questions concerning the right to vote and stand for elections have also been raised in connection with equality, as have questions concerning the autonomy of political parties. Parallel to this situation, legally sanctioned quotas or parity in political representation have also raised questions from the perspective of citizenship and

---

[1] Only 18.5 percent of all members of parliaments, combining upper and lower houses, are women. The Inter-parliamentary Union (IPU) has gathered data provided by national parliaments since September 2009. The data are available at the IPU's website, www.ipu.org (last visited Oct. 8, 2009).

[2] We distinguish parity measures – understood as measures to achieve an even, balanced, or comparable presence of both sexes (for example, approximately proportionate to the gender distribution in the population) – from quota measures that seek to guarantee a minimum presence of women in representative bodies (e.g., a minimum of 25 or 30 percent).

democratic theory, notably whether they are inconsistent or compatible with, or actually required by, the constitutionally sanctioned system of general and unitary representation that underlies political representation in modern states.

In this chapter we examine the range of possible constitutional approaches to legally imposed gender parity and gender electoral quotas and analyze their constitutional implications. We first discuss the rights perspective approaches, to argue then that the proper discussion should be much more about the requirements of citizenship in a representative democracy. We will analyze these discussions relying on some of the most recent cases brought concerning such types of measures in several countries, including France, Italy, Switzerland, Colombia and, most recently, Spain. Finally, we take the position and defend that gender political quotas can best be justified under a distinct parity democracy model.

I. THE RIGHTS MODEL

Constitutional reasoning that centers on the notion of formal equality is incompatible with either quotas or parity insofar as it aspires to a legal system that does not draw distinctions based on suspect criteria, including sex. The right to formal equality in political representation is commonly defended along with the traditional model of democratic elected representation. Indeed, in the political domain, the right to formal equality and the right to vote appear as defining elements of a representation model in which every citizen has one, and only one, vote and can freely choose among citizens who freely and equally enjoy their right to run for office without constraints of any sort. This general, abstract, unitary, and procedural model of representation is, in brief, not easy to reconcile with either electoral quotas or parity.

An eloquent implementation of the idea that formal equality should prevail in political representation, as part and parcel of the general, unitary model of representation, is the decision of the French *Conseil Constitutionnel* on gender quotas from 1982.[3] In this decision, the *Conseil* was for the first time confronted with the constitutionality of mandatory electoral gender quotas. After a decade of discussions in France, and after the French Socialist Party had adopted the first voluntary gender quotas in the 1970s, Parliament passed an act in 1982 that obliged electoral ballots in municipal elections to have at least 25 percent of candidates be of each gender.[4]

---

3 *See Conseil Constitutionnel* [CC] [Constitutional Court] decision No. 82–146DC, Nov. 18, 1982, J.O. 3475 (Fr.). For a thorough discussion of the French debate, see Blanca Rodríguez-Ruiz & Ruth Rubio-Marín, *The Gender of Representation: On Democracy, Equality, and Parity*, 6 INT'L J. CONST. L. 287, 287–93 (2008).

4 Loi modifiant le code électoral et le code des communes et relative à l'élection des conseillers municipaux et aux conditions d'inscription des Français établis hors de France sur les listes électorales [Act Amending the Electoral Code and the Code of Municipalities Concerning the Election of Municipal Councillors and the Conditions for Inclusion in Electoral Registers of French Nationals Residing outside France], Law No. 82–974 of Nov. 19, 1982, Journal Officiel de la République Française [J.O.] [Official Gazette of France], Nov. 20, 1982, p. 3487.

Sixty delegates from the opposition challenged the act before the *Conseil Constitu-tionnel*, which declared the law unconstitutional. Faithful to the universalist notion of citizenship prevalent in France, the *Conseil* held that the principles of equality before the law, of national sovereignty, and the indivisibility of the electoral body, recognized in the French Constitution[5] and in the Declaration of the Rights of Man and the Citizen of 1789,[6] all preclude any person or group from claiming the exclusive exercise of national sovereignty and that they confer on every citizen an equal right to vote and to stand for elections, without any qualifications or exceptions, other than those that may stem from such conditions as age or incapacity.[7]

The Italian Constitutional Court reached a similar conclusion in 1995 in the context of a constitutional challenge brought against two laws, Law No. 81/1993 and Law No. 277/1993.[8] Law No. 81/1993, regulating local and provincial elections, stipulated that neither gender could have a presence of less than 25 percent on lists in municipalities of up to 15,000 inhabitants, and not less than 33 percent in those of more than 15,000. Similarly, Law No. 277/1993, regulating elections to Congress, provided that the political parties must present electoral ballots in alternating gender order ("zipper list") for elections to seats subject to the proportional system (i.e., for 25 percent of seats). To be sure, the Italian Constitution does enshrine a substantive approach to the principle of equality in Article 3.2,[9] yet this provision was not found to support the adoption of affirmative action measures in the political field.[10]

---

[5] Article 3 of the French Constitution from 1958 reads (our translation),

> [1] *National sovereignty resides in the people, who exercise it through their representatives and by means of referendum.* [2] *No one sector of the people or single individual shall claim its exercise.* [3] *Suffrage may be direct or indirect in the conditions set forth by the Constitution, and shall always be universal, equal and confidential.* [4] *According to the law, electors are all French nationals of both sexes, who are of age and enjoy full exercise of their civil and political rights.*

[6] Article 6 of the Declaration of the Rights of Man and the Citizen of 1789 reads (our translation),

> *The law is the expression of general will. All citizens have the right to contribute to its making, either personally or through their representatives. As all citizens are equal before the law, they are likewise all equally eligible for any public office, position or employment, according to their abilities and with no distinction other than their virtues and talents.*

[7] Based on this 1982 decision, in 1999 the *Conseil Constitutionnel* also invalidated the law regulating elections to the Corsican Assembly, which would have introduced strict parity on electoral ballots. *See* CC decision no. 98–408DC, Jan. 20, 1999, J.O. 1028 (Fr.).

[8] Corte cost., n. 422/1995, Foro It. For a thorough discussion of the Italian debate, see Rodriguez-Ruiz & Rubio-Marín, *supra* note 3, at 294–96.

[9] According to Article 3.2, "It is the duty of the republic to remove all economic and social obstacles that, by limiting the freedom and equality of citizens, prevent full individual development and the participation of all workers in the political, economic, and social organization of the country" (our translation). Note that Article 3.2 only refers to *economic and social* obstacles, not to obstacles *in general*, which would include obstacles of a normative kind, as we will see is the case in Article 9.2 of the Spanish Constitution. Unlike this article, moreover, the Italian provision refers to the duty of the republic to *remove* obstacles for political participation, but not to *promote* the conditions for real and effective equality.

[10] Corte cost., n. 422/1995 (Italy).

This interpretation of strict formal equality in the political domain was also behind the decision of the Swiss Federal Supreme Court to strike down a popular initiative to pass a law reserving men and women an equal number of seats in all elected offices in the legislative, executive, and judicial branches in the canton of Solothurn. More precisely, the idea was to have all positions earmarked for the underrepresented sex until men and women would achieve a representation that mirrored their proportion in the canton's population (i.e., 50.74 percent for women).[11] The court found that the legislation violated the prohibition of discrimination between men and women.[12] Citing its French and Italian counterparts the Swiss Court reasoned that to the extent that the measure involved authorities directly elected by the people, it violated the equal right to vote and be voted. The principle of general, free, and equal voting rights, said the court, is an absolute principle, subject only to distinctions and limitations necessary to organize the electoral system.[13] Sex differentiations could never be a valid differentiation criterion.[14]

The way to electoral gender quotas in Italy and gender parity in France, though not in Switzerland, was opened through constitutional amendments that explicitly introduced the logic of substantive equality in the political field. In 1999, the French Constitution was amended to allow for affirmative action seeking gender equality in political representation.[15] After this constitutional amendment, the Law on Equal Access of Women and Men to Elective Offices and Functions was enacted on June 6, 2000, to introduce gender parity in political representation.[16] The law was challenged before the *Conseil Constitutionnel*. Yet this time the *Conseil* upheld its constitutionality on the basis of the constitutional amendment, which, the *Conseil* stated, nuanced the principle of indivisibility of the electorate, inasmuch as it introduced

[11] *See* Bundesgericht [BGer] [Federal Court] Mar. 19, 1997, 123 Entscheidungen des Schweizerischen Bundesgerichts [BGE] I 152 (Switz.).

[12] At the time Art.4.Abs.2. 1BV (see BGE 123 I 152 S. 157) (Switz.).

[13] BGE 123 I 152 S. 173.

[14] BGE 123 I 152 S. 174.

[15] The Constitutional Law No. 99–569 of July 8, 1999, introduced a fourth paragraph in Article 3 of the French Constitution, whereby "the law shall favour equality among women and men to have access to electoral mandates and hold elective office." It also amended Article 4 so as to provide that political parties "shall contribute to the application of the principle set forth in the last section of Article 3 in accordance with the provisions of the law." *See* Law No. 99–569 of July 8, 1999, J.O., July 9, 1999, p. 10175.

[16] Law No. 2000–493 of June 6, 2000, J.O., June 7, 2000, p. 8560. This law required, under penalty of disqualification, that all parties in elections employing lists include 50 percent of candidates of each gender (± 1) on their ballots. This included elections to municipal office (in towns of fewer than 3,500 inhabitants), regional office, the Corsican Assembly, the Senate (in those cases where the system of proportional representation applied), and the European Parliament. For legislative elections based on the system of single-member districts, the law stipulated a penalty in public financing proportionate to the degree of noncompliance for any party that failed to include an equal number of candidates of each gender (allowing for a 2 percent margin of error). The system established by this law has recently been perfected. *See* Law No. 2007–128 of Jan. 31, 2007, J.O., Jan. 31, 2007, p. 1941 ("tendant à promouvoir l'égal accès des femmes et des hommes aux mandats électoraux et fonctions électives" [to promote equality between women and men regarding access to electoral positions and functions]).

a substantive understanding of the principle of equality and allowed for affirmative action to afford men and women equal access to representative positions.[17]

Also in Italy, constitutional amendments were introduced to move from a formal toward a substantive understanding of equality in the political domain.[18] As in France, these amendments provoked a change in the attitude of the Constitutional Court toward mandatory electoral gender quotas, a change that occurred, interestingly enough, even before Constitutional Law No. 1/2003 went into effect. Thus when the government challenged the constitutionality of Valle d'Aosta Law No. 21/2003, which required that ballots for Regional Council elections include candidates of both genders, the Italian Constitutional Court rejected the challenge.[19]

Supporters of quotas mostly rely on this notion of substantive equality, whereby the constitutional principle of equality is not conceived as ensuring a neutral legal system, but as grounding the state's duty to remove obstacles so that people can actually and equally enjoy the rights and freedoms formally granted to them. This can be done either by ensuring equality of opportunities in the starting position or, at least to some degree, by guaranteeing equality of results.[20] Applied to the political domain, substantive equality implies the state's duty to ensure that all, in our case men and women, have similar opportunities to access political power and not just the same formal right to run for office.

This was also the approach the Colombian Constitutional Court took to gender quotas in its March 2000 decision, on an automatic review of constitutionality of a bill on gender quotas passed by the Colombian Congress in June 1999.[21] The piece of legislation was designed to implement the requirement of Article 40 of the Colombian Constitution that "the authorities will guarantee the adequate and effective participation of women at the decision-making levels of Public Administration."[22]

---

[17] CC decision no. 2000–429DC, May 30, 2000, J.O. 8564 (Fr.).

[18] Constitutional Law No. 2/2001 provided that electoral laws in regions with a special autonomy statute must promote electoral gender parity. Constitutional Law No. 3/2001 added the following seventh paragraph to Article 117 of the Constitution: "Regional laws shall suppress any hindrance of full equality between men and women in social, cultural, and economic life and shall promote parity of access to elective office between men and women." Finally, Constitutional Law No. 1/2003 added a second sentence to Article 51.1, which now reads, "Citizens of one or the other sex are eligible for public office and for elective positions under equal conditions, according to the rules established by law. To such ends, the Republic shall use special measures to promote equal opportunities among men and women" (our translation).

[19] Corte cost., Decision No. 49/2003.

[20] As has been noted, "If the discussion of substantive equality is to be taken seriously, it is impossible to fully rule out that some variants of equality... may be based on measures in some way geared toward... the outcome." Antonio D'Aloia, *Le "quote" electtorali in favore delle donne*, in LA PARITÀ DEI SESSI NELLA RAPPRESENTANZA POLITICA 51, 60 (our translation). In this line, Article 23 of the Charter of Fundamental Rights of the European Union allows for the possibility of adopting "*measures providing for specific advantages* in favor of the underrepresented sex" – this is so of course as long as the measures are reasonably justified. *See* 2007 O.J. (C 303) 7 (emphasis added), *available at* http://eur-lex.europa.eu/RECH_reference_pub.do (search by citation).

[21] Corte const., Mar. 29, 2000, Sentencia C-371/00 (Colom.).

[22] *Id.*

To this end, it established a 30 percent quota for women in high-level, decision-making positions in the public sector. These provisions were examined and found, for the most part, constitutional as temporary affirmative action measures compatible with the notion of substantive equality, as sanctioned in Article 13.2 of the Colombian Constitution,[23] and based on a proportionality test analysis that requires quotas to pursue a legitimate aim through means that are effective, necessary, and proportionate. The court, however, distinguished between executive appointments and elected positions and ruled out the possibility of mandatory electoral quotas on the grounds that the autonomy of political parties prevailed in the electoral field.

Like the Colombian Constitutional Court, the Swiss Federal Supreme Court interpreted the Swiss Constitution as already enshrining substantive equality, but said that women's substantive political equality could not be achieved through illegitimate means or through means disproportionate to the purported aim. Earmarking elected positions for the underrepresented sex was unconstitutional because it established equality of results and not just of opportunities.[24] Nor could the measure be considered necessary, because women's chances to get elected had naturally and gradually increased since the early 1990s and there were less intrusive mechanisms to enhance women's representation (including continuing education programs, increasing options for part-time employment, or number of crèches and school facilities for children).[25] Finally, the measure was considered disproportionate because the strict nature of the quota precluded men's access to certain governmental, legislative, and judicial positions regardless of qualifications.[26]

Little more than a year later, the court had the opportunity to fine-tune the types of affirmative action measures that could be validly adopted to enhance women's presence in political bodies under the substantive equality logic.[27] At stake this time was the initiative in Uri canton to amend the canton's constitution. The court insisted that freedom and equality in voting constitute fundamental principles in a democratic state that, it added, can only be limited for compelling reasons. Interestingly, protecting regional or linguistic minorities counted as one such compelling reason, whereas electoral gender quotas were considered incompatible with free and equal voting.[28] Specifically, the court declared unconstitutional a proposal that in elections following a majority system and seeking to appoint two candidates, one candidate would have to be male and another female.

---

[23] "The state will promote the conditions necessary in order that equality may be real and effective and will adopt measures in favor of groups which are discriminated against or marginalized" CONSTITUCIÓN POLÍTICA DE COLOMBIA [C.P.] art. 13.2 (our translation).

[24] BGE 123 I 152 S. 165 (Switz.).

[25] BGE 123 I 152 S. 167 & 168.

[26] BGE 123 I 152 S. 170–71.

[27] Bundesgericht [BGer] Oct. 7, 1998, 125 Entscheidungen des Schweizerischen Bundesgerichts [BGE] I 21 (Switz.).

[28] 125 I 21 S. 33 *in* BGer Oct. 7, 1998, 125 BGE I 21.

The initiative also included a provision whereby "approximately half" but "at least one third" of members of public boards and institutions elected by the people must be women. The court held this provision unconstitutional,[29] except when referring to political offices elected not by the people but by the canton's legislature as, the court argued, the right to vote only covers citizens' direct input on the formation of the political will.[30] This is so, moreover, as it was a temporary and limited compensatory measure: an obligation of results was imposed only by a one-third quota, which allowed the principle of merit and qualification to prevail for the most part.[31]

Another proposed amendment concerned local elections for the Uri regional parliament in councils that relied on proportional representation. It ruled that the difference between male and female candidates included in electoral lists (generally three or more candidates) could not be more than one. The court found this provision constitutional, arguing that it did not automatically privilege women over men, especially as the system relied on open ballots, but simply enhanced women's opportunities to get elected.[32] The aim of enhancing women's chances to get elected, the court argued, justified a (small) limitation of the principle of voting equality and the freedom of parties to nominate their candidates.[33]

The logic of substantive equality was also controlling in the January 2008 decision of the Spanish Constitutional Court upholding mandatory electoral gender quotas.[34] The Spanish Organic Law 3/2007 on the Effective Equality of Women and Men[35] introduced mandatory gender quotas on electoral ballots, whereby these must include not less than 40 percent of candidates from each gender. It introduced, in other words, what we could call a system of gender parity with a margin of flexibility, as it relies on minimum presence percentages for each sex, like the quota system, but endorses percentages that come very close to 50 percent. The Spanish Constitutional Court faced the constitutionality of this law as a result of a double challenge. One was put forward by a judge who confronted the ironic question of whether the invalidation of two electoral lists of the conservative *Partido Popular* (Popular Party) containing more than 60 percent female candidates was in conformity with the Constitution. The other was an abstract challenge brought forward

[29] 125 I 21 S. 33.

[30] 125 I 21 S. 37.

[31] *Id.*

[32] 125 I 21 S. 39.

[33] 125 I 21 S. 40. Interestingly, none of the proposed measures were adopted. The proposal was submitted to popular referendum in Uri and defeated by 84 percent of the popular vote on June 13, 1999. *See* Anne Peters & Stefan Suter, *Representation, Discrimination, and Democracy: A Legal Assessment of Gender Quotas in Politics, in* GENDER EQUALITY: DIMENSIONS OF WOMEN'S EQUAL CITIZENSHIP 175 (Linda C. McClain & Joanna L. Grossman eds., Cambridge University Press 2009).

[34] *See* S.T.C., Jan. 29, 2008 (S.T.C., No. 12/2008) (Spain).

[35] Ley orgánica para la igualdad efectiva entre mujeres y hombres (B.O.E. 2007, 71). Organic Laws are laws the approval, modification, or repeal of which require an absolute majority of the House of Representatives in a final vote on the entire bill. The Spanish Constitution requires that some matters, including some fundamental rights such as political rights, be regulated by Organic Law.

by fifty conservative Congressmen. In a nutshell, the plaintiffs questioned whether the law contradicted the equality principle[36] in relation to the right to participate in public affairs,[37] the freedom of association[38] in the context of political parties,[39] including their right to self-organization and their ideological freedom,[40] and free speech.[41] More generally, the plaintiffs also questioned whether the law contradicted the principle of the unitary sovereignty of the Spanish nation.[42] The Constitutional Court upheld the constitutionality of this provision, based mostly on a substantive approach to the constitutional principle of equality as enshrined in Article 9.2[43] and on the related possibility of adopting affirmative action measures in the political domain (a possibility that Article 9.2 explicitly contemplates).

The challenged provisions, said the court, do not compromise citizens' right to vote and stand for elections because citizens have no right to be included in electoral lists, or to have specific candidates included in them. Nor do they compromise the freedom of ideology and of expression of political parties. Parties are not required to share the values that underlie parity democracy; they can even pursue a change in the electoral laws on gender parity. What gender parity does restrict is the autonomy of political parties. Yet, the court notes, their autonomy is subject to limitations imposed by the Constitution and laws. It can be and already is modulated by the legislature in manifold ways, as when it sets out nationality, age, or residency requirements for valid candidatures or as when it opts for a system of closed and blocked lists. In this case, the legislator has decided to restrict this autonomy to assert substantive equality in the political field. The court then concluded that this restriction passed a test of proportionality, as it pursued a legitimate aim (effective gender equality) and is proportionate to that aim.

In his dissenting judgment, Justice Rodríguez Zapata expressed the skeptical view about the reach of the principle of substantive equality to limit the well-established notions of unitary representation. Linking substantive equality to the adoption of affirmative action measures, it raised a series of questions, many of which resonate with the Swiss Court's decision, such as these: Why is affirmative action implemented only with respect to sex and not other politically marginalized groups? Why are temporary measures not sufficient? Why is gender parity strictly

---

[36] CONSTITUCIÓN ESPAÑOLA (C.E.) art. 14.

[37] *Id.* art. 23.

[38] *Id.* art. 22.

[39] *Id.* art 6.

[40] *Id.* art. 16.

[41] *Id.* art. 20.

[42] *Id.* art. 1.2.

[43] "It is the responsibility of the public authorities to promote conditions ensuring that freedom and equality of individuals and of the groups to which they belong are real and effective, to remove the obstacles preventing or hindering their full enjoyment, and to facilitate the participation of all citizens in political, economic, cultural and social life." *Id.* art. 9.2, *available at* www.lamoncloa.ed/IDIOMAS/9/Espana/ElEstado/LeyFundamental/titulo_preliminar.htm.

necessary, there being other measures that could also enhance women's equality, hence their opportunities in the public domain? The dissent pointed to measures that allow women to reconcile work and motherhood, and that combat gender violence, sexual harassment, or any form of discrimination at work, in the media, or in the educational system. Moreover, political parties can ensure the inclusion of women in their lists and could possibly be encouraged to do so, for example, through financial aid from public authorities in proportion to the percentage of women on their ballots. In the end, how can a bidirectional rule that could in some instances have restrictive effects on women in some lists qualify as an affirmative action measure in favor of women's effective equality with men?

In sum, electoral gender quotas and parity are inadmissible under a formal understanding of the equality principle, while they may well be, and indeed often are, justified under a substantive equality model as a type of affirmative action measure. This is so at least until women can be said truly to enjoy equal opportunities to access representative positions. Under a substantive equality model, however, it may be difficult to explain why only women and no other politically underrepresented groups (such as ethnic, religious, or other minorities) should not enjoy similar quotas. Also under the substantive equality logic, measures that enhance opportunities might be easier to justify than those that guarantee certain results. Similarly, temporary measures can be better justified than measures that are open-ended in time. Although the goal of enhancing opportunities might justify quotas that ensure a minimum representation threshold for women (25 to 30 percent), it is not clear why parity measures (i.e., quotas that apply to both sexes and that set the threshold at 50 percent or something close to it) would pass a proportionality test. It would be hard, though not impossible, to argue that nothing short of a guaranteed representation of women that is strictly proportional to the female population is needed to remove whatever systemic obstacles there may be for women to run for office. Moreover, on the basis of substantive equality and the logic of affirmative action it would be difficult to justify that parity measures apply not only to women, but also to men. In the end, embracing the logic of affirmative action/substantive equality to support electoral gender quotas or parity is at odds with the unitary representation model and the notion of electoral formal equality that it represents.

II. FROM RIGHTS TO DEMOCRATIC REPRESENTATION

Democratic representation models move us away from the logic of rights and of substantive equality and into the requirements of citizenship in a representative democracy. This, we argue, is a necessary move if we wish to understand the significance and constitutional implications, both of women's low presence in political representative bodies and of the constitutional questions that legal measures aimed at correcting this state of affairs continue to raise. Indeed, in order to be fully able to account for what has happened in countries where either gender parity or some form of gender (but no other marginalized groups) quota has been established – such as France, Italy, or Spain – one has to move beyond both the rights discourse and address questions concerning the contours of our representative democracy.

As noted earlier, the traditional representation model, the model of unitary general representation that came hand in hand with the liberal state inaugurated with the French Revolution, is antithetical to both parity and any conceivable form of quotas that would defy the notion of a unitary electoral body (conceived as abstract citizens coming together to exercise their individual right to suffrage). This model subscribes to the prevalence of formal equality in the electoral field and has been appealed to in order to support and supplement the argument that electoral gender quotas and/or parity go against electoral rights, including electoral equality understood as formal equality, and against the autonomy of political parties. By the same token, gender quotas and/or parity defy the traditional, liberal model of unitary general representation, as they question the notion of both abstract citizens and abstract representatives, on which basis individuals are regarded equally well represented by any elected body of representatives, regardless of who is in them. In particular, gender quotas and/or parity suggest that elected bodies integrated mostly by male representatives do not adequately represent a citizenry composed of men and women in roughly equal numbers, as they cannot represent women as well as they do men. Justified on the grounds of substantive equality, electoral gender quotas and/or parity set to correct the differences in political representation between women and men. However, in as far as a particular constitution enshrines, or is read as enshrining, a model of unitary representation, mandatory electoral gender quotas and/or parity based on a substantive reading of the principle of equality in the electoral field face unconstitutionality challenges. By the same token, constitutional provisions that allow for electoral gender quotas and/or parity as forms of affirmative action are in tension with, indeed they come to qualify, the logic of unitary representation.

Substantive equality, in sum, does not suffice to justify electoral gender quotas and/or parity, both for reasons pertaining to the logic of affirmative action, as discussed in the previous section, and because of the limits imposed by the logic of unitary general representation. A full-blown justification must be couched within a model of representative democracy that allows for or even requires electoral gender quotas and/or parity. The need for such a model has not been sufficiently acknowledged in constitutional decisions on the matter. The French decision from 2006 approached the question, as we have seen, from a rights perspective. To be sure, the *Conseil Constitutionnel* noted that sex is a unique differentiation criterion because it cuts across all others; but it provided no clue about where the political relevance of such a fact specifically lies.[44]

[44] *See supra* note 17 and accompanying text.

In a similar vein, the decision of the Colombian Constitutional Court from 2000[45] opens with a series of considerations on the type of democratic system constitutionally entrenched. The court observes that, as stated in Article 1 of the Constitution,[46] Colombia is a unitary, participatory, and pluralist democratic republic. It goes on to recall that nowadays a democracy that tolerates the marginalization and the clear underrepresentation of half of its citizenry is no longer conceivable. "Participation in politics means that people as human beings are bound to decide and can't and ought not to delegate the decisions that affect them. Doing so would mean accepting their objectification, hence their dehumanization."[47] Furthermore, Article 2.1[48] emphasizes, among the goals of the state, the need to facilitate the participation of all in the decisions that affect them and the corresponding duty of the state to remove whatever obstacles hinder women's full participation in the democratic life of the country. As a result of the pluralist nature of the constitutionally sanctioned democratic model, and because men and women are both biologically and functionally different, "political decisions adopted without taking account of women's perspective, a perspective that is conditioned by manifold biological and sociological specificities, would be biased and partial and hence, contrary to the general will that embodies the common interest."[49]

Despite these opening considerations, however, the court declared electoral gender quotas unconstitutional, as against the autonomy of political parties and the principle of popular sovereignty. This is so, even though the statistics presented to the court show that between 1991 and 2000, the proportion of women never surpassed 13.42 percent in the Senate and 12.7 percent in the Chamber of Representatives,[50] and despite the court's opening considerations on the requirements of a participatory and pluralist democratic model. In the end, furthermore, the court for the most part upheld the quota system in appointed public positions, not for reasons pertaining to the democratic system, but based on substantive equality and on a proportionality test analysis.

Also the decision of the Spanish Constitutional Court from 2008[51] introduced considerations on gender parity that go beyond the rights perspective and pertain to

---

[45] See *supra* note 21 and accompanying text.
[46] "Colombia is a legal social state organized in the form of a unitary republic, decentralized, with the autonomy of its territorial units, democratic, participatory and pluralistic, based on respect of human dignity, on the work and solidarity of the individuals who belong to it, and the predominance of the general interest." C.P. art. 1 (our translation).
[47] See *supra* note 21.
[48] "The essential goals of the state are to serve the community, promote general prosperity, and guarantee the effectiveness of the principles, rights, and duties stipulated in the Constitution; to facilitate the participation of all in the decisions that affect them and in the economic, political, administrative, mid cultural life of the nation; to defend national independence, maintain territorial integrity, and ensure peaceful coexistence and the enforcement of a just order." C.P. art. 2.1 (our translation).
[49] See *supra* note 21.
[50] Id.
[51] See *supra* note 34 and accompanying text.

democratic theory. This court departed from the notion that the provisions under examination are not affirmative action measures that rely on a majority/minority logic and aim to favor an underrepresented minority. Rather, they are measures that account for the uniqueness of sex as a differentiation criterion and introduce equality in political representation through bidirectional mechanisms that favor neither men nor women, but that seek a balanced presence of both in electoral lists. Soon after these considerations, however, the court turned to the substantive understanding of equality enshrined in Article 9.2 of the Spanish Constitution to make it the touchstone of its decision. Nevertheless, the court continued to draw on considerations of democratic representation, as substantive equality revealed itself insufficient to justify parity democracy – an insufficiency discussed by the dissenting opinion. The dissenting opinion reasoned that the Constitution enshrines a unitary elected representation model and considers mandatory gender parity a departure from this model that would require a constitutional amendment. Without such an amendment, it argued, mandatory gender parity violates the right to equality in relation to the right to stand for elections, recognized in Articles 14 and 23 of the Spanish Constitution.[52]

In the end, all these decisions appear as missed opportunities to tease out and address the questions of democratic representation raised by electoral gender quotas or parity. As long as these questions remain unaddressed, justifications based on the logic of rights, namely on the logic of substantive equality and affirmative action, will remain open to criticisms of the kind raised by the Swiss decisions or by the dissenting opinion to the decision of the Spanish Constitutional Court.

III. PARITY DEMOCRACY MODEL: A PROPOSAL

This brings us to the model of parity democracy that we propound in this chapter. Under the logic of this model, both the distinctive treatment of gender as a category in the electoral field and the different logics underlying quotas and parity become clear. The parity democracy model sustains that democracy strictly interpreted cannot be anything other than parity democracy. To understand the logic behind this conclusion, this model takes us back to the origins of the state and representative democracy and to the ideology of the social contract and of the sexual contract on which this rests.[53] It is this social–sexual contract that draws the modern boundary between the public and the private terrain as respectively masculine and feminine – both symbolically and functionally. The parity democracy model rests

---

[52] "Spaniards are equal before the law and may not in any way be discriminated against on account of birth, race, sex, religion, opinion, or any other personal or social condition or circumstance." C.E. art. 14. "1. Citizens have the right to participate in public affairs, directly or through their representatives freely elected in periodic elections by universal suffrage. 2. They likewise have the right to access on equal terms to public office, in accordance with the requirements to be provided by law." C.E. art. 23.

[53] *See generally* CAROLE PATEMAN, THE SEXUAL CONTRACT (1988).

on the realization that the gendered identification of these two areas is neither circumstantial nor a mere oversight, but rather that the disqualification of women as active citizens – as members of the public sphere – is a structural feature of the modern state. This is so because the social contract reflects the liberal view of the subject as an autonomous being defining his own life project, a view upheld by the modern myth of the independence of the individual.

This picture of the individual leaves no room for dependency, nor does it reconcile personal autonomy and taking on the responsibility of dependency – both one's own and that of others. Dependency is not seen as a defining aspect of the person, but as an external enemy against which man, naturally free, must defend himself.[54] Thus conceived, independence becomes an essential attribute of the individual in the modern interpretation thereof, an attribute that the liberal state erects as a prerequisite for access to the public sphere and active citizenship, and that the democratic state presumes in theory and aspires to in practice. The problem is that, because independence is a myth, the state can only assume the individual to be independent if it goes to the effort of removing all manifestations of individual dependency. Such a construct was possible to the extent that the individual was conceived as male, whereas women were cast out of that concept and of the ideal of independence and assigned the tasks associated with man's dependency. In performing these tasks, women enabled men's physical, social, and cultural survival, allowing the ideal of men as independent citizens and actors in the public sphere to work in practice. Men thus achieved an appearance of independence by shifting toward women, in a pact of fraternity,[55] the weight of their own dependency. As a foundational myth of the state, the social–sexual contract thus constructs the public sphere as a space for the interaction of citizens, conceptualized as independent individuals and as males. It pushes dependency, and women, beyond the state's area of concerns. As managers of their own and other people's (men's) dependency, women are constructed, in an ironic twist, as dependent, hence as unfit for active citizenship. Their citizenship is constructed as indirect, a result of their relationship with men, and as passive, as it rests on their dependency on men and/or the state for sustenance and protection. Democracy, citizenship, and representation are constructed, in brief, as the field of independence. It is independence, conceptualized as male, which representative democracy was supposed to represent.

This is the situation that parity democracy proposes to rectify. By including an equal number of men and women in the public–representative realm, parity democracy provides the basis for the state to cease being the exclusive venue of individuals perceived as independent and allows it to be open to dependence – managed mainly by women. With parity democracy, dependence is moved into the public realm, not as an obstacle to the ideal of individual independence or autonomy, but as an equally

---

[54] *See* Jean-Jacques Rousseau, *Discourse on the Origin and Foundations of Inequality Among Mankind*, *in* THE SOCIAL CONTRACT AND THE FIRST AND SECOND DISCOURSES 69 (Susan Dawn ed. & trans., 2002).

[55] PATEMAN, *supra* note 53, at 109.

important facet of ordinary life. Once human dependence ceases to be perceived as an obstacle to participation in public affairs, political representation can go beyond the masculine ideal of individuals to embrace aspects that the sexual contract traditionally ascribed to women. The state can then go on to represent all individuals in all their complexity. Moreover, introducing dependency in the public sphere redefines human autonomy as aspired to under the liberal ideal. The autonomy paradigm can no longer be the dependence-free individual, but rather the person who takes responsibility for his or her own dependence, as well as for those who depend upon him or her, as natural limitations on any life project. The paradigm of autonomy thus becomes, not independence, but interdependence. Dependence and its management, caring and being cared for, thus find a dignified space within the public sphere, not as deviations from, but as defining elements of the ideal of the individual and the citizen. (Inter)dependency and care become constituent components of citizenship.[56]

The model of parity democracy is then in line with the dismantling of the sexual contract. This qualifies, although does not necessarily break with, the idea of unitary representation. It is not about women who will only represent women and men who will only represent men. Yet it questions the functionally and symbolically male premises of the system of general representation, based on a paradigm of autonomy as independence, and demands that individuals' dependency, constructed as both functionally and symbolically female, be introduced to the public/political domain and be represented on an equal footing with the ideal and the manifestations of independence. Indeed, it aims to redefine the subject of political representation as both dependent and independent by redefining autonomy as interdependence. The parity democracy model, in brief, articulates a justification of gender parity that rests on the idea that there is something distinctive, both structural and foundational, about the political exclusion of women that needs to be addressed in its own idiosyncrasy – something that reflects the sexual contract upon which the modern patriarchal state rests and politics is defined. This does not mean that the exclusion or underrepresentation of other groups is irrelevant or insufficiently expressive of some other democratic deficit, a deficit that challenges the model of unitary general representation from a different corner and also deserves attention. It means rather that parity has its own democratic logic, a logic that is distinct from, although compatible with, the logic of representation quotas of minority groups.

Parity democracy is then an enterprise concerned with redefining the state, popular sovereignty, democracy, and (men's and women's) citizenship in such a way that human interdependence gains a central place in the public sphere. As such, no constitutional amendment is strictly needed to justify it. Rather, parity democracy should be read into the constitutionally enshrined principles of democracy and popular sovereignty, as an interpretation thereof to move beyond the undemocratic

---

[56] *See* Joan Tronto, *Care as the Work of Citizens. A Modest Proposal, in* WOMEN AND CITIZENSHIP 131, 140–143. (Marilyn Friedman ed., Oxford University Press 2003).

implications of the sexual contract. Certainly, one could at the same time defend gender parity and the need of quotas for other marginalized groups, but one would need to do so through different grounds.

The unique logic of gender parity in representation needs to be acknowledged in a sufficiently articulated way. A move needs to be made from the liberal approach to representative democracy – that leaves the implications of the sexual contract unquestioned – to parity democracy. Rightly understood, democracy requires that such a move be made and the implications of the sexual contract corrected. This leaves us with gender parity as a requirement not so much of substantive equality but of a consistent understanding of representative democracy. It leaves us with gender parity as a democratic requirement.

Beyond the soundness of the normative conception articulated here, the fact remains that the presence of women in politics is gradually coming to be seen as a *sui generis* democratic matter. First, the rhetoric of parity democracy is increasingly enshrined in instruments of soft law both at a regional and international level.[57] Second, electoral gender quotas are on the rise worldwide (much more so than other forms of political quotas) and have in some instances triggered successful processes of constitutional reform and/or come to be constitutionally enshrined,[58] sometimes through the reservation of parliamentary seats for women.[59] Finally, ensuring the

---

[57] Comm. on the Elimination of Discrimination Against Women (CEDAW), *General Recommendation No. 23*, ¶ 14, U.N. Doc. CEDAW/C/1997/II/5 (May 30, 1997), asserted that "[s]ocieties in which women are excluded from public life and decision-making cannot be described as democratic. The concept of democracy will have real and dynamic meaning and lasting effect only when political decision-making is shared by women and men and takes equal account of the interests of both."

Within the European Council in the First Ministerial Conference on Men's and Women's Equality held in 1986, member-states pointed to the increasing presence and participation of women in the public sphere as an important concern of democracy and social justice. In 1988, the Declaration of Equality between Women and Men called upon the European Council to design policies and strategies to incorporate women into the political arena. More recently, in its recommendation of March 12, 2003, on equal participation of women and men in decision-making processes both in the political and public sectors, the European Council's Committee of Ministers invited member-states to adopt measures, including constitutional and/or legislative amendments, that promote the equal participation of women and men in political and public decision making.

The European Parliament, in its resolution of Sept. 16, 1988, urged political parties to adopt quotas to guarantee an equal presence of men and women in positions of political representation. In the 1990s, this type of statement would begin to be aimed, not at political parties, but directly at the member-states, as in Council Recommendation 694/1996 and Parliamentary Resolutions of Jan. 18, 2001 and Oct. 7, 2003. The Athens Declaration, issued on November 3, 1992, by a European Summit on Women and Power asserted that "a democratic system should entail equal participation in public and political life," that a "balance between women and men" contributes "to building a meaningful and lasting democracy" and that "[e]quality requires parity in the representation and administration of Nations."

[58] Electoral gender quotas exist in 100 states and in at least 15 states they are constitutionally entrenched; figures from the International Institute for Democracy and Electoral Assistance (International IDEA) (Stockholm, Sweden), *Global Database of Quotas for Women, available at* www.quotaproject.org (last visited Oct. 8, 2009).

[59] INDIA CONST. art. 234 T(2); UGANDA CONST. art. 78(1)(b); RWANDA CONST. art. 76 (2); and AFG. CONST. art. 83(6).

political participation of women, often by sanctioning gender quotas, has become a signifier of democratic credentials for countries transitioning from authoritarianism and/or conflict to democracy.[60] It is our understanding that any theory justifying or challenging gender electoral quotas should aim to account for what underlies such developments.

[60] U.N. Security Council Resolution 1325 on Women, Peace, and Security urges "Member States to ensure increased representation of women at all decision-making levels in national, regional and international institutions and mechanisms for the prevention, management and resolution of conflicts," U.N. Security Council, *Resolution 1325 on Women, Peace and Security,* ¶ 1, U.N. Doc. S/RES/1325 (Oct. 31, 2000). The new constitutions of some of these countries in transition foresee gender quotas for the national parliaments, regarded as an important component of the new regime's legitimacy. *See* AFG. CONST., Jan 2004, art. 83(6) and IRAQ CONST., Oct. 2005, art. 47(4) (*see* Peters & Suter, *supra* note 33, at 178 n. 24, for further examples).

11

Women's Involvement in International Constitution-Making

Elizabeth Katz

In 1776, Abigail Adams pled with her husband to please "remember the ladies" as he left to participate in the U.S. Constitution's all-male drafting process.[1] Centuries later, many women around the world remain uninvolved in their constitutions' creation and revision, leaving their rights in men's hands.

More than half of current national constitutions were drafted or revised over the last several decades,[2] so it is no surprise that there has been an accompanying explosion of scholarly inquiries into the drafting processes. These publications suggest that constitutions share core elements that transcend differences in cultures, geography, history, and other variables. Taken together, these studies offer a framework for the most successful constitutions in terms of both substance and process. Thus, scholars have been able to offer suggestions for future constitution-drafting processes. Often, however, like the constitution-drafting processes they describe, they omit any discussion of women's involvement. This chapter addresses the significance of that absence and begins to fill the void.

Many questions regarding women's participation in the creation and revision of constitutions remain unanswered. Which countries have included women? How meaningful were those inclusions? Does the involvement of women substantively change the text of the final document? Is women's involvement correlated with a constitution's perceived legitimacy? Although the available resources are limited, the small group of scholars that have discussed women's participation in individual countries make it possible to begin answering these questions.

This chapter addresses women's involvement through careful analysis of the available examples. First, it presents case studies of four countries' constitution-drafting processes with a focus on women's involvement or lack thereof: Afghanistan,

---

[1] Letter from Abigail Smith Adams to John Adams (Mar. 31, 1776), *in* Familiar Letters of John Adams and Abigail Adams During the Revolution, at 148–50 (Charles Francis Adams ed., 1876).

[2] Alicia L. Bannon, Note, *Designing a Constitution-Drafting Process: Lessons from Kenya*, 116 Yale L. J. 1824, 1826 (2007).

Colombia, Kenya, and Nicaragua. Using these examples, with supplemental information from other countries, this chapter then concludes that women's involvement is important for substantive and symbolic reasons. As will be shown, women's participation substantively changes constitutional text, brings unique and often taboo issues into the national spotlight, and empowers women participants.

I. CASE STUDIES

Although traditions, culture, and history vary by country, core constitutional features transcend national boundaries.[3] Consequently, international constitutional discourse has long been a useful part of constitution drafting.[4] The value of comparison extends beyond the constitutional text to the processes that created it.[5] This section describes the constitution-making process in several countries with a focus on women. It is not intended to be a comprehensive narrative of the drafting processes; rather, it seeks to provide a useful summary of the ways in which women were included or excluded. It also does not include subsequent history beyond the most immediate developments, but focuses instead on the processes themselves. The case studies were selected primarily based on available information and with the goal of surveying across regions to the extent possible. The included countries are Afghanistan, Colombia, Kenya, and Nicaragua.

A. Afghanistan

Afghanistan's most recent constitution-drafting process followed the fall of the Taliban, an Islamist group that took control of the country in 1996 and instituted what one scholar has called "a system of gender apartheid." Under the Taliban regime, both men and women were severely restricted. For women, these restrictions included denial of basic health care and education, enforcement of strict dress codes, and exposure to extreme violence.[6] These conditions changed drastically beginning with the defeat of the Taliban in 2001.

[3] A. E. Dick Howard, *The Bridge at Jamestown: The Virginia Charter of 1606 and Constitutionalism in the Modern World*, 42 U. RICH. L. REV. 9, 35 (2007); Vijayashri Sripati, *Constitutionalism in India and South Africa: A Comparative Study from a Human Rights Perspective*, 16 TUL. J. INT'L & COMP. L. 49, 56 (2007); EDWARD MCWHINNEY, CONSTITUTION-MAKING: PRINCIPLES, PROCESS, PRACTICE xii (University of Toronto Press 1981).

[4] A. E. Dick Howard, *How Ideas Travel: Rights at Home and Abroad*, in CONSTITUTION MAKING IN EASTERN EUROPE 10 (A. E. Dick Howard ed., 1993). On incorporation and rejection of "borrowed" constitutional ideas, *see generally*, Kim Lane Scheppele, *Aspirational and Aversive Constitutionalism: The Case for Studying Cross-Constitutional Influence Through Negative Models*, 1 INT'L J. CONST. L. 296 (2003); Julius O. Ihonvbere, *How to Make an Undemocratic Constitution: The Nigerian Example*, 21 THIRD WORLD Q. 343, 347–48 (2000).

[5] Robert A. Goldwin & Art Kaufman, *Introduction* to CONSTITUTION MAKERS ON CONSTITUTION MAKING: THE EXPERIENCE OF EIGHT NATIONS 1, 1–2 (Robert A. Goldwin & Art Kaufman eds., 1988).

[6] Holly Taylor, *The Constitutions of Afghanistan and Iraq: The Advancement of Women's Rights*, 13 NEW ENG. J. INT'L & COMP. L. 137, 144–46 (2006).

Women were at least somewhat involved in all stages of Afghanistan's constitutional-drafting process, beginning with the pre-constitution phases. At the Bonn Conference, which began the country's transitional period and established the interim government, two of twenty-three delegates were women, and many other women attended informally.[7] According to the Bonn Agreement, the delegates chose members of the interim administration "with due regard to . . . the importance of the participation of women."[8] Furthermore, the Agreement was intended to create a "broad-based, gender-sensitive, multiethnic and fully representative government" by 2004.[9] In the 2002 Emergency Loya Jirga, 220 of 1,500 delegates were women. However, the number of women allowed to speak was limited, and many were restricted to only five minutes. The conversation was dominated by warlords and commanders, stifling women's voices.[10] At the Constitutional Loya Jirga in 2003, 20 percent of the 500 delegates were women, and seven of thirty-five Constitutional Commission members were women. Unfortunately, though, the warlord intimidation experienced at the Emergency Loya Jirga continued to limit women's political participation. For example, one female delegate required special security during and after the convention because of her strong "criticism of warlord dominance." Such risks may have deterred other women from even participating.[11]

Women were also active outside the formal political process. Prior to the Constitutional Loya Jirga, a nongovernmental organization (NGO) called Women for Afghan Women (WAW) held its third annual meeting and decided to draft a Women's Bill of Rights.[12] The ethnically diverse group of women settled on twenty-one essential rights to improve women's status, increase their participation in economic, civil, and public life, and enhance their well-being. These rights included mandatory education through secondary school, equal pay for equal work, modern health services, and equal representation in government. WAW distributed copies of its Bill of Rights throughout the country. It also presented copies to President Karzai, the Constitutional Commission, and the Minister of Women's Affairs, who all seemed amenable to incorporating the demands except a provision involving the legal age of marriage. Despite the apparent support, however, the provisions women suggested were largely ignored. Nevertheless, many important women's rights were included.[13]

---

[7] Laura Grenfell, *The Participation of Afghan Women in the Reconstruction Process*, 12 Hum. Rts. Brief (Issue 1) 22, 23 (2004).

[8] *Id.* (quoting Article III (3) of the Bonn Agreement).

[9] *Id.*

[10] Taylor, *supra* note 6, at 146–47; Grenfell, *supra* note 7, at 23.

[11] Grenfell, *supra* note 7, at 23; Michael Schoiswohl, *Linking the International Legal Framework to Building the Formal Foundations of a "State at Risk": Constitution-Making and International Law in Post-Conflict Afghanistan*, 39 Vand. J. Transnat'l L. 819, 842 (2006).

[12] Grenfell, *supra* note 7, at 23; Nusrat Choudhury, Commentary, *Constrained Spaces for Islamic Feminism: Women's Rights and the 2004 Constitution of Afghanistan*, 19 Yale J. L. & Feminism 155, 167 (2007).

[13] Choudhury, *supra* note 12, at 167; Grenfell, *supra* note 7, at 23.

The women delegates to the Constitutional Loya Jirga successfully opposed the clerical Speaker and Islamist warlords to add the words "whether women or men" to the provision providing citizens with "equal rights and duties before the law." They also insisted on doubling their quota of lower house seats to 25 percent,[14] and were guaranteed 17 percent of appointed seats in the Upper House. Women's education and the end of "bad blood price" were also included.[15]

Ultimately, the failure to guarantee women a place in the judiciary may pose the greatest risk to women's rights. A tension may exist between the article that guarantees equal rights to men and women and an article that empowers the Supreme Court with the ability to overturn laws that it believes contravene the tenets of Islam. Because the judiciary historically has been dominated by hard-line Islamist jurists, the judiciary may undermine advances made by the Afghan Parliament and consequently stifle women's rights.[16] Women's political involvement is also hampered more directly by forces and threats in daily life. The lack of security interferes with women's ability to vote and to report violence. Women face resistance from families and are often deterred from voting by the lack of separate women's polling sites. The quotas that guarantee women places within the government do not guarantee that political parties will allow them to participate equally or hold positions of responsibility.[17]

In sum, women in Afghanistan have achieved mixed results in their constitution-drafting process. The completed constitutional text provides tools for Afghan women to use in securing women's rights, but these tools are weakened by textual vagueness and the power of the judiciary to thwart change. Scholars therefore consider it, "a limited step in the right direction."[18] One scholar explains, "[i]t expands Afghan women's ability to advocate for their rights from the extremely narrow spaces available in immediately preceding regimes even as it limits the breadth of that expansion."[19]

B. *Colombia*

Women have been involved in politics throughout modern Colombian history, yet they made few gains until the 1900s and continued to fall short of their goals in the most recent Colombian constitutional-drafting process. Instead, the Columbian Constitution continued the trend of gradual progress in the realm of women's rights.

---

[14] Saïd Amir Arjomand, *Constitutional Developments in Afghanistan: A Comparative and Historical Perspective*, 53 Drake L. Rev. 943, 956 (2005).

[15] Choudhury, *supra* note 12, at 167; Grenfell, *supra* note 7, at 23.

[16] Choudhury, *supra* note 12, at 156–57; Taylor, *supra* note 6, at 138.

[17] Taylor, *supra* note 6, at 149–50; Grenfell, *supra* note 7, at 24.

[18] Choudhury, *supra* note 12, at 179.

[19] *Id.*

The previous constitution in place was from 1886, making it the oldest uninterrupted constitution in Latin America. Despite numerous revisions, it lacked many of the standard guarantees of modern constitutions, such as equal protection of the laws. Several attempts at revision in the last few decades ended in failure.[20] The most recent successful effort was initiated by law students under the slogan, "We can still save Colombia," following the assassination of a Liberal senator and presidential candidate in 1989. A nonbinding special ballot showed that two million voters supported the creation of a constitutional assembly, so the president placed the issue on the ballot in the upcoming presidential election. That May, approximately 89 percent of voters voiced their support in favor of a constitutional assembly. The new president, César Gaviria Trujillo, then issued a decree calling for the election of a Constituent Assembly, a constitutionally questionable move that was approved by the Supreme Court.[21]

The court decision was reached only three weeks before the election, leaving limited time for preparation. This rush led to low participation of women, who were not fully prepared. All organizations were permitted to field a list of candidates for the seventy seats as long as they secured ten thousand signatures. The representatives were to be chosen based on proportional representation beginning with the candidates listed first. Women disagreed about whether to support the all-female list introduced by a feminist organization or lists that merely included some women. Ultimately only 8 of 119 lists began with women, leading to the election of only four women. Blame for this failure was placed on both a lack of serious media coverage of women candidates and the women's own lack of organization and consensus.[22]

"Colombian women's groups faced the recent constitutional process ill-prepared to play strong leading roles as 'founding mothers.'" Colombian women first made significant progress in securing their rights in the 1930s and 1940s, when elite women began advocating for civil and political rights with limited success. Women did not gain the right to vote until 1953, during the country's only military dictatorship. In the last few decades, progress has been made in laws regarding consensual unions or *de facto* marriages, paid maternity benefits, and employment discrimination. However, many of the changes disproportionately benefit elite women. Although Colombia ratified CEDAW in 1981, it was not implemented until 1990. Women comprise about half of voters, but before the new constitution held 1 percent of Senate seats and 5.3 percent of House seats, with similarly low participation in local office. They have experienced greater success in obtaining judicial posts, largely because of a "perception that women judges are more honest."[23] No strong women's movement

---

[20] Martha I. Morgan & Monica Maria Alzate Buitrago, *Constitution-Making in a Time of Cholera: Women and the 1991 Colombian Constitution*, 4 YALE J. L. & FEMINISM 353, 370–71 (1992).

[21] *Id.* at 366–68, 371–73.

[22] *Id.* at 373–74.

[23] *Id.* at 364.

has developed, and the existing feminist organizations are generally small groups of urban professionals and intellectuals.[24]

When the Constitutional Convention convened on February 5, 1991, the members met in five commissions divided by subject matter to review draft reforms. A group of women from Cali was concerned by the few women representatives and by April decided more women's participation was needed. They sent a letter to women throughout the country, calling on them to agree on strategies for the issues most important to women and inviting them to a meeting. This effort resulted in the formation of the Women and the Constituent Assembly National Network (Network). The Network – which eventually grew to include more than seventy organizations – stressed "free motherhood" (rather than focusing on abortion access) and pushed for gender equality, compensatory actions for marginalized groups, the incorporation of CEDAW into the constitution, equal participation in decision making, social security for domestic work, gender neutral language, and other related demands. In sum, they wanted "Democracy in the Country and in the Home."[25]

When the Assembly convened in May, it faced more than six hundred draft articles approved by the commissions. The articles showed some support for women's demands, such as not defining when life started and the recognition of civil divorce for all marriages. The Network circulated its list of proposals and publicized its demands through the radio, press conferences, lobbying, and a letter-writing campaign. Following two debates, the Assembly ultimately approved the Constitution on July 4, 1991. It contained 380 articles, making it one of the longest constitutions in the world.[26]

Although certainly many of the changes were supported by both women and men, the adopted articles show some clear evidence that women's involvement mattered in issues of equality, church–state relations, family law, and reproductive rights. A Network founder estimated that women achieved about half of their goals. Additionally, even where women's groups failed to secure the inclusion of language they desired, they were able to use the process to educate the country and set the foundation for later efforts.[27]

The principles of equality women sought were largely included, even tracking the exact language proposed by women leaders and women's organizations in some portions. Women secured promises of equality in family relations, employment, and more generally. One particularly promising article states that "[t]he authorities will guarantee the adequate and effective participation of women in the decision-making levels of Public Administration." However, other equality-related suggestions were less successful. Some portions use weaker language than women hoped. Women were also only partially successful in making the constitutional language gender

[24] Morgan & Buitrago, *supra* note 20, at 359–65.
[25] *Id.* at 377–78.
[26] *Id.* at 379.
[27] *Id.*

neutral: the constitution does not use the term "men" generically to mean "people," but it is generally written with masculine articles.[28]

Women were also partially successful in pushing for changes in church–state relations that they considered important. The old constitutional preamble had included a reference to Catholicism and God as the source of authority since 1886, language many women wanted removed. The new constitution reached a compromise position, retaining language referring to God as the nation's protector. Aside from the changed preamble language, the constitution provided new guarantees for freedom of conscience and worship, legal equality for all religious beliefs, and the prohibition of compulsory religious education in public schools.[29]

Both women and men perceived a need for change in the realm of family law. Because of the relationship between the Catholic Church and the nation since the late 1800s, no marriages performed by the Catholic Church could legally end in divorce. Even though civil marriages were introduced in 1973, with divorce allowed in 1976, 80 percent of marriages were still conducted by the Catholic Church without the possibility of divorce. The Constitutional Assembly approved the move allowing both civil and Catholic married couples to obtain civil divorces. However, the Assembly stopped short of making the new rule apply retroactively. The Assembly agreed to a milder expansion of the definition of family than women's groups had sought, and it promised to support women heads of household. It also departed from previous legislation by demanding punishment for domestic violence.[30]

Finally, abortion was the most contentious issue discussed during the constitution-drafting process. Colombia had the strictest abortion law in Latin America, with all abortions punishable by jail time. Nevertheless, abortions were widely available and even advertised. Because of the strong Catholic influence, many women who had themselves obtained abortions remained opposed to legalization. From 1975 through 1989, four unsuccessful attempts were made to bring the law into conformity with the lived experiences of Colombian women. The constitutional process provided a new forum for the debate. A subcommittee presented a draft article to the Assembly for free choice of motherhood, but it decided to withdraw it because of its controversial nature. Even the four women members of the Assembly disagreed about abortion rights. Although the Network pressured for change, the Assembly decided not to include language about abortion in the constitution because they feared creating tensions and using too much of their limited time. However, other types of family planning are expressly protected.[31]

Upon passage of the constitution, President Gaviria called the Assembly's work a "truly peaceful revolution." Whether it would be a revolution for women remained

---

[28] *Id.* at 380–83.
[29] *Id.* at 383–85.
[30] *Id.* at 385–88.
[31] *Id.* at 388–96.

an open question. Consequently, women's groups remained focused on the consti-tutional provisions. The Network, recognizing that the new Congress would imple-ment the constitution's guarantees and potentially address omitted issues, focused their efforts on the upcoming 1994 election. They educated women about their rights and prepared them to influence Congress. Still, only 14.7 percent of candidates in the election were women.[32]

Several lessons about women's participation can be gleaned from the Colom-bian experience. First, women's representation in the Constitutional Assembly was insufficient. The four women "played active roles as individuals, but their numbers were far too small – and their politics too varied – to exert significant influence as a group." Three of the four did not identify as feminists, and none saw herself as exclusively representing women. Second, although the Network was ultimately successful in many ways, the late organization of women's groups limited their effec-tiveness. The Network was also weakened by lack of involvement from working-class and poor women; the groups represented by the Network were diverse, but only middle- and upper-class women took active roles and served as leaders. This weak-ness was hidden in lobbying efforts, in which printed materials suggested widespread involvement, but the weakness showed in the lack of women candidates and elected representatives.[33]

A crucial future goal for the Colombian women's movement is to make the law experienced by women match the law promised on the books, especially because constitutional guarantees generally are not self-executing in the Colombian civil law system. Thus, the women's movement will need to continue moving toward a diverse, effective, and persistent organization to educate and organize Colombians and guarantee enforcement of women's rights. Success also depends on the country's ability to end violence. The "paper" guarantees provided in the new constitution provide a starting point for these continuing efforts.[34]

C. Kenya

Kenya's constitutional-drafting process provides a striking counterexample to the success of participatory constitution-making observed in other countries. Despite a "people-driven" approach to the constitutional review process situated within a broader democratic reform movement, after eight years of development the Kenyan Constitution was ultimately defeated by a significant margin in a nation-wide referendum.[35] This failure has attracted more attention to the Kenyan process than to many other constitution-drafting processes; articles by Alicia L. Bannon

---

[32] *Id.* at 396–400.
[33] *Id.* at 402–404.
[34] *Id.* at 358, 404–407, 412–13.
[35] Bannon, *supra* note 2, at 1829–30.

and Athena D. Mutua are particularly helpful in analyzing the shortcomings of the Kenyan process.

The constitution in place, negotiated in London on Kenya's independence in 1963, is seen by many as a symbol of "both British colonialism and domestic political oppression." The ruling party has repeatedly amended the constitution to maintain its control, even banning opposition parties. Thus, Kenya has been a "repressive one-party state throughout most of its history."[36] Elite Kenyans began seeking constitutional reform and multiparty elections, among other changes, in 1990. Although the president permitted some changes to be made, the reformers were unsatisfied by the progress and by 1994 began advocating for a new constitution. Their efforts led to the enactment of the Constitution of Kenya Review Act (Review Act) in 1997 to consider the possibility of creating a new constitution.[37]

The Review Act called for a three-part process: (1) a public consultation within every constituency, a first draft written by a small review commission, and circulation of the first draft among the public; (2) revisions to the draft by the National Constitution Commission (NCC), a large nationally elected body; and (3) ratification by Parliament without the possibility of amendment.[38] As Bannon observes, the act is "[s]trikingly . . . consistent with many of the preconditions that scholars have argued are necessary for successful constitution-writing." It was designed "to ensure that the document was home-grown and would create a sense of ownership, and it included checks to ensure that the government would neither control nor unduly influence the process."[39] Unfortunately, this model process was "hijacked" by politicians who rewrote it for their own benefit numerous times after its passage, severely undermining it.[40]

Although the first step of the review process successfully began in late 2001 and was completed partway through 2002 with the Review Commission's production of a draft, the next steps were derailed by the president's dissolution of Parliament and a contentious election in which a new party took hold of the presidency in December 2002. Consequently, the second stage was postponed for half a year. The NCC ultimately required three sets of contentious and divisive negotiations, lasting until March 2004.[41] The bitter debate was then passed to Parliament. Kenya's High Court then ruled that the constitution would require ratification through a national referendum. When Parliament amended the Review Act to accommodate the ruling, it controversially proceeded to further amend the Review Act to allow

[36] *Id.* at 1830.
[37] *Id.* at 1831–32; James Thuo Gathii, *Popular Authorship and Constitution Making: Comparing and Contrasting the DRC and Kenya*, 49 WM. & MARY L. REV. 1109, 1117 (2008).
[38] Bannon, *supra* note 2, at 1832–34.
[39] *Id.* at 1832 (internal quotations and citations omitted).
[40] Sripati, *supra* note 3, at 81.
[41] Bannon, *supra* note 2, at 1835–37; Athena D. Mutua, *Gender Equality and Women's Solidarity Across Religious, Ethnic, and Class Differences in the Kenyan Constitutional Review Process*, 13 WM. & MARY J. WOMEN & L. 1, 3–4, 59 (2006).

itself to change the draft. Parliament then debated changes and finalized a new draft in July 2005, with the referendum to take place in November 2005. The referendum was proceeded by violence and strategizing by political parties. When the votes were tallied, 57 percent of Kenyans had voted to reject the draft. Nevertheless, Kenyans still desired a new constitution.[42] The future is unclear, as severe violence erupted in 2007.[43]

Women's involvement in the process deserves attention. Kenyan women have long been subordinated to men through limited land and property ownership, violence, and less education.[44] Women face a patriarchal society and additional tensions common in postcolonial countries.[45] The Kenyan Constitution currently in effect legitimates women's subordinate status. Although it contains a provision against sex discrimination, this protection does not apply to many areas of "personal law" most relevant to women, such as adoption, marriage, divorce, and inheritance. Additionally, some areas of personal law (such as marriage) are covered by differing customary and religious laws because of the legal pluralism demanded by the constitution. The constitution also discriminates based on sex in the context of citizenship: Kenyan men's citizenship automatically passes to their foreign wives and foreign-born children, but the same is not true for Kenyan women. Finally, women have been severely underrepresented in politics. Since independence in 1963, they have never exceeded 5 percent of national representatives, and they have been similarly underrepresented at the local level.[46]

Despite their subordination, Kenyan women have long created women's groups for mutual support. Often apolitical, these groups have sometimes mobilized around significant national issues such as the war of independence. Given that Kenya was created from forty independent and quasi-independent nations, it is not surprising that Kenyan women are divided ethnically, racially, religiously, and otherwise, making their unification difficult.[47] Unification was not impossible, however. After Parliament rejected a woman delegate's proposal to increase women's participation in Parliament through quotas in 1997, the Women's Political Caucus (WPC) emerged and unified many of the other women's groups. The WPC submitted a document titled "The Women's Reforms Initiative" during the early stages of constitutional reform, demanding that women comprise half the constitutional reform body, that 30 percent of Parliamentary seats be reserved for women, that the government enact legislation in conformity with two international provisions involving women, and that a gender equality commission be created.[48]

---

[42] Bannon, *supra* note 2, at 1838–41.
[43] Gathii, *supra* note 37, at 1137.
[44] Mutua, *supra* note 41, at 14–15.
[45] *Id.* at 5–6, 60–61.
[46] *Id.* at 15–17, 23–25.
[47] *Id.* at 7.
[48] *Id.* at 49–51.

The WPC's advocacy had some early success when the Commission was being formulated. The initial Commission's twenty-five positions explicitly reserved five spaces for representatives of women's groups, and legislation authorized the WPC to pick the five members. However, the WPC's choices caused extreme protest from the government and some women because all five women were seen as elite and urban, and none came from the largest province in the country. The issue was ultimately mooted because Parliament amended the Review Act again and created a fifteen-member Commission, which included three women. The new Commission was so controversial that it caused a split in which Civil Society created a parallel review process. The WPC then split over which process to support and was significantly weakened by the division even after the review processes were merged.[49] Other differences arose between Muslim and non-Muslim women regarding the continuance of the Kadhi courts, between women of different ethnic groups regarding executive power, and among women of different classes regarding whether elite women could adequately represent women's interests broadly.[50]

Women achieved different levels of success during the three phases of the process. The first draft of the constitution, which followed an investigation of women's rights and submissions from women's groups, was seen as a "watershed" document for women's rights and gender equality. A provision obligated the state to ensure women's participation in political, social, and economic life. Another ensured personal security from both public and private violence. The draft also guaranteed women one-third of elected and appointed provisions. It enforced equal citizenship for both sexes and equal rights. In contrast to the constitutions of nearby countries such as South Africa and Uganda, however, it failed to commit to equality as a value.[51]

Following the explosive 2002 election, women's groups again formed a coalition, this time to maintain the advances of the October 2002 first draft. The brainchild of a team composed of scholars, NGO representatives, and religious leaders in conjunction with the Federation of Women Lawyers of Kenya and the League of Kenya Women Voters, the coalition created the "Campaign for Safeguarding the Gains of Women in the Draft Constitution." The Campaign was committed to women's solidarity and empowerment across ethnic groups. Its activities included creating a manual to explain its principles, suggesting language for the constitution, training delegates in conference procedures to increase their effectiveness, teaching lobbying skills, and educating people about the purpose of the constitution.[52] The campaign pushed for three principles: "social justice, gender mainstreaming, and gender equality."[53] "Social justice" included affirmative action for women, support

---

[49] *Id.* at 52–56.
[50] *Id.* at 11–12, 30.
[51] *Id.* at 57, 62–66.
[52] *Id.* at 83–90.
[53] *Id.* at 36–37, 66–71.

of women's Parliamentary seats, and outreach to minority communities. "Gender mainstreaming" involved securing an independent gender commission. "Gender equality" was the furthest reaching and was defined as the "equal valuing by society of women and men." It was aimed at traditions and practices that lead to gender hierarchies in which women are subordinated. The remedy was equality under the law, equal opportunities, and equal outcome through affirmative action.[54] As one of the first groups to publicize its positions after the election, the coalition had significant influence.[55]

According to Mutua, women's efforts can be seen as a "qualified success."[56] The first draft was a significant move toward gender equality, but the later divisions among women held them back from making other advances. Not surprisingly, issues that women had long advocated for and that society generally accepted were more successfully integrated into the constitution than newer proposals. For example, the Gender Commission, the one-third provision, and affirmative action for women had all been supported for the previous decade and were included in the final drafts. Various provisions to eliminate gender discrimination were also included, although the final draft represented a reduction in those provisions as compared to the previous draft. Women had less success in dictating the language of the provisions, as focus on the language was a more recent goal. Consequently, the language is weaker and more ambiguous in some areas than the women wished. Even when an issue had been central to women's efforts before the constitution-drafting process, if the women did not highlight it in the context of constitutional reform, it fell by the wayside. So, for example, a change in the age requirements for marriage, abortion rights, and same-sex marriage were all defeated. Mutua suggests, "[t]hese results point to the necessity of an independent women's movement with organizations and opportunities for women to consult one another across their diversities and that are capable of articulating and fighting for women's gendered interests."[57]

The Kenyan constitution-drafting process provides a number of lessons.[58] It illustrates "the critical importance of having a women's movement that is committed over time to developing, articulating, and acting on behalf of women's interests in all their diversities." To successfully secure and advance women's rights, the women's movement must help mediate the tensions between diverse groups of women and secure solidarity through "creative compromise." Women must seek social equality among themselves, rather than simply focusing on equality between men and women. The views of all women within the society must be respected and incorporated into the women's movement's constitutional goals.[59]

---

[54] *Id.* at 73–90.
[55] *Id.* at 4–5, 31–32, 36–37.
[56] *Id.* at 13.
[57] *Id.* at 121–27.
[58] Bannon, *supra* note 2, at 1871–72.
[59] Mutua, *supra* note 41, at 12.

D. *Nicaragua*

Women's involvement in the Nicaraguan constitution-drafting process was rooted in their support of the nationalist revolution of 1979. The story of their participation, told in great detail by Martha Morgan, provides an excellent model for other countries. Women in Nicaragua, as in other Latin American countries, have historically been restricted by both machismo and traditional Catholic patriarchal views, which together produce rigid gender stereotypes. At the same time, women have been reluctant to identify as feminists because feminism is perceived as linked to middle-class women and women in more "developed" societies. In their country's constitution-drafting process, however, Nicaraguan women were able to navigate these obstacles to provide both influential and symbolic participation.[60]

Nicaraguan women were not allowed to vote until 1955, but they were often involved in other political activities such as protesting and were involved in their country's successive revolutions. Their involvement in the 1979 nationalist revolution, in which the Sandinista National Liberation Front (FLSN) overthrew the Somoza dictatorship, was particularly strong. Although the Sandinistas did not invite any women to sit on their nine-member directorate, women comprised 25 percent of their membership and held 27 percent of their leadership positions. The Sandinistas had long been involved with the country's women's movement and were committed to ending economic, political, and cultural discrimination against women. Additionally, the party was supportive of the creation of the women's organization that was the predecessor of the very influential Luisa Amanda Espinoza Association of Nicaraguan Women (AMNLAE).[61]

The day after the Sandinistas overthrew the Somoza dictatorship in July 1979, the provisional governing body issued a Fundamental Statute that abrogated the 1974 constitution and established the framework for an interim government. A National Assembly was elected to draft a new constitution in November 1984 and seated in January 1985. The National Assembly included ninety-six representatives from seven political parties, plus their alternates. Fourteen representatives and fifteen alternates were women. Of the women, all but one representative and two alternates ran on the FLSN ticket. Many of these FLSN women delegates were mothers of the revolution's heroes and martyrs, and women who had themselves taken leadership roles in the revolution. They included peasant leaders, organization leaders, market vendors, a beautician, teachers, lawyers, and others.[62]

In April 1985, the National Assembly appointed a Special Constitutional Commission to prepare the first draft of the constitution. Of the twenty-two members on the Commission, there were originally two women, with two additional alternate

---

[60] Martha I. Morgan, *Founding Mothers: Women's Voices and Stories in the 1987 Nicaraguan Constitution*, 70 B.U. L. Rev. 1, 4–5, 11–13 (1990).

[61] Id. at 3, 7–9, 11–12.

[62] Id. at 20–22.

women participating at times. The Commission divided into three subcommittees: one prepared the initial outline and draft, one traveled to other countries to learn from their constitutions, and one organized a national consultation to involve the public.[63]

The national consultation was organized in two phases. The first part, held from August to October 1985, was a time for leaders of political parties, unions, businesses, religious groups, and women's organizations such as AMNLAE to present their views to the Commission. The Commission then completed the first draft and distributed 150,000 copies throughout the country for the people's evaluation. The second phase, which was held from May through June 1986, consisted of seventy-three open forums. AMNLAE helped women prepare to participate in these forums by holding meetings in which they explained the constitutional process in terms specifically designed for women. For example, they described the constitution as the "Mother Law" and ordinary statutes as its "children."[64] The forums drew 100,000 participants, of whom 2,500 spoke and 1,500 submitted written comments. Seven of the forums were held specifically for women, and women did not hesitate to raise controversial issues at these and other forums.[65]

Following the public forums, the Assembly created a twenty-member group, Comisíon Dictaminadora, to review comments and prepare a report and second draft for the Assembly's evaluation and approval. After ten weeks of debate, the Assembly adopted the constitution, and it became official on January 9, 1987. Despite some delays in the constitution going into effect, the document was profoundly important for the nation. Morgan describes the final version as "[a] product of compromise and pragmatism" that "combines revolutionary rhetoric, liberal democratic principles, and recognition of individual, social, and economic rights." The constitution was seen by Nicaraguans as "our commitment to the future," and carried great symbolic value.[66]

Women stressed three areas of concern throughout the process: equality, dignity, and reproductive freedom. Equality had long been a focus of the women's movement, but the discussion about dignity and reproductive freedom brought traditionally taboo topics to the forefront.[67] In many regards the women's efforts were successful. First, largely because of women's demands in the open forums, the constitution contains several provisions guaranteeing equality and prohibiting gender-based discrimination. Women were also successful in pushing for an article that removes the dichotomy between the public and the private and in securing a

---

[63] *Id.* at 22–23.

[64] *Id.* at 19.

[65] *Id.* at 23–24; Jules Lobel, *The Meaning of Democracy: Representative and Participatory Democracy in the New Nicaraguan Constitution*, 49 U. Pitt. L. Rev. 823, 851 (1988).

[66] Morgan, *supra* note 60, at 25–29.

[67] *Id.* at 19.

broader and more inclusive definition of "family." They changed gendered provisions they found offensive and removed discrimination against children born out of wedlock. Even where progress was not made, such as in divorce law and treatment of homosexuality, the forums were helpful in sparking discussions. Women also pushed for equality at work and to varying degrees accomplished goals such as equal pay for equal work, equal training opportunities, and equality within military services.[68]

Under the umbrella of dignity, women sought an end to domestic violence and rape. Consequently, the constitution contains an article guaranteeing "the right to respect for their physical, psychological, and moral integrity."[69] Involuntary servitude and the slave trade were forbidden. Another provision recognized the media's social responsibility for its portrayal of women.[70]

The discussion about motherhood freely chosen was extremely contentious. Many women and groups such as AMNLAE wished to expand the availability of abortion, which was only available for therapeutic reasons under existing law. AMNLAE formally presented its ideas on the topic to the Commission, but they were countered by the Catholic Church, a feeling that the nation was underpopulated, general cynicism toward family planning, and the perceived financial weakness of the health system. Women on both sides of the issue discussed abortion and the related issues of contraception and sex education at the open forums, and the media devoted great attention to these discussions. Ultimately, the Assembly decided constitutional debates were not the appropriate forum to reach an abortion decision, so no abortion provision was included. Still, the constitutional debate had provided a new platform to discuss reproductive freedom. Additionally, the adopted constitution did contain protections for pregnant women and mothers, such as protection against employment discrimination.[71]

The influence of women's participation has extended beyond the initial promulgation of the constitution. The issues they raised continue to be discussed and acted upon. For example, divorce and abortion remained on the agenda – a 1988 law made Nicaragua the first Latin American country to allow either party to divorce if desired.[72] Women have also remained involved in the political process. In the 1990 elections, women participated in constructing party platforms; fifteen women and twelve alternates were elected to the National Assembly, and a woman was even elected president.[73]

---

[68] Id. at 32–42; Lobel, *supra* note 65, at 852–53.
[69] Morgan, *supra* note 60, at 48 (quoting CONSTITUCIÓN POLÍTICA DE LA REPÚBLICA DE NICARAGUA art. 36).
[70] Id. at 44–51.
[71] Id. at 52–66.
[72] Id. at 70–85.
[73] Id. at 89–92, 104–107.

Many clear benefits were derived from women's participation in the Nicaraguan constitution-drafting process. The open forums were an educational opportunity for the entire country to learn about women's societal roles. Women brought issues to the table that had formerly been considered outside the public realm or taboo. Active involvement in meetings empowered women in ways they had never experienced before.[74] Morgan concludes that the constitution's "founding mothers" demonstrated the value of including women in the constitution-drafting process. "The example of their participation shows that when women's voices are included in the law, it tells a more complete – and more complex – story of who we are and who we want to be."[75]

II. LESSONS AND TRENDS

The case studies and information gleaned from other sources provide a forum for addressing lessons and trends. Based on this information, it seems clear that women's involvement in constitution-drafting processes significantly influences the regulative, constitutive, and transformative aspects of constitution drafting. Successful women's participation changes the constitutional text, raises significant issues, and is a source of empowerment for women.

First, women's voices influence the final content of constitutions. Women's advocacy and suggestions both alter and add constitutional provisions, ranging from the editing of constitutional language to the insertion of equality and nondiscrimination provisions. For example, discussions of gender equality throughout the South African constitution-drafting process led to the usage of gender-neutral language. The sole exception is in the context of appointment to political office, where the text says "women and men" may be elected to avoid the potential that gender-neutral language would lead to continuing stereotypes that exclude women.[76] Another common example is that women's involvement may help secure a portion of national candidate slots or legislative seats for women. For instance, Rwandan women's push for legislative seats resulted in their constitution devoting 30 percent of the seats in parliament to women. According to one scholar, this provision was the only notable difference between the Rwandan participatory constitution and those created by elites.[77] Rwanda's parliament is now 45 percent women, the second highest proportion in the world.[78]

---

[74] *Id.* at 67–85, 89–92, 104–107.
[75] *Id.* at 103.
[76] Christina Murray, *A Constitutional Beginning: Making South Africa's Final Constitution*, 23 U. ARK. LITTLE ROCK L. REV. 809, 828–29 (2001).
[77] Angela M. Banks, *Challenging Political Boundaries in Post-Conflict States*, 29 U. PA. J. INT'L L. 105, 105 n.2 (2007).
[78] *Id.*

Women's involvement also raises unique issues. This results in the discussion of formerly taboo "private" issues in public forums and increases society's awareness of the issues women face. This was clearly shown in the case studies describing Nicaragua and Colombia, where issues such as divorce and abortion were raised for the first time in public forums. Women extend the "societal self-examination and redefinition" that is crucial to a fully successful drafting processes.[79] Even though controversial issues may remain unresolved, their introduction expands societal dialogue and provides a framework for later progress.

Third, the very act of pursuing rights is a source of empowerment for women.[80] The significance of constitution drafting draws formerly politically inactive women into a nationwide discussion of society's goals and values. Feminist scholars note, "The assertion of rights can exude great symbolic force for oppressed groups within a society and it constitutes an organizing principle in the struggle against inequality."[81] Male leaders' decision to actively encourage women's participation shows that they value women's input and that they perceive women's contributions as valuable. It also suggests that they recognize that women's interests may diverge from their own, just as may be the case with racial or religious minority groups. In countries where women have been subordinated both socially and legally, this development has the potential to be profoundly meaningful and transformative.

Women's meaningful involvement requires two primary ingredients: women members of the constitution-drafting body; and an active, organized, and inclusive national women's group. The election or appointment of women to the body tasked with creating and revising drafts gives women an official platform for advocacy of women's rights. It also symbolizes the nation's commitment to including women and respecting their interests. However, merely appointing women to the constitution-drafting bodies is insufficient, as seen in the Colombian case study, because women delegates often have loyalties that trump or overshadow women's rights. Successful strategies for securing women membership on constitution-drafting bodies are important issues that merit further study.

The most vital ingredient in women's meaningful participation is an effective women's organization. The women's group must overcome religious, ethnic, economic, and other diversities to unite women around common goals they can all accept.[82] This may require delegating controversial issues to smaller groups. Once the common goals have been adopted, they should be published and distributed

---

[79] Morgan, *supra* note 69, at 70.

[80] Laboni Amena Hoq, Note, *The Women's Convention and Its Optional Protocol: Empowering Women to Claim Their Internationally Protected Rights*, 32 COLUM. HUM. RTS. L. REV. 677, 724 (2001).

[81] Hilary Charlesworth, Christine Chinkin, & Shelley Wright, *Feminist Approaches to International Law*, 85 AM. J. INT'L L. 613, 638 (1991).

[82] Mutua, *supra* note 41, at 127. *See, e.g.*, Hallie Ludsin, *Putting the Cart Before the Horse: The Palestinian Constitutional Drafting Process*, 10 UCLA J. INT'L L. & FOREIGN AFF. 443, 459–66 (2005).

among women and those in power.[83] The group should also focus on pushing for women representatives within the drafting body. The importance of this effort is clearly illustrated by the constitution-drafting process in South Africa, where demonstrations by the Women's League led to South Africa being the first country in which women and men sat in equal numbers in the constitution-making body.[84] As the process continues, the women's group should educate women delegates and citizens to increase their efficacy in advocating for women's rights and provide resources for women and their allies.

International women's groups are no substitute for a domestic organization because groups viewed as Western or feminist may seem foreign and illegitimate.[85] Instead, women in other countries can provide resources and support less directly through NGOs. NGOs may help existing women's groups form a coalition and serve as neutral organizers to assist the new coalition in selecting its unifying goals. NGOs may also act independently to reinforce international pressure on national governments to remember their obligations under CEDAW.[86] Extending beyond the drafting process, NGOs can join with domestic women's organizations to target other impediments to women's political involvement such as "traditional thinking and customary law, poverty, fear, lack of education, and racial and economic impediments."[87] Once again, the intricacies of this suggestion deserve greater attention and will hopefully be addressed by other scholars.

Effective women's participation also requires several specific conditions that may be outside women's immediate control both during and after the drafting process. First, safety must be secured to the extent possible. The threat of violence disproportionately harms women's interests because it discourages women from participating and may require political compromises that sacrifice women's rights. For example, because of the ongoing instability in Palestine, the current draft of its constitution was strongly influenced by fundamentalist Islamist groups that likely would be weaker in times of peace. Status law and equality are the areas most affected by the participation of Islamic fundamentalists so, as one scholar explains, "[i]n the current draft, women's rights are a sacrificial lamb to the cause of stability and security."[88] If a

---

[83] For example, South African women successfully distributed a Women's Charter. Penelope E. Andrews, *From Gender Apartheid to Non-Sexism: The Pursuit of Women's Rights in South Africa*, 26 N.C. J. INT'L L. & COM. REG. 693, 717–18 (2001).

[84] Sripati, *supra* note 3, at 89–90.

[85] Adrien Katherine Wing, *Constitutionalism, Legal Reform, and the Economic Development of Palestinian Women*, 15 TRANSNAT'L L. & CONTEMP. PROBS. 655, 696–98 (2006).

[86] Berta Esperanza Hernádez-Truyol, *Women's Rights as Human Rights – Rules, Realities and the Role of Culture: A Formula for Reform*, 21 BROOK. J. INT'L L. 605, 676 (1996); Hoq, *supra* note 80, at 705; Sripati, *supra* note 3, at 79.

[87] Stacy R. Sandusky, *Women's Political Participation in Developing and Democratizing Countries: Focus on Zimbabwe*, 5 BUFF. HUM. RTS. L. REV. 253, 260 (1999). For a discussion of women's political involvement internationally, *see generally* Jane S. Jaquette, *Women in Power: From Tokenism to Critical Mass*, 108 FOREIGN POL'Y 23 (1997).

[88] Ludsin, *supra* note 82, at 487, 500.

country is unable to ensure safety and stability, it should wait to draft its constitution so the harmful effects of the instability are not permanently enshrined in its highest law.

Women's constitutional rights are also jeopardized in some countries by the entrenchment of conservative men in the judiciary.[89] For example, in Iraq women fill only fifteen of thousands of judgeships.[90] Depending on the government created, the judges on a nation's highest court may be able to overturn legislation designed to benefit women, while judges in lower courts may reinforce traditional ideas about women's roles. Judges may further find international obligations, such as CEDAW, to be in violation of their nations' constitution.[91] Thus, the continuing participation and empowerment of women requires substantive or other checks on the judiciary, such as clear statements of rights that remove judicial discretion or the guarantee of women's positions within the judiciary.[92]

CONCLUSION

Women, much like minority groups, have unique interests in the drafting of their nations' constitutions. Women's participation is thus crucial to ensuring that women's rights and priorities are included or at least addressed in a nationwide dialogue. Women's involvement results in substantive textual changes, a broader and more inclusive discussion, and the empowerment of women. To achieve the benefits of women's involvement, countries must formally include women on their constitution-drafting bodies and develop a cohesive and organized women's group. This chapter argues that the very legitimacy of a constitution should turn on whether women are meaningfully involved in their constitutions' creation and adoption. It is time women seized upon the promise Abigail Adams made so many years ago: "If particular care and attention is not paid to the ladies, we are determined to foment a rebellion, and will not hold ourselves bound by any laws in which we have no voice or representation."[93]

---

[89] Ruthann Robson, *Achieving Sexual Freedom Through Constitutional Structures: The Problem of Judicial Review, in* Law and Rights: Global Perspectives on Constitutionalism and Governance 101 (Penelope E. Andrews & Susan Bazilli eds., 2008).

[90] Taylor, *supra* note 6, at 154.

[91] Schoiswohl, *supra* note 11, at 857–58.

[92] Makau Mutua, *The Iraq Paradox: Minority and Group Rights in a Viable Constitution,* 54 Buff L. Rev. 927, 954 (2006). On the increasing power of judiciaries caused by constitutional reform, *see generally* Ran Hirschl, Towards Juristocracy: The Origins and Consequences of the New Constitutionalism 1 (2004).

[93] Adams, *supra* note 1.

12

Between Constitutional Jurisdiction and Women's Rights Organizations*

Women, War, and the Space of Justice in Colombia

Carolina Vergel Tovar

On April 14, 2008, the Colombian Constitutional Court produced a decision that seems amazing given the local context: *Auto* [Statement] 092/2008 (Statement) for the protection of internally displaced women (IDW).[1] After 248 pages, the Constitutional Court declared that the disproportional effect of forced displacement on women's lives was a fact, meaning that the overwhelming majority of victims of displacement are statistically female. The court established two "constitutional presumptions" to make the procedural evaluation of the effects of this kind of crime easier. The court also ordered the government to create thirteen special programs to assist IDW as well as to undertake specific measures of protection that are considered, through this same statement, a response to 600 complaints.

The surprising novelty of this decision goes beyond its extension and the statistics analyzed by the court.[2] This statement is not a typical decision, what is known in Colombia as an *"acción de tutela."*[3] The process begins, formally speaking, with an examination of facts, which could be a violation or a serious menace to civil rights (an effective damage is not necessary; just a threat justifies the use of the action) and finishes with a decision to stop the menace and restore the right issued from this examination. Statement 092 also develops a thorough study on the impact of the

---

* Given the time between conception and publication of this article, a warning is needed: This article was conceived during the government of Alvaro Uribe Vélez (2002–2006; 2006–2010) and the comments are limited to this period.
[1] Corte Constitucional [C.C.] [Constitutional Court], Auto 092/2008.
[2] But, just to have a small statistical reference: since 1991 (year of its creation) and up to 2001, the Constitutional Court had emitted twenty decisions of *tutela* in relation to the cases of forced displacement, and had not referred explicitly to the situation undergone by women. *See* CAROLINA VERGEL, LA TUTELA JURÍDICA DE LOS DESPLAZADOS POR LA VIOLENCIA EN COLOMBIA (Universidad Externado de Colombia 2001).
[3] CONSTITUCIÓN POLÍTICA DE COLOMBIA art. 86. This action of constitutional order is a recourse of an exceptional nature that one can address to all the judges of the Republic to protect a fundamental right that is violated or simply threatened. Its procedure and decision must have priority.

war on the life of Colombian women, in particular the problems related to forced displacement and sexual assault.

In order to argue and give a theoretical foundation to its decision, the court defines and contributes to Colombian jurisprudence's history a new field of terms and concepts (particularly, those concerning the "gender" question). This statement also marks an important moment for women's rights organizations and associations of IDW, the principal actresses of the process before the decision. Given the social importance of this experience, the exploration of these two questions will guide my analysis.

First of all, my main interest is not to evaluate whether this decision could be a concrete example of "gender justice" because this type of theoretical framework requires a preestablished concept of what such kind of justice should be. Instead, I am interested in exploring what meaning the Colombian Constitutional Court has given to such a justice. However, this may at some point raise some difficulties, because a purely theoretical analysis of the statement is insufficient. This is basically because there is a strong relationship between the concepts employed by the court and the particular interpretation it gives to the IDW situation in the Colombian conflict. On the other hand, it seems to me that in this decision, the political mobilization of women has been specifically crucial as well. Therefore, some key points of this case are analyzed to understand the relationship between the "cause of women victims of the war" and the problem of justice in general.

I. BEHIND THE COURT STAGE

The first documentary track of Statement 092/2008 is the call to an audience, made by the Constitutional Court in another statement[4] in response to a previous requirement of *La Casa de la Mujer* (The Woman's House), a feminist nongovernmental organization (NGO) in Colombia.[5] To this audience, the court publicized its concern for the IDW situation and declared its intention to make a decision on it. Main organizations of women's rights defense, and associations representing women victims of the conflict, not only took advantage of this new institutional space to make a call to the victims nationwide, but also criticized the governmental policies addressing this issue by asking to be included as beneficiaries of the measures ordered by the court to settle the problems of IDW as a priority.[6]

In fact, the legal background of this decision is a little longer. Statement 092 is a decision of "follow-up" measures ordered in a different judgment delivered

---

[4] C.C., Apr. 27, 1007, Statement 102.

[5] *La Casa de la Mujer* is an NGO founded in the 1960s. It is one of the most important feminist organizations in Colombia and it was, during the sixties and seventies, the major meeting point of feminists in Bogotá. Information resulting from interviews, conducted and recorded by author, with Colombian feminists (June and August 2008) (records are on file with author).

[6] Interview with Olga Amparo Sánchez, director of the NGO (Bogotá, August 28, 2008).

also by the court.[7] It declared the question of forced displacement in Colombia an "unconstitutional status quo," as a response to 108 complaints, presented by 1,150 households of internally displaced people (IDP); these households were composed on average of four members, generally with a woman as head of family, elderly, and children.[8] The complaints were expressly accumulated by the court to compare the poor institutional responses to the overwhelming number of cases on violations to humanitarian law.[9] Clearly enough, for the court, the traditional political response was unable to address and contain this humanitarian crisis. In order to adjust the public policies of assistance to the IDP, the court set up a Citizen Commission, responsible for following up and examining the effective implementation of the judgment. We can consider the result of these actions a roadmap for constructing a new public policy to address the issues of those victims of the forced displacement phenomena.[10]

The Commission is not a completely new figure in the field of constitutional law.[11] In the perspective of comparative law, we found a relatively similar juridical figure in the case of the "impartial third," understood as a progressive implementation of a concrete measure of protecting fundamental civil rights.

I would like to make a note on the "accumulation of complaints" made by the court *motu propio*. This enormous wave of legal actions is not a class-action suit or a coordinated strategy by the multitude of displacement victims.[12] Vis-à-vis the amount of cases, the court made use of a mechanism that we can call "procedural economy." This strategy aimed not only to resolve each case by grouping the decisions that would be useful for several of them, but, above all, the court deduced by this accumulation the reality of a general problem and actually proposed a policy of assistance to all the

---

7   C.C., Statement T-025 of 2004.
8   The number of IDP is a controversial point between the government and specialized NGOs. The United Nations declares based on official statistics that there are some three million IDPs; the NGOs declare that there are almost four million. In any case, according to the United Nations, Colombia suffers from the biggest humanitarian crisis, coming second only to Sudan. Human Rights Council, *Report of the United Nations High Commissioner for Human Rights on the Situation of Human Rights in Colombia*, ¶ 54, U.N. Doc. A/HRC/7/39 (Feb. 29, 2008).
9   This position takes sides against the government's official point of view, which denies the character of armed conflict to the situation in the country. However, the court had actually recognized the pertinence and the constitutional legitimacy of the Humanitarian Treaties application. *See* C.C., Decision C-574 of 1992.
10 The follow-up Commission to Statement T-025 of 2004 is composed of renowned academics, recognized human rights activists, lawyers, and international agencies. It already produced six reports on progress and the difficulties of executing the decision, and it proposed a whole system to evaluate and follow up with public policy on the IDP. *La Consultoría para los Derechos Humanos y el Desplazamiento* (CODHES) is responsible for coordinating the Commission. The latest reports by the Commission can be found on CODHES' website, www.codhes.org/index.php?option=com_content&task=view&id=39&Itemid=52.
11 *See* A LA RECHERCHE DE L'EFFECTIVITÉ DES DROITS DE L'HOMME 19–20 (Véronique Champeil-Desplats & Danièle Lochak eds., Université de Paris X 2008).
12 However, one of the fundamental features of the dynamics of the associations of victims of forced displacement is precisely the transmission of a judicial "know-how" to be recognized as a victim and to obtain humanitarian assistance.

IDP in Colombia. I want to stress that the court did not act only with the plaintiffs in mind. The court completely built this policy idea from its appreciations of the cases as a whole.[13] Qualifying it as a "humanitarian crisis" would be the element of "legitimacy" the court needed to set up this policy, which would be evaluated by a Commission whose composition and dynamics would also be defined by the constitutional court judge. By transforming a considerable amount of single complaints into a humanitarian crisis, categorized by a proper concept ("unconstitutional status quo") that deserves and requires care in a permanent way, the court makes a commitment to the victims of forced displacement and provides a concrete answer to their needs as well.[14]

Organizations for the defense of women's rights really noticed the potential of this legal commitment. In March 2007, *La Casa de la Mujer* and *La Ruta Pacífica de las Mujeres* (The Women's Peaceful Way)[15] organized a conference to publicize the results of an education and community work program with women and associations of IDW from fifteen districts in Bogota.[16] One of the invitees of this key event was Judge Manuel José Cepeda, one of the appointed writers of the Statement. He attended the whole conference. According to Olga Sánchez, chairperson of "The House," the magistrate seemed to have been deeply affected by the oral testimonies; he listened to the testimonies of IDW attendees, who were victim to all kinds of violence.[17]

At this point, the strategy seemed to work. Women's organizations succeeded in transmitting a message on two concrete aspects of the victims and forced displacement issues: 1) the particularity of the "cause of displaced women"; and 2) the affirmation of their confidence in the legal mechanism installed by the court based

---

[13] *See* La FONCTION POLITIQUE DE LA JUSTICE (Jacques Commaille & Martine Kaluszynski eds., La Découverte 2007).

[14] In fact, the magistrate who authored the 092/2008 decision published a text about judges' commitment in the Colombian context, Manuel José Cepeda, *The Judicialization of Politics in Colombia: The Old and the New*, *in* THE JUDICIALIZATION OF POLITICS IN LATIN AMERICA (A. Angell et al. eds., 2005). In my opinion, a particularity of this position is the feeling of being part of a judiciary "new age," responsible for developing a political and law project included in the constitutional text.

[15] This network of women associations from different areas of the country was created at the beginning of the 1990s, aiming to denounce the effects of the war on women's lives. This network is recognized, among other things, by its capacity for public mobilization and by the diversity of associations that it gathers.

[16] This initiative was called *Red de mujeres en acción hacia el futuro* (Network of Women in Action Towards the Future). The Women's House published a note about the decision of the court where the organization gives an account of this process, CORPORACIÓN CASA DE LA MUJER, *Implicaciones del auto de la Corte sobre mujeres en situación de desplazamiento forzado*, CENTRO DE MEDIOS INDEPENDIENTES DE COLOMBIA (Aug. 9, 2008), *available at* http://colombia.indymedia.org/news/2008/08/91279.php.

[17] Sánchez was pleased with the effect generated by the methodology chosen for the meeting: "the voice of the women" above all, according to their own words. Instead of presenting analysis or statistics, the meeting focused on the narration of testimonies by the victims themselves. Interview with Olga Amparo Sánchez, *supra* note 6.

on its first decision thereof. After the meeting, the magistrate declared his commitment to and recognition of the claims of women's organizations. He formalized this
commitment by communicating to an audience that the court would take measures
in connection with these women's situation. Manuel José Cepeda delivered a two-
pronged message: 1) the commitment comes from the court (and not only from one
judge alone); and 2) this commitment is to IDW in general, and not only to those
present at that particular conference. Summing up, the court remained a policy
actor while sharing this key role with women's organizations that, in this particular
case, made use of legal procedures to make the cause visible[18] and to provoke social
reforms.[19]

However, taking a closer look at the contents of Statement 092/08, we can obtain a
more precise dimension of the dynamics of judicialization on those public policies
that aimed to address the issues facing IDP in Colombia, especially the IDW.

II. THE SPOTLIGHT MOMENT: FUNDAMENTAL POINTS
OF THE DECISION OF THE COURT

In addition to the story "behind" the decision, another characteristic to highlight
is the study made by the court on the situation of IDW in Colombia. This is particularly evident in the terms that the court chose to speak of forced displacement.
The court uses two types of arguments. The first set can be called the "legal authority arguments" (those that are considered by lawyers and law experts as legitimate
juridical "sources"). These arguments refer to three basic types of texts: 1) human
rights protection treaties; 2) Inter-American Court of Human Rights decisions;[20]
and finally, 3) the court's own previous constitutional jurisprudence on the
matter.

Despite the symbolic charge of the inputs,[21] these arguments would have been
sufficient, in purely legal terms, to ground a "traditional" decision of *tutela*. However,
the court chose to also ground its decision on a synthesis of the reports developed

---

[18]   The distinction between "complaints" and "causes" as steps of a strategy of social mobilization seems
    useful for certain cases. However, in the Colombian example of the IDW it would have to be adapted
    because it is a cause that makes use of complaints to gain legitimacy and support. *Cf.* E. Claverie,
    Procès, Affaire, Cause. Voltaire et l'innovation critique, 26 POLITIX 76–85 (1994).
[19]   *Compare* Anne Revillard, *Entre arène judiciaire et arène législative. Les stratégies juridiques des mouve-
    ments féministes au Canada, in* LA FONCTION POLITIQUE DE LA JUSTICE 145–163 (Jacques Commaille
    & Martine Kaluszynski eds., La Découverte 2007).
[20]   *Cf.* Comisión Interamericana de Derechos Humanos (CIDH), *Las mujeres frente a la violencia y
    la discriminación derivadas del conflicto armado en Colombia*, Doc. OEA/Ser.L/V/II.Doc67 (Oct. 18,
    2006).
[21]   The effective use (by all the levels of judiciary) of treaties on the protection of the human rights
    remains a problems of really implementing this type of legal instrument in Colombia. Otherwise,
    the use by the Constitutional Court of its own decisions as "precedents" is, in fact, one of the most
    controversial points in the political field. *See* DIEGO LÓPEZ, EL DERECHO DE LOS JUECES (2nd ed.
    Legis 2006).

by organizations for the defense of women's rights,[22] in particular on the reports focused on those issues related to women victims of the war.[23]

The court points out a number of precise determinations. The originality of the Statement's considerations and its resolutions need to be studied within each of these points; thus, the most important aspects are shown to understand the stakes of the court's decision.

A. *The Disproportionate Effect of Displacement on Women*

According to the court, forced displacement has a disproportionate effect on women's lives mainly because of two factors, which it identified and explained as the "gender risks" and the "gender aspects" of this issue. This "disproportion" is thus the conclusion of the court's detailed analysis on these identified factors. "Disproportion" implies a situation of vulnerability for these women, which justified differential treatment, in addition to the adoption of institutional measures exclusively conceived for women.

The court added to this interpretation of war effects the particular status of a "factual presupposition" as a starting point of its argument. However, it seems to me that the court could reinforce this demonstration thanks to two elements. The most explicit and with a concrete formal significance in the legal sphere would be the formulation and definition of this disproportionate character in the Inter-American Commission Report of Human Rights already mentioned.[24] Even though the second factor is more subtle, it shows the disproportionate character of forced displacement as one of the objectives of women's organizations that specialize in the denunciation of violations of women's rights among victims of the war in Colombia.[25] To explain the choice of this concept in constructing the cause of the displaced women would require quite a long time. I would limit myself here to show the overlap of the preceding documentations of the situation of women victims of the

---

[22] *Cf.* Amnesty International, *Colombia. Cuerpos marcados, crímenes silenciados. Violencia sexual contra las mujeres en el marco del conflicto armado*, Index AI: AMR 23/040/2004 (October 2004).

[23] The court makes reference for example to the report of the *Mesa de Trabajo Mujer y Conflicto Armado* (Women and Armed Conflict Group). This group is composed of almost all of the NGOs for women's rights protection and activists specialized in this subject. Thanks to the research work from its members, the group elaborated on the *Special Rapporteur on Violence Against Women* at the United Nations. The report the court referred to is MESA DE TRABAJO MUJER Y CONFLICTO ARMADO, VI INFORME SOBRE VIOLENCIA SOCIOPOLÍTICA CONTRA MUJERES, JÓVENES Y NIÑAS EN COLOMBIA, 2002–2006 (Bogotá 2006).

[24] The Commission did a general report about the problems of the Colombian women vis-à-vis the war whose recommendations concerned also the Judiciary. CIDH, *supra* note 20.

[25] For example, this argument can be very useful to justify an action at the International Criminal Court. The clearest example of this argumentation in the Colombian activist field would be the documents elaborated by the *Observatorio de los Derechos Humanos de las Mujeres* (Observatory of the women's rights), project of NGO *Sisma Mujer*. This organization is characterized for its emphasis on legal advocacy.

war in Colombia with the text of the decision itself.[26] This overlap, one of the characteristics of the court's argument, would show the court's clear sensitivity to some feminist critics against the "neutrality" of legal reasoning (and particularly against its way of establishing the relevant facts in a lawsuit)[27] and its strategic use of the feminist NGOs' arguments to further bolster its decision. Perhaps the court's argument would show them both, which in fact are not mutually incompatible.

"Gender risks," another concept the court elaborated in its argument, is one of the structural elements in the practical appreciation of the problems faced by IDW. I insist on this "structural character" because the disproportional effect is admissible as a presumption because gender risks could materialize and, indeed, they often do.

B. *Gender Risks*

Each gender risk the court identified is a concrete form of violence against IDW.[28] According to the court, there are ten factors of vulnerability, to which the women are exposed because of their feminine condition within the framework of the armed confrontation in Colombia. These factors, which do not touch the men, explain, when taken as a whole, the disproportionate impact of forced displacement of women. The detailed list of gender risks concerns the risk of sexual violence, sexual exploitation, or sexual abuse within the armed conflict; the risk of exploitation or enslavement to perform roles considered feminine tasks; the risk of forced recruitment of their children (in particular the women alone with children); the risks of any personal contact with members of the armed forces; risks arising from their leadership and advocacy work in human rights; the risk of persecution and murder and of coercive control strategies of public and private behavior; the risks of the murder or disappearance of their financial provider or by the disintegration of their family groups and their networks of social and material support; the risk of being dispossessed of their land and assets more easily; the risks of discrimination and the condition of special vulnerability of indigenous and black women; and finally, the risk of the loss of a partner or financial provider during the displacement process.

The court seems here to introduce a "differentialist" perspective between feminine and masculine situations in the war, not like an a priori condition, but rather like an assessment derived from appreciating and analyzing the facts denounced by victims. According to this vision the dynamics of war forces both women and men, but has

---

[26] Moreover, in the corpus of decision T-025/2004 we can find many references of the reports of the situation of the IDW as sources or evidence of this "unconstitutional *status quo*."

[27] *Cf.* Katherine O'Donovan, *Engendering Justice: Women's Perspectives and the Rule of Law*, 39 U. Toronto L. J. 127–48 (1989).

[28] C.C., Auto 092/2008 (p. 53).

two different perspectives of the risk.[29] That is why the "differentialist" perspective is highlighted by quotation marks.

It is interesting that the link to a specific type of discrimination against women of a structural kind is reinforced by war and multiplies the social masculine profits of the war;[30] however, it will be used more like in an argument built from another concept, also mentioned by the court: the "gender aspect" of forced displacement.

C. *The Analysis of Forced Displacement Starting from the Identification of the Gender Aspects*

The court identified eighteen gender aspect of forced displacement, that is, the aspects of displacement that have a differential impact, specific and accentuated for women, because of their feminine condition in the context of the Colombian armed conflict. The eighteen gender aspects also include "(1) recurring forms of violence and structural gender discrimination . . . , previous to the displacement, but which are reinforced or worsened and aggravated because of the conflict itself. . . . These are (2) specific problems of displaced women, a product of the conjunction of factors of vulnerability that they suffer and that are not the same for nondisplaced women, or for displaced men[31] (translations are mine).

Some examples of the first type of gender aspect of this situation in the Colombian case could be the various manifestations of "gender violence," that is, the violence exerted against women just because of "being women" and the general difficulties in all social backgrounds for women to be able to enjoy their rights. To the second type belong the institutional weaknesses, both administrative and procedural, to meet the specific needs of women victims of the armed conflict (e.g., the absence of trained people capable of dealing with women victims of sexual assault).

It is difficult to give a concrete dimension to the legal consequences that court recognition of structural discrimination toward women can have. This recognition is not formulated in an abstract way. To the contrary, it is described starting from a catalog of rather precise examples, and this detail gives a particular conclusive force to the argument. However, from the point of view of women organizations, the perspective can be completely different. It will be necessary to follow how these organizations will interpret and use the concepts of the court's decision. Meanwhile, the possibility of widening the implementation of the gender risk concept remains an open question and rather casuistic. The court's decision listed a fixed number of criteria and showed a systemic effort to contain a rather complex set of problems

---

[29] In spite of the differences of the specific context of each war, this bond between war violence and gender violence are a common feature of wars in general. *Cf.* Women and Civil War: Impact, Organizations, and Actors (Krishna Kumar ed., Lynne Rienner Publishers 2001).

[30] *Cf.* Joshua S. Goldstein, War and Gender: How Gender Shapes the War System and Vice Versa (Cambridge University Press 2001).

[31] C.C., Auto 092/2008 (pp. 5–6, 17–19).

to take measures; at the same time, it took into consideration precisely this complexity by recognizing a structural discrimination against women. In my opinion, a more concrete result of this recognition was the court's order to the government to introduce specific programs for IDW.

D. *The Creation of Thirteen Programs in Favor of Female Victims of Forced Displacement*

The programs to be created are – in general – a response to each gender risk. These programs seek to provide effective assistance to all aspects of the IDW's life (e.g., security, education, sexuality, health care, access to land), and are adapted to the IDW's social characteristics (e.g., their race or age, or their situation as single mothers, women activists).

These programs must be structured following a minimum "criteria of reasonability."[32] This concept, outlined by the court, includes evaluation, particularly of results, as well as of the basic elements of any public policy: clear objectives, activities, timeline, institutional arrangements, and financial resources allocation. The court gathers international parameters for humanitarian aid (in particular, the Guiding Principles of Forced Displacements[33]) as well as specific criteria commonly linked to public policies.

I will not consider whether defining these concepts falls within the court's jurisdiction or if it constitutes an abusive interference in the functions of the executive. Taking a side on this doctrinal and political debate is useless for the current analysis;[34] however, to remark on the use of some definitions is relevant[35] in the social, political, and legal context of Colombia.[36] I simply stress the point that this court decision can be considered a step forward, after a series of decisions that described and denounced the government's insufficient response to the situation of IDW[37] especially given the permanence of the armed conflict. In other words, the court's decision could be the

---

[32] See *id.* at 126.

[33] Comm. on Human Rights, *Report of the Representative of the Secretary-General, Mr. Francis Deng, submitted pursuant to Commission resolution 1997/39. Addendum: Guiding Principles on Internal Displacement.* U.N. Doc. ONU E/CN.4/1998/53/Add.2 (Feb. 11, 1998).

[34] For a historical reconstruction of this debate in the Colombian context, see LÓPEZ, *supra* note 21.

[35] *Cf.* Jacques Chevallier, *Pour une sociologie du droit constitutionnel, in* L'ARCHITECTURE DU DROIT. MÉLANGES TROPER 281–97 (Economica 2007).

[36] Decisions like Statement 092 gave rise to many critics. To give a more concrete idea of the stakes of the debate, the current government presented this argument as one of the factors that justify a constitutional reform that would reduce the competences of the Constitutional Court. *Cf.* Rodrigo Uprimny, *La justice au cœur du politique: potentialités et risques d'une judiciarisation en Colombie, in* Commaille & Kaluszynski eds., *supra* note 13, at 229–50.

[37] An intermediate point in the evolution of the decisions of the court toward a more detailed and relevant response vis-à-vis the situation of the IDW is C.C., Statement 218 of 2006. This decision recognizes as urgent a measure "to adopt a differential, specific approach which recognizes the fact that displacement has appreciably different and distinct effects according to the age and gender factors."

result of a process *in crescendo* of denunciations on one side, and judicial decisions and judgments on the other one, both related to the protection of IDP.

However, besides this, one could say that with the decision of the court, one approaches a new type of affirmative action, already distinguished by the vocabulary of legal doctrine: the "structural approach" and "procedural positive action."[38] Both types of affirmative action give more emphasis to the means of regulation than to the general or standard norm of defining discrimination. More concretely, according to Mizumachi, these approaches aim at the interaction of three actors: "the establishment, the law, and the intermediaries; and it depends basically on the voluntary character of measurement."[39]

Although the order given by the Colombian Constitutional Court to the government is nonnegotiable, in practice, establishing the follow-up Commission for Statement T-025/04 (which widened and accommodated the problems of women in Statement 092/08) could be translated into what the doctrine names as "proceduralization of the law."[40] "This model . . . is based on the enlarged concept of 'procedural reason,' according to which one faces the problem, one acts looking for consensus, and one solves the concrete problems by means of open and continuous negotiations."[41]

This negotiated character when executing the court's order appears more clearly if we follow the information of this Commission's reports, which detail the progress and shortcomings of installing the court-ordered institutional "programming" measures. In contrast with the establishment of constitutional protection, as an ongoing process, it is remarkably the creation of two "presumptions," both constitutional in nature, to expedite administrative and legal procedures for women.

E. *The Creation of Two Constitutional Presumptions for Internally Displaced Women*

The first presumption was that of the "aggravated vulnerability of displaced women": the main objective of this presumption is to facilitate access to the various services of the *Sistema Nacional de Asistencia Integral a la Población Desplazada* (SNAIPD; National System of Integral Assistance to the Displaced Population). To this point, the court added the compulsory mandate for civil servants to be attentive to the multiple violations of fundamental rights of which displaced women might be victims. This also implied a formal prohibition to require proof elements or administrative approaches without taking into account this particular state of vulnerability

---

[38] Cf. Y. Mizumachi, *Une analyse réflexive des théories de la 'positive action' de type procédural, in* EGALITÉ DES SEXES: LA DISCRIMINATION POSITIVE EN QUESTION 139–48 (Danièle Lochak & Miyoyo Tsujimura eds., Gender Law and Policy Center, Société de législation comparée 2006).

[39] For more information about the structural approach, *see id.* at 141–43.

[40] Champeil-Desplats & Lochak eds., *supra* note 11.

[41] Mizumachi, *supra* note 38, at 143.

explained by the court. In other words, the "state of vulnerability" became a parameter to evaluate proofs and to examine the respect of the due process.

The second presumption was the necessity of permanent renewal of humanitarian aid,[42] which must thus be maintained in an integral and continuous way. There is, in this context, no need to make visits, or specific checks for this renewal (contrary to current general practices).[43] Moreover, authorities would have to demonstrate that the woman in question is self-sufficient, mainly in economic terms, and that her situation was restored with dignity before being able to justify a decision to end any assistance.

The mechanism of the presumptions materializes what I called the differentialist approach of the court. The court recognized a particular and serious impact of forced displacement (and of war) on women beyond a pure declaration and created concrete procedural measures.

In addition to intervening and modifying the protocols that public administration responsible for these affairs should follow, the court mentioned values like autonomy and dignity to guide this public responsibility. The reasons for this axiological framework are not very clear: does the court mean autonomy in response to the classical feminist claim and dignity because we are talking about a vulnerable population? I do not have the time to analyze the axiological uses of the court. Nevertheless, the court seemed more interested in a pragmatic answer. I can say that the court – relating here to MacKinnon's thesis – tried to shorten the gap between women's lived experience and the crucial moment of appreciating the facts.[44] This obviously tries to avoid perverting the claim for the proof of the "permanent reality of vulnerability" on behalf of the victim alone. As for the cases concerning sexual crimes, the court also takes measures that will have procedural consequences.

F. *Cases of Sexual Assault: Responsibility for the Attorney General*

Finally, the court decided to transfer the eighty-six files concerning rape cases or sexual assaults in general to the office of the Attorney General, so that it would carry out the necessary inquiries. The Attorney General must consequently return to the court a report on the progress of each case at the end of a six-month period.

---

[42] According to Law 387 of 1997, this assistance consists of the right to receive food and a housing subsidy for three months. Decision T-025/2004 of the court widened this time until the end of the situation of vulnerability. Nevertheless, the burden of proof remained on the displaced persons; that is, it was the population victim who was to prove that he or she still needed the assistance.

[43] The public authorities responsible for giving this assistance to the IDP had established the domiciliary visits as a mechanism to check their living conditions and also the permanence of their condition of vulnerability. This mechanism encountered several difficulties and generated unjust treatments due to the high fluctuation of the families (almost always living in irregular housing).

[44] Catharine MacKinnon, *Feminism, Marxism, Method, and the State: Toward Feminist Jurisprudence*, 8 Signs 635 (1983).

The schematic idea of the court's decision can be thought of as a structure with a particular "logical" formulation divided in two great parts (if such a thing can be even imagined): it begins with a diagnosis that identifies elements of discrimination against women, then makes the distinction between those elements – those of a structural nature, those derived from war or such, and those that affect women disproportionately in a particular way, in a context of dual vulnerability against women: as an IDP and as a woman.

It is rather obvious that all the elements set up by the court to build its analysis and justify its legal measures had a direct relationship with the concept of "gender." In this way, the court gave an example of gender justice. I adopt here a functional concept of "gender justice" – a legal action that intervenes on a situation, defined in some way by a situation of "sex discrimination," to improve the situation and condition of the plaintiff woman involved. Gender justice also refers to a juridical operation that tries to avoid discrimination against women.[45]

From my point of view, this peculiar notion of gender justice describes the direction of the court's work. Although it is not a radical break from the universality of human rights,[46] a distinction nevertheless exists: 1) on the level of the appreciation of the facts (the disproportionate impact of displacement for women's lives, gender risks, and gender aspect of displacement situation); and 2) on the level of the answer to the problems (affirmative actions of a legal, procedural, and political nature).

Finally, one could stress that the Colombian Court's analysis granted concrete direction to the methodological and political premise to "take into consideration the gender perspective" in the constitutional protection of human rights. In any case, although it is not the first act recognizing women's terrible situation in the Colombian conflict,[47] this decision marks a radical change in the legal response to the complaints of women victims of the Colombian armed conflict. It is now necessary to present the initial reactions to the decision for a better understanding of its range and political scope.

III. AFTER THE "PREMIÈRE"

On July 24, 2008, three months after the Constitutional Court's Statement 092, I find myself in a conference room in Medellin.[48] I came here to attend a *Colloquium* on Statement 092/2008, organized by the *Ruta Pacífica de las Mujeres.* Auxiliary

---

45 For a gender-sensitive analysis of justice, see Joan Williams, *Igualdad sin discriminación, in* GÉNERO Y DERECHO 75–97 (Alda Facio & Lorena Fríes eds., La Morada ediciones 1999).

46 MacKinnon, *supra* note 44.

47 Indeed, C.C., Decision T-025 of 2004, crucial for the legal answer to the problems of forced displacement, had already granted women the character of "subjects of special constitutional protection." This character justifies the adoption of measures of positive discrimination, by considering their special conditions of weakness and vulnerability.

48 Located in the northeast portion of the country, Medellin is the capital of Antioquia and is one of the main cities of Colombia for its population and economy size.

judge to the Constitutional Court Federico Guzmán wrote an exposition on the decision that was to be the "main course" of this meeting. When he came in, we had a real surprise. The judge, rather young (in his early thirties) and dressed in jeans and a patterned shirt, definitively did not correspond to the "typical" profile of a judge (we were expecting at least a tie). The head of a project for land's protection, who happened to be sitting next to me, expressed her opinion about the judge with sympathy.

However, in his defense, one could not qualify the event as informal or casual. The meeting's attendees (about fifty people) consisted mainly of three different types of groups. First are civil servants, who work at the municipal and regional government, responsible for various programs for IDP or for women. This group brings back the formality that the magistrate's jeans want to make disappear. Second are members of several feminist NGOs. Finally, there is a group of women victims of forced displacement representing various victims' associations. There are very few men, four in all, the magistrate included.

What I found more astonishing was Guzmán's presentation. It seemed to me an honest effort to make the decision accessible and to invite women victims' associations and the feminist NGOs in particular to take an active part in the planning of the thirteen programs outlined by the court.[49]

Then, suddenly, one of the most striking questions to me came from the public (to be precise, from a public servant): why had the court decided to make the question of the situation of women a priority? The magistrate's response was something similar to this: quite simply that the court had received too many reports, complaints, information, and inquiries on the matter and it could not do otherwise. In addition, for that reason too, the court decided to convene the technical audience (see *supra*) to inform themselves at the best possible level about the matter and, of course, to take the most urgent measures. Successful strategy, it seems, but were the NGOs interested in this "displaced women cause" to some degree satisfied with the results?

To answer this question, it might be useful to identify the stakes and the problems for the formal "author" of the decision as well as others. The invitation and posterior notification to NGOs sent by the court appear to have a particular meaning to the Statement's implementation. The court was supposed to respond to this massive mobilization of women's organizations that was drawing the attention of the judge. However, the court did not limit itself to take into account NGOs' recommendations and requests. It also used the "Follow-up Commission of the Decision T-025/04"

---

[49] The memories of another meeting confirm this appreciation. The same judge took part with a text whose same objectives occupy a central place. *See* Federico Guzmán Duque, *Mujeres y niñas desplazadas por el conflicto armado: la dimensión femenina de la tragedia humanitaria en Colombia*, *in* Taula Catalana por la paz y los derechos humanos en Colombia, Ayuntamiento de Barcelona – Centro de Estudios Jurídicos, IV Jornadas sobre Colombia. Mujeres y conflicto en Colombia (Apr. 17–19 2008).

to truly allow these organizations to participate in the process by helping to create public policies. Therefore, by asking them to take part in the construction of a public policy specifically addressed to women, the court changed the organization's role and their position from one of denunciation to participation.

In my opinion, the court did this to try and establish a twofold pact of legitimacy: on the one hand, to reinforce the legitimacy of the decision as a legal act with a political dimension supported by domestic mobilized lobbies and by the international authorities, particularly the Inter-American Commission and the Inter-American Court of Human Rights; and, on the other hand, to reinforce the legitimacy of the work of women's NGOs. This is a very significant recognition, especially when we consider the mistrust and sometimes the official aggressive stance of the government toward women's NGOs. As seen on several occasions, the government did not even hesitate to discredit these NGOs by associating them with "terrorists" (the generic term systematically used by the Executive to refer to the guerrillas).[50]

Paradoxically, even though the court gave full recognition of their work and accomplishments in very clear language, one of the initial reactions I could observe from some feminists when they received the invitation of the *Agencia Presidencial para la Acción Social y la Cooperación Internacional* (Presidential Agency of Social Action and International Cooperation; the principal national authority responsible for coordinating the public-policy assistance to the IDP), to take part in the discussions on executing Statement 092/08, reflected, in my eyes, a negative perception of any official initiative. This is another effect of the court's decision to be considered seriously. A brief anecdote would clarify this idea. While attending a meeting with other experts on war effects on women's lives, I heard a feminist activist saying that "it [was] really necessary to pay attention to this participation, because quite easily one was going to end up 'legitimating' the government's policy." She thought, even after Statement 092/2008, about not attending the meetings organized by the court as a way to test the capacity of responsible authorities to manage the problems "without the help of feminist NGOs," which, in her opinion, had already done a great deal of the job. However, the wide recognition made by the court and the importance of the statement were not questioned. In short, what at first appearance is a successful strategy involves other complex questions.

Setting up of the decision of the court was also a more complex exercise when having to directly face the IDW. In that sense, the most direct effect or, better said, the effect with the least intermediation was that of the decision to transmit the sexual assault cases to the prosecutor, because the case would not go through the design and construction of any public policy. The court here was less innovative: it did

---

[50] Office of the High Commissioner of the Human Rights (HCHR), Human Rights First Front Line, FIDH et OMCT, Presentation of the HCHR, universal periodic examination in Colombia, Session 3 (Dec. 1, 2008).

nothing different than communicate the case to a concerned judge, with the less "traditional" order of forcing the judge to report the results back to the court.

It is not, however, the particular work of the Attorney General that I would like to stress here, but the concrete effect that this situation will have on the women involved with these crimes. Insofar as the court's decision impels these lawsuits (and transforms the actions of *tutela* into denunciations of a criminal nature), it places the women on a new "register" of victims facing the practical implications of each procedure. Indeed, it is not the same thing to prepare the documentation that must be used as a support of an action of *tutela* (the evidence as well as the text that comprises the request) to be committed to a criminal trial, and to be ready, as a victim, to testify and "to hold on" until the end.

Tutela is a legal action that is rather easy to engage: it is expeditious as an action to be always solved in priority, it is subject to minimal formalities, it requires only one summary proof of the violation or of the threat of the fundamental right in question, and it does not require representation by a lawyer.[51]

Some of the IDWs do not realize that they are victims of a crime and demand only humanitarian aid. In Colombia, if we consider the procedural requirements, expenses, and time needed to raise a complaint, the emotional stress and, sometimes, the serious risk to personal safety, it is more than obvious why victims of the war insist and concentrate their actions via this constitutional *tutela* way. This is a very clear example of what Revillard calls the margins of action on the "structures of political and legal opportunity"[52] – that is, the context that makes a political or juridical action in a particular case possible (not in a formal, but practical way). In this case, the action was on the activists of the cause of displaced women in Colombia.[53]

However, for the NGOs defending women's rights, as well as for the displaced women, the request, even by this constitutional way of *tutela*, also relates to and remains a question about the access to justice: women claim and require tangible results (inquiries, judgments, punitive damages).[54] The court thus does not transform a request into something else. The court's reply is not limited to rule each case (although in fact it does), but it may propose an integral solution of the IDW's problems. According to this approach, we could even reverse the question: precisely

---

[51] In comparison, for example, with the public action of "tort law" (standard action to initiate a tort lawsuit of State responsibility), one needs a lawyer, evidence, and especially the possibility of waiting approximately ten years to have a final decision. This legal logic of the ordinary way is not adapted for the context of armed conflict or vulnerability in general.

[52] Revillard, *supra* note 19, at 145–63.

[53] This analysis is beyond what I develop here. I only suggest the possibility of this kind of framework.

[54] I do not advance here a thorough analysis of the form in which this "cause for the women victims of the war" – as I call it – is posed. I limit my analysis to remark that the way of judicial activism of this cause, at least for this statement process, which I comment on here, follows the formal criteria of the system.

insofar as the decision of the court for the cases of sexual assault was more traditional, we can imagine that this resolution was more foreseeable for its actresses.

To sum up, the inquiries concerning sexual assault and abuses will require the concerned women's organizations, and the direct victims, to prepare for this new procedure. If I recall once again the meeting at Medellin, this particular concern was not addressed at that time. These NGOs were even unaware of which cases concerned women living in Medellin. The situation in Bogotá was quite different. In Bogotá, the organizations participating and inspiring Statement 092/2008 were preparing to train litigation teams to accompany these lawsuits, among other legal actions. It is extremely probable that, at least at the beginning, there will be cases the court will denounce to the Attorney General; for example, cases by women who have no access to any support of this kind and who could show the weakness of their support from NGOs. In a less predictive tone and to summarize a complex situation, this allows us to notice how the stakes of the decision changes coming from the perspectives of women's organizations or the victims directly, and how that perspective also can change depending on the context.

CONCLUSION

To write a broad conclusion on a decision whose effects are still growing and developing would be, in my opinion, a useless effort.[55] However, I would like to recall the objective at the beginning of my analysis and to reaffirm this transcendental character and, at the same time, this very complex decision of the court. These two characteristics reaffirm the perspective that can contribute to developing a sociology of constitutional law, according to which the scientific interest is not only directed to the uses and mobilizations of the law for the "users" of the legal system, but also to the judges themselves. The surprising commitment of the Colombian Constitutional Court to the "women displaced by violence" has been hardly recognized in the country, and this leaves us without some elements that could help to explain the reasons of the court's commitment.[56]

My short commentary of this historical decision of the Colombian Constitutional Court allows me to emphasize some interesting elements to be studied when concentrating on "the question of the explanation of the choice and the legal strategy

---

[55] In fact, the court produced another decision (C.C., Statement 237/2008) because it found the government's response unsatisfactory. I decided nevertheless to stop my analysis at the same time when my empirical research had to stop.

[56] I would limit myself here to mention the two principal theories in connection with the new role of the constitutional judge in Latin America. A first theory, built starting from a sociopolitical analysis of the history of the ideas, is DIEGO LÓPEZ, LA TEORÍA IMPURA DEL DERECHO (Editorial Legis 2003). For a continental perspective, *see* YVES DEZALAY & BRYAN GARTH, THE INTERNATIONALIZATION OF PALACE WARS: LAWYERS, ECONOMISTS, AND THE CONTEST TO TRANSFORM LATIN AMERICAN STATES (Chicago Series in Law and Society 2002).

adopted by social movements."[57] Between two great legal strategies corresponding to great traditions of making law, strong legal action on the one hand and lobbying for legislative reforms on the other, the activists of the cause of women displaced by violence in Colombia appear to have found a certain point of balance and finally found a tool for social reforms, particularly in the action of *tutela*.

[57] Revillard, *supra* note 19.

13

The Promise of Democratic Constitutionalism

Women, Constitutional Dialogue, and the Internet

Tsvi Kahana and Rachel Stephenson

I. INTRODUCTION

Mainstream constitutionalism has been slowly but surely turning its back on the courts. For many years, the notion of a constitution was synonymous with the notion of judicial review. Conventional wisdom held that we have a constitution to restrain majorities and legislatures. At the birth of a nation, or at some pivotal point in its history, the polity determines long-term principles to guide it for generations to come. These principles must be put in general terms to allow for adaptability and adjustments over time. They also limit the power of the government, and therefore must be enforced by an external institution, one that is not a directly publicly accountable part of government. This institution is the courts. When constitutional principles are not clear, the courts are charged with interpreting them. However, such conventional wisdom is no more. Many scholars across the globe have been advocating the replacement of judicial supremacy-based constitutionalism with what we call democratic constitutionalism. Unlike constitutional models that exemplify legislative supremacy, democratic constitutionalism favors a supreme and entrenched constitution. However, unlike under a system of judicial supremacy, democratic constitutionalism leaves the final word on constitutional matters in the hands of the elected lawmakers.

The merits of this middle-ground model of constitutionalism have been the subject of much debate in the literature. However, the relationship between democratic constitutionalism and feminism has not yet been explored. In this chapter, we offer a first reflection on this topic and argue that democratic constitutionalism provides important opportunities for the direct participation of women in discussions of constitutional issues.

Today, an important tool through which this dialogue can occur is one of tremendous significance to women – the Internet. The Internet allows for inclusionary participation free from the oppressive and embodied restraints of the physical world. It offers a mode of text-based communication that is uniquely fluid and flexible. Consequently, the Internet allows the type of back-and-forth, inclusive, and ongoing participation that other modes of communication lack.

This chapter proceeds in four parts. Part II introduces democratic constitutionalism and points to important questions that feminism will need to address to fully evaluate this concept. Part III demonstrates the way in which democratic constitutionalism brings about a direct dialogue between the representative and the represented about the meaning of the constitutional text. Part IV, the lion's share of the chapter, introduces the Internet as a potential medium for pursuing this dialogue, due to the faceless, communal, and textual nature of Internet communication. We suggest that the type of dialogue and the mechanism through which it can take place, the Internet, are particularly conducive to the participation of women in constitutional interpretation. By engaging in dialogue through the Internet, women have the opportunity to disembody their opinions, thereby freeing themselves from the type of instant gender bias that can result from face-to-face encounters. With women's use of online social networking systems on the rise, the Internet is uniquely able to draw new female perspectives into constitutional debate and interpretation. Indeed, the faceless nature of the Internet may be of value to all minority groups who have traditionally felt or been alienated from formal political mechanisms by virtue of their "otherness," something that disappears in cyberspace. This part concludes by making the connection between the textual nature of the Internet and the textual nature of constitutions, generally, and proposes the idea of constitutions and the Internet together, creating a sort of textual living tree. Part V introduces the various challenges that our account meets if one wishes to turn it from a theoretical journey into a practical platform. The chapter concludes by noting the possibility of what we call feminist democratic constitutionalism.

II. DEMOCRATIC CONSTITUTIONALISM AND WOMEN

The debate about the legitimacy of judicial review of legislation has dominated constitutional theory for more than a century. Traditionally, the two polar choices in the debate were American-style constitutionalism, with judicial review at its center, and Commonwealth-style legislative supremacy, with no constitutional texts safeguarding basic rights and no judicial review of legislation. In the past two decades or so, scholars have enriched this debate with subtlety and nuance, supporting a paradigm that would combine both judicial and legislative engagement with the Constitution. Embodying what Frank Michelman refers to as "judicial leadership without judicial finality,"[1] this new paradigm does not oppose judicial review

---

[1] Frank Michelman, *Judicial Supremacy, the Concept of Law, and the Sanctity of Life, in* JUSTICE AND INJUSTICE IN LAW AND LEGAL THEORY 139 (Austin Sarat & Thomas R. Kearns eds., 1996).

altogether; rather, it opposes judicial supremacy. Proponents of this view argue that although the courts should have a say in constitutional issues, they should not have the final or exclusive say. They advocate that the constitutional powers exercised by the courts should be weakened in favor of granting greater constitutional powers to nonjudicial institutions, particularly legislatures.[2]

Beyond theory, novel constitutional instruments have appeared in the world of institutional design. New bills of rights, such as the Canadian Charter of Rights and Freedoms[3] and the British Human Rights Act,[4] provide for significant judicial involvement in rights protection, but leave the final word on these matters to legislatures. The Charter, for example, gives the judiciary the power to strike down legislation, but includes a "notwithstanding" mechanism, allowing legislatures to create legislation notwithstanding the Charter.[5] The British Human Rights Act does not give courts the power to strike down legislation, but rather allows for a judicial declaration that legislation is incompatible with rights, leaving the final decision of whether to repeal such legislation to the English Parliament.

Advocates of democratic constitutionalism offer a variety of arguments in its support. Some of these arguments are instrumental and are based on the conviction that true partnership between courts and legislatures generates better public discourse and, ultimately, better decisions.[6] Other democratic constitutionalists maintain that legislatures are just as qualified to interpret the Constitution as the courts and that despite what advocates of judicial supremacy argue, interpretation by legislatures is not anarchic, irrational, or tyrannical.[7] To the extent that legislative decisions

---

[2] *See id.; see also* Stephen Gardbaum, *The New Commonwealth Model of Constitutionalism*, 49 Am. J. Comp. L. 707, (2001); Christopher P. Manfredi, Judicial Power and the Charter: Canada and the Paradox of Liberal Constitutionalism (2nd ed. 2001); Robert C. Post, *The Supreme Court, 2002 Term – Forward: Fashioning the Legal Constitution: Culture, Courts, and Law*, 117 Harv. L. Rev. 4, (2003); Robert C. Post & Reva B. Siegel, *Legislative Constitutionalism and Section Five Power: Policentric Interpretation of the Family and Medical Leave Act*, 112 Yale L. J. 1943,(2003); Larry D. Kramer, The People Themselves: Popular Constitutionalism and Judicial Review (2004); Sanford Levinson, *Constitutional Engagement "Outside the Courts" (and "Inside the Legislature"): Reflections on Professional Expertise and the Ability to Engage in Constitutional Interpretation*, in The Least Examined Branch: The Role of Legislatures in the Constitutional State 378 (Richard Bauman & Tsvi Kahana eds., 2006); Keith E. Whittington, Political Foundations of Judicial Supremacy: The Presidency, the Supreme Court, and Constitutional Leadership in U.S. History 4 (2007); Mark Tushnet, Weak Courts, Strong Rights: Judicial Review and Social Welfare Rights in Comparative Constitutional Law (2008).

[3] *Canadian Charter of Rights and Freedoms*, Part I of the *Constitution Act, 1982*, being Schedule B to the *Canada Act 1982* (U.K.), 1982, c.11 [hereinafter, *Charter*].

[4] *Human Rights Act 1998*, c.42.

[5] For various approaches on the notwithstanding mechanism, *see* Tsvi Kahana, *What Makes for a Good Use of the Notwithstanding Mechanism?*, 23 Supreme Ct. L. Rev. 191 (2004).

[6] *See, e.g.,* Christine Bateup, *The Dialogic Promise: Assessing the Normative Potential of Theories of Constitutional Dialogue*, 71 Brook. L. Rev 1109, 1109 (2006); Gardbaum, *supra* note 2, at 748.

[7] *See, e.g.,* Whittington, *supra* note 2, at 835–836, 839; Tushnet, *supra* note 2, at 157. In the United States, some scholars rely on what they believe to be the true historical understanding of the principle

are irrational, judicial interpretation suffers from the same flaw. In any case, advocates of democratic constitutionalism argue that the difference between the two institutions is largely insignificant.[8] Other influential writers are motivated by a democratic, participatory, and antielitist political vision embodied by democratic constitutionalism.[9] They argue that it is simply unfair to grant judges the power to interpret the Constitution and that this power should rest with the people or their representatives. Finally, some democratic constitutionalists rely heavily on structural arguments, based on the view that a constitution is not a legal document in the simple sense of the word but rather a political statement – a rhetorical, deliberative, and discursive device around whose majestic generalizations the polity, individuals, and institutions should organize their arguments.[10]

Is democratic constitutionalism good for women? To date, this has remained unexplored. Nevertheless, some inferences can be drawn from existing feminist literature on judicial review, and judicial or legislative supremacy. The starting point is the perennial question of which institution is better for women – courts or legislatures. Several arguments have been made for both sides.

Feminist advocates of courts argue that courts protect rights, including women's rights, better than legislatures.[11] They note that women's groups can initiate and participate in litigation,[12] and that the public discourse around high-profile rights cases mobilizes public support of women's and feminist issues[13] while legitimizing

---

of checks and balances between the branches of government – a principle that has been a building block of the American constitutional tradition. *See, e.g.,* Kramer, *supra* note 2, at 228; JOHN AGRESTO, THE SUPREME COURT AND CONSTITUTIONAL DEMOCRACY 79–95 (1984).

[8] Agresto, *supra* note 7, at 79; Kramer, *supra* note 1, at 240; Peter H. Russell, *Standing Up for Notwithstanding,* 29 ALBERTA. L. REV. 293, 301 (1991).

[9] *See, e.g.,* Gardbaum, *supra* note 2, at 739–740; Kramer, *supra* note 2, at 8.

[10] *See, e.g.,* Larry D. Kramer, *Forward: We the Court,* 115 HARVARD L. REV. 5, 10 (2001); Agresto, *supra* note 7, at 71.

[11] *See* Karen O'Connor & Lee Epstein, *Beyond Legislative Lobbying: Women's Rights Groups and the Supreme Court,* JUDICATURE, 1983–1984, at 134, 143 (arguing that, "while women's groups' efforts often have been frustrated in legislative forums, the Supreme Court has served as a source of expanded women's rights," and concluding that women's groups should continue to utilize the courts in the future). The same is true of course with regard to disadvantaged groups generally. *See* WILLIAM A. BOGART, COURTS AND COUNTRY; THE LIMITS OF LITIGATION AND THE SOCIAL AND POLITICAL LIFE OF CANADA (1994).

[12] *See, e.g.,* F. L. Morton & Avril Allen, *Feminists and the Courts: Measuring Success in Interest Group Litigation in Canada,* 34 CANADIAN JOURNAL OF POLITICAL SCIENCE 55, 56 (2001) (asserting that "no group has been more active in using litigation than organized feminists," and that "feminists played an influential role in the framing and adoption of the Charter"); *See also* O'Conner & Epstein, *supra* note 11, at 148.

[13] *See, e.g.,* Diana Majury, *The Charter, Equality Rights, and Women: Equivocation and Celebration,* 40 OSGOODE HALL L. J. 297, 302–303 (2002) ("The Charter is seen as providing a forum for raising issues; for developing more sophisticated analysis and argument for public, judicial, and political education; and for mobilizing and politicization ... "). For the same point with regard to these disadvantaged groups generally, *see* Bogart, *supra* note 11, at 53.

women's and feminist goals, values, and causes.[14] Conversely, feminist advocates of legislatures remind us that judges often favor the powerful, such as men or corporations, over those who actually need their protection.[15] They argue that courts are generally more conservative leaning and favor the status quo,[16] and that judges are elitist and do not represent the diversity of groups in society.[17] Additionally, they note that rights discourse and litigation polarize public debate and contaminate it with legalese.[18] According to this view, litigation offers an illusion of change that monopolizes activists' time and resources while preventing actual progress from occurring.[19]

---

[14] *See, e.g.,* Morton & Allen, *supra* note 12, at 83 ("Litigation can also serve the corollary purposes of legitimating a group and consolidating support for a[n] existing policy. . . . Favourable judicial rulings can have an incremental effect on public and elite opinion."). *See also* JOEL F. HANDLER, SOCIAL MOVEMENTS AND THE LEGAL SYSTEM: A THEORY OF LAW REFORM AND SOCIAL CHANGE 209 (1978).

[15] *See* Lois G. MacDonald, *Promoting Social Equality through the Legislative Override,* 4 N.J.C.L. 1 (1994).

[16] *See, e.g.,* Majury, *supra* note 13, at 301 (arguing that "it is more likely that rights will be interpreted to reproduce existing power relations and protect the status quo than to challenge and redress inequities"); A. Wayne MacKay, *The Legislature, The Executive and the Courts: The Delicate Balance of Power or Who is Running this Country Anyway?* DAL. L.J., Fall 2001, at 37, 54 (arguing that, "[b]y nature judges are conservative"); A. Wayne MacKay, *Fairness After the Charter: A Rose By Any Other Name,* 10 QUEEN'S L.J. 263, 335 (1985) ("the Bench is an unlikely habitat for revolutionaries").

[17] *See, e.g.,* Majury, *supra* note 13, at 299 (citing the leftist critique of the Charter concerning "the power the Charter cedes to the courts, that is, to elite, unelected judges who are largely unaccountable"); GWEN BRODSKY & SHELAGH DAY, CANADIAN CHARTER EQUALITY RIGHTS FOR WOMEN: ONE STEP FORWARD OR TWO STEPS BACK? 3 (1989) ("By and large, judges are white, middle-aged, middle-class men with no direct experience of disadvantage"); Joel Bakan, *Constitutional Interpretation and Social Change: You Can't Always Get What You Want (Nor What You Need),* 70 CAN. BAR. REV. 307, 319 (1991) ("Biographies and statistics demonstrate convincingly that members of the judiciary do not represent the Canadian population, not in terms of class, race, ethnicity, gender, culture, or education.").

[18] *See* MARY ANN GLENDON, RIGHTS TALK: THE IMPOVERISHMENT OF POLITICAL DISCOURSE, 171 (1991) ("Our stark, simple rights dialect puts a damper on the processes of public justification, communication, and deliberation upon which the continuing vitality of a democratic regime depends. . . . It impedes creative long-range thinking about our most pressing social problems. Our rights-laden public discourse easily accommodates the economic, the immediate, and the personal dimensions of a problem, while it regularly neglects the moral, the long-term, and the social implications").

[19] *See* GERALD N. ROSENBERG, THE HOLLOW HOPE: CAN COURTS BRING ABOUT SOCIAL CHANGE? 339–340 (1991) (footnote omitted). "In the abortion field, reliance on the Court seriously weakened the political efficacy of pro-choice forces. After the 1973 decisions, many pro-choice activists simply assumed they had won and stopped their pro-choice activity. . . . The political organization and momentum that had changed laws nationwide dissipated in celebration of Court victory. The pro-choice movement was harmed in a second way by its reliance on Court action. . . . By winning a Court case 'without the organization needed to cope with a powerful opposition,' pro-choice forces vastly overestimated the power and influence of the Court. A further danger of litigation as a strategy for significant social reform is that symbolic victories may be mistaken for substantive ones, covering a reality that is distasteful. Rather than working to change that reality, reformers relying on a litigation strategy for reform may be misled (or content?) to celebrate the illusion of change." Bogart similarly notes that "[l]itigation's ability to produce symbolic as opposed to actual change can be one of its most troubling illusions. This is an issue that surfaces in the discussion of women's issues, particularly abortion and related questions" (BOGART, *supra* note 11, at 45).

Also, access to the courts is largely available only to the well off[20] and courts do not have a great record in facilitating social change.[21]

In the past, these arguments have not been made specifically about democratic constitutionalism, but rather with regard to constitutionalism, generally – that is, with regard to the general choice between courts and legislatures. To examine the adaptability of these arguments to democratic constitutionalism one can proceed in two ways. First, one could assume that because democratic constitutionalism is a middle ground between a system of judicial supremacy and a system of legislative supremacy, all of these arguments remain relevant for democratic constitutionalism but with modified force. Consider, for example, the matter of rights protection by the courts. Some feminists believe that judicial focus on individual rights has merit because it protects individual women from legislation made by a male or a male-oriented majority. Others, however, believe that legislatures understand and better protect collective issues, such as the need to limit the rights of the accused when women's rights are concerned. Both of these camps would object to democratic constitutionalism but would view it as a lesser evil than legislative supremacy and judicial supremacy, respectively.

The second way to approach the relationship between democratic constitutionalism and feminism is to look at democratic constitutionalism not as a middle ground, but as a freestanding institutional paradigm and to compare it to both judicial supremacy constitutionalism and legislative supremacy constitutionalism. Consider the issue of accessibility. Advocates of judicial supremacy constitutionalism believe that litigation is a more useful tool for women's issues than legislation, which is controlled by political majorities. On the other hand, advocates of legislative supremacy believe that litigation can help only those who are already well off. Arguably, under democratic constitutionalism, both avenues are open to women because both branches of government are involved in constitutional interpretation.[22]

---

[20] *See, e.g.*, BRODSKY & DAY, *supra* note 17, at 137–138 (arguing that "[w]omen simply do not have the money, resources, and power necessary to use the law that is there to protect and support them"); Bakan, *supra* note 17, at 318 ("The oppressed and disempowered groups who are the supposed beneficiaries of progressive Charter litigation will, because of their lack of resources, be the least likely to have genuine access to the courts").

[21] *See, e.g.*, BRODSKY & DAY, *supra* note 17 (arguing that "women and other disadvantaged groups would be wiser to put their efforts into the democratic system, trying to change conditions of disadvantage through political rather than legal means"); ROSENBERG, *supra* note 19, at 338 (similarly argues that "U.S. courts can *almost never* be effective producers of significant social reform. At best, they can second the social reform acts of the other branches of government").

[22] Arguments of this type would require some fleshing out in order to be robust. For example, it is not obvious that women would be able to utilize both legislation and litigation. Resources are limited, and therefore a choice of allocation might have to be made as to what avenue to choose. The more polished version of this argument would be that the marginal benefit of either litigation or legislation, beyond a certain point, is relatively low. Therefore, distributing participation resources to both litigation and legislation would yield better results than would either allocating all resources to litigation or to legislation. Another polished version of the argument would be that because some resources are

In this chapter, we seek to undertake the second type of analysis and argue that, in one sense, democratic constitutionalism allows for participation of women and other disempowered groups of society in ways that neither legislative supremacy nor judicial supremacy constitutionalism do. To make this point, we must first explore the relationship between representation and constitutional interpretation.

III. A DIRECT AND TEXTUAL CONSTITUTIONAL DIALOGUE

Several authors view democratic constitutionalism as dialogic in nature because, rather than hegemony, it produces a dialogue between courts and legislatures on constitutional issues.[23] In this chapter, we also set forth from the notion of dialogue. However, we have in mind a more important dialogue – that between the representative and the represented – about the meaning of the Constitution. This dialogue can exist in a system of democratic constitutionalism in a more meaningful way than under either legislative or judicial supremacy constitutionalism. Under judicial supremacy, where final word on constitutional issues is judicial, individuals not participating in litigation are unable to directly engage in dialogue with the judges who interpret the Constitution. Under legislative supremacy, there may be such direct dialogue between the polity and the legislators, but this dialogue is not textual. It will not be related to the values enshrined in the Constitution because, under legislative supremacy, there is no constitution. Only under democratic constitutionalism can this dialogue be both direct and textual.

Suppose the following question of constitutional interpretation arose: Is legislation that allows for same-sex unions but not for same-sex marriage constitutional? Under this legislation, people of the same sex may create a legal union identical to marriage but it would simply be referred to as "a union." The legislation is created as a compromise between advocates of gay marriage and those who oppose any legal recognition of gay marriage. Let us suppose, as well, that the relevant provision in the country's Constitution protects "equality" and "freedom of religion" and deems that these rights may be limited only in a "reasonable" way. There are many ways to go about examining the constitutionality of the new law but perhaps the most obvious would be to ask the following questions of constitutional interpretation: Does depriving gay people of legal title rather than a concrete legal benefit amount to a violation of equality? Does endowing gay couples with the title "marriage" violate the freedom of religion of those for whom a homosexual relationship

---

available only to litigation (e.g., pro bono time) or only to legislation (e.g., neighborhood connection with a legislator), the net amount of resources will increase under democratic constitutionalism, both as compared to judicial supremacy constitutionalism and as compared to legislative supremacy constitutionalism. The two types of arguments are not mutually exclusive, although the inquiries they propose might lead to different empirical findings.

[23] For excellent survey and analysis of dialogue theories in constitutional theory, *see* Bateup, *supra* note 6.

is a sin? In addition, if the answer to either question is yes, does the compromise arrived at by the legislature provide for "reasonable" limits on the relevant right?

Under a legislative supremacy regime, this question will be answered without any reference to a constitutional text, even if it exists. The terms "equality," "freedom of religion," and "reasonable" might come up in public discussion about the matter, but the question will not be "What does the Constitution say?", but rather, "what do we, as a polity, prefer?" In a system of judicial supremacy, the ultimate interpretation of this question, and therefore the decision concerning the constitutionality of the "unions yes, marriage no" compromise would be entirely up to the court and its understanding of the Constitution. Democratic constitutionalism presents an attractive alternative to both of these approaches. Under democratic constitutionalism, courts may voice their opinion about the matter, thus participating in public discourse and giving individuals their day in court, but the final decision on the "unions yes, marriage no" compromise will remain with the legislature. Under democratic constitutionalism, the legislature ultimately decides on the meaning of "equality," "religion," and "reasonable."

However, if legislators (i.e., the representatives) get to decide on the matter, then surely the represented (i.e., the polity) should be involved in the process as well. Democratic constitutionalism endorses a partnership between courts and legislatures that is, all other things being equal, preferable to judicial supremacy. However, there is no reason to stop at the institutional level – we can go all the way back to the polity itself. Under democratic constitutionalism, not only would legislators have the opportunity to interpret the Constitution but so would the people themselves. That is, they too would have a platform to express their views not only about the merits of the "union yes, marriage no" compromise, but also about whether this compromise is consistent with the Constitution.

The fact that the engagement would revolve around the text of the Constitution is at the heart of the difference between the public dialogue about constitutional issues under a supremacy of parliament regime and the public dialogue about constitutional issues under a democratic constitutionalism regime. Under the former, the discussion would be one of preference; under the latter, the discussion has the potential to be about interpretation.

Taking the interpretive dialogue to this next level seems like a natural progression for democratic constitutionalism. Public involvement in constitutional interpretation not only fulfills the obvious aspirations for civil participation and republican involvement in governance, but is needed to preserve public attachment to the Constitution. Moreover, public involvement is warranted because courts sometimes need information about public views on constitutional matters.[24] For example, courts may need to articulate what is or is not acceptable to the polity, and without public

---

[24] See Tushnet, *supra* note 2.

deliberation about and pronouncement on constitutional matters, courts are deprived of this information.

Involving the public in constitutional interpretation may not only be suitable for democratic constitutionalism; it may also be necessary to make democratic constitutionalism legitimate. A strong objection to constitutional interpretation being done by legislatures stems from "public choice skepticism" about legislators' incentive to engage in interpretation in a manner that is appropriately detached from the policy preferences of their constituents. If a legislator's primary motive is reelection, he or she may have to adopt a constitutional interpretation that is in line with his or her constituents' policy preferences rather than engaging in a more unbiased form of interpretation. In such cases, contradicting the constituents' preference would be political suicide. However, if we take seriously the possibility that the public itself is interested in constitutional interpretation, this objection is significantly weakened as the public will be more likely (albeit, this is certainly not guaranteed) to respect a legislator whose interpretation of the Constitution differs from their own. Furthermore, if the public choose not to reelect the representative, it might be because of differing views on the Constitution and not the public's naked policy preferences.

Democratic constitutionalism does not support replacing legislative interpretation of the Constitution with "direct interpretation" by the polity in a referendum, citizens' assembly, or other mechanism of direct democracy. Although interesting, such direct interpretation would be susceptible to all of the traditional problems of direct democracy, such as the tyranny of the majority, simplification of public discourse, and information deficits.[25] Rather, democratic constitutionalism condones polity involvement in the interpretive process similar to the way in which the polity is involved in the legislative process under any system of constitutionalism. Democratic constitutionalism seeks to encourage public participation in legislative decision making with regard to the interpretation of the Constitution rather than to replace the latter with the former. Such polity involvement may contribute to a more sincere and comprehensive constitutional dialogue, because the polity lacks a similar incentive to give way to majority sentiment. Thus, ideally, a dialogue that is facilitated between the representative and the represented would lead to a more honest, inclusive, and antielitist model of constitutionalism.

Dialogue between the representative and the represented has been done for many years through town hall meetings, primary elections, surveys, phone conversations, letters, and so on. In this chapter, we focus on the Internet as a venue for such dialogue. As the next section explains, the Internet possesses some unique characteristics, which makes it especially appropriate for the participation of women in the direct and textual discourse that democratic constitutionalism envisions.

---

[25] It should be noted, however, that at least some of the problems will not be as severe given that the polity will be somewhat limited by the four corners of the Constitution.

IV. FEMINISM, CONSTITUTIONAL INTERPRETATION,
AND THE INTERNET

A. *Introduction*

People are increasingly engaging with representatives, institutions, and political issues online.[26] On Facebook, Twitter, and individual and group blogs, people have established forums to discuss political issues. For example, a simple Google search for "reproductive rights" leads to thousands of blogs on various issues, including reproductive tourism, contraception, and adoption. These blogs range widely in sophistication. Some are authored by academics in the field of reproductive technology while others are written by users of the technology or even teenagers voicing their cultural and religious views. Similarly, there exists a wide range of forums on Facebook, with groups and pages, such as a group devoted to gender equality in reproduction, a page in honor of Dr. Henry Morgentaler, Canada's abortion pioneer,[27] and a page asking people to sign a petition against a proposed bill. Many of these sites use hyperlinks to direct Internet users to more information, often information on government websites. These sites are also interactive, providing users with the option of leaving comments or posting new hyperlinks to other sites of interest.

Although these sites are important and informative, they are not concerned with interpretation. They address various policy and ideological issues, sometimes about constitutional matters, but in a way that is not directly connected to the text of the Constitution. Indeed, although there is considerable lively literature on cyberfeminism and participation of women and minorities online, the question of interpretation of the Constitution online has not been discussed. In this part of the chapter, we argue that the Internet's special qualities make it an especially appropriate medium for a dialogue about constitutional interpretation. The Internet is unique in that it allows disembodied participation, it expands the idea of the political, and it is a textual medium. These characteristics of the Internet are addressed in this part.

Section B addresses the possibility of disembodied participation in constitutional interpretation, thereby allowing liberation and avoiding prejudice and stereotypes. Section C discusses the way in which the Internet has blurred the distinction between what is political and what is nonpolitical, thereby bringing in more groups and communities to partake in political discourse. Section D focuses on the textual nature of the Internet that makes it especially suitable to the activity of interpretation. The first two characteristics – disembodiment and the expansion of politics – are not unique to interpretative participation, and are true of participation online generally. Nevertheless, it is important to show how these characteristics may be applied to

[26] See Jane Schacter, *Digitally Democratizing Congress? Technology and Political Accountability*, 89 B. U. L. Rev. 641, 652 (2009).
[27] See Celia Milne, *Catching Up With . . . Dr. Henry Morgentaler: A Tale of Nine Lives*, 43 Med. Post, 1–3 (2007).

interpretation. The third characteristic, the textual nature of the Internet, is of special advantage to the interpretation.

B. *Disembodied Participation: Liberation and Inclusiveness*

In the 1990s, when the Internet was relatively new to the majority of the population, the leading feminist view was that this new technology was male-dominated. By the early 2000s, ideas had changed and feminist scholars began to point out that the technology was not quite as androcentric as popular perception had held. Justine Cassel and Henry Jenkins' research, for example, documents the rise of the "game grrlz" movement in the late 1990s.[28] These female gamers challenged the gender stereotypes that marked the Internet industry at the time, excelling at fighting games that were typically considered masculine domain.

At the same time, other feminist scholars began to argue that the Internet was a new subversive medium, one that could mesh well with women's voices. The Internet had grown into a global community – one defined by webs, networks, and connections. These communities of webs and networks lend themselves well to the qualities of collaboration, communication, and consensus often associated with women. For example, cyberfeminist[29] Sadie Plant conceptualized the Internet as a liberating place for women, particularly because of its textual nature. In her book *Zeroes and Ones*,[30] Plant symbolically renders zeroes as "female" and ones as phallic and "male," predicting that the digital future is feminine, distributed, and nonlinear – a world in which "zeroes" are displacing the phallic order of the "ones."[31]

Currently, cyber- or technofeminists are still divided on the Internet's value for new political involvement.[32] Some cyberfeminists, such as Fereshteh Nouraie-Simone, argue that the Internet enables a subversion of traditional hierarchies of power.[33] Others, like Lori Kendall, argue that the Internet merely reproduces already existing hierarchies.[34] We suggest that the Internet is a tool for subversion, as well as a space that allows freedom from physical identity (when that is what the user desires). Consider, for example, a commentator on a website. He or she is not instantly marked with the same biases that present themselves in face-to-face encounters.

---

[28] See Henry Jenkins, *Voices from the Combat Zone: Game Grrlz Talk Back, in* FROM BARBIE TO MORTAL KOMBAT: GENDER AND COMPUTER GAMES 328 (Justine Cassell and Henry Jenkins eds., 1999).

[29] Jessie Daniels, *Rethinking Cyberfeminism(s): Race, Gender, and Embodiment*, 37 WOMEN'S STUD. Q. 101, 117–118 (2009).

[30] SADIE PLANT, ZEROES AND ONES: DIGITAL WOMEN AND THE NEW TECHNOCULTURE (1997).

[31] *Id.* at 104.

[32] *Id.* at 101–124.

[33] See Fereshteh Nouraie-Simone, *Wings of Freedom: Iranian Women, Identity, and Cyberspace, in* ON SHIFTING GROUND: MUSLIM WOMEN IN THE GLOBAL ERA, 61 (Fereshteh Nouraie-Simone ed., 2005).

[34] LORI KENDALL, HANGING OUT IN THE VIRTUAL PUB: MASCULINITIES AND RELATIONSHIPS ONLINE (2002).

Thus, marginalized groups can enter the virtual public space of the Internet without facing the barriers that exist in physical public spaces.

Nouraie-Simone writes in the context of women in Iran, but we suggest that her point about disembodiment can be extended to all female Internet users. She finds that "[t]he absence of the physical body in electronic space and the anonymity this offers have a liberating effect on repressed social identity, as 'electronic technology' becomes a 'tool for the design of freely chosen identities.'"[35] Nouraie-Simone takes her notion of disembodiment even further, seeing it as empowering women to create new identities – an idea often called "identity tourism." Similarly, Sherry Turkle suggests that the ability to play with gender in cyberspace can also help shape a person's real-life understanding of gender.[36] These inspiring ideas deserve elaboration because it is useful in demonstrating the concrete ways in which the Internet may allow inclusive and authentic participation of the people on questions of constitutional interpretation.

Online, those who are usually constrained by their physicality are free from the biases that taint their expression in real life. Turkle writes about what it means to be disembodied in cyberspace, and the opportunities this disembodiment creates. She explores the experiences that her interview subjects have with gender play and disembodiment online, and suggests that these experiences have implications that extend into RL (real life).[37] Turkle notes that online, multiple identities are available – one can be who one IRL (in real life) is not.[38] In beginning her discussion of her online experience, Turkle tells of how, when filling out a profile to participate in an online game, she neglected to fill in the gender box. When someone questioned her about her gender she considered that being a virtual man might actually be more comfortable than being a virtual woman.[39] It turns out that "gender swapping" is common in online communities, especially within the complex world of online role-playing games that Turkle explores.[40] Performing a different gender online offers people the "opportunity to explore conflicts raised by one's biological gender" in a place that is safe and anonymous.[41] The experience of being another gender is accessible online, and has value in that it encourages reflection on the way in which gender shapes our expectations of others. Gender is a powerful force in society, something that Turkle suggests, attractive women know all too well. RL attractive women experience greater social ease by describing their online characters in ways that are traditionally unattractive, or take things even further by creating male personas online.[42] Coming back to RL from these disembodied experiences

---

[35] Nouraie-Simone, *supra* note 33, at 61–62 (footnote omitted).
[36] SHERRY TURKLE, LIFE ON THE SCREEN: IDENTITY IN THE AGE OF THE INTERNET (Phoenix, 1997).
[37] *Id.* at 12.
[38] *Id.* at 179.
[39] *Id.* at 210.
[40] *Id.* at 213.
[41] *Id.*
[42] *Id.* at 215.

has an impact. As Turkle suggests, "[h]aving literally written our online personae into existence, we are in a position to be more aware of what we project into everyday life. Like the anthropologist returning home from a foreign culture, the voyager in virtuality can return to a real world better equipped to understand its artifices."[43]

Disembodiment in the context of the public's participation in constitutional interpretation on the Internet may enhance the likelihood of involvement by women and minorities. First, they may feel more free to participate and less constrained by traditional biases when the physical body is removed from the equation. Second, the anonymity of the Internet may decrease the danger of discouraging the views based on stereotypes against women, and thus contribute to increased political participation by women.[44] Moreover, although full objectivity is impossible, a traditional distinction between preference-stating (i.e., political discourse) and constitutional interpretation (i.e., legal discourse) is that the latter aspires to be more objective. Indeed, for some constitutional theorists, what makes the courts so appropriate for constitutional adjudication is that they are the "the forum of principle."[45] Disembodying oneself may affect not only the way one is perceived, but also the way one thinks. To the extent that disembodiment brings us closer to objectivity, it is a welcome technique for the constitutional interpretation, which aspires to objectivity.

C. *Expanding Politics: New Communities*

Through disembodiment and identity tourism, the Internet allows for the expansion of participation in politics. However, it does more than that: it actually expands politics. We may say that because of disembodiment, more people may be brought to politics and, because of collapsing the wall between what is conceived as political and what is conceived as nonpolitical, the politics are brought to the people.

Anita Harris, in canvassing studies of young Australian women, states that young women "feel more alienated from, and less entitled to participate in, formal political activities than young men, but are more likely to be engaged in informal, localized politics or social-conscience-style activism."[46] Harris discusses how young women are already engaged in political activities online, but that the forums they tend to use are not traditionally seen as political.[47] The young women Harris discusses are arguably a group that would respond positively to our vision of online constitutional

---

[43] *Id.* at 263.

[44] It is clear that anonymous online participation is not free of problems. For example, it provides a forum for offensive expression, often abusive to minority groups. See Dan Gillmor, "Fix for anonymous sleaze is in our attitudes, not laws: It's vital to protect anonymous speech; start by cleaning up the online cesspools," SALON, January 5, 2011, *available at* www.salon.com/life/internet_culture/?story=/tech/dan_gillmor/2011/01/05/fixing_anonymity (last visited Jan. 26, 2011).

[45] *See* Ronald M. Dworkin, *The Forum of Principle, in* A MATTER OF PRINCIPLE 33 (1985).

[46] Anita Harris, *Young Women, Late Modern Politics, and the Participatory Possibilities of Online Cultures*, 11 J. YOUTH STUD. 481, 481 (2008).

[47] *Id.* at 482.

interpretation. Not only are these women using the new technologies that we envision as venues for interpretation, but as Harris suggests, they are hungry for new ways in which to become politically involved and have their voices heard. In this way, we see these women as ideally situated to use the Internet as a venue for the facilitation of involvement in constitutional interpretation.

Nowhere is the blurring of the traditional distinction between the political and the nonpolitical more clear than in the increasingly widespread use of social networking sites such as Facebook and Twitter. Typically, individuals join these sites for social connectedness or entertainment. However, in today's online world, information cannot be neatly compartmentalized. In the past, the average politically disengaged person may not have cared to pick up a newspaper or read a political magazine, therefore avoiding political information. On social networking sites, the exposure to politics may not be purposeful but it does draw in, at least somewhat, those that would otherwise be disengaged. Feminism has challenged for many years the division between the personal and the political, and this observation is even more obvious in the online world.

For example, Hillary Clinton, the current U.S. Secretary of State, has 17,869 followers on Twitter, most of whom we can assume are already politically engaged. Clinton has taken full advantage of Twitter and other social media as a political tool to get the U.S. government's message across.[48] Much more popular, actor Ashton Kutcher has 6,379,741 followers.[49] Given Kutcher's résumé, it may be safe to assume that his fan demographic is not predominantly the most politically engaged individuals. However, mixed in with "tweets" about sports or his irritation with his new smartphone, Kutcher criticizes politicians, and raises issues of human trafficking and modern-day slavery. If Kutcher is a celebrity from the entertainment world who also expresses his views on political issues, Sarah Palin is an example of the opposite – a political celebrity who actually prefers online platforms to express dissatisfaction with the attitudes of traditional media, and who sometimes tweets about family and personal matters.[50] Technology makes political engagement possible in a way that flipping through the newspaper every day, skipping past the news to reach the comics, never did.

Research on the exact impact of social networking sites on politics and participation is still in its infancy, but some evidence has begun to emerge on the potential of online political participation. For example, a U.S. study that surveyed college students in the month prior to the 2008 presidential election found that "lightweight" political activity on Facebook, along with high levels of political activity among Facebook contacts, actually predicted participation in other political venues. As a user's

---

[48] *See* Andrew Quinn, *Tweet Like an Egyptian – Hillary Clinton Tries it Out*, Reuters, February 23, 2011, http://blogs.reuters.com/frontrow/2011/02/23/tweet-like-an-egyptian-hillary-clinton-tries-it-out/.

[49] As of Feb. 27, 2011.

[50] Pete Cashmore, *Sarah Palin Shuns Press: Talks to Twitter, Facebook Instead*, Mashable, July 4, 2009, http://mashable.com/2009/07/04/sarah-palin-facebook/ (last visited Jan. 15, 2011).

political activities on Facebook increased, so did his or her political participation elsewhere.[51]

Beyond changing the nature of politics, the Internet also facilitates the evolvement of new communities and the creation of "new cultures."[52] The Internet provides a plurality of domains in which social actors may engage in deliberation on social issues. This engagement facilitates the creation of shared interpretations about how such issues should be approached.[53] Each domain or sphere is its own community – similar to nonvirtual communities. The members of these communities may or may not belong to the same physical communities, gender, ethnicity, or socio-economic groups, and this diversity may serve to enhance the diversity of virtual political involvement in our proposed scheme. Virtual communities could participate in politics, just as physical communities often do, without suffering from the same homogeneity associated with physical groups that are separated by geography, ethnicity, and socioeconomic status.[54] However, virtual social groups are still manifestations of physical social groups, and as such, should be taken seriously, regardless of their status as mediated through cyberspace. Thus, online communities can facilitate democratic deliberation.[55]

D. *The Internet, Text, and the Living Tree*

Online discourse is especially appropriate for constitutional interpretation by the polity, as envisioned by democratic constitutionalism. First, both the Internet and

---

[51] *See* Jessica Vitak, Paul Zube, Andrew Smock, Caleb T. Carr, Nicole Ellison, & Cliff Lampe, *It's Complicated: Facebook Users' Political Participation in the 2008 Election*, 14 CYBERPSYCHOLOGY, BEHAVIOR, AND SOCIAL NETWORKING 107 (2011). Critics, however, argue that "lightweight" online political involvement, or "slacktivism," (the clever combination of the words slacker and activism), are irrelevant for the real world. *Id.*

[52] WOMEN@INTERNET: CREATING NEW CULTURES IN CYBERSPACE (Wendy Harcourt ed., Zed Books 1999).

[53] *See, e.g.*, Deva Woodly, *New Competencies in Democratic Communication? Blogs, Agenda Setting and Political Participation*, 134 PUBLIC CHOICE 109, 121 (describing blogs as "a communicative space characterized by dialogue among interested peers – a form of political communication that is distinctly different from the communicative capabilities exhibited by or suited to traditional media").

[54] *See, e.g.*, Barry Wellman & Milena Gulia, *Virtual Communities As Communities: Net Surfers Don't Ride Alone*, *in* COMMUNITIES IN CYBERSPACE 167, 184 (Mark A. Smith & Peter Kollock eds., 1999) (noting that "relaxation of constraints on the size and proximity of one's 'communication audience' on the Net can increase the diversity of people encountered" and that the "lack of in-person involvement... allows relationships to develop on the basis of communicated shared interests rather than be stunted at the onset by perceived differences in social status"); Jenny Preece & Diane Maloney-Krichmar, *Online Communities: Design, Theory, and Practice*, JOURNAL OF COMPUTER-MEDIATED COMMUNICATION, July 2005 (online) (noting that "[u]ntil the advent of telecommunications technology, definitions of community focused on close-knit groups in a single location" and "social relationships took place with a stable and limited set of individuals").

[55] *See, e.g.*, AARON BARLOW, BLOGGING AMERICA: THE NEW PUBLIC SPHERE 66 (2008) ("bloggers do see themselves as broadening conversation... they are all trying to do something to expand the public sphere").

Constitution are text based. Moreover, the Internet brought about a sort of deformalizing and democratization of text, in the same processes that democratic constitutionalism wishes the Constitution to undergo.

The Internet is not only about text – much of it has images and sounds. However, it is said that, thanks to the Internet, never before have people written or read so much.[56] An increase in Internet use has resulted in an increase in our consumption and output of text. Internet users are clearly not intimidated by the written word, and they may even prefer the virtual written word to print. Our proposal for constitutional engagement embraces Internet users' comfort with the virtual written word. Like any text-based Internet communication, online constitutional interpretation would be interactive, nonlinear, and would have the unique capacity to be nonelitist in nature.[57]

An example of the potential fluidity and flexibility of text can be seen in the ways in which Internet users have created new Internet-based communications such as emoticons and Internet slang. In this way, Internet communication is perhaps more akin to oral communication than the traditional written word.[58] Further, users share a new Internet language in which parentheses and semicolons [;)] convey a meaning ("a wink") and are not just a jumble of punctuation.

The Internet not only allows a textual dialogue about the text of the Constitution, it actually creates what may be called a dialogical text. Users can jump from one document to another simply by clicking on a hypertext link. For example, a person can make a short, ten-word post in a tweet on Twitter or as a status update on Facebook that leads readers to an in-depth article, which in turn could send the user to even more links to more text.[59] Bloggers on the Internet often link to original source documents, enabling their audience to go directly to the documents at issue. This can be done instantly, and without the user incurring expense. The flexibility and ease that Internet communication offers simply does not exist with traditional oral or paper communication.[60] By following links and clicking from site to site, users of the Internet make an informational tree as they surf the web. The unique nonlinearity of the Internet allows users to build their own trees of information and communication.

[56] *See* ROGER E. BOHN & JAMES E. SHORT, HOW MUCH INFORMATION? 2009 REPORT ON AMERICAN CONSUMERS (Global Information Industry Center, University of California, San Diego, 2009), http://hmi.ucsd.edu/pdf/HMI_2009_ConsumerReport_Dec9_2009.pdf, at 18.

[57] For a view that feminism welcomes the shift from more traditional text to hypertext, *see* Barbara Page, *Women Writers and the Restive Text: Feminism, Experimental Writing, and Hypertext*, 6 POSTMODERN CULTURE 196 (1996).

[58] *See* Beverly A. Lewin and Yonatan Donner, *Communication in Internet Message Boards*, 18 ENGLISH TODAY, 29, 29–30 (2002).

[59] "Ironically, the same technologies derided by some for contributing to a lack of literacy – Facebook and Twitter – are full of recommendations of things to read." Eliot Van Buskirk, *Study: Rumors of Written-Word Death Greatly Exaggerated*, Wired, December 29, 2009, *available at* www.wired.com/epicenter/2009/12/reading-expands-study/ (accessed January 15, 2010).

[60] *See* Schacter, *supra* note 26, at 650.

Perhaps related to the emergence of text as a nonelitist instrument, we witness a reimagining of the nature of textual communication. Text on the Internet is playful and interactive. Users are not constrained by traditional formalities of language as they were prior to the Internet – the Internet seems not to have any formal requirements for text. Typos and poor grammar abound, but do not negate or devalue the message of the text as they may in a more traditional medium.[61] When formalities like grammar and form no longer carry any weight, everyone's views on constitutional interpretation begin as equally legitimate. Constitutional interpretation would no longer be limited to those citizens with legal education and to those who have the skills or resources to participate in litigation or the legislative process. On the Internet, anyone with a blog or a Twitter account could provide a source of public consultation.

The notion that constitutions do not remain frozen to the time of their creation is widespread and very familiar in constitutional theory. In Canada, for example, Lord Sankey famously coined the phrase that the Canadian Constitution is "a living tree capable of growth and expansion within its natural limits."[62] This means that the Constitution's text, as well as its meaning, is not stagnant – instead, it is meant to change along with the values of society.

The living tree metaphor can be extended to the people's involvement in constitutional interpretation. The text of constitutions acts as the roots of the tree, and the dialogue between the represented and their representatives helps the tree to grow and branch out. This growth results in an interpretation of the Constitution that is not constrained by text or elitist judicial interpretation, but one that is responsive to the very people that the Constitution is meant to serve and protect. Interpretation will grow out of the dialogue between the legislatures and the people and continue to branch off of the views of the polity. Thus, just as judicial interpretation creates new branches of meaning for the text of the Constitution by building off of earlier decisions and interpretations, the people, through the interactive medium of the Internet, can build their own branches.

V. CHALLENGES AND AGENDA FOR RESEARCH

Our analysis, thus far, has portrayed an idealized and somewhat stylized picture of the Internet and its potential for women's participation. However, the study of the Internet is still in its infancy and several questions must be addressed before we

---

[61] See Lewin and Donner, *supra.* note 57, at 29. See also Eugene Volokh, *Cheap Speech and What It Will Do*, 104 YALE L. J. 1805, 1806–07 (1995):

> The new media order that these technologies will bring will be much more democratic and diverse than the environment we see now. Cheap speech will mean that far more speakers – rich and poor, popular and not, banal and avant garde – will be able to make their work available to all.

[62] *See* Dworkin, *supra* note 46.

can comfortably convert our theoretical argument into a practical platform. Several matters require future research.

The first field of research is empirical studies about women's participation online in various forms. It may be reasonably argued that the Internet is not a tool of the underincluded. Although we see the Internet as a tool that can be used to reach out to marginalized groups, critics of this idea argue that it remains to be seen if this new technology will make previously disengaged citizens more likely to consume political information. They argue that it is possible that the same informational and participation imbalance that is seen in "real-world" politics will be reproduced, and that educated, wealthy, white men will continue to dominate the political discourse, be it Web-based or not.[63]

Moreover, emerging research on women's participation online reveals that across several areas of online interaction, women tend to participate less than men. For example, one of the symbols of the Internet revolution is Wikipedia, whose contributors are 90 percent men and only 10 percent women. On the other hand, as is always the case with social science, one must be very careful not to draw general conclusions from specific studies. For example, Deborah Halbert suggested that the masculine construction of knowledge focuses on industrialized labor, which exists within a system of production that generates knowledge in the abstract sense.[64] By contrast, "[w]omen's labor networks people together in social structures by moving beyond labor as a commodity to labor as an act of care."[65] Thus, a "feminist way of knowing emphasizes the relationships built, rather than dominion over others."[66] It may very well be the case that sharing thoughts and ideas about the interpretation of the Constitution is closer to the notions of knowledge sharing, networking, and community building than to the development of a concrete, sometimes profitable,

---

[63] *See* Schachter, *supra* note 26, at 657 ("[t]he internet has created new tools for the segment of the electorate that was already politically engaged before the advent of the internet"). Clear and authoritative information about woman's access to the Internet is not available. In the United States – and quite possibly throughout the developed world – there is parity among males and females although there are gender differences in terms of usage, agency, and representation with technology. *See* Cindy Royal, *Framing the Internet: A Comparison of Gendered Spaces*, 26 Soc. Sci. Computer Rev. 152 (2008). However, in developing countries, the gender disparity in access to the Internet is typically more apparent. One study found that for women and girls in many developing countries and remote regions, access to the Internet may be limited or nonexistent due to financial and cultural barriers, as well as lack of resources, home and family obligations, and education. *See* Helen Aitkin, *Bridging the Mountainous Divide: A Case for ICTs for Mountain Women*, 22 Mountain Res. & Dev. X?, 225–229 (2002). Similarly, UNESCO states that "[p]redominant among those currently excluded from the IT revolution are women." United Nations Educational, Scientific and Cultural Organization (UNESCO). *Community Multimedia Centres (CMC) and Gender.* Accessed February 4, 2011 (www.unesco.org/webworld/cmc).

[64] Debora Halbert, *Feminist Interpretations of Intellectual Property*, 14 Am U. J. Gender Soc. Policy & L. 431 (2006).

[65] *Id.* at 439.

[66] *Id.* at 440.

online enterprise. Therefore, women are more likely to participate in constitutional interpretation than in the creation of a database such as Wikipedia.

Secondly, not all scholars believe in the advantages of online deliberations as compared to real-life discourse. For example, Richard Davis notes how users often tend to speak past one another and do not connect as a deliberative group, but merely collect together as isolated individuals.[67] Davis attributes this "absence of engagement" to the depersonalized and often chaotic settings of the Internet forum. Similarly, authors argue that rather than simply making participation more accessible, the Internet forum provides "new ways to interact with information that can confuse and overwhelm people taught to extract meaning from only conventional print."[68]

Finally, the technical ways in which the representatives are to engage with the polity about interpretation needs to be carefully considered. For example, should legislators canvass only the opinions of the polity, directly addressing interpretive questions? Or should they also consider polity opinions about policy matters that indirectly reveal interpretive views? Should every legislator employ an individual with some type of legal or constitutional expertise?[69]

It is clear that much work needs to be done before our theoretical argument can be applied in actual political systems. However, we hope that future researchers will take it upon themselves to study some of these questions, keeping in mind the potential we see in including women and minorities in a direct and textual dialogue between representatives and represented about the meaning of the Constitution.

VI. CONCLUSION: TOWARD FEMINIST DEMOCRATIC CONSTITUTIONALISM

In conclusion, let us briefly reintroduce the contours of the conceptual excursion we took. We started with the idea of democratic constitutionalism and showed that under this paradigm, legislatures rather than courts have the final authority over constitutional issues. This is in contrast to both the traditional American-style judicial supremacy style and the once-British model of parliamentary sovereignty. We then explained that taking democratic constitutionalism seriously means including in the constitutional dialogue not only the representatives, but also the represented –

---

[67] RICHARD DAVIS, THE WEB OF POLITICS: THE INTERNET'S IMPACT ON THE AMERICAN POLITICAL SYSTEM 177 (1999).

[68] Julie Coiro, *Reading Comprehension on the Internet: Expanding Our Understanding of Reading Comprehension to Encompass New Literacies*, 56 READING TEACHER 458, 458 (2003).

[69] Clearly, there is no way to ensure that the public indeed engages with the Constitution and does not merely express its political preferences; however, this is the case whenever there is a constitution, regardless of the agent or institution. Judges may dress political preference as interpretive judgments; so may legislators and the polity. At the end of the day, any model of constitutionalism requires trusting interpretive agents to be able to distinguish, and be interested in distinguishing, between preference-stating and interpretation.

namely the polity. The bulk of the chapter showed the ways in which the Internet has the potential to empower women through participation on constitutional issues.

We demonstrated that the Internet allows for a direct and textual dialogue between the polity and their representatives. We also demonstrated that political participation on the Internet may be disembodied and, therefore, bring about more liberation and inclusiveness. In addition, we discussed how the Internet has the potential to create new communities especially suitable for women and other disempowered groups. We also pointed out both the promise and the perils of online political participation.

As is often the case with conceptual analysis, there is more to the theoretical force of the argument than meets the eye. The analysis in this chapter demonstrates how analyzing constitutionalism from a feminist perspective allows us to think about not only the interaction between feminism and constitutionalism, but also about some of the fundamental concepts of constitutionalism. In that sense, this chapter provides first thoughts on what may be referred to as feminist democratic constitutionalism.

This becomes evident if we consider the notion of a textual living tree, a central element of our analysis. Using the notion of online communities emerging from the literature on cyberfeminism, we portrayed a tree whose growth is rooted not only in the hegemonic and elitist judiciary, but also in the polity itself, allowing for participations of disempowered groups. In a telling way, this line of thinking is applicable to constitutionalism in general. A common criticism of the notion of a living tree does not apply when the growth of the tree is done by the polity. The criticism is that if the judges are responsible for the growth of the tree, then with every adjustment to the scope of constitutional provisions, the legislature's law-making authority diminishes.[70] However, under the model of feminist democratic constitutionalism, this criticism no longer has any significance. Through dialogue between the represented and representing, the people are part of the growth of the Constitution. If the Constitution is a living tree, and the interpretations of the court and legislature are the branches of that tree, then dialogue on the Internet about the Constitution could be imagined as the soil that nourishes it. In fact, not only are the represented part of the growth, they help the Constitution bloom.

---

[70] Davis, *supra* note 66, at 7.

PART IV

The Constitutionalism of Reproductive Rights

14

Pregnancy, Equality, and U.S. Constitutional Law

Jennifer S. Hendricks

A recurring problem in sex equality law is the law's tendency to treat men's experiences as the norm and women's as the exception. In one context, however, U.S. constitutional law does the opposite: U.S. Supreme Court precedent treats pregnancy as the prototype – the norm – for constitutionally protected parental rights. The Court's model of pregnancy as a parental relationship was developed in the context of adjudicating the rights of unwed fathers, but it can be generalized to develop a broad feminist theory of reproductive freedom that encompasses a woman's full range of reproductive decisions, from abortion to parenting. This chapter develops that theory in two contexts: surrogacy contracts and the right to abortion.[1]

When the U.S. Supreme Court first confronted the parental claims of unwed fathers, it declined to fully embrace the patriarchal view that a man's "seed" establishes rights over any child made with that seed.[2] Instead, the Court developed a test for parental rights that encompassed both a biological tie and a caretaking relationship. Pregnancy was the model for this test. The unwed father precedents therefore suggest that the woman who gives birth to a child has a caretaking relationship with the child and should be recognized as the child's "constitutional parent."[3] In surrogacy arrangements, the separation of genetic and gestational motherhood challenges this conceptual scheme. Nonetheless, the result should be the same: the woman who gives birth to the child should have constitutionally protected parental rights.

---

[1] For a more extensive discussion of the surrogacy issue, *see* Jennifer S. Hendricks, *Essentially a Mother*, 13 Wm. & Mary J. Women & L. 429 (2007), and for the abortion issue, *see* Jennifer S. Hendricks, *Body and Soul: Pregnancy, Equality, and the Unitary Right to Abortion*, 45 Harv. C. R.-C. L. L. Rev. 329 (2010).

[2] Barbara Katz Rothman, Recreating Motherhood 35 (1989) ("In a patriarchal system, a person is what grows out of men's seed.").

[3] This phrase is Gary Spitko's. *See* E. Gary Spitko, *The Constitutional Function of Biological Paternity: Evidence of the Biological Mother's Consent to the Biological Father's Co-Parenting of Her Child*, 48 Ariz. L. Rev. 97, 99 (2006).

This model of pregnancy as a parental relationship raises concern for many feminists, who worry that it stereotypes women as nurturers and could undermine the right to abortion. I claim that the opposite is true. Denying the relational component of pregnancy cuts abortion off from other issues of reproductive freedom, distances the abortion discourse from women's reproductive experiences, and undermines women's legal claims in other contexts. Recognizing pregnancy as both a biological condition and a caretaking relationship provides a solid foundation for analyzing women's reproductive freedom and equality.

PREGNANCY AS PROTOTYPICAL PARENTHOOD

U.S. equality law has long struggled over the treatment of pregnancy. The Supreme Court has a strong preference for formal theories of equality, insisting that the state treat like things alike but having little to say about the state's response to sex differences. The observation that women are often unfairly disadvantaged because of their capacity for pregnancy is surprisingly difficult to translate into the doctrinal requirements for a claim under the Equal Protection Clause of the Fourteenth Amendment.

The Supreme Court has dealt with claims involving pregnancy and equality primarily in two contexts: first, workplace discrimination against pregnant (or potentially pregnant) women and second, state laws making women but not men the legal parents of their children born out of wedlock. In the workplace discrimination cases, the Court used a superficial theory of formal equality to hold that women's biology need not be accommodated. In the parental status cases, however, the Court protected men's rights by adopting a more flexible and accommodating theory of equality. In doing so, the Court also recognized pregnancy as both a biological status and a caretaking relationship.

The most famous of the workplace cases is *Geduldig v. Aiello*.[4] The plaintiffs in *Geduldig* were state employees who claimed that the exclusion of pregnancy from their disability insurance plan constituted sex discrimination. They argued that an employee's need for disability benefits and the cost to the state of providing those benefits were the same regardless of whether the disability was caused by pregnancy or, say, prostatectomy, gout, or circumcision – conditions that were covered for men. Because men received comprehensive income protection for disability, a substantive theory of equality would require comparable protection for women, including coverage of a pregnancy-related disability.

The Court, however, used a theory of formal equality to conclude that the statute was not discriminatory. Men, just like women, were denied benefits for pregnancy-related disabilities. The Court saw the statute as distinguishing not between men

---

[4] 417 U.S. 484 (1974).

and women but between "pregnant . . . and nonpregnant persons."[5] Although the Court acknowledged that women were unequally burdened, it blamed biology rather than law. Women, according to the Court, were saddled by nature with the disproportionate burden of reproduction. This burden inherently inhibited women's ability to participate in the workforce. Formal equality did not require the state to make up the difference.

In a workplace case like *Geduldig*, pregnancy looks like a disadvantage: it hinders women's ability to participate in the workplace, especially on the terms that men have set. In the context of parental rights, however, pregnancy looks like an advantage. A mother and father are differently situated with respect to a newborn child, and the mother's claim is intuitively stronger. Before the Supreme Court got involved, most state laws codified this intuition by recognizing an unwed mother but not an unwed father as a legal parent. Under the formal equality theory of *Geduldig*, the fact that men and women are differently situated with respect to parenthood would end any equality analysis of such laws. Just as *Geduldig* was not about men and women but about pregnant and nonpregnant persons, parentage laws would be deemed to be not about men and women but about persons who have grown and birthed babies in their bodies and persons who have not. Women's unequal, but natural, burden in the workplace would become men's unequal, but natural, status in the family.

The Supreme Court reached a different result for unwed fathers by pursuing substantive rather than formal equality. The Court did not limit its analysis (as it did in *Geduldig*) to the observation that women and men are differently situated and therefore may be treated differently. Instead, having admitted to a biological difference between the sexes, the Court considered the implications of different treatment, and it demanded parity of results that would make up for men's biological disadvantage. To achieve this parity, the Court used motherhood as a model to craft a "biology-plus-relationship" for fathers' parental rights. As the Court later explained, it gave the man the ability to acquire parental rights comparable to a mother's by creating a test modeled on pregnancy but "in terms the male can fulfill."[6]

The Court began to develop this test in *Stanley v. Illinois*.[7] *Stanley* was the first case to declare that an unmarried, biological father could have a constitutional right to be recognized as a legal parent of his offspring. At the same time, the decision

---

[5] *Id.* at 496 n. 20.

[6] *Nguyen v. INS*, 533 U.S. 53, 67 (2001) (describing Congress's effort to give male citizens means to obtain citizenship for foreign-born children). *See also* Mary L. Shanley, *Unwed Fathers' Rights, Adoption, and Sex Equality: Gender Neutrality and the Perpetuation of Patriarchy*, 95 COLUM. L. REV. 60, 88–90 (1995) (stating that the model parent is a pregnant woman but that "different biological roles of men and women in human reproduction make it imperative that law and public policy 'recognize that a father and a mother must be permitted to demonstrate commitment to their child in different ways.'"; quoting *Recent Developments: Family Law – Unwed Fathers' Rights – New York Court of Appeals Mandates Veto Power Over Newborn's Adoption for Unwed Father Who Demonstrates Parental Responsibility*), 104 HARV. L. REV. 800, 807 (1991).

[7] 405 U.S. 645 (1972).

emphasized that biological paternity, standing alone, did not confer constitutionally protected parental rights.

The Supreme Court's starting point in *Stanley* was its agreement with the State of Illinois that unwed mothers and unwed fathers were differently situated:

> [O]n the basis of common human experience, . . . the biological role of the mother in carrying and nursing an infant creates stronger bonds between her and the child than the bonds resulting from the male's often casual encounter. . . . Centuries of human experience buttress this view of the realities of human conditions and suggest that unwed mothers of illegitimate children are generally more dependable protectors of their children than are unwed fathers.[8]

Stanley, however, was "a somewhat unusual unwed father" in that he had "loved, cared for, and supported these children from the time of their birth until the death of their mother."[9] Although biological paternity appeared to be a prerequisite to Stanley's claim, his relationship with and history of caring for the children were critical. Only because he was an "unusual" father who had been involved in parenting did he acquire the parental rights that the mother gained at the time of birth.

Later cases fleshed out the biology-plus-relationship test and confirmed that a man acquired constitutionally protected parental rights only if he had participated in rearing his genetic offspring. Both the mother and the father have a biological tie to the child, and the father's participation in childrearing was treated as the counterpart to the mother's pregnancy and delivery. Thus, a distinction in parental rights between mothers and fathers was appropriate with respect to newborns, but the mother's advantage faded as the child grew if "the father ha[d] established a substantial relationship with the child and ha[d] admitted his paternity."[10]

The importance of the relationship requirement was demonstrated in a case called *Lehr v. Robertson*.[11] Jonathan Lehr was the biological father of a baby whose mother disappeared with the child shortly after the birth. She married another man, who petitioned for an adoption. In the meantime, Lehr had been searching for the child. He had hired private investigators and filed a petition to obtain a declaration of paternity and visitation rights. Despite knowing of that petition, the mother, her husband, and the judge finalized the adoption without giving Lehr notice of the proceeding.[12]

---

[8] *Id.* at 665–66 (Burger, C. J., dissenting). Although the quoted passage is from the dissent, the majority did not dispute this characterization of mothers and fathers but argued that men's typical irresponsibility should not control an individual case. *Id.* at 654–55.

[9] *Id.* at 666 (Burger, C. J., dissenting).

[10] *Caban v. Mohammed*, 441 U.S. 380 (1979).

[11] 463 U.S. 248 (1983).

[12] *Id.* at 250; *id.* at 268–69 (White, J., dissenting). Under New York law, Lehr would have received notice of the adoption proceeding if he had listed himself on the state's putative father registry. However, "[t]he sole purpose of notice [was] to enable the person served . . . to present evidence to the court relevant to the best interests of the child." *Id.* at 252 n. 5 (quoting N.Y. Domestic Relations Law §111-a). Lehr would not have been able to block the adoption if the judge determined it to be in the child's

The Supreme Court upheld the state's denial of Lehr's parental rights. Under the biology-plus-relationship test, Lehr had failed to establish an *actual*, day-to-day, family relationship with the child. The Court drew a "clear distinction between a mere biological relationship and an actual relationship of parental responsibility": "Parental rights do not spring full-blown from the biological connection between parent and child. They require relationships more enduring."[13] The mother's connection through pregnancy and birth was presumed to be such a "more enduring" relationship. In addition, the mother's automatic parental relationship allowed her to "place a limit on whatever substantive constitutional claims might [arise] by virtue of the father's actual relationship with the children."[14] *Lehr* thus allowed states to give unwed mothers veto power over the father's ability to establish parental rights.[15]

The background assumption of the fatherhood cases is that a mother's rights are established by the birth of the child. The Court perceived the father as differently situated at the time of birth and held that he remains differently situated unless and until he establishes a caretaking relationship with the child. Once that relationship is established, however, the father's parental rights are protected *as a matter of sex equality*. Although *Lehr* demonstrates that the relationship requirement has teeth, the standard is not as high as it might have been. The Court did not require that the father's contribution be precisely equivalent to pregnancy: the father need not have endured risks or burdens comparable to those of pregnancy. Instead, the relationship prong of the biology-plus-relationship test is satisfied by ordinary parental behavior that is appropriate to men's more limited biological abilities.

This substantive approach to equality acknowledges that men and women are not similarly situated but seeks comparable treatment that produces fair results. A woman acquires parental rights through pregnancy and birth; a man acquires similar rights by caring for his biological offspring after they are born. The criteria are roughly

---

best interests, and his parental rights, if any, would have been terminated without any showing that he was unfit. The presence of a putative father in the proceeding thus required the court to listen to an argument against the adoption, but it did not alter the substantive legal standard allowing the adoption to be granted if in the child's best interests.

[13] *Id.* at 259–60 (quoting *Caban*, 441 U.S. at 397 (Stewart, J., dissenting)) (emphasis omitted).

[14] *Caban*, 441 U.S. at 397 (Stewart, J., dissenting).

[15] After *Lehr* it is unclear whether the father is entitled to some form of notice and, if so, what form. In 1994, the Supreme Court refused to hear a case more directly raising the question of a father's rights when the mother had prevented him from forming a relationship with the child. *See In re Doe (Baby Boy Janikova)*, 638 N.E.2d 181 (Ill.), *cert. denied*, 513 U.S. 994 (1994), *cited in* Shanley, *supra* note 6, at 74–75, 77–85 (arguing that fathers should not have such a right). Nonetheless, many have interpreted *Lehr* to mean that at least this minimal notice to unwed fathers is constitutionally required, or even that he has the right to block the adoption. *See* June Carbone, *The Legal Definition of Parenthood: Uncertainty at the Core of Family Identity*, 65 LA. L. REV. 1295, 1322 (2005) ("[M]any states now confer parental status on the basis of biology alone"); Leslie Joan Harris, *Reconsidering the Criteria for Legal Fatherhood*, 1996 UTAH L. REV. 461, 468 ("[U]nder the statutes and case law of many states, custodial claims of unwed fathers are protected to a far greater extent than the Supreme Court has said is constitutionally necessary, even when this protection comes at the price of disrupting functional, but not biologically related, families.").

comparable but tailored to the biological condition of the sexes. In contrast to *Geduldig* – where formal equality allowed the state to define the male body as the norm and to deem the disadvantage of pregnancy natural and thus beyond legal redress – the parental rights cases used substantive equality to insist that the state make up the difference for men who lack the ability to become pregnant.

In addition to this novel use of substantive equality, the parental rights cases for the first time set out a constitutional definition of parenthood. Although the Supreme Court had long used the Fourteenth Amendment to protect parental rights, it had never before defined the prerequisites for constitutional parenthood. The biology-plus-relationship test on which the Court settled was modeled on pregnancy, which the Court saw as the prototypical parental relationship. The unwed father cases thus implicitly set out a constitutional understanding of pregnancy as well. That constitutional understanding has implications for emerging issues created by reproductive technology and for issues of women's reproductive freedom, particularly the right to abortion.

WOMEN SEEKING MOTHERHOOD: PREGNANCY AND REPRODUCTIVE TECHNOLOGY

The unwed father cases established a constitutional understanding of parenthood that is based on biological relationship and the formation of a caretaking relationship. That understanding should persist even in different kinds of disputes over parentage. In particular, it should persist when motherhood rather than fatherhood is in question. Although the unwed father cases took motherhood as a given, new reproductive technologies and the market they have spawned have clouded the definition of motherhood and whether its essence lies in genetics, gestation, or something else. The unwed father cases, and the biology-plus-relationship test they developed, provide important guidance for such questions. Correctly applied, they require courts to continue to recognize pregnancy as the prototypical basis for parental rights.

Consider how the biology-plus-relationship test might apply to a woman. A woman who conceives and gives birth to a child is plainly a parent according to the test: she is the biological parent in all senses, and she is presumed to have a relationship with the child. Because she was the prototype for the biology-plus-relationship test, it is not surprising that she easily passes it. It is important, however, to realize that she passes it because of pregnancy and birth themselves – that is, her status need not depend on her genetic tie to the child.

The unwed father cases established that the genetic tie alone is insufficient to confer parental rights. If genetics were controlling, then the genetic fathers in *Stanley* and *Lehr* would have had parental rights automatically. Despite the rough equality of genetics, the Supreme Court saw a difference between how a woman becomes and is a mother and how a man becomes and is a father. The parenthood protected by the Constitution had to include a caretaking relationship analogous to gestation.

That does not mean, however, that a gestational mother who lacks a genetic tie necessarily fails the biology prong of the biology-plus-relationship test. In recent years, couples who seek children through surrogacy contracts have increasingly been advised to use *in vitro* fertilization of their own or a donated egg, rather than artificial insemination of the gestational mother's egg. The theory is that avoiding a genetic tie to the gestational mother weakens her claim if she changes her mind about giving up the child. If she is not the genetic mother, courts will more likely conclude that she is not the "biological" mother and thus not a legal mother. Such conclusions, however, are based on an inappropriately narrow conception of biological connection and on failure to correctly apply the biology-plus-relationship test.

Consider again the prototype for parental rights – the woman who is both a genetic parent and the gestational parent of the child. For nine months, she shares diet, digestion, blood, movements, sleep, and a range of other physical and emotional functions with the child. To give parental rights to men in the unwed father cases, the Court looked to this prototype and saw two important traits: biology and caretaking. The Court translated those traits into terms men could fulfill. It would be strange indeed to insist that women satisfy this test on the new, male terms. Men satisfy the "biology" prong of the test merely by contributing genes because that is all they *can* do. A father's "relationship" with his child may be motivated by biology, but the relationship develops separately from any biological connection. For the mother, there is no such dichotomy between "biology" and "relationship." Her initial relationship with the child flows from biological connection, and that connection goes well beyond the transmission of DNA. To limit women to fulfilling the biology requirement with genes and the relationship requirement with gestation is to adopt the male experience as the norm, even though the test was originally based on women's experience.[16] A gestational mother has both a biological connection to the child and the same caretaking relationship as the prototypical mother. Even if she lacks the genetic tie, she has as strong a claim to parental rights as a genetic father who establishes a caretaking relationship after birth.[17]

Cases arising from the use of reproductive technology often involve several possible mothers, including the genetic mother, the gestational mother, and the contractually intended mother. Disregarding the unwed father cases and their emphasis on caretaking relationships, U.S. courts have frequently privileged genetic ties over other factors when choosing among multiple mothers. For example, *In re Baby M*[18]

---

[16] *Cf.* ROTHMAN, *supra* note 2, at 34 ("In a patriarchal system, when people talk about blood ties, they are talking about a genetic tie, a connection by seed. In a mother-based system, the blood tie is the mingled blood of mothers and their children.").

[17] Consider, too, the alternative: if the gestational mother does not have parental rights to the child of a surrogacy arrangement at the time of birth then, at least so far as the Fourteenth Amendment is concerned, no one does. The genetic parents have not yet established a relationship on which to base a claim. In theory, that leaves the state free, at the time of birth, to recognize none of their claims.

[18] 537 A.2d 1227 (N.J. 1988).

was the first well-publicized dispute over a surrogacy contract in the United States. The New Jersey Supreme Court threw out the surrogacy contract and concluded that the gestational mother, Mary Beth Whitehead, was the legal mother only because she was also the genetic mother, not merely the gestator. By contrast, when the intended mother has provided the egg for another woman to carry, courts often recognize her as the legal mother on the basis of that genetic connection. In a California case, *Johnson v. Calvert*,[19] the court likened the gestational mother to a foster mother and held that the legal parents were those who had provided the egg and sperm for the gestational mother to carry.

The primacy of genetics continues even where there is no contract purporting to assign legal rights away from the gestational mother in favor of the genetic parents. In the New York case of *Perry-Rogers v. Fasano*,[20] two couples were trying to achieve pregnancy through *in vitro* fertilization at the same clinic. One of the Perry-Rogers' embryos was mistakenly implanted in Donna Fasano. Fasano gave birth to twins, one of whom was the genetic child of each couple.[21] Defining parenthood solely as a genetic tie, the court held that Fasano was a legal stranger to the second child, and that the Perry-Rogers were his parents.

These early decisions on reproductive technology and surrogacy contracts wrongly privileged genetic ties over the caretaking relationship that was a key component of the biology-plus-relationship test. Treating DNA as the essence of biological parenthood ignores that biological motherhood comprises multiple biological functions. Focusing solely on DNA imposes the male experience of biological fatherhood on the definition of motherhood. This narrow focus undermines the law's interest in the caretaking aspects of parenthood, with particular harm to families with adoptive, same-sex, or other nontraditional sets of parents.[22] Moreover, a genetic preference in surrogacy law will encourage riskier *in vitro* practices over artificial insemination, solely for the sake of weakening the gestational mother's legal claim to the child.[23]

---

[19] 851 P.2d 776 (Cal. 1993).

[20] 715 N.Y.S.2d 19 (App. Div. 2000).

[21] It seems likely that racial differences between the couples influenced the court's emphasis on genetics. *See* Leslie Bender, *Genes, Parents, and Assisted Reproductive Technologies: ARTs, Mistakes, Sex, Race, and Law*, 12 COLUM. J. GENDER & L. 1 (2003).

[22] In future work, I will address this relationship from the perspective of the children, including children who may someday be brought to term in artificial wombs. For other analysis from the child's perspective, see Mary Pat Byrn, *Which Came First, the Parent or the Child?*, 62 RUTGERS L. REV. 305 (2010) (arguing that children have a right to have their parents recognized by law, and basing identification of the correct legal parents on the children's best interests); ROTHMAN, *supra* note 3, at 91, 257 ("By the time they are born, they have been here, in this world for nine months: not as children, not as people, but as part of their mothers' bodies. A baby enters the world already in a relationship, a physical, social, and emotional relationship with the woman in whose body it was nurtured"; arguing that every child has a right to have a human mother recognized by law).

[23] *See* ROTHMAN, *supra* note 3, at 36 ("[T]he central concept of patriarchy, the importance of the seed, was retained by extending the concept to women.").

Courts should instead return to the biology-plus-relationship test and its model of the pregnant and birthing woman as prototypical parent.

Genes alone do not confer constitutional status as a parent. Pregnancy and birth satisfy the biology-plus-relationship test. They also provide a clear and well-recognized means for establishing parentage in the face of new technologies that continue to increase the number of biological parents, including the possibility of more than two or fewer than two genetic parents. Gestation and birth should therefore be sufficient to establish constitutional parental rights. Retaining that foundation, and a constitutional definition of parenthood modeled on pregnancy, would provide a better basis than genetics or contract for resolving new questions of family formation presented by reproductive technology.

PREGNANCY AS PARENTING: A DANGEROUS PATH?

Using pregnancy as the model for the biology-plus-relationship test assumes that gestation and birth establish a caretaking relationship between a woman and the child she bears. That premise raises a theoretical and a practical concern for feminists. The theoretical concern is that treating pregnancy as a form of parenting stereotypes women as mothers and as inherently nurturing. The practical concern is that this view of pregnancy implies that a fetus is already a child, thus undermining the right to abortion. Next I argue that to the contrary, existing justifications for abortion rights are flawed to the extent they fail to incorporate both the biological and the relational aspects of pregnancy. Although the unwed father cases at times reflected gender stereotypes, rejecting these stereotypes does not require rejecting any distinction between biological motherhood and biological fatherhood. Concern about stereotypes or the right to abortion should not lead to an unrealistic account of pregnancy that jars with many women's experience and weakens a pregnant woman's claim to eventual parental rights.

Recognizing that a woman who gives birth has satisfied the biology-plus-relationship test does not imply that women are inherently more nurturing or ought to shoulder more parenting responsibilities after birth. The unwed father cases emphasized whether the father had been involved in the child's care, not whether he did so lovingly or resentfully or whether the children were psychologically dependent on him. Instead, the Supreme Court focused on whether the father was part of the child's everyday life; whether his influence was good or bad would be the concern of fitness and custody proceedings.[24] Similarly, regardless of whether a pregnant woman takes affirmative steps to enhance the eventual child's welfare,

---

[24] *Cf.* Katharine K. Baker, *Property Rules Meet Feminist Needs: Respecting Autonomy by Valuing Connection*, 59 OHIO ST. L. J. 1523, 1564 (1998) ("Parents transmit values not so much by what they say, but by what they do, how they live, and how they interact with others.").

she is, for better or worse, the child's everyday life. As with fathers, the question of parental fitness is distinct from the question of initial parental status. If the biology-plus-relationship test is sufficient for a man to gain parental rights, then pregnancy and birth ought to be sufficient for a woman.

WOMEN AVOIDING MOTHERHOOD: THE RIGHT TO ABORTION

Political discourse about women's rights has long connected sex equality with reproductive freedom generally, and with abortion in particular. In legal discourse, arguments for drawing this connection tend to emphasize either the bodily imposition of forced pregnancy or the disproportionate burdens of the parent–child relationship on women compared to men. Each argument thus focuses only on one part of the biology-plus-relationship understanding of pregnancy. Neither a body-focused nor a burdens-of-motherhood approach is fully satisfactory, because each neglects an important aspect of pregnancy. A fuller account of abortion rights and their role in women's reproductive freedom must incorporate both aspects of pregnancy, as well as pregnancy's connection to parenthood.

FOCUSING ON THE BODY: GOOD SAMARITAN ARGUMENTS FOR ABORTION RIGHTS

Several scholars have developed arguments for a woman's right to not carry the physical burden of the state's claimed interest in potential life. These arguments apply to the physical burden of pregnancy, even where it is presumed not to present a greater than average risk. Their main feature is an analogy between pregnancy and other situations in which the law declines to impose similar physical burdens. The limits of these analogies illustrate the limits of focusing solely on the physical aspect of pregnancy.

The most famous of these body-focused arguments is Judith Jarvitz Thomson's *A Defense of Abortion*.[25] Thomson's essay presents an ethical case against requiring women to be Good Samaritans, even assuming that a fetus has the same moral status as a born person. Among several other analogies, Thomson asks us to consider a person's rights and duties if she is kidnapped by the Society of Music Lovers and turned into a life support system for a famous violinist. The violinist can survive only if the kidnapping victim remains hooked up for nine months. Thomson argues that she has the right to unplug herself, even if doing so will cause the violinist's death.

Eileen McDonagh has translated Thomson's ethical argument into legal terms.[26] Like Thomson, she accepts, for purposes of argument, the premise that the fetus is a person. Nonetheless, she argues that abortion restrictions impose Good Samaritan

---

[25] Judith Jarvitz Thomson, *A Defense of Abortion*, 1 PHIL. & PUB. AFF. 47 (1971).
[26] *See* EILEEN McDONAGH, BREAKING THE ABORTION DEADLOCK (1996).

duties on pregnant women that exceed any such obligations legally imposed on men, thereby violating the Equal Protection Clause.

The strength of Thomson's violinist analogy lies in its demand that we contemplate the physical risks and burdens of pregnancy in a new context, where background assumptions about the normalcy of pregnancy do not apply. Stripped of these assumptions, the health risks of pregnancy clearly exceed the burdens the law ordinarily imposes on unwilling individuals, even to further the state interest in the life of another. Translating this analogy into the language of equal protection, McDonagh makes a convincing case for an affirmative obligation on the part of the state to provide (pay for) abortions, just as it pays for law enforcement that responds when one person attempts to capture and make use of the body of another. Although a pregnant woman who seeks an abortion may be a legally justified bad Samaritan, a woman who cannot afford an abortion is a "captive Samaritan" to whom the state owes the same duty of rescue as other captives.[27]

The Good Samaritan argument has not taken hold in either court decisions or popular discourse about abortion. This failure is because of three related levels of resistance to Thomson's analogy. First is the entrenched naturalness of pregnancy and caretaking as women's social role. It is opponents, not advocates, of abortion who paint the right as a right to walk away from rendering needed, life-saving aid to another. Second, important branches of feminist thought resist the law's embrace of bad Samaritanism generally.[28] And third, despite its resonance with traditional sex roles, resistance to the Good Samaritan analogy is also grounded in women's experiences of pregnancy, reproduction, and abortion. Women who would otherwise want a child do not have abortions because of the physical burdens of a typical pregnancy; women have abortions to avoid motherhood.[29] For that reason, the Good Samaritan argument is unable to provide a complete account of abortion rights as human rights for women, even if the argument ought to be doctrinally sufficient to call into question the constitutionality of abortion bans.

The Good Samaritan argument reveals the extent of the burden forced pregnancy places on women. In doing so, however, the argument characterizes pregnancy and abortion in ways designed to maximize their similarity to men's lives rather than their place in women's lives. What makes the Good Samaritan argument incomplete is that the right to have an abortion is not *just* about the body. It is about the whole

---

[27] *Id.* at 145.

[28] *See, e.g.,* Leslie Bender, *An Overview of Feminist Torts Scholarship,* 78 CORNELL L. REV. 575, 580–81 (1993) (using relational feminist concepts to argue against the bad Samaritan principle that a person has no duty to rescue a stranger in distress).

[29] In a study published in 2005, 74 percent of the respondents stated that they had abortions because "having a baby would dramatically change my life," 73 percent said they couldn't afford a baby, and 48 percent didn't "want to be a single mother or [were] having relationship problems." Lawrence B. Finer et al., *Reasons U.S. Women Have Abortions: Quantitative and Qualitative Perspectives,* 37 PERSP. ON SEXUAL & REPROD. HEALTH 110, 112 (2005).

course of one's life – it is about relationships, especially the parenting relationship that will arise if the pregnancy is carried to term.

THE BURDENS OF MOTHERHOOD: AN INCOMPLETE ACCOUNT
OF REPRODUCTIVE RIGHTS

Perhaps because of the limits of the body-focused approach, arguments that focus on the whole life's course rather than the nine months of pregnancy have become more prevalent in feminist thought, public discourse, and the Supreme Court's own explanations for the abortion right. Rather than comparing pregnancy to other physical invasions, these arguments make a straight sex equality argument by comparing the social burdens of motherhood to the social burdens of fatherhood.

Burdens-of-motherhood arguments have evolved over the years. They began in a relatively simple form that had its roots in the formal equality theory of second-wave legal feminism, which saw a path to equality in being like a man – that is, free of caretaking responsibility for children. This approach accepted the assumption that having children was incompatible with a woman's professional advancement, thus necessitating a right to abortion.[30] More recent incarnations of this approach reject the assumption that women are the natural caretakers of children. They blame socially enforced gender roles for pressuring women to sacrifice participation in the public sphere for the sake of caretaking. These newer arguments also contextualize the abortion right in women's lived experiences of intersecting inequalities. In doing so, however, they detach the abortion right from women's bodies and suggest that the right is contingent on the persistence of those inequalities. This form of equality argument is thus important for illuminating the operation of sex inequality in society, but it is incomplete as an account of reproductive freedom as a human right.

This newer version is exemplified by Jack Balkin's recent article, *Abortion and Original Meaning*,[31] which attributes the incompatibility between motherhood and public participation to social pressure to conform to a particular vision of motherhood. This version of the burdens-of-motherhood argument highlights the fact that the problem lies in society rather than biology.

Social inequality, however, is a shaky basis for establishing a fundamental right. The Supreme Court continues to give the state great latitude in responding to the uniqueness of pregnancy. States can choose to level the playing field *or* to leave women in their "naturally" unequal state. The same is true for other forms of "natural" inequality – that is, inequality not directly attributable to the state from the narrow perspective of state action doctrine.[32] Doctrinally, the government has

---

[30] *See Planned Parenthood of Southeastern Pa. v. Casey*, 505 U.S. 833, 846 (1992).

[31] Jack M. Balkin, *Abortion and Original Meaning*, 24 CONST. COMMENT. 291, 323–24 (2007).

[32] For a more extensive discussion of the parallel treatment of biological disadvantage and social inequality, see Jennifer S. Hendricks, *Contingent Equal Protection: Reaching for Equality after* Ricci *and* PICS, 16 MICH. J. GENDER & L. 397 (2010). The state action doctrine makes the government accountable

no duty to design its laws to respond to *de facto* inequality, whether that inequality lies in reproductive capacity or in the social organization of childrearing. If the state has decided on a policy to protect fetal life, the state action doctrine means that the unequal status of mothers in society will not provide a basis for rejecting that policy.

Even setting aside the state action problem, however, abortion is an unconvincing response to the problems of female poverty and inequality. Pro-choice advocates are quick to point out that they, rather than their pro-life opponents, are more likely to support social welfare programs for poor women. Nonetheless, the availability of abortion is a "pathetically inadequate remedy"[33] for a pregnant woman complaining that she lacks the material resources to rear a child. Nor is it an adequate response to the woman who may be pregnant involuntarily but whose own beliefs lead her to choose sacrifice of her own wishes over abortion. The fact that abortion opponents have not offered better solutions to those problems does not alter the grossness of the disparity.

Focusing on the inequalities that constrain women's lives can explain why the right to abortion is sometimes an important means of asserting some control over a woman's own life. Moreover, there is compelling evidence that abortion restrictions are in fact largely motivated by concerns about women's sexuality and enforcing the maternal role.[34] As with the body-focused arguments, that evidence should be enough, as a legal matter, to strike down abortion bans based on their current effect and interaction with inequality. However, using abortion as a backstop to avoid the worst impositions of inequality does not provide a full justification of abortion as a human right regardless of the woman's social condition.

The emphasis on existing social inequality, moreover, suggests a sunset clause for abortion rights. If the right to avoid becoming a mother through forced pregnancy and childbirth flows from society's disproportionate expectations of mothers, then abortion will no longer be needed once the Supreme Court concludes that equality is at hand. The Court has already forecasted the end of structural race inequality;[35] the practical end of sex inequality cannot be far behind. Many women in the United States already experience greater levels of equality and privilege – absolutely, relative to men, and relative to other women – than any other women in recorded history.

---

only for harms linked through a tight chain of causation to specific, illegal acts of discrimination by the government. Everything else is societal discrimination or structural inequality. When the purportedly natural workings of society result in inequality, the government may choose whether to act as a counterweight. The difficulty of establishing an affirmative right to government help is that government is not required to act without proof of fault and immediate causation.

[33] Robin West, *Opinion Concurring in the Judgment*, in WHAT ROE V. WADE SHOULD HAVE SAID: THE NATION'S TOP LEGAL EXPERTS REWRITE AMERICA'S MOST CONTROVERSIAL DECISION 141 (Jack M. Balkin ed., 2005).

[34] *See* Reva Siegel, *Reasoning from the Body: A Historical Perspective on Abortion Regulation and Questions of Equal Protection*, 44 STAN. L. REV. 261 (1992).

[35] *See Gratz v. Bollinger*, 539 U.S. 244, 342–43 (2003) (predicting that affirmative action in higher education will not be needed after about twenty-five years).

Moreover, those are the very women who actually, in practice, have a protected right to abortion. Although feminist lawyers must continue to work to demonstrate the disparate impact of abortion restrictions on various groups of women, we need a theory of abortion rights that accounts for the right we currently have as well as the one we seek.

The focus on the social rather than the biological aspect of motherhood also lends support to the development of a general "right to avoid parenthood," a right about which feminists should be cautious. That right, for example, has been applied to enforce the wishes of a husband seeking to destroy frozen embryos over his wife's protest.[36] It also lends credibility to claims for a so-called male right to abortion.[37] The latter claim is not for a man's right to force a woman to have an abortion but his right to avoid child-support obligations if he exercised reasonable care to avoid becoming a father. When the right to abortion is premised largely on the postbirth consequences of motherhood, it is not entirely unreasonable to argue that it is unfair for women to have a clean-up period to avoid motherhood after pregnancy has begun, while sexual intercourse for men is a strict liability affair. Resting the right to abortion entirely on the social context of parenthood is an invitation to claims of equal rights for men.

Finally, as with the body-focused arguments, we must return to women's lived experiences – this time, their experiences of motherhood. Burdens-of-motherhood arguments emphasize the incompatibility of intense caretaking with participation in the public sphere. *Casey* appeared merely to assume that whenever a child was born that conflict would fall on the mother. More sophisticated versions of the argument agree that the burden will fall disproportionately on the mother but explain that phenomenon in terms of social pressure to conform to gender roles. This explanation requires too much false consciousness about the reasons mothers devote huge amounts of time, money, and energy to caring for their children. Without denying the social pressure on mothers, it is good that someone feels responsible for the children, and not unreasonable to think that even in our nonsexist future, women will feel disproportionately attached (relative to men) to their biological children.[38]

---

[36] *See Davis v. Davis*, 842 S.W.2d 588 (Tenn. 1992).

[37] *See, e.g.*, Ethan J. Leib, *A Man's Right to Choose: Men Deserve a Voice in the Abortion Decision*, 28 LEGAL TIMES 1 (Apr. 4, 2005) (arguing that a man who is not negligent with respect to conception should be able to avoid a child support obligation by requesting that the woman abort).

[38] *See* Hendricks, *Essentially a Mother, supra* note 2, at 458–61, 468–73 (discussing the concrete connection between parent and child as one reason for recognizing parental rights and criticizing the Supreme Court for moving away from recognition that such a connection exists between a birth mother and her newborn). My claim is not that the bond between a biological mother and child is unequaled by other love between parents and children (or that the bond is always love) but that the fact of pregnancy and birth is reasonably associated with a parent–child relationship such as the relationships that the Supreme Court says men develop when they are the biological father *and* play a substantial caretaking role in the child's life. Pregnancy is *both* a biological relationship and day-to-day caretaking.

The ability to act on that attachment without sacrificing material security is as much a part of reproductive freedom as the right to abortion.

Burdens-of-motherhood arguments respond to the lived experiences of pregnancy and inequality that structure the circumstances under which many women seek abortions. By focusing on the social burden of motherhood as compared to fatherhood, however, they disconnect the abortion right from women's bodies, instead constructing it as a right to avoid parenthood under conditions of inequality. This account of abortion rights is not adequate for a construction of women's reproductive human rights that looks forward to the elimination of that inequality.

A UNITARY APPROACH

The leading equality arguments for abortion rights are incomplete because they each focus on a single dimension of pregnancy. Each gives only a partial view of how forced pregnancy diminishes human dignity. This partiality is, to a great extent, a function of the search for a basis for comparison to male experience on which to ground an equal protection analysis. In analyzing reproductive rights, pregnancy should be analyzed on its own terms as a biological and social process, as it was in the unwed father cases. Analogies to male experience should incorporate both aspects as well. This section explores analogies that attempt to integrate the biological with the social.

The burdens-of-motherhood argument criticizes society for forcing women to "become mothers" by imposing disproportionate responsibility for taking care of children after they are born. A more unified perspective on pregnancy and birth is that pregnant women have already become mothers – in the social as well as biological sense – when they give birth. Regardless of pressures created by society as a whole, the law does not force men to become fathers in the same sense. Forced pregnancy can thus usefully be compared to the types of duties that family courts will and will not require the parents of born children to perform. A second comparison, which more thoroughly integrates the physical and the social, is to a different kind of intimate relationship: one known as Stockholm syndrome, which may arise when a person is held physically hostage to the needs of another.

Whereas legal fatherhood triggers a technical duty to support, courts are loathe to impose a physical caretaking burden on parents other than pregnant women. Through child support requirements, the state forces only liability, not parenthood, onto noncustodial parents. Visitation, and the caretaking relationship it implies, is considered a right, not a duty.[39] Faced with custodial parents' requests that another

---

[39] Daniel Pollack & Susan Mason, *Mandatory Visitation: In the Best Interest of the Child*, 42 FAM. CT. REV. 74 (2004). *See also* Barbara Bennett Woodhouse, *Talking About Children's Rights in Judicial Custody and Visitation Decision-Making*, 36 FAM. L. Q. 105, 131 (2002) (citing the protection of the parent's visitation rights rather than the child's right to be visited (or to refuse the visit) as an example of myopia toward the rights of children).

parent be required to take advantage of visitation rights, courts have recoiled: "A court simply cannot order a parent to love his or her children, or to maintain a meaningful relationship with them."[40] Although the law imposes child support obligations based on a tort-like notion of causation, it does not force noncustodial parents to engage in the caretaking work that is likely to produce an emotional bond.

The mandatory visitation analogy improves on the burdens-of-motherhood arguments because it draws a comparison between state enforcement of pregnancy and state enforcement of a postbirth relationship with children. It also shows the shortcoming of the "male abortion" argument focused on child support, which misses the point about forcing an actual relationship as opposed to financial liability. It suffers, however, from some of the same flaws previously discussed. First, it requires one to embrace the questionable premise that a person has no legal duty to provide direct care for his or her child. It thus suffers from the same tension with relational feminism that was discussed in connection with the Good Samaritan argument. Second, although the prospect of forced visitation attempts to raise a specter of physical coercion, it is not comparable to the invasion of bodily integrity involved in forced pregnancy.

To bring the body back into play, one could turn to the oft-cited example of organ donation or other medical procedure. No court or legislature in the United States has ever ordered a parent to submit to a medical procedure for the benefit of a born child. Yet they have so ordered pregnant women for the benefit of fetuses, both through abortion bans that mandate childbirth and through court-ordered cesareans and other surgery.[41] These comparisons, however, lack the relational element of pregnancy – even forced organ donation to a child would not impose the intimate caretaking relationship of pregnancy. The offense lies in the invasion of bodily integrity, again neglecting the relational aspect that is an important part of the right to abortion.

A better analogy may be to supplement Thomson's violinist hypothetical with information about the likely nonphysical effects on the person serving as the violinist's life-support system. In a psychological phenomenon known as the Stockholm syndrome, people who find themselves physically hostage to the interests of another have been known to come to identify and sympathize with those interests.[42] During the period of physical risk, this phenomenon is considered a natural, adaptive method for surviving and for coping psychologically with the captive state.[43] Enforced pregnancy creates similar conditions. The pregnant woman is physically hijacked to serve the interests of the state, which purports to be acting on behalf of the fetus.

---

[40] *Id.*

[41] *See generally* Beth A. Burkstrand-Reid, *The Invisible Woman: Availability and Culpability in Reproductive Health Jurisprudence*, 81 COLO. L. REV. 97 (2010).

[42] *See* THOMAS STRENTZ, PSYCHOLOGICAL ASPECTS OF CRISIS NEGOTIATION 243–245 (2006).

[43] *See id.* at 245–46.

This circumstance forces her to develop a psychological posture toward the fetus and the eventual child. Our violinist's life-support system is thus not merely physically kidnapped for nine months' service. She is put in a position in which it is likely that she will identify with, care for, and develop a long-term emotional bond with the violinist. For the involuntarily pregnant woman, that adaptation to the captive state is reinforced by personal beliefs and social norms about motherhood. If she is prevented from having an abortion, it is preferable – not diagnosable as a "syndrome" – that she develop a positive identification with the child, whether to rear herself or to find a different home.

This analogy also provides a useful example of the need to distinguish what is natural from what is desirable. A hostage's identification with her captors is natural in that it is recognized as a normal, adaptive psychological response to physical captivity. The response is adaptive in that it may actually increase the odds of survival. "Natural," however, does not mean "inevitable": many hostages do not experience Stockholm syndrome. Moreover, once the period of captivity is over, the response is no longer considered desirable. To the contrary, it becomes a "syndrome" in need of treatment.

With pregnancy, the social response is reversed: even after the period of physical "captivity," society usually favors and promotes the mother's identification with the infant's needs.[44] As I have said, I agree with that societal preference; it bears emphasizing that this analogy does not imply that a pregnant woman's attachment to a fetus or infant is a pathology. A woman seeking an abortion, however, can be understood as analogous to a hostage seeking to avoid the development of an attachment analogous to Stockholm syndrome. This analogy shows why the relationship theory of pregnancy is consistent with a right to abortion: "When a woman chooses abortion, she is choosing not to enter into a maternal relationship. Women want access to safe abortions as quickly as possible, before quickening, before a relationship can begin."[45] The harm of forced pregnancy is not only the physical invasion evoked by Thomson's violinist analogy but also the creation of a strong emotional relationship of identification.

Neither mandatory visitation nor the Stockholm syndrome is, of course, a perfect or even a very good analogy to forced pregnancy. They have the advantage, however, of combining the physical and the social aspects of pregnancy. They are therefore somewhat truer to the experience of pregnancy. They are also consistent with the Supreme Court's use of pregnancy as the prototypical form of parenthood in the unwed father cases. This resonance creates opportunities for developing a broader-based constitutional vision of reproductive freedom.

---

44 Unless perhaps she has previously signed a contract to turn the child over to others. *See In re Baby M*, 537 A.2d 1227 (N.J. 1988).
45 ROTHMAN, *supra* note 3, at 243.

CONCLUSION

The U.S. Supreme Court, strongly committed to formal theories of equality in most circumstances, crafted the biology-plus-relationship test to achieve substantive equality for men despite their biological limitations. Biology-plus-relationship is a woman-centered theory of pregnancy on which feminists can build. It values pregnancy as the prototypical parental relationship, supporting women's claims for rights arising from gestation itself. At the same time, it recognizes that the biological and relational aspects of pregnancy are inextricably intertwined, a perspective largely missing from feminist analysis of abortion law. This model of pregnancy can thus provide a consistent theory for examining pregnancy and reproductive freedom over a wide range of issues.

15

Federal Spending and Compulsory Maternity

Nicole Huberfeld

Congress has long had the power to spend for the general welfare as well as the authority to attach conditions that the recipient, whether state or individual, must accept to receive the funds. The Court's major decision regarding conditional spending, *South Dakota v. Dole*, focused on the federal–state relationship in setting forth a test for understanding the constitutional boundaries limiting Congress's ability to place conditions on funds. That benchmark facilitated a disconnect, however, that analytically separates the individual from the conditional spending program, a divide that allows Congress to impinge on individual rights when it could not otherwise do so.

An example of this disconnect is found in the Court's decisions allowing state and federal governments to burden the privacy right to obtain abortion by withholding funds in public health-care programs, particularly Medicaid. The import of programs such as Medicaid cannot be overstated,[1] but using their power to blockade exercise of constitutionally protected rights demands consideration of the individual affected by the legislative conditions accepted by the state. This role of the third party is played not only by women, but also by physicians and other health-care providers who are most affected by conditions on spending. Together, they highlight the gap that exists between conditional spending jurisprudence and the impact conditional spending has on individuals participating in federal health-care programs (and sometimes individuals with private insurance).

This chapter examines the disconnect between Spending Clause jurisprudence and women's reproductive rights, ultimately suggesting that the focus on the federal–state relationship is too narrow. The chapter concludes that the *Dole* test could protect the interests of individuals when applied in full, which is not the Court's current practice, and that Congress should cease inserting such funding limitations

---

[1] *See* Sara Rosenbaum, *Medicaid at Forty: Revisiting Structure and Meaning in a Post-Deficit Reduction Act Era*, 9 J. HEALTH CARE L. & POL'Y 5 (2006).

in health-care legislation not only because they may be unconstitutional, but also because they hinder access to necessary, legal medical services.

I. CONDITIONS IN THE CASE LAW

The case law is better understood through three background components: the structure and intent of the Medicaid program, the "greater includes the lesser" theory, and the debate over positive and negative rights. Congress enacted the Medicaid Act as companion legislation to Medicare in 1965.[2] Medicaid was structured to provide medically necessary care to the "deserving poor," people who fit within certain eligibility categories such as pregnant women, dependent children, the elderly, blind, and disabled, and who also met the government's definition of poverty. The Medicaid Act requires states to ensure that all Medicaid enrollees, statewide, have access to certain mandatory medical services, which include inpatient and outpatient hospital care, physician services, long-term care, and laboratory and radiology services. Medicaid was designed to provide consistent access for these essential categories of medical care (and allows states to choose from many more optional categories, such as prescription drugs).

Medicaid is often described as an "entitlement" program, which implicates certain theories of public spending and its enforceability. One such theory is the positive/negative rights theory of constitutionally protected individual rights, meaning that the government must refrain from impinging certain rights protected by the constitution (negative rights), but it need not facilitate the exercise of those rights (positive rights).[3] The negative/positive dichotomy is a convenient way to describe how the Constitution was drafted, but it is an anachronism considering the amount of money the federal government spends with conditions designed to influence behavior. The active/inactive distinction seems crude in the modern era, when the reach of government "has extended far into areas previously reserved to the family, market, and church, and this extension confounds easy definition of positive and negative rights."[4] In the context of the power to spend, wholesale acceptance of the positive/negative rights distinction seems particularly dangerous, as the government uses this power to manipulate beneficiaries.

The positive/negative rights theory overlays the "greater includes the lesser" theory of government spending.[5] The Court has stated that Congress is not required to

---

[2] ROBERT STEVENS & ROSEMARY STEVENS, WELFARE MEDICINE IN AMERICA 51–53 (1974).

[3] Susan Frelich Appleton, *Beyond the Limits of Reproductive Choice: The Contributions of the Abortion-Funding Cases to Fundamental-Rights Analysis and to the Welfare-Rights Thesis*, 81 COLUM. L. REV. 721, 734–38 (1981).

[4] Seth F. Kreimer, *Allocational Sanctions: The Problem of Negative Rights in a Positive State*, 132 U. PA. L. REV. 1293 (1984). *See also DeShaney v. Winnebago County Dept. of Social Services*, 489 U.S. 189, 203–205 (1989) (Brennan, J. dissenting) (rejecting majority's description of and reliance on the positive/negative rights distinction).

[5] Cass R. Sunstein, *Why the Unconstitutional Conditions Doctrine Is an Anachronism (With Particular Reference to Religion, Speech, and Abortion)*, 70 B.U. L. REV. 593, 597–98 (1990).

spend on certain programs and therefore can attach conditions as it chooses to any program when it decides to spend. The greater includes the lesser theory supports the notion that indirectly infringing rights is permissible so long as the vehicle is conditions on federal funding, which proponents argue can be accepted or rejected by the beneficiary of the spending. Governmental infringement becomes a choice to waive a right rather than an impermissible burden.[6]

These background points illuminate the themes that emerge in the case law. Conditional federal funding clearly has had an impact on state law; as is discussed later, *Dole* focuses only on the federal–state relationship. When the state does not deliver, individuals have been prevented from enforcing the benefits created by the conditions the federal government imposed on the state, leaving no recourse when the state's failure harms the individual.[7] Under the greater includes the lesser theory, and for those jurists that adhere to a negative rights theory of the Constitution, this is the desired outcome. The Court's rejection of individual enforcement efforts emphasizes the problem: the individual is removed from the conditional spending analysis, even when Congress intended that the individual benefit from the spending scheme.

Much litigation has followed the 1973 decision in *Roe v. Wade*, but one facet of it can be singled out – the government funding decisions. *Singleton v. Wulff* began this line of cases by discussing the import of funding to both the physician and the patient involved in an abortion.[8] Evaluating a state prohibition on use of Medicaid funds for "nontherapeutic" abortions, the Court noted that a "woman cannot safely secure an abortion without the aid of a physician, and an impecunious woman cannot easily secure an abortion without the physician's being paid by the State. The woman's exercise of her right to an abortion . . . is therefore necessarily at stake here."[9]

Four years after *Roe*, the Court heard the companion cases *Beal v. Doe* and *Maher v. Roe*.[10] *Beal* held that the Medicaid Act did not require states to pay for nontherapeutic abortions.[11] *Maher* involved a Connecticut law that limited state

---

[6] *See Rust v. Sullivan*, 500 U.S. 173, 193 (1991); *see also* Lynn A. Baker, *The Prices of Rights: Toward a Positive Theory of Unconstitutional Conditions*, 75 CORNELL L. REV. 1185, 1190–91, n.12 (1990) (describing longstanding use of the doctrine to indicate that "the State's 'greater' power not to bestow the benefit or privilege at all incorporates a 'lesser' power to provide it conditionally").

[7] *See Blessing v. Freestone*, 520 U.S. 329 (1997); Nicole Huberfeld, *Bizarre Love Triangle: The Spending Clause, Section 1983, and Medicaid Entitlements*, 42 U.C. DAVIS L. REV. 413, 428–38 (2008).

[8] *Singleton v. Wulff*, 428 U.S. 106 (1976).

[9] *Id.* at 117.

[10] *Beal v. Doe*, 432 U.S. 438 (1977); *Maher v. Roe*, 432 U.S. 464 (1977). *See also Poelker v. Doe*, 432 U.S. 519 (1977) (public hospital refusal to provide abortion services did not violate Equal Protection Clause based on *Maher v. Roe*).

[11] Pennsylvania limited payment for abortions to those certified as "medically necessary" by three physicians, meaning a threat to the health of the mother, fetal defects, rape, or incest. *See Beal v. Doe*, 432 U.S. at 441–42. The Court held that the Medicaid Act did not oblige Pennsylvania to pay for all legal abortions, even though it required states to provide access and payment for certain categories of medical care. *Id.* at 444; *see also* 42 U.S.C. § 1396d(a).

Medicaid benefits to medically necessary first trimester abortions. The majority held that states do not violate the Equal Protection Clause if they refuse to fund nontherapeutic abortions in their Medicaid programs, the implication of which was that a state that pays for childbirth need not also pay for abortion in its Medicaid program.

Allowing states to shun one particular medical procedure that would otherwise be covered as a physician service or an outpatient hospital service ignored the statutory framework and the purpose of the Medicaid Act. Medicaid was created to secure equal medical assistance for individuals "whose income and resources are insufficient to meet the costs of necessary medical services."[12] Every woman seeking abortion must have the help of a physician to pursue her medical goals, just as women giving birth seek medical care for prenatal services, labor, and delivery. Denying Medicaid payment effectively foreclosed indigent women from obtaining this medical care.[13] The Court's analysis separated the right to obtain abortion from realization of the right, which reflects the greater includes the lesser theory of spending.[14]

The misconceptions regarding the Medicaid program and individuals' reliance on it continued a few years later in *Harris v. McRae*.[15] The Court analyzed the most restrictive version of the Hyde Amendment, which permitted federal Medicaid funding for abortions only when the life of a mother was endangered. The Court held that states were not required to pay for services that the federal government would not fund and relied heavily on its decision in *Maher*, comparing the Hyde Amendment to Connecticut's funding moratorium and reiterating that refusal to fund does not place an "obstacle" in the path of women seeking abortion. The Court decided that refusal to fund was not a "penalty," even though medically necessary services were not being covered. Justice Brennan's dissent responded that refusal to pay is deliberate prevention of the exercise of a constitutionally protected right[16] and described the Hyde Amendment as a withdrawal of funds for medically necessary services that would otherwise be paid for by Medicaid. The Court had ignored the legislative history of the amendment, which supported Justice Brennan's assertion that in both "design and effect it serves to coerce indigent pregnant women to bear children they would otherwise elect not to have. . . . "[17] The lack of legislative history analysis is startling given that the Hyde Amendment's proponents were blunt about

---

[12] *See* STEVENS & STEVENS, *supra* note 2, at 57; *see also* 42 U.S.C. § 1396.

[13] *See Maher*, 432 U.S. at 454 (Marshall, J., dissenting). Justice Marshall revealed the legerdemain: "As the Court well knows, these regulations inevitably will have the practical effect of preventing nearly all poor women from obtaining safe and legal abortions." *Id.*

[14] *See id.* at 462 (Blackmun, J., dissenting).

[15] *Harris v. McRae*, 448 U.S. 297 (1980).

[16] *Id.* at 330 (Brennan, J., dissenting).

[17] *Id.* at 330–31.

their desire to stop women from exercising constitutional rights.[18] Representative Hyde stated that he knew poor women would not access abortion if Medicaid did not pay for it.[19]

Rust v. Sullivan relied on the "authority" that the government possesses under *McRae* and *Maher* and held that Congress could refuse to fund both abortions and abortion counseling to promote childbirth.[20] The Court engaged in a greater includes the lesser analysis, stating that this limitation was not the same as a penalty and that women were in the same position as if the federal funding did not exist. The Court also reiterated that indigency is not created by the government and thus not its duty to change. Justice Blackmun's dissent argued that this was no different than if the federal government "banned abortions outright."[21]

A year after *Rust*, the Court decided *Planned Parenthood of Southeastern Pennsylvania v. Casey*,[22] which also built on *Maher* and *McRae*. Although not a Spending Clause case, *Casey's* analysis of governmental interference is significant. Justice O'Connor's plurality reduced the standard of review to an "undue burden" analysis and attempted to describe what would constitute an undue burden by the state on a woman's exercise of her privacy right, relying in part on *Maher* and *McRae*. The joint opinion stated, "The fact that a law which serves a valid purpose, one not designed to strike at the right itself, has the incidental effect of making it more difficult or more expensive to procure an abortion cannot be enough to invalidate it."[23] The Court again ignored the burden placed on women of no means when abortion becomes more expensive and the state's intent clearly is to "strike at the right itself."[24] Paradoxically, Justice O'Connor also wrote, "Finding of an undue burden is a shorthand for the conclusion that a state regulation has the purpose or effect of placing a substantial obstacle in the path of a woman seeking an abortion of a nonviable fetus."[25]

Fifteen years later, *Gonzales v. Carhart* built on the foundation of these precedents.[26] Justice Kennedy "assumed" that *Roe* and *Casey* remained good law, and in so doing, also relied on the obstacle language from *Casey* that drew from *Maher* and *McRae*.[27] The Court continued not to recognize that failure to fund

[18] *See* Michael J. Perry, *Why the Supreme Court Was Plainly Wrong in the Hyde Amendment Case: A Brief Comment on Harris v. McRae*, 32 STAN. L. REV. 1113, 1123 (1980).

[19] Statement of Representative Henry Hyde, House CONG. REC., June 17, 1977, at 19,700–19,701.

[20] *Rust v. Sullivan*, 500 U.S. 173 (1991).

[21] *Id.* at 218 (Blackmun, J. dissenting).

[22] *Planned Parenthood of Se. Pa. v. Casey*, 505 U.S. 833 (1992).

[23] *Id.* at 874.

[24] The law was the Pennsylvania Abortion Control Act, and the state had been attempting to limit access to abortion since *Roe*. *See* Brief for Petitioners and Cross-Respondents at 2–5, *Planned Parenthood of Se. Pa. v. Casey*, 505 U.S. 833.

[25] *Casey*, 505 U.S. at 877–78.

[26] *Gonzales v. Carhart*, 550 U.S. 124, 127 S. Ct. 1610 (2007).

[27] *Id.* at 1626–27.

is a state action that acts as an obstacle to the individual who seeks to exercise constitutionally protected rights.

The spending-related cases expose at least two trends. First, in contrast to constant tinkering with the *Roe* precedent, the doctrine from *Maher* and *McRae* has remained steady, allowing an ongoing impact on the exercise of individual rights. Unwavering reliance on *Maher* and *McRae* has permitted the Court to continue a fallacy that the government does not unduly burden a woman's privacy right by refusing to pay for abortion in federal spending programs while favoring childbirth. Such an analysis exists by virtue of the greater includes the lesser theory and is reinforced by continued interest in the positive/negative rights dichotomy. Both theories ignore the reality of modern government, the power of which derives not only from the deterrent effect of criminal punishment but also from pervasive, influential spending.

Second, these precedents afford Congress exceptionally broad power to employ conditions on spending to prohibit use of federal funds for abortion, thereby influencing state policy, private policy, and the rights of women and their physicians. However, the authority created by *Maher* and *McRae* has grown beyond its original context, as Congress has created not only pure funding statutes that prohibit payment for abortion, but also conscience-clause funding statutes that prohibit recipients of federal funds from controlling the medical behavior of their health-care providers.

II. LEGISLATIVE LEGACY

Many conditional spending statutes have sprouted from the fertile soil of *Maher* and *McRae*. I call the first type "pure funding statutes," meaning laws that forbid use of federal funds for abortion procedures or counseling. I dub the second type "conscience-clause funding statutes," meaning laws that forbid recipients of federal funds from discriminating against those health-care providers who refuse to participate in abortion or abortion counseling. These two varieties of statute have given *Maher* and *McRae* broad influence that reaches into general reproductive services, including contraception and sterilization, for women in public programs and for those who have private insurance. These laws also reveal the breadth of Congress's power to place conditions on federal funds in ways that run afoul of current Spending Clause jurisprudence and reflect the permissiveness of the greater includes the lesser model for conditional spending.

A. *Pure Funding Statutes*

The Hyde Amendment affects two major conditional spending programs, Medicaid and the Children's Health Insurance Program (CHIP).[28] It was first passed in 1976 in

---

[28]   42 U.S.C. § 1396 (2006) (Medicaid); 42 U.S.C. § 1397ee(c)(1) (2006) (SCHIP).

response to *Roe v. Wade*[29] and has always attached to the funding for the Department of Health and Human Services (DHHS).[30] Representative Hyde stated during the floor debate, "I would certainly like to prevent, if I could legally, anybody having an abortion, a rich woman, a middle-class woman, or a poor woman. Unfortunately, the only vehicle available is the HEW medicaid [sic] bill."[31] The Hyde Amendment is important to understand because it has spawned other pure funding statutes.

Medicaid is a cooperative federalism program by which the federal government matches funds that states spend to provide "medical assistance" to certain very poor citizens.[32] States must provide medical assistance for enrollees in certain categories of medical care and generally the same benefits to all enrollees,[33] including costs for both outpatient hospital services and physician services.[34] Despite these requirements, the Hyde Amendment has attached as a condition on federal funding for Medicaid since 1977. Although the Hyde Amendment addresses DHHS distribution of federal funds, under *McRae* states need not pay for services that the federal government will not fund,[35] rendering the Hyde Amendment a condition on Medicaid spending at the state and federal levels.

Many women depend on Medicaid for access to medical care, and the policies implemented through Medicaid spending have a disproportionate impact on women. Women enrolled in Medicaid tend to be of childbearing age, poor, less educated, minorities, and parents.[36] The impact of the Hyde Amendment (and other such funding restrictions) is clear from the fact that Medicaid pays for more than 40 percent of all births nationally and covers family planning, prenatal care, childbirth, and postnatal services.[37] Before the Hyde Amendment was passed, thirteen states had enacted abortion funding bans; but by 1979, forty states had terminated state coverage for abortions not covered by federal Medicaid funds. Currently, seventeen states provide coverage for abortions that are not paid for with federal funds.[38] Before Congress ended federal funding, Medicaid paid for almost one-third of all abortions; after, the federal government has paid for almost none.[39] Even though the rate of abortion has been decreasing nationally, it has been increasing for all poor

---

[29] Pub. L. No. 94–439, §209, 90 Stat. 1418 (1976).

[30] *See, e.g.*, Pub. L. No. 108–447, div. F, tit. V, §§507(a), 508(a) (2004); *see* Pub. L. No. 103–112, §509, 107 Stat. 1082, 1113 (1993); Pub. L. No. 98–619, § 204 (1984); Pub. L. No. 97–12, § 402 (1981); 42 C.F.R. §§ 441.200–208.

[31] CONG. REC. H19698, 19700 (June 17, 1977) (statement of Rep. Hyde).

[32] 42 U.S.C. § 1396 (2006).

[33] 42 U.S.C. § 1396a(a)(10)(B) (2006).

[34] *See* 42 U.S.C. § 1396d(a)(2) & (a)(4).

[35] 448 U.S. at 308.

[36] KAISER FAMILY FOUNDATION, WOMEN AND HEALTHCARE: A NATIONAL PROFILE 16 (2005), www.kff .org/womenshealth/7336.cfm.

[37] 42 U.S.C. § 1396a(l).

[38] Kaiser Family Foundation, *Abortion in the U.S.: Utilization, Financing, and Access*, 1 (2008), www .kff.org/womenshealth/3269–02.cfm.

[39] CONG. REC. H19698, 19709 (June 17, 1977) (statement of Rep. Weiss). *See also* ADAM SONFIELD ET AL., GUTTMACHER INSTITUTE, PUBLIC FUNDING FOR FAMILY PLANNING, STERILIZATION AND ABORTION

women since 1994.[40] As abortion has become more concentrated among women
enrolled in Medicaid, it has become clear that women must divert money for rent,
food, utilities, and other necessities to financially access the procedure.

Congress has denied funding for abortion coverage in many other federal programs. For example, CHIP provides block grants to states to provide health-care
coverage to low-income, uninsured children and their families.[41] When CHIP
was enacted in 1997, Hyde language was written into the legislation, and as with
Medicaid, CHIP funds may not be used for abortion except in extraordinary
circumstances.[42] Other pure funding statutes that build on the Hyde Amendment
example include federal employee health benefits, federal prisoners, military personnel and families, Native Americans, Peace Corps volunteers, and foreign-aid
programs.

Pure funding statutes primarily act on the enrollees in federal health-care programs, although health-care providers are affected too because they are limited in
the services they can provide to women. This dual effect highlights at least two concerns regarding the current status of conditional spending. The first is the idea that
the federal government may place conditions on federal spending if the conditions
are clear to the recipient, which generally means the state, discussed further later
in the chapter. The second involves the greater includes the lesser theory that the
federal government may impose regulations by virtue of spending that it could not
otherwise implement. In programs such as Medicaid, the state accepts the condition on behalf of its citizens, who have no ability to influence the decision. This
underlines the disconnect between the existing conditional spending doctrine and
its impact on individuals; if the greater includes the lesser theory holds that citizens
can waive their rights when conditioned funds are offered, then the theory is also
incorrect, because such waivers are made on their behalf by states that negotiate
with the federal government.

B. *Conscience-Clause Funding Statutes*

Conscience-clause funding statutes prohibit health-care providers that accept federal funds from discriminating against those who refuse to participate in abortion,
sterilization, and related services. These statutes greatly extend the reach of the Hyde
Amendment language authorized by *Maher* and *McRae*; three major conscience-
clause funding statutes serve as examples.

SERVICES, FY 1980–2006 18 (2008), www.guttmacher.org/pubs/2008/01/28/or38.pdf (federal government contributed to the cost of 191 abortion procedures in 2006).

[40] HEATHER D. BOONSTRA ET AL., GUTTMACHER INSTITUTE, ABORTION IN WOMEN'S LIVES 26–28 (2006),
www.guttmacher.org/pubs/2006/05/04/AiWL.pdf.

[41] 42 U.S.C. § 1397aa (2006).

[42] 42 U.S.C. § 1397ee(c)(1) (2006); 42 U.S.C. § 1397jj(a)(16) (2006).

The Church Amendment applies to federal funds related to the Public Health Service Act, Community Mental Health Centers Act, and the Developmental Disabilities Services and Facilities Construction Act.[43] It states that federal fund recipients are not required to provide abortion or sterilization and prevents health-care providers and other individuals from experiencing discrimination by recipients of DHHS funds on the basis of their refusal to perform or participate in such health-care services. The Church Amendment protects both sectarian hospitals that oppose abortion and sterilization procedures and the employees of such hospitals who do not share their employers' religious convictions.

The Danforth Amendment to the Public Health Service Act (Title X) prohibits "abortion-related discrimination in governmental activities regarding training and licensing of physicians."[44] This amendment prevents federal, state, and local governments receiving federal funds from discriminating against health-care providers who refuse to provide abortion-related services and protects doctors, medical students, and health-training programs. It also prevents medical-training programs from losing accreditation status (which would jeopardize federal funding) if they refuse to train residents in abortion and sterilization. The Danforth Amendment protects refusals to participate in abortion or related services for any reason; it is not limited to religious objections.[45]

Congress passed the Weldon Amendment in 2004 as part of an omnibus appropriations bill and, like the Hyde Amendment, it has become a rider to the annual DHHS/Labor/Education appropriations legislation.[46] The Weldon Amendment allows all federally funded health-care entities to refuse to "provide, pay for, provide coverage of, or refer for abortions."[47] This amendment is even broader than the Hyde Amendment, as not all health-care providers accept Medicaid reimbursement, but most accept Medicare funds. Also, like the Danforth Amendment, the Weldon Amendment does not specify that an objection need be religious.

These amendments formed the foundation for a Bush Administration regulation that would have required all health-care providers who receive federal funds to certify that they were complying with the terms of these amendments (the "conscience regulation").[48] The conscience regulation would have affected approximately 572,000 health-care providers, but the Obama Administration eliminated it.[49] Nevertheless, it serves to illuminate how conditional funding is wielded in ways that aggrandize the power to spend and create individual rights dilemmas. The pure funding statutes prohibit programs such as Medicaid from paying for most abortions,

---

[43] 42 U.S.C. § 300a–7 (2006).

[44] 42 U.S.C. § 238n (2006).

[45] *See* Robin Fretwell Wilson, *The Limits of Conscience: Moral Clashes over Deeply Divisive Healthcare Procedures*, 34 AM. J. L. & MED. 41, 49 (2008).

[46] Pub. L. No. 108–447, §508(d)(2005), 42 C.F.R. § 59.5(a)(5); Pub. L. No. 109–149, §508(d) (2006).

[47] Consolidated Appropriations Act, 2008, Pub. L. No. 110–161, Title V, §508.

[48] 73 Fed. Reg. 78072 (Dec. 19, 2008).

[49] 76 Fed. Reg. 9968 (Feb. 23, 2011).

while the conscience-clause funding statutes permit health-care providers to turn women away with no obligation to provide an alternative. Even if Medicaid paid for abortions, poor women would still face the difficulty of providers being excused from performing reproductive medical services. Conversely, when Medicaid does not pay, it is harder for a poor woman to find a health-care provider who will help to pursue her medical options because of the conscience-clause funding statutes. By the mechanism of conditions on spending, the federal government maneuvers around *Roe* and *Casey*. The conscience regulation distended the *McRae* and *Maher* precedents by placing an obstacle in the path of *all* who seek abortion, sterilization, or contraceptive use. *McRae* and *Maher* applied only to federal programs. The conscience-clause funding statutes and conscience regulation use the federal spending power to narrow access to reproductive care for all women, even in private payment situations, because the laws affect all health-care providers who accept any form of federal reimbursement. Conditions on federal funds can affect not only individuals who are the beneficiaries of the conditional funds but also those who are not.

III. RECONNECTING SPENDING CLAUSE JURISPRUDENCE

Congress created the statutory spending conditions that lead to the benchmark *Maher* and *McRae* decisions, and it can remove those conditions. Congress could cease creating pure funding statutes and conscience-clause funding statutes, or at least modify the most broadly worded existing laws, so that the individual is not negotiated out of the federal–state relationship. Termination of Hyde-type legislative language would help erase the peculiar legacy of *Maher* and *McRae*. Even so, the conditional spending authority that facilitated the Hyde Amendment would remain, so the Court's analysis should be revisited.

The Court did not delineate a test for evaluating the constitutionality of conditions placed on federal funds until 1987 in *South Dakota v. Dole*.[50] The *Dole* decision created a five-part test that focused on the federal–state relationship and allowed the federal government to regulate states indirectly through conditional spending in ways that it might not be able to do directly. The focus on the federal–state relationship is problematic because programs like Medicaid do not solely command state compliance with federal law; they also benefit particular individuals by creating a federal scheme that is followed and administered by the states. The *Dole* test fails to account for the ultimate beneficiary of the federal scheme.

The first prong of the *Dole* test demands that the government spend only for the "general welfare."[51] The Court clarified that it would defer to Congress's judgment

[50] South Dakota v. Dole, 483 U.S. 203 (1987).
[51] The Spending Clause provides, "Congress shall have Power . . . to pay the Debts and provide for the common Defence and general Welfare of the United States. . . ." Art. I, Sec. 8, Cl. 1.

rather than second-guess whether spending is actually for the general welfare.[52] As a whole, the Medicaid Act can be described as providing for the general welfare by providing health-care services to people who could not otherwise afford them. However, if the spending activity is narrowed to placing limits on use of federal funds to prevent paying for abortion, the benefit for the general welfare is muddied; forcing poor women to birth children, or to forgo life necessities to seek a legal, safe abortion, do not appear to be outcomes that serve the general welfare. Nevertheless, the Court has essentially rendered this element of the *Dole* test a political question, and observers consider it useless.[53]

The second prong asks if the federal government has provided "clear" notice of conditions on spending, meaning whether a "state official who is engaged in the process of deciding whether the State should accept . . . funds and the obligations that go with those funds . . . would clearly understand . . . the obligations of the Act."[54] As an example for the pure funding statute model, consider the Medicaid Act. The Hyde Amendment contains plain language that is unambiguous. The *Dole* analysis ends there, which is part of the conundrum. The state accepts certain federal conditions as a quid pro quo for much needed federal funds. The Court has long held that the federal government may do indirectly through spending what it may not do directly through other powers.[55] However, this prong of the *Dole* test only asks if the state understands the conditions and does not question the constitutionality of the condition or the impact on beneficiaries. If the state and the federal government are complicit in violating a constitutional right by means of conditional spending, it is insufficient to simply confirm that the condition is "clear."[56] Further, the Medicaid Act as a whole may not provide state officials with clear notice given the ever-changing nature of the program and the long-term state reliance on Medicaid funding.[57]

The exercise of this particular right, like the Sixth Amendment right to assistance of counsel, requires the assistance of a professional. Denial of payment to the health-care provider is denial of the right itself, whether or not the funding condition is clear to the state accepting the federal funds.[58] Both the health-care provider and

---

[52] *Dole*, 483 U.S. at 207.

[53] *See, e.g.,* Lynn A. Baker & Mitchell N. Berman, *Getting off the Dole: Why the Court Should Abandon Its Spending Doctrine, and How a Too-Clever Congress Could Provoke It to Do So,* 78 IND. L.J. 459, 464–65 (2001).

[54] *Dole*, 483 U.S. at 207; *Arlington Central Sch. Dist. Bd. of Educ. v. Murphy,* 548 U.S. 291, 296 (2006).

[55] *Dole*, 483 U.S. at 207.

[56] *See* Laurence H. Tribe, *The Abortion Funding Conundrum: Inalienable Rights, Affirmative Duties, and the Dilemma of Dependence,* 99 HARV. L. REV. 330, 333 (1985).

[57] *See* Nicole Huberfeld, *Clear Notice for Conditions on Spending, Unclear Implications for States in Federal Healthcare Programs,* 86 N.C. L. REV. 441, 488 (2008).

[58] *See* Kenneth Agran, *When Government Must Pay: Compensating Rights and the Constitution,* 22 CONST. COMMENTARY 97, 101–102 (2005).

the Medicaid enrollee are affected by the state's decision to accept the condition of spending but are unaccounted for in the clear statement rule.

The clear notice requirement is also inadequate in the conscience-clause funding statute context. A hospital, for example, accepts federal funds when it participates in Medicaid and accepts the conditions attached thereto. The clear notice requirement does not protect the hospital, as it focuses on a state's acceptance of conditions. Further, it does not protect individuals who seek treatment in the hospital and who have no control over the conditions on federal spending that may affect their care.

The third *Dole* requirement is that "conditions on federal grants might be illegitimate if they are unrelated 'to the federal interest in particular national projects or programs.'"[59] Justice O'Connor's dissent would have given this prong teeth: "The Court can draw the line between permissible and impermissible conditions on federal grants.... 'The appropriate inquiry, then, is whether the spending requirement or prohibition is a condition on a grant or whether it is regulation.'"[60] Germaneness should be about more than simply how funds are spent. For example, even though the Medicaid Act facilitates medical care for the indigent, the Hyde Amendment deliberately withholds care to the indigent. The statistics are well known: half of all pregnancies in the United States are unintended; one-third of all women of childbearing age will terminate pregnancy; more than one-fifth of all women will have an abortion by the end of their reproductive years.[61] Abortion is one of the most commonly performed medical procedures in the United States, and a medical professional must participate to safely perform the procedure either medically or surgically. Pure funding statutes such as the Hyde Amendment fail the germaneness test by denying to women medically necessary, nonexperimental medical assistance, a direct conflict with the goal of the Medicaid Act. The privacy right protected by *Roe, Casey,* and (perhaps) *Gonzales v. Carhart* need not be raised to come to this conclusion. Refusal to fund a legal, common, and necessary medical procedure for a certain portion of the population is not rationally related to funding medical assistance for that portion of the population.

The *Dole* majority held that "Congress conditioned the receipt of federal funds in a way reasonably calculated to address this particular impediment to a purpose for which the funds are expended."[62] The "reasonably calculated" standard is also flawed when considering the conscience-clause spending statutes. For example, the Danforth Amendment is attached to the Public Health Services Act, which is intended to facilitate "family planning facilities."[63] It stretches the bounds of

[59] 483 U.S. at 207.
[60] *Id.* at 215–16 (O'Connor, J., dissenting).
[61] *See* Guttmacher Institute, *Facts on Induced Abortion in America* (2010), www.guttmacher.org/pubs/fb_induced_abortion.html.
[62] 483 U.S. at 209.
[63] 42 U.S.C. § 300 (2006).

reason to consider the condition to that act allowing health-care providers to opt out of abortion, sterilization, and contraception to be a condition that is "reasonably calculated" to furthering the congressional goal of providing family planning. Yet this is what the conscience-clause funding statutes do; they attach conditions to spending that are anathema to the goal of the spending itself.

Further, the conscience-clause funding statutes attach conditions such that individuals who do not receive federal spending are also subject to their limitations. All patients in a hospital, regardless of whether they rely on public or private insurance mechanisms, are subjected to rules that protect health-care providers who refuse to participate in abortion or sterilization. The Court's failure to apply germaneness has facilitated this violation of the rights of nonpublic insurance patients.

The fourth prong of the *Dole* test states, "Other constitutional provisions may provide an independent bar to the conditional grant of federal funds."[64] Chief Justice Rehnquist clarified that the spending power cannot be used "to induce the States to engage in activities that would themselves be unconstitutional."[65] The majority used the example that the federal government could not condition receipt of federal funds on the state inflicting cruel and unusual punishment. The unconstitutional conditions doctrine is unpredictable, and many authors have observed that the Court applies the doctrine unevenly.

The *Dole* description of the independent constitutional bar would seem to reverse *McRae* and *Maher*, as they permitted the federal government to impose conditions on federal funds that require the state to either pay for reproductive services without a federal match or require that women who want Medicaid assistance waive their right to access abortion. The former is not necessarily the imposition of an independent constitutional bar, but it does implicate coercion, discussed next. The latter does amount to an independent constitutional bar, but *McRae* and *Maher* have not been overruled, the result of which is the statutes discussed herein.

Dole focuses solely on the relationship among the federal government, the condition, and the state, but that standard analysis does not account for all parties to the transaction. Admittedly, the Court has chipped away at *Roe* so that its analysis has been twisted into a different kind of fundamental right.[66] Nevertheless, the precedent stands, and yet Congress has bypassed it by paying for medical assistance in every other situation in which medical care is necessary, including childbirth, except this one.

---

[64] 483 U.S. at 208.

[65] *Id.* at 210.

[66] The strict scrutiny test was applied in *Roe*, at least pre-viability. *See Roe v. Wade*, 410 U.S. at 155. *Casey* lowered the level of scrutiny to an "undue burden" standard, which was mentioned in other abortion-related cases but had not been applied to fundamental rights. *See Casey*, 505 U.S. at 874, 877–78. The undue burden standard was eroded by *Gonzales v. Carhart*, which applied a hybrid undue burden/rational basis review. *See Gonzales v. Carhart*, 550 U.S. 124, 127 S. Ct. 1610, 1634–35 (2007).

Dole created a fifth element: that congressional coercion can become impermissible compulsion.[67] This "coercion" element has been little interpreted and, as a result, lower federal courts have been unwilling to apply it.[68] Some guidance exists, though, as the Court found relevant the amount of federal funding offered and the amount jeopardized for noncompliance. In the pure funding statute context, states rely very heavily on Medicaid funds, which promise a federal match ranging from 50 percent to 83 percent.[69] Every state has participated in Medicaid since the early 1970s, and the poorest states are often the richest recipients of Medicaid funds. Given the degree to which states rely on Medicaid funding, it appears that federal compulsion exists. States have participated in Medicaid for more than forty years, and choosing to reject Medicaid funds based on certain conditions, such as the Hyde Amendment, is improbable, especially knowing that states could not otherwise shoulder the burden of their low-income and chronically ill patients.[70] Although courts emphasize that states can "choose" to refuse Medicaid funds if they dislike the conditions imposed on them, this analysis is unrealistic.

Likewise, poor individuals have the "choice" of being uninsured, a barrier to medical care, or being enrolled in Medicaid (assuming they meet the eligibility requirements). The Court in *McRae* and *Maher* indicated a belief that women could still access those services that the government refused to fund through Medicaid, but Medicaid beneficiaries are extraordinarily poor and rely on Medicaid for all of their medical assistance. Justice Blackmun recognized this in *Singleton v. Wulff*,[71] as did Justice Brennan in his *Maher* dissent,[72] and it is still true today. Such realities make the idea of coercion, and the individual's disconnect from the funding conditions, more concrete.

The conscience-clause funding statutes further the idea of coercion and help to highlight the missing piece in conditional spending. For example, the Danforth Amendment prevents Title X recipients from counseling abortion as a form of family planning, and this restriction must be accepted to continue to receive funding. Once an entity has accepted Title X funding, it would be extremely difficult to decline that funding without closing a clinic. The Court's coercion analysis involves the state, an actor that has more bargaining power with the federal government than most others have. The assumption that the party faced with the conditions on spending can simply choose to reject the conditions (and the money) seems particularly erroneous when the power imbalance between community nonprofit and federal government is considered.

---

[67] 483 U.S. at 211.

[68] *See, e.g., West Virginia v. United States Dept. of Health and Human Svcs.*, 289 F.3d 281 (4th Cir. 2002).

[69] *See* 42 U.S.C. § 1396d(b).

[70] *See* Rosenbaum, *supra* note 3, at 6, 27–30.

[71] *Singleton v. Wulff*, 428 U.S. at 117.

[72] *Maher*, 432 U.S. at 454 (Brennan, J., dissenting).

Applied with teeth, the *Dole* test reveals that both the pure funding statutes and the conscience-clause funding statutes are impermissible exercises of the federal power to spend. The Court has read the power to spend broadly, but it has created a test that facilitates stronger scrutiny. Given that the Roberts Court has been willing to revisit precedent but has taken incremental steps in the area of the Spending Clause, the *Dole* test is worth another look.[73]

The Rehnquist Court limited congressional power, yet the Court avoided narrowing its interpretation of the Spending Clause, thereby allowing Congress to circumvent constitutional rules by imposing conditions on spending. This leniency seems inconsistent with the Rehnquist Court's revitalization of federalism and limitations on Commerce Clause power,[74] although it is consistent with the greater includes the lesser theory of conditional spending.

The Court has not addressed the contours of congressional power under the Spending Clause often. With limited decisions to mine, determining the boundaries of the power to spend becomes a bit of an exercise in clairvoyance. Nevertheless, given the Roberts Court's pattern of revisiting precedent, and the fact that the Court has slightly modified the standards for conditions on spending, this chapter endeavors to determine how impact on individuals can be reflected better in the conditional spending analysis. The Roberts Court thus far has limited individual rights and read statutory language narrowly, a tricky combination for contemplating how conditions on spending can be evaluated with an eye toward protecting individuals.[75]

Dole's focus on the federal–state relationship creates tension with the reality that federal conditions on spending impact more than just the states. The only canon that appears to cover the federal government–individual relationship is the unconstitutional conditions doctrine. This doctrine represents the Court's analysis of the federal government's ability to influence individual behavior through "spending, licensing, and employment."[76] In other words, "government may not condition the receipt of its benefits upon the nonassertion of constitutional rights even if receipt of such benefits is . . . a 'mere privilege'. . . . "[77] The doctrine has been applied inconsistently, sometimes protecting fundamental rights and individual liberties, and sometimes not, although the basic idea is that an individual can litigate governmental action that "inhibits or penalizes the exercise of constitutional rights."[78]

The unconstitutional conditions doctrine is an uncomfortable fit for both pure funding statutes and conscience-clause funding statutes because of the various levels at which the funding and attendant conditions operate. The pure funding statutes

---

[73] *See* Samuel R. Bagenstos, *Spending Clause Litigation in the Roberts Court*, 58 DUKE L. J. 345 (2008).

[74] *See Dole*, 483 U.S. 203 (1987); *New York v. United States*, 505 U.S. 144 (1992); *Lopez v. United States*, 514 U.S. 549 (1995); *Printz v. United States*, 521 U.S. 898 (1997); *United States v. Morrison*, 529 U.S. 598 (2000).

[75] *See* Erwin Chemerinsky, *Turning Sharply to the Right*, 10 GREEN BAG 2d 423 (2007).

[76] Sunstein, *supra* note 7, at 593–94.

[77] LAURENCE H. TRIBE, AMERICAN CONSTITUTIONAL LAW, § 10–8, 681 (2d ed. 1988).

[78] *Id.*

reflect federalism; the state can accept or reject the funding depending on whether the elements of the *Dole* test are met. However, a second level exists at which the individual who relies on the federal spending program is subjected to the conditions that were accepted by the state. This second level is unrepresented in either the *Dole* analysis or the traditional unconstitutional conditions analysis. In the first, only the federal–state relationship is discussed. In the second, the Court assumes a direct bargaining relationship between the federal government and the individual that does not exist.

Consider again the Medicaid program. Its legal entitlement extends to the state and the individual enrollee. Many of the Medicaid funding conditions require the state to adhere to certain rules regarding the administration of the program. However, those conditions also may benefit or burden the state's Medicaid enrollees, who have no part in the state's acceptance of the federal conditions, as well as the health-care providers who agree to treat enrollees.[79] Although the Court undertook an unconstitutional conditions analysis in *McRae* and *Maher*, it failed to account for the nature of the conditional spending. The conscience-clause funding statutes magnify the issue; in exchange for federal funding of any kind, health-care providers must permit unspecified moral objections to reproductive health services. Both models permit indirect violation of constitutional rights, particularly women's reproductive rights, and the incursions are deliberate.

The question is how to connect the Spending Clause jurisprudence to the individual so that intentional, indirect attacks by conditioned federal funds are at least recognized if not prevented. One avenue would be to apply the existing *Dole* framework to the individual, not just the state, meaning that the Court should apply the *Dole* test conjunctively rather than selectively. The analysis herein indicates that *Dole* may be up to the task. This would require the Court to analyze germaneness and coercion, which has occurred, although only occasionally. For instance, in a decision heard during the same term as *Dole*, the Court considered conditions placed on landowners who wanted to build a home that would block public beach access.[80] Although a property case, the majority analyzed the state's imposition of the condition (an easement) using a germaneness analysis. The Court held that, because the condition was required for obtaining the necessary building and land use permits, the state was able to "extort" the easement out of the property owner without paying for the taking of the property; and, the permit condition did not serve the same governmental purpose as the development ban, thereby eliminating any nexus between the ban and the condition. In other words, germaneness did not exist because the condition was not tailored closely enough to the goal of the law. The

---

[79] Professor Farber refers to "third-party effects," meaning that the government bargains with an intermediary (here, the state) who may not actually represent the interests of the individual whose constitutional rights are at issue. *See* Daniel A. Farber, *Another View of the Quagmire: Unconstitutional Conditions and Contract Theory*, 33 FLA. ST. U. L. REV. 913, 935 (2007).

[80] *Nollan v. Ca. Coastal Comm'n*, 483 U.S. 825 (1987).

Court often determines whether or not a law is properly tailored to a governmental goal, especially when the government infringes individual rights in pursuit of that goal. The spending power should not be exempt from this kind of nexus analysis.

Some have asserted that coercion is not judicially determinable, but *Dole* seems to indicate otherwise, as the majority indicated that proportionality should be considered. In the case of Medicaid, Title X, and CHIP, failure to comply with conditions can result in complete withdrawal of funding. States have asserted that they cannot reject federal conditions because they need the federal funds; imagine then the position of the individual benefiting from the federal program. Only the poorest and most vulnerable citizens even qualify for Medicaid funding. The notion that they could negotiate with the federal government regarding conditions on federal funds seems absurd; that they are being coerced seems more than possible.

CONCLUSION

South Dakota v. Dole facilitated an analytical separation between the individual and the conditional spending program, a divide that has allowed Congress to impinge on individual rights when it could not do so using other enumerated powers. At a micro level, the Court's decisions have allowed government to burden the privacy right to obtain abortion by withholding funds in public health-care programs. At a macro level, the power to place conditions on spending has created an end-run that has been quite successful, as exhibited by the pure funding statutes and conscience-clause funding statutes that result from *McRae* and *Maher*. The gap that exists here could exist in any federal spending program, but the case of Medicaid is particularly notable given the fragility of its enrollees.

If the federal government is to restructure health-care programs in an effective, nondiscriminatory manner, the boundaries of its power to spend should be explored and better defined. Underlying doctrines such as the greater includes the lesser theory and the positive/negative rights theory tend to ignore the reality of modern government, which wields influence through benefits. The *Dole* test can facilitate drawing such boundaries if all of its elements are actively analyzed. The current focus on the federal–state relationship does not protect individuals in federal health-care programs, nor does it particularly protect states. Although individual rights have not appeared important to the majority of the Roberts Court, protecting states through active federalism doctrine may be. Additionally, Congress can change this trend by eliminating the Hyde Amendment and other pure funding statutes and by balancing conscience-clause funding statutes. The latter would be unconstitutional under a revitalized *Dole* regime, as the ability to affect private-pay patients through federal spending far exceeds the bounds of the spending power.

16

Challenges for Contemporary Reproductive Rights Advocacy

The South African Example

Rachel Rebouché

INTRODUCTION

South Africa's Choice on the Termination of Pregnancy Act of 1996 (CTOPA)[1] is heralded as one of the most progressive abortion laws in the world.[2] An outlier from its African counterparts, the CTOPA gives a woman of any age the right to a government-funded abortion until the twelfth week of pregnancy. Women's rights activists, as part of the South African movement to eradicate the discriminatory policies of apartheid and to incorporate international human rights norms, exerted significant influence in drafting the CTOPA and rights in the Constitution. Reflecting a leading strategy in reproductive health advocacy, proponents of the CTOPA relied on the autonomy and equality rights expressed in documents agreed to at the International Conference on Population and Development (ICPD) in 1994 and the Fourth World Conference on Women (FWCW) in 1995. The CTOPA is emblematic, in this way, of the recognition of the modern relationship between reproductive health care, including abortion, and women's human rights.

The implementation of the CTOPA, however, is not as inspiring. The number of illegal terminations has not changed significantly since the CTOPA's enactment.[3] Although rates of maternal mortality associated with illegal abortion have decreased,

---

[1] Act 92 of 1996, amended by the Choice on Termination of Pregnancy Amendment Act 92 of 2008 [hereinafter CTOPA]. The 2008 amendment to the CTOPA allows all facilities with 24-hour maternity wards to perform terminations, irrespective of whether the Minister of Health approved of their use for abortion. Additionally, the Amendment allows nurses who complete a Medical Controls Council training course to provide abortions. The amendment first passed Parliament in 2004 but was successfully challenged in *Doctors for Life v. Speaker of the National Assembly*, 2005 Case CCT 12/05, for failure to adequately consult provinces.

[2] *See* Charles Ngwena, *An Appraisal of Abortion Laws in Southern Africa from a Reproductive Health Rights Perspective*, 32 J. L. Med. & Ethics 708, 713 (2004) (describing the CTOPA as "exemplary") [hereinafter Ngwena I]; Audrey Haroz, *South Africa's 1996 Choice on Termination of Pregnancy Act: Expanding Choice and International Human Rights to Black South African Women*, 30 Vand. J. Transnat'l L. 863, 903 (1997) (describing the CTOPA at the "forefront of defining human rights").

[3] Banwari Meel & Ram P. Kaswa, *The Impact on the Choice on Termination of Pregnancy Act of 1996*, 36 Afr. J. Primary Health Care & Fam. Med. 1, 1 (2009).

indications of maternal morbidity (illness or negative health effects) remain fairly constant.[4] Contradicting the expectations of the CTOPA's drafters, the passage of a law that enunciates a right to abortion services has not substantially improved women's reproductive health.

This chapter explores how the CTOPA's implementation has been limited by the very controversies that its drafters sought to avoid. Legislation focused on liberalizing the grounds for legal abortion may be well suited to a project in which the primary and most important aim is to create a rights based framework. Yet it may not be responsive to implementation problems, help ensure delivery of health services, or take account of the unique context in which those services will be rendered. The first part of this chapter describes the regulation of and public reaction to abortion during apartheid. The second part considers the influence of the international campaign for gender equality on the South African constitutional drafting process, which facilitated the incorporation of reproductive rights. The third part addresses the strategies for drafting the CTOPA and charts how transnational reproductive rights movements are influenced by U.S. case law and activism. The fourth part examines the treatment of parental involvement in minors' abortion decisions as an example of the unintended consequences of the CTOPA advocacy strategy. The chapter concludes by suggesting considerations that contemporary reproductive rights reform projects might incorporate in pursuit of a more responsive, and less reactive, approach.

I. ABORTION LAW DURING APARTHEID

Since the CTOPA took effect on February 1, 1997, the reproductive health landscape in South Africa has changed dramatically in some ways, and minimally in others. Prior to 1975, South Africa's abortion law was based on Roman–Dutch common law, which criminalized abortion except to save the life of the mother.[5] South African courts relied on the interpretation of England's Offences Against the Person Act of 1861 to permit abortion that preserved a pregnant woman's physical or mental health.[6] Other reproductive health services consisted mainly of maternal and child health care and provision of contraceptives for certain segments of the population (for the racist purposes mentioned later).[7]

---

[4] Rachel Jewkes et al., *Prevalence of Morbidity Associated with Abortion before and after Legalization in South Africa*, 324 Brit. Med. J. 1252 (2002).

[5] *See* Charles Ngwena, *The History and Transformation of Abortion Law in South Africa*, 30 Acta Academica 32, 35–36 (1998) [hereinafter Ngwena II].

[6] South Africa recognized an exception for mental health if continuing a pregnancy would make the woman a "mental wreck" as set out in the English case, *R v. Bourne*, 1 K.B. 687 (Central Criminal Court, London, 1938).

[7] Diane Cooper et al., *Ten Years of Democracy in South Africa: Documenting Transformation in Reproductive Health Policy and Status*, 12 Reprod. Health Matters 70, 71 (2004).

In passing the Abortion and Sterilisation Bill of 1975 (the 1975 Act), the apartheid government intended to clarify the application of the common law and to foreclose any discussion of making legal abortion available on additional grounds.[8] The 1975 Act provided for abortion in very restricted circumstances,[9] permitting terminations only when there was a serious threat to a woman's physical or mental health, serious risk of disability of the fetus, or in instances of rape or incest.[10] Legal abortion required the approval of two medical practitioners (in addition to the practitioner performing the abortion) and a hospital superintendent.[11] The district surgeon and a magistrate had to certify abortion for reasons of rape or incest.[12] Abortion on the ground of mental health required the assessment of a state-registered psychiatrist or a court order.[13] Violations of the law could result in a fine of 5,000 rand and a five-year prison term.[14]

Despite the threat of criminal prosecution, before and under the 1975 Act, law had little to do with most women's abortion decisions. Gaining access to designated state hospitals, multiple doctors, psychiatrists, or courts was financially and logistically impossible for many,[15] particularly "poor, black, rural, or young women."[16] Only about one thousand legal abortions were reported in twenty years of the 1975 Act's operation,[17] or less than 1 percent of total (legal and illegal) abortions.[18] In contrast, the estimated number of annual illegal abortions was high. One study cites 200,000 illegal abortions per year under the 1975 Act,[19] and two other studies cite ranges from 100,000 to 500,000.[20] Although estimates of the number of illegal abortions varied, the health consequences for women were clear.[21] An oft-cited study conducted by the Medical Research Council (MRC) found that in one year more than 44,000 women visited hospitals with complications from induced terminations and 425 women died.[22]

---

[8] *Ngwena II, supra* note 5, at 35–36.
[9] Jeremy Sarkin-Hughes, *A Perspective on Abortion Legislation in South Africa's Bill of Rights Era*, 56 Tydskrif vir Hedendaagse Romeins-Hollandse Reg 83, 87 (1993).
[10] The Abortion and Sterilisation Act 2 of 1975 § 3 as amended by Act 48 of 1982 and repealed by CTOPA, *supra* note 1 (the 1982 Amendment did not make substantive changes to the 1975 Act).
[11] *See id.* §§ 3–7.
[12] Haroz, *supra* note 2, at 881.
[13] Sally Guttmacher et al., *Abortion Reform in South Africa: A Case Study of the 1996 Choice on Termination of Pregnancy Act*, 24 Int'l Fam. Planning Persp. 191, 191 (1998).
[14] The Abortion and Sterilisation Act 2 of 1975 § 10.
[15] Cooper, *supra* note 7, at 71.
[16] Catherine Albertyn, *Reproductive Health and the Right to Choose – Policy and Law Reform on Abortion, in* Engendering the Political Agenda: A South African Case Study 17 (Catherine Albertyn ed., 1999) (noting "[o]fficial statistics throughout the 1970s and 1980s demonstrate that access to legal abortions under the act was largely determined by race and class").
[17] *Id.* at 8; *see also* Sarkin-Hughes, *supra* note 9, at 84.
[18] Guttmacher et al., *supra* note 13, at 192.
[19] Barbara Klugman & Sanjani Jane Varkey, *From Policy Development to Policy Implementation: The South African Choice on Termination of Pregnancy Act, in* Advocating for Abortion Access: Eleven Country Studies 251–82 (B. Klugman & D. Budlender eds., 2001).
[20] Sarkin-Hughes, *supra* note 9, at 83; Guttmacher et al., *supra* note 13, at 192.
[21] Jeremy Sarkin, *Suggestions for a New Abortion Law*, 9 S. African L. J. 125, 138 (1996).
[22] Guttmacher et al., *supra* note 13, at 192.

Perhaps of more importance than law were the norms of some communities in which women lived. Although differing from group to group, customary law dealt with abortion as a family matter that potentially warranted moral disapproval but not criminal punishment.[23] Abortion was prevalent, and there was no uniform policy sanctioning it. For example, the Sotho community historically relied on family councils to settle the issue on a case-by-case basis.[24] Abortion as governed by customary law reveals the tension between centralized state power embodied in national legislation and local governance shaped by custom, a theme that emerges clearly in the context of the CTOPA's implementation.[25]

National surveys before the passage of the CTOPA revealed significant ambivalence about the liberalization of abortion law. In 1994, as the CTOPA was being debated, 34 percent of respondents stated they were against abortion in all circumstances, 45 percent supported retaining the 1975 Act, and 21 percent supported broader access to legal abortion.[26] Those aligned against abortion came from both conservative and progressive backgrounds. Abortion politics in the progressive community were divisive for a number of reasons; for example, many anti-apartheid activists opposed abortion because of their religious beliefs.[27]

The relationship between women's rights and anti-apartheid movements was also complicated.[28] Sexist attitudes were not necessarily challenged by the leaders of the early struggle against apartheid, despite the many women who were involved in anti-apartheid activism.[29] Some apartheid leaders viewed the feminist movement (and groups like the Abortion Reform Action Group [ARAG], the primary organization pushing for repeal of the 1975 Act during apartheid),[30] as fixated on an agenda for white, middle-class women and detached from the concerns of black South Africans. This was, in no small part, because of the deeply racist family-planning policies of the apartheid government.[31] Population-control laws encouraged white women to bear children through tax incentives and public appeals to their "duty" to ensure the

---

[23] *Ngwena I, supra* note 2, at 711.

[24] *Ngwena II, supra* note 5, at 35–36 (1998). *See also* Bernard Dickens & Rebecca Cook, *Development of Commonwealth Abortion Laws*, 28 INT'L & COMP. L. Q. 424, 427 (1979).

[25] For a discussion of the role of customary law in South Africa, see T. W. BENNETT, CUSTOMARY LAW IN SOUTH AFRICA 38 (2004).

[26] Albertyn, *supra* note 16, at 16 (citing D. Budlender & D. Everatt, *How Many For and How Many Against? Private and Public Opinion on Abortion*, 40 AGENDA 101, 102 (1999)).

[27] Guttmacher et al., *supra* note 13, at 193.

[28] Penelope Andrews, *The Stepchild of National Liberation: Women and Rights in the New South Africa*, *in* THE POST-APARTHEID CONSTITUTIONS: PERSPECTIVES ON SOUTH AFRICA'S BASIC LAW 327 (2001) [hereinafter Andrews I]; *see also* Saras Jagwanth & Christina Murray, *"No Nation Can Be Free When One Half of It Is Enslaved:" Constitutional Equality for Women in South Africa*, *in* THE GENDER OF CONSTITUTIONAL JURISPRUDENCE 231 (Beverley Baines & Ruth Rubio-Marín eds., 2004).

[29] Albertyn, *supra* note 16, at 12.

[30] Guttmacher et al., *supra* note 13, at 191.

[31] Kelly Blanchard et al., *Abortion Law in South Africa: Passage of a Progressive Law and Challenges for Implementation*, 139 GAC MED MEX 109, 110 (2003).

survival of the only "Christian and Western country on the continent of Africa."[32] In contrast, policies designed to "control" the black population promoted broad and free use of contraceptives and sterilization.[33] Black women were injected with the contraceptive drug Depo-Provera, sometimes without their consent, at three times the recommended dosage.[34]

Against this backdrop of opposition and skepticism from diverse quarters, one might imagine that repealing the 1975 Act and enacting new legislation would take time and require a significant change in popular opinion. However, the transition from apartheid to a democratic republic, with a new constitutional ethic and commitment to human rights, gave reproductive rights advocates an opportunity to pursue reform on their terms.

II. THE FOUNDATION OF REPRODUCTIVE RIGHTS ADVOCACY

This section describes the critical juncture in which feminist activists exerted considerable influence in constitution drafting and legislative reform. This influence ultimately resulted in the ratification of a constitution that provided unprecedented reproductive rights and the passage of the CTOPA.

Support for reproductive rights gained momentum as leaders of the anti-apartheid movement began to assemble the structure for a constitutional, representative democracy. Architects of the new legal order relied heavily on international human rights to build consensus and to strengthen the legitimacy of the "government-in-waiting," led by the African National Congress (ANC).[35] Advocates worked with key members of the ANC to translate a commitment to human rights into an agenda that included gender equality and reproductive rights.[36]

By the start of constitutional negotiations, South African advocates had formed influential organizations in civil society[37] – a "well-orchestrated campaign" of a "global feminist endeavor."[38] These advocates made a case for explicit and extensive equality rights that would not only address the segregationist legacy of apartheid

[32] Jerome Singh et al., *South Africa a Decade after Apartheid: Realizing Health through Human Rights*, 12 GEO. J. POVERTY L. & POL'Y 355, 373 (2005) (citing a speech delivered by the apartheid government's Minister of Bantu Administration and Development).
[33] *Id.*
[34] Barbara Brown, *Facing the Black Peril: The Politics of Population Control in South Africa*, 12 J. S. AFR. STUD. 256, 259–60 (1987). *See also* Cooper et al., *supra* note 7, at 71.
[35] Kieran McEvoy & Rachel Rebouché, *Mobilizing the Professions: Lawyers, Politics, and the Collective Legal Conscience*, in JUDGES, TRANSITION, AND HUMAN RIGHTS 275 (John Morrison et al. eds., 2007).
[36] Albertyn, *supra* note 16, at 18.
[37] *Andrews I*, *supra* note 28, at 346. Tracy Higgins et al., *Gender Equality and Customary Marriage: Bargaining in the Shadow of Post-Apartheid Legal Pluralism*, 30 FORDHAM INT'L L. J. 1653, 1654 (2007).
[38] Penelope Andrews, *Striking the Rock: Confronting Gender Equality in South Africa*, 3 MICH. J. RACE & L. 307, 307, 310 (1998) [hereinafter *Andrews II*].

but also recognize all forms of discrimination as equally repugnant.[39] Human rights treaties like the United Nations Convention on the Elimination of Discrimination Against Women, interpreted as recognizing substantive equality, reinforced arguments for a constitution with expansive rights for women.[40] Substantive equality recognizes equality as a norm that can both level the playing field for men and women and justify the redistribution of resources in ways that take into account women's historic disadvantage. Although still a concept needing "conceptualization, concretization, and indigenization," substantive equality has been described as the centerpiece of post-apartheid jurisprudence because of its perceived potential to address wealth and resource disparities between South Africans.[41]

Advocates also found support in the constitutional processes of other countries that relied on human rights principles to define the domestic treatment of gender equality. Helen Irving describes how Canada and Australia, for example, incorporated concepts such as disparate impact or constitutional language such as "equality of benefit" to emphasize substantive equality principles.[42] The extent to which the South African Constitution includes gender equality is a testament to the persuasiveness of the "well-orchestrated campaign" of feminist activists.[43] Section 9, "Equality Rights," includes "equal protection and benefit of the law;" nondiscrimination on the grounds of sex, gender, sexual orientation, marital status, and pregnancy; and protection for positive action to redress past disadvantage.[44]

South African advocates were a part of the international movement that linked inequalities between men and women to the state's control of women's reproductive capacity and childbearing decisions.[45] Then-recent activism around the ICPD[46] (as well as the FWCW) helped advocates set out an international approach to reproductive rights:[47] "The [ICPD and FWCW] and the parallel discourse around them in many ways smoothed the way for the formal adoption of similar constitutional guarantees and for the efforts to implement them in South Africa."[48]

---

[39] *Id.* at 309.

[40] *Id.* at 314–15; Ruth Rubio-Marín & Martha I. Morgan, *Constitutional Domestication of International Gender Norms, in* GENDER AND HUMAN RIGHTS 121 (Karen Knop ed., 2004).

[41] Charles Ngwena, *Accessing Abortion Services under the Choice on Termination of Pregnancy Act*, 25 J. JURIDICAL SCIENCE 19, 25 (2000) [hereinafter *Ngwena III*].

[42] HELEN IRVING, GENDER AND THE CONSTITUTION: EQUITY AND AGENCY IN COMPARATIVE CONSTITUTIONAL DESIGN 168–78 (2008).

[43] *Andrews I, supra* note 28, at 310.

[44] S. AFR. CONST. 1996, § 9.

[45] *See* Rebecca Cook & Susannah Howard, *Accommodating Women's Differences under the Women's Anti-discrimination Convention*, 56 EMORY L.J. 1039, 1045 (2007) (emphasizing the ways in which equality principles in international human rights documents like CEDAW should be used to support reproductive health rights).

[46] United Nations International Conference on Population and Development, Cairo, Egypt, 5–13 Sept. 1994, A/CONF.171/13 [hereinafter ICPD].

[47] Platform for Action of the Beijing Declaration, Fourth World Conference on Women, Beijing, China, 4–15 Sept. 1995, United Nations Department of Public Information, DPI/1766/Wom (February 1996) [hereinafter *Beijing Platform*].

[48] *Andrews I, supra* note 28, at 346.

ICPD provisions spoke to the ways in which reproductive decision making was central to women's ability to realize their full equality.[49] The prior conventions on population and development dealt with reproductive health in terms of controlling the world's birthrate and allowing parents to decide whether to have children. The Mexico City Population Conference held in 1984, for example, framed reproductive health as a demographics concern. International family-planning measures could help alleviate poverty by reducing family size and relieve pressures on environmental resources by reducing use by large populations of people.[50]

As advocates across the world responded to abuses committed by states in enforcing population policies, expressed often in laws that required sterilization of certain populations or penalized the use of contraceptives,[51] the approach to family planning changed. Substantial research highlighted how laws that stigmatized ending or prohibiting pregnancy correlate with high maternal morbidity and mortality rates. The 1994 ICPD Programme for Action marked the shift in focus from population control to individual well-being, women's empowerment, and gender equality[52] – a rights-based approach that has become the dominant framework for reform in international reproductive health.[53] Interestingly, the ICPD does not itself include a right to abortion, but stresses the need for safe, effective, and affordable health services.[54] The omission of the right to an abortion (in contexts where abortion is illegal) was the result of compromise.[55] However, the presence or absence of laws liberalizing abortion access has become a readily identifiable means to assess whether states are committed to women's rights.[56] The FWCW, for example, draws on the wording and general intent of the ICPD to urge states to reconsider laws criminalizing abortion as a means to improve women's health.[57]

Activism around the ICPD and FWCW influenced the ANC's decision to include reproductive rights in the Constitution, and proved instrumental in countering the objections of Constitutional Assembly members who opposed constitutional language supporting reproductive rights.[58] By 1994, the ANC Health Plan included the statement, "(e)very woman must have the right to choose whether or not to

---

[49] Cooper et al., *supra* note 7, at 71–72.

[50] Rebecca Firestone, Laura Reichenbach, & Mindy Jane Roseman, *Conceptual Successes and Operational Challenges to ICPD: Global Reproductive Health and Rights Moving Forward, in* REPRODUCTIVE HEALTH AND HUMAN RIGHTS: THE WAY FORWARD 221 (2009).

[51] Mindy Jane Roseman & Laura Reichenbach, *Global Reproductive Health and Rights: Reflecting on the ICPD, in* REPRODUCTIVE HEALTH AND HUMAN RIGHTS: THE WAY FORWARD 7–8 (2009).

[52] Firestone et al., *supra* note 50, at 221–22.

[53] This is not to suggest that the rights framework is the only approach in the field of global reproductive health, or is not in conflict with other models. Roseman & Reichenbach, *supra* note 51, at 17–18.

[54] ICPD, *supra* note 47, ¶ 8.25.

[55] ADRIENNE GERMAIN & TERESA KIM, EXPANDING ACCESS TO SAFE ABORTION: STRATEGIES FOR ACTION 3–4, 6 (1998).

[56] *Id.* at 3–4.

[57] *Beijing Platform, supra* note 48, ¶ 106(k).

[58] Albertyn, *supra* note 16, at 19.

have an early termination of pregnancy according to her own individual beliefs."[59] The Constitutional Assembly ultimately agreed to language securing a right to make decisions concerning reproduction (Section 12(2)(a)) and a right to reproductive health care services (Section 27 (1)(a)).[60] With these provisions, South Africa became the first and only country to explicitly recognize a positive right to both reproductive decision making and reproductive health care in its Constitution.[61]

With these new provisions, the state's role changed from limiting women's choices through the law to one of noninterference and promotion of an individual's rights.[62] The South African movement for post-apartheid gender equality, like feminist activism elsewhere,[63] "envisions the legal levers it pulls as activating a highly monolithic and state-centered form of power."[64] However, with rights come certain costs.[65] The expression of a right may become an end in itself and may be overly dependent on state recognition and enforcement.[66] As the conversation shifted from writing a constitution to drafting legislation, advocates focused on removing restrictions on how, when, and which women could decide to have an abortion. Less of a focus was how policies might help secure practical access to abortion care and a broader range of reproductive health services.[67] The CTOPA's Preamble references the need for comprehensive reproductive health services; its text does not.

The repeal of the 1975 Act and its replacement with substantive and state-centered rights to abortion may have been the likely starting place.[68] However, the approach of the CTOPA, the primary piece of legislation pursued by advocates on the heels of constitutional change, may have "crowded out" issues other than the right to abortion and "attract[ed] institutional energy and resources that would otherwise flow elsewhere."[69] The course that legislative reform took, described next, was shaped

---

[59] *Id.* at 20.

[60] *Id.* at 28.

[61] IRVING, *supra* note 42, at 199.

[62] *See* MICHEL FOUCAULT, SECURITY, TERRITORY, POPULATION: LECTURES AT THE COLLEGE DE FRANCE 1977–78 352–55 (Michel Senellart ed., Graham Burchell trans., 2007) (discussing a shift in governmental control from prevention to promotion in modern economies).

[63] *Andrews I, supra* note 28, at 331.

[64] Janet Halley et al., *From the International to the Local in Feminist Legal Responses to Rape, Prostitution/Sex Work, and Sex Trafficking: Four Studies in Contemporary Governance Feminism,* 29 HARV. J. L. & GENDER 335, 341 (2006).

[65] *See Ngwena I, supra* note 2, at 716; *see also* Rebecca Cook, *The Elimination of Sexual Apartheid: Prospects for the Fourth World Conference on Women, in* ISSUE PAPERS ON WORLD CONFERENCES No. 5 19 (American Society of International Law, 1995) ("a unifying theme in feminist analyses is that women cannot control their choices in life unless they can control their reproductive health.").

[66] *See* David Kennedy, *The International Human Rights Movement: Part of the Problem?,* 15 HARV. HUM. RTS. J. 101, 109–10 (2002).

[67] Note that the right to reproductive health care is part of a broader right to health and complemented by a state duty to "take reasonable legislative and other measures, within its available resources, to achieve the progressive realization" of that right. S. AFR. CONST. 1996, § 27(2).

[68] Halley et al., *supra* note 64, at 330–32. *See also* Rubio-Marín & Morgan, *supra* note 40, at 117.

[69] Kennedy, *supra* note 74, at 108.

by reproductive rights movements elsewhere, particularly in the United States. As a consequence, the structure and scope of the CTOPA reflect the trajectory of U.S. reproductive rights activism, and may not adequately address obstacles to implementation specific to South Africa.

III. DRAFTING LEGISLATION: AN AMERICAN ANTI-MODEL

This section illustrates how reproductive rights reform projects, and the international principles that underpin them, transplant the American experience of abortion law and politics in interesting and indirect ways.[70]

A. *What the CTOPA's Drafters Wanted*

The United States' involvement in the diffusion of rights generally is the subject of varied attention.[71] Much has been written about how an American rights-based system of adjudication helped fortify an international human rights culture.[72] Human rights advocacy in promoting autonomy, equality, choice, and secularism draws support from U.S. legal traditions of equality and state noninterference.[73] Scholarship, notably in the field of law and development, has also detailed the American influence on the transplantation of law reform projects and the migration of law in a global economy.[74]

American activists and organizations promoting reproductive rights played an important role in the development of an international movement and specifically in the drafting of ICPD and FWCW documents.[75] A representative of the Department of State stated the U.S. position on the ICPD Programme for Action: "Advancing the roles and rights of women is a critical common thread that must be woven through recommendations and implementation of our goals from [the ICPD and FWCW] . . . [Sustainable development] cannot be realized when women are denied

---

[70] *Cf.* Gerald L. Neuman, Casey *in the Mirror: Abortion, Abuse, and the Right to Protection in the United States and Germany*, 43 Am. J. Comp. L. 273 (1995).

[71] Nadine Taub, *International Conference on Population and Development*, *in* Issue Papers on World Conferences No. 1 12 (American Society of International Law ed., 1994).

[72] Heinz Klug, *Model and Anti-Model: The United States Constitution and the "Rise of World Constitutionalism*," 2000 Wisc. L. Rev. 597, 600. *See* Duncan Kennedy, *The Three Globalizations of Legal Thought*, *in* The New Law and Development: A Critical Appraisal (David Trubek & Alvaro Santos eds., 2006) (describing the role of U.S. constitutionalism and rights balancing as the basis of modern globalization and diffusion of law).

[73] *See, e.g.*, Sally Engle Merry, *New Realism and the Ethnography of Transnational Law*, 31 L. & Soc. Inquiry 975 (2006).

[74] David Kennedy, *The Mystery of Global Governance*, 34 Ohio N. U. L. Rev. 827, 829 (2008); Laura Nader, *The Americanization of International Law*, *in* Mobile People, Mobile Law: Expanding Legal Relations in a Contracting World 207–208 (Franz von Benda-Beckmann et al. eds., 2005).

[75] Julia L. Ernst et al., *The Global Pattern of U.S. Initiatives Curtailing Women's Reproductive Rights: A Perspective on the Increasingly Anti-Choice Mosaic*, 6 U. Pa. J. Const. L. 752, 763–64, 785 (2004).

the choices that spring from access to a full range of primary and reproductive rights."[76]

The constitutional protection of privacy in *Roe v. Wade*[77] also provided a catalyst for reframing reproductive decisions in terms of autonomy and equality rights.[78] *Roe* "both informed and was informed by a larger global movement to recognize reproductive health and self-determination as integral components of women's equality."[79] The decision does not make extensive reference to autonomy or equality rights, and instead grounds the right to abortion in privacy.[80] However, the influence of *Roe* extends well beyond its text: It helped set the stage for a rights approach by supporting and encouraging legislative and judicial decisions to liberalize abortion laws across the world.[81] The CTOPA adopts a trimester approach inspired by *Roe*, and, as noted by a South African activist, "ground[s] it in the right to freedom, dignity, and autonomy of the woman."[82] The CTOPA also seeks compromise by recognizing "changing moral attitudes of women towards developing fetal life."[83] Reflecting this compromise, ARAG drafted a proposal that allowed abortion for any reason up to fourteen weeks of pregnancy and from week fourteen to twenty-four under certain conditions, which included the health of the woman and fetus, age, socioeconomic reasons, and family size.[84]

Advocates exerted substantial influence in shaping the legislative process, as reflected by the final act, which retains the structure and most of the substance of the draft put forward by ARAG. When the ANC's ad hoc Committee on Abortion and Sterilization publically consulted on a new abortion law,[85] women's rights groups (both local and international), academics, and civil rights organizations formed the Reproductive Rights Alliance to lobby the Committee and to provide it with resources and expertise.

The Committee recommended to the Portfolio Committee of the Department of Health (responsible for drafting the legislation) that the 1975 Act should be repealed

---

[76] Taub, *supra* note 71, at 12–13 (citing Address by Timothy E. Wirth, Counselor, U.S. Department of State (Mar. 30, 1994)).

[77] 410 U.S. 113 (1973).

[78] Ernst et al., *supra* note 75, at 755, 760.

[79] *Id.* at 753.

[80] *See* Ruth Ginsburg, *Some Thoughts on Autonomy and Equality in Relation to* Roe v. Wade, 63 N.C. L. REV. 375 (1985). *See also* Reva Siegel, *Reasoning from the Body: A Historical Perspective on Abortion Regulation and Questions of Equal Protection*, 44 STAN. L. REV. 261, 348–78 (1992).

[81] Reed Boland & Laura Katzive, *Developments in Laws on Induced Abortion: 1998–2007*, 34 INT'L FAM. PLANNING PERSP. 110, 117 (2008); CENTER FOR REPRODUCTIVE RIGHTS, ROE V. WADE AND THE RIGHT TO PRIVACY 54–58 (3d ed. 2003). *See also* Naomi Cahn & Anne T. Goldstein, *The Constitution, Reproductive Rights, and Feminism:* Roe *and its Global Impact*, 6 U. PA. J. CONST. L. 695 (2004).

[82] CENTER FOR REPRODUCTIVE RIGHTS, INTERNATIONAL VOICES: THIRTY FACES OF ROE (2002), *available at* www.crlp.org/crt_roe_30_inter.html#ca_2#ca_2.

[83] Albertyn, *supra* note, 16 at 17.

[84] *Id.* at 21–22.

[85] *Id.* (citing AD HOC SELECT COMMITTEE ON ABORTION AND STERILISATION, REPORT OF THE AD HOC SELECT COMMITTEE ON ABORTION AND STERILISATION ¶ 3 (1995)).

and that the bill should include ARAG's proposal.[86] Advocates got most but not all of what they wanted. The final version of the CTOPA allows abortion for any reason until twelve, rather than fourteen, weeks of pregnancy.[87] It retained the ARAG draft's broad grounds for abortion in the second trimester (including if continued pregnancy would "significantly affect the social or economic circumstances of the woman").[88] Terminations after twenty weeks are also permitted with the advice of two medical practitioners and if continued pregnancy would 1) endanger the woman's life, 2) result in "a severe malformation of the fetus," or 3) pose a risk of injury to the fetus.[89]

B. *What the CTOPA's Drafters Sought to Avoid*

The influence of human rights and of the United States is evident in the issues the drafters of the CTOPA decided to take off the table. As stated by a key member of the Reproductive Rights Alliance, "[r]eproductive rights advocates in South Africa learned from the U.S. abortion rights movement's mistakes as well as from its successes."[90] Kim Lane Scheppele describes this comparative method of law reform as "knowing who you are by what you are not" – the process of rejecting the practices of another country by drafting legislative language intended to preclude those undesirable outcomes.[91] In the same vein, Heinz Klug described the United States as an "anti-model" for South African constitutionalism,[92] elaborating that "by and large United States jurisprudence has been increasingly used as a counterexample, as a source of distinction, or merely distinguished as inapposite."[93]

More generally, opposition to U.S. policies helped fortify a rights approach. As *Roe* inspired legislative reform that liberalized grounds for terminations in many places, *Roe* also fostered opposition to abortion at home, which translated to policies effecting abortion laws abroad.[94] For example, the now-rescinded "global gag rule" (or the Mexico City Policy) prohibited recipients of U.S. foreign aid, such as nongovernmental organizations working outside of the United States, to perform abortions unless there was a threat to the woman's life, rape, or incest; provide counseling or referral for abortion; or lobby for liberalized abortion laws.[95] International reproductive rights activists (especially those based in the United States) have relied

[86] *Id.* at 23.
[87] *Id.* at 35.
[88] CTOPA, *supra* note 1, § 2(2).
[89] *Id.* § 2(1)(c).
[90] CENTER FOR REPRODUCTIVE RIGHTS, *supra* note 82 (quoting Catherine Albertyn).
[91] Kim Lane Scheppele, *Aspirational and Aversive Constitutionalism: The Case for Studying Cross-Constitutional Influence through Negative Models*, 1 INT'L J. CONST. 296, 300, 303–305 (2003).
[92] Klug, *supra* note 72, at 599.
[93] *Id.* at 607.
[94] Ernst et al., *supra* note 75, at 761.
[95] *Id.* at 774–75, 786–87.

on women's human rights arguments to oppose the restrictive policies of the U.S. government.[96]

For women's rights advocates outside the United States, domestic opposition to abortion became a warning to avoid polarization around the issue. By the time the CTOPA was drafted, U.S. states had passed numerous laws that cut back on the right to abortion. Parental involvement laws, protections for health provider refusals, regulation of health facilities where abortions are performed, and state-mandated counseling (in some instances intended to dissuade women from abortion) are examples of laws that limit when and how to obtain an abortion.[97] Underpinning this regulation is the rejection of the premise that liberalized abortion leads to improvements in women's health or equality.[98] The 1992 decision of the U.S. Supreme Court in *Planned Parenthood v. Casey* affirmed and facilitated state laws that restrict access to abortion.[99] Although *Casey* preserved constitutional protection for abortion, the decision rejected *Roe's* trimester framework and gave states much more discretion to restrict access to abortion and to extend protections for fetal life. The Court held that states may limit abortion access so long as the state does not create an undue burden on the woman's choice to have an abortion. In practice, however, the Court's undue burden standard upholds state laws that make abortion logistically and financially difficult.[100]

The drafters of the CTOPA wanted the rights approach first set out in *Roe*, but not the resulting controversies and obstacles to abortion associated with U.S. regulation. South African advocates used their lobbying power to defeat amendments that would have restricted access to abortion in the ways that laws upheld by *Casey* did. The debate around parental involvement in minors' abortion decisions illustrates this strategy. The ARAG draft originally proposed that minors be advised but not be required to have counseling.[101] The Reproductive Rights Alliance fought against the inclusion of mandatory counseling for minors in the Committee's draft and tried to diffuse public pressure for a parental involvement requirement.[102] Central in this campaign was the U.S. experience of parental consent and notice for minors' abortions, and the research documenting the emotional, physical, and financial costs of requiring consent from potentially absent, unsympathetic, unsupportive, or

[96] James Gathii, *Exporting Culture Wars*, 13 U. C. DAVIS J. INT'L L. & POL'Y 67, 70, 79 (2006).

[97] For a comprehensive treatment of the many developments in American abortion law, *see* THE REPRODUCTIVE RIGHTS READER: LAW, MEDICINE, AND THE CONSTRUCTION OF MOTHERHOOD (Nancy Ehrenreich ed., 2008). For a summary of the types of laws that restrict abortion access, *see* CENTER FOR REPRODUCTIVE RIGHTS, OVERVIEW OF TYPES OF ABORTION RESTRICTIONS IN THE STATES (2007), *available at* http://reproductiverights.org/.

[98] Gathii, *supra* note 96 at 67. *See also* Robert Post & Reva Siegel, Roe *Rage*, 42 HARV. C. R.-C. L. L. REV. 373, 377 (2007).

[99] 505 U.S. 833 (1992).

[100] *See* Linda Wharton & Sue Frietsche, *Preserving the Core of* Roe: *Reflections on* Planned Parenthood v. Casey, 18 YALE J. L. & FEMINISM 317 (2006).

[101] Albertyn, *supra* note 16, at 18.

[102] *Id.* at 26.

abusive parents.[103] The extent to which drafters succeeded in neutralizing the debate on parental involvement is questionable and the focus of the next section.

IV. THE CTOPA IN PRACTICE

The final version of the CTOPA passed in November 1996 by a vote of 209 to 87.[104] As an alternative to legislation, the 1975 Act could have been challenged in court as unconstitutional, as other laws from the apartheid era were. Advocates pressed instead for a statutory right to abortion that they could draft so as to avoid court interpretation of what that right included, "reacting to what we thought was a problem in the U.S."[105]

The first court challenge to the constitutionality of the CTOPA, *Christian Lawyers Association v. Minister of Health* (*Christian Lawyers I*), underscores the strategy of avoiding U.S.-associated outcomes.[106] A high court rejected privacy as the basis of its decision upholding the law, and relied on common law definitions of when life begins to determine that a fetus is not a rights-bearer.[107] The judgment quotes from *Roe* in support of a general consensus that the fetus does not have a right to life because granting such a right would infringe on women's rights to equality and security of person.[108] *Christian Lawyers I*, however, describes *Roe* as if it were frozen in time, ignoring the existence of state statutes in the United States that protect the fetus post-*Roe*. Examples include laws that criminally or civilly punish harming a fetus – upheld by and large as not imposing an undue burden on a woman's abortion decision.

A similar pattern surfaces in the second case challenging the CTOPA. *Christian Lawyers Association v. Minister of Health* (*Christian Lawyers II*) – a challenge to minors' access to abortion without parental consent – quotes from *Roe* at length to show support for a "right of a woman to determine the fate of her pregnancy."[109] *Casey* is cited as "affirm[ing] the essential findings of *Roe* including the constitutional principle that women have a constitutional right to determine the fate of their

---

[103] *See generally* HELENA SILVERSTEIN, GIRLS ON THE STAND: HOW COURTS FAIL PREGNANT MINORS (2007).

[104] The ANC resisted pressure from members to allow a conscience vote and, instead, voted collectively. However, had the ANC allowed a conscience vote, the CTOPA might not have passed in its current form (or at all). Guttmacher et al., *supra* note 13, at 193.

[105] CENTER FOR REPRODUCTIVE RIGHTS, *supra* note 82 (quoting Catherine Albertyn).

[106] Klug, *supra* note 72 at 613.

[107] *Id.* at 612.

[108] *Christian Lawyers Association v. Minister of Health* 1998 (11) BCLR 1434 (S. Afr.) [hereinafter *Christian Lawyers I*]. The court held that the drafters of the Constitution did not intend to extend a right to life to the fetus, and that "the finding that the foetus is not a person and does not enjoy a constitutional right to life has been generally accepted [among other countries]." *Id.* at 1444.

[109] *Christian Lawyers Association v. Minister of Health* [2004] 4 All SA 31, 42 (S. Afr.) [hereinafter *Christian Lawyers II*].

own pregnancy."[110] The decision fails to mention that *Casey* upheld Pennsylvania's parental involvement law, which required the consent of a parent before an abortion could be performed.

Christian Lawyers II demonstrates that advocates neither avoided controversy by taking limitations on minors' access to abortion off the table, nor cemented a standard of noninterference in minors' abortion decisions. Petitioners argued that women under the age of eighteen were incapable of giving informed consent, as defined by the CTOPA, without parental involvement.[111] Judge Mojapelo held that the capacity of a minor to give informed consent should be determined by the mature minor standard developed in common law – a minor "mature enough to form an intelligent will" may seek health care without parental involvement.[112] If a minor lacks "emotional and intellectual maturity," then the CTOPA requires health professionals to refuse to provide a termination.

However, the case does not offer guidance to medical professionals on how to determine maturity. The court's reliance on the common law would suggest that common law decisions would be informative on the point. However, the mature minor standard can be as frustrating to a minor's agency as parental involvement laws by requiring a third party (the doctor) to approve a minor's abortion decision.[113] In this way, the decision creates a maturity test that potentially resembles the U.S. standard for waiver of parental involvement. Under American parental involvement laws, a minor may avoid giving notice to or obtaining consent from a parent if a court, or in three states a physician, finds that she is both mature and well informed or that an abortion would be in her best interests.[114] The wide discretion this test affords to courts is well documented, as is the bias that some judges express because of their attitudes about abortion. Courts can (and do) systematically deny most or all petitions heard or, conversely, grant almost all petitions.[115]

Arguably, doctors, like judges, could apply their discretion to the detriment of minors if they believe *most* adolescents are immature. Judge Mojapelo's decision

---

[110] *Id.* at 43.

[111] B. Bekink & M. Bekink, *Aspects of Rape, Statutory Rape, and the Choice on the Termination of Pregnancy Act 92 of 1996: Do We Protect Our Minor Women?*, 69 Tydskrif vir Hedendaagse Romeins-Hollandse Reg 14, 22 (2006).

[112] *See Gillick v. West Norfolk and Wisbech Area Health Authority*, [1985] 3 All E.R. 402 (H.L.).

[113] Joanna Erdman, *Moral Authority in English and American Abortion Law, in* Constituting Equality: Gender Equality in Comparative Constitutional Rights 107, 110 (Susan Williams ed., 2009).

[114] *Casey*, in upholding Pennsylvania's parental consent statute, reiterated the conclusion of the U.S. Supreme Court's decision in *Belotti v. Baird*. In *Belotti*, the Court held that a parent may not have an absolute veto of their child's abortion decision. If a minor does not want to obtain parental consent (or cannot obtain parental consent), states must provide an alternative process that allows the minor to show she is mature and well informed or it is in her best interests to have an abortion. *Belotti v. Baird*, 443 U.S. 622, 644 (1979).

[115] *See* Carol Sanger, *Regulating Teenage Abortion in the United States: Politics and Policy*, 18 Int'l J. L., Pol'y & Fam. 305, 309 (2004) ("Judges tend to fall into two categories: those who grant no petitions, and those who rubberstamp most.").

attempts to dismiss this possibility by stating that health professionals are not allowed to set age thresholds for minors seeking abortions.[116] However, providers, as part of their discretion to determine maturity, could still set impossibly high thresholds for young women to evidence "an intelligent will." This concern is heightened in light of South African health professionals' demonstrated reluctance to terminate the pregnancies of women of any age.[117] For example, a study conducted in the Transkei region showed that only 12.5 percent of capable practitioners were willing to perform abortions.[118]

Judge Mojapelo's opinion highlighted minors' right to reproductive decision making in Section 12 of the Constitution, but interestingly, the decision contains no discussion of how the constitutional rights of children in Section 28, which applies to persons under eighteen, might inform a mature minor standard. The best interest principle in Section 28(2), which states, "a child's best interests are of paramount importance in every matter concerning the child," has been held by the Constitutional Court of South Africa to be a stand-alone and enforceable provision.[119] The Constitution grants the minor a right to parental care in Section 28(1)(b), suggesting that the right to parental care derives from the Constitution's protection of the minor's well-being rather than a parent's right to direct the upbringing of a child. This interpretation would be consistent with the decision of the Constitution's drafters to omit any reference to parental rights or to the right to found a family.[120] The best interest standard understood in this way may be in tension with the mature minor doctrine, and suggests that the benchmarks for how doctors should treat minors seeking abortions are far from certain.

Subsequent legislative interventions related to minors' consent have not clarified the standard. When *Christian Lawyers II* was decided, the Child Care Act governed parental consent for minors' medical treatment and surgical procedures.[121] Under the act, any surgical procedure for a child under eighteen needed a guardian's approval.[122] This contradicted the CTOPA, which requires no such consent for

---

[116] *Christian Lawyers II*, [2004] 4 All SA at 39–40 (S. Afr.).

[117] Sanjani Jane Varkey, *Abortion Services in South Africa: Available Yet Not Accessible to All*, 26 Int'l Fam. Planning Persp. 87, 88 (2000). *See also* Diana McIntyre & Barbara Klugman, *The Human Face of Decentralisation and Integration of Health Services: Experience from South Africa*, 11 Reprod. Health Matters 108–19 (2003).

[118] G. A. Buga, *Attitudes of Medical Students to Induced Abortion*, 79 East African Med. J, 259–62 (2002).

[119] *Minister of Welfare and Population Development v. Fitzpatrick and Others* 2000 (3) SA 422 (CC), 2000 (3) BCLR 713 (CC) (S. Afr.) (stating that section 28(2) "creates a right that is independent of those specified in section 28(1)"); *Sonderup v. Tondelli* 2001 (1) SA 1171 (CC) (S. Afr.) (section 28(2) as "an expansive guarantee that a child's best interests will be paramount in every matter concerning the child").

[120] D. Marianne Blair & Merle Weiner, Family Law in the World Community: Cases, Materials, and Problems in Comparative and International Family Law 1138 (2003).

[121] Child Care Act, No. 74 of 1983. F. F. W. Van Oosten, *The Choice on Termination of Pregnancy Act: Some Comments*, 116 S. Afr. L. J. 60, 71 (1999).

[122] Bekink & Bekink, *supra* note 111, at 21.

surgical abortion. The Children's Act of 2005, which replaced the Child Care Act, changed the requirement of guardian approval, but does not necessarily abrogate the court's mature minor standard.[123] Subject to the CTOPA, the Children's Act permits a child to consent to a surgical operation if she is over the age of twelve, and "is of sufficient maturity and has the mental capacity to understand the benefits, risks, social, and other implications of the surgical operation."[124] The act does not define who would make the maturity determination and requires parental "assistance" unless the parent refuses to assist the minor "by reason only of religious or other beliefs."[125]

Drafters of the CTOPA may have assumed that eliminating regulation of minors' abortion choices would guarantee better access to abortion. However, in light of *Christian Lawyers II* and the Children's Act, the lack of clarity surrounding a maturity standard is one of the major impediments to young women's ability to exercise their rights under the CTOPA.[126] The CTOPA may have created rights for women, but it did little to change the governance of institutions and communities that control access to health resources. Ten years after the CTOPA's enactment, less than half of health facilities authorized to perform abortions actually did so,[127] and abortion care is absent from the general medical curriculum for primary care providers.[128] Reliance on the creation of a positive right may inadvertently eclipse policy solutions that, although difficult to negotiate, could help deliver better reproductive health care to women.

CONCLUSION

The rights-based template most readily available to those seeking to repeal restrictive abortion laws may marginalize strategies that could accomplish advocates' larger aim of improving women's lives. The CTOPA establishes a legal right to abortion, but it may not help mediate difficult debates about the attitudes of health care providers, the role of family oversight in abortion decisions, or the present limitations of the primary health care system.

There may be room for compromises or creative solutions that would not be possible or wise in the United States. Strategies could have, for example, tapped

---

[123] The Children's Act, No. 38 of 2005.

[124] *Id.* § 129(1)–(3).

[125] *Id.* § 129(10).

[126] This chapter does not describe the substantial research on the lack of facilities (and the amendment to the CTOPA), lack of training and education, the role of provider refusals, and continuing stigma that continues to plague the implementation of the CTOPA. For further analysis of the relationship between the drafting of the CTOPA and the obstacles to its implementation, see the longer version of this chapter in volume 63 of the Alabama Law Review, "The Limits of Reproductive Rights in Improving Women's Health."

[127] Cooper et al., *supra* note 7, at 75.

[128] *See also* Varkey, *supra* note 117, at 87.

into the customary governance of abortion. The circumvention of law evident in the number of illegal abortions before and after the CTOPA suggests that many women make their reproductive decisions outside of the law's reach. Reproductive health legislation should build on and seek to incorporate the community-based resources that now shape women's access to abortion. Concentrating less on what outcomes legislation should avoid, and more on the particularized problems of infrastructure that make reform complicated, might help advocates discover new ways to use state power to improve women's reproductive health.

PART V

Women's Rights, Multiculturalism, and Diversity

17

Constitutional Rights of Women under Customary Law in Southern Africa

Dominant Interventions and "Old Pathways"

Chuma Himonga

In the same way that modern law is not always progressive for women, tradition is not always backward for women. We decided that we had to rethink custom.[1]

Tensions between customary law and human rights – whether contained in a country's constitution or in international human rights instruments – are an established fact. This tension is accentuated in countries whose constitutions protect inherently conflicting rights, such as the rights to gender equality, dignity, and security of the person, on the one hand, and the right to participate in one's culture of choice and customary law rights, on the other hand. Several constitutions on the Continent now carry these kinds of provisions.[2]

The main approaches to resolving these conflicts in Southern Africa are legislative and judicial interventions to which we refer as dominant interventions. However, it seems that preoccupation with these interventions has for a long time diverted the attention of women's rights scholars and activists both from 1) their limitations and 2) the needs to search for, and recognize, alternative approaches identified by studies on the rights of women in the region. Specific reference is made in this chapter to the approach identified with Women and Law in Southern Africa Research Project (WLSA) of engaging with customary law to protect the rights of women. We have labeled this approach the "old pathways." This label is intended to underscore the point that, although the WLSA approach goes as far back as 1988, it has not featured prominently in current strategies and interventions for protecting women's rights in the region in the same way that the dominant interventions have.

In 1988, WLSA launched a series of studies on women and law in Southern Africa involving the participation of seven countries – Botswana, Lesotho, Malawi,

---

[1] Alice Armstrong, *Rethinking Culture and Tradition in Southern Africa: Research from WLSA*, in GENDER AND SOCIAL JUSTICE 87 (Ann Stewart ed., London Blackstone Press 2000).

[2] Malawi, Uganda, and Namibia, *see* S. AFR. CONST. 1996 §§ 30, 26, 37 & 19, respectively.

Mozambique, Swaziland, Zambia, and Zimbabwe. Among others, these studies yielded the idea of using custom, tradition, and culture (customary law) to improve the legal situation of women.

In this chapter we suggest that there is a need to revisit this idea so that it can be used to provide an alternative to the dominant methods of protecting women's rights in the region. In doing this we question the apparent preoccupation with the dominant interventions to the exclusion of other equally legitimate strategies. We locate the "old pathways" in discourses that view universal human rights in cultural contexts, but without compromising the universality of rights. We refer to these discourses as the dialogic human rights analytical framework.

The arguments advanced in this chapter begin with an appraisal of the current dominant methods of implementing the rights of women in Southern Africa. The second part highlights the limitations of these interventions that justify the need to consider alternative approaches. The third part discusses the notion of engagement with customary law within the dialogic human rights analytical framework. The fourth part examines the "old pathways" as a model of engagement with customary law. The conclusion to the chapter reflects on concerns that have a bearing on the "old pathways."

I. DOMINANT INTERVENTIONS OF IMPLEMENTING WOMEN'S RIGHTS

In many parts of Southern Africa, governments, nongovernmental organizations (NGOs), units of academic institutions, and individuals are making tremendous efforts in their respective countries to advance the rights of women in both the private and public spheres. The most commonly mobilized interventions in these pursuits are legislation and litigation.

An interesting dimension in South Africa is how these two interventions reinforce each other in rooting out discriminatory customary laws. On the one hand, the courts engage in some form of statutory law – making law by amending discriminatory pieces of legislation,[3] as well as temporarily replacing major components of discriminatory laws with existing legislation.[4] On the other hand, the legislature reaffirms the decisions of the courts concerned, especially those of the Constitutional Court, on a given subject by enacting legislation that endorses them.[5] Our concern here is not to evaluate the appropriateness of these approaches. The point we are making is simply that there are concerted, reinforced state undertakings in some countries to protect women's human rights through legislative and litigation strategies.

---

[3] *Gumede v. President of the Republic of South Africa* 2009 (3) BCLR 243 (CC) (S. Afr.).
[4] *Bhe v. Magistrate Khayelitsha* 2005 (1) SA 580 (CC) (S. Afr.).
[5] See Reform of Customary Law of Succession and Regulation of Related Matters Act 11 of 2009 (in force on 20 September 2010).

Similarly, civil society attaches tremendous value to these strategies in its view of how to deal with customary law in relation to women's rights. This is evident from efforts made to ensure that the "right" provisions to protect women's rights are included in regulatory frameworks when various subjects of customary law are reformed.[6] Another example is civil society's increasing interest in conducting research to facilitate litigation on women's rights.[7]

These efforts have yielded significant results in the field of customary law. The continental legal scene is not devoid of legislation: proposed legislative reforms and jurisprudence seeking to promote and protect the rights of women in areas that are predominantly regulated by customary law. The areas of marriage, inheritance, traditional leadership, and access to land have been the major targets. This development is particularly visible in countries that have ratified women's human rights treaties, or have constitutional entrenchments of human rights that concern women.

In the next section we provide recent examples of these interventions, especially from South Africa.

A. *Legislative Intervention*

Recent examples of this form of intervention in South Africa are the Recognition of Customary Marriages Act (RCMA),[8] the Reform of Customary Law of Succession and Regulation of Related Matters Act (RCLSA),[9] and the proposed Traditional Courts Bill.[10]

As declared in its Preamble, the RCMA was designed to implement, among other things, gender equality in various aspects of marriage. This is reflected in a number of its provisions, such as Section 6, which changed the status of married women. Until this section, official customary law[11] ascribed minority status to married women, thereby subjecting them to the guardianship of their husbands. Now a wife has legal status and legal capacity equal to that of her husband.[12]

Furthermore, although the Act accords explicit recognition to the controversial notion of polygyny, it mitigates the unequal position in which it places men and women in this respect. It does this by prescribing a special procedure requiring men

---

[6] *See* Chuma Himonga & Rashida Manjoo, *The Challenges of Formalisation, Regulation, and Reform of Traditional Courts in South Africa*, 3(2) Malawi L. J. 157–181 (2009).

[7] The ongoing research by Law Race and Gender Unit at the University of Cape Town on women's access to land is a current example.

[8] Act 120 of 1998.

[9] Act 11 of 2009.

[10] 2008, Bill 15–2008.

[11] The term "official customary law" is used to designate the body of customary law that is applied by the courts and state institutions, but may be different from the customary law that regulates the people in their daily intercourse. The latter is known as living customary law.

[12] *See* Act 120 of 1998 § 6.

wishing to enter into polygamy to indirectly seek the consent of all the co-wives in respect of the regulation of the future proprietary consequences of the marriage.[13]

Presumably, a wife in a monogamous marriage who does not wish to be part of the polygamous marriage will oppose the approval of the property contract, and thereby frustrate the husband's intended subsequent marriage(s). Furthermore, a recent decision of the North Gauteng High Court, Pretoria, has enhanced the monogamous marriage by holding that a subsequent (polygamous) marriage that had been entered into without the contract approved by the court to regulate the matrimonial property of the spouses in terms of the RCMA (i.e., Section 7(6)) was void and null *ab initio*.[14]

In *Gumede v. President of the Republic of South Africa*,[15] the Constitutional Court affirmed the implementation of the rights of women as the primary purpose of the RCMA. It stated that "[T]he Recognition Act [i.e., RCMA] must be given a meaning that extends optimal protection to a category of vulnerable people who, in this case, are women married under customary law, in order to give effect to the equality and dignity guarantees of the Constitution. *That, after all, is the primary purpose of the Recognition Act.*"[16]

Similarly, the RCLSA's Preamble states gender equality as one of the reasons for the enactment of the Act as follows:

> Section 9 of the Constitution provides that everyone has the right to equal protection and benefit of the law; . . . the Constitutional Court has declared that the principle of male primogeniture, as applied in the customary law of succession, cannot be reconciled with the current notions of equality and human dignity as contained in the Bill of Rights.

The RCLSA generally follows the decision taken by the Constitutional Court in *Bhe v. Magistrate Khayelitsha*[17] of "reforming" the customary law of succession via the Intestate Succession Act (ISA). The court extended the application of the ISA to all estates previously governed by customary law. The premise was that because this Act already achieved the principle of gender equality in respect of noncustomary law estates, it could be applied to achieve the same goal in respect of customary law estates. However, it should be observed that the court modified the application of the ISA to customary law estates to accommodate polygamous marriages. This raises the controversial question of whether, in making special provision for this customary practice, the court considered it to be compatible with the Constitution. We will return to this question.

The Traditional Courts Bill has been included in this section of the chapter for the sole purpose of illustrating the importance attached to legislative intervention as

---

[13] *Id.* § 7(6)(8).
[14] *Mayelane v. Ngwenyama and Another* 2010 (4) SA 286 (S. Afr.).
[15] *Gumede v. President of the Republic of South Africa* 2009 (3) BCLR 243 (CC) (S. Afr.).
[16] *Id.* ¶ 43.
[17] *Bhe v. Magistrate Khayelitsha* 2005 (1) SA 580 (CC) (S. Afr.) (emphasis added).

a strategy for implementing the rights of women. The case in point is the ongoing opposition from civil society to the enactment of the Bill due to its failure, among other things, to adequately address issues of women's rights.[18] Specifically, the Bill has been contested because it does not sufficiently protect women's rights in terms of their appointment to preside in the proposed courts and their participation in court proceedings in other respects.

The Bill seeks to officially recognize the authority and jurisdictional limits of traditional courts under the new constitutional dispensation. Equally important, the Bill seeks to reform customary law to advance respect for democratic principles, and the rights of women and other vulnerable groups guaranteed by the Constitution.

However, owing to its shortcomings noted earlier, it is unlikely that the Bill will pass into law. If it passes without meeting the demands of civil society, especially on women's rights, its constitutionality will most likely be challenged in court. This brings us to the role of courts in protecting women's constitutional rights.

B. *Judicial Interventions*

It is remarkable that the Constitutional Court in South Africa has maintained the stance it adopted in 2005 in *Bhe* against discriminatory customary law. In that case, the court upheld Ms. Bhe's challenge of the discriminatory rule of male primogeniture, which excluded her female children from inheriting their father's estate in preference for a male heir. This rule had been codified by Section 23 of the Black Administration Act.[19]

The court ruled that Section 23 and its regulations were unconstitutional and invalid because they discriminated unfairly, *inter alia*, on the grounds of gender contrary to Section 9(3) of the Constitution. Furthermore, it held that the principle of male primogeniture violated women's right to dignity, contrary to Section 10 of the Constitution. It accordingly struck down the statutory provisions concerned. It then declared the deceased's female children to be the sole heirs to their father's estate.

This judgment is said to have been effectively enforced, and has improved the lives of Ms. Bhe and her daughters.[20] Thus, the judgment is not only one on paper, as many judgments tend to be, but one that has actually changed the situation of the women concerned for the better. However, the extent to which this and other precedents discussed in this section will positively impact other women's lives is not guaranteed: it will largely depend on how individual women are affected by the operation of the factors discussed in Part II of this chapter.

Within about three years of *Bhe*, the Constitutional Court struck at two other core elements of customary law in the areas of marriage and succession to status in

---

[18] Himonga & Manjoo *supra* note 6.
[19] Black Administration Act 38 of 1927.
[20] *Women's Legal Trust*, 1 WOMEN'S LEGAL CENTRE NEWS 6 (2008).

Gumede v. President of the Republic of South Africa [21] and *Shilubana v. Namitwa*,[22] respectively.

Gumede is discussed at length because it shows both the vulnerability of many women during and upon termination of a customary marriage, and it was the first case involving the RCMA to reach the Constitutional Court. Mrs. Gumede was in the process of getting divorced from her husband as per the official customary law – as codified by the KwaZulu Act on the Code of Zulu Law[23] and the Natal Code of Zulu Law[24] (the Codes) – under which she was married. She applied to the High Court to determine the constitutional issues concerning the parties' matrimonial property rights.

Mrs. Gumede was married before the RCMA came into force. Consequently, the proprietary consequences of her marriage were governed by the Codes.[25] The relevant customary rules were set out in Sections 20 and 22 of these Codes. Section 20 stated,

> The family head [a male] is the owner of the family property in his family home. He has charge, custody, and control of the property attaching to the houses of his several wives and may in his discretion use the same for his personal wants and necessities, or for general family purposes or for the entertainment of visitors. He may use, exchange, loan, or otherwise alienate or deal with such property for the benefit of or in the interests of the house to which it attaches.

Section 22 provided that "The inmates of a family home [including the wife] irrespective of sex or age shall in respect of all family matters be under the control of and owe obedience to the family head."

In contrast, the proprietary consequences of customary marriages entered into after the Act came into force were governed by relatively egalitarian matrimonial property regimes imported from the law governing civil marriage.[26] These property regimes usually take the forms of a marriage out of community and of profit and loss (with or without the accrual system), and a marriage in community of property and of profit and loss[27] (unless excluded by an antenuptial contract).

Mrs. Gumede, with the assistance of the Women's Legal Centre Trust,[28] challenged the constitutionality of the codified customary law rules previously mentioned

---

[21] *Gumede* 2009 (3) BCLR 243.

[22] *Shilubana v Namitwa* 2009 (2) SA 66 (CC) (S. Afr.).

[23] Act 16 of 1985.

[24] Proc R151 of 1987.

[25] This was in consequence of Section 7(1) of the RCMA. It provided that the proprietary consequences of a customary marriage entered into before the commencement of the act continued to be governed by customary law.

[26] This was in consequence of Section 7(2) of the RCMA, which stated, *inter alia*, that a monogamous customary marriage entered into after the commencement of the act was a marriage in community of property.

[27] This means each spouse retains both the estate and property he or she owned before the marriage and that which he or she acquires during the marriage.

[28] This organization was also admitted as *amicus curiae*.

and Section 7(1)(2) of the RCMA.[29] She alleged that they were unfairly discriminatory on the grounds of race and gender.

All of the impugned provisions were held to be inconsistent with the Constitution
and invalid because each of them unfairly discriminated against the applicant on the
ground of gender. The Constitutional Court invalidated[30] Sections 20 and 22 of the
Codes, as well as section 7(1) of the RCMA as it related to monogamous customary
marriages. It also severed a part of Section 7(2) of the RCMA, which restricted
the application of the marriage in community of property regime to monogamous
marriages entered into after the commencement of the RCMA. With regard to the
codified customary law, the court reasoned that

> There can be no doubt that the marital property system contemplated by
> the . . . Code strikes at the very heart of the protection of equality and dignity our
> Constitution affords to all and to women in particular. That marital property system
> renders women extremely vulnerable by not only denuding them of their dignity
> but also rendering them poor and dependent. This is unfair. The Constitution itself
> places a particular premium on gender equality by providing that if discrimination
> is based on gender as one of the listed grounds, it is presumed to be unfair.[31]

It is also interesting that the fact that existing rights and duties of spouses married
before the RCMA came into force would be affected retrospectively did not deter
the court from making a retrospective order. In its reasoning it stated, "[A] prospective
order would not grant any . . . relief to wives in marriages concluded before the start of
the Recognition Act. . . . The provisions of ss [section] 7(1) and (2) of the Recognition
Act are improperly underinclusive. The discrimination they spawn is so egregious
that it should not be permitted to remain on our statute books by limiting the
retrospective operation of the order we are to make. . . . The recognition of the equal
worth and capacity of all partners in customary marriages is well overdue."[32]

In this respect, the court went further in protecting women's rights than it did in
Bhe. There, its decision was applied retrospectively but only up to April 1, 1994, the
date when the interim Constitution on which Ms. Bhe relied came into force.

The overall result of this decision is that the proprietary consequences of women
married monogamously before the RCMA came into force are no longer governed by
customary law, but by the more favorable provisions of the RCMA. Furthermore, the
decision shows how legislation (i.e., RCMA) aimed at implementing women's constitutional rights is itself closely censured to ensure that it meets constitutional muster.

The last case to be analyzed, *Shilubana*, is the first gender equality dispute concerning succession to status to reach the Constitutional Court to date. The court
rejected the opposition to Ms. Shilubana's succession to the status of Hosi (a form

---

[29] See *supra* notes 25 & 26.
[30] S. AFR. CONST. 1996 § 167(5) requires the Constitution Court to confirm any invalidation of legislation
    by a court.
[31] *Gumede v. President of the Republic of South Africa* 2009 (3) BCLR 243 (CC) ¶ 36 (S. Afr.).
[32] *Id.* ¶ 51.

of traditional authority) from which she had been excluded after her father's death on account of her being a woman. Instead, it held that the Valoyi, Ms. Shilubana's ethnic group, had – through the decision of its royal family to install a female as a traditional leader – developed its customary law in accordance with the Constitution.[33]

The human rights dimension of the Valoyi Royal Family's resolution that influenced the court's decision is worthy of note. It stated, "[T]hough in the past it was not permissible by the Valoyis that a female child be heir, in terms of democracy and the new Republic of South Africa Constitution, it is now permissible that a female child be heir since she is also equal to a male child."[34] Thus, the court upheld the development of the customary law of the Valoyi, by the Valoyi, because such development aligned the customary law to the constitutional principle of equality.

The value of this case in respect of the implementation of women's rights should be understood in relation to the court's role in the development of customary law. Unlike *Bhe* and *Gumede* that invalidated customary law to protect the rights alleged to have been violated, *Shilubana* passively recognized as constitutional a rule that had been instituted by a traditional institution itself.

In our view, recognizing that a community can align its customary law with constitutional rights encourages the protection of women's rights from a bottom-up rather than a top-down approach. The former is more likely to have the support of the community, with no cost to women. Otherwise, the community's opposition makes it harder, if not impossible, to implement women's rights by any mechanism.

The kind of development of customary law achieved in *Shilubana* relied on the specific provision of the South African Constitution, which requires the courts to develop customary law in accordance with the spirit, purport, and objectives of the Bill of Rights.[35] However, there is no reason why courts in countries where there is no explicit provision to this effect should not equally be able to develop customary law in accordance with the spirit of their respective constitutions. Moreover, such development is consistent with the nature of customary law as an evolving system of law.

Another significant dimension of both *Gumede* and *Shilubana* should be mentioned before we conclude this section of the chapter, namely the responsibility of the State to pay the cost for litigating women's rights. In this respect, a large portion of Ms. Shilubana's litigation costs were borne by the State through representation by a State Attorney.[36] In *Gumede*, the court ordered the State to pay the applicant's costs in the High Court and Constitutional Court. In light of the problem of women's access to courts discussed in the next section, these are positive gestures by the State

---

[33] *Shilubana v. Namitwa* 2009 (2) SA 66 (CC) ¶¶ 49, 55, 73 & 75 (S. Afr.).
[34] *Id.* ¶ 4.
[35] S. Afr. Const. 1996 § 39(2).
[36] *Shilubana*, 2009 (2) SA 66 ¶ 92.

and the court. More of these initiatives would greatly promote the protection of women's rights through the dominant strategy.

In this section, we have evaluated the dominant interventions used to implement women's rights. We have shown how these interventions have aggressively obliterated major elements of customary law in some countries to the benefit of women. However, it is trite that these interventions play a very minimal role, if any at all, in the protection of the women's rights in some countries. For example, in Malawi, where 82 percent of the population lives in rural areas,[37] there are apparently no superior court decisions on the implementation of women's rights.[38] In the next section we highlight some of the reasons for this state of affairs in the region.

II. LIMITATIONS OF THE DOMINANT INTERVENTIONS

In this section we maintain that the dominant interventions do not benefit the majority of African women who are governed by customary law. In fact, we could argue that, paradoxically, they create, in two ways, a negative or hostile political environment in which to implement women's rights. Firstly, the interventions can be used to advance arguments that portray African women as their own stumbling blocks to the protection of their rights. That is, these women have their human rights secured by law (i.e., legal provisions and court judgments) and yet they do not use this law to their benefit. In other words, this argument places the blame on the women themselves.[39] Secondly, the high-profile nature of these interventions may create an illusion in the minds of relevant government officials and members of civil society that they have achieved the goal of protecting women's rights. However, in reality, women's lives have remained much the same as before the interventions stepped in.[40]

The WLSA studies confirmed the reality of women's situations in relation to legal reforms. They discovered that even though reforms of customary succession law had been accomplished by legislation in some countries, in reality nothing had changed for women.[41] Similarly, it has been observed that the "model of state generated rights has been tried and found wanting for too long."[42] This has been attributed to the fact that these rights "are predicated upon decontexualization and the severance of

---

[37] Thoko Kaime, The African Charter on the Rights and Welfare of the Child: a Sociolegal Perspective 5 (Pretoria University Press, 2009).

[38] This is evident from the absence of any mention of such cases in the Malawi Commission's Report on the review of the laws of marriage and divorce. We also gathered this impression on our field research visit to Malawi in October 2009.

[39] Mary Maboreke, *Understanding Law in Zimbabwe, in* Gender and Social Justice 101, 116 (Ann Stewart ed., London Blackstone Press, 2000).

[40] Chuma Himonga, *African Customary Law in South Africa – Many Faces of Bhe v. Magistrate Khayelitsha*, 2005 Recht in Africa 163, 170–172.

[41] Armstrong, *supra* note 1.

[42] Maboreke, *supra* note 39, at 112 (citing Stewart).

women from their contexts when in fact the aim should be "to find ways to strengthen women's position within the existing contexts."[43]

The following have been identified elsewhere[44] as possible reasons why the dominant interventions do not benefit many women in African contexts: 1) the reluctance of States to enforce court judgments in favor of women; 2) the fact that judicial interventions focus on official customary law, as opposed to living customary law; 3) the inaccessibility, complexity, and alien nature of the laws they generate; and 4) the contestation about the use of Eurocentric solutions.

The issue of access to courts needs further discussion with respect to the implications of the adversarial system of adjudication. This mode of adjudication requires courts to determine and rule on only those matters that are before them. The value of precedent as a source of law is also tied to this aspect of adjudication.

As apparent from *Gumede*, some of the official customary law that the courts deal with to protect women's rights has been codified. Invalidating unconstitutional legislation in many countries requires litigation in superior courts. In others, the confirmation of the highest court, such as the Constitutional Court, is also required.[45] What does this mean for women seeking to vindicate their rights against the offensive customary law through litigation? The answer is obvious: They must repeatedly go to the courts concerned for each and every aspect of customary law that allegedly violates their rights. This in turn multiplies the cost of litigation. *Bhe* may be used to illustrate this point in relation to the issue of polygyny.

Although this issue is widely known to be controversial and potentially raises constitutional questions, the Constitutional Court did not question its constitutionality in that case, presumably because it was not before it. In other words, the court glossed over this practice in a manner that gave it its implicit recognition until such a time that another woman challenges its constitutionality. In this respect, the court accommodated polygyny in its remedy by amending the Intestate Succession Act so as to make it applicable to polygamous marriages as well. Thus, the court protected the rights of women in polygamous marriages in respect of their inheritance rights, but it did not at the same time question the practice of polygyny itself.

The effect of the court's silence on this practice is that if women have any quarrel about it in relation to their rights, as some of them probably do, they must bring another action in court. To the degree that this practice is codified (i.e., by the RCMA), a woman seeking to invalidate it would necessarily need to approach the superior courts, including the Constitutional Court! The obvious question is how many women in Africa, let alone those who are subject to customary law, can afford these repeated journeys to the superior courts?

---

[43] *Id.*

[44] Chuma Himonga, *Law and Gender in Southern Africa, in* THE UNCERTAIN PROMISE OF SOUTHERN AFRICA 289–90 (Y. Bradshaw & S. Ndegwa eds., Indiana Press, 2000).

[45] *See* S. AFR. CONST. 1996 § 167(5).

Because of the inaccessibility of these forums to many a woman governed by customary law, litigation is the preserve of a few – like Ms. Bhe, Mrs. Gumede, and Ms. Shilubana, who were lucky enough to be assisted by NGOs or the State to surmount the legal representation costs. For this reason, it may be argued that 1) the adversarial system of adjudication is inappropriate in African contexts because it creates too many hurdles for women to jump over to vindicate their rights, and 2) the courts could assist to reduce the repeated use of this costly intervention. One way of doing the latter would be to use *obiter dicta* to address the constitutionality of aspects of customary law that are related to matters before them. In *Bhe*, the court could perhaps have considered using its wide powers[46] to raise potential constitutional matters that had not been raised by the parties in the matter before it. In this respect, the court is to be commended for the way it dealt with the controversial interpretation of Section 8(4)(a) of the RCMA in *Gumede*.

Essentially, this section, read with the provisions of the Divorce Act,[47] deals with the just and equitable distribution of matrimonial property on divorce. It gives the court power to order one spouse to transfer his or her property to the other in appropriate circumstances in a civil marriage if the parties were married out of community of property. The controversy[48] about this section is whether or not it applies to customary marriages as well.

What is of concern is the argument advanced on behalf of Mrs. Gumede – that is, urging the court not to "decide the proper meaning of the section because the equality claim can be adjudicated upon without deciding the interpretive question."[49] In other words, this was a plea to the court to take a narrow view of the matter before it, deal only with the equality claim, and leave interpretation of the provision concerned for a future time.

It was unfortunate that the NGO and Mrs. Gumede's legal representatives did not see the broader cost implications for women who would have to bring an action in the future to determine the meaning of this controversial section. The stance taken by the court on this issue is preferable precisely because it recognized the plight of women in this regard. In our view, D. C. J. Moseneke was right:

> My view is that the meaning of s. 8(4)(a) is germane to the justification enquiry and must be decided. And what is more, this is a question of importance in the adjudication of divorces relating to customary marriages. We have heard full argument on the interpretation of the provision and there is no reason why we should not decide the issue. *Another important consideration is that it is not always feasible or affordable for litigants in divorce proceedings, particularly those relating to customary*

[46] François du Bois, *Sources of Law: Overview and Constitution, in* Wille's Principles of South African Law 33, 37–38 (François du Bois ed., Juta & Co. 2007).

[47] Act 70 of 1979.

[48] *See Gumede v. President of the Republic of South Africa* 2009 (3) BCLR 243 (CC) ¶ 41 (S. Afr.).

[49] *Id.*

marriages, to approach this court for the determination of a proper interpretation of a legal provision that affects them so close.[50]

This is the correct approach for courts if the dominant interventions are to benefit more women than only those who are able to receive assistance from NGOs or the State to vindicate their rights.

This discussion of the limitations of the dominant interventions has attempted to show that only a few women in Southern Africa currently benefit from the dominant methods of implementing women's rights. There is, therefore, a need for women's rights scholars and activists to seriously consider human rights discourses that engage with customary law as one of the possible solutions to women's rights violations. In the next section, we conceptualize the idea of engagement with customary law (as contemplated by WLSA) within a dialogic human rights analytical framework.

III. CONCEPTUALIZATION OF ENGAGEMENT WITH CUSTOMARY LAW WITHIN THE HUMAN RIGHTS FRAMEWORK

The point of departure for the human rights discourse that engages with customary law is the acknowledgment that customary law can be used to advance women's rights. WLSA's concept of engagement with customary law centers on rediscovering and using custom, tradition, and culture[51] that valued women and their role in society to protect women's rights. At the same time, this idea rejects those aspects of custom and tradition that allowed men to control women and resources. Central to this notion of engagement with customary law also is the idea that women have different interests, needs, and expectations with regard to both their rights and their cultures.

Fundamentally, this engagement entails a view of customary law as part of the solution to the violation of women's rights. Whereas the top-down dominant interventions seem to view customary law as the "villain" and "the problem" that must be "fixed," engagement with this system of law capitalizes on its potential as a source of solutions.

Furthermore, engagement, in its ordinary parlance, connotes a dialogue, in this context a dialogue between normative systems – the systems of customary law and human rights – that is aimed at improving women's rights without compromising on the universality of these rights. Thus the tenor of engagement is dialogic rather than antagonistic. The human rights analytical framework espoused by An-Na'im, which I refer to as the dialogic framework, provides a home for this idea of engagement with customary law.

---

[50] *Id.* (emphasis added).
[51] The term "custom" includes customary law whereas "culture" is used to reflect evolving customs. "Tradition" connotes customs that are static and rooted in the past. *See* Armstrong, *supra* note 1, at 100.

It is beyond the scope of this chapter to discuss the dynamics of the dialogic framework fully. However, in essence, the framework promotes cultural dialogues in the implementation of human rights. In this respect, it defies the dichotomous discourses of relativism and universalism in relation to the implementation of human rights. The gist of this framework is mediating the paradox of human rights normative universality through processes of internal discourse and cross-cultural dialogue. The aim of this internal discourse and cross-cultural dialogue is to broaden and deepen genuine and substantive consensus over the formulation, interpretation, and implementation of international human rights norms.[52]

The paradox of normative universality itself is the result of the development of the modern notions of human rights in the political, cultural, and ideological history of the West. In this respect, An-Na'im argues that although international human rights are considered to be universal, their universality is not based on true universal normative consensus. This is so because of the limited participation (for various reasons) by non-Western societies in formulating and articulating human rights norms contained in various treaties.[53] The result is that international human rights (and their national extensions in the form of constitutional human rights) do not fully or substantially reflect the indigenous experiences, realities, and contexts of non-Western societies.[54] Seen from this perspective, "the universal normative consensus is an elusive concept."[55] This also leads to the basic problem that any conceptualization of issues relating to human rights in Western and non-Western societies "will probably be limited by the cultural conditioning of its author."[56] However, An-Na'im is far from advocating abandoning normative universality of human rights. Instead, his objective is to identify the difficulty associated with the conceptualization of rights as universal because of cross-cultural communication. More importantly, his objective is "to emphasize the need to take that difficulty into account in seeking to achieve human rights normative universality."[57]

In its focus on internal discourse and cross-cultural dialogue, the dialogic framework denies the existence of "a simplistic dichotomy between folk models and international standards, which installs one as the definitive norm by which the other is to be judged."[58] Rather, there is a dynamic interaction between the two, which An-Na'im sums up as follows: "On the one hand, international standards [of human rights norms] should be premised on fundamental global ethical, social, and political values and institutions, and thereby have an inspiring, elevating, and informative influence on popular perceptions of existing folk models. These models

---

[52] *See* Abdullahi An-Na'im, *Cultural Transformation and Normative Consensus on the Best Interests of the Child*, 8 INT'L J. L. & FAM. 62, 64–71 (1994).
[53] *Id.* at 65.
[54] *Id.*
[55] *Id.*
[56] *Id.* at 66.
[57] *Id.* at 67.
[58] *Id.* at 71.

and their rationale, on the other hand, should be seen as a source of the values and institutions which legitimatize the international standards. Both aspects of this dynamic interaction . . . should be mediated through the processes of discourse and dialogue."[59]

When located in this analytical framework, engagement with customary law should serve to protect women's human rights rather than seek to preserve custom, tradition, and culture for their own sakes. The engagement should seek to use custom, tradition, and culture to protect the rights of women within cultural contexts, but in a manner that does not deny the universality of women's human rights. This kind of engagement with customary law provides a sound alternative to the dominant interventions for protecting women's rights.

However, this is not a suggestion for two competing alternatives. Rather, the two methods should complement each other in serving the diverse interests and needs of women in African contexts. In the next section, I outline the WLSA model of engagement with customary law, which I commend for serious consideration in future endeavors to promote and implement women's rights in customary law in Southern Africa, and probably in the rest of the Continent.

IV. WLSA "OLD PATHWAYS"

WLSA was conceived to have both research and activist objectives for improving women's legal status.[60] In our view, the studies on inheritance and maintenance were most influential in WLSA's understanding of customary law in relation to women's rights, and in shaping its "pathways." This partly explains why most illustrations concerning this model are drawn from the areas of inheritance and maintenance.

The clearest articulation of the idea or model of engagement with customary law by using custom and tradition that is connected to WLSA is by Armstrong in a chapter entitled "Rethinking Culture and Tradition in Southern Africa: Research from WLSA."[61] This model may be summarized under seven headings, featuring its essential elements.[62]

A. Custom as a Political Tool

This element entails taking the good aspects of custom, tradition, and culture that incorporated values and protections for women in the past to emphasize the protection rather than the control of women under customary law. Thus, custom "can be

---

[59] *Id.*

[60] For a fuller discussion of the WLSA research project, *see* Chuma Himonga, *Women and Law in Southern Africa Research Project: Bridging the Divide between Scholarship and Action*, in GENDER AND IDENTITY IN AFRICA 197–214 (Mechthild Reh & Gudrun Ludwar-Ene eds., Lit Verlag 1995).

[61] Armstrong, *supra* note 1.

[62] *Id.* at 95–100.

used as a political tool by re-stating it in ways that emphasize the protections and rights offered to women rather than the control offered to men [by custom]."[63]

B. *Custom as a Way of Communication*

This element can be used to communicate "legal rights" that have a Western ring or that sound individualistic in the language of custom. Custom can, therefore, be used as a tool of communication in programs aimed at promoting women's rights, such as public legal education programs.

C. *The Use of Customary Law Institutions to Enforce Rights*

As noted in the discussion of the dominant interventions earlier, most women do not use state institutions to protect their rights. Instead, they use the family. The extended family and the community should therefore be used to enforce the rights women had under custom in traditional society, as well as those that have evolved in modern conditions.

   These institutions should also be recognized as sites of legal decisions and solutions. These propositions require that state institutions be made to look like the family – they must be less formal and include the family in the process. However, there is a need to ensure that the inclusion of the family in decision-making processes is not affected by gender and age hierarchies to the detriment of the woman in certain situations.

D. *The Use of Custom to Critique Western Legal Solutions*

Most Western feminist legal solutions seek to make women more independent, autonomous and, in our view, more individualistic. Yet most women who participated in the WLSA research did not seek these values in isolation to other equally important relational values. "They did not want to be controlled by the extended family, but they did want to be part of it. They did not want to be dependent but neither did they want to be alone."[64]

   Armstrong illustrates the alienating nature of Western feminist solutions with the following instances: giving the widow the right to inherit her deceased husband's property disconnects her from the good supportive aspects of her husband's extended family; giving her the right to marry without family consent means that she loses the family's support in the event of the marriage breaking down; giving her individual ownership of property means that she loses her claim to rights in her extended

---

[63] *Id.* at 95.
[64] *Id.* at 96–97.

family's property, which she may need in difficult times.[65] Thus, "all of these western solutions alienate her from the family which may at times be oppressive but is also at times supportive."[66]

It is clear from these examples that rights-protection strategies should focus on "solutions which allow a woman to be connected but not dependent, to belong but not be controlled. For example, we could talk of the *involvement* of the family in the marriage process, while emphasizing that the control of the family must be eliminated."[67]

E. *Using Custom to Understand Women's True Position*

As seen from the preceding element, the value women place on certain aspects of custom conflicts with the rights they have under Western feminist solutions. As a result, they may not claim their rights under those solutions. Thus, custom can be used in this context to understand the true position of African women and why Western legal rights do not work for them.

In other words, using custom in this way may prevent misunderstandings of African women's position. These seem to be represented by the following statement that describes the situation of women under customary law in Namibia in some of the current women's rights discourses: "Even more surprising . . . was being confronted with a major stumbling block to the pace of change, namely that the women themselves . . . glossed over and justified such [traditional cultural] practices as iconic symbols of their culture, even though these customs had laid the very foundations of their subjugation. . . . It was also clear that the idiosyncrasy of women, defending practices to their own detriment in the name of culture, could only have come about through having been indoctrinated over generations, being stripped of an own opinion, a voice, a choice, their dignity, or any claim to human rights."[68]

F. *The Use of Custom as an Evolving System*

Customs change and the conditions under which traditions arose pass on. The process of change sometimes gives way to individualization of interests in different areas of people's lives, such as ownership of land and inheritance. As a result, "some of the group orientation of the customary law has trouble responding."[69]

---

[65] *Id.* at 95–100.

[66] *Id.* at 97.

[67] *Id.*

[68] Veronica de Klerk, *Women's Action for Development: 15 Years of Experience with Customary Practice in Rural Namibia, in* WOMEN AND CUSTOM IN NAMIBIA CULTURAL PRACTICE VERSUS GENDER EQUALITY 33, 34 (Oliver C Ruppel ed., Macmillan Education Press, 2008).

[69] Armstrong, *supra* note 1, at 90–91.

The fact that custom evolves can be used to direct some of the changes to benefit women. A classic example is that of the WLSA research group in Botswana, which used the evolving nature of custom to get men to maintain their children. It is reported that "Instead of simply rejecting the customary law and calling for Western-oriented women's rights, WLSA held meetings with customary chiefs and explained how the colonial process and the rise of individualism, property ownership, and capitalism has changed the way that the customary law is perceived and stated. In this process they emphasised the respect that the customary law had for women and the protection that the customary law gave to women and children – customary values."[70]

G. *Rejecting Custom*

This element recognizes that "the capacity for custom, customary law, tradition, and culture to change in ways which benefit women is equalled by their capacity to change in ways which oppress women."[71] It also acknowledges undesirable elements of patriarchy in customary law. Furthermore, while some women may want to be protected by traditional means, others reject the control of traditional institutions. For these and other reasons, it is inevitable that custom must at times be rejected as a means for solving women's legal problems.[72]

The gist of the model of engagement with customary law outlined under these elements is summed up by Armstrong in the following statement:

> [I]t is necessary to act on two fronts. We need to rediscover and use the aspects of custom and tradition that acknowledged and valued women and their role in society, and at the same time we need to reject the aspects of custom and tradition which allowed men to control women and resources, remembering all the time that there are different women with different needs and expectations. It is important neither to reject both sides of custom and tradition nor to accept both sides. It is important to recognise the contradictions for women in custom and tradition, to analyse both the good and the bad, to embrace the former and reject the latter. . . . This is how women act in practice. They pick and choose from traditional law and modern law, creating their own version of hybrid law that meets their immediate needs.[73]

Thus, methods of protecting women's rights should be informed by and include the strategies that women who are subject to customary law have themselves implemented. The WLSA "old pathways" may have something to offer our search for effective ways of implementing women's rights in legally, socially, and culturally pluralistic societies, such as those of Southern Africa.

[70] *Id.* at 98.
[71] *Id.*
[72] *Id.* at 99.
[73] *Id.*

CONCLUSION: REFLECTIONS ON CONCERNS

In concluding this chapter, I dispel any idea that the WLSA model of protecting women's rights is perfect. To the contrary, there are dangers that should be guarded against in using this model. Maboreke identifies two of these dangers that are particularly worthy of note with respect to the WLSA "pathways."[74]

The first is the danger of disregarding women's multiple identities as individuals with individual interests on the one hand, and as cultural beings belonging to their cultural groupings on the other hand. Disregarding women's multiple identities could lead to the legal self-understanding of women, which is essential to protecting their legal rights, being eclipsed by their cultural being. The second danger is what Maboreke calls "gagging the gender critique."[75] Essentially, this consists of the refusal by the nation's citizenry or government authorities to problematize culture and to find solutions to aspects of it that violate women's rights. At the center of this issue is the view that culture is immutable. These are serious issues, and unless properly guarded by the WLSA "pathways," these issues will be a methodological approach to exploit women and violate their human rights – the exact opposite of what these "pathways" purport to be.

However, the WLSA "pathways" seem to stay clear of these dangers in four ways. First, they are located within the dialogic human rights framework outlined in this chapter. This framework entails an internal discourse along with the cross-cultural dialogue. The former means that the people whose cultures are affected participate in the discussion of the meaning and implications of human rights norms. Within this framework, exploitative aspects of culture can be dealt with by the women and their agencies. Second, the "pathways" acknowledge the multiple identities of women by recognizing that women are at different levels in relation to their customs and culture – some customs or elements of culture that are good for some women are not good for others.[76] The question of multiple identities calls for what Armstrong refers to as the "need [for] a multiplicity of solutions for a multiplicity of women with a multiplicity of needs."[77] In other words, there is little or no room for the one-size-fits-all approach. Third, the WLSA "pathways" are premised on the important idea that customs (and culture) are continually evolving and therefore not immutable.[78] Thus, women's rights should be interpreted within the framework of changing cultures. Fourthly, the "pathways" recognize the need to reject custom and tradition when they do not promote women's interests.

The models of engagement with customary law, such as those proposed by WLSA and outlined in this chapter, constitute legitimate methods of protecting women's

---

[74] Maboreke, *supra* note 39, at 109–113.
[75] *Id.* at 110.
[76] Armstrong, *supra* note 1, at 94.
[77] *Id.* at 95.
[78] *Id.* at 90–91.

rights in different situations in Southern Africa. They should therefore inform the implementation of constitutional and other universal human rights of women in this region. Furthermore, precisely because most African women's lives are embedded within familial relationships (and this is not necessarily a bad thing), approaches to protecting their rights that operate at the level of these relationships and within women's social and cultural contexts should be acknowledged and supported.

The "old pathways" approach assures the protection of women's rights as individual women, with individual interests and needs, rather than as an elusive, homogenous group. Depending on their interests, needs, and social capacities, some women may choose the protection of legal rights strategies offered by the top-down dominant interventions discussed in this chapter, while others may prefer interventions embedded within their culture, traditions, and customs.

18

Minority Women

A Struggle for Equal Protection against Domestic Violence

Puja Kapai

Feminist legal scholars, long distraught over the failure of the law and its institutions to account for their impact on the realities that women experience, have fought hard against the masculinity and patriarchal representations of the law given its detrimental and discriminatory effects on women.[1] As a result, society's norms, systems, culture, and practices have come under strict scrutiny to address the inequalities perpetuated through these systems.[2]

With the feminist movement having gained pace over the last century, the world has united in condemning discrimination against and the subjugation of women, particularly as manifested in its most debilitating form, violence against women.[3] Although family violence has been recognized as a growing social problem, domestic violence has been recognized as a distinct form of violence affecting women as a class.[4] Given that violence against women has been noted as the single most pervasive form of human rights violation[5] in addition to being the most

---

[1] Note the works of important feminist scholars of the last half century who have engaged a wide array of audience in various fields in attempts to display the masculine nature of society, its norms, and its systems. See FEMINISM Vols I & II (Susan Moller Okin & Jane Mansbridge eds., Edward Elgar Publishing Limited, 1994).

[2] Leti Volpp, *Feminism Versus Multiculturalism*, 101 COLUM. L. REV. 1181–218 (2001).

[3] The World Health Organization revealed in its World Report on Violence and Health that between 40 percent and 70 percent of women who are murdered are victims of an ongoing abusive relationship and are killed by existing or former partners. WORLD HEALTH ORGANIZATION, WORLD REPORT ON VIOLENCE AND HEALTH (2002), *available at* www.who.int/violence_injury_prevention/violence/world_report/factsheets/en/ipvfacts.pdf (last visited Oct. 10, 2009).

[4] *See* United Nations Center for Social Development and Humanitarian Affairs, *Strategies for Confronting Domestic Violence: A Resource Manual* 7, U.N. Doc. ST/CSDHA/20 (1993). Initiatives for eliminating violence against women took center stage with the historic passing of the Convention for the Elimination of All Forms of Discrimination Against Women, Adopted UNGA Res. 34/180 Dec. 18, 1979, 1249 U.N.T.S. 13, (entered into force Sept. 3, 1981; acceded to by 186 states (as of May 2009)), *available at* www2.ohchr.org/english/law/cedaw.htm [hereinafter CEDAW].

[5] UNIFEM, UNIFEM United Kingdom Annual General Meeting 2008 News Release, *UNIFEM Supports New Initiatives to End Violence against Women* (Nov. 12, 2008), *available at* www.unifemuk.org/news-2008–11-12-UNIFEM-supports-new-initiatives-to-end-violence-against-women.php.

costly[6] to society, at least eighty-nine state parties have introduced legislation to address domestic violence against women in furtherance of their international obligations.[7]

Article 2(1) of CEDAW recognizes and condemns violence against women as a rampant form of perpetual discrimination against women that obstructs the protection of their fundamental freedoms. State parties to CEDAW are required[8] to address violence against women through measures that are effective and relevant to counter historically embedded discriminatory treatment of women in light of CEDAW's guarantee of substantive equality,[9] including the prevalence of violence by nonstate actors in the domestic sphere.[10]

In 1993, the United Nations General Assembly passed the Declaration on Elimination of Violence Against Women (DVAW).[11] Recognizing the discriminatory effect of violence against women that works against the equal enjoyment of rights by women,[12] DVAW Article 4 implores states to condemn violence against women in any of its forms by exercising due diligence through preventive, investigative, and legislative measures to punish such acts whether occurring in the public or private sphere.[13] It further requires that states should develop comprehensive strategies[14] to protect women against any form of violence and particularly to guard against the revictimization of women because of insensitive legal or administrative measures.[15]

In light of the international condemnation of domestic violence, governments have put into place civil and criminal[16] remedies to provide relief to domestic

---

[6] See SYLVIA WALBY, THE COST OF DOMESTIC VIOLENCE (Department of Trade and Industry, 2004), *available at* www.womenandequalityunit.gov.uk/research/cost_of_dv_Report_septo4.pdf.

[7] See Division for the Advancement of Women of the Department of Economic and Social Affairs of the United Nations Secretariat, Report of the Secretary General, In-depth Study on All Forms of Violence Against Women, U.N. Doc. A/61/122/Add.1 (July 6, 2006), *available at* http://reliefweb.int/rw/lib.nsf/dbgoosid/HVAN-6UFSCZ/$file/UNGA-women-jul2006.pdf?openelement.

[8] Arguably, the norms espoused in CEDAW have now obtained a *"jus cogens"* or *"peremptory norm"* status. Save for persistent non-objectors, states not party to CEDAW are equally bound by the obligations therein. *See* Legal Status and Rights of Undocumented Migrants, Advisory Opinion 18, Advisory Opinion OC-18/03, Inter-Am. Ct. H.R, ¶ 101 (Sept. 17, 2003).

[9] See generally SANDRA FREDMAN, HUMAN RIGHTS TRANSFORMED (Oxford University Press 2008).

[10] See Secretary General, Report of the Secretary General on the In-Depth Study on All Forms of Violence Against Women, delivered to the General Assembly, ¶¶ 255–57, U.N. Doc A/16/122/Add.1 (July 2006).

[11] Declaration on the Elimination of Violence against Women, G.A. Res. 48/104, 48 U.N. GAOR Supp. No. 49, UN Doc. A/48/49, at 217 (1993).

[12] *Id.* Preamble, ¶ 3.

[13] *Id.* Art 4(c)–(e).

[14] For example, legal, political, administrative, and cultural measures. *See id.* Art. 4(f).

[15] *Id.* Art. 4(g).

[16] Many states have not yet criminalized domestic violence, marital rape, incest, sexual harassment, and harmful traditional practices. *See* Study of the Secretary General, *Ending Violence Against Women: From Words to Action, A Factsheet* (Oct. 9, 2006), *available at* www.un.org/womenwatch/daw/vaw (last visited May 2, 2009) [hereinafter *From Words to Action*].

violence victims and their families. In some jurisdictions, the call for a more comprehensive system of protection has led to the development of specialized domestic violence courts and batterer-intervention programs to rehabilitate perpetrators of violence.

Although these global and local efforts are commendable, there is much debate over their adequacy and effectiveness[17] in light of increasing rates of violence against women, particularly in the domestic sphere, due to poor implementation, underreporting, inadequacy of the laws, or lack thereof.[18] Given these failings, governments are required to reexamine their laws and policies pertaining to domestic violence to provide an environment to enhance women's safety, autonomy, and participation in their public and private lives and to root out violence in all its manifestations, cultural, religious, political, and otherwise.[19]

Presently, there is a critical failure at the implementation level because of a lack of resources and commitment. Law enforcement officers, clinicians, psychologists, judges, lawyers, and activists have also struggled to reconcile the notion of a victimized woman continuing to live with or love the batterer, often concluding that the victim must be fabricating the abuse, its prevalence, or seriousness.[20] Work done by feminist and other scholars reveals the impact of social and judicial perceptions about women who fail to leave their batterers despite the assistance rendered[21] on the likelihood of victimized women successfully obtaining relief. These problems are

[17] Critics argue that criminal justice approaches against perpetrators of domestic violence fail to do justice because their arrest or imprisonment strains relations between the perpetrator and victim, increasing the risk of a more violent attack on release. Others have argued that costs for restraining orders are insurmountable and discriminate against impoverished women. *See, e.g.*, Taskforce on Local Criminal Justice Response to Domestic Violence, Domestic Violence: Keeping the Promise 2–9 (2005), www.safestate.org/documents/dv_report_ag.pdf.

[18] This is reflected by the fact that where is legislation, there is a lack of regulations or clear procedures for health and law enforcement officials to implement legislation. Low prosecution and conviction rates and high dismissal rates are telling of the inadequacies of these measures. *See, From Words To Action, supra* note 16.

[19] The CEDAW Committee has issued twenty-six general recommendations targeting, *inter alia*, gender-based violence, equality in marriage and family relations, the participation of women in public life, women's health issues, and most importantly, temporary special measures. *See also* Article 5(a) of CEDAW requiring that state parties take measures to modify cultural and social patterns to eliminate gender-based prejudicial treatment.

[20] Nan Seuffert, *Critique and Comment: Domestic Violence, Discourses of Romantic Love and Complex Personhood in the Law*, 23 Melb. U. L. Rev. 211, 211–12 (1999), noting that such "tolerance" and "love" for an abuser is perceived as inconsistent with feminist ideology and its vision of gendered relations. Indeed, this inconsistency is given the guise of incredibility in trials of defendant women who turn into aggressors and kill their batterers. *See id.* at 212. The myth of the autonomous woman who, unless she is "masochistic," would never stay with her abuser has been disputed by many feminists as an erroneous construction. *See, e.g.*, R. Emerson Dobash & Russell P. Dobash, Women, Violence, and Social Change 158, 223–38 (1992).

[21] *See* Merle Weiner, *From Dollars to Sense: A Critique of Government Funding for the Battered Women's Shelter Movement*, 9(2) L. & Equality: J. Theory & Prac. 185, 186–89 (1991).

compounded by the lack of a holistic approach despite the existence of legislation and institutional provisions.

Aside from examining alternative approaches to addressing domestic violence, a more critical discussion has emerged regarding the viability of the "one-size-fits-all" approach. Research has revealed that women experience and respond to domestic violence differently depending on various factors.[22] The reasons for this differential response are multifold.[23] Research findings show that general laws fail to adequately protect the interests of all groups of women.[24] Women belonging to minority groups are singled out as most unlikely to use existing systems of protection. How victims respond to violence invariably depends on user capacity, the willingness to report, and cultural response systems. In light of the recognition that minority, ethnic, indigenous, refugee, and migrant women are especially vulnerable to violence and discriminatory practices,[25] the assumptions inherent in the laws and institutional mechanisms to assist victims in fact perpetuate power dynamics in a patriarchal society. The measures are racialized and class- and culture-specific. Despite this fact, no equality-based challenge has been brought with respect to domestic violence laws and their inadequacies with respect to meeting the specific needs of this group.

Intersectionality has gained extensive prominence in the writings of feminist scholars working in numerous fields because of its contribution toward a more comprehensive feminist discourse that seeks to locate knowledge within realities of women whose experiences are not singularly shaped by their gender, but rather by a multiplicity of factors such as race, class, sexuality, identities, and other phenomena. These experiences help us better define our capacities for dominance or to be dominated as a woman (or man).[26] This theory delineates sites of oppression horizontally as opposed to the paradigmatic depiction of oppression as hierarchical. Intersections analysis[27] implores us to view multiple layers of experience as informative of an

---

[22] *See* Roberta Lee et al., *Intimate Partner Violence and Women of Colour: A Call for Innovations*, 92 AM. J. OF PUB. HEALTH, 530, 531 (2002), arguing that compared to white women, African American, American Indian, and Hispanic women experience domestic violence differently in terms of the forms of violence and the nature of the injury. The former are less likely to seek medical care whereas Hispanic immigrants' fear of authorities in their home jurisdictions inhibits reports of violence. *See* Mary Ann Dutton et al., U.S. Department of Justice, *National Evaluation of the Rural Domestic Violence and Child Victimization Enforcement Grant Program*, Volume I 59 (2002), *available at* www.ncjrs.gov/pdffiles1/nij/grants/198128.pdf (last visited Sept. 13, 2009).

[23] Some of these are rooted in distrust of authorities due to past experiences with officials or the experience of oppression during colonialism, while others stem from reluctance (sometimes, inability) to share family problems, considered very private in some cultures.

[24] Swati Shirwadkar, *Canadian Domestic Violence Policy and Indian Immigrant Women*, 10 VIOLENCE AGAINST WOMEN 860 (2004).

[25] DVAW, *supra* note 11, Preamble; CEDAW Committee's General Recommendation No. 19, ¶ 11, U.N. Doc. No. A/47/38 (1992), *available at* www.un.org/womenwatch/daw/cedaw/recommendations/recomm.htm.

[26] WENDY K. KOLMAR & FRANCES BARTKOWSKI, FEMINIST THEORY: A READER 49 (McGraw-Hill 2005).

[27] Some have called intersectionality "interlocking systems of domination" or "multiple jeopardy." *See* Deborah King, *Multiple Jeopardy, Multiple Consciousness: The Context of a Black Feminist Ideology*,

overall pattern of domination that requires deconstruction as a whole. It is argued that this deconstruction is all the more important to further the project of substantive equality to protect all women against domestic violence.

Kimberle Crenshaw was one of the first scholars to examine the "story" of the racialized battered woman, exposing the intersection between race and gender in the context of domestic violence.[28] Crenshaw has argued that for dominant systems to be challenged, those resisting dominance are forced to categorize their demands in terms of the logic of the dominant system itself. Inability to do so results in exclusion from the discourse for change.[29] It is here, she argues, that intersections analysis can prove groundbreaking in addressing the needs of the marginalized woman who is neither accommodated within the feminist discourse nor within that of antiracism completely.[30] Third World feminists have similarly posited that intersections analysis offers a new site for the production of knowledge, arguing that "difference" constitutes a resource through which feminist knowledge can be reorganized.[31]

Failure to integrate user-specific information into models of intervention and to account for culture-based beliefs and systems of information and worldviews will necessarily limit and undermine the effectiveness of the legal and social frameworks combating violence in the domestic sphere. Furthermore, they will remain inept at recognizing high-risk groups, providing appropriate intervention services, and meeting the needs of marginalized groups experiencing domestic violence.

To the extent that domestic violence legislation is in existence and implemented through a framework of multidisciplinary measures in a country, this chapter focuses on the extent to which such services are accessible to a routinely marginalized group of women who, despite advancements in the law relating to domestic violence, continue to fall through the gaps. By examining the assumptions underlying existing models of prevention and intervention against domestic violence, this chapter outlines the source of these gaps and investigates the reasons for the continued failure of domestic violence policies in some countries to safeguard the interests and rights of a neglected community of ethnic minority[32] and immigrant women in countries where such laws and policies are relatively advanced in their development. Although ethnic groups have long been residing in Western countries, migrant worker and sponsorship schemes have increasingly attracted such groups in larger numbers since

---

14 SIGNS 42 (1988); BELL HOOKS, AIN'T I A WOMAN? BLACK WOMEN AND FEMINISM (1981); and BELL HOOKS, FEMINISM: A TRANSFORMATIONAL POLITIC (1989).

28 Kimberle Crenshaw, *Mapping the Margins: Intersectionality, Identity Politics, and Violence Against Women of Colour*, 43 STAN. L. REV. 1241–99 (1991).

29 Kimberle Williams Crenshaw, *Race, Reform, and Retrenchment: Transformation and Legitimation in Antidiscrimination Law*, 101 HARV. L. REV. 1331 (1989).

30 Crenshaw, *supra* note 28, at 1244.

31 *See* GENDER AND FEMINIST THEORY IN LAW AND SOCIETY, xi–xxiii (Madhavi Sunder ed., Ashgate 2007).

32 The term *ethnic minority* refers to any woman who is a member of an ethnic or racial group that is a minority as compared to the dominant ethnic or racial group in the country concerned.

the last half of the century. This chapter seeks to critically examine the assumptions underlying preventive and interventionist measures against domestic violence and question their validity, drawing on the cultural, racial, and socio-economic attributes of these women to argue the need for a varied and systemic response that specifically provides for the needs of ethnic and immigrant women.

Both immigrant and ethnic minority women share certain commonalities in their experience with law and social policies relating to domestic violence. The cultural and socioeconomic attributes of ethnic minority and immigrant women make them less receptive to law and policy relating to domestic violence. Their capacities to play an active role in the preventive and legal mechanisms for protection are closely tied to their "cultural" equipment. This chapter highlights the different ways in which the "location" of ethnic minority and immigrant women within their cultural, racial, and socioeconomic backgrounds affects their perceptions and actions particularly when recognizing and responding to domestic violence.

The Western liberal democratic society is selected as the context for analysis due to the rights-oriented framework of the law, which affords human rights and constitutional rights protection for all people. As such, it can be assumed that there is a degree of development of human rights and constitutional principles, such as equality and nondiscrimination, which imposes on a government the obligation to offer substantive and equal protection to all women.

The following sections of this chapter argue that ethnic minority and immigrant status are yet to be applied as relevant differentials in the context of developing effective strategies for addressing domestic violence within the ethnic minority community. Using intersections analysis, it is argued that ethnic minority and immigrant women face obstacles on various counts, including class, language, ethnicity, culture, and experiences.

This chapter argues first that domestic violence response systems in many countries in the West are predicated on basic assumptions about user capacity and cultural attributes; second, these assumptions are flawed to the extent that they are based predominantly on the information and experience of the white woman; third, given the assumptions underlying such legislation and policy, their effectiveness in addressing domestic violence against minority women is questionable because a significant proportion of such women are excluded from equal protection against violence in the home; fourth and in conclusion, that equal protection demands standards exacted by the doctrine of substantive equality be applied here. In light of this, the lack of suitable mechanisms to account for the impact that ethnicity and culture have on accessibility to law and social resources renders the law inept and discriminatory in that it fails to achieve substantive equality in its protection of all women against domestic violence. It is argued that new initiatives and a more holistic approach toward combating domestic violence through user-oriented, culturally informed legislative policy measures designed to achieve substantively equal protection are required to ensure equal access to ethnic minority and immigrant women.

I. THE ROLE OF FEMINISM

The assumption that a woman's subjectivity is constructed only by her gender rather than her membership in other communities[33] is gradually being displaced. Post-feminism has facilitated this shift in feminism's focus from equality to difference.[34] Recognizing the need to traverse the emphasis on "white, Western, middle-class" subjectivity of "northern hemispherical women,"[35] postfeminism has spearheaded engagement with postmodernism, poststructuralism, and postcolonialism to pro-vide useful frameworks through which to challenge modernism, patriarchy, and imperialism.[36] Feminisms have since consciously included the voices of those at the margins to strengthen their theoretical foundation and practical relevance, placing identity and locality at the core and theorizing from the point where these inter-sect with other critical realities of women.[37] Postfeminism became the harbinger of hope for marginalized, diasporic, colonized, or indigenous groups and paved the way for a "nonhegemonic" feminist discourse that would account for their unique experiences of oppression.[38] The application of MacKinnon's consciousness-raising method to women's lived experiences would serve to enhance the relevance of law and policy for women of color. At the same time, however, it is worth heeding Katherine Bartlett's call to ensure that consciousness-raising transcends this lived reality rather than merely reproduces it so that a new imagined reality becomes possible for women in the future.[39]

II. MAPPING THE FRAMEWORK: PROTECTION AGAINST DOMESTIC VIOLENCE

Men have long perpetrated various forms of violence against women, sometimes in the pursuit of control and at others, as chastisement. Feminists have correctly identified violence as a tool to exert control or power over another. Taking cue from the macrocosm of social structures and the power dynamics represented therein, the microcosm of the family replicates these power differentials and inequalities. In the family context, domestic violence has been used to exert coercive control.[40]

---

[33] Volpp, *supra* note 2, at 1199.

[34] Difference-based theories in feminism have benefited greatly from the influences of philosophers of difference like Derrida or Lacan.

[35] ANN BROOKS, POSTFEMINISMS: FEMINISM, CULTURAL THEORY, AND CULTURAL FORMS 4 (Routledge 1997).

[36] *Id.*

[37] Indeed, modern-day identity politics are borne out of this encounter of feminist legal scholarship with distinct identity groups' campaigns for recognition and redistribution of power within the world. *See* Sunder, *supra* note 31, at xii.

[38] *Id.*

[39] *Id.* at xv (citing Katherine T. Bartlett, *Feminist Legal Methods*, 103 HARV. L. REV. 829, 830 (1990)).

[40] R. EMERSON DOBASH & RUSSELL DOBASH, VIOLENCE AGAINST WIVES: A CASE AGAINST PATRIARCHY 24 (Free Press 1979).

Although physical violence against women is the norm, more recently, emotional and psychological violence have also been categorized as types of domestic violence.

The traditional responses to domestic violence in many liberal democratic societies tend to include civil remedies such as injunctions or protection orders, while the machinery of the criminal law is also made available for more serious incidents of violence. Criminal law pertaining to assault, battery, and grievous bodily harm are used to address instances of physical violence. Some countries have criminalized domestic violence and created an alternative machinery to deal with assault and injury in the context of the family.

Apart from legal remedies, shelters, victim support centers, and hospitals provide basic needs, counseling, and medical support for victims. The success of these measures in protecting victims against violence and preventing repeat violence depend extensively on the subjective attributes of the woman experiencing the violence. Although factors external to her gender[41] constitute her attributes, her cultural beliefs about her role, the expectations others have of her, her knowledge of available resources, and her basic cultural equipment are constitutive of her personality and capacity in that they shape every thought and consequent action. The singular focus of most domestic violence legislation and services tends to be based on gender rather than the numerous other factors that are constitutive of a woman's reality, which may or may not relate to her gender. Such a focus has serious limitations[42] and could potentially and has indeed perpetuated inequalities experienced by racialized and immigrant women. The inherent assumptions underlying these systems of protection are first, that the victims are aware that they are victims of violence that is wrongful; second, that they want to seek relief from such violence; third, that they have the psychological, physical, and monetary capacities to seek such relief; fourth, that they will seek such relief; and fifth, that they will seek such relief from state and nonstate resources. The following section addresses each of these assumptions, arguing that they exclude cultural equipment and attributes in the assessment of the

---

[41] Inderpal Grewal suggests, "it is necessary to understand gender as a highly contingent and diverse formation" and the binary presentation of feminism as *opposed to* multiculturalism is a falsely premised assumption in that it presumes that women's subjectivities are constructed only by their gender. *See* Inderpal Grewal, *"Women's Rights as Human Rights": Feminist Practices, Global Feminism, and Human Rights Regimes in Transnationality*, 3 CITIZENSHIP STUD. 337, 342 (1999) and Inderpal Grewal, *On the New Global Feminism and the Family of Nations: Dilemmas of Transnational Feminist Practice*, *in* TALKING VISIONS: MULTICULTURAL FEMINISM IN A TRANSNATIONAL AGE 501, 519–20 (Ella Shohat ed., 1998).

[42] *See* Norma Alarcon, *The Theoretical Subject(s) of this Bridge Called My Back and Anglo-American Feminism*, *in* MAKING FACE, MAKING SOUL: HACIENDO CARAS 356, 360 (Gloria Anzaldua ed., 1990) where she writes, "The inclusion of other analytical categories such as race and class becomes impossible for a subject whose consciousness refuses to acknowledge that 'one becomes a woman' in ways that are much more complex than in a simple opposition to men. In cultures in which 'asymmetric race and class relations are a central organizing principle of society,' one may also 'become a woman' in opposition to other women."

usability and accessibility to these services. It is this ignorance that beckons the failure of legal and social support systems to assist ethnic minority women experiencing
domestic violence.

III. CONSTITUTIVE REALITIES AND CULTURAL COMPETENCE

A. *Defining and Identifying Violence*

Culture-based traditional gender roles have routinely permitted the abuse of
women.[43] Both genders have intimated the cultural acceptability toward physical
chastisement of a wife by her husband as a rebuke.[44] This applies to ethnic minority
and immigrant women alike. Communities differ extensively on what constitutes
violence and more importantly, unacceptable violence. For example, in Japan physical battering is considered less egregious than overturning a dining table at home.[45]

One of the prime difficulties is definitional. Physical violence has been broadly
defined as including kicking, burning, biting, choking, hitting, shaking, pushing,
rough handling, assaulting or restraining with a weapon, or threats to do any of
these.[46] Although most forms of physical aggression are almost universal in their
infliction of pain, their "acceptability" varies considerably across cultures.

A separate but related issue pertains to the determination of sexual violence within
intimate relationships, the threshold for which also varies across cultures. Many Asian
countries reject the idea of rape within marriage and consider sexual intercourse
within marriage to be implicitly consensual. Among Haitian women, any woman
alleging sexual abuse perpetrated by her husband would be disbelieved because all
women are expected to be willing partners.[47]

Ethnic and immigrant groups in the United States have been identified as
particularly at risk given the higher rates of male-to-female partner violence and

[43] Hoan Bui & Merry Morash, *Domestic Violence in the Vietnamese American Community*, 5 VIOLENCE AGAINST WOMEN 769–95 (1999); Merry Morash, Hoan Bui, & Anna M. Santiago, *Gender Specific Ideology of Domestic Violence in Mexican Origin Families*, 1 INT'L REV. OF VICTIMOLOGY 67–91 (2000); and Carolee GiaoUyen Tran & Kunya Des Jardins, *Domestic Violence in Vietnamese Refugee and Korean Immigrant Communities, in* RELATIONSHIPS AMONG ASIAN AMERICAN WOMEN 71–96 (Jean Lau Chin ed., American Psychological Association 2000).

[44] Kimberly A. Huisman, *Wife Battering in Asian American Communities: Identifying the Service Needs of an Overlooked Segment of the U.S. Population*, 2 VIOLENCE AGAINST WOMEN 260–83 (1996); Anahid Dervartanian Kulwicki & June Miller, *Domestic Violence in the Arab American Population: Trans-forming Environmental Conditions Through Community Education*, 20 ISSUES IN MENTAL HEALTH NURSING 199–215 (1999); and YOUNG I. SONG, BATTERED WOMEN IN KOREAN IMMIGRANT FAMILIES: THE SILENT SCREAM (Garland 1996).

[45] Kumaralingam Amirthalingam, *Women's Rights, International Norms, and Domestic Violence: Asian Perspectives*, 27 HUM. RTS. Q. 683 (2005).

[46] Department of Justice, Canada, *Spousal Abuse: A Fact Sheet from the Department of Justice Canada* (2005), *available at* http://canada2.justice.gc.ca/en/ps/fm/spouseafs.html (last visited Oct. 10, 2009).

[47] Rachel E. Latta & Lisa A Goodman, *Haitian Immigrant Women*, 11 VIOLENCE AGAINST WOMEN 1441, 1447–48 (2005).

female-to-male partner violence among Blacks and Hispanics compared to Whites.[48] One study, for example, examined the extent of agreement between heterosexual couples[49] as to male-to-female and female-to-male physical, psychological, and sexual violence, revealing disagreements about the occurrence or absence of violence. The study also found that women were less likely to identify themselves as victims of violence.[50] Assessing for differences across sex and ethnicity, rates of male-to-female and female-to-male minor physical violence appear twice as high among Blacks and Hispanics compared to Whites.[51] Ethnicity and sex also affect whether an act is classified as sexually coercive.[52]

These findings reaffirm the need to refine models of intervention to better understand the complex set of circumstances, including ethnicity and sex, that interact with patterns of violence and affect identification of violence, reportage,[53] and use of services.

B. *Cultural Information and Culture as Capacity*

Studies have shown that ethnic minority and immigrant women do not benefit much from traditional measures to combat domestic violence. In this section, I argue that the various legal and social institutions deployed to protect women from domestic violence generally fail to adequately and effectively address the distinct needs of ethnic minority and immigrant women given their lack of attention to the specific cultural context within which the minority woman is engaged.[54] In light of findings that culture and social structures affect immigrant and ethnic minority women's recognition of and responses to domestic violence,[55] this section examines cultural and social factors and how they impact help-seeking behavior and receptivity to interventions in the context of domestic violence.

[48] Caetano et al., *Intimate Partner Violence, Acculturation, and Alcohol Consumption Among Hispanic Couples in the United States*, 15 JOURNAL OF INTERPERSONAL VIOLENCE 30–45 (2000); and Schafer et al., *Rates of Intimate Partner Violence in the United States*, 88 AM. J. OF PUBLIC HEALTH 1702–04 (1998). *See also* Anita Raj & Jay Silverman, *Violence Against Women: The Roles of Culture, Context, and Legal Immigrant Status on Intimate Partner Violence*, 8 VIOLENCE AGAINST WOMEN 367–98 (2002).

[49] Caetano et al., *Agreement on Reporting of Physical, Psychological, and Sexual Violence Among White, Black, and Hispanic Couples in the United States*, JOURNAL OF INTERPERSONAL VIOLENCE 1–20 (2008).

[50] *Id.* at 9.

[51] *Id.* at 7.

[52] *Id.* at 11.

[53] *Id.* at 16.

[54] Within immigrant and ethnic communities, the gendered nature of the woman's role both justifies abuse and increases a woman's vulnerability to abuse through their micro-systems that keep them isolated and subservient to men, particularly given their self-sacrificial tendencies. *See* M. S. George & L. Rahangdale, *Domestic Violence and South Asian Women*, 60 N. C. MED. J. 157–59 (1999).

[55] MARGARET ABRAHAM, SPEAKING THE UNSPEAKABLE: MARITAL VIOLENCE AMONG SOUTH ASIAN IMMIGRANTS IN THE UNITED STATES (Rutgers University Press 2000). *See also* Y. I. Song, *Domestic Violence Against Women in Korean Immigrant Families*, *in* KOREAN AMERICAN WOMEN LIVING IN TWO CULTURES 134–60 (Y. I. Song & A. Moon eds., Academia Koreana 1997).

Culture consists of language and other tools that have been referred to by some as "cultural equipment." Cultural equipment serves to inform communication between and within groups and affects the ability and capacity of the individual to interact with the structures and institutions in society. Language, norms of order, and other social customs come together to dictate our notions of justice, our roles, and our understanding of things around us generally.[56]

Whether individuals are capable of making effective use of judicial and social institutions depends on their cultural equipment instilled through upbringing, education, and attachment to cultural or religious norms and communities. These ideas materially affect belief systems, the assessment of facts and life experiences, and one's responses to life's events.

It has long been thought that there are sufficient cultural factors that necessarily affect the prevalence of domestic violence within Asian and other immigrant communities. The similarities between Asian cultures, for example, have been linked to Confucian ideals that have embedded patriarchy within societal and filial structures, particularly across China, Vietnam, and Korea.[57] Other culture or religion-based norms across Asian societies have also been known to create and perpetuate patriarchal societies.

These attitudes are also rooted in the lack of legislative provisions against such abuse in victims' countries of origin. For example, in Japan, until 2001, there was no legislation that specifically recognized spousal violence or provided any support measures for victims of such violence.[58] Even in Asian countries where such legislation has recently been enacted, it remains underused given the very low reportage of domestic violence claims by victims themselves.

Chow has documented how Asian women are confronted with a clash of values that inhibit reportage of abuse, affecting help-seeking behavior. They struggle between the expectation of obedience,[59] self-sacrifice in the familial or collective interest, and their desire for independence or self-expression.[60] Similarly, Haitian

---

[56] Although culture is never static nor uniform, and cultural beliefs and practices vary across communities, the lack of cultural homogeneity does not bar the identification of central traits that define a culture and its core value system. Culture here is used as a general term referring to shared cultural attributes, beliefs, and norms embraced by members in their strict or diluted versions. *See* Margaret Abraham, *Ethnicity, Gender, and Marital Violence: South Asian Women's Organisations in the United States*, 9 GENDER & SOCIETY 450–68 (1995) and BODY EVIDENCE: INTIMATE VIOLENCE AGAINST SOUTH ASIAN WOMEN IN AMERICA (Shamita Das Dasupta ed., Rutgers University Press 2007).

[57] Merry Morash et al., *Getting Out of Harm's Way: One-Year Outcomes for Abused Women in a Vietnamese Immigrant Enclave*, 14 VIOLENCE AGAINST WOMEN 1413, 1414 (2008).

[58] Yoshiyuki Takano, *Coping with Domestic Violence by Japanese Canadian Women*, in HANDBOOK OF MULTICULTURAL PERSPECTIVES ON STRESS AND COPING 319 (Paul T. P. Wong & Lilian C. J. Wong eds., 2006)

[59] Ko-Li Chin, *Out of Town Brides: International Marriage and Wife Abuse Among Chinese Immigrants*, 25 J. COMP. FAM. STUD. 53–69 (1994).

[60] Esther Ngan-Ling Chow, *The Feminist Movement: Where are All the Asian American Women?*, in MAKING WAVES 362–77 (Asian Women United of California eds., Beacon 1989).

immigrant victims of domestic violence reported that having witnessed violence perpetrated by men against women in their communities publicly contributed to behaviors of acceptance, endurance, and nonintervention.[61] Transgressions against these cultural expectations attract rebukes, which legitimize violence.[62]

An additional factor is the cultural emphasis on filial loyalty, a particular imperative for the woman in the family. For Indian victims, reporting one's husband to the police is contrary to the very essence of being a "good Hindu wife," a label predicated on being self-sacrificial as opposed to self-preserving.[63] The cultural upbringing primarily teaches women to see themselves as instruments, to be subservient to the needs and demands of others. As a result, from the outset, very low value is placed on a woman's self-worth in these communities.[64] In the circumstances, any abuse directed at them is accepted with resignation that this must be "fate."[65] The lack of legislative and social support measures and apathy toward complaints of violence combine with other cultural factors diluting women's awareness of their own plight and their imperative to act against abuse.[66] Immigrant women's cultures, contexts, and legal status contribute to their increased vulnerability to abuse and control by the batterers and create barriers against help-seeking.[67]

---

[61] Latta & Goodman, *supra* note 47, at 1447.

[62] Nilda Rimonte, *Domestic Violence Among Pacific Asians, in* MAKING WAVES 327–37 (Asian Women United of California eds., Beacon 1989). Similar patterns of acceptability toward abuse at the hands of male partners have been observed in Latino populations in the United States. *See* Julia Perilla et al., *Culture and Domestic Violence: The Ecology of Abused Latinas,* 9 VIOLENCE AND VICTIMS 325–39 (1994) and Julia L. Perilla, *Domestic Violence as a Human Rights Issue: The Case of Immigrant Latinos,* 21 HISP. J. BEHAV. SCI. 107–33 (1999) [hereinafter *Domestic Violence as a Human Rights Issue*].

[63] The self-preserving notion based on individuality and autonomy is largely underscored by most frameworks of protection against domestic violence. *See* Rashmi Goel, *Sita's Trousseau: Restorative Justice, Domestic Violence, and South Asian Culture,* 11(5) VIOLENCE AGAINST WOMEN 639, 640 (2005), arguing that the restorative justice model advocated for dispute resolution against domestic violence is ill-suited to the South Asian cultural context.

[64] AZRU KANA-DEUBA, A SITUATIONAL ANALYSIS OF VIOLENCE AGAINST WOMEN AND GIRLS IN NEPAL 3 (SATHI and The Asia Foundation 1997).

[65] Satya P. Krishnan et al., *Lifting the Veil of Secrecy – Domestic Violence Against South Asian Women, in* A PATCHWORK SHAWL: CHRONICLES OF SOUTH ASIAN WOMEN IN AMERICA 145–69 (Shamita Das Dasgupta ed., Rutgers University Press 1998).

[66] Bui & Morash, *supra* note 43; Nancy Luke et al., *Exploring Couple Attributes and Attitudes and Marital Violence in Vietnam,* 13 VIOLENCE AGAINST WOMEN 5–27 (2007); Jae Yop Kim & Clifton Emery, *Marital Power, Conflict, and Norm Consensus, and Marital Violence in a Nationally Representative Sample of Korean Couples,* 18 J. INTERPERSONAL VIOLENCE 197–219 (2003); Jae Yop Kim & Kyu-taik Sung, *Conjugal Violence in Korean Families: A Residue of the Cultural Tradition,* 15 J. FAM. VIOLENCE 331–45 (2000); and Shamita Dasgupta & Sujata Warrier, *In the Footstep of 'Arundhati': Asian Indian Women's Experience of Domestic Violence in the United States,* 2 VIOLENCE AGAINST WOMEN 238–59 (1999).

[67] *See* Anita Raj & Jay Silverman, *Violence Against Immigrant Women: The Role of Culture, Context, and Legal Immigrant Status on Intimate Partner Violence,* 8 VIOLENCE AGAINST WOMEN 367 (2002).

C. *(Re)constituting Realities: The Ethnic or Immigrant Woman*

In addition to the cultural factors that impact a woman's response to domestic violence, there is a need to examine her situational context carefully. Although empirical studies have positively correlated culture to the incidence of domestic violence,[68] many have argued that the violence is characteristic of the socioeconomic conditions of the community rather than culture per se.[69]

An assessment of the victim's and the perpetrator's community life and socioeconomic backgrounds is indispensible to capture how their experiences, expectations, and needs combine to determine the viability of a particular legal or social response system. Based on several research studies that have shown the impact that the combination of culture and other socioeconomic factors can have on the effectiveness of domestic violence response measures, there is a need to reexamine how host countries can provide more culturally sensitive sites for adjudication in the context of family violence so that the outcomes can resonate more strongly with the lived realities of these women.[70]

i. Language

Language poses a significant hurdle for ethnic minority and immigrant women, affecting several aspects of their immigrant experience. First and foremost, their ability to access basic resources and services is severely limited given their inability to communicate their needs.[71] Language directly impacts access to services because it limits awareness and knowledge of the existence of protection and other measures against domestic violence. This poses the additional burden of depending on someone to communicate these needs. This presents a risk of mismatch between needs articulation and service provision. Because of the numerous languages and dialects around, shelters find it difficult to accommodate all ethnicities.[72]

---

[68] *Id.* at 372–73.

[69] For example, a study by Malla et al. establishes the connection between economic impoverishment and rates of violence against women. *See* Sapana Malla et al., *Violence Against Women and Girls in Nepal, in* BREAKING THE SILENCE: VIOLENCE AGAINST WOMEN IN ASIA 139–51 (Fanny M. Cheung et al. eds., Elite Business Service 1999).

[70] *See id.* at fn. 128. *See also* Huisman, *supra* note 44, detailing the failings of a lack of community outreach programs and the lack of culturally tailored services that do not reflect the values immigrant or ethnic women consider most important in their decision to seek shelter outside the home.

[71] For example, one Korean social worker was of the view that at times, circumstances in shelters were more frightening than those experienced in the home where the victim was subject to abuse. *See* Huisman, *supra* note 44, at 267.

[72] Although some shelters have tried to provide multilingual access, interpreters are often not trained in issues arising in an abusive setting and may be unaware of subtleties that might be relevant to accurately mapping the problem and designing appropriate interventions. Female interpreters ought to be secured where this would likely enable a more candid sharing of events. *See* Huisman *supra* note 44, at 268.

Sometimes, a woman's access to a new language is restricted by the abusive spouse to limit her ability to function independently of the spouse.[73] This presents problems relating to economic and social dependency and creates limitations that inhibit accessibility to resources and services.

ii. Economic and Immigration Status

Economic independence comes with education and employment. Sometimes, despite access to either of these, the flourishing of women's conditions may be constrained by cultural or social systems. In some cultures, patriarchal norms dictate that men are the traditional breadwinners in the family and as such, women are unlikely to have the benefit of receiving education or employment is unlikely or prohibited. These beliefs serve to constrain an ethnic minority or immigrant woman's financial independence by diminishing her accessibility to resources, including any prospects for training or inclusion in the workforce and social activities.

Similarly, language incapacity acts as a handicap against employment or confines prospects of employment to particular industries, directly impacting independence.[74] This impedes integration given the limitations to skills training, mobility, economic prospects, and social networking. This handicap is further exacerbated by enclave dwelling in which immigrant and ethnic minority women see little need to learn a new language.

Immigrant women awaiting sponsorship for citizenship by their husbands are clearly in a vulnerable position. Usually, these comprise the "mail-order" brides or those who have had their marriages arranged. With her immigration status dependent on her sponsoring spouse, such a woman may be even further restrained in her mobility and access for a number of reasons and would feel culturally and practically obliged to comply with her husband's expectations and would unlikely lodge a complaint in light of her complete financial dependence on her spouse and the dim prospects for her own financial independence in the future.[75]

These women also lack legal rights unless they are aware of them and have availed of them in special cases.[76] The resolve to endure violence as opposed to challenge it may be further strengthened by cultural taboos associated with divorced and separated women and particularly so if they have children. They would also exercise refrain for fear of losing them if deported.[77]

---

[73] Perilla, *Domestic Violence as a Human Rights Issue, see supra* note 62; George & Rahangdale, *supra* note 54.

[74] Swati Shirwadkar's study on immigrant women in Canada illustrates how education and linguistic affluence of immigrant women impacts awareness of legal rights, Shirwadkar, *supra* note 24.

[75] Perilla, *Domestic Violence as a Human Rights Issue, supra* note 62.

[76] Orloff L. E., *Access to Public Benefits for Battered Immigrant Women and Children*, 33 CLEARINGHOUSE REV. J. POVERTY L. & POL'Y 237 (1999).

[77] Perilla, *Domestic Violence as a Human Rights Issue, supra* note 62.

Puja Kapai

Cultural stereotypes pertaining to law-enforcement authorities also prevent access to justice on account of distrust toward police, social services, and law enforcement officers, particularly where the women have experienced racism, ridicule, or ignorance.[78] As a result, an ethnic or immigrant woman's choices or alternatives are severely reduced when men maintain economic control in the relationship or can impact immigration status.[79]

iii. Rurality and Spatiality

A further reality that characterizes the lives of ethnic minority and immigrant women is rural residence, poor conditions within the urban space, and isolation. Rural neighborhoods are typically characterized by spatial isolation. Women may live in areas where transport systems are generally underdeveloped and distance already isolates communities from help centers, which are usually located in metropolitan or urban areas.[80] This contributes to ignorance of available services and protective measures. Pruitt has extensively documented[81] how rurality and spatiality isolate women and distance them from available help and services.[82]

Immigrant enclave dwellings within rural or urban settings strengthen neighborhood ties but at the same time, given the shared social, cultural, and moral fabric and the community bonding, women in trouble may be even more reluctant to speak out against violence.[83] Enclave dwelling therefore entrenches these infirmities by limiting prospects of effective acculturation into the host community.

Even where ethnic minority and immigrant women are living within urban areas, their economic and social circumstances share some of the difficulties characteristic

---

[78] Latta & Goodman, *supra* note 47, at 1447.

[79] *See* Abraham, *Speaking the Unspeakable: Marital Violence Against South Asian Immigrant Women in the United States,* 5 INDIAN JOURNAL OF GENDER STUDIES 215–41 (1998).

[80] *See* Deborah Weissman, *The Personal is Political – and Economic: Rethinking Domestic Violence,* BYU. L. REV. 387, 407–27 (2007) and Gary L. Bowen et al., *Neighborhood Characteristics and Supportive Parenting Among Single Mothers, in* FAMILIES, CRIME, AND CRIMINAL JUSTICE 183, 184 (Greer Litton Fox & Michael L Benson eds., 2000), arguing that individuals become increasingly unwilling to intervene in their neighbors' affairs as relational networks decline. *See also* Michael L. Benson et al., *Neighborhood Disadvantage, Individual Economic Distress, and Violence Against Women in Intimate Relationships,* 19 J. QUANTITATIVE CRIMINOLOGY 207, 210 (2003), linking isolation from social structures and increased incidence of domestic violence.

[81] Lisa Pruitt, *Toward a Feminist Theory of the Rural,* UTAH L. REV. 421–88 (2007).

[82] *See* particularly the cases *Stete v. Oldenburg,* 628 NW 2d 278, 289 (Nev. Ct App 2001) and *Moyer v. Moyer* No. 03–03-00751-CV, 2005 WL 2043823, at 1 (Tex. App. Aug. 26, 2005), both cited in Pruitt, *id.* at 452–53 to illustrate the aggravated vulnerabilities of rural women, arguing that such considerations are relevant and ought to be accounted for in determining cases brought by the state against abused women for their crimes.

[83] Community and religious leaders or elders often implore women to stay in the relationship and not to speak about private affairs concerning the family in public. Perpetrators of violence are well aware of the constraints of cultural contexts and the law and use both to maintain control over their spouses. The gaps in services strengthen their confidence that they will never be found out. *See* George & Rahangdale, *supra* note 54.

of rural lifestyles given cultural, economic, educational, and linguistic barriers. This isolation is particularly entrenched in patriarchal communities that bar employment and schooling, enforcing both physical and psychological isolation. Oftentimes, the women are distanced from their family and friends back home[84] but may be residing with or close to the husband's family. This context often exacerbates exposure to or legitimatization of violence against women and perpetrators may include the spouse or in-laws.[85] Culturally enforced isolation limits socialization[86] into different cultures and norms[87] and perpetuates "infirmities."

The impact of "psychological spatiality" typifies the sense in which ethnic minority and immigrant women share their experience of spatiality with rural women. Current social and legal mechanisms largely ignore the burdens of rurality and spatiality. The systems are inherently biased toward catering to the needs of an urban populace and thus, fail to locate ethnic minority and immigrant women within their realms of assistance.[88]

iv. Racial Discrimination

In addition to the numerous barriers that affect accessibility to resources, employment, and education, ethnic minority and immigrant women fear that discrimination and inequality will reign over their future if they attempt to live life on their own. Their fears come from their experiences of discrimination and ill treatment and greatly affect their assessment of the prospects for a life independent of one's community.

Many of the aforementioned factors breed an extensive level of dependency that is crippling, particularly for battered women, who may suffer from other inhibiting characteristics, physical and mental, which curtail their actions.[89] Their dependence on their communities results in a resignation to community expectations. The loss

---

[84] In some instances, this contact is limited or controlled entirely by the partner. *See* Meeta Mehrotra, *The Social Construction of Wife Abuse: Experiences of Asian Indian Women in the United States*, 5 VIOLENCE AGAINST WOMEN 619–40 (1999).

[85] *Id.*

[86] George & Rahangdale, *supra* note 54, detailing how friendship with "Americans" is limited by spouses of South Asian women.

[87] However, studies have shown that as the number of years of residence increase, the adherence to traditional patriarchal values is reduced, albeit marginally when compared to attitudes of their nonimmigrant counterparts. *See* S. B. Yim, *Korean Battered Wives: A Sociological and Psychological Analysis of Conjugal Violence in Korean Immigrant Families*, in KOREAN WOMEN IN A STRUGGLE FOR HUMANISATION 171–199 (Harold Hakwon Sunoo & Dong Soo Kim eds., 1978).

[88] Pruitt, *supra* note 81, at 438–40. *See also* JUDITH BAER, OUR LIVES BEFORE THE LAW 55–66 (1999).

[89] *See* LENORE WALKER, THE BATTERED WOMAN 88–89 (1979), and ELIZABETH SCHNEIDER, BATTERED WOMEN AND FEMINIST LAW MAKING 185–86 (2000), on theories relating to why abused women fail to leave their batterers, the impact of sustained abuse on women's physical and psychological capacities to protect themselves against further domestic violence, and the conditions of learned helplessness and battered woman syndrome, which help explain the psyche of the battered woman where she fails to leave a relationship of abuse or turns aggressor.

of face and concept of shame operate powerfully to restrain vulnerable women from talking about their problems. The circumstances consequent on reportage are frightening for many immigrant and ethnic women given the cultural, familial, and other burdens placed on them.

Legislative and other interventions fail to account for the unacceptability of the consequences of interventions such as injunction, arrest, imprisonment, or divorce. Miscast as "solutions," they are ill suited to the context of ethnic and immigrant women because each of these challenges the cultural mores of the women concerned and would result in their ostracism from the community. This interdependence between the individual and the community is critically unaccounted for in existing interventions against domestic violence in the West.

Traditional responses to domestic violence entail approaching law-enforcement authorities to obtain civil remedies such as injunctions, projection orders, prosecution for battery, assault, or rape, or alternatively to enlist police protection and social support from shelters and hospitals providing basic needs and medical care. They espouse particular cultural choices that reflect norms considered appropriate to address particular social ills. The fundamental assumption underlying any of these options is that the woman correctly perceives herself as a victim of violence. However, she may not at all identify herself as a victim.[90] This would govern and limit awareness of mechanisms to prevent abuse and, ultimately, her access to any systems of assistance.

Obstructions to availing oneself of traditional response mechanisms to combat violence result not only from definitional issues, but are a direct result of the woman's specific constitution of herself as situated within her cultural or religious context, which I refer to as her "self-concept," her beliefs about gender roles and family life.[91] Her self-concept leads her to act and react in a particular manner to certain life events.[92] The current system, which depends extensively on victim-initiated complaints, is seriously flawed because it fails to address the needs of women who culturally lack any sense of an autonomous self and, even if they see themselves as separate from their family, they lack the capacity to exercise autonomy.

The Hindustani woman residing in the Netherlands, for example, turned to suicide as her only respite from the violence in the belief that her life would be condemned by her community should she speak ill of her husband or have him

---

[90] *See* Farah Ahmad et al., *Patriarchal Beliefs and Perceptions of Abuse among South Asian Immigrant Women*, 10 VIOLENCE AGAINST WOMEN 262–82 (2004).

[91] Floretta Boonzaier & Cheryl de la Rey, *'He's a Man and I'm a Woman.' Cultural Constructions of Masculinity and Femininity in South African Women's Narratives of Violence*, 9(8) VIOLENCE AGAINST WOMEN 1003–1029 (2003).

[92] The critical impact and relevance of the self-concept as informed by culture or religion on a woman's capacity to act to bring herself out of cycles of domestic violence is illustrated by the case of an Indian woman residing in the Netherlands. *See* Sawitri Saharso, *Female Autonomy and Cultural Imperative: Two Hearts Beating Together, in* CITIZENSHIP IN DIVERSE SOCIETIES 224 (Will Kymlica & Wayne Norman eds., Oxford University Press 2000).

arrested. This belief stems from a very strong set of values that see marriage as an eternal bond that carries over into the afterlife. Clearly, liberal democratic responses based on restorative justice, where access is primarily premised on the assumption that the abused woman has the cultural equipment required to give her the capacity to undertake the actions needed, have overlooked the lack of correlation between these systems and the realities of the women concerned. Even when immigrant and ethnic minority women recognize their victimized status, internalized cultural and religious structures have led them to develop and apply coping mechanisms, none of which resonate with and, indeed, are contrary to the available social and legal structures. The result of seeking assistance must be one that is culturally consonant with an immigrant or ethnic minority woman's lived reality.

The current gaps in accounting for the numerous factors that exacerbate the plight of abused women operate to enmesh abused immigrant and ethnic women in a vicious cycle where the very law and social networks that are there to protect the victims act as oppressors by relegating such women to a situation of irrelevance. Accessibility to the law and social services requires positive capacities in almost *each* of the categories described earlier. There is a critical need to work toward building these capacities through networking with ethnic minority and immigrant communities to raise awareness, knowledge, and basic life skills to dilute isolation and to penetrate the situational context of these women.

IV. EMPOWERMENT THROUGH RECOGNITION: A METHOD OF CONSCIOUSNESS-AWARENESS

Given that research that has critically examined the causes of violence against women has recognized cultural and social factors as major contributors to the perpetuation of such violence, a culturally informed perspective would further the cause of protection of minority women within their cultural frameworks. The more changes are introduced in a manner that is culturally sensitive, the more viable these changes will be, making the systems of protection that much more effective at preventing and dealing with violence. By exploring the coping mechanisms used by women in different cultures, women subject to domestic violence may be assisted through a culturally sensitive approach that resonates with their cultural beliefs. There is a further need to systematically design systems to raise consciousness and begin a process of diversity mainstreaming that can accompany gender mainstreaming in law and policy to cultivate a multicultural approach toward tackling social problems.

V. APPLYING THE DOCTRINE OF SUBSTANTIVE EQUALITY TO FRAMEWORKS OF PROTECTION AGAINST DOMESTIC VIOLENCE

The fight for equality in law and social policy has been fought on many fronts. The feminist discourse has contributed tremendously to the project of equality and, at the same time, it has highlighted the inadequacies of equality as a formal concept, through its exclusion of voices of marginalized women. There is an urgent need, therefore, to incorporate the experience of marginalized women to enhance the accuracy and productivity of the feminist discourse in addressing the plight of women. In addition to a heightened discourse of constitutionalism, gendered constitutionalism,[93] and mainstreaming, there is a need for a transformative notion of equality to apply to govern the rights of abused women in a manner that addresses the problem at all its levels.

The doctrine of substantive equality can be applied in interventions against domestic violence to strive for the recognition and affirmation of difference through the cultivation of legally and socially inclusive frameworks of governance. Sandra Fredman has illustrated how substantive equality disrupts the traditional discourse of "rights" and "recognition" to force considerations of social context in any equation of inequality and redistribution. Theories of multiculturalism and the experience of social exclusion have challenged even the concept of substantive equality, traditionally rooted in redistributive discourse to orient itself toward a rights-based view of redistributive measures.[94]

Here, there is a need to expand the discourse to develop substantive equality as including positive duties as opposed to the traditionally "negative" conception of the duty of restraint. This includes extending substantive equality to include social rights. In this sense, the dual dimensions of equality need to be recognized through re-grounding substantive equality in redistribution and rights as opposed to just one or the other.

The lack of appropriate mechanisms to account for the impact that ethnicity has on accessibility to law and social resources renders the law inept and discriminatory in that it fails to achieve substantive equality in its protection of all women, particularly women of color, against domestic violence. These findings clearly beckon for an alternative critical discourse in law and social policy. The embrace of law and its democratization requires that its foundation be firmly grounded in a dialogue of inclusiveness and an expansive array of voices.[95]

This can only be achieved by targeted initiatives to ensure greater access to ethnic minority women by applying a transformative vision of substantive equality to assess their needs based on their situational context (economic, social, cultural, and religious). Without the development of comprehensive tools to determine this context, the state would fail in its obligations to protect all women against discrimination under CEDAW, and also their most basic duties of nondiscrimination on grounds of race, national origin, and other factors. Such an approach would be transformative

---

[93] *See generally* THE GENDER OF CONSTITUTIONAL JURISPRUDENCE (Beverly Baines & Ruth Rubio-Marín eds., 2005).

[94] Catherine Albertyn, Sandra Fredman, & Judy Fudge, *Special Issue: Substantive Equality, Social Rights, and Women*, 23 SOUTH AFRICAN J. HUM. RTS. 209, 210 (2007).

[95] The phrase "democratization of law" is borrowed from Sunder ed., *supra* note 31, at xii.

because it would challenge the traditional approaches and boundaries of law and social policy that perpetuate existing norms pertaining to universal attitudes toward gender-based violence and effective responses. It would foster a more inclusive dialogue through facilitating an understanding of systemic inequalities, cultural biases, and inherently non-universal concepts that perpetuate formal outcomes, thereby inhibiting transformative change. This chapter concludes by recommending that a more holistic approach to combat domestic violence be designed, through user-oriented, culturally informed legislative and policy measures, to achieve transformative substantive equality. Accounting for the role and impact of such exogenous factors in the development of law is critical to cultivate carefully deliberated models of intervention to better protect and empower ethnic minority and immigrant women in their fight against domestic violence.

CONCLUSION

Although the end of the last century has seen greater strides in the application of constitutionalism and, through it, the concept of substantive equality, there is a long road ahead in terms of fully utilizing these standards to their fullest potential to achieve justice, dignity, and equality. Although equality and nondiscrimination principles have been broadly interpreted and applied in constitutional discourse, both gendered constitutionalism and substantive equality demand a more exacting inquiry than that which presently unfolds in the application of existing frameworks to women in marginalized contexts. Intersectional theory has been a pioneer in highlighting the importance of multicontextual assessments. It has been said that "de facto rights cannot be secured unless the interlocking relationships among gender, class, race, ethnicity, national identity, and the structures of state power are taken into account."[96] There is a critical need to assess the interaction between these different traits in their combined impact on knowledge, awareness, and accessibility to the law and social services. Without accounting for the specific contexts and realities of women at the "margins," constitutionalism or even gendered constitutionalism does not go far enough. Without a comprehensive approach to addressing multiple marginalizations, protection measures will remain inadequate.

A participatory and democratic mechanism through which minority women can voice their needs can be developed through cross-cultural and bi-national studies. The laws of the country of origin, the reliability of social work and legal officers, the self-concept of the victimized woman within her cultural setting would all serve to better inform service providers of her specific needs. This would enable the identification of culturally viable and relevant models of intervention for such women, providing substantive protection of their rights.

---

[96] *See* Donna Sullivan, *Gender Equality and Religious Freedom: Toward a Framework for Conflict Resolution*, 24 N.Y. J. INT'L L. & POL. 795, 803 (1992).

Moreover, stakeholders including minority and immigrant women should be involved in the discussion. Without democratization, the viability of new intervention models as well as the principles of dignity, justice, and equality would be threatened. Focused research and careful design can help realize a vision of equality and constitutionalism that is not only gendered but also substantive and transformative.

19

Watch GRACE Grow

South African Customary Law and Constitutional Law in the Equality Garden

Jewel Amoah

The reputed reference to constitutions as "living trees" suggests that constitutional provisions grow and evolve in accordance with changing social, political, and legal contexts. As a living tree, a constitution is rooted in a nation's history and culture; it shapes the nation's future and influences the interaction of its citizens in the present. As the tree blossoms, it provides shade for those who seek refuge under the umbrella of constitutional protection. Constitutional jurisprudence is the fruit of careful judicial pruning and fertilizing of constitutional rights.

South Africa's 1996 Constitution[1] is heralded as one of the world's most progressive, and it is no exception to the living tree metaphor. Judicial interpretation and application of the Bill of Rights in South Africa's Constitution involves drawing from the deep roots of culture to harvest the fruit of a new country nourished by hope and sustained by the promise of equality. The living tree metaphor can be expanded to apply to African customary law as it also grows and develops with changing social context.

This chapter considers the living trees of the South African Constitution and customary law, as they exist in what is constructed herein as the Garden of Equality. The quest for equality is at the heart of the Constitution, and specific provision is made in Section 9 of the Constitution's Bill of Rights.[2] The metaphor of living trees in the Garden of Equality includes yet a third three. This third tree represents the

---

[1] S. Afr. Const. 1996.
[2] See id. s. 9.

   (1) Everyone is equal before the law and has the rights to equal protection and benefit of the law.
   (2) Equality includes the full and equal enjoyment of all rights and freedoms. To promote the achievement of equality, legislative and other measures designed to protect or advance persons, or categories of persons, disadvantaged by unfair discrimination may be taken.
   (3) The state may not unfairly discriminate directly or indirectly against anyone on one or more grounds, including race gender, sex, pregnancy, marital status, ethnic or social origin, colour, sexual orientation, age, disability, religion, conscience, belief, culture language and birth.

common law: the legislation and case law that govern the lives and interactions of South African citizens who are not otherwise governed by customary law. The Constitution provides that any discord between customary law and common law notions of equality be resolved by deference to the provisions and principles contained in the Constitution.

The vision of harmonious coexistence of the trees in the Garden of Equality advanced in this chapter is inspired by select equality rights jurisprudence from South Africa's Constitutional Court that reflects an inclination toward judicial development of customary law. This development provides an opportunity to bring customary law in line with contemporary notions of equality, and yet still preserve the distinct status of customary law. The development of customary law will ensure its continued existence and enhanced respect and consideration both within and outside of customary communities. The cases of *Bhe v. Khayelitsha Magistrate*[3] and *Shilubana v. Nwamitwa*[4] reflect multiple perspectives on how to negotiate between the common law and African customary law.

In relying on the metaphor of the Garden of Equality and the living trees of constitutional, common law, and customary law, this chapter develops and applies an analytical tool in the form of the acronym **GRACE**, to represent an African girl child whose gender, race, age, and culture intersect to impact on her experience of equality.[5] In proposing the Garden of Equality as a metaphorical tool to address GRACE's struggle for equality in contemporary South Africa, this chapter is divided into four parts. Part I examines the notion of intersectionality and explains why an intersectionality analysis is required to gain insight into who GRACE is and where she is situated in contemporary South African society, as well as to illustrate the value of an intersectionality analysis in securing GRACE's right to equality.

(4) No person may unfairly discriminate directly or indirectly against anyone on one or more grounds in terms of subsection (3). National legislation must be enacted to prevent or prohibit unfair discrimination.

(5) Discrimination on one or more of the grounds listed in subsection (3) is unfair unless it is established that the discrimination is unfair.

[3] *Bhe and Others v. Magistrate, Khayelitsha and Others (Commissioner for Gender Equality as Amicus Curiae); Shibi v Sithole and Others; South African Human Rights Commission and Another v. President of the Republic of South Africa and Another* 2005 (1) SA 580 (CC) [hereinafter *Bhe*].

[4] *Shilubana and Others v. Nwamitwa* 2009 (2) SA 66 (CC) [hereinafter *Shilubana*].

[5] GRACE is an analytical model developed by the author in the course of her doctoral dissertation, focusing on equality rights for the girl child under South African customary law. Reference to GRACE appears in previous published work, including Jewel Amoah, *At the Crossroads of Equality: The Convention on the Rights of the Child and the Intersecting Identities of GRACE, An African Girl Child,* in Proceedings of the Conference on the International Rights of the Child 313, 313–37 (Collins et al., eds., 2008); Jewel Amoah, *Building Sandcastles in the Snow: Meanings and Misconceptions of the Development of Black Feminist Theory in Canada,* in Theorizing Empowerment: Canadian Perspectives on Black Feminist Thought 95, 95–118 (Notisha Massquoi & Njoki Wane eds., 2007); Jewel Amoah, *The World on Her Shoulders: The Rights of the Girl-Child in the Context of Culture and Identity,* 4 Essex Hum. Rts. Rev. 1 (2007).

Part II briefly reviews select equality rights cases to demonstrate that the female perspective and influence is becoming an increasingly prominent factor in equality rights jurisprudence. Part III discusses legal pluralism and the coexistence of the common law and customary law in the Garden of Equality. Part IV explains that development of the customary law in accordance with equality principles in general, and the Constitution in particular, is vital for GRACE's enjoyment of equality.

I. INTERSECTIONALITY

The last decade of the twentieth century saw the emergence of Critical Race Theory, an American academic genre focusing on the intersection of race and sex, and the nature of the discrimination that is rooted in the intersection of these two aspects of identity.[6] In addition, Critical Race Feminism[7] examines the discrimination and oppression experienced by those whose racial identity along with their gender relegate them to the position of "other," and locates them at the margin rather than the (political, economic, and/or social) center of society. Intersectionality[8] was the term given to a method for identifying and addressing concurrent discrimination along these two axes of race and sex. The basic premise of intersectionality is that the world is experienced at the point where aspects of identity meet or intersect.[9] An intersectional analysis acknowledges that race and sex (as well as other identity

---

[6] *See* Kimberle Crenshaw, *Mapping the Margins: Intersectionality, Identity Politics, and Violence Against Women of Color*, 43 STAN. L. REV. 1241 (1991) [hereinafter Crenshaw, *Mapping the Margins*]; Kimberle Crenshaw, *Demarginalizing the Intersection of Race and Sex: A Black Feminist Critique of Antidiscriminatory Doctrine, Feminist Theory, and Antiracist Politics*, 1989 U. CHI. LEGAL F. 139; Paulette M. Caldwell, *A Hair Piece: Perspectives on the Intersection of Race and Gender*, 40 DUKE L. J. 365 (1991); Trina Grillo, *Anti-Essentialism and Intersectionality: Tools to Dismantle the Master's House*, 10 BERKELEY WOMEN'S L. J. 16 (1995).

[7] In explaining the origins of critical race feminism and where it is situated in the broad field of critical legal studies, Crooms says that

> Critical race feminism, as a legal theoretical stance, not only has roots in the oppositional discourses of Critical Legal Studies, Critical Race Theory, and Feminist Legal Theory, but also represents an analysis that is, itself, oppositional within these discourses. Its method includes multiple consciousness and a bottom-based focus, which illuminates the position of the ignored and disempowered to challenge the biases and privileges left unaddressed by Critical Legal Studies, Critical Race Theory, and Feminist Legal Theory.

Lisa A. Crooms, *Indivisible Rights and Intersectional Identities or "What Do Women's Human Rights Have to Do with the Race Convention,"* 40 HOWARD L. J. 619, 620 n.6 (1997).

Although Critical Race Theory and Critical Race Feminism are theoretical constructs of Western – primarily American – legal academics it will be argued that the principles of these theoretical constructs can be applied to an African human rights context. The reason for this transferability is that there is much commonality in theories and analysis related to addressing the framework of marginalization and disadvantage – much of this is able to transcend boundaries of culture and geography.

[8] Crenshaw, *Mapping the Margins, supra* note 6.

[9] Ideally, this meeting point is an intersection, a crossing, with one avenue/axis running through another, and it is unnecessary and impossible to determine which of the two avenues is the primary one.

factors) collectively impact upon the way one experiences the world, and the way one is perceived in the world.

Equality for GRACE, the African girl child, is an appropriate context to apply intersectionality as an analytical framework. The African girl child is, at one and the same time, African (which brings culture into the equation[10]), female (specifically gendered as a girl), and a child (under eighteen years of age). The African girl child who is the primary subject of this equality analysis is referred to herein as **GRACE**, a name that reflects the collective impact that **G**ender, **R**ace, **A**ge, and **C**ulture have on her experience of **E**quality in the world.

The intersectionality analysis is fundamental to explaining identity. Crenshaw describes her understanding of intersectionality as

> a provisional concept linking contemporary politics with postmodern theory. In mapping the intersections of race and gender, the concept does engage dominant assumptions that race and gender are essentially separate categories.... While the primary intersections that [are] explore[d] here are between race and gender, the concept can and should be expanded by factoring in issues such as class, sexual orientation, age and color.[11]

The acknowledgment that intersectionality can be expanded into multiple dimensions gives way to the notion of multiplicity. On the subject of multiplicity, culture[12] is an aspect of identity that intersects along with race, age, and gender to form a particular experience. However, it could also be considered that culture is not simply another aspect of intersecting identity, but rather, culture is the backdrop, or the dimension within which the intersection occurs. If culture is part of the intersectionality analysis, then culture – which would include customary law – is a necessary component of the attainment and enjoyment of equality for GRACE.

Where culture is an aspect of identity, Volpp explains that "[c]ulture is constantly negotiated and is multiple and contradictory. The culture we experience within a particular community will be specific and affected by our age, gender, class, race, disability status, and sexual orientation."[13] So, not only does culture affect identity,

---

[10] This emphasis on cultural location suggests that the African girl child is different from the Asian, American, or European girl child. This chapter seeks to demonstrate that this difference is a fundamental aspect of identity. It is an aspect that influences who one is as well as how one sees one's self in relation to others.

[11] Crenshaw, *Mapping the Margins*, *supra* note 6, at 1244–45 n. 9. This list of factors to which intersectionality applies is not exhaustive, and can also include disability and religion.

[12] Although culture is not specifically defined, for the purposes of this chapter, the dissenting judgment of Justice Ngcobo in *Bhe* attempts to give content and context to culture as it applies in that case. For the purposes of African customary law, the "concept of ubuntu – *umuntu ngumuntu ngabantu* – [is] a dominant value in African traditional culture. This concept encapsulates communality and the interdependence of the members of a community.... [I]t is a culture which regulates the exercise of rights by the emphasis it lays on sharing and co-responsibility and the mutual enjoyment of rights. It is this system of reciprocal duties and obligations that ensured that every family member had access to basic necessities of life such as food, clothing, shelter, and health care." *Bhe*, 2005 (1) SA ¶ 163.

[13] Leti Volpp, *Feminism versus Multiculturalism*, 101 COLUM. L. REV. 1181, 1192 (2001).

but aspects of identity also impact on the perception and experience of culture. In the case of GRACE, the African girl child, because culture and gender are so fundamental to her identity, any attempt to analyze this identity may result in what Volpp refers to as a battle between feminism and multiculturalism.[14] The juxtaposition of feminism and multiculturalism pits gender against culture. Such an oppositional framework leaves no room for the idea of cultural constructions of feminism or feminist constructions of culture – both of which are attainable through intersectionality.

II. REVIEW AND ANALYSIS OF SELECT SOUTH AFRICAN EQUALITY RIGHTS JURISPRUDENCE

A. *Common Law Interpretations of Gender-Equality Rights*

The cases discussed in this section reflect a challenge to gendered roles and perspectives. This challenge is based on constructing a notion of equality that embodies the full potential of the Constitution.

i. President of the Republic of South Africa v. Hugo[15]

Early in his term of presidency, Nelson Mandela, acting under powers provided for in the Constitution of the Republic of South Africa, 1993,[16] issued Presidential Act No. 17, providing for the release of certain categories of prisoners.[17] One of these categories was "mothers in prison on May 10, 1994, with minor children under the

---

[14] *See generally id.*
[15] *President of the Republic of South Africa v. Hugo* 1997 (6) BCLR 708 (CC) [hereinafter *Hugo*].
[16] S. AFR. (Interim) CONST. 1993, s. 82(1)(k). The 1993 Constitution is referred to as the Interim Constitution, and the 1996 Constitution is the Final Constitution.
[17] See *Hugo, supra* note 15 at ¶ 2. Presidential Act No. 17 provided that special remission of the remainder of their sentences would be granted to

> All persons under the age of eighteen (18) years who were or would have been incarcerated in 10 May 1994; (except those who had escaped and are still at large)

All mothers in prison on 10 May 1994, with minor children under the age of twelve (12) years; All disabled persons in prison on 10 May 1994 certified as disabled by a district surgeon.

Presidential Act No. 17 further provided that no special remission of sentence would be granted for the following offences:

murder
culpable homicide
robbery with aggravating circumstances
assault with intent to do grievous bodily harm
child abuse
rape
any other crimes of a sexual nature
trading in or cultivating dependence producing substances

age of twelve years." The effective date of May 10, 1994, was also the date on which
Nelson Mandela was inaugurated as South Africa's first Black African president,
signifying the dawn of a New South Africa: one that would no longer be shackled by
the injustices of racism and apartheid. The selection of certain categories of prisoners
to be released demonstrated an effort on the part of the government to give some
a second chance at a new life in the new South Africa. The rationale behind the
particular category of mothers of children under twelve years of age was "motivated
predominantly by a concern for children who had been deprived of the nurturing
and care which their mothers would ordinarily have provided."[18] This is not to say
that fathers did not have a role to play in the nurturing and care of children, but
that "there are only a minority of fathers who are actively involved in nurturing and
caring for their children, particularly their preadolescent children. There are, of
course, exceptions to this generalization, but the *de facto* situation in South Africa
is that mothers are the major custodians and the primary nurturers and care givers
of our nation's children."[19]

John Hugo challenged the pardon afforded to mothers of children under twelve
on the basis that it constituted discrimination on the ground of sex. He argued that
the pardon provided to mothers was an advantage that was not "afforded to fathers
of small children."[20] Only women who were parents of children under twelve were
released; women who did not have children were not released, and neither were
men, like Hugo, who were parents of children under twelve. In framing his claim of
discrimination, Hugo further argued that the Presidential Act provided for pardons
based on the intersecting identities of gender and parenthood of children under
twelve. John Hugo felt that he was disadvantaged by the law because he was not, nor
could he be, located at this particular intersection.

In writing for the majority, Justice Goldstone considered the affidavit evidence of
the president and child welfare experts in arguing that mothers played a particular
role in childrearing, and that the remission granted to women of children under
twelve was an effort to recognize this special role. The reasoning of the Constitutional
Court demonstrated that although Hugo could not locate himself at the targeted
intersection of sex and parenthood in order to receive early remission of his prison
sentence, this did not constitute unfair discrimination. The categories of remission established under the legislation represented broad generalizations; and as is
often the case with generalized categories where the majority is targeted, there is
often a minority who ought otherwise to qualify but does not fit within the parameters
of the generalizations. There was no outright entitlement to a remission of prison
sentence for Hugo, or for any of the mothers who fell properly within the category.
Hugo could not argue unfair discrimination on the basis of an advantage that he

[18]   *Id.* ¶ 36 (affidavit of Nelson Mandela).
[19]   *Id.* ¶ 36 (affidavit of Helen Starke, National Director of the South African National Council for Child
       and Family Welfare).
[20]   *Id.* ¶ 33.

was not in any event entitled to. The Constitutional Court reasoned that Hugo was not unfairly denied early release from prison, as the legislation provided that such release fell within the president's discretion. Moreover, granting remission of prison sentence to mothers of children under twelve did not prevent Hugo or anyone else from seeking an individual pardon from the president on compassionate grounds.

ii. Fraser v. Children's Court Pretoria North[21]

The *Fraser* case involved a challenge to Section 18(4)(d) of the Child Care Act[22] that required a Children's Court to obtain both parents' consent before it issued an adoption order of a "legitimate" child, but did not require the father's consent in the case of an "illegitimate" child. Lawrie Fraser was the unmarried father of a child put up for adoption by his former partner. The adoption application was granted by the Children's Court, but Fraser, who wanted to be able to adopt the child himself, applied to have it set aside.

The basis of the challenge begins with the distinction that is made between "legitimate" and "illegitimate" children. The definition of legitimacy in the Child Care Act included those children who were born of customary marriages in accordance with the Black Administration Act,[23] but excluded children born of Islamic marriages, as these were potentially polygamous marriages, and therefore not recognized unions.[24] In writing for a unanimous court, Justice Mohamed explained that the distinction made between children born of customary marriages (deemed legitimate) and children born of Islamic/religious marriages (deemed illegitimate) meant that "fathers of children born from Black customary unions have greater rights than similarly placed fathers of children born from marriages contracted according to the rites of religions such as Islam."[25] Apart from the distinction that is made between some marital unions, Justice Mohamed was of the opinion that the Child Care Act would in any event be in violation of the constitutional provision for equality in that it unfairly discriminated against certain fathers based on their gender and marital status. Regardless of whether the inequality is based on the form of union entered into by the parents, or whether it is based simply on gender and marital status, the Child Care Act hinged its need of parental consent to adoption on particular intersections. Lawrie Fraser did not fall within any of the identified intersections, but he successfully argued that his mere status as a parent – irrespective of his marital

---

[21] *Fraser v. Children's Court Pretoria North* 1996 (8) BCLR 1085; 1997 (2) SA 218 [hereinafter *Fraser*].

[22] Child Care Act 74 of 1983 s.18(4)(d).

[23] The Black Administration Act of 1927 provided much of the legislative foundation for the separate legal existence of South Africa's Black population. This act has been repealed on a piecemeal basis over the last decade concluding in 2011.

[24] Although the Recognition of Customary Marriages Act, Act 120 of 1998, had led to the formal recognition of customary law marriages, legislation to recognize Islamic marriages in South Africa has been drafted but not enacted.

[25] *Fraser, supra* note 21 at ¶ 23.

status – should entitle him to the opportunity to consent to (or refuse) the adoption of his own child.

This case raises similar issues of gender stereotype as were raised in *Hugo*, but the two cases differ with respect to the role of fathers in the lives of their children. Both *Hugo* and *Fraser* associate the equality rights being claimed by the father with the best interests of the child. Framing rights in this way reflects an acknowledgment that equality rights need not necessarily be based on the identity of the individual, but rather accrue to the individual by virtue of his or her position in a familial relationship. *Hugo* and *Fraser* dealt with equality rights challenges by men (fathers) to the way in which certain laws appointed rights to women. Successful in *Fraser*, but unsuccessful in *Hugo*, the male applicants challenged the legal locations of women at particular intersections and the exclusion of men from these intersections.

B. *Developing Equality Rights in African Customary Law*

The female equality rights applicants in the *Bhe* and *Shilubana* cases are located at the intersection of customary law and gender. Being located at an intersection of customary law at first instance disadvantages female claimants. However, the common disadvantage can be alleviated if the intersection is reconceptualized to promote equality rather than stay rooted in traditional constructions of inequality.

In customary law the family is the central unit of society. Attaining equality in a customary law context is largely dependent on one's identity or status within the family. Both *Bhe* and *Shilubana* challenge male primogeniture, a traditional customary law rule that succession occurs through the male line.[26] Historically, this rule was the best way of ensuring that male heirs would meet their responsibilities in caring for the deceased's family.[27] However, increasingly in modern times, there has been a movement away from the duties that are traditionally associated with succession.

iii. Bhe v. Khayelitsha

This case involves a constitutional challenge to the rule of male primogeniture as it applies in the African customary law of succession. The application in the *Bhe* case was brought on behalf of the two minor daughters of Ms. Nontupheko Bhe and Vuyo Mgolombane. Mr. Mgolombane died intestate in 2002. The couple had lived together from 1990 until the time of his death. Because no customary marriage

---

[26] For a thorough discussion of the customary law of succession, the history of the rule of male primogeniture and its evolving contemporary application, *see Bhe*, 2005 (1) SA ¶¶ 167–75 (Ngcobo, J., dissenting) and T. W. BENNETT, CUSTOMARY LAW IN SOUTHERN AFRICA 334–56 (2004).

[27] The same could not be said for female heirs, because traditionally women would leave their own families to take up residence with their husband's family. Thus a female heir could not guarantee that the property of the deceased would remain with the intended family.

union had taken place, Justice Langa, writing for the majority, found it necessary to include an analysis of the rights of the Bhe daughters as if they were deemed illegitimate. Similar to *Fraser*, the "legitimacy" of the child figures as an axis in the intersection, and impacts on the equality analysis and entitlement.

During the period of cohabitation, Ms. Bhe was a domestic worker and Mr. Mgolombane was a carpenter. They lived in a temporary informal shelter in Khayelitsha, Cape Town. Mr. Mgolombane obtained state housing subsidies that he used to purchase the property on which the family lived, as well as materials to build a house. At the time of his death, the youngest of the Bhe children lived with her parents in the temporary shelter, and the oldest child lived with Mr. Mgolombane's father, Maboyisi Mgolombane. The estate of the younger Mr. Mgolombane was comprised of the temporary informal shelter and the property on which it stood, and various items of movable property that Ms. Bhe and Mr. Mgolombane had acquired over the years, including the building materials for the house they intended to build. When Mr. Mgolombane died, his father, who lived several hundred kilometers away, was appointed representative and sole heir of his estate, in accordance with Section 23 of the Black Administration Act, the legislation governing private laws of Black South Africans. The elder Mr. Mgolombane indicated that he intended to sell the property to offset his son's funeral expenses. This decision did not seem to consider the consequences on Ms. Bhe and her daughter(s). In seeking to prevent the property's sale, Ms. Bhe argued that the automatic application of customary law and the rule of male primogeniture unfairly discriminated against her daughters by preventing them from inheriting their father's estate.

The majority judgment held that in light of the new era of nondiscrimination, estates that would previously have devolved according to the Black Administration Act and the customary law rule of male primogeniture must now devolve according to the Intestate Succession Act, which was the legislation that typically applied to estates that did not fall under customary law and consequently the jurisdiction of the Black Administration Act. Justice Langa was of the opinion that it was not the judiciary's responsibility to develop customary law. His solution was to remove the Bhe daughters from the operation of customary law in order to secure their right to equality. However, this has the effect of removing culture as an aspect of identity.

In dissent, Justice Ngcobo expressed that courts have a constitutional obligation to develop indigenous law to bring it in line with the Bill of Rights, in particular, the right to equality. He reasoned that the principle of primogeniture should not be struck down, but should be developed in line with the right to equality by allowing women to succeed the deceased. Development of the customary law as proposed by Ngcobo enables the judiciary to observe customary law practices as they are currently being applied in the communities. The resulting analysis likens the customary law to a living tree. Rather than being a system of rigid and archaic rules, which is not consistent with the contemporary notion of equality that pervades the Garden of

Equality, development of the customary law allows it to coexist with the common law in the same social context.

If the *Bhe* case were to be viewed as the fruit of judicial pruning within the Garden of Equality, then the result in the case reflects a careful balancing of "constitutional equality and rights to culture. The *Bhe* court engaged in a rights-balancing exercise, albeit one that places more weight on equality rights than rights to culture. . . . [T]his 'weighted balancing' is an appropriate approach that recognizes and values the positive aspects of culture but ultimately subjects that culture to foundational equality norms."[28] Without supplanting equality rights, the reasoning in *Bhe* reflects the special consideration and status that is increasingly being applied to culture.

In discussing what she terms the "weighted balancing" approach applied by the majority judgment in *Bhe*, Joanna Bond explains that such an approach is ideal because

> [i]t does not do so at the expense of women's equality rights. In addition, the rights-balancing approach allows judges to acknowledge the ways that customary law has changed over time. Judges who reject a rigid rights-trumping approach may, when appropriate, recognize the "living" customary law and the ways in which it conforms to human rights standards.[29]

Bond is correct in that the weighted balancing approach is laudable for the promotion it gives to women's cultural rights; however, even if these cultural rights are trumped by equality, this approach does have its shortcomings. The weighted balancing approach is still somewhat artificial, in that it is a method of analysis that is conducted in a system foreign to the customary law community. A more appropriate method of analysis would allow for the development of customary law, such that the balancing approach is done at the community level and not by the judiciary, whose members are removed from the community.

Although the Constitutional Court's result was favorable for the Bhe family applicants, the process was less than ideal as considerations of equality and culture were imposed on the community from outside rather than negotiated within the community itself. The further removed the equality consideration is from the affected community, the less likely that the proper balance is given to contemporary community constructions of culture and equality – both of which are located at particular intersections within a community and influence the identities of the citizens of that community. Even if for reasons of conflict of interest, the community itself is not able to come up with a desirable situation – which may for instance be the case if there is a split in the community with respect to weight that should be afforded to traditional interpretations of culture vis-à-vis contemporary notions of equality – it would be appropriate to have the matter determined by the local magistrate. This

[28] Johanna E. Bond, *Constitutional Exclusion and Gender in Commonwealth Africa*, 31 FORDHAM INT'L L. J. 289, 336–7 (2008).
[29] *Id.* at 340.

was the order of progression of events in the *Bhe* case. However, when the magistrate's decision to strictly interpret the historical notion of the primogeniture rule as permitting the Bhe daughters to be disinherited, notwithstanding the new era of equality in South Africa, it was clear that this decision could not go unchallenged. Nelson Tebbe argues that the magistrate erred by not applying "the rules of succession with sensitivity to the social context." He argues that the eventual ruling prevented parliamentary debate that might have led to a "workable compromise between customary law and the equality provisions of the constitution."[30]

Had the magistrate taken note of the developments in customary law Tebbe suggests, then there may not have been such a fracas around the issue of judicial development of the customary law. Instead, what may have happened is that there would have been the quiet fertilizing of the customary law tree, to enable it to bloom to its full potential within the Garden of Equality.

On the surface, the tension in *Bhe* is best described as being between gender equality – as in the rights of the Bhe girl children to inherit from their father versus strict observance of the traditional customary law rule of male primogeniture – as in the rights of the grandfather to have sole discretion to dispose of his son's property, without any obligation toward the well-being of the wife and children left behind. But the issues and the tension at play here are so much more complex than what this binary oppositional framework suggests. The complexity that arises from the *Bhe* case is not simply about a choice between culture and gender equality, but rather about how best to incorporate and balance these rights in the fragmented identities of the citizens of South Africa.

A full intersectional approach is suggested as a means to address this fragmentation. Intersectionality provides for the coexistence of competing rights and interests (such as gender and culture), yet it does not require that one be chosen over the other. Justice Ngcobo's dissent, although not a perfect reflection of an intersectionality approach, is not a hard binary choice of one over the other. Justice Ngcobo argued that the court had

> an obligation to apply customary law and to participate in the development of customary law in a way that was consistent with the Constitution. Instead of striking down the rule of primogeniture altogether, he would have modified the customary law rule to preserve inheritance by the eldest child, thus allowing female as well as male children to succeed to the position of family head. This interpretation of customary law, in his view, would preserve the valuable function of the customary successor while eliminating the gender discriminatory aspects of the rule.[31]

---

[30] Nelson Tebbe, *Inheritance and Disinheritance: African Customary Law and Constitutional Rights,* J. RELIGION 466 at 492 (2008).

[31] Tracy E. Higgins, Jeanmarie Fenrich, & Ziona Tanzer, *Gender Equality and Customary Marriage: Bargaining in the Shadow of Post-Apartheid Legal Pluralism,* 30 FORDHAM INTL L. J. 1653, 1667 (2007).

In seeking to modify or develop customary law to acknowledge and reflect contemporary practice as opposed to traditional strongholds, Justice Ngcobo's dissent reflects
a harmonious rather than a hierarchical approach to competing rights. Higgins,
Fenrich, and Tanzer refer to this hierarchical approach as the "choice paradigm."[32]
In instances where an intersectional approach requires some element of choice, it
is not a choice between entities where there is a hierarchical construction of preference, but rather the choice may be one of necessity of outcome. In this analytical
process, all intersecting identity factors are considered, as are the consequences of a
particular choice.

iv. Shilubana and Others v. Nwamitwa[33]

Like *Bhe*, the issue in *Shilubana* involved the right to succession. However, in
this case, it was succession to the title and office of chief. The facts of the case
span four decades, during which time there were changes in community practice
and ideology as well as the law and ideology of South Africa itself. Also similar to
Bhe, the *Shilubana* case involved a battle between family members with respect
to the equality principles in the Constitution and the principle of male preference
that is the foundation of the customary law rule of primogeniture. The analysis in
Shilubana is not simply a matter of equality trumping culture, but one of discerning
the precise content of the equality and cultural rights for the community concerned.

In 1968, Ms. Shilubana's father, Hosi Fofoza Nwamitwa of the Valoyi community,
died without a male heir. As customary law at the time did not permit a woman to
become Hosi,[34] Ms. Shilubana did not succeed him although she was his eldest
child. Instead, Hosi Fofoza was succeeded by his brother, Richard Nwamitwa.
During 1996 and 1997, the traditional authorities of the Valoyi community passed
resolutions deciding that Ms. Shilubana would succeed Hosi Richard, because in the
new constitutional era women were equal to men and so gender should no longer
be a bar to chieftainship. However, following the death of Hosi Richard in 2001,
Sidwell Nwamitwa, son of Hosi Richard and cousin to Ms. Shilubana, challenged
her succession. Sidwell claimed that the tribal authorities had acted unlawfully and
that he, as Hosi Richard's eldest son, was entitled to succeed his father.

In writing for the full court, Judge Van Der Westhuizen recognized that the community itself had incorporated the spirit and principles of the new constitutional era
into its practices, by appointing Ms. Shilubana as chief. In this case, the judicial
development of customary law simply involved acknowledging the application of
equality that was currently taking place at the community level. This approach is

---

[32] *Id.* at 1664 and 1691–3.

[33] *Shilubana and Others v. Nwamitwa*, 2009 (2) SA 66 (CC).

[34] A Hosi is a chief or traditional leader.

considerably less intrusive than what was adopted in *Bhe*, as it reflects an acknowledgment by the judiciary that the courts might not be in the best position to determine
the practices and intentions of the community. By giving primary consideration to
what is actually going on in the community and acknowledging the adoption and
application of constitutional equality rights by the community, the judgment serves
to elevate the status of culture.

Shilubana did not involve a binary matter of culture versus equality, but rather,
judicial consideration of the extent to which one is reflected in the other. There is a
recognized intersection between the cultural practices of the community and its own
willingness to adapt these practices in keeping with new constitutional principles.
Such development of customary law at the community level alleviates the need
for judicial development of customary law to be imposed on the community. The
Constitutional Court in *Shilubana* noted that when fulfilling its role as the final
arbiter of customary law and equality principles, deference should be given to what
is actually taking place at the community level.[35]

If customary law is understood as a life force that grows and develops along with
the people whose lives it governs, then it is seen as something to be negotiated with, as
opposed to a stagnant, ossified concept that is superseded by contemporary notions
of equality. "Customary law is an independent and original source of law. Like
the common law it is adaptive by its very nature. By definition then, while change
annihilates custom as a source of law, change is intrinsic to and can be invigorating of
customary law."[36] The adaptability of customary law enables it to be more responsive
to and reflective of changing social, political, and environmental contexts than the
common law. This adaptability was demonstrated in the decision of the Valoyi
community to embrace the possibility of a female Hosi – a concept reflective of
both the traditional royal bloodline, as well as the constitutional principles of gender
equality.

Development of the customary law is an ongoing process, and the judiciary must
be ever vigilant to discern and apply the relevant customary law for the community
at issue. Such vigilance is done in recognition that

> [t]he destructiveness of apartheid in South Africa has left the country with daunt-
> ing social welfare problems that demand urgent attention. To ensure the efficient
> administration of justice, while at the same time guaranteeing a right to culture,
> the architects of the new order should follow an integration model. This approach
> requires the greatest possible integration of customary law and the [common]
> law.... [L]egal integration is more viable in the near future because it will bring
> together laws of diverse origins without destroying them and minimize social dis-
> location. Legal integration would allow the varying laws to continue to exist, but
> would standardize their effects and remove conflicts among them.[37]

[35] *Shilubana, supra* note 33 ¶ 49.
[36] *Id.* ¶ 54.
[37] Lynn Berat, *Customary Law in a New South Africa: A Proposal*, 15 FORDHAM INT'L L. J. 92, 124 (1992).

This desired integration is dependent on open channels of communication between the judiciary, which imposes an official, tangible character on the law, and the community, which is responsible for the lived reality of the law.

III. LEGAL PLURALISM

Legal pluralism is akin to the Garden of Equality in that both provide for a legal landscape in which various normative orders, such as customary law and the common law, can coexist.

Unlike the common law, as reflected in case law, or codified in legislation, customary law is not readily discernible and ascertainable to those other than to whom it is intended to directly apply. Customary law reflects a community code: it is a system of beliefs and practices developed by the community, applied and interpreted by the community and adapted, where necessary, by the community. As Bennett explains, "Customary law derives from social practices that the community concerned accepts as obligatory."[38] This element of obligation implies that customary law is more than a series of community beliefs and observations; it is a system of laws by which community members must abide or face appropriate sanction. Because customary law is a creation of the community in which it resides, it is not directly accessible to outsiders.[39] Anyone seeking to discover a particular customary law can only do so through a method of questioning community members or by closely observing the activities of members of the community. Such social science methods of fact determination result in "a construction of reality that is coloured by the preconceptions of the informants and the researchers."[40]

African customary law "primarily regulates personal, familial issues, or relationships between private persons. It consists of largely unwritten rules or laws that may be applied informally by traditional leaders or, in some cases, by the courts."[41] The regulation of personal and family issues constitutes a broad range of issues related to the day-to-day lives of community members. Traditional gender roles that become part of habitual community practice and identity are often hard to alter. Customary law is typically no exception. *Shilubana* is unique for its reflection of a community that saw the gender inequality inherent in its customary law and took steps to correct it. The problem arose where those who sought to maintain the gender inequality for their own benefit challenged the right of the community to progressively develop its own laws to conform to modern social context. Higgins et al. demonstrate that

---

[38] BENNETT, *supra* note 26, at 1.

[39] A. J. Kerr argues that "few courts can feel confident that they are able to correctly determine what a particular rule of customary law is, . . . because the courts do not have access to all the sources of customary law." A. J. Kerr, *The Role of Courts in Developing Customary Law*, 1999 OBITER 41, 44.

[40] BENNETT, *supra* note 26, at 1.

[41] Bond, *supra* note 28, at 296.

[t]he resistance of customary practices to legal regulation stems in part from the very wide acceptance – if not endorsement – of such practices by people living under customary law. Approximately twenty million South Africans live under traditional authority in rural areas. In urban areas, though formally under the jurisdiction of district courts and municipal and state authority, most African people still consider themselves living within the fold of tradition.[42]

Although historically, the formation and application of customary law did not include input from women in the community, women have spearheaded contemporary efforts to incorporate equality principles into customary law. In both the *Bhe* and *Shilubana* cases, the named litigants were women – women seeking the assistance of the courts in promoting and protecting their right to equality within a customary law context. Apart from initiating the litigation, women's groups and gender-equality advocates were also included as secondary parties and *amicus curiae* in these cases.[43] In commenting on the sense of empowerment to be garnered from broader female participation in the *Bhe* litigation, Johanna Bond states that the case

represents significant progress for the many women who are subject to customary law in South Africa. It reminds us that when women have the opportunity to promote gender equality from within their cultural communities, they will use the constitution, among other things, to do so. The constitution becomes an important, although not the only, vehicle through which to redefine and reshape cultural meaning, allowing women to challenge dominant cultural norms without abandoning culture altogether. Constitutional agency thus provides women a voice and often initiates a societal dialogue about shared norms and values.[44]

Customary law can be defined in terms of what characteristics of the common law it does not possess. This method posits the common law as the benchmark for a workable system of laws, and anything that deviates from this is considerably less workable and less valuable. This highlights one of the key aspects of customary law: it is typically only considered valuable to those who operate within it. Outsiders, who cannot appreciate its various nuances and hold it up against the benchmark of Western-styled common law systems do not appreciate the inherent value and worth of customary law. This problem is magnified when a Western-styled and influenced judiciary attempts to interpret and develop customary law.

In theory, legal pluralism provides for the coexistence of both the common law and customary law. However, in practice, this is not a coexistence of equals. Although legal pluralism is touted as a means of promoting the existence of customary law, and recognizing its importance in various facets of the lives of the majority of South

---

[42] Higgins, Fenrich, & Tanzer, *supra* note 31, at 1697–8.
[43] In *Bhe*, 2005 (1) SA the Women's Centre Legal Trust and the Commission for Gender Equality were listed as parties. In *Shilubana*, 2009 (2) SA the National Movement of Rural Women and the Commission for Gender Equality were listed as parties.
[44] Bond, *supra* note 28, at 329.

Africans, legal pluralism functions as a means of reinforcing the hierarchy between the common law and customary law. The increasing recognition of the impact of customary law on the majority of South Africans, and as reflected in the *Shilubana* judgment, the willingness of the judiciary to acknowledge the community's role in developing customary law, suggests that there is a movement toward deference to the community perspective – at least where discerning customary law is concerned.

Even though the South African Constitution recognizes and protects customary law,[45] it is also important that the community safeguard its own law. Customary law can be more reflective of equality rights than the common law, given the ease and speed with which customary law can be adapted. As was evident in the *Shilubana* case, there are instances where the community itself is able to identify and adapt to gender-equality principles. Where this is not the case, and change is reluctant to come from within the community, then redress can be sought from the judiciary. Although this is an increasingly relied-upon method, it is not the most desirable because it does not come directly from the community. If women in the community had a greater opportunity to contribute to the development of customary law in their communities, recourse to the judiciary for the recognition and enforcement of equality rights would become an option of last resort.

Although women's participation in the development of customary law is desirable, it is not always practical. In seeking to incorporate principles of gender equality into customary law, women often have to choose between their culture and their gender. This notion of binary choice leaves little room to recognize that most women reside at the intersection of both. Seeking to infuse equality into customary law should not be described as a choice of one system over the other, but rather an attempt to create an option that is truly reflective of and responsive to the various intersecting identities of the contemporary African woman who lives subject to customary law. This woman may be a housewife, or a teacher, or an engineer or lawyer. She has benefited from the progress and advancements of contemporary society, and she is able to govern her private family matters in accordance with customary law. She should not be disadvantaged for living in plural societies – instead, she should reap the benefits of a plural legal system that supports the dual character of her life. In supporting this duality, Nyamu explains that

> [i]n plural contexts, responses to cultural legitimization of gender hierarchy must take account of the symbiotic relationship between formal law and culture and the role of formal institutions in the shaping of culture. Formal law may lend a natural appearance to dominant articulations of custom, and custom may be invoked to lend legitimacy to formal law. The symbiotic relationship between law and custom

---

45 S. AFR. CONST. 1996 s. 211 (3) reads: "The Courts must apply customary law when that law is applicable, subject to the Constitution and any legislation that specifically deals with customary law."

is exemplified by the special accommodation of customary laws in the national constitution of some African countries.[46]

Where the relationship is not symbiotic and culture and the constitution do not mutually to feed off of one another, but are instead in a constant battle to assert their hierarchy, Banda explains that

> [f]rom an African women's perspective one of the problems of the whole human rights enterprise is the individualized nature of human rights. Women in many parts see themselves and are identified as being part of a collective.[47]

The choice between customary law and the common law is often a matter of the community versus the individual. A truly plural system that is reflective of an intersectionality analysis will help to alleviate this individual versus group dilemma by allowing the respective rights to coexist rather than compete with one another.

IV. THE GROWING STATUS OF CUSTOMARY LAW IN THE GARDEN OF EQUALITY

The attainment of substantive equality for GRACE requires that considerations of customary law as part of her cultural context be informed by an intersectional analysis. Customary law exists in the Garden of Equality alongside the common law. Although this coexistence takes place with a presumed deference to the constitutional principles that laden the branches of the constitutional tree, there is no readily discernible hierarchy within the Garden. The harmony as opposed to hierarchy that exists in the Garden is reflective of the intersections of the common law, constitution, and customary law that impact on the daily lives of many South Africans. The true attainment of equality in this society of intersecting laws may require that GRACE be able to exercise the choice to move within and between systems; just as one meanders through the different paths in a garden, there must be a similar flexibility to shift between systems of law.

This flexibility, however, cannot be without its certainties. The coexistence of the common law and customary law provides an element of choice, but this choice is also predicated on patterns of predictability. Johanna Bond explains that meandering through the garden and systems of law is not unheard of, and in fact it provides a way for women and girls to seek to apply their own sense of self-determination to attain equality.

> Throughout much of Commonwealth Africa, women have the power to exit their cultural communities. In many countries, a woman may, for example, marry according to statutory law; she may choose to abandon other aspects of custom as

---

[46] Celestine I. Nyamu, *How Should Human Rights and Development Respond to Cultural Legitimization of Gender Hierarchy in Developing Countries?*, 41 HARV. INT'L L. J. 381,417 (2004).

[47] Fareda Banda, *Global Standards: Local Values*, 17 INT'L J. L. POL'Y & FAM. 1, 15 (2003).

well. Other women may cherish aspects of their cultural identity and community but seek equality *within* that community. These women who seek change without exiting their cultural communities must have the option of using the constitution to redefine personal and customary law in a way that reflects equality norms.[48]

What Bond describes as the redefinition of personal and customary law is essentially about choice as to how one will navigate a path through the Garden of Equality. Where the rights claimant is unable to make this choice for herself, or has been denied the privilege of choice by the power system within her own community, then it is appropriate for judicial intervention to develop the customary law in a way that permits blending of the various systems of law. Judicial development of customary law is not about replacing it with the common law, but rather about interpreting it consistently with the Constitution, yet still permitting the character of the customary law to be evident. In this way, the cultural link, familiarity, and acceptance between an equality rights claimant such as GRACE and her customary law community are maintained. The unique character of customary law is that it is by its nature "a constantly evolving system. In the past this development was frustrated and customary law stagnated. This stagnation should not continue, and the free development by communities of their own laws to meet the needs of a rapidly changing society must be respected and facilitated."[49]

The *Bhe* and *Shilubana* cases address a choice of gender equality in keeping with the Constitution, over culture rights reflected in customary law. The inference in this is that a preference for culture or customary law is a choice against equality. This translates to a choice between culture and equality, and suggests that the two concepts cannot coexist. This suggestion is of course highly controversial. In commenting on the *Bhe* case, Johanna Bond cautions against a straight binary (or hierarchical) selection of gender over culture. Instead, she stresses that what is needed is more of a careful balancing approach, which may tip the scales slightly in favor of one element, while still acknowledging the importance of the other element. Bond explains that such an approach "reflects an intersectional understanding of identity, one that perceives women [and girls] as potentially rights-seeking feminists and as members of cultural communities."[50] In this balanced approach, gender rights are not necessarily preferred over cultural rights, but rather, gender rights are seen to inform tradition and culture, such that there is a distinct cultural component to gender-equality rights. Such a balancing approach will hopefully spawn a "commitment to the positive aspects of culture without pandering to custom and tradition. It will value customary law but require that customary law conform to individual rights and guarantees."[51]

---

[48] Bond, *supra* note 28, at 332–3.
[49] *Shilubana supra* note 33 ¶ 45.
[50] Bond, *supra* note 28, at 340.
[51] *Id.* at 340–1.

Contrary to this balancing approach, which uses constitutional principles as the arbiter in the prioritizing of equality rights over cultural rights, Omotola argues that the problem lies in the constitutional provisions themselves. Omotola argues that constitutions, as creations of Western culture and Western law, pose a significant threat to the future of African customary law. She argues that African governments should focus more on maintaining African culture by preventing constitutional provisions that override it.[52]

Nelson Tebbe offers yet another approach to resolving the battle between gender equality and cultural rights. Tebbe proposes

> a more gradual and deliberative process in Parliament, in local and provincial governments, and, most critically, in African communities themselves. Courts have an important role to play in ensuring that progressive constitutional commitments to equality and dignity are ultimately enforced.... Yet widespread and lasting acceptance of egalitarian values may best be achieved not through imposition by unelected judges but instead through democratic advocacy and local deliberation. Low-level constitutionalism may be particularly appropriate in the case of customary law, which purports to reflect the evolving norms of living people.[53]

Such an approach acknowledges and respects the need for community participation in the process of developing the customary law. At the same time, it incorporates a modern deference to entrenched democratic processes. This approach was evident in the *Shilubana* case, which

> suggests that traditional communities may well be willing to adapt customary law to the core principles of the constitutional democracy. If that is so, then progressive jurists might be wise to encourage the internal development of indigenous law in an egalitarian direction, at least in the first instance, rather than imposing it from the outside using the force of government and power.[54]

The "progressive" work of the Valoyi community in *Shilubana* only came to light because it was challenged from within. It is possible that many communities have adopted a similarly progressive approach to developing the customary law in line with the Constitution, but such development is not publicized outside of the community, because it has been relatively uncontroversial. The quiet acquiescence of the blending of customary law and constitutional principles is akin to a pleasant walk through the Garden of Equality. The Garden of Equality is a space in which the trees of constitutional law, common law, and customary law exist and flourish together and have the ability to produce fruit to nourish and sustain those who draw from the garden. GRACE's enjoyment of the Garden of Equality is enhanced by

---

[52] Jelili Omotola, *Promogeniture and Illegitimacy in African Customary Law: The Battle for Survival of Culture*, 15 INDIANA INT'L & COMP. L. REV. 115, 144 (2004).

[53] Tebbe, *supra* note 30, at 469, 495.

[54] *Id.* at 488.

the ability and willingness of the judiciary to develop the particular customary law rule at issue. The development of customary law, and the consequent respect for this system of law in contemporary society, has the effect of safeguarding GRACE's right to equality while maintaining her culture and her identity.

CONCLUSION

Gender-equality rights case law in South Africa has evolved from claims for male access to ameliorative programs to particularized claims for gender-equality rights within a customary law context. The reliance on such a context necessarily introduces an element of tension between cultural rights and gender-equality rights. Although cultural rights are presumed to have as much weight and import as equality rights, cultural rights are not completely synonymous with customary law. The obligation on courts to apply customary law where appropriate is found in Section 211(3) of the Constitution, and this obligation itself cautions that the application of customary law is subject to the Constitution. It all seems a bit circular, but any development of customary law is not so much about developing an independent system of laws and principles, but rather about adapting this system to conform to the Constitution.

The preservation of the customary law depends on recognition of its inherent ability to develop and change with social context. Adherence to customary law in this form is truly reflective of a democratic constitutionalism process, where those whose lives are most affected by the law are given an opportunity to offer their contemporary interpretations of that customary law, in light of the constitutional provision for equality.

Culture can function as either the backdrop to the intersection or as an axis of the intersection itself. For purposes of this chapter, culture is the contextual background for the identity of GRACE, the African girl child. Bearing in mind the notion of multiplicity, and the multiple dimensions on which the identity operates, culture is not a flat or stagnant background. But rather, culture is broad and it is deep, and it is fluid. It brings dynamism to the context of identity.

The Garden of Equality is an idyllic place for GRACE to explore the full benefits of equality that come with an understanding of her intersecting identity. This can easily be done if the judiciary continues to not only develop the customary law, but also to acknowledge and respect development of customary law that takes place at the community level. Such development will enable the customary law tree to blossom and bear the life-sustaining fruit of equality. In this way, the idyllic is also possible.

20

Critical Multiculturalism

Vrinda Narain

A policy of multiculturalism is an integral part of the state's commitment to protecting group life. Yet, it also tests the limits of accommodation and interrogates the state's own ideology and its adherence to principles of equality and religious freedom. In multiculturalism policies, the status of women has been a common site of contestation and negotiation. Practices such as veiling, underage marriage, polygamy, and religious family law test the limits of tolerance. Debates around gender in the politics of difference serve simultaneously to name certain communities as backward and majority culture as the norm. A feminist critique of multiculturalism is critical to bring hidden perspectives into the dialogue between the community and the state, to highlight the gendered dimension of this issue, and to ensure that the community and state include subaltern voices in their dialogue on the accommodation of difference.

In this chapter, I discuss the idea of critical multiculturalism to better understand how pluralist democracies can formulate a policy that respects group difference while upholding gender equality. I consider these issues through the lens of Muslim women who are situated at the intersection of a religious community and secular state, making them a compelling category of analysis. Muslim women experience discrimination along multiple axes – as women, as Muslims, and as Muslim women. Their situation illustrates the paradox of multicultural vulnerability where the state's commitment to protecting minority rights can result in subordinating women's interests within the group. This raises questions of state legitimization of a differentiated citizenship through the creation of a parallel system of law that is explicitly discriminatory.

I argue that it is necessary to craft an understanding of multicultural citizenship that allows for the possibility of difference without exclusion and pluralism, and without a totalizing narrative. Rather than a simplistic acknowledgment of cultural relativism that may justify all manner of subordination, multiculturalism has to be reimagined in a way that brings a fresh perspective to rearticulating women's rights, a perspective that crafts meaningful responses to women's exclusion from equal citizenship and that evaluates the potential of constitutional rights as the legitimate arena in which to reclaim women's selfhood.

The contemporary context in which debates about multiculturalism are taking place is one of increasing anti-Muslim prejudice, a fear of the "Other," and anxieties about illiberal practices that immigrants bring to mainstream society.[1] In India, minority rights discussions focus on Muslim minority rights in particular singling out Muslim personal law as backward and in need of reform. This focus on the Other obfuscates issues of concern within mainstream society such as systemic discrimination, and structural inequality. At the same time, this focus is one-dimensional in that it deals only with discussions on the politics of cultural difference rather than examinations of the exclusion of minorities because of structural injustices such as racism, unemployment, and lack of access to education and justice.[2] The purpose here is to engage in critical reflections on the issues implicated, acknowledging the fraught political context.

I. THE LOCATION OF MUSLIM WOMEN

The Constitution of India guarantees equality and freedom from discrimination.[3] It also guarantees religious freedom and the protection of minority rights.[4] In sharp contrast to these equality guarantees, Muslim women are subject to explicit

---

[1] Will Kymlicka, *The New Debate on Minority Rights* (and Postscript), *in* MULTICULTURALISM AND POLITICAL THEORY 25, 54 (Anthony Simon Laden et al. eds., Cambridge University Press, 2007).

[2] Joan W. Scott, *Multiculturalism and the Politics of Identity*, *in* 61 OCTOBER 12, 13 (Summer 1992), reprinted in THE IDENTITY IN QUESTION 3 (John Rajchman ed., Routledge 1995).

[3] INDIA CONST arts. 12–35. The fundamental rights are provided in Part III of the Constitution in Articles 12 through 35. Article 14: Equality before law. – The State shall not deny to any person equality before the law or equal protection of the laws within the territory of India. *Id.* art. 14

The relevant provisions of Article 15 are: A.15. – Prohibition of discrimination on the grounds of religion, race, caste, sex, or place of birth. – (1) The State shall not discriminate against any citizens on grounds only of religion, race, caste, sex, place of birth or any of them.... (3) Nothing in this article shall prevent the State from making any special provision for women and children. (4) Nothing in this article or in clause (2) of article 29 shall prevent the State from making any special provision for the advancement of any socially or educationally backward classes of citizens or for Scheduled Castes and Scheduled Tribes. *Id.* arts. 15(1), (3), & (4).

[4] *Id.* art. 25. Freedom of conscience and free profession, practice and propagation of religion. – (1) Subject to public order, morality and health and to other provisions of this Part [The fundamental rights chapter] all persons are equally entitled to freedom of conscience and the right freely to profess, practice and propagate religion. – (2) Nothing in this article shall affect the operation of any existing law or prevent the State from making any law – (a) regulating or restricting any economic, financial, political or other secular activity which may be associated with religious practice; (b) providing for social welfare and reform or the throwing open of Hindu religious institutions of a public character to all classes and sections of Hindus.

discrimination in the family, which is regulated by religious personal laws.[5] These laws discriminate on the basis of both religion and gender. The religious personal laws are justified under the right to religious freedom and the state's commitment to protecting group life. This explicitly discriminatory system and the contradictions between public formal equality and private discrimination are a compelling demonstration of the reluctance of the state to uphold gender equality when it is presumed to conflict with group interests. In this way, then, the public–private dichotomy underpins the religious–secular binary, where the state is committed to a policy of secularism in the public sphere but does not interfere with religious law in the private sphere, even when these laws conflict with constitutional guarantees. Indeed, for Muslim women, cultural relativism seems to be equality's nemesis.[6] Muslim women are simultaneously included and excluded from equal citizenship, as the state's guarantee of equality does not extend to the private sphere of the family. Thus Muslim women are explicitly discriminated against within the family, and the state does nothing to enforce constitutional guarantees of equal citizenship in the family as part of its commitment to multiculturalism, which includes accommodating Muslim group rights.

The state has created a differentiated citizenship whereby it has differing obligations and duties to citizens based on both gender and religious identity. This was illustrated by the controversial *Shah Bano* case and the subsequent enactment of the Muslim Women's Protection of Rights on Divorce Act.[7] The *Shah Bano* case, dealing with spousal support for divorced Muslim women, brought postcolonial India to the brink of a constitutional crisis.[8] Shah Bano was a seventy-three-year-old Muslim woman whose husband left her. She then sued him for spousal support under India's secular law and was successful.[9] However, her husband then divorced her unilaterally under the Muslim personal law. Mohammed Ahmed Khan appealed the support order, claiming that as a Muslim he was not required to pay support for more than forty days and that the religious personal law absolved him of all support duties beyond this period known as *iddat*. The Supreme Court, however, ruled in Shah Bano's favor. This provoked a strong reaction from religious leaders who were unwilling to enlarge women's rights and who characterized the Supreme Court decision as an unwarranted interference in the Muslim personal law that violated Muslim minority rights and religious freedom. The religious leaders prevailed, and the government of that time abrogated the Supreme Court decision and enacted a new law, regulating Muslim women's access to spousal support, that absolved

5 Family relations in India are governed by religious personal laws, which are laws based on religious norms and rules, common law precedent, custom and tradition, as well as legislated initiatives. These are the only laws in India that apply on the basis of religious identity.
6 Beverley Baines, *Equality's Nemesis?*, 5(1) J. L. & EQUALITY 57 (2006).
7 *Mohammed Ahmed Khan v. Shah Bano Begum*, A.I.R. 1985 S.C. 945.
8 Zakia Pathak & Rajeswari Sunder Rajan, *Shah Bano*, 14 SIGNS 558, 558 (1989).
9 CODE CRIM. PROC., § 125 (India).

husbands of the duty to support; this moved Muslim women further away from equal citizenship.[10]

This case resonated far beyond the courtroom and the classroom, raising questions of gender justice, minority rights, and the accommodation of difference. It tested constitutional rights and fundamental organizing principles of India's multicultural democracy – secularism, religious freedom, and women's equality. The state absolved itself of responsibility for enforcing constitutional principles in the "private sphere" of the family, abandoning Muslim women to greater regulation by male religious leaders. The *Shah Bano* controversy tells us about the limits of constitutional rights and their emancipatory potential. It also tells us of the danger of an uncritical accommodation of difference and the paradox of multicultural vulnerability.

In Canada, more recently, the Sharia law debates raised similar questions on the appropriate role of the state, the perceived tension between religious freedom and gender equality, and the accommodation of difference. In 2003, there was a proposal by Syed Mumtaz Ali, a retired lawyer and one of the founders of the Islamic Institute of Civil Justice, that Muslims should use the Ontario Arbitration Act to set up a form of Sharia court to regulate family relations according to Muslim law. A number of Canadian feminist organizations and Canadian Muslim feminist organizations responded to this proposal by expressing their concern for women's rights. The Ontario government appointed former Attorney General Marion Boyd to conduct a study. The Boyd Report recommended the introduction of faith-based arbitration for Muslims using Sharia Muslim law.[11] Women's groups lobbied strongly against the Report's recommendations and ultimately Ontario Premier Dalton McGuinty announced a ban on all religious family arbitration.

My interest in foregrounding these two examples is to illustrate the way in which mainstream narrative frames and constructs the figure of Muslim women as the Other. Focusing on the complex interface between public and private law and the impact of constitutional law on women's rights in the family, I am interested in better understanding the ways pluralist democracies seek to balance seemingly competing rights of religious freedom, gender equality, and minority rights. The *Shah Bano* case and the Sharia law proposal put women in the position of choosing between their rights and their religion and served to reinforce either/or binaries. Particularly in the context of the aftermath of 9/11, anti-Muslim sentiment has caused anxiety among Muslim communities. Inevitably, a politicized religious identity is an inextricable part of the defensive reaction of minority groups to perceived and real majority hostility.

---

[10] The Muslim Women's (Protection of Rights on Divorce) Act, 1986 (Act No. 25 of 1986), Gazette of India, Extraordinary, pt. 2, sec. 1 (May 19, 1986).
[11] MARION BOYD, DISPUTE RESOLUTION IN FAMILY LAW: PROTECTING CHOICE, PROMOTING INCLUSION (Ontario Attorney General 2004).

In postcolonial India, the question of women's rights was framed as central to the modernizing project of nationalism. The construction of the modern Indian woman as a sign of civilizational advance was the self-conscious return of the imperial gaze that had cast India as backward, hopelessly hierarchical, and divided along lines of religion, caste, and gender. The abysmal status of women in India was used to justify the imperial project; in postcolonial India, women's equal citizenship was meant to signify India's new status as a modern, civilized country. Yet, particularly for Muslim women, their unequal status within the family and the refusal by the state and the community to reform Muslim personal law were inextricably a part of the postcolonial dilemma of ensuring women's rights while respecting group integrity. These were and continue to be issues embedded within a complex legacy of colonialism and a history of religious strife fraught with political tensions between competing constituencies of religious leaders and a centralizing state.[12]

Muslim women in India have to fight for both formal equality de jure rights that they lack, as well as for substantive equality rights to hold the state accountable for enforcing constitutional guarantees. The perceived tension between gender equality and group rights is often mediated by an understanding that group interests take precedence over women's equality. The *Shah Bano* controversy and the Sharia debates presented women's rights and group rights as inimical to each other. The notion of prioritizing gender equality over religious freedom was premised on the understanding that racialized women and in particular, Muslim women, have to be saved from their barbaric cultural practices that subordinated them. This assumption must be linked to discursive strategies of imperialism and colonialism.[13]

Rather than being simply a deconstructive project, my aim is to interrogate binaries that shape discussions on the relationship between women's equality, group rights, and the accommodation of difference. I argue that it is necessary to construct a more nuanced understanding of what constitutes the identity of Muslim women in India, and in the Canadian context, to situate these women within their cultural context without seeing or classifying them as either victim or agent, while acknowledging the important role that culture plays in their lives.

II. CHALLENGING DUALISMS

The situation of Muslim women, the accommodation of group difference, and the protection of minority rights are invariably viewed through categories of analysis that serve to obfuscate the material reality of Muslim women's everyday lives, focusing on

---

[12] Deniz Kandiyoti, *Between the Hammer and the Anvil: Post-Conflict Reconstruction, Islam and Women's Rights*, 28(3) THIRD WORLD Q. 503, 504 (April 2007).

[13] *See* Leti Volpp, *Feminism versus Multiculturalism*, 101 COLUM. L. REV. 1181 (2001) and Sherene Razack, *The 'Sharia Law Debate' in Ontario: The Modernity/Premodernity Distinction in Legal Efforts to Protect Women from Culture*, 15 J. FEMINIST LEGAL STUD. 3 (2007).

the politics of cultural difference rather than on structural injustice.[14] Some of the simplistic Manichean categories that have to be challenged are those of group rights versus women's rights, public versus private, religious versus secular, East versus West, and modernity versus tradition.

Often Muslim women's rights are presented as oppositional to group rights and feminism is perceived as being contradictory to multiculturalism. Minority women are viewed as victims of their culture and gender subordination is located in racialized communities and cultures.[15] The assumption is that women are oppressed by their cultures and so would be better off by shedding their cultures.[16] In India, controversy rages over claims to reform Muslim personal law. In the Canadian context, the notion of the subordinating impact of culture on women crystallized around issues such as the Sharia law proposal in Ontario and the controversy over the status and dress of Muslim women in the reasonable accommodation debates in Quebec.

Pitting multiculturalism against feminism results in certain assumptions, implicit and explicit, about minority cultures and cultural values delivered from the point of view of the neutral objective viewer. Constructing an either feminism or multiculturalism dichotomy obscures the forces that actually shape culture, denies women agency within patriarchy, and discounts the notion that women have as much a stake as men do in the continuance of the culture of their group. Moreover, it discounts the level of systemic gender discrimination in the wider society and Muslim women are seen as more subordinated and more oppressed by their cultures.[17] In resorting to cultural explanations, we must be wary of essentializing the group to avoid understanding these as "natural trends" of Muslim culture.

Another binary deployed is that of the true Muslim woman versus the Westernized feminist.[18] In India, conservative religious leaders condemned Shah Bano for straying from the path of true Islam and betraying the community.[19] In the Sharia law initiative, it was asserted that true Muslim women would opt for Sharia law to regulate their family life. The proposal was framed as an effort to save Muslim women from the intrusion of the norms of the wider society and to bring them back to the path of true Islam.

Significantly, however, what may appear to be victories for feminists may in fact be somewhat ambivalent successes. The *Shah Bano* case was hailed as a victory for women and for secular citizenship over narrow sectarian interests. Yet there were problematic aspects of this judgment. By singling out Muslim family law as in need of reform and in violation of constitutional principles, the decision "otherized" the

[14] Iris Marion Young, *Structural Injustice and the Politics of Difference*, *in* Multiculturalism and Political Theory 60, 63 (Anthony Simon Laden et al. eds., Cambridge University Press 2007).

[15] Susan Moller Okin, *Is Multiculturalism Bad for Women?*, *in* Is Multiculturalism Bad for Women? 7 (Joshua Cohen et al. eds., Princeton University Press 1999).

[16] Volpp, *supra* note 13, at 1187.

[17] Volpp, *supra* note 13.

[18] Pathak & Sunder Rajan, *supra* note 8, at 564.

[19] *Id.* at 572. Asghar Ali Engineer, Shah Bano Controversy 211, 211–12 (Orient Longman 1987).

Muslim community by questioning its commitment to the postcolonial, secular democratic ideal. It also took the focus away from gender discrimination in other personal laws in India. The court constructed the figure of the Muslim woman as a helpless victim needing to be saved from the obscurantist forces of religious personal law. The state also used the discourse of rescue. The state, by enacting the Muslim Women's Act, claimed to be saving true Muslim women by giving back their religion to them in much the same way as the British colonial authorities claimed to be giving back to the natives their true, rediscovered traditions and laws.

The defeat of the Sharia Law proposal similarly was hailed as a victory for women's rights, and for universal citizenship over a differentiated citizenship, and yet this too had mixed results. Sherene Razack makes a compelling argument that the response of Canadian feminists to the Sharia law proposal, in their efforts to protect Muslim women from "their" culture, served to reinscribe a modernity/premodernity binary.[20] In their anxiety to counter conservative patriarchy within Muslim communities, Canadian feminists utilized a trope that reinscribed the binary understanding of East versus West, and a framework of religious and modern.[21] In so doing, they may have inadvertently helped sustain an understanding of state control in which the Muslim woman as victim is used to control Muslim communities, while simultaneously serving to defuse a more radical feminist and antiracist critique of the wider society and the community itself.

Feminists' responses to issues like *Shah Bano* in India and the Sharia proposal in Canada illustrate the dangers of fueling a conservative agenda by reinscribing majority anxieties of the illiberal practices of the minorities. This fear of "backward" practices is a significant factor in anti-Muslim hostility.[22] The double-edged nature of rights and the reality that they can be co-opted by conservative groups and appropriated to their own agenda is demonstrated by the Sharia debates and the *Shah Bano* issue. In both cases the conservative right came uncomfortably close to the feminist position on women's equality and universal citizenship, subverting the rights discourse to its own anti-Muslim agenda.

In the face of anti-Muslim hostility, it is very difficult for women within Muslim communities to sustain progressive politics and pursue gender justice for fear that this might promote an agenda that undermines group integrity. It forces them to make a choice between their rights and their group's culture/rights/interests. Yet, even when living in patriarchal societies, women do exercise agency. These women are aware of patriarchy and their resistance to it can be found in different places and in different ways. The fact that women like Shah Bano exercise their rights and make claims under the secular law should be a signal to the state and to the community that they are demanding change. Civil society, Muslim communities,

[20] Razack, *supra* note 13.
[21] *Id.* at 6.
[22] Kymlicka, *supra* note 1.

and the state must recognize this diversity and dissent within the group and must work toward inclusion of these voices in the formulation of public policy. If the state claims to represent all its citizens, it must craft an understanding of democratic multiculturalism that responds to the claims and aspirations of all members of the Muslim community.

The public/private split, whereby the state concedes authority over the group to decide matters of personal law, abandons women to the authority of those who are least likely to address their vulnerability and disadvantage. In such a situation, too much power and authority over the group is ceded to community leaders, and this may result in in-group subordination and the paradox of multicultural vulnerability.[23] Questioning the public/private distinction has profound implications for the role of the state in its efforts to reconcile the reality of social diversity with the necessity of balancing respect for group difference with gender equality.

A simplistic policy of multiculturalism arguably promotes a safe state-sponsored community identity, endorsed by dominant leaders. Such a policy endorses definitions of culture, group difference, and the presumed interests of the group that buttress existing structures of authority within the community. The struggles of women and other disadvantaged groups within the community are not acknowledged either by the state or by the community leaders. Differences are obscured and commonalities emphasized as the state accepts a projection of this unitary identity and a static understanding of "ethnic" culture. It also serves to homogenize groups and rigidify group boundaries, strengthening conceptions of "Us" and "Them," and raising critical questions of representation, authenticity, and the construction of identity.

III. TOWARD A CRITICAL MULTICULTURALISM

Invariably the debate on women's equality and the accommodation of group difference focuses on misleading oppositional constructions of public/private, Westernized feminist/true Muslim woman, East/West, modernity/tradition, and cultural relativism/universalism. Challenging these dualisms is critical to the inquiry because the terms of the debate today are so highly dichotomized. They abstract and decontextualize the material realities of the everyday lives of Muslim women.

Iris Young has articulated concern that a focus on culture and on the politics of cultural difference has narrowed the groups of concern to ethnic, national, and religious groups while limiting the issues of justice at stake.[24] Debates invariably decontextualize the structural privileges of the majority as well as the social and

---

[23] Nira Yuval-Davis, *Identity Politics and Women's Ethnicity, in* IDENTITY POLITICS AND WOMEN: CULTURAL REASSERTIONS AND FEMINISM IN INTERNATIONAL PERSPECTIVE 408, 419 (Valentine Moghadam ed., Westview Press 1994).

[24] Young, *supra* note 14, at 60.

economic disadvantages of the minorities. Issues of structural injustice are displaced to focus instead on issues of culture. Not surprisingly, questions of poverty and unemployment among Muslims are ignored while simultaneously magnifying issues related to religion and culture.[25] This understanding is demonstrated by *Shah Bano* and the Sharia law debates. In these cases, much time was spent discussing cultural practices of the "Other," but little time was spent on discussing gendered structural difference or racialized gender inequality. Invariably, the terms of the accommodation of difference are set by mainstream culture and norms. Granting recognition based on the terms of the majority community does little to challenge the hegemonic discourse or to displace structures of domination.[26]

Current multiculturalism policies do not pay sufficient attention to distributive justice or to institutionalized structures of disadvantage. Beyond granting affirmative rights, it is crucial to address the political economy of disempowerment and marginalization. Analyses of marginalization and responses to disempowerment have to go beyond cultural difference, to understand how to dismantle the structural aspects of oppression.[27] Moving toward a policy of critical multiculturalism would entail recognizing that culture is not the fundamental organizing principle of racialized/immigrant women's lives. A principal focus on culture prevents a critique of racism, systemic gender subordination in mainstream society, the impact of globalization and neoliberalism, the lack of access to employment, access to justice, and economic vulnerability. This could result in the creation of a permanently disenfranchised racialized underclass, cut off from the economic gains of wider society.[28]

Certainly, culture and religion play an important role also in the lives of women in the community, and supporting a link with culture is a central aspect of multiculturalism. Women have as great an interest as men do in the culture of the group. Culture affirms an individual's and a group's choice, autonomy, and identity. However, it is necessary to have a critical understanding of culture, rejecting any claims to a pure cultural authenticity; acknowledging the hybridity of culture and the modernity of tradition; and recognizing that cultures are fluid and changing.[29] It is crucial to demystify arguments of culture to understand whose interests are being served and whose are being denied by particular interpretations of culture.

At the same time, we must be wary of drawing too sharp an opposition between cultural difference and structural difference. Indeed, it is necessary to craft a policy of multiculturalism that can both take into account cultural differences and respond

---

[25] *Id.* at 83.
[26] Glen S. Coulthard, *Subjects of Empire: Indigenous Peoples and the "Politics of Recognition" in Canada*, 6 CONTEMPORARY POLITICAL THEORY 437, 439 (2007).
[27] *Id.*
[28] Kymlicka, *supra* note 1, at 58.
[29] HOMI BHABHA, THE LOCATION OF CULTURE 5, 159–172 (Routledge 1994); Stuart Hall, *Culture, Community, Nation*, 3 CULTURAL STUD. 349–63.

to structural injustice. A policy that focuses on cultural difference can reduce ethnic, religious conflict by recognizing distinct cultures and practices. Attention to structural injustice is important as it highlights the depth and systemic basis of inequality that keeps people and groups in subordinate positions. The intention is not to reject altogether the politics of cultural difference, but rather to emphasize the importance of group difference arising not only from cultural difference, but also from structural disadvantage, from the gendered division of labor, from the construction of normal and deviant ideas, and ultimately from the way they mediate tensions between minority groups and the wider society.[30]

Policies of multiculturalism are a way of state control over immigrant/racialized communities and a method of governmentality. The focus on cultural difference implies a constant engagement with what is permissible by the state and what is not, for example, the *kirpan*, the *hijab*, Sharia law for family law arbitration, and so on. As a result, civil society as a site of struggle is potentially obscured. It is possible that "multiculturalism by design" can result in a formal instrumentalism whereby only state-recognized groups are regarded as legitimate, and state-recognized group representatives are accepted as the sole spokesmen for the group, and women's voices are marginalized. Such a policy on the protection of minority rights can lead to the consolidation and legitimization of patriarchal interests that are less likely to enlarge women's rights and are less enthusiastic about women's political and economic participation.[31]

The problem with such a conception of multiculturalism is that it precludes an understanding of the differences within cultures and of the transformative impulse in minority cultures. It also suppresses traditional forms of resistance and negates feminist critiques of patriarchy, as well as dissent, from within. It is in this way that minorities are ghettoized into their groups and are seen as a monolithic, homogenous entity, undifferentiated by class, gender, or sexual orientation. In India, in accommodating Muslim group rights, women's rights were ignored. For the state, Muslim women had a prior religious and gendered identity and the state presumed that Muslim group interests would take precedence over Muslim women's equality.

Uncritical policies of the protection of minority rights conceptualize the imperiled Muslim woman as an "object of regulatory power, as the subject of racial, cultural, national representation."[32] Muslim women are viewed with ambivalence by mainstream society, seen both as a threat and as a victim, resulting in the reproduction of a neo-colonialist discourse within the rhetoric of multiculturalism.[33] The situation of Muslim women illustrates the paradox of multicultural vulnerability whereby the

[30] Young, *supra* note 14, at 78–79.
[31] Kandiyoti, *supra* note 12, at 514.
[32] Homi Bhabha, *Of Mimicry and Man: The Ambivalence of Colonial Discourse*, in RACE CRITICAL THEORIES: TEXT AND CONTEXT 113, 119 (Philomena Essed & David Theo Goldberg eds., Blackwell Publishing 2002).
[33] *Id.* at 121.

state's commitment to protecting minority rights can result in the subordination of women's interests within the group. Ayelet Shachar proposes the idea of joint governance as a way of giving voice to minority groups and to minorities within these groups.[34] Joint governance seeks to create a more dynamic division of power between the state and community authorities, avoiding situations where women are forced to choose between their rights or their cultures. Ideally it would provide a greater chance for authorities, either the state or community leaders, to respond to claims for change. However, community leaders have invariably been reluctant to enlarge women's rights.

The difficulty with this model is that it assumes that women may freely choose between the state or religious community authority, and that there is equal participation and representation in the dialogue both between the state and the group and within the group itself. In addressing minority women's vulnerability, any analysis of the accommodation of group difference has to take in to account the diversity within the group. Furthermore, it cannot be assumed that all groups are progressive and committed to internal reform. A further difficulty is that the group may not comply with constitutional guarantees and norms of the wider society.[35] This raises questions of state legitimization of a differentiated citizenship through the creation of a parallel system of law that is explicitly discriminatory. In India, the state has explicitly endorsed discrimination against Muslim women within the family, privileging group interests over women's rights as an essential part of the state's commitment to minority rights. Perhaps an alternate way to accommodate group difference would be to posit a greater role for the state. Despite charges of paternalism, arguably the state must act positively to enforce rights of equality and freedom from discrimination. The state must be held accountable for women's equality and to ensure compliance with constitutional guarantees. In deciding which aspects of culture are to be accommodated and which ought not, Will Kymlicka's model of internal restrictions and external protections is useful. Following Kymlicka's distinction, we can better understand how laws aimed at safeguarding group identity may in fact lead to imposing greater restrictions on women and minorities within the group.[36] Muslim women must be included in the dialogue between the state and the community on balancing seemingly opposing rights of gender equality and religious freedom.

Feminists are committed to democratic dialogue and deliberative democracy, seeking to displace the public/private split, and to craft a more inclusive democratic dialogue embracing and modifying the Habermasian notion of the public sphere as an emancipatory space from which discrimination and disadvantage can

---

[34] A. Shachar, *Religion, State, and the Problem of Gender: Reimagining Citizenship and Governance in Diverse Societies*, 50 McGILL L. J. 49–88 (2005).

[35] *See* WILL KYMLICKA, MULTICULTURAL CITIZENSHIP 151 (Clarendon Press 1995).

[36] VRINDA NARAIN, GENDER AND COMMUNITY: MUSLIM WOMEN'S RIGHTS IN INDIA 102 (University of Toronto Press 2001).

be challenged. Jurgen Habermas's idealized notion of the public sphere assumes that this rational deliberation would be based on reason and would bring about transformation and the end of dominance. It assumes that those engaged in this dialogue would participate as equals; that particular interests and identities would be bracketed in their deliberations; and finally, that there would be free access to this public sphere.[37] Feminist scholars question whether the idea of the dialogic public sphere as developed by Habermas can in fact be liberating or whether it might not be, on the contrary, subjugating.[38] Evaluating the possibility of modifying Habermas's idea of public space and dialogue to be more inclusive of disempowered voices, Nancy Fraser asserts the importance nonetheless of using this Habermasian notion of democratic dialogue and an emancipatory public sphere as a conceptual resource critical to feminist inquiry.[39] Feminist critiques of Habermas question the notion of equal access of all groups to the public sphere, noting the significant and continued exclusions of disempowered groups from the public sphere.[40] The possibility of excluding or bracketing particular identities and engaging in dialogue as equals is also questioned. In fact, these differences are noteworthy as being markers of social inequality. Further, this idealized notion sees the public sphere as somehow culture free and neutral, not recognizing the persistent existing hierarchies and power relations. Fraser's understanding of the public sphere as being constituted by many "publics" rather than a singular one as formulated by Habermas and others is significant.[41] This understanding better reflects the reality of diverse societies where the discursive relations between differentially empowered groups may take the form not merely of deliberation but also of contestation. Finally, Fraser challenges the exclusion of private issues or interests from public discussion, arguing that for a multiculturalism policy to respond to discrimination and disadvantage, it must recognize the way in which social inequality limits the possibility of free dialogical engagement. Further, labeling some issues as "private" screens them off from public scrutiny and debate.[42]

Seyla Benhabib's idea of deliberative democracy is particularly attractive here as a modification of both the Rawlsian notion of the public sphere and the Habermasian understanding of dialogic engagement.[43] Benhabib's conception of

---

[37] *See* Jurgen Habermas, "The Public Sphere: An Encyclopedia Article (1964)" *New German Critique* No. 3 1974 49–55, Jurgen Habermas, The Public Sphere: An Inquiry into a Category of Bourgeois Society 35–37 (Thomas Burger & Frederick Lawrence trans., MIT Press 1989).

[38] Alev Cinar, *Subversion and Subjugation in the Public Sphere: Secularism and the Islamic Headscarf, in* 33(4) Signs: J. Women in Culture & Soc. 891, 892 (2008).

[39] Nancy Fraser, *Rethinking the Public Sphere: A Contribution to the Critique of Actually Existing Democracy*, 25/26 Social Text 56, 57 (1990).

[40] *Id.* at 63.

[41] *Id.* at 68.

[42] *Id.* at 77.

[43] Seyla Benhabib, *Beyond Interventionism, and Indifference: Culture, Deliberation, and Pluralism*, 31(7) Phil. & Soc. Criticism, 753, 759 (2005).

deliberative democracy pays more attention to the role of civil society in the constitution of the public sphere. Questioning the public/private split, she recognizes the power relations inherent in democratic deliberations.[44] Benhabib calls for the reconstituting of the "liberal" public sphere that pays attention to nonstate dimensions. She argues for a deliberative democracy that recognizes more than the official public sphere of state bureaucracies and institutions but includes as well a focus on social movements, civil, cultural, religious, artistic, and political associations of the "unofficial" public sphere as well.[45] This is a useful way of looking at the politics of multiculturalism that might avoid the "We" setting the norms for the "Others." The process might also include a critical inquiry into mainstream institutions, recognizing that in public debates and dialogical engagement, there is a reflection of existing power reflections and the Others have a weakened position. Thus the politics of structural difference engenders more than mere tolerance but respect. From the perspective of gendered subalterns, this insight underscores the need to think harder about the opposition between public and private, and religious and secular, to recognize the deliberate discursive construction of the public sphere through the use of secularism and modernity norms. The opposition between the public and the private sphere is less interesting than a critical feminist multicultural reclaiming of the public sphere with the understanding that a public/private division is inherently flawed.

It is necessary to begin by thinking critically about the terms in which the opposition between religion and women's equality has been framed rather than presuming that women in "patriarchal" minority communities are subordinated by their cultures and therefore would be better off if they exited from their cultural communities and assimilated into mainstream society.[46] Homi Bhabha suggests that the perceived conflict of interest between feminism and multiculturalism and liberal feminists' focus on the "conflict" itself produces a monolithic understanding of minority cultures as antiwomen and a stereotypical characterization of racialized communities.[47] Invariably the images evoked are those of violence against women, polygamy, and dowry deaths, all of which underscore the passivity and victim-status of minority racialized women.[48] Not surprisingly, mainstream culture is contrasted as free, liberal, and liberated particularly for women. By positing feminism as oppositional to multiculturalism, such arguments evolve into a comparative judgment on minority cultures and strip away agency from racialized women, further subordinating them. It is only by putting the context of the material reality of these women back into the

[44] *Id.* at 757.
[45] Benhabib, *supra* note 43, at 756. SEYLA BENHABIB, THE CLAIMS OF CULTURE: EQUALITY AND DIVERSITY IN THE GLOBAL ERA 118–21 (Princeton University Press 2002).
[46] *See* Volpp, *supra* note 13 and Okin, *supra* note 15.
[47] Homi K. Bhabha, *Liberalism's Sacred Cow*, BOSTON REV., Oct.–Nov. 1997, *available at* www.bostonreview.net/BR22.5/bhabha.html (last visited Nov. 6, 2009).
[48] *Id.*

discussion that we can begin to situate women within minority and racialized communities in a way that better understands their exclusion from equal citizenship.[49]

Too often minorities are perceived as hostile to mainstream society, preserving their "culture" against the onslaught of progress. This view is disconcertingly close to the orthodoxy of religious leaders who use the public/private split superimposed on the religious–secular binary to reinforce their authority over the community, saving it from the hegemonic norms of the assimilationist majority.[50] Underscoring the continuity of the colonial past with the postcolonial present, the liberal agenda of saving Muslim women from their barbaric communities and backward laws is not very different from the colonial civilizing mission. Such an understanding of minority communities "obscures indigenous traditions of reform and resistance, ignores 'local' leavenings of liberty, flies in the face of feminist campaigns within nationalist and anticolonial struggles, leaves out well-established debates by minority intellectuals and activists concerned with the difficult 'translation' of gender and sexual politics in the world of migration and resettlement."[51]

For Muslim women, whether in India or in immigrant, diasporic communities in the West, the challenge has been to contend with community structures of authority both political and religious "while strategically negotiating their own group autonomy in relation to the paternalistic liberalisms of colonial modernity or Westernization."[52] It is necessary to close the gap between religious and secular: it might not be realistic to draw too sharp an opposition between the two. Arguably, secularism itself is a way of controlling religion. We need to recognize that religious law is fluid and changes over time. Muslim law in India has been modified by the colonial encounter, by parliamentary legislative initiatives, by custom and tradition, and by a secular judiciary. Indeed, Muslim law in India is very much a product of modernity where tradition has been selectively reinterpreted and discursively negotiated.[53] A related imperative is to question the secularism discourse and its inflexible association with modernity. Particularly in Nehruvian postcolonial India, secularism was associated with modernity and viewed as the opposite of communalism. Yet the two are more closely linked than it might seem.[54]

An uncritical top-down version of state multiculturalism treats identities and cultures as monolithic and unchanging.[55] Such a policy ignores the assimilation of cultures to the mainstream and it creates a political, divided reality.[56] By asserting

---

[49] Id.
[50] Id.
[51] Id.
[52] Id.
[53] VRINDA NARAIN, GENDER AND COMMUNITY: MUSLIM WOMEN'S RIGHTS IN INDIA 35 (University of Toronto Press 2001).
[54] GYANENDRA PANDEY, THE CONSTRUCTION OF COMMUNALISM IN COLONIAL NORTH INDIA 241 (Oxford University Press 1990).
[55] Scott *supra* note 2, at 14.
[56] Id.

an essential identity and a notion of a universal state/national culture, this version of multiculturalism ignores how this core value system and the secular public sphere are themselves constructed through certain specific exclusions and inclusions.[57] Difference becomes the basis of discrimination, demonstrating the usefulness of contextualization and historicization strategies in situating identities within certain political and social formations. In reflecting on multiculturalist policies that seek to reflect "diversity" it becomes important to theorize diversity, the construction of identity, and the politics of difference. Historicization understands and acknowledges relations of power and of force; it interrogates the notion of an essentialized identity and claims of authenticity, representation, and agency.[58] As Joan Scott compellingly argues, "[o]ddly enough, given the charges of incoherence and anarchy made against multicultural approaches, historicizing the question of identity offers the possibility of a more unified view than that of liberal pluralists."[59] The framing of difference in individual terms rather than group difference results in closing the structures of historical, group-based disadvantage from scrutiny. It is framed in protective language that individualizes the complaint and discrimination, and it strips the individual victim of agency.[60] Scott insists that we need to treat identity as fluid and changing. We need to acknowledge that identities are not simply given but are historically constructed and that there are multiple identities, some of which become politically salient for a time in certain contexts.[61] This insight acknowledging the constructedness of identity and its discursive mediation leads to the recognition that multiculturalist policies must be strategized in such a way that goes beyond simplistic identity groups and that, as a political strategy, the project of multiculturalism should not to be to reify a simplistic understanding of identity.[62]

It is necessary to better understand group differences as they are generated from structural power and the constructions of normal and deviant as they also reflect cultural and religious differences.[63] The challenge is to craft a policy of multi-culturalism that can respond to the differences among groups while retaining an understanding of the universal norms of equality and freedom from discrimination; to refocus attention on and to reinsert gender equality in the negotiations between groups and the state in the accommodation of difference.

These questions have implications for the community itself. Moving away from a focus on the state as the site of antiracist critique, and of recognition and "tolerance" of difference, what is the responsibility of the Muslim community itself? Frantz Fanon argued that for the colonized to challenge their subject status they needed

[57] *Id.*
[58] *Id.* at 16.
[59] *Id.*
[60] *Id.* at 17.
[61] *Id.* at 19.
[62] *Id.*
[63] Young, *supra* note 14, at 88.

to engage in critical self-reflection of their own history, traditions, and culture to return the subjectifying gaze.[64] This critical self-examination can be a source of empowerment within communities of resistance and can also be a way of asserting a nonessentialist identity for Muslim women.[65] It becomes imperative to formulate a notion of multiculturalism that contains within itself a challenge to the hegemonic project and an internal logic of self-empowerment of marginalized groups and their agency. Such a conception resists looking to mainstream society for validation and recognition but seeks engagement in a constructive manner.[66] This understanding would result in a move away from the rigidly Manichean understanding of power relations, culture, women's rights, and group rights, giving Westernized feminists and true Muslim women a more nuanced recognition of the complexities involved in the contest over respect for women's equality and the recognition of group difference.

[64] FRANTZ FANON, BLACK SKIN, WHITE MASKS 222 (Grove Press 1967).
[65] *Id.*
[66] BELL HOOKS, YEARNING: RACE, GENDER, AND CULTURAL POLITICS 22 (South End Press 1990). Glen S. Coulthard, *Subjects of Empire: Indigenous Peoples and the "Politics of Recognition" in Canada*, 6 CONTEMP. POL. THEORY 437, 454 (2007).

21

Democratic Theory, Feminist Theory, and Constitutionalism

The Challenge of Multiculturalism

Susan Williams

This chapter addresses a particular subset of issues in the study of multiculturalism: issues concerning the treatment of disadvantaged groups within a minority culture. The problem is well recognized in the literature and is often referred to as an issue of "internal minorities"[1] or as the "paradox of multicultural vulnerability."[2] The difficulty is that accommodations of the minority culture by the larger society sometimes result in serious harms to vulnerable groups within the minority culture. In the many controversies in liberal democracies over issues of accommodation, the vulnerable group that is hurt is often women. This chapter will argue that a central concern in such situations should be using the accommodation to encourage internal dialogue within the minority culture and to increase the capacity and opportunity for the vulnerable group to influence and challenge the dominant interpretation of their own culture. In other words, accommodation of the minority culture should be transformed from a threat to such vulnerable internal groups into a tool for strengthening their voices.

This issue in political theory has important implications for a range of issues in constitutional interpretation and design. One's view on the ways in which a legal order should protect minority cultural or religious groups and their practices – or, conversely, protect the vulnerable people within those groups against such practices – will deeply shape one's choice and/or interpretation of particular provisions in the constitution. For example, a strong position for protecting vulnerable internal minorities could lead to the adoption or interpretation of provisions addressing

---

[1] *See* Leslie Green, *Internal Minorities and Their Rights, in* THE RIGHTS OF MINORITY CULTURES 257 (Will Kymlicka ed., Oxford University Press 1995); *see generally* MINORITIES WITHIN MINORITIES: EQUALITY, RIGHTS, AND DIVERSITY (Avigail Eisenberg & Jeff Spinner-Halevy eds., Cambridge University Press 2005).

[2] *See* AYELET SHACHAR, MULTICULTURAL JURISDICTIONS: CULTURAL DIFFERENCES AND WOMEN'S RIGHTS 3 (Cambridge University Press 2001).

I would like to thank Christina Clark for her research assistance on this project.

gender equality that require positive action on the part of government to eliminate gender discrimination in the private realms of family and community. On the other hand, a strong position for providing protection for cultural and religious minority groups could lead to the adoption or interpretation of provisions protecting cultural or religious rights that require accommodation of minority group practices. And, an attempt to harmonize disparate systems of cultural or religious norms and institutions with the state-based system through constitutional recognition for plural legal systems can facilitate either accommodation of the minority culture or intrusion by the larger society into the practices of the minority community. So, taking a particular position on the appropriate response of the state to the problem of internal minorities will have significant constitutional implications.

The chapter will begin with a brief description of the problem, including the range of common responses in the literature on multiculturalism and why those responses are unsatisfactory. Part II canvasses the work of some feminist theorists who have attempted to generate more satisfactory answers by turning to a constructivist view of culture and a dialogic model of democracy. I will argue that this move is very valuable, but incomplete, because the theorists tend to focus on the dialogue that takes place between majority and minority cultures rather than on the dialogue within the minority culture. Part III examines the dialogic model of democracy in more detail and suggests that a full account requires a focus on the role of disruption and challenge as crucial to addressing the inevitable reintroduction of domination. In Part IV, I apply this approach to the issue of women as vulnerable internal minorities and generate a framework for addressing these problems. By focusing on how the choices of the majority can support and encourage such internal challenge, we open up a new range of possible responses to issues of multicultural accommodation in these difficult cases.

I. THE PROBLEM OF VULNERABLE INTERNAL MINORITIES

The problem of vulnerable internal minorities arises when a minority religious or cultural group requests an accommodation for its practices from the state and those practices cause significant harm to a group within the minority community. This problem may come up in a broad range of circumstances and involve a number of different sorts of internal minorities, but in many cases the vulnerable group that is hurt is women. So, for example, the accommodation of Orthodox Jewish family law can lead to harm to women whose husbands refuse them a religious divorce and thereby bar them from remarriage, or the accommodation of First Nation or Native American membership rules can lead to harm to women whose children are denied membership benefits because their mothers married outside of the tribe.

As Ayelet Shachar describes in her book *Multicultural Jurisdictions*, the literature has tended to resolve the problem of vulnerable internal minorities by going to one extreme or the other. Some theorists would allow a minority group to restrict or discriminate against its own members with very few limits beyond a guarantee that those members have freedom to exit.[3] At the other extreme, some theorists would refuse to allow any discrimination or restrictions that violate the liberal rules applicable within the majority culture.[4] Both of these extreme responses are highly problematic.

The problem with relying on exit as the basis for allowing mistreatment of internal minorities is twofold. First, to function as a justification here, exit cannot simply be a theoretical possibility; it must be a practical possibility. However, economic, social, and emotional realities often make exit a less than meaningful option for vulnerable people.[5] And second, even if exit is truly possible, this approach forces a woman faced with such cultural practices to choose between her rights as a citizen and her culture: because the only way to vindicate the former is to exit from the latter, she cannot have both.[6]

The alternative approach, by insisting that no minority community can be accommodated in any practice that violates the liberal norms of the majority, leaves no room for the existence of minority communities that dissent from this majority culture. One might value multiculturalism for a variety of different reasons: the contribution of cultural communities to individual autonomy,[7] the role of such communities in providing the goods of belonging,[8] or the value of dissenters in the democratic dialogue in the larger society.[9] However, whatever the reason, much of the value will be lost if minority cultures are squeezed out by the majority in this

3 Chandran Kukathas, *Are There Any Cultural Rights?*, in THE RIGHTS OF MINORITY CULTURES, *supra* note 1 at 247–48.
4 *See, e.g.*, SUSAN MOLLER OKIN, IS MULTICULTURALISM BAD FOR WOMEN? 9–24 (Princeton University Press 1999); *see generally* BRIAN BARRY, CULTURE AND EQUALITY: AN EGALITARIAN CRITIQUE OF MULTICULTURALISM (Harvard University Press 2002).
5 *See* SARAH SONG, JUSTICE, GENDER, AND THE POLITICS OF MULTICULTURALISM 161–62 (Cambridge University Press 2007) (describing psychological and practical conditions for meaningful exit); Savitri Saharso, *Female Autonomy and Cultural Imperative: Two Hearts Beating Together*, in CITIZENSHIP IN DIVERSE SOCIETIES 230–31 (Will Kymlicka & Wayne Norman eds., Oxford University Press 2000) (describing how culture can limit the capacity for autonomy). *See generally* Oonagh Reitman, *On Exit*, in MINORITIES WITHIN MINORITIES, *supra* note 1, at 192–204 (arguing that exit cannot play the protective and transformative roles assigned to it).
6 *See* SHACHAR, *supra* note 2, at 70–71. Gurpreet Mahajan has also pointed out that exit is not a very meaningful option if the larger society continues to regard you (perhaps because of the color of your skin or the ethnicity of your name) as a member of the minority community even after you leave. *See* Gurpreet Mahajan, *Can Intra-Group Equality Co-exist with Cultural Diversity? Re-examining Multicultural Frameworks of Accommodation*, in MINORITIES WITHIN MINORITIES, *supra* note 1, at 102.
7 *See* WILL KYMLICKA, MULTICULTURAL CITIZENSHIP: A LIBERAL THEORY OF MINORITY RIGHTS 76, 89 (Clarendon Press 1995).
8 *See generally* JAMES TULLY, STRANGE MULTIPLICITY: CONSTITUTIONALISM IN AN AGE OF DIVERSITY (Cambridge University Press 1995).
9 *See* MONIQUE DEVEAUX, CULTURAL PLURALISM AND DILEMMAS OF JUSTICE 34 (Cornell University Press 2000).

way.[10] In other words, this approach is really only possible for those who do not regard the inclusion of minority cultures as an important priority of justice. So, how might a society respect and include minority communities while also protecting and respecting the vulnerable minorities within those communities? A number of feminist theorists have turned to a more complex understanding of culture and to dialogic models of democracy to provide a method for recognizing and promoting both of these goals.

II. FEMINIST RESPONSES

Many feminists have decried the "billiard ball" model of culture and insisted on a constructionist approach instead. The billiard ball model sees cultures as mutually exclusive, having clear boundaries and determinate contents.[11] This essentialized model of culture, while explicitly rejected by everyone, often seems to be implicit in the claims of both multiculturalists and their opponents.[12] In opposition to this model, feminist theorists offer a constructivist account in which "[c]ultural communities have long interacted and shaped one another in their interactions, and they have been internally heterogeneous from the start."[13] Groups and the members who identify with them are produced and continually reproduced through interaction, both within the group and with others.[14] Sarah Song describes four elements of this constructivist model: 1) "cultures are the products of specific and complex historical processes, not primordial entities"; 2) "cultures are internally contested, negotiated, and reimagined by members, who are sometimes motivated by their interactions with outsiders"; 3) "cultures are not isolated but rather overlapping and interactive"; and 4) "cultures are loose-jointed . . . the loss or change of one strand does not necessarily bring down the entire culture."[15]

This constructivist approach to culture shifts the focus in multicultural issues in several ways. Most important for the purposes of this chapter, recognizing the internally contested nature of cultures suggests "the need for greater attention to the *politics* of cultural construction, change, and maintenance."[16] All of the feminist theorists working with this constructivist model of culture emphasize the need for

[10] *Cf.* Jeff Spinner-Halevy, *Autonomy, Association, and Pluralism, in* MINORITIES WITHIN MINORITIES, *supra* note 1, at 165 ("If all private groups are remade in the image of the state, then everyone's choices are reduced.").

[11] *See* TULLY, *supra* note 8, at 10 (describing and criticizing this model); *see also* Iris Marion Young, *Together in Difference: Transforming the Logic of Group Political Conflict, in* THE RIGHTS OF MINORITY CULTURES 157–61 (Will Kymlicka ed., Oxford University Press 1995).

[12] *See* ANNE PHILLIPS, MULTICULTURALISM WITHOUT CULTURE 8–9 (Princeton University Press 2007).

[13] SONG, *supra* note 5, at 31; *see also* SEYLA BENHABIB, THE CLAIMS OF CULTURE: EQUALITY AND DIVERSITY IN THE GLOBAL ERA 5–7 (Princeton University Press 2002); PHILLIPS, *supra* note 12, at 45.

[14] Young, *supra* note 11, at 159–61.

[15] SONG, *supra* note 5, at 32.

[16] *Id.* at 35 (emphasis in original).

sensitivity to the power dynamics within a culture and the ways in which the minority group's interaction with the majority affects the status, power, and resources of sub-groups within the minority community. As many theorists have recognized, certain forms of accommodation – such as group political representation and incorporation of traditional norms into the state legal system – can have a systematic effect of supporting traditional authority figures in the community, and their views of the culture, at the expense of the power and perspectives of more marginalized groups, often including women.[17] There is no neutral position for the state here: action and inaction both have consequences for the distribution of power and status inside the minority community. Focusing on the internally contested nature of culture directs our attention to these consequences.

Many of the feminist theorists struggling with the issues of vulnerable internal minorities also embrace a dialogic model of democracy as a useful tool for deal-ing with difficult cases. Anne Phillips suggests that dialogue is the most promising approach because it recognizes both difference and the possibility of intercultural understanding and can encourage internal transformation of the community.[18] Sim-ilarly, Seyla Benhabib uses a deliberative model of democracy to describe the inter-action between majority and minority cultural groups and how it can give rise to workable solutions to some of these issues.[19] Iris Marion Young's well-known defense of certain forms of group rights is based on a dialogic model of democracy.[20] Monique Deveaux develops "a more robust conception of democracy,"[21] which is a dialogic model with some important modifications.[22] Sarah Song asserts that demo-cratic deliberation must have a central role in determining which accommodations are required by justice in multicultural societies.[23] And Judith Squires endorses a vision of diversity politics focused on contextual impartiality and democratic deliber-ation as the basis for bringing feminism and multiculturalism together.[24] Although there are many real disagreements among these theorists about the specific form and implementation of a dialogic democratic approach, they all see this model as offering a better basis for dealing with multicultural issues than either a liberal individualist approach or a communitarian approach.

---

[17] See PHILLIPS, *supra* note 12, at 163 (criticizing consociationalism for increasing power of elites), 169 (criticizing the incorporation of traditional legal systems as making one interpretation of norms authoritative).

[18] See *id.* at 161. She cautions, however, that the dialogue must be structured carefully or it will tend to increase the power of authority structures within the community, for example by endorsing traditional leaders as spokespersons in the dialogue, *id.* at 161–62.

[19] See BENHABIB, *supra* note 13, at 105–46.

[20] See generally IRIS MARION YOUNG, INCLUSION AND DEMOCRACY (Oxford University Press 2000).

[21] DEVEAUX, *supra* note 9 at 3 (rejecting a requirement of consensus and insisting that deliberative democracy is not neutral but based on specific norms, which must be made explicit and justified).

[22] See *id.* at 140–41.

[23] See SONG, *supra* note 5, at 10.

[24] Judith Squires, *Culture, Equality, and Diversity, in* MULTICULTURALISM RECONSIDERED 120 (Paul Kelly ed., Polity Press 2005).

A dialogic model of democracy is a good starting place for thinking about issues of multiculturalism in liberal, democratic societies. The focus on equal respect and inclusion provides a foundation for both the accommodation claims made by minority communities and the possible grounds for limiting those claims. And I agree with these theorists that a democratic dialogue between the many groups in such a pluralist society is an important part of the process for resolving the difficult cases concerning accommodation.[25] The particular observation I want to offer here is that a dialogic, democratic approach to the problem of vulnerable internal minorities requires additional attention to the dynamics *within* the minority community and not only to dialogue between the community and the larger society. Although all of the theorists I am describing recognize this issue, none of them has focused her attention on it.[26] Their focus is on the nature of the dialogue within the larger society: the conditions under which that dialogue can take place, the role of the minority community in that conversation, and the ways in which the dialogue might contribute to the solution of hard cases.

These theorists all recognize the need for dialogue among the subgroups within each community[27] and the risks that accommodations may pose in terms of

---

[25] It is interesting to note the high level of consensus among the theorists I am describing on the identification of a category of claims that are not so difficult and that all of them would reject. These are claims where the harm visited on the vulnerable member because of cultural practices is severe, generally physical, and in clear violation of the generally applicable criminal laws. For example, all of these theorists agree that the "cultural defense" should not excuse a man who kills his wife or other female family member in a so-called honor killing. If such a defense were accepted, that would effectively function as an exemption for members of that cultural group from the usual criminal laws on murder. Although the writers I describe offer different views about why these defenses should not have this result, and also differ on what other relevance (if any) such cultural information might have in a criminal case, they all agree that no exemption is appropriate here. Perhaps one might say that these cases form an "overlapping consensus" among feminists who are sympathetic to the claims of minority communities about where the limits of those claims lie.

[26] Monique Deveaux has given the most attention to this issue in her essay A *Deliberative Approach to Conflicts of Culture*, in Minorities within Minorities, *supra* note 1 at 340. There, she offers a clearer statement of her conviction that democratic processes must apply within the cultural minority community, and not just between that community and the larger society, *id.* at 343. She also offers some guidelines for the dialogue that are useful for internal as well as external purposes, *id.* at 350–51 (nondomination, political equality, and revisability). Nonetheless, the example she uses to illustrate the process is still an external conversation – between community members, outside experts, and representatives of the larger society – rather than the ongoing, internal process of cultural construction, interpretation, and implementation, *id.* at 356–61 (describing the process of public consultation preceding the passage of the South African Customary Marriage Act of 1998). In addition, she does not consider the use of accommodation as itself a mechanism for encouraging internal dialogue. In this chapter, my goal is to add those missing elements.

[27] *See, e.g.*, Phillips, *supra* note 12, at 161 (recognizing need for internal transformation), 178 ("Institutions should be developed that will better enable individuals to articulate what they want"); Song, *supra* note 5, at 82–83 ("The government's role should be focused on strengthening the position of the vulnerable in decision-making procedures . . . The state should lean toward an option that recognizes the contested nature of cultural practices"), 134; Ayelet Shachar, *Should Church and State be Joined at the Altar? Women's Rights and the Multicultural Dilemma*, in Citizenship in Diverse Societies, *supra* note 5, at 220–21 (women are still struggling for access to power to interpret texts and make rules

undermining this internal dialogue.[28] Yet they give no systematic attention to the ways in which accommodations might be used to support or encourage such dialogue. This missing element is, I believe, crucial to an adequate approach to the problem of vulnerable internal minorities.

III. THE NEED FOR CHALLENGE: DEMOCRATIC THEORY

In this section of the chapter,[29] I want to step back from the specific problem of vulnerable internal minorities and take a broader view of democratic theory. I will argue that a dialogic model of democracy requires attention to the role of disruption and challenge in preventing the reintroduction of oppression. Such disruption and challenge is crucial and cannot simply be assumed – incentives and support for it must be built into the democratic structure. The conclusion I will draw is that one important aim of accommodation in multicultural contexts should be to provide support for such challenge by vulnerable internal minorities within the community's dialogue. Indeed, I believe that this approach is necessary, although not sufficient, to any long-term solution to the difficulties posed by claims for accommodation that cause substantial harm to vulnerable internal minorities.

In a dialogic model of democracy, the purpose of democratic politics is to form a political community in which people can seek a way forward together.[30] Participants engage in a collective process of deliberation to seek this path. Their role is to bring their particular perspectives and expertise to this deliberation and to listen carefully to the contributions of the other deliberators so as to reach agreement on the best path forward. Their ideas, and even their perceptions of their interests and situations, are expected to be changed in this process.

A number of democracy theorists, including Bonnie Honig, Jane Mansbridge, and Nancy Fraser, have recognized the dangers of a dialogic or deliberative model of

---

in religious communities); DEVEAUX, *supra* note 9, at 134–35 ("importance of debate, discussion, and dissent within cultural communities.").

[28] *See, e.g.,* PHILLIPS, *supra* note 12, at 139 (arguing that there is a trade-off between exit and voice that discourages internal change).

[29] The argument in this section of the chapter closely follows the argument offered in Susan H. Williams, *Equality, Representation, and Challenge to Hierarchy: Justifying Electoral Quotas for Women, in* CONSTITUTING EQUALITY: GENDER EQUALITY AND COMPARATIVE CONSTITUTIONAL LAW 53–72 (Susan H. Williams ed., Cambridge University Press 2009). In that chapter, I apply this framework to the issue of electoral gender quotas for women.

[30] In some versions, the goal of this deliberation is to seek the common good of the community. *See* Cass R. Sunstein, *Beyond the Republican Revival*, 97 YALE L. J. 8 (1988). In other versions, the dialogic process itself is the goal, understood as "free and reasoned deliberation among individuals considered as moral and political equals." Seyla Benhabib, *Toward a Deliberative Model of Democratic Legitimacy, in* DEMOCRACY AND DIFFERENCE: CONTESTING THE BOUNDARIES OF THE POLITICAL 67, 68 (Seyla Benhabib ed., Princeton University Press 1996). I intend my description of the category of dialogic democracy to cover both of these versions.

democracy that does not reckon seriously enough with the ineradicability of power.[31] Difference is inevitable, and there is a constant pressure for people with power to use that difference to generate or reinforce hierarchy. The risk of a deliberative model of democracy is that we will too quickly assume that our deliberative processes are free of coercion (when they are not), or that our dialogue has resulted in a good that is common (when it is not). The ideal of a politics free of power and domination is an ideal worth embracing, but if we think that any actual politics has achieved that ideal, then we are allowing ourselves to be led astray by the dream.

What is necessary, then, is not that we abandon these ideals, but that we supplement them with elements specifically designed to keep our eyes open to the dangers in these valuable goals. We must build in mechanisms for calling our attention to the ways in which our efforts at deliberation have resulted in or relied on coercion, or our efforts to build commonality have succeeded only in denying or suppressing difference. Our theory must include strong and explicit attention to the processes through which our ideals fail or are subverted.

Think about an analogy to efforts to cure a particular endemic disease. The primary concern, of course, is to initiate the public health reforms needed to eliminate the disease, perhaps cleaning up water supplies or providing inoculations. However, it is also essential to ensure that you have good mechanisms for detecting the reemergence of the disease. And it is necessary to be vigilant about the possibility that your public health efforts may themselves be generating problems, such as antibiotic resistance or damaging side effects. Moreover, the two projects here may not necessarily overlap: the programs necessary to eliminate the disease may not by themselves provide you with adequate warning about the risks of reemergence or side effects.

I want to suggest that dialogic democracy is like the goal in a disease eradication plan. It is a picture of the sort of society we hope to create and a model of the legal and political institutions that might help to get us there. I am arguing that we need to add to this model a strong element analogous to the watchdog function of the disease-detection program: a part of the model devoted to recognizing and calling attention to the reemergence of the problems these models are designed to address, whether in the same old form or in a new guise generated by our reform efforts themselves. The focus here is on the act of recognizing and resisting evil rather than on constructing something good.

The evil can come through many different mechanisms. Sometimes, hierarchy and oppression reemerge simply because we have failed to implement our ideals

[31] Bonnie Honig, *Difference, Dilemmas, and the Politics of Home,* in DEMOCRACY AND DIFFERENCE, *supra* note 30, at 257–77; Jane Mansbridge, *Using Power/Fighting Power: The Polity,* in DEMOCRACY AND DIFFERENCE, *supra* note 30, at 46–66; Nancy Fraser, *Rethinking the Public Sphere: A Contribution to the Critique of Actually Existing Democracy,* in HABERMAS AND THE PUBLIC SPHERE 123 (Craig Calhoun ed., MIT Press 1992).

effectively. We know what we are trying to do, but the plan we adopt is ineffective. To continue the disease metaphor, the plan may be ineffective either because it fails to eradicate the disease or because it causes new problems, such as side effects. Such failures can be the result of ignorance or laziness or unwillingness to bear the costs that real change requires.

Sometimes, hierarchy and domination are generated because we don't really understand our goals. We have a mistaken idea about what dialogic democracy would look like in a particular context and we are aiming for the wrong goal. Again, this failure can lead to our program being ineffective in both of the ways described earlier: it may fail to eradicate existing problems and it may cause new or additional problems.

And sometimes, the evil sneaks back in because people with power are (consciously or unconsciously) resisting the loss of that power. All too often, such people are able to cripple the reforms intended to challenge their power or even to pervert the reforms into a mechanism for reinforcing their power. The important point here is that even our best efforts – when we have understood the ideal well and implemented it effectively – always contain the possibility that they will be undermined in this way. The insidiousness of power is such that we can never guarantee that our reform efforts will not become the vehicles for the very oppression they were designed to combat.

In fact, I believe that we must accept that our efforts will always be subject to all three of these failings, although the degree of each may vary. The methods we choose will never be perfectly effective. Our understanding of our ideals will always be incomplete and imperfect. And power will always sneak back in through whatever mechanisms we adopt to try to restrain it. Because we will always fail in all of these ways, to one degree or another, we must build into our theory explicit attention to these dangers. The element of challenge requires us to be vigilant for all of these different means through which hierarchy and oppression can be reintroduced. It requires us to direct our attention to mechanisms for detecting and resisting this reintroduction. In other words, we must provide support and encouragement for challenging oppression as a central part of our commitment to dialogic democracy.

Such challenge cannot be effective unless the people most likely to suffer from the reintroduction of oppression have a strong voice in the dialogue and a meaningful opportunity to be heard. Those who are not themselves the victims of oppression can, of course, oppose it. Men can be feminists. But it would be a poor disease-detection program indeed that did not give a central place to the persons most likely to experience the symptoms of the disease. If we want an effective mechanism for calling our attention to the reemergence of domination, we must ensure that those who are most vulnerable to the danger play a central role in the democratic dialogue.

IV. DIALOGIC CHALLENGE AND THE PROBLEM OF VULNERABLE
INTERNAL MINORITIES

The basic claim I wish to make is that the majority's deference to and accommodation of the practices of a minority group is more warranted as the group demonstrates more willingness to carry on an internal dialogue in which challenge is possible. Taking this approach is not the same as asking whether the cultural practices that are at issue in the accommodation claim are consistent with liberal individual rights. Here we are focused not on the specific practices at issue in the accommodation, but on the methods through which such practices are created, interpreted, and implemented. If those methods – and the background conditions under which they operate – allow for meaningful challenge, then the larger society should offer a greater degree of accommodation to the community's practice, even if the practice includes some illiberal features.[32]

Openness to challenge is not an all-or-nothing matter. There is a minimum level of dialogic openness that is required of all communities, in the form of bans on extreme coercion, such as imprisonment.[33] But, beyond this minimum, the larger society should continue to encourage the development of more inclusive and open dialogic conditions within the community. And, to ensure that the internal dialogue within a community includes challenge to inequality and domination, the vulnerable members of that community must have a meaningful voice in the dialogue.

I suggest that the larger society should approach issues of accommodation by thinking about three different mechanisms for encouraging and supporting internal dissent and challenge. First, the larger society can increase the capacity for challenge by internal minorities by giving them recognition and social capital. Second, the larger society can increase the capacity of internal minorities by redistributing practical resources, such as economic power and education, to them. And third, the larger society can increase the opportunity for internal minorities to challenge hierarchy within their own communities by making accommodation conditional on the adoption of internal dialogic practices that provide opportunities for such challenge. The first two mechanisms are aimed at ensuring that vulnerable internal minorities have the resources and capacity for making challenges; the third mechanism is aimed at ensuring that they have the opportunity to use that capacity.

---

[32] *See* Deveaux, *supra* note 26, at 359. We hope and believe, of course, that such procedures will, in time, lead to greater protection for individual rights, but that may be a slow and gradual process and its end-point within a given minority culture may never exactly match the list of rights endorsed by the majority culture.

[33] *See id.* at 353 n. 10. Thus, exit, while inadequate, is clearly a necessary protection for vulnerable members. And, there are surely also other minimum protections for the welfare of individuals, particularly children, that cannot be waived, *see supra* note 25 (describing the generally accepted limits imposed by serious criminal laws.)

In implementing all three of these methods, however, it is important for the state to enlist the cooperation of traditional community leaders as much as possible. Otherwise, the state's support and encouragement for the vulnerable internal minority will simply lead the rest of their community to reject and demonize that minority as a tool of the oppressive majority culture. This dynamic is amply demonstrated in the many examples of women's groups charged with being purveyors of Western ideals when they push for equality within their own non-Western cultures. There is probably no way to avoid this problem completely, but the more that the traditional leaders' interests and status can be tied to the recognition and empowerment of the internal minorities, including women, the less powerful this response will be. I will, therefore, offer suggestions in each of the sections that follow of methods for trying to forge this tie and encourage the accompanying support of traditional leaders.

A. Recognition

The state and the majority culture need to seek out and raise up multiple representatives and spokespeople for the vulnerable internal minorities. This can often be best achieved in the realm of public debate and discussion, outside of the particular arena of government. For example, mainstream news media should routinely look for representatives of women's groups internal to minority communities for comment on issues concerning that community. Civil society organizations seeking input from representatives of a particular community should do the same. And government also should seek out and invite participation by women's groups internal to minority cultural communities as part of any consultation process.

It is difficult to enlist the traditional community leaders in this process because they are very likely to endorse women's representatives who are less critical of traditional authority, which would, of course, undermine the purpose of supporting challenge. So, it is probably not useful to attempt to involve these traditional leaders in the process of identifying the women's representatives. It is, however, extremely useful to bring the traditional leaders together with the women's representatives in conversations about the community's needs and concerns. If these conversations take place in contexts in which both sets of leaders are representing the community's interests to the larger society, then there is the possibility for a positive dynamic. It is likely that in many cases they will agree on at least some of the goals of the community and the opportunity to discover such common ground in the context of presenting the community's desires to the larger society can help to build trust and cooperation between these leaders.[34]

---

[34] *See* Deveaux, *supra* note 26, at 358 & n. 20 (describing how women, along with traditional leaders, supported some customary practices in the discussion over the South African Customary Marriage Act.)

B. *Redistribution*

The state needs to offer practical support to vulnerable internal minorities that will increase their power to speak up and challenge the hierarchy in their own communities. In the case of women, such support might take the form of opportunities for education, economic development, and protection from domestic and other forms of intra-community violence. As many observers have noted, the reason that exit is an insufficient solution is that women often experience very substantial barriers to exit, in the form of economic, educational, and social limitations that dramatically raise the cost of leaving. At a minimum, the state can provide support that reduces the impact of such limits.

The state should also try to enlist the support of traditional community leaders for programs that provide resources to the women of the community. The goal is for these leaders to see such programs as benefiting the community as a whole. One way to encourage that view would be to offer the benefits (e.g., education, economic development support) to both men and women in the community but to increase the amount of support based on the percentage of recipients who are women. For example, the state might offer scholarship aid to members of a disadvantaged group, and the total amount available for scholarships might increase as the percentage of women participating in the scholarship program increases. Or the state might enlist women by using their traditional roles (e.g., as mothers) to give them resources and training (e.g., on organizing and teaching) that will increase their capacity more generally. Another method is for the government to provide public recognition for the traditional leaders in communities with high rates of female participation in such programs. The goal is to come up with mechanisms that create incentives for the community leaders to encourage women to take advantage of these opportunities.

C. *Accommodation Tied to Dialogue*

Finally, and most importantly, the state should tie accommodation of minority cultural practices to the development and support of internal dialogic practices that are inclusive and open to challenge. If the state specified the precise dialogic practices required, it would be very likely to create a backlash of what Ayelet Shachar has called "reactive culturalism": where the minority community hardens its own cultural barriers to equality in response to pressure by the majority to be more egalitarian.[35] To minimize this dynamic, I suggest that the majority should set out the general goals of this dialogic practice and then leave it to the minority community to come up with the precise mechanisms for promoting those goals. When a minority community requests an accommodation, the community would

[35] *See* SHACHAR, *supra* note 26, at 35–37.

then bear the burden of showing that its internal dialogue included the necessary openness to challenge to justify that accommodation.

I envision this justification as a precondition that must be met before the accommodation claim goes forward to the type of democratic dialogue in the larger society envisioned by the feminist theorists on whom I have been relying. In other words, the issue raised by the vulnerable internal minority should be seen as creating an independently necessary (although not sufficient) criterion for accommodation: an accommodation that imposes costs on such an internal minority can go forward to the regular process of consideration only if the community requesting it first meets this requirement of open internal dialogue.

This justification should operate on a sliding scale. If the accommodation of the practice does not create issues with respect to a vulnerable internal minority, then the requirement of internal dialogue should be minimal. For example, where the issue is an exemption from helmet laws for Sikh motorcyclists who cannot put the helmet over their turbans, there is little worry about the accommodation causing particular harm to a vulnerable internal minority. So, as long as the community meets the minimum standard for allowing members to participate in the shaping of its cultural practices, such an accommodation request could go forward to the dialogue with the larger society.

But as the accommodation of a particular cultural practice becomes more problematic in terms of its harm to a vulnerable minority within the community, the degree of inclusiveness and openness to challenge required of the internal dialogue will be higher. So, for example, when the issue is an exemption for Muslim girls to allow them to wear headscarves to school, there is a more serious concern about the impact on girls and women within the community who might be coerced into continuing a cultural practice they wish to challenge.[36] There is also, on the other side, the worry that enforcing the secular dress code may lead a significant number of Muslim families to remove their daughters from the public schools and place them in Islamic schools where they may have even less opportunity to challenge cultural practices.[37]

One important piece of the puzzle in resolving such difficult issues is to ask the community to demonstrate that it has strong internal mechanisms to allow such challenges to be made, heard, and considered, so that its cultural practices have the capacity to adapt over time to the needs, desires, and values of its members.

---

[36] Such pressures on other girls were, apparently, one of the reasons why some government officials in France opposed allowing the headscarf. *See* SONG, *supra* note 5, at 174. Of course, the other reason was the commitment to laicite as a principle of the French Republic. *See* Katherine Pratt Ewing, *Legislating Religious Freedom: Muslim Challenges to the Relationship Between Church and State in Germany and France, in* ENGAGING CULTURAL DIFFERENCES: THE MULTICULTURAL CHALLENGE IN LIBERAL DEMOCRACIES 70–71 (Richard A. Shweder, Martha Minow, & Hazel Rose Markus eds., Russell Sage Foundation 2002). This second reason falls into the category of other concerns that might (or might not) justify refusing accommodation.

[37] *See* SONG, *supra* note 5, at 175.

Many commentators have noted the contested and perhaps changing meaning of the practice of veiling in Islamic communities in many countries.[38] The central question, then, is whether women have a realistic opportunity to challenge this cultural practice and/or change its meaning within the particular communities affected by the policy.

The general guidelines or goals for such an inclusive and open internal dialogue should include at least three parts. First, the process must allow information about alternatives to the current practice. There must be opportunities for people to hear about how other communities handle similar issues and about alternative interpretations of this community's traditions and practices. The presentation of this information, moreover, cannot be monopolized by the traditional leaders: people who actually support these alternative practices must be allowed to speak in favor of them. I realize that some communities would prefer that their members not be aware of alternative practices or interpretations, but such ignorance is inconsistent with any robust model of dialogue, particularly once we see challenge as a central part of dialogue. If challengers are limited to making arguments against the current orthodoxy, without being able to present alternatives to it, they will be seriously disadvantaged. Thus, the community must show that it allows the presentation of alternatives to justify its accommodation claims where there are important consequences for vulnerable internal minorities.

Second, the dialogue must include broad participation by dissenters. Those who wish to challenge the traditional practice, or the traditional leaders' interpretation of that practice, must be given meaningful opportunities to do so. A meaningful opportunity would generally mean at least that 1) different groups within the community must be allowed to speak for themselves and cannot be forced to be represented by spokespersons not of their choosing; and 2) the dissenters must be heard by a broader audience than just the traditional leaders of the community.[39] The point here is that the dissenters must be given the chance to affect the culture of their community.[40]

---

[38] See, e.g., Katherine Bullock, Rethinking Muslim Women and the Veil: Challenging Historical and Modern Stereotypes (Int'l Inst. of Islamic Thought 2002); Faegheh Shirazi, The Veil Unveiled: The Hijab in Modern Culture (University Press of Florida 2003).

[39] Monique Deveaux proposes that one of the requirements of the dialogue is political equality between participants: the opportunity to participate in and influence the outcome of the dialogue cannot be affected by other sorts of inequalities, such as wealth, power, gender, and so on. See Deveaux, *supra* note 26, at 350–51. Although I believe this is a wonderful ideal, I am afraid that it is likely to be unattainable in most communities – majority as well as minority – for the foreseeable future. As a result, a more limited and more specific set of concerns would be more useful as guidelines for resolving these issues. The requirements discussed here are intended as a first cut at such specific guidelines for an adequate level of guaranteed participation.

[40] There may be additional procedural requirements that are necessary to allow the voices of vulnerable internal minorities to be heard effectively. For example, if women are afraid to speak up publicly because of the risk of retribution, then there would need to be anonymous mechanisms for participation. The specific conditions necessary for honest participation will vary with the circumstances of different communities of women. So, the suggestions in text, while necessary, may not be sufficient as conditions for ensuring adequate dialogue.

And third, the community's ultimate decision on the practice at issue must demonstrate some recognition of and concern for the views of dissenters. This does not mean that the community must necessarily adopt the views of the dissenters, but it must show that it has considered them and attempted to accommodate them to some extent. One aspect of this concern is captured by Monique Deveaux's requirement that the outcomes of such dialogue must be revisable – they must be seen as capable of being reopened and altered in the future.[41] Revisability is necessary to assure dissenters that their concerns have not been permanently foreclosed, but it may not be sufficient for the purposes of the requirement I am describing. In addition to revisability, the community must demonstrate some understanding of and sympathy for the concerns of dissenters. In other words, the community must demonstrate some of the same willingness to accommodate its own minorities that it is requesting from the larger society.[42]

I recognize that imposing this model of dialogic democracy on minority cultures may seem to be just as intrusive as the imposition of liberal standards for individual rights that I condemned earlier in the chapter. After all, some of these minority communities reject democratic procedures at least as vehemently as they reject any of the specific rules of the larger society from which they are seeking to depart. Why should it be acceptable to impose democratic procedures on them if it is not acceptable to impose the substantive rules regarding behavior that are at issue in accommodation claims?

First, some minority communities do, in fact, accept the need for some degree of democratic consent as the basis for communal authority. In other words, many groups purport to be democratic, even if they don't envision democracy as being tied to elections, and they would themselves rely on the consent of their members as the foundation for their claims. The presence of internal dissent is some evidence that these views exist in a community.[43] For such groups, it is reasonable to ask them to think hard about the opportunities through which their members can express consent (or the lack thereof). Thus, for a subset of communities, the requirement of dialogic democracy can be seen as calling them to a deeper attention to values they share.

Second, the state must impose these democratic processes as a condition for accommodation or its own legitimacy is threatened. All of the commentators on multicultural issues seem to agree about the need for the state to prevent the most egregious forms of violence against members of minority communities – such as honor killings – because the state would violate its commitments to its citizens if it failed to do so. In other words, there is consensus on the idea that the state owes a minimum level of protection to all of its citizens. Accommodations that violate

---

[41] *See* Deveaux, *supra* note 26, at 350–51.
[42] *See* Green, *supra* note 1, at 269.
[43] *See* Deveaux, *supra* note 26, at 361.

that minimum threaten the legitimacy of the state itself.[44] If one adopts a dialogic approach to democracy, as proposed in the earlier sections of this chapter,[45] then the legitimacy of the liberal democratic state rests on the claim that authority derives from the democratic consent of the governed as manifested in such a dialogue. When the state makes the choice to exercise its power, in the form of an accommodation that supports the practices of a minority community, it must do so in accordance with this basic requirement of legitimacy. From the perspective of the state, then, the issue of democratic dialogue within the minority community is made central and crucial by the state's own commitments, regardless of whether or not those commitments are shared by the particular minority community at issue.[46]

CONCLUSION

In closing, I address two dangers associated with the approach to accommodation suggested in this chapter. First, the burden of justification placed on minority cultural communities by this approach might be seen as setting up a double standard: the majority culture, which in every liberal democratic country also contains practices that harm women, will generally be able to ensure that the legal system reflects those practices through normal democratic processes, without having to meet a similar burden of justification.

I do, indeed, intend to apply the same moral standard to both majority and minority cultural practices that harm women. The justification offered for this standard –

[44] From the perspective of a liberal, rights-based model of democracy, that minimum would probably include the specific individual rights and entitlements concomitant to citizenship. The risk of this approach is that, as our vision of individual rights and entitlements becomes richer, the space available to dissenting minority cultures might become smaller. A dialogic approach, on the other hand, allows the majority culture to develop a rich and broad conception of rights while accommodating alternative views by a minority community as long as the minority community meets the requirements for a meaningful internal dialogue about these issues. A similar inflation of the requirements for the dialogue is, of course, also possible, but it would still leave space for greater variation in the end result, thus better protecting the value of multiculturalism.

[45] Proposed, but not defended. This chapter does not address the much larger question of defending the choice of a dialogic model as against other, more liberal rights-based models of democracy. The purpose of this chapter is simply to suggest that the dialogic model of democracy offers important insights that are crucial to understanding and resolving the problem of vulnerable internal minorities. Nonetheless, the usefulness of the dialogic model in addressing this challenge could provide one argument in favor of its adoption over competing models that have proven less useful in this context.

[46] I recognize that this argument blurs the line between public and private to some extent, by holding the state accountable for the internal practices of a private community, but I believe that it is possible to adopt this position without reaching the question of whether the public/private distinction should be abandoned entirely. Whatever one thinks of the coherence or desirability of this distinction in general, it is particularly weak in cases where the government is being asked to take positive action to allow or support the acts of the private community that are harming the individual. Even if ordinary private action is not seen as implicating the legitimacy of state power, private action that was specifically authorized or supported by a positive grant of state power clearly does so. That is the type of private action at issue in an accommodation claim.

its roots in a dialogic model of democracy – makes it plain that there is no reason for distinguishing between the majority and minority in terms of the basic moral requirements for the legitimacy of power. There may, however, be some differences in the way this moral requirement is brought to bear through law and legal institutions. To the extent that the majority's cultural practices are encapsulated in legal rules, those rules will be subject to the constitutional requirement of gender equality. Thus, a vibrant and substantive conception of gender equality can and should be developed within the constitutional doctrine and should be used directly to address those majority practices that are made the basis for law. In particular, the constitutional doctrine of gender equality, which will apply to majority practices incorporated into the law, should include consideration of whether women had a meaningful opportunity to participate in and challenge the adoption and interpretation of such laws. In other words, a legal/political system without adequate representation of and participation by women should be seen as casting serious doubt on the legitimacy of rules that harm women.

Majority cultural practices that are not encapsulated in the law, on the other hand, may not be directly reviewable under the constitutional standard. Such practices will probably not require an accommodation because the law is generally designed not to interfere with the practices of the majority. As a result, there will be no opportunity for direct review of such practices unless the legal system recognizes some form of horizontal application of rights. The goal of even-handed application of this moral standard, to both majority and minority communities, would therefore support drafting or interpreting the constitutional provisions on gender equality as including such horizontal application. In short, applying this standard equally to both majority and minority cultures will require the development of specific constitutional doctrines that can extend the reach of the dialogic democracy model (and its attendant need for challenge) to include the practices of the majority culture.

The second problem with relying on internal community dialogue to deal with the issue of vulnerable internal minorities is that the cultural evolution that this model hopes to encourage is often a very slow process and, in the meantime, the women in these communities will be harmed by the persistent gender inequalities enforced by customary law. I do not in any way wish to minimize the costs that women will bear during the time it takes for them to gradually change their cultures. There are two reasons why I believe that this approach is, nonetheless, the best path to a future of greater equality.

First, it is a mistake to think that we can avoid these costs by imposing the majority culture's rules on the minority culture. In case after case around the world, the result of such efforts to impose greater equality has regularly been that the women in the cases are worse off afterward. Sometimes the women are put under tremendous pressure by their communities to renounce the benefits that the larger society is trying to extend to them, such as in the *Shah Bano* case in

India.[47] Sometimes the community forces the girls or women out of the public institutions in which the more equal practice is enforced, as was the case of the French Muslim schoolgirls who were removed from public schools that would not allow them to wear a headscarf.[48] Sometimes the girls are subjected to harsher practices within their own communities than would have been the case if the majority institution had been willing to cooperate with the minority community, as was the case with girls sent to traditional practitioners of female genital cutting when the doctors in a Seattle hospital were not allowed to perform a less damaging form of the procedure.[49] If the goal is to help the actual individual women whose welfare is at stake in such cases, it is not at all clear that an intransigent position by the majority refusing to accommodate the minority practice does in fact help them.

Second, in the long run, the welfare of the women in the community more generally depends on their ability to participate effectively in the shaping of their culture. The only way to avoid reactive culturalism and to make stable progress toward equality is for the cultural community to move toward this future through mechanisms it understands to be voluntary. Otherwise, even if a particular case can be resolved to help an individual woman, the cultural reaction generated by the imposed solution will mean that other women in the community will pay the cost: their efforts at cultural challenge and growth will be set back. In the long run, opening up the channels for internal change is a necessary part of reaching greater equality. Accommodation must therefore be transformed from a threat to vulnerable internal minorities into a mechanism through which the state and larger society can encourage more open dialogues within minority cultural communities.

[47] *See* Martha Nussbaum, *India, Sex Equality, and Constitutional Law, in* THE GENDER OF CONSTITU-TIONAL JURISPRUDENCE 191 (Beverly Baines & Ruth Rubio-Marín eds., Cambridge University Press 2005).
[48] *See* SONG, *supra* note 5, at 175.
[49] *See id.* at 166–68.

PART VI

Women between Secularism and Religion

22

Secular Constitutionalism and Muslim Women's Rights

The Turkish Headscarf Controversy and Its Impact on the European Court of Human Rights

Hilal Elver

POINT OF DEPARTURE

In recent years, there have been major public debates in several European countries about the acceptability of Muslim females wearing a headscarf or *hijab*. Excluding religiously devoted Muslim women from education and public services in some countries raises serious human rights violations in societies that would otherwise qualify as liberal democracies. In this chapter I explore the recent Turkish headscarf controversy that led Turkey to political turmoil to show its complex implications on domestic and transnational legal order. The Turkish headscarf controversy is one of the earlier and deeply complex cases. Furthermore, the Turkish reliance on secularism to justify denying women who wear headscarves into public spaces became a model legal argument for European courts. Turkey is a unique example from the perspective of secularism and religiosity because despite its "strictly secular" governmental structure, the overwhelming majority of its population adheres to what I call "societal Islam."

The headscarf controversy also situated freedom of religion in context of gender claims and Islamic culture. Articulating the specific problem in relation to Muslim women raises complex arguments about the supposed incompatibility between women's rights and Islam. Especially after the 9/11 attacks on the United States, stereotyping of Islamic societies became widespread and fear of political Islam created a real concern in mainstream American and European public opinion. The general public has engaged in racial profiling, which has produced incidents of violence, including attacks on women wearing headscarves.[1] This eventually gave rise to racialization of Muslims by way of construction of the "Muslim women's outlook."[2] Judicial cases provide an undeniable argument that emerging *Islamophobia* in the

---

[1] Leti Volp, *The Citizen and the Terrorist*, 49 UCLA L. REV. 1575 (2002).
[2] For very negative views about Islam and women's rights, *see, e.g.*, AYAAN HIRSI ALI, INFIDEL (Free Press 2007); IRSHAD MANJI, THE TROUBLE WITH ISLAM (St. Martin Press 2003).

West and elsewhere negatively affects Muslim women's daily life, education, and participation in the workplace. There are a range of policy outcomes and various degrees of tolerance and/or discrimination against Muslim women because of uneven domestic political matters, cultural differences, and constitutional orders of various countries.[3]

In Europe and in the United States, the headscarf controversy extended beyond an individual's freedom of religion and gave rise to the sociopolitical consequences of being an "other." In Turkey, however, the debate is embedded in its unique historical struggle to establish and maintain a secular democracy in a religious society. I begin the chapter with the current political crises associated with the headscarf controversy, taking into account the controversy's social, political, and legal ramifications. In the second part, I evaluate the pivotal role of the European Human Rights Court (ECHR) decisions that uphold national bans on headscarf cases. These cases are good examples of how judicial action turned a seemingly domestic debate into a transnational issue. Evaluating and interpreting these cases, I conclude that the role of judges as interpreters of human rights principles and constitutional order in domestic and international courts is crucial.

I. TURKEY

A. *Current Headscarf Controversy*

Turkey is the only country where students who wear headscarves are not allowed to attend universities. This continues even though 99 percent of the population is Muslim, approximately 64 percent of Turkish women wear a headscarf, and 70 percent of Turks think that the headscarf ban should be lifted at universities.[4] The headscarf debate in Turkey is deeply emotional and political, dividing society sharply into two uncompromising camps.

In July 2007, when the Justice and Development Party (AKP), sympathetic to Islam, came to power for the second time, the headscarf debate became a priority on the country's political agenda. In April 2007 during the presidential election, the legal and political atmosphere transformed into chaos because the presidential candidate's wife wore a headscarf. The attacks focused on a single question: how dare a First Lady wear a headscarf, a symbol of Islam or more crudely, "a symbol of backwardness"? Secular citizens organized street demonstrations, meetings, TV ads, art exhibitions, and dance and music performances to show how Turkish women would be captured, imprisoned, and victimized by Islamic tradition if they wore a headscarf.

---

[3] In Europe, for instance, while France issued a law against wearing "ostentatious religious symbols" in secondary schools, in Germany the Constitutional Court permitted "Landers" to enact a law against wearing headscarves if they wish.

[4] Headscarf Report 2007, *available at* www.mazlumder.org (last visited February 2009).

These secular demonstrations also conveyed that Turkey would be going backward if it lifted the headscarf ban at universities. Following the collapse of the six-hundred-year, longest, and last remaining Islamic empire, the Ottoman Empire, Kemal Atatürk's reforms in the 1920s represented a historically unique and significant attempt to make Turkey modern, European, and Western. Secularists believed and feared that the freedom to wear headscarves in universities would defy Atatürk's vision, and be the first step toward the downfall of secular Turkey and the inevitable return to the dark days of the Ottoman period.

The underlying issue here was not only about secularism, modernity, and fear of Islamization, but more importantly, it was about losing political power. The urban secular elite were uneasy about sharing public space with an emerging Anatolian middle class and a new political and business elite. In this anti-AKP campaign, secular feminists played an enormous role. In many urban centers of Turkey, secular women's organizations in solidarity with the opposition party CHP and the military leadership conducted huge public demonstrations called "Republic Protests" in support of the Kemalist ideal of state secularism.

The tipping point came in February 2008 when the newly elected Turkish government, to keep their election promise, enacted a constitutional amendment to lift the headscarf ban in universities.[5] Instead of solving the ongoing problem, the amendment created outcry and confusion in universities and in the public opinion because of the polarized societal structure. Soon after, the CHP took the headscarf question to the Constitutional Court.[6] Although legal arguments persisted on the headscarf case, an unexpected development occurred in March 2008 when the chief prosecutor filed a case against the governing party, asking the Constitutional Court to close down the AKP and ban the prime minister and the president from politics.[7]

Soon after, the Constitutional Court handed down its historical twin decisions. In the first case, the court ruled against lifting the headscarf ban at universities. This was expected given the court's earlier jurisprudence on the issue.[8] This time however, the court articulated the judgment carefully to discourage any future legislative attempt

[5] The constitutional amendment on February 9, 2008, added few words to Article 10 (principle of equality) and Article 42 (freedom of education) to lift the headscarf ban in universities. For detailed information, *see* Hilal Elver, *Lawfare and Wearfare in Turkey, in* THE MIDDLE EAST REPORT (April 2008), http://merip.org/mero/interventions.

[6] On February 19, 2008, CHP members applied to the Constitutional Court, asking that the court invalidate Law No. 5737, dated Feb. 9, 2008. The CHP argued that the law violated the secularism principles and was contrary to Articles 1, 2, 3, 4, 6, 7, 8, 9, 24, 42, 138, 153, 174, and the Preamble of the Constitution.

[7] The Turkish Constitutional Court is notorious for its activism in the area of political party closures. In the court's history, there are twenty-four party closure cases. Many of these parties were religious parties, and some of them were ethnically oriented Kurdish parties.

[8] The decisions of 1989 and 1992 of the Constitutional Court on headscarf bans in universities are clear indications of the court's view on the headscarf issue, and this view was repeated in recent cases.

to amend the Constitution as a prelude to lifting the headscarf ban.[9] The second decision on the AKP party's closure was highly political and created international outrage and domestic pressure. The governing party escaped closure by a narrow margin. The Constitutional Court's twin decisions effectively blocked democratic channels not only to lifting the headscarf ban in Turkey but also to any future parliament-initiated constitutional reform. The court, as an unelected institution, designated itself as the sole arbiter of its own authority.

This recent political and legal turmoil shows that the Turkish headscarf controversy has an impact not just on female university students but on the society at large. It goes back to the historical period when the Ottomans heavily regulated citizens' clothing as an indication of ethnic and professional background. Clothing had always been political, a tool that displaced power relations causing important social, economic, and legal consequences in society. The Turkish Republic inherited this preoccupation when it transformed from an Islamic empire to a secular republic. During and after the transformation period, Turkish women were an agency of modernity and Western-oriented secularism, and they provided a representation of the new secular state and modern society.

As inspired by European models, the Cultural Revolution became integral to the nation-building effort to transform the society into a unified and homogenized social entity. Turkish reformers believed that the real basis of European political superiority was embodied in its culture and legal system and sought to Europeanize Turkish society through law. In this process of Westernization, secularism was the overarching objective, to which all other goals were subordinated. The transformation also included achieving the Cultural Revolution's aim not only in the Republic's public sphere and political life, but also in the private sphere of Republic's social fabric.[10]

Atatürk imposed legal reforms, designed to alter the daily lifestyles of ordinary Turkish people, on Turkish society. These reforms affected their alphabet, style of dress, calendar year, and much more. Atatürk's aim was to transform the outlook from its supposed backwardness that was identified with anything related to Islam, to modernity, which was associated with being European. Nevertheless, Atatürk was very careful not to touch the headscarf issue, knowing that this piece of dress had an important cultural meaning beyond religious duty. He did not hesitate to ban the *fez*, a certain type of headgear for men, and also the wearing of religious dresses in public outside of religious ceremonies. Sensitivity about the headscarf during the most dramatic cultural reform gives us an understanding of how important its cultural meaning was for Turkish women. Even though Turkish women were a major agency to represent modernity and the transformation to Western lifestyle, tradition was too strong to ban the headscarf. The founders of the secular Turkish

---

[9] For structural consequences of the headscarf decision, see Hilal Elver, *The Headscarf as an Instrument of Political Suicide in Turkey*, TODAY'S ZAMAN, Nov. 19, 2008, *available at* www.zaman.com.

[10] For a detailed discussion on Westernized public/private spheres, see FEROZ AHMED, THE MAKING MODERN TURKEY (Routledge 1993).

State preferred to encourage women not to wear a headscarf indirectly by way of media, endless pictures, and speeches.

The Turkish State, through its secular policies and Westernization programs, threatened the Muslim value system without providing a satisfactory ideological framework that had sufficient mass appeal to replace Islam. Turkey did not enjoy as smooth of a transition to modernity as the Kemalist seculars claim. Almost 99 percent of the population was Muslim, with the great majority of it living in rural areas. Only a small minority of the population who belonged to the middle and upper classes and who lived in urban areas adopted the Western outlook and mentality. Unofficially, local Islamic tradition continued to survive despite all the State's attempts to eliminate religious elements from the legal system.[11]

This bipolar social structure begun to change in the 1980s when Turkey became part of the global economy by shifting its system from a state-planned economy to free-market capitalism. Economic prosperity triggered domestic immigration to city centers, where previous residents of villages and small towns were demanding education, jobs, political participation, and the modern lifestyles that had previously been reserved for the urban elite. The economic and social transformation was most noticeable to secular urbanites through young females who demanded a university education with their elegantly worn headscarves. The headscarf was a symbol of old bad days, Islam, patriarchal family structure – anything that secular Turks wanted to forget, but that the neo-conservative new middle class tried to bring back as their never-abandoned reality.

B. *The Headscarf Conflict in Turkish Courts*

In the 1950s, encouraged and supported by the modernization project, women's participation in public life and female student enrollment in universities significantly increased. Among the admitted female students, only a few wore a headscarf. Therefore, until the end of 1960s, very few students were expelled from the universities for wearing a headscarf.

In 1980, military coup and its legal and structural consequences brought the headscarf controversy to the Turkish political scene. Under the influence of the Iranian Revolution, political Islam gained power in Turkey and religion became one of the prominent alternative ideologies available in the Cold War era. At the same time, the social and economic conditions in the country triggered internal and external migration from villages and small Anatolian towns to urban centers. As a result, headscarf use in universities increased. Turkish women quickly became the first victims of an image war between Islamists and secularists that centered mainly on the headscarf. During the Cold War period, Muslim students, especially

---

[11] Ihsan Yilmaz, *Nonrecognition of Post-Modern Turkish Sociolegal Reality and the Predicament of Women*, 30 BRITISH JOURNAL OF MIDDLE EASTERN STUDIES 26 (2003).

females, were not considered as much of a threat to the Turkish State. At the same time, however, it was very difficult for the military, as self-proclaimed representatives of Kemalist ideology, to allow a Muslim presence. In the political arena there was uncertainty about the status of wearing a headscarf. It was neither legally banned nor socially accepted.

Government was rather reluctant to issue a law to ban headscarf use in universities, worrying that it would create political backlash against their electoral gain. However, this was not the case for the judiciary, who was very secular and had no fear of political gain. The Highest Administrative Court (HAC) was the pioneer in the headscarf battle, and the Constitutional Court followed in its footsteps. In its decisions against headscarf use between 1983 and 1989, the HAC kept repeating the same reasoning, predominantly based on Turkish modernity, secularity, and Atatürk's reforms. More strikingly, the HAC in one of its earlier decisions categorized girls into two groups: "Uneducated, traditional, innocent girls who wear turbans because they follow others; or educated, but their world view is against freedom of women and [the] foundational principles of [the] Turkish Republic."[12] The HAC repeated this argument in several cases without any hesitation despite the discriminatory or gender-sensitive language.

In 1989, the Turkish Constitutional Court delivered its landmark decision on the headscarf question. It annulled the statute that allowed headscarf use in universities, arguing that secularism had a unique history in Turkey and the legislative body could not introduce a legal measure that took religious convictions into account.[13] This was the first comprehensive Constitutional Court decision against headscarf use, and became a major legal precedent for future cases in Turkey and eventually abroad. The decisions' reasoning was more political than legal. The Constitutional Court emphasized the primacy of the secularism principle over any other democratic principles in the Constitution, and did not make any effort to protect an individual's right of freedom of religion, or education. Rather, the court strongly emphasized the protection of students who did not wear headscarves in case they might face social pressure.

The existing legal ambiguity and difficulty of implementing such rules literally left it up to the individual discretion of university administrations. For many years, students and administrators tried to find creative solutions. For instance, some universities created "persuasion rooms" at the entrance of the schools to convince students to abandon their headscarves to gain entrance. Some students agreed, while others replaced headscarves with wigs, hats, or many other creative disguises. Although many students used these loopholes, some decided instead to give up their education.

---

[12] *See* Danistay 8th Section judgments (cited in SEMIH GEMALMAZ, TURK KIYAFET HUKUKU VE TURBAN [Turkish Dress Code and Turban]), 1214 (Legal Yayincilik 2008).

[13] E.1989/I, K. 1989/12, T. 7.3.1989, JCC 1991 at 25. The court in its decision annulled the Higher Education Statute No. 2547, Article 44.

In 1997, when the religious Welfare Party was a coalition partner of the government, the military demanded the resignation of the Deputy Prime Minister by "electronic ultimatum" because of his desire to lift the headscarf ban. In 1998, after being pushed out of the governing position, the Constitutional Court dismantled the Welfare Party, emphasizing that the Party's support of the freedom to wear a headscarf was the major reason for the decision.

In 1999, a confrontation about the headscarf took place in the Turkish Parliament. Newly elected parliamentary member Merve Kavakci, from the new Islamic Party Virtue (a continuation of the dismantled Islamic Welfare Party), wanted to enter Parliament wearing a headscarf. Fellow Parliament members from secular parties accused her of mounting a political attack on secularism and Turkish democracy. The incident received international media attention and triggered a move for the abolition of the Virtue Party by the Constitutional Court. Furthermore, Kavakci lost her Turkish citizenship because of a technical violation of the Turkish Citizenship Law. In sum, the headscarf became a political and legal tool to attack two democratically elected Islamic parties and expel them from politics.

In the 2000s, when the secular parties were in power, they implemented what was proclaimed as "zero tolerance to the headscarf." The Minister of Education declared, "[Wearing a headscarf] is a crime, the punishment is dismissal from the civil service. Everybody must comply with this rule. If they don't, they have no place among us."[14] Against the strict implementation of this ban, thousands of students and civil servants filed court applications. Although some of these applications were settled in favor of them in lower courts, they were consistently rejected by the higher courts. In the 2002 election when the AKP came into power, the headscarf ban was a sensitive political matter. Despite their religious-friendly stance, the current Turkish government, fearful of strong secular forces, has refrained from giving favor to the headscarf issue until the 2008 incident that brought the country political turmoil.

C. Invisible Women

For almost four decades, this ongoing power struggle has caused two generations of religiously devout women to lose educational and professional opportunities. These women have been set aside, pushed out, and humiliated by seculars, university administrations, and government bureaucracies. The first generation of women who were expelled from universities are now grandmothers. These women could not hold position in public offices, those who were lawyers were not allowed to represent their clients before courts, and some even had difficulties gaining access to court buildings.[15] Despite this, there is still a lack of sympathy in secular public debate for women who wear headscarves.

---

[14] Turkish Daily News, Feb. 11, 2000.
[15] *Come Without Headscarf* (translation), Yeni Safak Daily Newspaper, Nov. 7, 2003.

The headscarf ban has been unjustly advocated and promoted using the concept of "public space," a phrase that is not derived from legal terminology.[16] By defining almost all places as "public," this concept has been used and abused to exclude Muslim women. Although excluding Islam from public spaces was difficult, it was possible at least to push away women with headscarves from public spaces to project an image of the secular Turkish State as Western and modern. For instance, the current president's and the prime minister's wives were excluded from national day celebrations and public events for wearing their headscarf; or women wearing headscarves were prosecuted in Turkey for participating in a workshop in Ministerial offices. Many strange things happened in Turkey that, while are amusing for outsiders, are heartbreaking for those victimized. Many administrators have claimed power to regulate public places to exclude women with headscarves without any legitimate foundation.

Despite there being no regulation against headscarf use, the ban in the public sector also influences the private sector, and women wearing headscarves are facing a variety of difficulties and discriminations when they attempt to find a job. Because the job market already offers limited positions, these women, if they are employed at all, are given unfairly low wages. However, the real danger was introducing this exclusionary concept in the courts. For instance, the Highest Administrative Court (*Danistay*) affirmed a decision by a lower court, which denied entry to citizens who wear headscarves into a public library. According to the *Danistay*'s decision, it was necessary to affirm the lower court's ruling as doing otherwise would make it difficult for the Constitutional Court and other high courts to establish a consistent jurisprudence on the headscarf in public spaces.[17]

Because the headscarf ban is practiced in an inconsistent manner at different times and in different forms depending on the political atmosphere in Turkey, it is very difficult to assess the scope of the ban, as well as find out the number of women who have been discriminated against. There are no reliable statistics on how many girls were expelled from universities because university administrations did not give reasons for expulsion. In fact, 90 percent of expelled female students who were not permitted to attend classes because of the ban on headscarves were expelled under the guise of absenteeism.[18] Since June 2000, allegedly 270,000 students out of 677,000 who were expelled from higher education institutions were victims of the headscarf ban.[19] There have been reports that approximately 5,000 female teachers

[16] For the concept of "public space," see JURGEN HABERMAS, STRUCTURAL TRANSFORMATION OF PUBLIC SPHERE (MIT Press 1991).
[17] 1st Administrative Court of Istanbul, 23/12/2003, 2002/1666 E; The High Administrative Court (*Danistay*) section 8, 7/2/2005, 2004/3421 E, 2995/460 K, *available at* www.liberal-dt.org.tr.
[18] Ali Bulac, *AIHM ve Basortusu* [The EHCR and Headscarf], 129 UMRAN DERGISI 33 (May 2005).
[19] Fatma Benli, *Assessment of the Women Condition in Turkey According to the Statistics and the General Impacts of the Ban on Women*, for Organization for Women's Rights against Discrimination (AKDER), Istanbul Turkey, 2007.

were fired for this same reason.[20] The economic, social, and more importantly, emotional consequences of such a ban on women and their families, generation after generation, will always be difficult to fully know.

The headscarf situation unfairly impacts women because it is acceptable for men to be religious without risking humiliation or exclusion from universities or public jobs. Indeed, it seems the only humiliation for a religious man is having a wife with a headscarf! It is almost impossible to understand why liberal, secular feminists do not appreciate such an important problem in Turkish society. The silence of the liberal intellectuals, with few exceptions, is disappointing. Aside from a few research projects and secular intellectuals, the great majority do not pay attention to the legal and social consequences of remaining silent. The Turkish government shows no current desire to help women with headscarves because of their experience with the Constitutional Court in 2008.

It seems that these women are forgotten now, at least until the next election. These women's political power is needed for elections, and only then. Not only the AKP, but other parties have discovered this power of women. Recently, the strong secularist opposition party CHP has accepted several women delegates who wear the *shador*, which is a more extreme religious dress than the headscarf. This move is widely considered as a symbolic political gesture only with no real desire to include such women in political life. The headscarf women are fearful that this more extreme image will be a setback to their existence and hurtful to their reformist agenda.

II. THE HEADSCARF DEBATE GOES TO THE EUROPEAN COURT OF HUMAN RIGHTS

Since as early as the 1990s, the European Human Rights Commission opened its doors as a last resort to assess appeal decisions from the member countries' domestic courts. In 1993, two female students applied to the European Human Rights Commission, claiming violations of the right to education and equality when one of the Turkish universities refused to give diplomas to female students who wore headscarves. The Commission simply followed the 1989 decision of the Turkish Constitutional Court, maintaining that the secular state had the right to restrict religious practices if to do so was consistent with a citizens' right to equal treatment and religious freedom. The Turkish educational establishment, the government, and judicial elite gladly relied on this 1993 Commission decision given the Commission's considerable prestige and authority to validate the ban.[21] The Commission, however,

---

[20] Mehmer Agar, *Would It Hurt if We Win Women Wearing Headscarf?* (translation), ZAMAN DAILY NEWSPAPER, Oct. 1, 2004.

[21] *See Lamia Karabulut and Senay Karaduman v. Turkish Government*, Admissibility Decision on Application No. 18783/91, May 3, 1993.

failed to deal correctly with existing laws, political complexity, and more importantly, the gender issue.

The decision did not discuss the unequal treatment between male and female students in relation to representing and practicing their religion. This was a disappointment for both the few liberal feminists and the many headscarf wearers. Although strictly secular Turkish courts clearly were not showing any mercy to headscarf wearers, the supranational human rights court, the European Commission of Human Rights, should have been the venue to protect such rights against oppressed governments – but it did not.[22]

The European Commission of Human Rights has been superseded by the full-time European Court of Human Rights (ECHR). Many headscarf victims have sought relief from the new court, including the wife of the current Turkish president, Abdullah Gul. Ironically, when Gul was the Minister of Foreign Affairs in 2002, his wife withdrew her complaint against the Turkish government.[23] The court is consistent in its treatment of controversies concerning the headscarf ban, deciding always in support of the Turkish government.[24] This was even true when the ECHR rejected the Islamic Welfare Party's application against the Turkish Constitutional Court's decision on the party's closure. After the disappointment of the Welfare Party case, another Islamic Party, *Fazilet Partisi* [Virtue], which was also dismantled by the decision of the Constitutional Court, decided to withdraw its application from the ECHR. These developments convinced a large portion of the Turkish public opinion that the ECHR's decision was biased against Islamic values in Europe and in Turkey, and that it acted politically rather than legally. In many other cases, however, especially on minority rights and due-process principles, the ECHR has taken strong positions in favor of the protection of human rights and has ruled against the Turkish government. The court's first and most famous decision in relation to headscarves was *Leyla Sahin v. Turkey*, which was delivered in 2005 by the Grand Chamber of the ECHR.

Next, I discuss and analyze a few headscarf cases that have reached the court from various member-states.

A. Dahlab v. Switzerland

This first case is a 2001 inadmissibility decision against a Swiss primary school teacher, Lucia Dahlab, in the canton of Geneva. Dahlab, who had converted to Islam, was prohibited from wearing a headscarf after performing her professional duties for four

---

[22] This 1993 decision, however, was consistent with the Commission's earlier and lesser-known decision on the headscarf controversy in Turkey. *See Yanasik v. Turkey* (Jan. 6, 1993, DR 74, p.14–28).
[23] *Tekin v. Turkey* No. 41556/98.
[24] *Kalac v. Turkey* (inadmissibility decision, June 23, 1997); *Dal and Ozen v. Turkey* (inadmissibility decision, October 3, 2002); *Akbulut v. Turkey* (inadmissibility decision, June 2, 2003).

years.[25] During that time there were no complaints from her colleagues, her pupils, or their parents. When her students asked her why she covered her head, she said it was to keep her ears warm.[26] She seemed to have been very sensitive about not proselytizing – so much so that she used this excuse "of keeping her ears warm" rather than identify herself as a Muslim to her students. Right after 9/11, the school inspector reported and the school's director general issued a direction requesting that Dahlab cease wearing these garments at school. She refused and challenged this decision in the Swiss courts, where she lost. She then brought the case to ECHR.

The ECHR upheld the government's request that she remove her headscarf. There are three key elements to the reasoning: 1) the wearing of an Islamic headscarf might have a proselytizing effect; 2) the headscarf is incompatible with gender equality; and 3) it is incompatible with tolerance and respect. The ECHR found that the ordinance did not target the plaintiff's religious belief, but rather it aimed "to protect other's freedom and security of public order" given that the young children in Dahlab's classes (ages four and eight) were "more easily influenced [than older children] by such a powerful external symbol."[27] The ECHR concurred with the Swiss Federal Court's view that the prohibition on wearing a headscarf in the context of the applicant's activities as a teacher was "justified by the potential interference with the religious beliefs of her pupils at the school and the pupils' parents, and by the breach of the principle of denominational neutrality in schools."[28]

None of these three major arguments in the *Dahlab* case were supported by the facts or by evidence. Instead, a woman with an excellent employment record who had spent years wearing Islamic clothing (with no complaints from her pupils or their parents) had been effectively sacked because of her religion. The case did not even receive full and proper consideration by the ECHR. In 2001, the judgment did not seem to be a particularly important; but when *Sahin* and *Dogru* were brought before the court, it became clear that the decision and its reasoning would have larger effects.

B. Leyla Sahin v. Turkey

In 2005, the Grand Chamber of the ECHR ruled that obstructing medical school student Leyla Sahin's education was permissible in a democratic society. The ECHR's interpretation of religious freedom (Article 9 of the European Convention of Human Rights [Convention]) in *Leyla Sahin v. Turkey* was a more serious case than in

[25] *Dahlab v. Switzerland*, App. No. 42393/98, 2001-V Eur. Ct. H.R. 447.

[26] *Id.* at 456.

[27] Carolyn Evans, *The "Islamic Scarf" in the European Court of Human Rights*, 7 MELB. J. INT'L L. 52, 64 (2006).

[28] The ECHR did not even consider that there would be Muslims among the pupils and their families too. Switzerland is a country that has significant immigrant populations, the majority of which are from Turkey. This decision might have a significant negative impact on Muslim minorities in this particular school region.

Dahlab, in that it went all the way to the Grand Chamber.[29] The court's basic argument was that the headscarf ban in Turkish universities does not necessarily violate the freedom of religion; rather, such a ban was legally acceptable given the prevailing conditions in Turkey. The ECHR did not hesitate to acknowledge concerns about Islamic extremism, even though there was absolutely no evidence that Leyla Sahin was part of any political movement of this kind;[30] in fact, the court itself accepted the claim that she wore a headscarf because of her religious beliefs. The decision came as a surprise to many liberal legal scholars and human rights organizations in Turkey, Europe, and the United States. Yet it was celebrated in the secular circle as the final result of the legal debate on headscarves; secularists claimed that there was no higher legal authority than the ECHR, and any further discussion should be curtailed.

Ms. Sahin, a twenty-four-year-old student, was a fifth-year student at the Faculty of Medicine of the University of Istanbul. In 1998, the university issued a circular declaring that students with headscarves must not be admitted to lectures, courses, and examination. Ms. Sahin was thus excluded from school because she refused to remove her headscarf and she participated in protests against these "dress code" rules. After she exhausted domestic legal remedies, she brought a suit against Turkey for upholding the university's decision to prohibit her from taking exams or attending lectures while wearing her headscarf. Although a general university amnesty released her from this penalty, she left the university and completed her studies in Austria.

In its decision of June 29, 2004, a seven-judge Chamber of the ECHR unanimously held that there had been no violation of Sahin's freedom of religion under Article 9. In reaching its decision, the ECHR Chamber drew on the Turkish Constitution, legal practices concerning Turkey's development as a secular state, as well as on the case law of the Constitutional Court. Importantly, the ECHR also drew on court decisions and legal debates on the Islamic headscarf and state education in some European countries without noticing that none of those countries had headscarf bans in universities. The ECHR explicitly quoted the French National Assembly's Bill of February 2004 (which became law in March 2004) banning "ostentatious" religious symbols in state primary and secondary schools. The ECHR also cited the September 24, 2003, *Ludin* case from the German Constitutional Court as an example of a legal position that seemed to run counter to that of other EU member-states.[31]

On September 27, 2004, Sahin requested that the case be referred to the Grand Chamber of the ECHR; one year later, a seventeen-judge panel handed down a decision, which included a separate "concurring opinion" of two judges, and a dissenting opinion. The majority decision of the Grand Chamber followed the lower Chamber's decision reaffirming that Turkey's political concern legitimized

---

[29] *Sahin v. Turkey*, App. No. 44774/98, [2005] E. Ct. H.R. (GC) 819.
[30] *Id.* ¶ 109.
[31] The leading case is Ludin, Bundesverfassungsgericht [BVerfG] [Federal Constitutional Court] Sep. 24, 2003, 108 Entscheidungen des Bundesverfassungsgerichts [BVerfGE] 282 (F.R.G.).

the interference with Sahin's freedom of religion. The ECHR did not emphasize the proselytizing effect of headscarves, as it did in *Dahlab*; rather, it emphasized pressure on other students who did not wear headscarves. However, as we mentioned earlier, the Grand Chamber relied in part on the *Dahlab* decision with respect to gender equality and tolerance, and cited the relevant portions of the *Dahlab* case in its conclusion.[32]

Key concerns in *Sahin* include 1) the possibility that an Islamic political party may rise in popularity and move to create a fully Islamic state in Turkey;[33] 2) that the headscarf is a sign of gender inequality; and 3) that the headscarf is an element of intolerance and threat to Turkish secularism.

Even though the reasonableness of the Turkish state's concerns was highly questionable, it was similar to those of European public opinion at the time. The ECHR thus took those concerns seriously. The ECHR also made clear that the legitimacy of a ban in terms of human rights was highly context specific. This left the door wide open for a different judgment in different sociopolitical circumstances, and many commentators have interpreted this as an implied reference to the French law that banned religious symbols in public schools.[34] The ECHR's referral gave legitimacy to the highly questionable French law. Even though the French legal system generally does not allow for judicial review of legislation, French citizens may still challenge the law by filing a complaint directly with the ECHR because France is a signatory of the European Convention of Human Rights.

In cases dealing with Article 9, the ECHR seems to have a somewhat consistent procedure for its analysis. It discusses first whether the state has interfered with the rights set forth in Article 9. If this is answered in the positive, it then decides whether the state can justify the restrictions placed on the specific act (in these cases, the ban on headscarf use) according to the criteria set out in Article 9(2) of the Convention. The ECHR first decided that Turkey interfered with Sahin's right to freedom of religion.[35] This part of the decision has been viewed as a big success, as the court significantly departed from its earlier decisions involving headscarves. The court then moved onto a more extensive analysis to find out what conditions are necessary to allow this limit on freedom of religion. According to Article 9(2), i) the restriction should be prescribed by law; and ii) it should be necessary in a "democratic society" in the interest of "public safety, for the protection of public order, health, or morals, or for the protection of the rights and freedom of others."[36]

The court first had to address how to interpret "prescribed by law." The court opted to give a generous interpretation to what "law" meant and effectively elevated a

---

[32] *Dahlab v. Switzerland*, 2001-V Eur. Ct. H.R. 447, at ¶ 46.
[33] See *Refah Partisi (Welfare Party) and Others v. Turkey*, 35 Eur. H.R. Rep. 3 (2002).
[34] See *Sahin*, [2005] E. Ct. H.R. (GC) 819, ¶¶ 115 & 136.
[35] *Id.* ¶ 78.
[36] European Convention on Human Rights, Article 9(2).

circular, provided by the Vice-Chancellor of Istanbul University, to law.[37] The court then proceeded to address the second portion of the Article 9(2) analysis, whether the limitation of religious freedom is "necessary in a democratic society."[38] This part of the decision was the most problematic part. Even though the ECHR interpreted and implemented various liberal principles while rhetorically following European human rights principles based on the Convention and the courts' jurisprudence, it did not bother to evaluate such principles in the context of specific cases.[39] Rather, literally, point by point it followed the Turkish government's defense. Doing so, the ECHR used the margin of appreciation principle,[40] a contested area of the human rights court.[41]

In delimiting the extent of the margin of appreciation, the ECHR regarded what was at stake, namely "the need to protect the rights and freedom of others, to preserve public order and the secure civil peace and true religious pluralism."[42] Referring to its earlier case *Karaduman*, the ECHR claimed that "measures taken in universities to prevent certain fundamentalist religious movement from exerting pressure on students who did not practice their religion or who belong to another religion were found to be justified by the Convention."[43]

According to Jeremy Gunn, "We would not normally expect a human rights tribunal to be more solicitous of the sensibilities of those who do not like religious expression (which is not guaranteed by the European Convention)."[44] Moreover, Turkey presented no evidence at all that the wearing of the headscarf in schools created social pressure on students who chose not to wear it. The court did not look for this evidence either. There are, however, numerous ways the ECHR could have looked for evidence of Islamist pressure on women to wear the headscarf in universities, including considering Ms. Sahin's story itself.

The ECHR oversimplified the use of headscarf in Turkey as merely an indicator of a polarizing opposition between the threat of fundamental Islamism to secularists seeking to retain a secular democracy and legal system. Wearing a headscarf has

---

[37] *Id.* ¶ 121.

[38] *Id.* ¶¶ 100–23.

[39] *Id.* ¶¶ 104, 106–108.

[40] Margin of appreciation refers to the level of scrutiny/deference afforded to national authorities by the ECHR to determine whether a particular interference with a right is necessary in a democratic society to protect health, morals, or other interests listed.

[41] The idea behind this principle is that national legal systems and democratically elected authorities are often better placed to address issues arising within their own territories. Therefore the "margin" is "variable in the sense that the closer you get to the core values of democracy, the narrower the margin will be." The "margin of appreciation" doctrine is somewhat similar to the American idea of a standard review; when the ECHR margin of appreciation is narrowed, the effect is similar to the heightening of an American court's level of scrutiny.

[42] *Sahin*, [2005] E. Ct. H.R. (GC) 819, ¶ 110.

[43] *Id.*

[44] Jeremy Gunn, *Religious Freedom and Laicite*, BYU L. REV. 422 (2004).

multiple meanings in modern Turkey, including tradition, religion, class and ethnicity, and even for the empowerment of women. Information on its uses is easily accessible. Moreover, there was no proof that women in Switzerland or Turkey were being forced to wear a headscarf. Indeed, a brief inquiry in the issue would reveal otherwise. In this circumstance, a more accurate description of the situation was that educated, intelligent women were adopting the headscarf as voluntary compliance with what they perceived to be a religious obligation.[45] The court also failed to discuss how clothing is viewed in different Muslim societies and by the different Muslim scholars. Instead, the ECHR adopted a vague, broad-brush approach to the issue and relied on the popular (misconceived) Western view that the Quran and Islam are generally oppressive to women. The court did not see any need to be more specific and, by doing so, inferred that wearing a headscarf must, by extension of this self-evident, shared Western understanding of Islam, be similarly oppressive to women.[46]

Although *Dahlab* and *Sahin* both deal with a ban on wearing a headscarf, the ECHR, with the exception of discussing the differences in the proselytizing effect, did not pay attention to the significant differences between them: The facts and consequences of *Dahlab* took place Switzerland, a predominantly Christian country, as opposed to *Sahin*, which took place in Turkey, a predominantly Muslim country; *Dahlab* was a teacher, *Sahin* was a university student. Regardless, the previously mentioned differences simply do not matter, and the court did not bother to prove its value judgments that seemed to be based on stereotype.

The ECHR then evaluated the concept of secularism and intolerance to justify the headscarf ban. The court did not make any effort to connect the applicants' acts in either judgment. Both applicants did not take part in any religious organizations or political movement that promoted Islamic fundamentalism, nor did they participate in any civil disobedience in their schools or workplace. At some level, the court seemed to be saying that anyone who is sufficiently serious about advertising the fact that they are Muslim must be fundamentalists and should not be tolerated. To do that, the ECHR equated Islam with intolerance, suggesting that the Islamic woman is under oppression. The ECHR then placed "intolerant" Islam opposite secularism, describing political Islam on one side and the classical liberal role of the state on the other.[47] However, it is not certain that secularism always works hand in hand with democracy and religious freedom. On the contrary, history is full of opposite examples that show otherwise and there was a wide range of literature available to the ECHR had the court been willing to explore it.[48]

---

[45] The ECHR literally used a language that is highly questionable: "appears to be imposed on women by a precept which is laid down in Koran," *Dahlab v. Switzerland*, 2001-V Eur. Ct. H.R. 447, 449.

[46] Evans, *supra* note 27, at 65.

[47] *Sahin*, [2005] E. Ct. H.R. (GC) 819, ¶ 107.

[48] Jeremy Gunn's view on the role of laicite and religious freedom in France and the United States provides an example of conflicts between the two: "But despite the popular beliefs that laicite and

Although promoting the concept of secularism in general is highly problematic, the ECHR took one further step to promote the even more problematic concept of *Turkish* secularism. The ECHR with its almost congratulatory tone found that Turkish secularism is consistent with the values underpinning the Convention. This was a rather important comment, because the ECHR as a European Institution has never given, in any of its earlier decisions, such confirmation to a Turkish constitutional order and its democracy.[49] Some commentators even opined that the ECHR's unjustified deference to Turkey's secularism principle was the most determinant factor affecting the *Sahin* case's outcome.[50] Many scholars harshly criticized the court's deference to Turkish secularism, pointing out that the ECHR's unqualified assumption that Turkey's headscarf ban, as well as its constitutional principles of secularism and equality, arose as the result of a democratic process, at best "systematically mislead[] the reader."[51] The ECHR never mentioned that several contradictory headscarf regulations had been issued during a period of political turmoil in Turkey. It never mentioned the military's effect and role on Turkish politics and secularism principles. The court did not recognize that the Turkish Constitution has no democratic tone but a militaristic color. The ECHR's general attitude toward Turkish cases was very critical. However, with respect to headscarf cases and because Islam was becoming a European problem, the ECHR knowingly preferred not to look critically at Turkish politics; rather the court preferred to condemn Islam using arguments from the Muslim world.

The ECHR's view of Turkish secularism as promoting gender equality, and as being guarantor of democratic values and the "meeting point of liberty and equality," are some of the reasons that the court approved of this form of secularism. To the court, there appeared to be an opportunity for women to be freed from religious restraints and societal pressures when Turkey became a secular state. The court needed further elaborate research before concluding such an authoritative result about gender development in Turkey. Although there has been significant development in women's legal status since the Republic's establishment, there has been a huge gap between legal rights in law books and the social structure in Turkey. This issue has initiated significant amount of research but there was no reference to this

---

religious freedom are founding principles that unite the citizens of their respective countries, they actually operate in ways that are more akin to founding myths. . . . In current controversies involving religion and the state, where the doctrines are cited for the ostensible purpose or resolving conflicts, they continue to be applied in ways that divide citizens on the basis of their beliefs and that belittle those whose beliefs do not conform to popular preferences." See Jeremy Gunn, *Religious Freedom and Laicite*, 2004 BRIGHAM YOUNG UNIVERSITY L. REV. 422.

49 *Sahin*, [2005] E. Ct. H.R. (GC) 819, ¶ 114.

50 Jennifer M. Westerfield, *Behind the Veil: An American Legal Perspective on the European Headscarf Debate*, 54 AM. J. COMP. L. 639 (2006); *See also*, among others, the works of Carolyn Evans, Jeremy Gunn, and Tore Lindholm.

51 T. Jeremy Gunn, "Fearful Symbols: The Islamic Headscarf and the European Court of Human Rights" *available at* www.strasbourgconference.org/papers.php.

matter in the judgment. Moreover, banning headscarves had a very negative impact on gender equality, an issue that the ECHR never articulated.[52]

Finally, the ECHR had to determine whether there was a reasonable relationship of proportionality between the means employed and the legitimate objectives pursued by the interference. It stated that, "[p]racticing Muslim students in Turkish universities are free, within the limits imposed by educational organizational constraints, to manifest their religion in accordance with habitual forms of Muslim observance."[53] This was simply not true; students with headscarves certainly were not free to observe their religion. Moreover, the ECHR did not have the prerequisite Islamic knowledge to decide whether the headscarf was a "habitual" form of Muslim observance. Like some courts in the United States,[54] the ECHR should, in the absence of an expert witness, accept an individual's interpretation about the content of observation in particular religion. As Judge Tulkens of the ECHR wrote in her dissenting opinion, "[i]t is not the Court's role to make an appraisal . . . of a religion or a religious practice."[55]

Moreover, the long and complex decision-making history for the regulations that banned the headscarf in universities in Turkey has been shown by the court as an example of "continued dialogue" between various groups with students. This dialogue has included establishing "convincing offices" to try to persuade students to remove their headscarves before entering university buildings.[56] This practice, however, was widely criticized in Turkey as being a coercive act and as creating extra burden and stigma for students instead of dialogue.

The court did not appreciate this internal political dynamic. The omission of relevant history rests uneasily with the very wide margin of appreciation that the court gave to Turkey's institutional determination.[57] Considering the questionable merit of these determinations, it is difficult to see how this judgment is proportional to the aims pursued, namely protecting the rights and freedoms of others and maintaining the public order. The ECHR should have explained their reasons for a ruling that effectively precluded an entire class of women from pursuing higher education in Turkey. "The Court never balanced the right of women to manifest their religion

---

[52] Elizabeth Chamblee, *Rhetoric or Rights? When Culture and Religion Bar Girls' Right to Education*, 44 Virginia J. Int'l L. 1072 (2004).

[53] *Sahin*, [2005] E. Ct. H.R. (GC) 819, ¶ 117.

[54] In the United States, the Supreme Court has likewise indicated that courts should not take into account or decide on whether a practice is "central" to an individual' religion. "It is not within the judicial ken to question the centrality of particular beliefs or practices to a faith, or the validity of particular litigants' interpretations of those creeds." See *Employment Div. v. Smith*, 494 U.S. 872, 887 (1990).

[55] *Sahin*, [2005] E. Ct. H.R. (GC) 819, ¶ 12 (dissenting opinion).

[56] *Id.* ¶ 120.

[57] Gunn, *supra* note 48; Westerfield, *supra* note 50.

by wearing headscarves against the right of other students to avoid proselytism."[58] Instead of providing evidence that there was ever an attempt to proselytize fellow students by wearing the headscarf, the court heavily emphasized the margin of appreciation for Turkey's institutional determination, and ignored a proportionality analysis.

C. Dogru v. France *and* Kervanci v. France

In December 2008, the ECHR came up with two decisions concerning restrictions on religious freedom, continuing the line of its previous jurisprudence. The cases involved two eleven-year-old Muslim girls who wore headscarves and were expelled from school in 1999.[59] Even though the issue was whether or not a headscarf or a hat was incompatible with physical education class, the ECHR upheld French secularism and found no violation of the girls' right to religion, saying that the girls had made an "ostentatious" display. The ECHR found that the expulsions were not disproportionate because the girls could continue their education by correspondence course, and did not even consider arguments that the girls' right to education was violated.

Even though these cases were decided after the enactment of the French law of 2004, the events unfolded way before the law's enactment. Therefore, the court was unable to consider the French law. The court noted that the domestic authorities justified the measures based on statutory and regulatory provisions, internal documents, and the decision of *Conseil d'Etat* on 1) the duty to attend classes regularly; 2) the requirements of safety and the necessity; and 3) the necessity of appropriate dress for sports practice.[60]

Then, the ECHR dedicated a long paragraph to the history of French *laicite* [secularism] dating back to 1789. It noted that from the 1980s the French secular model was confronted with integrating Muslims into society, particularly schools. Quoting a paragraph from the Stasi Commission, the court stated that "[i]n France, the troubles have given rise to various forms of collective mobilization regarding the question of the place of Islam in Republican society."[61]

In *Dogru*, the ECHR did rely on its earlier decisions, particularly *Sahin*. Except for a few paragraphs about safety that was specific to Dogru's situation, the decision did not reflect any new arguments or any adjustments despite the case involving subjects that were eleven-year-old girls. To prove that the interference was "necessary in a

---

[58] Benjamin D. Bleiberg, *Unveiling the Real Issue: Evaluating the European Court of Human Rights Decision to Enforce the Turkish Headscarf Ban in Leyla Sahin v. Turkey*, 91 CORNELL L. REV. 129–62 (2005).
[59] *Dogru v. France*, App. No.27058/05, [2008] Eur. Ct. H.R. 1579; *Kervanci v. France*, App. No. 31645/04, [2008] Eur. Ct. H.R. *See* Registrar of the ECHR press release, Dec. 4, 2008, *available at* www.echr.org.
[60] *Id.* ¶ 51.
[61] *Id.* ¶¶ 17–22.

democratic society," the ECHR formulated a common argument, recommending that the "same solution [as *Sahin*] be adopted in the recent case, having regard to the fact that the measure in question had mainly been based on the constitutional principles of secularism and gender equality."[62] Furthermore, the court stated "[i]n France, as in Turkey and Switzerland, secularism is a constitutional principle, and founding principle of the Republic . . . the attitude which fails to respect that principle will not necessarily be accepted as being covered by the freedom to manifest one's religion and will not enjoy protection of Article 9 of the Convention."[63]

This is a monumental paragraph proving that Turkish cases, involving either the headscarf or political party closure, play a pivotal role in formulating the court's jurisprudence in cases related to Islam.[64] It is rather astonishing that Turkey, with a bad reputation in the ECHR in terms of caseloads (second largest after Russia) and noncompliance, received such attention from the court. As of 2007, Turkey has only won 10 percent of its cases in the ECHR.[65] Interestingly, cases in which Turkey has been successful have been about the expulsion of students and teachers because of the headscarf or employment discrimination, expulsion from the military because of religion,[66] and dismantlement of religious parties.

CONCLUSION

Taken together, the ECHR decisions in relation to the headscarf (and to a certain extent to Islam) raise crucial questions. There is no doubt that in any future ECHR case in relation to Islam, no matter which country is involved, the result will be very predictable. The court clearly stated that Article 9 on religious freedom is not applicable to Islam. However, no court can openly say that living together with Muslims, whose culture and religion is dramatically different from others, is just unacceptable. Therefore, the ECHR made the right tactical choice when they implemented a wider margin of appreciation, by relying heavily on the Turkish

---

[62] *Id.* ¶ 37.

[63] *Id.*

[64] See the discussion on *Refah Partis and others v. Turkey* in *Dogru, id.* ¶ 72.

[65] Turkey has been responded in more cases involving the right to life, torture, liberty and security, fair trials, free expression, free association, and the right to an effective remedy before a national authority. According to statistics of the ECHR, between 1995 and 2004, there were only five judgments on Article 9, and only one of which is an adverse judgment. For more information, *see* Thomas W. Smith, *Leveraging Norms: The ECHR and Turkey's Human Rights Reforms, in* HUMAN RIGHTS IN TURKEY, 262–74 (Zehra Arat ed., University of Penn. Press 2007).

[66] In *Kalac v. Turkey*, App. No. 20704/92, 27 Eur. H.R. Rep 552 (1997), the court upheld the Supreme Military Council's decision to dismiss a judge advocate in the Turkish Air Force who allegedly, through his conduct and attitude, "revealed that he had adopted unlawful fundamentalist opinions." The application was denied in *Tepeli and Others v. Turkey*, App. No. 31876/96 (Sep. 11, 2001), *available at* www.echr.coe.int/eng, in which forty-one former members of the armed forces claimed they were purged for their religious beliefs. In *Erdem v. Turkey*, App. No. 26328/95 (Sep. 11, 2001), *available at* www.echr.coe.int/eng, the court blocked about twenty petitions involving military life, and religious observance and dress.

court's argument. For many Europeans and Turks who are strictly secular and fearful about Islam, the decisions set just the "right tone." It was celebrated both in Europe and the secular sector of Turkey. Only a few liberal human rights organizations and scholars (mainly from the United States) offered criticism of the problematic *Sahin* case, seeing the damage done by the ECHR to human rights and secularism.

Immigration, multiculturalism, and religious diversity in the twenty-first century pose a special challenge to judicial method and policy conclusions. Whenever human rights courts reach a judgment on fundamental issues, such as freedom of religion and discrimination against Muslim women, it will have important consequences. These consequences will have cross-geographical and cross-cultural impacts. The headscarf judgments, including dissenting opinions, raise an important question about the connections between national courts and international tribunals. It illustrates the growing tensions inherent in the globalization of certain legal principles.

Furthermore, these cases seem to reflect the influence of various political developments. Particularly, supranational courts have a future impact on the larger adjudication environment and on the legal policy that is disclosed by their jurisdictional limits. The developments in various countries after the *Sahin* decision indicate that this decision was successful in paving the road for many regulatory arrangements in comparable European countries. France has already claimed that the *Sahin* decision makes clear that the French law banning conspicuous religious dress from schools is consistent with the Convention. It is not very encouraging that, by now, instead of accommodating freedom of religion especially for minorities, the decision-making trend is going in a direction that is likely to cause social conflict rather than promote tolerance and acceptance.

Unfortunately with respect to headscarf cases, the ECHR has adopted an approach that allows states to violate the rights of members of specifically non-Christian religions who wish to wear clothing in public for religious reasons. The ECHR's approach over a series of cases has failed to give proper weight to the need for states to have strong justifications for such restrictions. The ECHR's decisions set a very low bar for states that seek to limit the rights of those within their jurisdiction. ECHR member-states find it difficult to move outside of religious paradigms that are most common in Europe (either broadly Christian or secular) and to deal with non-Christian religions in a manner that is respectful and culturally sensitive.[67]

---

[67] *See generally* CAROLYN EVANS, RELIGIOUS FREEDOM UNDER THE EUROPEAN CONVENTION ON HUMAN RIGHTS 117–23 (2001); PAUL TAYLOR, FREEDOM OF RELIGION: UN AND HUMAN RIGHTS LAW AND PRACTICE (2005); Evans, *supra* note 27.

23

On God, Promises, and Money

Islamic Divorce at the Crossroads of Gender and the Law

Pascale Fournier

I. INTRODUCTION

If liberalism is committed to the individual and individual choice, it is also conventionally taken to be committed to freedom and equality. Giving effects to such principles often creates tensions: the "free" acts of individuals will sometimes produce inequality; and state enforcement of equality will likely reduce individual freedom. Beyond that, despite statutory – even constitutional – guarantees of equality, systemic slants lead to gendered inequalities that almost invariably subjugate or disempower women, either individually or collectively. When faced with the claims of subordinated groups, liberalism is asked to make concessions in which these collisions intensify and multiply. In fact, if the mandate to address the rights or interests of groups is not perfectly consistent with liberalism's commitment to individuals, such group accommodation may, however, be necessary if individuals in those groups are to be treated liberally – that is, accorded liberty or equality. And the mandate to address the subordination of groups generates new collisions between liberty and equality: de facto freedom for subordinated groups may require their specific regulation, while equality of their members may require active distributions in their favor. The "politics of recognition" invoked by subordinated groups within liberalism is thus an inherently contradictory project, exposing in practice the ideals of liberty and equality as fundamentally paradoxical.

Through the journey of one symbolic legal institution – *Mahr* (a form of dowry) – I will follow the ways in which Islamic marriage travels, offering a panoply of conflicting images, contradictions, and distributive endowments in the transit from Islamic family law to Western adjudication in Canada, the United States, Germany, and France. I insist on the importance that distributive consequences rather than recognition occupy central place in the assessment of the legal options available to Muslim women in Western courts. In family law matters, the enforcement of *Mahr* by Western courts carries considerable distributive power, although *Mahr* is often treated as mere religious recognition by the judiciary. Moreover, the distributional impact is far from homogeneous and predictable. At times, *Mahr* that is institutionally transferred by Western courts imposes an exceptional penalty on the Muslim husband (courts add the amount of *Mahr* to the division of family assets and to spousal support), whereas sometimes it becomes an exceptional penalty for the Muslim wife (through conflict of laws, *Mahr* replaces alimony and equitable division of property). Still other times, the unenforceability of *Mahr* for an economically dependent wife leads to an exceptional bonus (through conflict of laws, *Mahr* is rejected as against "public order" and Western equity standards are applied instead). The plurality of receptions and interpretations *Mahr* receives in Western courts parallels the distinct ways *Mahr* is conceived in its place of residence, here represented by Egypt, Tunisia, and Malaysia, three countries that incorporated Islamic law into their national legal frameworks. Identifying variations in *Mahr*'s point of departure serves to illustrate that it is both internally plural as well as externally plural – at its point of arrival in Western courts, illustrated by an analysis of representative case law from Canada, the United States, France, and Germany.

To represent this distributive framework, I introduce four short scripts in which a fictional Leila embarks in a bargaining tactic with her husband Samir on divorce and uses *Mahr* as its central object. In offering the many conflicting faces of *Mahr* as bonus and penalty, I assess the interaction between Islamic law and Western law, as well as the subjective gains and losses predicted by Leila in relation to the enforceability of *Mahr*. This chapter implicitly addresses the stakes of conceiving *Mahr* as an autonomous legal institution, rather than as a dynamic part in a larger marital web of rights and duties. Ultimately, I claim that the stakes are the constitution of a romantic subject in the former (the husband offers a gift to the wife on marriage to express his love for her and his respect for God; this gift must travel as a legal transplant to Western states), and a calculating subject in the latter (*Mahr*, inherently plural, is used by the parties to gain something from the other; this institution is always-already resisting claims of "true" and "authentic" Islamic law). A distributional analysis of *Mahr* is crucial, I argue, because *Mahr* is encountered by actual parties and often used by them as a tool of relative – and gendered – bargaining power in the negotiation of contractual obligations related to the family. Despite the seeming (and often genuine) difference in bargaining power between the husband and the wife in the negotiation of the marriage contract, case law shows that Muslim wives are not content merely to let their *Mahr* slip away. On the contrary, some of them argue fiercely – although not always successfully – in Western courts to hold on to what they believe is theirs. Moreover, Islamic law travels with a multiplicity of voices, and it is this complex hybridity that will be mediated through Western law upon adjudication.

II. THE PLACE OF DEPARTURE: MAHR'S INTERNAL PLURALISM

Mahr, meaning "reward" (*ajr*) or "nuptial gift" (also designated as *sadaqa* or *faridah*), is the expression used in Islamic family law to describe the "payment that the wife is entitled to receive from the husband in consideration of the marriage."[1] *Mahr* is usually divided into two parts: that which is paid at the time of marriage is called prompt *Mahr* (*muajjal*), and that which is paid only on the dissolution of the marriage by death or divorce or other agreed events is called deferred *Mahr* (*muwajjal*).

Three forms of Islamic divorce (*Talaq, Khul,* and *Faskh*) can be used by the parties involved in a marital relationship. Islamic family law determines the degree to which the husband and wife may or may not initiate divorce and the different costs associated with each form of divorce.[2] *Talaq* (repudiation) is a unilateral act that dissolves the marriage contract through the declaration of the husband only.[3] What comes with this unlimited "freedom" of the husband to divorce at will and on any grounds is the (costly) obligation to pay *Mahr* in full as soon as the third *talaq* has been pronounced.[4] In this regulatory regime, there is no shortcut for a wife who wants to obtain a divorce but who cannot obtain the consent of her husband. A wife may unilaterally terminate her marriage without cause only when such power has been explicitly delegated to her by her husband in the marriage contract.[5] Otherwise, she may apply to the courts either for a *Khul* or a *Faskh* divorce. *Khul* divorce can be initiated by the wife with the husband's prior consent; however, the court (*qadi*) must grant it, and divorce by this method dissolves the husband's duty to pay the deferred *Mahr*.[6] In the case of a *Faskh* divorce, a fault-based divorce initiated by the wife, she must demonstrate to the court that her case meets the limited grounds under which divorce can be granted,[7] in which case she will be entitled to *Mahr*.

This description of classical Islamic family law, however, is expressed differently in contemporary jurisprudence. To demonstrate the internal plurality of *Mahr*, I develop the Islamic legal framework within which *Mahr* is conceived in three different countries – Egypt, Tunisia, and Malaysia. It is not, as the proponents of

---

[1] JOHN L. ESPOSITO & NATANA J. DELONG-BAS, WOMEN IN MUSLIM FAMILY LAW 23 (2d ed., Syracuse University Press 2001).

[2] Pascale Fournier, *In the (Canadian) Shadow of Islamic Law: Translating Mahr as a Bargaining Endowment*, 44 OSGOODE HALL L. J. 649–77 (2006).

[3] DAWOULD SUDQI EL ALAMI & DOREEN HINCHCLIFFE, ISLAMIC MARRIAGE AND DIVORCE LAWS OF THE ARAB WORLD 22 (Kluwer Law International 1996).

[4] ASAF A. A. FYZEE, OUTLINES OF MUHAMMADAN LAW 133 (4th ed. Oxford University Press 1974); JOSEPH SCHACHT, INTRODUCTION TO ISLAMIC LAW 167 (Clarendon Press 1982); NOEL J. COULSON, A HISTORY OF ISLAMIC LAW 207 (Edinburgh University Press 1964); JUDITH E. TUCKER, WOMEN IN NINETEENTH-CENTURY EGYPT 54 (Cambridge University Press 1985); ESPOSITO & DELONG-BAS, *supra* note 1, at 36.

[5] Zahra, M. A., *Family Law, in* LAW IN THE MIDDLE EAST 140–41 (Majid Khadduri & Herbert J. Liebesny eds., Middle East Institute 1955).

[6] EL ALAMI & HINCHCLIFFE *supra* note 3, at 27–28; Abdal-Rahim, A. R., *The Family and Gender Laws in Egypt during the Ottoman Period, in* WOMEN, THE FAMILY, AND DIVORCE LAWS IN ISLAMIC HISTORY 105 (Amira El Azhary Sonbol ed., Syracuse University Press 1996); TUCKER, *supra* note 4, at 54.

[7] EL ALAMI & HINCHCLIFFE *supra* note 3, at 29.

the formalist school would argue,[8] a static institution derived solely from God and spiritually detached from society.

A. Mahr *in Egypt*

Egypt typifies the dichotomy of dual legal systems through its retention of both Western-inspired national law and Islamic personal law.[9] During the nineteenth century, Islamic law was progressively replaced by European legal systems. Eventually, only family law remained within the direct application of Islamic law,[10] and, in 1956, the Islamic courts were integrated into the national court system.[11] Islamic law has, nonetheless, remained very influential and is considered the principle source of law,[12] especially in family law matters.[13] Despite rising divorce rates in Egypt since the 1970s,[14] it has proven difficult for Egyptian women to obtain a divorce. For example, under Egyptian Law No. 100 (1985), a wife could only obtain a *Faskh* divorce on the following grounds: her husband habitually failed his duty to provide her maintenance, he suffered from a serious disease, he was absent for a lengthy period, he was imprisoned for a long-term sentence, or she suffered "harm" as inflicted by her husband.[15] In response to lobbying by women's rights activists, the Egyptian legislature adopted Egyptian Law No. 1 of 2000,[16] which now allows women to apply

---

[8] In all of the English and French literature on Islamic family law that I have studied, *Mahr* is described as a single, separate, autonomous, and historically static institution. Afzal Wani, a well-known Islamic scholar and specialist on the legal institution of *Mahr*, presents *Mahr* as if it were a European code: "The law of *mahr* as it exists today is well developed like the law relating to other Muslim law institutions. It covers all the relevant matters like: subject matter of *mahr*, amount of *mahr*, mode of its payment, when it becomes due, widowed and divorced women's claims to *mahr* and so on." *See* M. Afzal Wani, The Islamic Institution of Mahr: a Study of its Philosophy, Working and Related Legislations in the Contemporary World 27 (1996).

[9] The Egyptian legal system developed from a mix of Roman, French, Ottoman, and Islamic law, as well as ancient, medieval, and customary Egyptian law. *See* Bharathi Anandhi Venkatraman, *Islamic States and the United Nations Convention on the Elimination of All Forms of Discrimination Against Women: Are the Shari'a and the Convention Compatible?*, 44 Am. U. L. Rev. 1950, 1984 (1995); Brenda Oppermann, *Impact of Legal Pluralism on Women's Status: An Examination of Marriage Laws in Egypt, South Africa, and the United States*, 17 Hastings Women's L. J. 65, 68 (2006).

[10] Lama Abu-Odeh, *Modernizing Muslim Family Law: The Case of Egypt*, 37 Vand. J. Transnat'l L. 1043, 1045–46 (2004).

[11] Lisa Hajjar, *Religion, State Power, and Domestic Violence in Muslim Societies: A Framework for Comparative Analysis*, 29 Law & Soc. Inquiry 1, 24 (2004).

[12] Clark Benner Lombardi, *Islamic Law as a Source of Constitutional Law in Egypt: The Constitutionalization of the Sharia in a Modern Arab State*, 37 Colum. J. Transnat'l L. 81, 86 (1998–1999).

[13] Abu-Odeh, *supra* note 10, at 1051, 1097, 1100; Oppermann, *supra* note 9.

[14] Abdullahi A. An-Na'im, Islamic Family Law in a Changing World 159 (2002).

[15] Abu-Odeh, *supra* note 10, at 1106.

[16] Law No. 1 of 2000 regulating certain litigation procedures in personal status, *Al-Jarida Al-Rasmiyya*, 22 Jan. 2000, No. 4 (Egypt) [hereinafter Law No. 1/2000]. The law was controversial and subject to considerable debate. *See* Amira Mashhour, *Islamic Law and Gender Equality – Could There be a Common Ground?: A Study of Divorce and Polygamy in Sharia Law and Contemporary Legislation*

for a somewhat modified version of the classical *Khul* divorce.[17] In fact, a wife can nowadays obtain a divorce without the husband's consent and without any specific ground except stating that the continuation of the marriage may cause her to violate God's law.[18] Whereas classical jurists have interpreted *Khul* divorce as requiring the return of the deferred *Mahr* only,[19] a wife who is seeking *Khul* divorce under the Egyptian Law No. 1 of 2000 must not only repay any prompt *Mahr*, but also renounce *all* of her postmarriage financial rights under Islamic law, which include the unpaid portions of deferred *Mahr* and maintenance.[20]

By March 2000, the Personal Status Court in Cairo alone had received more than three thousand applications for a *Khul* divorce.[21] Given the considerable length of time and difficulty of proving harm to obtain a *Faskh* divorce, studies show that only women of means are requesting such divorces.[22] In fact, the return of paid prompt *Mahr* and any payments made on a deferred *Mahr* may act as a deterrent against divorce for poorer women.[23]

B. Mahr *in Tunisia*

The Tunisian legal system is based on French civil law and Islamic law. Although the Constitution states that the country is Muslim, this provision does not require all laws to conform with Islamic law.[24] Habib Bourguiba, the first president who administered the country from 1956 to 1987, was very influential in the development of women's rights as part of his efforts toward modernization and development.[25] In 1956, the Personal Status Code created major reforms in the legal system based on

---

in Tunisia and Egypt, 27 Hum. Rts. Q. 562, 583 (2005); Mulki Al-Sharmani, Recent Reforms in Personal Status Laws and Women's Empowerment: Family Courts in Egypt 9–10 (2007).

[17] Law No. 1/2000, *supra* note 16, art. 20: "The two spouses may agree between themselves upon khul', but if they do not agree mutually and the wife files a claim requesting it [khul'], and ransoms herself and releases herself by khul' (khala'at zawjaha) by forfeiting all of her lawful financial rights, and restores to him [her husband] the dower he gave to her [upon marriage], then the court is to divorce her from him."

[18] Lynn Welchman, Women and Muslim Family Laws in Arab States: A Comparative Overview of Textual Development and Advocacy 115 (2007).

[19] Mashhour, *supra* note 16, at 584.

[20] Additional rights given up include the right to postdivorce maintenance (*nafaqat il idda*) and any postdivorce compensation (*mu'ta*). *See id.* at 583–84; Welchman, *supra* note 18, at 112; Azizah Al-Hibri, *The Nature of Islamic Marriage: Sacramental, Covenantal, or Contractual?, in* Covenant Marriage in Comparative Perspective 201 (J. Witte Jr. & E. Ellison eds., 2005).

[21] An-Na'im, *supra* note 14, at 159.

[22] Al-Sharmani, *supra* note 16, at 8.

[23] Welchman, *supra* note 18, at 115; Abu-Odeh, *supra* note 10, at 1102.

[24] *See* Mounira M. Charrad, States and Women's Rights: The Making of Postcolonial Tunisia, Algeria, and Morocco 222 (2001); Laurie A. Brand, Women, the State and Political Liberalization: Middle Eastern and North African Experiences 202 (1998).

[25] Brand, *supra* note 24, at 177.

Qur'anic reasoning,[26] including the criminalization of polygamy.[27] Tunisian family
laws make divorce proceedings more equitable for women, providing them with the
same access as men under Islamic law.[28] Only courts can grant a divorce, so *Talaq*
outside the court is not considered a legal divorce.[29] Moreover, the traditional *Faskh*
divorce is not applied.[30] Divorce may be obtained by mutual consent, at the request
of one of the parties without specific grounds,[31] or because of abuse.[32]

Mahr remains an integral component of a valid marriage.[33] Without paying
prompt *Mahr*, a husband cannot legitimately consummate the marriage.[34] Deferred
Mahr is payable immediately on divorce or death, and is considered an unsecured
debt against a husband's estate if unpaid.[35] Unlike many other Muslim countries,
a wife does not need to remit her *Mahr* in seeking divorce.[36] In practice, however,
Mahr amounts are quite low and there is no obligatory minimum.[37] Bourguiba
used the occasion of his own marriage in 1962 to break with tradition by giving his
wife a singular "symbolic dinar" as *Mahr* instead of a substantial amount.[38] The
1993 Amendments to the 1956 Personal Status Code further cemented the trend by
removing the requirement that *Mahr* not be "trifling."[39]

---

[26] As one Tunisian scholar commented, "The CSP [Personal Status Code] is a more powerful symbol
of Tunisia than the Constitution," CHARRAD, *supra* note 24, at 309.

[27] For this reform to be implemented, it was reasoned that the Quran favors monogamy and, as with
slavery, polygamy no longer constitutes a necessary or acceptable practice. Moreover, the government
adopted Muslim scholarly arguments stating that it was impossible to treat multiple wives equally and
that polygamy was historically justified only because of the decrease in the male population following
the particular context of war, Venkatraman, *supra* note 9, at 1980–81; Quran Sura 4 (129) and Sura
4 (Verse 3); Mashhour, *supra* note 16, at 585; Andrea Barron, *Tunisia as an Arab Women's Rights
Leader*, THE GLOBALIST, July 11, 2007, *available at* www.theglobalist.com/StoryId.aspx?StoryId=6306
(last visited Mar. 12, 2009). Those who defy this law are subject to a fine and/or imprisonment: BRAND,
supra note 24, at 208.

[28] Adrian Morse Jr. & Leila Sayeh, *Tunisia: Marriage, Divorce, and Foreign Recognition*, 29 FAM. L. Q.
701, 719 (1995).

[29] Mashhour, *supra* note 16, at 585–86; Morse & Sayeh, *supra* note 28, at 712; BRAND, *supra* note 24, at
178.

[30] WELCHMAN, *supra* note 18, at 128; Mashhour, *supra* note 16, at 586.

[31] WELCHMAN, *supra* note 18, at 128; Mashhour, *supra* note 16, at 585–86; AN-NA'IM, *supra* note 14, at
159; Morse & Sayeh, *supra* note 28, at 714; Abu-Odeh, *supra* note 10, at 1107–09.

[32] Code du Statut Personnel, Art. 31, Jurisite, *available at* http://jurisitetunisie.com/tunisie/codes/csp/
Menu.html [herein after CSP]; BRAND, *supra* note 24, at 208; Morse & Sayeh, *supra* note 28, at 713–14.

[33] Order No. 13/1956 on the promulgation of the Code of Personal Status, Al-Jarida Al-Rasmiyya, 17 Aug.
1956, No. 66, Art. 32 (Egypt) [hereinafter Order No. 13/1956]; AN-NA'IM, *supra* note 14, at 158–59.

[34] Morse & Sayeh, *supra* note 28, at 709.

[35] *Id.* at 713; Abu-Odeh, *supra* note 10, at 1107–1109.

[36] Rubya Mehdi, *Facing the Enigma: Talaq-e-tafweez a Need of Muslim Women in Nordic Perspective*
33 INT'L J. SOC. L. 133, 140 (2005).

[37] Lilia Labidi, *From Sexual Submission to Voluntary Commitment: The Transformation of Family Ties
in Contemporary Tunisia*, in The New Arab Family, in CAIRO PAPERS IN SOCIAL SCIENCE 24, 122
(Nicholas S. Hopkins ed., 2003).

[38] *Id.* at 121–22.

[39] WELCHMAN, *supra* note 18, at 91–92.

C. Mahr *in Malaysia*

The Malaysian legal system is derived from three sources: English common law, Islamic law, and *Adat*, the latter being defined as Malay customary law preexisting Islam. *Adat* has had a significant influence on Islam, mostly in ensuring greater freedom, rights, and public participation for Muslim women in Malaysia.[40] The official legal system incorporates common law and Islamic law, with civil courts responsible for most areas of the law and *Adat* influencing certain areas of law.[41] The Islamic court system governs family law, charitable endowments, bequests, inheritance, and various offenses including those against Islam.[42]

A Malaysian woman is provided with a number of legal options for divorce. First, she can request a *Faskh* divorce if her husband has disappeared for more than one year, if he failed to maintain her for three months, or if she did not consent to marriage.[43] Second, she can negotiate a *Khul* divorce with the consent of her husband;[44] in so doing, she must give up her claim to any outstanding *Mahr* and return whatever portion was given to her on the solemnization of the marriage, or must pay an agreed-upon amount. If the parties cannot agree, Syarian Court judges may determine the amount "in accordance with *Hukum Syarak*, the amount, having regard to the status and the means of the parties."[45] Through the process of *hakam*,[46] a woman can also ask the court to declare a *Talaq* divorce.[47]

In Malaysia, *Mahr* is known as *Mas Kahwin*, which literally means "marriage gold."[48] At the time of marriage, it can be given as money actually paid or as something that can be valued, or acknowledged as a debt.[49] Amounts are traditionally

---

[40] Rebecca Foley, *Muslim Women's Challenges to Islamic Law: The Case of Malaysia*, 6 INT'L FEMINIST JOURNAL OF POLITICS 53, 56 (2004); Noraida Endut, *Malaysia's Plural Legal System and Its Impact on Women*, in MUSLIM WOMEN AND ACCESS TO JUSTICE 20 (Maznah Mohamad ed., 2000).

[41] In Malaysia, non-Muslim family law is regulated by federal law that allows for some level of consistency across states, whereas Islamic family law falls under state jurisdiction. However, the federal government has developed model laws such as The Islamic Family Law (Federal Territories) Act 1984 (Act 303), Malaysia Act 303.50a [hereinafter Act 303] that states can choose to adopt either entirely or with modifications, Endut, *supra* note 40, at 37.

[42] In these matters, no intervention of the civil courts is allowed. Nik Noriani Nik Badli Shah, *Legislative Provisions and Judicial Mechanisms for the Enforcement and Termination of the Islamic Marriage Contract in Malaysia*, in THE ISLAMIC MARRIAGE CONTRACT (A. Quraishi & F. E. Vogel eds., 2009).

[43] MUSLIM FEMINISM AND FEMINIST MOVEMENT: SOUTH-EAST ASIA 52 (Abida Samiuddin & R. Khanam eds., 2002); Endut, *supra* note 40, at 44, 65; AN-NA'IM, *supra* note 14, at 271.

[44] Act 303, *supra* note 40, §49(1); AN-NA'IM, *supra* note 14, at 255.

[45] Act 303, *supra* note 40, §49(3); Noor Aziah Mohd Awal, *Malaysia: Family Laws in Malaysia: Past, Present, and the Future*, in THE INTERNATIONAL SURVEY OF FAMILY LAW 189 (Bill Atkin ed., 2007).

[46] Under Islamic law, the first step is generally a form of counseling; if this is unsuccessful, arbitration by *hakam* based on the Quran takes place and, as a final option, the Islamic court presides, Endut, *supra* note 40, at 45–46.

[47] Act 303, *supra* note 40, §§49(3), 47(2) & (11).

[48] M. G. PELETZ, ISLAMIC MODERN: RELIGIOUS COURTS AND CULTURAL POLITICS IN MALAYSIA 305 (2002).

[49] The standard definition is "the obligatory marriage payment due under *Hukum Syarak* [Islamic Law according to any recognized Mazhab] by the husband to the wife at the time the marriage is

quite low, and maximum rates are set by law[50] depending on region and a woman's status (i.e., an unmarried woman or a divorcée).[51]

III. THE PLACE OF ARRIVAL: MAHR'S EXTERNAL PLURALISM

My analysis of how the law captures claims based on identity within the liberal framework suggests that in adjudicating *Mahr*, courts have characterized this Islamic institution in three different ways: the Legal Pluralist Approach, the Formal Equality Approach, and the Substantive Equality Approach.[52] I classify these three disciplinary discourses within the wider expression of liberalism because they all share, in both their normative and descriptive dimensions, the same commitment to individuals' autonomy and liberty. Along this spectrum of ideology, *Mahr* has been the subject of competing aesthetic and political representations, from a form of religious family affiliation under legal pluralism, to a space of mere secular contract under formal equality, and finally to the projection of a gendered symbol under substantive equality. I focus on adjudication and case law because courts present themselves as invested in the technical enterprise of applying the law in a nonideological manner. In Table 23.1, I briefly introduce the three forms of adjudication.

IV. A LEGAL REALIST SHIFT: MAHR AS CONTRADICTIONS

A legal realist shift exposes the contradictory nature of the adjudicative process. Case law analysis reveals two contradictions that have accompanied *Mahr*'s journey to Western liberal courts. The first is the "Doctrine–Outcome Contradiction": as the legal doctrine adopted by the court projects the mandate to recognize or not to recognize, the resulting outcome from that recognition does not follow the doctrine as would logically be expected; instead, it often reverses it. The second is the "Ends–Means Perversity Contradiction": the probability that the legal means available to judges to achieve a given end cannot, in a globalized context of rules, produce the anticipated result. Moreover, the parties involved in the dispute over the enforcement of *Mahr* act out this contradiction, individually and relationally, in related but somewhat different terms. The aim of this section is to acknowledge, yet eventually attempt to transcend, the complexities of the binaries that organize the disciplinary fields in which *Mahr* is projected and produced.

solemnized, whether in the form of money actually paid or acknowledged as a debt with or without security, or in the form of something that, according to *Hukum Syarak*, is capable of being valued in terms of money." Act 303, *supra* note 40, §2(1).

[50] There is considerable variance in the permissible maximum amounts set, likely because of the economic capacity in each region, JAMILA HUSSAIN, ISLAM: ITS LAW AND SOCIETY 82 (2004).

[51] *Id.*

[52] For a detailed analysis of how legal pluralism, formal equality, and substantive equality play out in the enforcement of *Mahr*, see Pascale Fournier, *Transit and Translation: Islamic Legal Transplants in North America and Western Europe*, 4 J. COMP. L. 1 (2009).

TABLE 23.1. *Three Forms of Adjudication*

	Legal Pluralism	Formal Equality	Substantive Equality
Mahr as . . .	Western State views *Mahr* under the umbrella of Islamic family law	Western State views *Mahr* under the umbrella of Western contract law	Western State views *Mahr* under the umbrella of Western family law
	The Western judge welcomes the imam as an expert witness: multiculturalist understanding of *Mahr*	The Western judge pictures the legal system as devoid of representative role for the minorities: secular understanding of *Mahr*	The Western judge engages in sexual identity politics: gendered understanding of *Mahr*
	Mahr is the expression of religious identity	*Mahr* is a contract irrespective of race, gender, or religion	*Mahr* is a religious custom that has an effect on substantive equality
Mahr is . . .	*Mahr* is enforceable as an Islamic custom. It is recognized on the basis of: • Manifestation of identity (Canada) • Islamic custom (France and Germany) • Related to a *Khul* divorce (Quebec and U.S.) OR *Mahr* is not enforceable because it is too "foreign" to be adjudicated by a Western (non-Muslim) judge. It is not recognized on the basis of: • Being utterly foreign (Canada)	*Mahr* is enforceable as a contract. It is recognized on the basis of: • Marriage agreement (Canada) • Antenuptial agreement (U.S.) • Legal debt (Germany) • Contractual condition of marriage (France) OR *Mahr* is not enforceable because it speaks to contractual exceptions. It is not recognized on the basis of: • Vagueness (U.S.) • Lack of consent (U.S.) • Abstractness (Germany)	*Mahr* is enforceable, but its amount must respect Western family law rules of equity. It is recognized on the basis of: • Readjusted alimony (Germany) • Being due even though the wife initiated the divorce (Quebec) OR *Mahr* is not enforceable because it violates gender equality: the equal division of community property on dissolution of the spouses' marriage is applied. It is not recognized on the basis of: • Equity (Quebec) • Unjust enrichment (Germany) • Substantial justice (Canada) • Public policy (France and U.S.)

(continued)

TABLE 23.1 *(continued)*

	Legal Pluralism	Formal Equality	Substantive Equality
Case Law	**Canada:** M.(N.M.) v. M.(N.S.) (2004); Nathoo v. Nathoo (1996); M.H.D. v. E.A. (1991); Kaddoura v. Hammoud (1998); I.(S.) v. E.(E.) (2005) **France:** Cour de Cassation, 1978–000137 (1978) **Germany:** OLG Bremen, FamRZ 1980, 606; Kammer-gericht (Berlin), Fam RZ (1988, 296); OLG Koeln IPRAx (1983, 73) **United States:** Akileh v. Elchahal (1996); Dajani (1988)	**Canada:** Amlani v. Hirani (2000) **United States:** Odatalla v. Odatalla (2002); Akileh v. Elchahal (1996); Aziz v. Aziz (1985); Habibi-Fahrich v. Fahnrich (1995); Shaban v. Shaban (2001) **Germany:** Hamm FamRz (1988, 516); Amtsgericht Buende, 7 F 555/03 (2004); IPRax 1988, 109–113, BGH (1987) **France:** Cour de Cassation, Dec.2, 1997 (Pourvoi)	**Germany:** IPRax, OLG Koeln (1983, 73); OLG Cell, FamRZ (1998, 374) **Canada:** M.H.D. v. E.A. (1991); M. F. c. MA. A. (2002); Vladi v. Vladi (1987) **France:** Arrêt de la Cour d'appel de Douai, January 8, 1976: N. 76–11–613 **United States:** Dajani (1988)

A. *The Doctrine–Outcome Contradiction*

The Doctrine–Outcome[53] Contradiction may well be the effect of the deeply con-tradictory nature of law in general and adjudication in particular.[54] This section tests the Doctrine–Outcome Contradiction by using concrete cases. It addresses the indeterminacy between the legal doctrine used by the judge, on the one hand, and the outcome of particular legal pluralist decisions as represented by the holding of the case, on the other. The legal pluralist camp exemplifies this contradiction as it frequently adopts the doctrine of Islamic law to interpret *Mahr*, and yet other doctrines and policies held by judges block the causal relationship between doctrine and outcome. To study the Doctrine–Outcome Contradiction, the Critical Legal Studies (CLS) indeterminacy thesis is invoked to capture the "spin" that the holding receives in relation to the doctrine. This thesis posits that the interpretation of legal doctrine by judges may, in a given case, support opposing outcomes.

IPRax (1983) is a German case that enforced *Mahr* as an Islamic custom by showing an ideological commitment to legal pluralism.[55] In the absence of any written or oral contract, the judge accepted the religious expert evidence arguing for the existence of

---

53 In this section, I use the term *outcome* to refer to the case ruling in a given decision.
54 DUNCAN KENNEDY, A CRITIQUE OF ADJUDICATION: FIN DE SIÈCLE (Harvard University Press 1997).
55 *IPRax* 1983 (Praxis des Internationalen Pivat – und Verfahrensrechts, 74–7 and 64–65).

an Islamic *Mahr al-mithl* (proper *Mahr*), to be determined by comparing "the *mahr* paid to other female members of the wife's family, for instance sisters, paternal aunts, and female cousins."[56] The wife argued that, given her privileged socioeconomic status, she should be awarded 75,000 Euros plus 4 percent interest as *Mahr al-mithl the Islamic way*. However, the judge recast *Mahr al-mithl* against the backdrop of the German national legal order, and more specifically that of the local Hamburg legal regime. He awarded 10,000 Euros as *Mahr al-mithl the German way*, divided into monthly payments of 1,000 Euros, based on what a similarly situated *German* woman living in Hamburg should receive. For the Muslim woman, the distributive consequences of such a shift of rules lowered her claim dramatically. Could those specific material stakes have motivated the "spin" of legal doctrine and hence the outcome that flew from it?

The second example, *Kaddoura*, exemplifies judges' choice of interpretation through policy analysis rather than through deductive legal reasoning. The Canadian court concluded that all the elements related to the definition and enforcement of a "domestic agreement" pursuant to Section 52(1) of Ontario's Family Law Act[57] were met; thus, *Mahr* could predictably have been enforced as a simple "domestic agreement." Yet, somehow, the chain of causality between the legal doctrine and the holding was broken down by the introduction of another legal doctrine: the (American!) principle of the separation of church and state.[58] Justice Rutherford compared *Mahr* to Christian marital commitments "to love, honour and cherish and to remain faithful"[59] and refused to enforce it on the basis that it constitutes a "religious" obligation, not a civil one.

B. *The Ends–Means Perversity Contradiction*

i. *Mahr* as a Culturally Transformed Legal Transplant?

The legal pluralist cases have all attempted to legally transplant *Mahr* – that is, to recreate it through many different routes of cultural recognition: as "a manifestation of identity" in Canada; as "an Islamic custom" in France and Germany; as "related to a *Khul* divorce" in Quebec and the United States. Along the way, however, Western courts transformed *Mahr*.

M.(N.M.)[60] exemplifies the Ends–Means Perversity Contradiction in that the court advanced an image of religion as an organized, comprehensive, and organic entity: Muslim subjects *chose* to be Muslims, and one consequence of Muslim

---

[56] David Pearl & Werner Menski, Muslim Family Law 180 (3d ed. Sweet & Maxwell 1998).
[57] Family Law Act, R.S.O. 1990, c.F.3 (ca.), pt. 1, s. 52(1) (Can.).
[58] *Kaddoura v. Hammoud*, [1998] O.J. No. 5054, 44 R.F.L. (4th) 228, 168 D.L.R. (4th) 503, 1998 CarswellOnt 4747, 83 O.T.C. 30, ¶ 26 (Can. Ont. Gen. Div.).
[59] *Id.* ¶ 25.
[60] M.(N.M.) v. M.(N.S.), 2004 BCSC 346, 26 B.C.L.R. (4th) 80 (Can. B.C. Sup. Ct.).

identity is the enforcement of *Mahr* by the court. Ironically, the *Mahr* that was institutionally transferred unfolded as an exceptional penalty imposed on the husband, a result that cannot be explained or legitimated from the point of view of the original Islamic milieu of departure. The court held that Muslim marriage agreements should not be governed by the same contractual principles that governed other secular contracts; thus the *Mahr* agreement in question would be valid. The British Columbia court added the "amount of $51,250 on account of the Maher"[61] to the $101,911 due by the husband on the division of family assets *and* to an additional $2,000 monthly in spousal support.

ii. *Mahr* as Projecting a "Religious" Contractual Intention?

The Ends–Means Perversity Contradiction also affects the formal equality cases. In following a mandate *not* to culturally recognize *Mahr*, the judicial narratives embracing formal equality have attempted to secularize *Mahr*, and merely to give effect to "the intention of the parties." Yet the contract law doctrinal analysis, as applied to the specific context of *Mahr* (were the parties capable of contracting *Mahr*? Was there a "meeting of the minds" between the two parties regarding prompt and deferred *Mahr*? Was there consideration, even in cases where no amount was specified [*Mahr al-mithl*]?, etc.), has carried a religious intention into the law and, in effect, although pretending not to, courts have opened the door to the existence of this "contractual/religious" intention of the parties.

Aziz, Odatalla, and Akileh have all denied this perverse relationship between means and ends. In fact, the three American decisions all insist on the fact that the religious character of *Mahr* is irrelevant: "Why should a contract for the promise to pay money be less of a contract just because it was entered into at the time of an Islamic marriage ceremony?"[62] asks *Odatalla*. "Its secular terms are enforceable as a contractual obligation, notwithstanding that it was entered into as part of a religious ceremony,"[63] responds *Aziz*. After all, suggests *Akileh*, the *Mahr* "agreement was an antenuptial contract."[64] Under the Formal Equality Approach, secular *Mahr* becomes an antenuptial agreement immediately enforceable as long as the conditions of contract law doctrine are met. The irony lies in the fact that, in interpreting *Mahr*, the *secular-promise-to-pay-money-in-the-form-of-an-antenuptial-agreement* can only be understood, contractually, contextually, by referring to the religious intentions of the Muslim parties. By a priori rejecting the pertinence of the Islamic shadow behind which husband and wife negotiate, bargain, and determine *Mahr* and its amount, courts have paradoxically refused an appreciation of contract law that would account for the parties' particular, peculiar private ordering regime,

---

[61] *Id.* ¶ 31.
[62] *Odatalla v. Odatalla*, 810 A.2d 93, 309 (N.J. Super. Ct. Ch. Div. 2002).
[63] *Aziz v. Aziz*, 127 Misc.2d 1013, 1013, 488 N.Y.S.2d 123 (Sup. Ct. 1985).
[64] *Akileh v. Elchahal*, 666 So.2d 246, 248 (Fla. Ct. App. 1996).

one that depends on their religious, gendered roles as much as it does on their contractual, "marketplace" roles.

iii. The Performance of the Contradiction by the Parties Themselves: Holmes' "Bad Man" and "Bad Woman"

In Holmes' The Path of the Law,[65] the legal system is depicted as "an instrument... of business" whose "prophecies" the lawyer attempts rigorously to predict and master. If adjudication is about judges' "duty of weighing considerations of social advantage," parties must know not only the adequate rules and precedents but also "the relative worth and importance of competing considerations" that are likely to affect judges. Emphasizing the existence of battles between individuals and/or groups, Holmes develops the famous "bad man" theory of the law, the individual who cares only about the material (and not the ethical) consequences of his act.[66]

Holmes' predictive theory of law and his advocacy of the bad-man perspective constitute powerful strategies undermining the misleading picture of law. In this section, I add another internal dimension to the Ends–Means Perversity Contradiction: the agency and active role of the Muslim parties themselves in relation to each other, as well as in relation to the Western court. Because of their individual motives, each spouse advocates or opposes the judicial enforcement of *Mahr* depending on how his or her interests would be affected. Is it possible that the *Muslim-husband-arguing-for-the-nonenforcement-of-Mahr-mainly-on-religious-grounds* is the equivalent of Holmes' "bad man," and the *Muslim-wife-arguing-for-the-enforcement-of-Mahr-mainly-on-secular-grounds* personifies a Holmesian "bad woman"?

a. The Muslim (Religious/Secular) Husband as the "Bad Man"?

In most of the matrimonial disputes analyzed in this chapter, Muslim parties made contradictory claims about Islam and the role of religion in a secular, Western state more generally. The Muslim husband typically argued that the obligations imposed by *Mahr* arose solely from religious/Islamic law and can therefore be interpreted only by reference to religious dogma.[67] In *Odatalla*, for example, Mr. Odatalla asked the court to *not* enforce *Mahr* – alleging that, according to his religious faith, *Mahr* could only be decided by an Islamic authority[68] – but, on the same account, requested "alimony and equitable distribution of certain jewelry, furniture, wedding

---

[65] Oliver Wendell Holmes, *The Path of the Law* (1897), *in* AMERICAN LEGAL REALISM 15–24 (William W. Fisher III et al. eds., Oxford University Press 1993).

[66] *Id.* at 17.

[67] *See* M.(N.M.), 2004 BCSC 346; *Kaddoura*, [1998] O.J. No. 5054; *Aziz*, 127 Misc.2d; and *Odatalla*, 810 A.2d.

[68] *Odatalla*, 810 A.2d. at 95.

gifts, and marital debt,"[69] demands that he could *not* have made under Islamic family law. Mr. Odatalla's adjudicative strategy is that of Holmes' "bad man" in that he uses law as a strategy to gain the most advantageous economic outcomes and material consequences while undermining the importance of religious law (Holmes' morality).

Can we imagine the Muslim wife behaving in the same fashion, alternatively drawing on and occasionally transcending the secular/religious performance – and bending perceived traditional gender roles in so doing? Can the Muslim wife, in asking for the enforcement of *Mahr* in Western courts, constitute a Holmesian "bad woman"?

b. The Muslim (Secular/Religious) Wife as the "Bad Woman"?

In most of the matrimonial disputes studied in this chapter, the Muslim wife claimed that nothing in law or public policy prevents judicial recognition and enforcement of the secular terms of *Mahr*. After all, *Mahr* is a contractual matter.[70] At times, however, in response to the Islamic argument that she should waive *Mahr* because she is the one asking for divorce (*Khul* divorce),[71] the Muslim wife donned the religious hat and presented a profoundly surprising description and analysis of Islamic law. The key to understanding the performance of the "bad woman" is to measure the *predicted* economic gains and losses of advocating the enforcement or nonenforcement of *Mahr* in a given situation, in relation to both Islamic family law *and* Western law. In response to the "waiver rule" of *Khul Mahr*, the "bad woman" has two options: either pretend that the "waiver rule" is *not* part of Islamic family law (the religious route), or suggest that the "waiver rule" is so discriminatory that it should be regarded as inherently contrary to "public order" in relation to international private law rules (the secular route). Either one of these options allows her to wield *Mahr* promises as weapons in order to emerge from the dissolution of her marriage with more than she would otherwise get.

A Quebec trial decision illustrates the point. In *M.H.D. v. E.A.*,[72] the Muslim wife embarked on a "secular" argumentation and convinced the court that Syrian Islamic law could not apply in Canada because its application would create a negative effect on Muslim wives availing themselves of the *Divorce Act*. The Muslim wife argued *Khul Mahr* as a legal institution violates substantive equality, in that it requires the Western state to punish a wife because *she* is the one initiating the divorce proceedings, an outcome that would not similarly apply to the husband. In the name of gender equality, such discriminatory Islamic traditions should be formally

---

[69] *Id.* at 94.
[70] *See* M.(N.M.), 2004 BCSC 346; *Kaddoura*, [1998] O.J. No. 5054; *Aziz*, 127 Misc.2d; and *Odatalla*, 810 A.2d.
[71] *Mahr* is attached to a wider regime of Islamic family law dictating in which cases it will be enforced: under a *Talaq* or *Faskh* divorce, but not so under a *Khul* divorce.
[72] *M.H.D. v. E.A.*, Droit de la famille – 1466, Sept. 23, 1991, No. 500–09–001296–896, (Can. Que. C.A.).

and rigidly *rejected* by the host legal system, despite rules of international private law incorporating Syrian Islamic law: "With all due respect to the beliefs of the religious authority as well as to those of the husband, the court believes that such traditions, customs, and doctrine put before us are not applicable to the wife, and that the court must consider the wedding present discussed above only with respect to the *Quebec Civil Code..*"[73]

V. MAHR AS BONUS AND PENALTY

In this section, I perform a distributive shift to argue that in the social life of Islamic marriages, *Mahr* is not unitary and autonomous but rather a functional institution that produces a series of inconsistent characteristics we can study. Through this distributive reading of *Mahr*, my hope is to offer a narrative concerned primarily with the social effects created by the judiciary as it claims to merely *translate Mahr* according to ideological preferences when in fact it *produces Mahr* as bonus or penalty. In an attempt to underline the complexity of *Mahr* as it moves from ideology to contradictions, I have deconstructed the *Muslim-woman-reacting-to-Mahr* into many conflicting players, situated in a continuum spectrum along the bonus/penalty lines. In every subsection, I present Leila in relation to her specific background rules and norms and situate how *Mahr* could be employed and deployed by her in strategic terms given that location. Although these perspectives are fictional, each Leila also reflects, directly or indirectly, the legal reasoning or outcome of real cases I have encountered and studied in my research.

A. *The Enforcement of* Mahr

i. *Mahr* as Penalty for Wife and Bonus for Husband: Leila, the German-Egyptian-"Foreign Bride"

Leila[74] has been married to Samir for fifteen years. Although of Egyptian origin and citizenship, she lives in Kreuzberg, the Turkish Muslim suburb of Berlin. She rarely goes out and makes contact with her German neighbors more hesitantly than her sons and her husband. However, in recent years, Leila has been exposed to the new wave of feminist critiques coming from German women of Muslim background, such as those of Necla Kelek's in *The Foreign Bride*.[75] In this work, Kelek addresses both the everyday violence of arranged marriages as well as the oppressive and sexist

---

[73] *Id.* ¶ 27 (translated from the original French by the author).

[74] This script is partly based on Oberlandesgericht [OLG] [Higher Regional Court] Bremen 1980, FamRZ 606, a 1980 German decision from the Higher Regional Court of Bremen, and NECLA KELEK, DIE FREMDE BRAUT [THE FOREIGN BRIDE] (2005).

[75] In her book, Kelek strongly criticizes both the so-called fundamentalist Muslim society for perpetuating a culture of female slavery, and the liberal German society, which in her opinion has adopted a hands-off approach based on tolerance. KELEK, *id.*

behavior of Muslim men in Germany. This book represented an ultimatum for Leila: she would either embrace women's rights (and other Western, German conceptions of freedom) or remain forever "a foreign bride" whose equality is constantly being jeopardized. Leila left Samir, her sons, her home – with perfect irresponsibility.[76]

Despite her sister Fatima's painful divorce experience in Egypt that left her heavily indebted to her ex-husband, Leila wasn't worried about suffering the same fate; German divorce law, she had been told, was much more favorable toward women. Faced with the impossibility of surviving with very limited economic resources, Leila reached the courthouse, confident that state alimony and division-of-property laws in Germany would guarantee her generous benefits. How wrong she was! Leila soon realized that, as a non-German citizen, Egyptian Islamic law would apply to her case! Because she had no claim under Egyptian law at the time to postdivorce alimony or to her share of the profits accruing to the marital property, the court held that *Mahr* constituted a substitute for postdivorce maintenance and division of the surplus of marital profits! Furthermore, because Leila was the one seeking the divorce, the court held that she had given up her right to deferred *Mahr* and was obligated to pay back the prompt *Mahr* she had been given at her wedding.

ii. *Mahr* as Penalty for Husband and Bonus for Wife: Leila, the Canadian-Pakistani-Journalist-Writing-as-a-Lesbian-Refusenik

Leila,[77] asserting herself as a Lesbian Refusenik living in British Columbia, Canada, acknowledges the freedom made possible by her surroundings: "The good news is I knew I lived in a part of the world that permitted me to explore. Thanks to the freedom afforded me in the West – to think, search, speak, exchange, discuss, challenge, be challenged, and rethink – I was poised to judge my religion in a light that I couldn't have possibly conceived in the parochial Muslim microcosm of the madressa."[78] Leila married Samir at the age of eighteen; he repudiated her three years later, as soon as she made her sexual preferences known to him. Leila is infinitely grateful to Canadian society, where one can become a lesbian and even

---

[76] I borrow this expression from Ralph Ellison, Invisible Man (1952), in which he argued that irresponsibility is, for subordinated groups, a consequence of their invisibility.

[77] This script is partly based on Irshad Manji's autobiographical book, Irshad Manji, The Trouble with Islam: A Muslim's Call for Reform in her Faith (2003), an international best seller that has been published in twenty-six countries (*see* www.muslim-refusenik.com). However, many of the facts that I have included in this story are purely fictional, including a first marriage with a man, and should not be interpreted as reflecting Manji's life. I chose this perspective because I believe it captures some of the anger of some Muslims who consider themselves as "Muslim Refusenik." I have also incorporated the outcome of two Canadian cases, namely *Nathoo v. Nathoo*, [1996] B.C.J. No. 2720 (Can. B.C. Sup. Ct.), and *M.(N.M.)*, 2004 BCSC 346.

[78] Irshad Manji, The Trouble with Islam: A Muslim's Call for Reform in her Faith 19 (St. Martin's Press 2004).

marry, write radical and provocative essays against Islam,[79] and choose an alternative path of life against the wishes of one's parents.

Leila is infuriated by proponents of multiculturalism who romanticize Islam and excuse brutality as a "cultural feature." Leila is angry, embarrassed at the fact that she was once "in the closet," married to Samir, sleeping next to Samir, faking with Samir, because one cannot be "a Muslim and a Lesbian": "You may wonder who I am to talk to you this way. I am a Muslim Refusenik. That doesn't mean that I refuse to be a Muslim; it simply means I refuse to join an army of automatons in the name of Allah."[80] Leila decides to ask the secular court for the enforcement of *Mahr*, in the amount of $50,000, as a calculated revenge. Given that "the parties chose to marry within the Muslim tradition,"[81] knowing "full well that provision for Maher was a condition of so doing,"[82] the court chose to enforce *Mahr* in addition to the $37,747.17 owed by Samir to Leila as a result of the division of family assets.

B. *The Nonenforcement of* Mahr

i. *Mahr* as Penalty for Wife and Bonus for Husband: Leila, the American-"Terrorist"-Convicted-under-the-Patriot-Act

On September 25, 2001, Leila[83] was arrested and detained on the basis of allegations that she constituted a threat to the security of the United States, by reason of her involvement in terrorist activities linked to Al-Qaeda. She was convicted soon after under the Patriot Act. Having recently married Samir, whom she had met a few months before being arrested, Leila remains in detention. In response to these unfounded suspicions linking her to terrorist groups, Leila finds peace in reading the Qu'ran and in writing letters to Samir, her soulmate. For her, *Mahr* symbolizes the beauty and purity of Samir's love, like "a bone in the upper part of the breast, or gristles of the ribs; or something presentable as a gift like a pearl."[84] Leila was a romantic. Last week, she received a letter informing her that Samir wishes to divorce her religiously, with no further explanation. Samir came on Sunday for his weekly visit and irrevocably pronounced the three *Talaq*. Leila was repudiated. Heartbroken, she asked a Californian lawyer to represent her in a claim for the enforcement of deferred *Mahr*, a symbolic amount of $1,700. She was informed that the court could not enforce *Mahr*. It held that the marriage contract must be considered as one designed to facilitate divorce, because with the exception of

[79] *Id.* at 35.
[80] *Id.* at 3.
[81] *Nathoo*, [1996] B.C.J. No. 2720, ¶ 24.
[82] *Id.*
[83] This script is partly based on *In re* Marriage of Dajani, 204 Cal. App. 3d 1387 (1988).
[84] M. Afzal Wani, The Islamic Law on Maintenance of Women, Children, Parents and Other Relatives: Classical Principles and Modern Legislations from India and Muslim Countries (Upright Study Home 1995).

prompt *Mahr* "the wife was not entitled to receive any of the agreed upon sum unless the marriage was dissolved or husband died. The contract clearly provided for wife to profit by divorce, and it cannot be enforced by a California court."[85] Leila was perplexed. How did *Mahr* provide *her* to profit from divorce? And how did it *clearly* do so? It was Samir who *religiously* divorced her! The least she could ask for is the enforcement of deferred *Mahr*, a condition of issuing *Talaq* in the first place! By distorting *Mahr*'s function, the court penalized Leila.

ii. *Mahr* as Penalty for Husband and Bonus for Wife: Leila, the *French-Member-of-Ni-Putes-Ni-Soumises*

Leila[86] is attempting to break her marriage to escape a hostile domestic environment. At nineteen, Leila would have never guessed where life would take her when she married Samir, a family friend, in Malaysia. At the time of the wedding, Leila was proud that she had garnered both a fairly high amount of *Mas Kahwin* (*Mahr*) as a young, unmarried woman, as well as an additional substantial amount of promised *Pemberian* (a customary form of dowry). The very idea of divorce seemed unthinkable at the time.

Leila and Samir moved to France seven years later so that Samir could pursue an advanced engineering degree. Bored with her life as a housewife, Leila decided to take night courses to become a secretary. She excelled in her course and blossomed in her new job working for a women's organization. Samir became more and more jealous and possessive after Leila started working. His physical abuse escalated and he started to make degrading remarks on how she became a "Western slut." He was particularly incensed that Leila had been introduced by a colleague to the organization *Ni Putes Ni Soumises* (Neither Whores Nor Slaves),[87] a French feminist movement founded in 2002 that has already secured the recognition of the French press and parliament. She eventually organized several conferences and publicly shared her experience of suffering with other Muslim women, especially those from her native Malaysia. Leila knew too well that Samir would never pronounce the three *Talaq* and she did not even attempt to negotiate a *Khul* divorce. One day, she

[85] *Id.*
[86] This script is partly based on the following French and Canadian decisions: Arrêt de la Cour d'appel de Douai, Jan. 8, 1976, No. 76–11-613 (Que.); and *Vladi v. Vladi*, 1987 Carswell NS 71, 7 R.F.L. (3d) 337, 79 N.S.R. (2d) 356; 196 A.P. R. 356, 39 D.L.R. (4th) 563 (N.S. Sup. Ct. Trial Div.).
[87] The French organization "Ni Putes Ni Soumises" [Neither Whores Nor Slaves] has become a nation-wide force, in France, of Muslim women refusing violence and submission. "Neither Whores Nor Slaves" is an expression that is meant to reflect the tragedy of Sohane Benziane, a nineteen-year-old girl who was set on fire and killed by a boy she knew in a run-down apartment estate in the outskirts of Paris in October 2002. The movement expresses its anger at the "tolerance" of French society toward the violence and stigmatization suffered by Muslim women in the name of Islamic tradition in the neglected French suburbs. The political platform of the organization can be found at www.niputesnisoumises.com.

simply walked away and never came back. She decided to reach the French court system though, to claim *Mahr*. She argued that, precisely because she is "neither a whore nor a slave," she should never have been submitted to the unequal and degrading treatment that the promise of *Mas Kahwin* and *Pemberian* represent: these foreign institutions should be declared contrary to *l'ordre public français* (French public order). The court agreed.[88] Thanks to the court's application of Western equity standards, Leila was awarded $253,000 instead of $0 under Islamic family law.

CONCLUSION

Whereas liberalism is one possible way of framing emancipatory claims made by minorities in Western societies, it has become, I have argued, the dominant approach underlying the way the legal system in Western liberal states deals with claims made by Muslims in general and Muslim women in particular. I have explored *Mahr's* internal and external pluralism from its place of departure under Islamic family law – illustrating that even there *Mahr* is not a static and monolithic religious institution – to its place of arrival under Western secular law, and analyzed *Mahr* as "adjudication" and "reception" by the Western liberal court, without inquiring into its subjective significance for the Muslim woman involved. A legal realist and distributive shift follow the way *Mahr* operates in the distribution of power and desire between the Muslim husband and the Muslim wife, as well as in the constitution of their respective identities through law.

In this chapter, I attempted to bring back into focus what has been hidden by the adjudicative discourse of *Mahr* as "recognition," as "equality," and as "fairness." My four Leilas demonstrate that the legal enforcement of *Mahr* as a legal rule has *asymmetric* economic effects *among* different groups of women. For one Leila, the enforcement of *Mahr* can be a bonus; for another, it is a penalty. For a third one, the unenforceability of *Mahr* is a penalty; for another one, it is a bonus. Leila's dilemma and negotiating strategies occupy different contexts, ranging from subversive uses of *Mahr* as a moral victory, a personal revenge, or an act of liberation. Such complex itinerary travels along with *Mahr* and reminds us too well that real women with real lives develop their own ways of bending gender roles to empower themselves as much as they can, despite the unpredictability of *Mahr's* reception in Western courts.

[88] I refer specifically here to Arrêt de la Cour d'appel de Douai, Jan. 8, 1976: No. 76–11-613.

24

Polygamy and Feminist Constitutionalism

Beverley Baines

FEMINIST CONSTITUTIONALISM'S DILEMMA

Polygamy poses a dilemma for feminist constitutionalism. Canada offers the perfect crucible for understanding this dilemma. Not only is polygamy a crime[1] but also Canada justifies criminalization on the grounds of protecting women and children, thereby attracting the attention and concern of feminists. For their part, constitutionalists will address polygamy because the constitutionality of criminalizing it has just been referred to the courts. However, feminists and constitutionalists will differ over the appropriate outcome for this case. Because most feminists believe polygamy is harmful to women, they will support continued criminalization. By definition, on the other hand, constitutionalists advocate limiting the powers of liberal states, meaning they will seek decriminalization. In sum, the issue of de/criminalizing polygamy polarizes feminists and constitutionalists, creating a dilemma for those who choose to subscribe to feminist constitutionalism.

Fortunately, feminist constitutionalism is a sufficiently novel concept that it is still under construction. In Canada, the relationship between feminism and constitutionalism has gone through several stages over the past quarter century. Constitutional scholar and feminist Donna Greschner typified the preliminary stage when she

---

[1] Canada. Criminal Code, R.S.C. 1985, C-46, s. 293 provides

293. (1) Every one who

(a) practises or enters into or in any manner agrees or consents to practise or enter into
   (i) any form of polygamy, or
   (ii) any kind of conjugal union with more than one person at the same time, whether or not it is by law recognized as a binding form of marriage, or

(b) celebrates, assists or is a party to a rite, ceremony, contract or consent that purports to sanction a relationship mentioned in subparagraph (a) (i) or (ii),

is guilty of an indictable offence and liable to imprisonment for a term not exceeding five years.

posed this provocative question: "Can constitutions be for women too?"[2] The second stage consisted of many feminist and constitutional scholars – indeed, too many to mention individually by name – applying feminist analysis to various issues of constitutional law. Thus scholarly research progressed from women to feminism and from constitutions to constitutionalism during these first two stages. For the current state, what remains is to elaborate the relationship between these "isms."

Because de/criminalization divides feminists and constitutionalists, it jeopardizes this relationship. In other words, polygamy provides a test case for the inclusivity of the concept of feminist constitutionalism. In this chapter, I propose to assess three legal strategies that might promote the requisite inclusivity. The first strategy has feminists inviting constitutionalists to incorporate the constitutional norm of sex equality into their argument. I refer to this approach as the feminist equality strategy. The second strategy calls for constitutionalists to ask feminists to subscribe to the reshaped proportionality test that surfaced recently in the opinions of the four women Justices currently on the Supreme Court of Canada. This approach is the women's proportionality strategy. In the final strategy constitutionalists and feminists, as well as courts, must listen to the voices of the women who live in polygamous relationships. This strategy is the polygamous wives' strategy.

The first two strategies are doomed to failure. On the one hand, constitutionalists will use their opposition to the original proportionality test – deference – to subvert the feminist equality strategy. On the other hand, feminists will not see any advantage to adopting the women's proportionality strategy. Yet both of these strategies are constructive. Who could quarrel with extending the reach of sex equality? Who could object to making the proportionality test more even-handed? Interestingly, the problem is not with these strategies per se. The difficulty is that both treat de/criminalization as a competing rights issue. Irrespective of whether the discourses of women's equality and proportionality are invoked, competing rights contests mandate zero-sum analyses with winner-take-all outcomes. In effect, they are more conducive to dividing feminists and constitutionalists than to bridging the gap between them.

However, I argue that the final strategy could obviate the need for a competing rights approach. In fact, it calls instead for other skills. Not only does it demand that constitutionalists and feminists hone their listening skills, more importantly, it requires them to recognize the constitutional citizenship of the women who live in polygamous relationships. Were they to listen to polygamous wives arguing criminalization infringes their right to sex equality, and I suggest there is every reason for them to make this argument, perhaps constitutionalists and feminists might acknowledge that these women embody both constitutionalism and feminism. My objective is to adapt Greschner's question to ask, can feminist constitutionalism be

---

[2] Donna Greschner, *Can Constitutions Be for Women Too?* in THE ADMINISTRATION OF JUSTICE, 20 (Dawn Currie and B. MacLean eds., 1986).

for women living in polygamy too? Polygamous wives may be, in short, a paradigm for feminist constitutionalism.

POLYGAMY BECOMES A CONSTITUTIONAL ISSUE

Before developing the three strategies for making feminist constitutionalism more inclusive, I want to explain how polygamy became a constitutional issue in Canada. According to historian Sarah Carter, this issue has its roots in late nineteenth-century Western Canada, a region that "was home to a diverse population with multiple definitions of marriage, divorce, and sexuality."[3] Before this time, the predominance of the Christian, heterosexual, and monogamous model of marriage "was not a foregone conclusion."[4] Carter describes the extensive efforts of policy makers who were determined to impose this new monogamous marriage model on white settler society, aboriginal peoples, and newcomers such as Mormon and Muslim immigrants.

Three late nineteenth-century lawsuits illustrate polygamous relationships between white male settlers and aboriginal women, as well as among aboriginal peoples. The issue in the first two cases was the validity of mixed marriages entered into by white male fur traders and aboriginal women according to the prevailing aboriginal customs in Alberta before the adoption of British common law.[5] In *Connolly v. Woolrich*,[6] thirty years after William Connolly had married Susanne "Pas-de-nom" in 1803, they moved to Quebec where, without ending the first marriage, he went through a Roman Catholic marriage ceremony in 1834 with a white woman, Julia Woolrich. Similarly in *Fraser v. Pouliot*,[7] fifteen years after Alexander Fraser married Angélique Meadows in 1788 or 1789, they also moved to Quebec where, during the currency of that marriage, he entered into successive conjugal relationships with Pauline Michaud and Victoire Asselin. The litigants were descendants fighting over succession to large estates.

Polygamy was raised in both cases. However, the courts did not treat it as a relationship that the white men instigated. Instead, it was addressed as an aboriginal custom that might invalidate the original customary marriages. The white male judges ruled that polygamy did not have any impact on the validity of Connolly's customary marriage because he had not practiced it while in Alberta. Then they

---

[3] Sarah Carter, THE IMPORTANCE OF BEING MONOGAMOUS: MARRIAGE AND NATION BUILDING IN WESTERN CANADA TO 1915 (2008) at 4.

[4] *Id.* at 4.

[5] See Constance Backhouse, PETTICOATS AND PREJUDICE: WOMEN AND LAW IN NINETEENTH-CENTURY CANADA (1991) 9–25 for a detailed narrative of these two cases.

[6] *Connolly v. Woolrich and Johnson et al.* (1867), 11 L.C. Jur. 197 (Lower Canada Superior Ct.), aff'd *Johnstone v. Connolly* (1869), R.J.R.Q. 266 (Que. C.A.).

[7] *Fraser v. Pouliot et al.* (1881), 7 Q.L.R. 149 (Que. Superior Ct.); *Fraser v. Pouliot et al.* (1884), 13 R.L.O.S. 1 (Que. Superior Ct.); *Fraser v. Pouliot et al.* (1885) 13 R.L.O.S. 520 (Que. Q.B.); *Jones v. Fraser* (1886), 12 Q.L.R. 327 (Que. Q.B.); *Jones v. Fraser* (1886), 13 S.C.R. 342.

referred to his second marriage not as polygamous but rather as bigamous and a nullity. In contrast, the appellate court dismissed the validity of Fraser's customary marriage using the fact of aboriginal polygamy as one reason. Unfortunately for Angélique Meadows' heirs, the lawyer who lost the polygamy argument in Connolly had become an appellate judge; and he was the one who wrote the majority decision in Fraser. His "memory of the bitter defeat in the *Connolly* case was long"[8] and it tainted his opinion in Fraser to the point where he "stepped far beyond the scope of the case before him."[9]

In the third case, *The Queen v. "Bear's Shin Bone,"*[10] polygamy was not a peripheral issue, likely because the accused, Bear's Shin Bone, was not a white male settler but rather a member of the Blood nation on the Kaini reserve. He was charged with polygamy under the Criminal Code because he had married two women, Free Cutter Woman and Killed Herself, who were also of the Blood nation. These marriages were according to the custom of the Blood Indians, which permitted polygamy. In a one-paragraph judgment, the white male judge held that the Blood Indian custom violated the polygamy prohibition enacted in 1890 and reenacted in the first Criminal Code in 1892.[11] This decision is the only recorded conviction for committing this crime in more than 110 years.

The uniqueness of the Bear's Shin Bone case raises two questions. First, why was he singled out for prosecution? On the surface, the answer is simple. At the instigation of Christian (specifically Anglican and Roman Catholic) missionaries, the Department of Indian Affairs (DIA) had spent most of the 1890s adopting a number of strategies, including forced residential schooling and denial of annuities, intended to encourage aboriginal peoples on the southern Alberta reserves to give up their second and subsequent wives. Because the DIA provided no mode of sustenance for these women, its efforts were largely unsuccessful. By late 1898, therefore, the DIA had decided to proceed with a test case "against Bear's Shin Bone, the most recent of the men to enter into a polygamous marriage."[12]

But why persevere against the aboriginal peoples in southern Alberta? The real reason had to do with the arrival of a sect of Christians (specifically Mormons and ex-Mormons) from Utah in 1887. Fleeing American anti-polygamy laws and led by Charles Ora Card, they had settled in southern Alberta, establishing the town of Cardston near to the Kaini (Blood) reserve.[13] As Carter writes, "There was concern that Mormons would encourage the Treaty 7 groups to continue to practice polygamy, and there was likely also concern to the opposite effect, that

---

8 Backhouse, *supra* note 5 at 24.
9 *Id.*
10 *The Queen v. "Bear's Shin Bone,"* [1898–1901] 4 Terr. L.R. 173; (1900) 3 C.C.C. 329 (N.W.T.S.C.).
11 An Act Further to Amend the Criminal Law, S.C. 1890, c. 37, s. 11. In 1892, the polygamy prohibition was incorporated in Canada's first Criminal Code, see: Criminal Code, S.C. 1892, c. 29, s. 278.
12 Carter, *supra* note 3 at 222.
13 *Id.* at 42–43.

the Mormons would learn that polygamy was in fact permitted in Canada."[14] It is more than curious, however, that after criminalizing polygamy in a provision that included explicit reference to prohibiting "what among the persons commonly called Mormons is known as spiritual or plural union,"[15] Canada launched the test case not against the Mormons in Cardston but rather against Bear's Shin Bone. Effectively, the government's choice discriminated both on religious and on racial grounds.

The second major question raised by the uniqueness of the Bear's Shin Bone case pertains to its consequences. Immediately after the case, aboriginal peoples who practiced polygamy did not abandon it, although concerted efforts by the DIA to abolish it "became less pronounced after 1903."[16] Nevertheless, aboriginal polygamy ended fairly early in the twentieth century.[17] It is likely that a similar timeline applies to Cardston Mormons whose adherence to polygamy was never very strong. However, in 1946, Harold Blackmore, a local convert to polygamy who was shunned by his fellow Cardston Mormons, moved his family to Lister, British Columbia, to found what one journalist recently dubbed "the polygamy capital of Canada."[18] Renamed Bountiful in 1984, it is now the focal point of the contemporary constitutional struggle over the de/criminalization of polygamy.

Bountiful Mormons are also known as members of the Fundamentalist Church of Jesus Christ of the Latter Day Saints (FLDS). There may be as many as 1,200 FLDS adherents residing in Bountiful,[19] not all of whom live in polygamous relationships. However, they may not be the largest group of polygamists in Canada. Despite criminal and immigration laws that prohibit polygamy, immigrants from countries in the Middle East, Asia, and Africa where polygamy is legal not only bring their actually polygamous families to Canada but also enter into polygamous relationships in Canada. Many are Muslims, although like Mormons, only a small number of Muslims may actually practice polygamy.

To illustrate, recently a Toronto Muslim imam told a newspaper reporter that in the past five years he had "officiated or 'blessed' more than 30 polygamous marriages."[20] Also, according to Tarek Fatah, founder of the Muslim Canadian Congress, there "are dozens of imams who have multiple wives, and who are conducting polygamous marriages and flaunting it."[21] Given the significant increase

---

[14] *Id.* at 206.

[15] Criminal Code, *supra* note 11, s. 278.

[16] Carter, *supra* note 3 at 229.

[17] Martha Bailey and Amy J. Kaufman, POLYGAMY IN THE MONOGAMOUS WORLD: MULTICULTURAL CHALLENGES FOR WESTERN LAW AND POLICY (2010) at 2–3.

[18] Daphne Bramham, THE SECRET LIVES OF SAINTS: CHILD BRIDES AND LOST BOYS IN CANADA'S POLYGAMOUS MORMON SECT (2008) at 9.

[19] *Id.* at 283.

[20] Noor Javed, *GTA's Secret World of Polygamy*, TORONTO STAR, May 24, 2008 at A10.

[21] Wendy Stueck, *Legal Experts Split over Constitutionality of Oppal's Move against Polygamy*, GLOBE AND MAIL, January 9, 2009, *available at* www.theglobeandmail.com/news/national/article965088.ece.

in Muslim immigration to Canada, therefore, polygamist Muslims may now out-number the polygamist Christians in Bountiful. However, as long as living in a polygamous relationship is a crime, polygamists outside of Bountiful are unlikely to self-identify. Outside of Bountiful, in other words, their numbers are unknown and unknowable.

Clearly, these unknown polygamists were not taken into account in January 2009 when British Columbia Special Prosecutor Terry Robertson charged James Oler and Winston Blackmore with the crime of polygamy.[22] Oler and Blackmore are rival leaders of two factions of the FLDS in Bountiful. However, these charges were quashed in September 2009 for procedural reasons.[23] No mention was made of the underinclusivity of these charges, perhaps because it might have made them vulnerable to an allegation of religious discrimination for prosecuting only Christians and not Muslims.

In October 2009, British Columbia launched a reference case to test the consti-tutionality of criminalizing polygamy.[24] A reference case enables a government to seek an advisory opinion about a constitutional question from a court. Provincially instigated reference cases are heard in provincial appellate courts (with provision for a further appeal to the Supreme Court of Canada), except in British Columbia where legislation permits this Province to initiate a reference case at the trial court level.[25] British Columbia chose to test the constitutionality of polygamy at the trial level because it will give the government "the option to introduce evidence and witnesses, which will put a human face on polygamy in contrast to the more abstract nature of a reference to the B.C. Court of Appeal."[26]

Sixteen groups and individuals have applied to intervene – to provide their opin-ions for or against criminalization – at the trial.[27] They include the Canadian Coali-tion for the Rights of Children; the Canadian Polyamory Advocacy Association; the Canadian Association for Free Expression; the B.C. Teachers' Federation; the Christian Legal Fellowship; the B.C. Civil Liberties Association; the David Asper Centre for Constitutional Rights; the Catholic Organization for Life and Family; the Knights of Columbus, B.C. and Yukon Chapter; West Coast Women's Legal

---

[22] *Charges Laid against B.C. Polygamist Leaders*, CANWEST NEWS SERVICE, 7 January 2009, *available at* www.nationalpost.com/news/canada/story.html?id=1151644.

[23] *Blackmore v. British Columbia (Attorney General)* 2009 BCSC 1299. Robertson was the third Special Prosecutor appointed by Attorney General Wally Oppal. Madam Justice Stromberg-Stein ruled that the decision of William Peck, the first Special Prosecutor, not to proceed with prosecution was final and binding on Attorney General Wally Oppal.

[24] British Columbia. Ministry of Attorney General, *Statement: Province to Seek Supreme Court Opinion on Polygamy, available at* www2.news.gov.bc.ca/news_releases_2009–2013/2009AG0012–000518.htm.

[25] Constitutional Question Act, R.S.B.C. 1996, c. 68, s. 1. Enacted in 1996, presumably the Legislature had polygamy in mind given this Province's longstanding efforts to combat it.

[26] British Columbia, Statement, *supra* note 24.

[27] *Religious, Children's, Civil Rights Groups Apply to Intervene in BC Polygamy Case*, BRITISH COLUMBIA NEWS, January 30, 2010, *available at* www.britishcolumbia.name/news/religious-childrens-civil-rights-groups-apply-to-intervene-in-bc-polygamy-case/.

Education and Action Fund; REAL Women of Canada; and Stop Polygamy in Canada, as well as Winston Blackmore and Oler.[28] Thereafter, Winston Blackmore pulled out when he was denied special status and funding to take part in the case, claiming he could not afford to participate.[29]

Strikingly absent from this lineup of potential interveners, likely also for funding reasons, are individuals or groups whose sole purpose is to represent women living in polygamous relationships. Moreover, none of the potential intervener groups are specifically denominated as representatives of Muslim women. These lacuna are serious deficiencies. The legislation permits courts to notify interested parties about their entitlement to be heard, but it cannot force them to appear.[30] Similarly, courts may appoint *amicus curiae* to represent the arguments that absentees might make, but their credentials are vulnerable to challenge if they are drawn from outside or do not have the support of the groups whose arguments they convey.[31] This case threatens to become limited to and mired in "the human face" of the male FLDS polygamists in Bountiful. To the extent that this happens, Mormon and Muslim women will be spoken about rather than having the opportunity to speak for themselves.

THE "COMPETING RIGHTS" APPROACH

Notwithstanding the absence of women, the court will hear claims about their right to sex equality. The state, officially the Attorneys General of British Columbia and Canada and perhaps those of other provinces, will unquestionably rely on women's equality rights to justify criminalization of polygamy. Lawyers for the state may try to bolster this claim by pointing to public or Canadian "values." However, they do so at their peril if they try to assert such "values" as an independent claim. On the one hand, if it is unpacked the values claim becomes redundant because it is founded on the claim for women's equality rights. On the other hand, it is likely that the court, at least the Supreme Court of Canada if it hears the appeal, will treat the polygamy issue as a "competing rights" case, not a rights versus values case.

What is a competing rights case? And why would it obviate a "values" claim that is not based on rights? The Ontario Human Rights Commission recently identified competing rights cases as a "developing area of law."[32] These cases may arise under the Canadian Charter of Rights and Freedoms,[33] or under human rights legislation.

---

[28] *Id.* See also: Ken MacQueen, *Making Their Bed*, MACLEANS, March 17, 2010, *available at* www2.macleans.ca/2010/03/17/making-their-bed/.

[29] James Keller, *Polygamy Court Case Will Proceed without Bountiful Leader, Says Lawyer*, THE CANADIAN PRESS, April 28, 2010, *available at* http://ca.news.yahoo.com/s/capress/100428/national/polygamy.

[30] Constitutional Question Act, *supra* note 25, s. 5.

[31] James Keller, *Blackmore Says Polygamy Lawyer Should Step Down over Political Donations*, THE CANADIAN PRESS, May 8, 2010, *available at* www.thewesternstar.com/index.cfm?sid=339260&sc=505.

[32] Ontario Human Rights Commission, *Process for Reconciling Competing Rights Claims, available at* www.ohrc.on.ca/en/resources/Guides/competingrights.

[33] Canadian Charter of Rights and Freedoms, Part I of the Constitution Act, 1982, being Schedule B to the Canada Act 1982 (U.K.), 1982, c. 11 [Hereinafter Charter].

However, the Commission was careful to distinguish typical Charter claims in which individuals challenge state action or law and typical statutory human rights claims in which individuals normally target an organization's policies or decisions; these are not competing rights cases. The Commission argued instead that this designation should be reserved for "situations where the rights of two individuals appear to be in conflict."[34] More illuminatingly, competing rights arise in conflicts that involve "religious, ethnic, and cultural diversity."[35] Therefore, only a rights-based and not a values-based claim will qualify as a possible justification for criminalizing polygamy if the courts treat the constitutional reference as a competing rights case.

Irrespective of whether Winston Blackmore appears in the courtroom, he and other polygamists maintain that prohibiting polygamy infringes the Charter right to freedom of religion.[36] Therefore, when British Columbia (and Canada) raise women's equality rights under Section 1 of the Charter,[37] the conflict will be joined and the polygamy reference will qualify as a competing rights case. Of course, someone may question the logic of juxtaposing sex equality to religious freedom because it sets polygamist against polygamist. What may be less transparent is, however, that the underlying conflict is Christian (Mormon, ex-Mormon, and FLDS) against Christian (mainstream Roman Catholic and Anglican), and/or even Muslim (if they step up to the plate) against Christian.

In fact, when conflicts between or among religious groups are played out under the Charter, they should not qualify as competing rights cases. Long ago, in *R. v. Big M Drug Mart Ltd*,[38] the Supreme Court of Canada made it clear that the state could not use its version of Christianity to justify infringing the religious freedom of adherents of minority religions. Canada cannot deny the consistency between the recently enacted Civil Marriage Act limitation of marriage to "two persons,"[39] and its common law precursor, *Hyde v. Hyde and Woodmansee*,[40] which relied on Christian values to limit marriage to "one man and one woman." Notwithstanding these concerns, I predict the reference will go forward as a competing rights case. What follows is a brief account of the arguments that will be made under this rubric.

Those seeking decriminalization will argue that the polygamy prohibition infringes their Charter right to freedom of religion.[41] Section 2(a) of the Charter

---

34 Ontario Human Rights Commission, *supra* note 32.
35 *Id.*, citing Beverley McLachlin at the Fourth Annual Human Rights Lecture of the Law Society of Ireland in May 2008, at 20.
36 Charter, *supra* note 33, s. 2(a).
37 *Id.*, s. 1.
38 *R. v. Big M Drug Mart Ltd.*, [1985] 1 S.C.R. 295 at ¶ 134.
39 Civil Marriage Act, S.C. 2005, c. 33.
40 *Hyde v. Hyde and Woodmansee* (1866), [1861–73] All E.R. Rep. 175.
41 They may also invoke their Section 7 rights to liberty and their section 15(1) religious equality rights. The former does not raise a competing rights issue; the latter may prove as difficult to sustain as most other section 15(1) cases. In this chapter, I intend to pursue only the religious freedom claim.

provides that "[e]veryone has...freedom of conscience and religion."[42] Mormon polygamists (especially those who are members of the FLDS) explain that their religious beliefs mandate them "to engage in plural or 'spiritual' marriage; this [is] essential to attaining the highest level of eternal salvation."[43] They claim "to be following the practice of the Old Testament prophets in order to be compliant with God's law."[44] In addition, they maintain that men need to marry at least three wives while women have only one husband whom they share among several wives.[45] Similarly, Islamic religious beliefs provide the grounding for polygamy among Muslims.[46] Not only was the Prophet Muhammed a practicing polygamist, but also the practice is mentioned in the Qur'an that allows up to four wives if a man has the means to support them equally.[47]

Given these beliefs, the effect of criminalizing polygamy is to place Mormon and Muslim polygamists who wish to marry and have families either in the position of violating their religious commitments or of forgoing marriage and family life. Absent plural marriages, their religious salvation is jeopardized if not completely denied. The criminal prohibition forces them to choose between adhering to their respective religious texts and having families, thereby limiting their religious freedom and violating Section 2(a) of the Charter. Under these circumstances, it is impossible to understand how the polygamists' claim for religious freedom might not meet the test for sincerity – they sincerely believe polygamy has a nexus with their religion – or the test for an interference that is more than trivial or insubstantial – the prohibition is intended to end their polygamous practices.[48] Thus, the court(s) should find that the polygamy prohibition violates polygamists' Charter right to freedom of religion in Section 2(a).

Still, John McLaren points to a worrisome tendency on the part of Canadian judges whose "instinct seems to be to limit and understate the domain of the sacred and religious in the public life of the secular state."[49] He might have pointed to *Alberta v. Hutterian Brethren of Wilson Colony* wherein the Supreme Court of Canada upheld the requirement that all drivers' licenses contain photos as an identity fraud prevention measure, even though it threatened the viability of the communal lifestyle of the minority religious respondents.[50] In the polygamy reference, religious claims may be diminished by judges opting to treat the issue as primarily one of marriage (and divorce) laws that, in turn, they deem secular. That they are wrong

---

[42] Charter, *supra* note 33, s. 2(a).

[43] Carter, *supra* note 3 at 41.

[44] *Id.*

[45] *Id.*

[46] Bailey and Kaufman, *supra* note 17 at 8.

[47] *Id.* at 9–10.

[48] *Alberta v. Hutterian Brethren of Wilson Colony* 2009 SCC 37 at ¶ 32 (McLachlin, CJC).

[49] John McLaren, *Protecting Confessions of Faith and Securing Equality of Treatment for Religious Minorities in Education*, in DIVERSITY AND EQUALITY: THE CHANGING FRAMEWORK OF FREEDOM IN CANADA (Avigail Eisenberg ed., 2006) 153 at 155.

[50] *Hutterian Brethren, supra* note 48.

on both counts would not preclude judges from holding otherwise. In effect, an ambitious judge might hold that monogamy is an unwritten constitutional value.

McLaren warns as well of "a tendency for judges to distinguish between respectable and nonrespectable religion."[51] Regrettably, it would not take much for judges to give into their distaste for polygamy by discounting the FLDS religious belief in it as the work of crackpots. They should not accede to stereotyping, even when such views are widely expressed among the citizenry. As a corrective, judges should ensure that Muslim polygamy is included in the frame. Globally, twenty-three percent of the world's population is Muslim, the large majority of whom "live in countries where polygamy, in accordance with Islamic law, is legal."[52] Recognizing that some Muslims practice polygamy might serve as a counter to the disrespect for and exclusion of the FLDS religious belief in polygamy. After all, the Criminal Code prohibits polygamy irrespective of which religious beliefs are held.

Assuming the court finds an infringement of religious freedom, can the state save the polygamy prohibition by asserting that its purpose is to protect women's equality rights? The Charter provides the state with the opportunity to justify infringing rights in Section 1.[53] Judges apply Section 1 using a four-pronged test originally set out in *R. v. Oakes*.[54] The state must show that 1) the objective of Section 293 of the Criminal Code is sufficiently important to warrant limiting religious freedom; 2) prohibiting polygamy is rationally connected to the objective of Section 293; 3) Section 293 minimally impairs religious freedom; and 4) the deleterious effects of criminalizing polygamy are not disproportionate to the salutary effects. Each of these claims is subject to controversy.

To win the controversy about the objective of Section 293, the state has to persuade the court that the original purpose, or the current purpose, or the purpose after the section was amended in 1954 is to protect women's equality rights. The first two claims are unlikely to be successful, the first because the original version of Section 293 explicitly referred to keeping Mormons out of Canada,[55] making the purpose religious, that is, to reinforce the views of the majority religions – Anglicanism and Roman Catholicism – that marriage had to be monogamous. The Supreme Court of Canada has already decided that a religious purpose that directly contradicted the Charter right to freedom of religion "could not be a purpose that justified limiting the right."[56] The second claim would also fail because, given the original purpose

---

[51] McLaren, *supra* note 49, at 155.
[52] Bailey and Kaufman, *supra* note 17 at 2.
[53] Charter, *supra* note 33, s. 1 which provides

    1. The Canadian Charter of Rights and Freedoms guarantees the rights and freedoms set out in it subject only to such reasonable limits prescribed by law as can be demonstrably justified in a free and democratic society.

[54] *R. v. Oakes*, [1986] 1 S.C.R. 103.
[55] Criminal Code, S.C. 1892, *supra* note 11.
[56] Peter W. Hogg, Constitutional Law of Canada (2007) at 35–23, referring to *Big M Drug Mart*, *supra* note 38.

(religious), any attempt to attribute a different purpose based on today's values (sex equality) would run afoul of the no-shifting-purposes rule set out in *R. v. Big M Drug Mart Ltd.*[57]

Only the third claim has the ghost of a chance. In 1954, Canada amended the polygamy provision in the Criminal Code by deleting the reference to Mormons.[58] This amendment was made at the behest of two Mormon men – John Blackmore and Solon Low – who sat in the federal House of Commons as the past and present leaders, respectively, of the Social Credit Party.[59] The state could argue that the amendment gave the prohibition of polygamy a new purpose, namely women's equality. However, merely deleting the reference to Mormons does not change the underlying Christian purpose of protecting and promoting only monogamous marriages. Under these circumstances, the state's claim will require evidence to substantiate it. Such evidence is likely to be difficult to find because women's equality rights did not really become a significant public issue until decades later, that is, well after the Royal Commission on the Status of Women issued its Report in 1970.[60]

The second prong of the Oakes test requires the state to show a rational connection between criminalizing polygamy and protecting women's equality rights. The state would have to counter the argument that the polygamy prohibition is overinclusive because there are studies that show some polygamous relationships do not harm women, either economically, or socially, or in terms of their well-being.[61] As well, the state would confront the contention that criminalizing polygamy is underinclusive because there are many ways in which the equality rights of women living in monogamous relationships are harmed without the state resorting to criminalizing those who cause the harm.

To meet the minimal impairment prong of the Oakes test, the state would explain why anything less than criminalization would not protect women's equality rights. This would be difficult given there was a gap of more than seventy years between the most recent polygamy prosecutions. That is, before the charges were laid in British Columbia in 2009, the previous case was *R. v. Tohurst and Wright,*[62] a 1937 decision in which the Ontario Court of Appeal quashed the convictions of James Tolhurst and May Wright on the ground that criminalizing polygamy did not make adultery a criminal offense. Moreover, decriminalizing polygamy would not result in converting it into a legal form of marriage. The state would have to amend the Civil Marriage Act, as well as many other pieces of legislation. Failure to make these

[57] *Big M Drug Mart, supra* note 38.
[58] Criminal Code, S.C. 1953–54, c. 51, s. 243.
[59] Bramham, *supra* note 18 at 49.
[60] Canada, REPORT OF THE ROYAL COMMISSION ON THE STATUS OF WOMEN (1970).
[61] Angela Campbell, *How Have Policy Approaches to Polygamy Responded to Women's Experiences and Rights? An International, Comparative Analysis* in POLYGAMY IN CANADA: LEGAL AND SOCIAL IMPLICATIONS FOR WOMEN AND CHILDREN (Status of Women Canada, 2005), *available at* http://epe.lac-bac.gc.ca/100/200/301/swc-cfc/polygamy-e/index.html.
[62] *R. v. Tolhurst and Wright* [1937] O.R. 570 (OCA).

changes would mean polygamists could marry religiously but not civilly. If the state were determined to express its disapproval of polygamy otherwise than as it does through the Civil Marriage Act, the federal, provincial, and territorial governments could agree to amend their statutory human rights laws to define polygamy as a discriminatory practice subject to civil penalties.

Finally, to assess the deleterious versus salutary effects of criminalizing polygamy as required by the fourth prong of the Oakes test, the state would have to argue that the benefits of protecting women's equality rights outweigh the deleterious effects on polygamists' religious freedom. This prong is seldom, if ever, analyzed in any depth when courts are dealing with competing group rights because the judges prefer to defer to governmental policy.[63] Only if British Columbia had proceeded with the criminal case would the deference rule have been superseded by a serious attempt at balancing effects.[64]

In sum, when the polygamy reference case is treated as a competing rights case in which the competition lies between the right to religious freedom and women's rights to sex equality, the judge(s) may opt for continued criminalization. Ultimately, this outcome may be driven less by the formulaic application of each prong of the Oakes test. Instead it may simply exemplify judicial conformity to the Oakes deference rule that applies in cases where the contest involves competing group rights. If this happens, feminists who support continued criminalization will be happy, while constitutionalists will not. Were decriminalization to prevail, feminists and constitutionalists would trade positions but still remain polarized. The chances for feminist constitutionalism appear remote.

STRATEGIES BRIDGING FEMINISM AND CONSTITUTIONALISM

In this part, I assess three strategies for bridging the gap between feminists and constitutionalists in the context of the issue of de/criminalizing polygamy. The three strategies are a feminist equality strategy, a women's proportionality strategy, and a polygamous wives' strategy. The feminist equality strategy represents a feminist perspective that is required of constitutionalists. The women's proportionality strategy is presented from the constitutionalists' perspective to feminists to persuade them to settle for it. Finally, polygamous wives could offer their perspective as a third strategy, presenting it to both feminists and constitutionalists.

Feminist Equality Strategy

Canadian feminism is not monolithic. For instance, feminist legal scholars are conflicted about polygamy. Although no one has surveyed us, from many conversations

---

[63] *Irwin Toy Ltd. v. Quebec* [1989] 1 S.C.R. 927, at 993.
[64] *Id.* at 994.

my sense is that most would agree with Professor Rebecca Cook and Lisa Kelly[65] when they conclude that polygamy is inconsistent with international law, if not the Charter, because it is harmful to women. Like Professor Margaret Sommerville,[66] they urge continued criminalization. Although others such as Professor Lorraine Weinrib[67] stop short of actually advocating criminalization, it would appear to be their objective when they resort to the prevailing rhetoric about polygamy's harms. These are the feminists who create what I have identified as feminist constitutionalism's dilemma, and whose concerns I endeavor to address in this chapter.

However, there is another side to feminist legal scholarship pertaining to polygamy. A number of feminist legal scholars deny that there is conclusive evidence of women being harmed by polygamy. These scholars include Professors Angela Campbell,[68] Lori Beaman,[69] Susan Drummond,[70] and Martha Bailey (writing with Amy Kaufman).[71] They do not deny that some women (and children) living in polygamous relationships suffer harm. Rather they argue that, given the criminalization of polygamy in Canada, it is impossible to conduct reliable research. While none have yet argued for legalization, they advocate decriminalization for a number of reasons, including to enable researchers to determine whether, and if so what, harm is a reality for women living in polygamous relationships. Clearly they do not contribute to feminist constitutionalism's dilemma.

Equally obviously, however, pro-decriminalization feminists do not represent all feminists. Because I am not willing to truncate feminism's full potential to address

---

[65] Rebecca J. Cook and Lisa M. Kelly, POLYGYNY AND CANADA'S OBLIGATIONS UNDER INTERNATIONAL HUMAN RIGHTS LAWS (Department of Justice Canada, 2006), *available at* www.justice.gc.ca/eng/dept-min/pub/poly/poly.pdf; Lisa M. Kelly, *Bringing International Human Rights Law Home: An Evaluation of Canada's Family Law Treatment of Polygamy*, 65 UNIVERSITY OF TORONTO FACULTY OF LAW REVIEW 1 (2007).

[66] Margaret Somerville, *If Same-Sex Marriage, Why Not Polygamy?* GLOBE AND MAIL, August 11, 2007, at A15.

[67] Lorraine E. Weinrib, *Shooting Down Polygamy Law not Necessarily a Slam Dunk*, University of Toronto Law School Faculty BLOG, January 13, 2009, *available at* http://utorontolaw.typepad.com/faculty_blog/2009/01/lorraine-e-weinrib-shooting-down-polygamy-law-not-necessarily-a-slam-dunk.html; Lorraine Weinrib, *Permissibility of Polygamy Put in New Light*, LAW TIMES, October 15, 2007 at 6.

[68] Angela Campbell, *Bountiful Voices*, 47 OSGOODE HALL LAW JOURNAL 183 (2009); Angela Campbell, *Wives' Tales: Reflecting on Research in Bountiful*, 23 CANADIAN JOURNAL OF LAW AND SOCIETY 121 (2008); Angela Campbell, *How Have Policy Approaches to Polygamy Responded to Women's Experiences and Rights? An International, Comparative Analysis, supra* note 61.

[69] Lori G. Beaman, *Doit-on criminaliser la polygamie au nom de la protection des droits des femmes?*, *in* RAPPORTS SOCIAUX DE SEXE/GENRE ET DROIT: REPENSER LE DROIT (Louise Langevin, ed., 2008) 149; Lori G. Beaman, *Who Decides? Harm, Polygamy and Limits on Freedom*, 10 NOVA RELIGIO 43 (2006); Lori G. Beaman, *Church, State, and the Legal Interpretation of Polygamy in Canada*, 8 NOVA RELIGIO 20 (2004); Lori G. Beaman, *Religion and the State: The Letter of the Law and the Negotiation of Boundaries*, *in* GLOBALIZATION, RELIGION, AND CULTURE (Peter Beyer and Lori G. Beaman eds., 2007), 393.

[70] Susan Drummond, *Polygamy's Inscrutable Criminal Mischief*, 47 OSGOODE HALL L. J. 317 (2009).

[71] Bailey and Kaufman, *supra* note 17.

polygamy, I propose to explore the possibility of forging a relationship between feminist legal scholars who support criminalization and constitutionalists who seek decriminalization. I have no intention of compromising the integrity of feminism, which depends on identifying and condemning behavior that harms women. Perhaps it follows that too much is at stake for feminists to compromise their support for criminalization. Constitutionalism may have to accommodate feminism by making an exception for polygamy.

While harm is a defining feature of feminism, so too is sex equality. Indeed, feminists are not conflicted about the pivotal status of sex equality. Thus I propose to shift the frame from harm to sex equality, asking whether the discourse of sex equality is something feminism and constitutionalism might have common. Feminists who support continued criminalization have little difficulty treating polygamy's harm as its violation of women's right to sex equality. For these feminists, in other words, criminalization protects sex equality. Thus focusing on sex equality maintains the integrity of their feminism.

In contrast, sex equality is not a defining feature of constitutionalism. However, women's equality rights share with other fundamental rights and freedoms the attribute of justifying limits on state power. Put differently, for constitutionalists it is deference to state power that is inconsistent with protecting sex equality rights. From their perspective, sex equality is served by decriminalization. Therefore, the discourse of sex equality leaves the polarization between constitutionalism and feminism in place. A feminist equality strategy cannot bridge the gap between them.

Women's Proportionality Strategy

In this strategy, the "women" are the four women currently sitting on the Supreme Court of Canada. If the polygamy reference case reaches this court, Chief Justice Beverley McLachlin and Justices Marie Deschamps, Rosalie Abella, and Louise Charron may hear it. Indeed, were the four to sit, they would constitute a majority on all but a nine-person bench.[72] In the next Part, I explore some of the factors that will influence how these four Justices and their colleagues perceive women living in polygamous relationships. In this Part, however, I turn to their recent jurisprudence to argue that they have collectively begun the process of reshaping the proportionality test that informs the application of Section 1 of the Charter. Effectively, their test is more onerous for the state because they put limits on the deference approach that has governed competing groups' cases to date. Although constitutionalists will approve, feminists who favor criminalization will be a hard sell.

Constitutionalists should recognize that the four female Justices have reshaped the Oakes test beginning with the religious freedom cases decided since 2006. Prior

---

[72] Benches may consist of five, seven, or nine Justices.

to this time, the second, third, and fourth prongs – rational connection, minimal impairment, and deleterious/salutary effects – of the Oakes test were known collectively as the proportionality test. In reality, however, the rational connection and minimal impairment – particularly the latter – prongs were paramount. Not only did they impose a test of reasonableness, or what became known as deference. More importantly, the test of reasonableness/deference obviated resort to the actual proportionality test in the fourth prong. Instead of independently balancing effects in the fourth test, mostly this prong was collapsed into the third or minimal impairment prong. In fact, deference became an all-but-irrefutable presumption in cases involving rights competitions among social groups.

However, three recent cases – *Multani v. Commission scolaire Marguerite-Bourgeois*,[73] *Bruker v. Marcovitz*,[74] and *Alberta v. Hutterian Brethren of Wilson Colony*[75] – have reinstated a proportionality test by emphasizing the autonomy of the fourth prong. In *Multani*, Justice Charron initiated the revival. First, she rejected the claim for internal limits to the right to freedom of religion in Section 2(a) of the Charter.[76] Then, in the context of her Section 1 analysis, Justice Charron adverted to the need for an assessment of the fourth prong even though the state had already lost at the third prong.[77] Chief Justice McLachlin adopted Justice Charron's opinion. Although Justices Deschamps and Abella authored a concurring opinion, they avoided taking a position on Section 1 by using an administrative rather than constitutional law approach to the issue of prohibiting kirpans in public schools.

Although *Bruker v. Marcovitz* is not a Charter case, it nevertheless constituted a second step in the road to reshaping the proportionality test. In *Bruker*, Justice Abella emphasized the need for a "balancing of competing rights and values" as an essential element of the equivalent provisions in the Quebec Charter.[78] She held (and the Chief Justice adopted her opinion) that the public interest in protecting the equality rights of a Jewish woman outweighed the religious freedom of her husband when he refused to honor his agreement to provide a religious divorce (*get*).[79] "Any infringement of Mr. Marcovitz's freedom of religion is," Justice Abella wrote, "inconsequential compared to the disproportionate disadvantaging effect on Ms. Bruker's ability to live her life fully as a Jewish woman in Canada."[80] There is no whiff of a reasonableness test here; a full-blown balancing or proportionality exercise was conducted despite the absence of the state as a party. In their dissent,

---

[73] *Multani v. Commission scolaire Marguerite-Bourgeois* 2006 SCC 6.
[74] *Bruker v. Marcovitz* 2007 SCC 54.
[75] *Hutterian Brethren, supra* note 48.
[76] *Multani, supra* note 73 at ¶ 25–30 (Charron J).
[77] *Id.* at ¶ 78 (Charron J).
[78] *Bruker, supra* note 74 at ¶ 77 (Abella J).
[79] *Id.* at ¶ 92 (Abella J).
[80] *Id.* at ¶ 93 (Abella J).

Justices Deshamps and Charron decided the claim was not justiciable;[81] hence, they did not undertake a Section 1 analysis.

Finally, although Chief Justice McLachlin acknowledges early in the *Hutterian Brethren* case that the court normally applies a reasonableness or deference test to social problems,[82] she nevertheless devotes eight paragraphs to reassessing the significance of the fourth, or proportionality of effects, prong.[83] The Chief Justice treats this prong as requiring a balancing test, returning to its origins in *Oakes* and citing former Chief Justice Dickson's explanation of its function:

> Even if an objective is of sufficient importance, and the first two elements of the proportionality test are satisfied, it is still possible that, because of the severity of the deleterious effects of a measure on individuals or groups, the measure will not be justified by the purposes it is intended to serve. The more severe the deleterious effects of a measure, the more important the objective must be if the measure is to be reasonable and demonstrably justified in a free and democratic society.[84]

Any suggestion that deference is determinative has disappeared.

To explain why she has to address the significance of the fourth prong almost twenty-five years after former Chief Justice Dickson accorded it so much importance, Chief Justice McLachlin first observes that "it has not often been used."[85] Then she attributes to senior constitutional scholar Peter Hogg the oppositional argument that the fourth prong "is actually redundant."[86] He had asked rhetorically how a law that has a pressing and substantial objective (i.e., passes the first prong) could have effects disproportionate to its objective.[87] Although Chief Justice McLachlin is too polite to come right out and say that Professor Hogg did not attend adequately to former Chief Justice Dickson's analysis in *Oakes*, her gravamen is clear.

The answer lies in the fact that the first three stages of the Oakes test are anchored in an assessment of the law's purpose. Only the fourth branch takes full account of the "severity of the deleterious effects of a measure on individuals or groups."[88] Continuing, she argues that analytical clarity and transparency call for distinguishing between the minimal impairment and proportionality of effects prongs because they "involve different kinds of balancing."[89]

According to the Chief Justice, the fourth prong "allows for a broader assessment of whether the benefits of the impugned law are worth the costs of the rights

---

[81] *Id.* at ¶ 106 (Deschamps J).
[82] *Hutterian Brethren, supra* note 75 at ¶ 37 (McLachlin CJC).
[83] *Id.* at ¶ 72–78 (McLachlin CJC).
[84] *Id.* at ¶ 74 (McLachlin CJC, citing *Dickson CJC* in *R. v. Oakes, supra* note 54 at 139–40).
[85] *Id.* at ¶ 75 (McLachlin CJC).
[86] *Id.*
[87] *Id.*
[88] *Id.* at ¶ 76 (McLachlin CJC).
[89] *Id.*

limitation."⁹⁰ She concludes the *Hutterian Brethren* case is one "where the decisive analysis falls to be done at the final stage of Oakes."⁹¹ The state satisfied the first three prongs leaving the court with the final question of "whether the deleterious effects are out of proportion to the public good achieved by the infringing measure."⁹² Although Chief Justice McLachlin and Justice Abella (dissenting) come to diametrically opposed conclusions about the outcome of this balancing test, they do not differ about the test itself.

In sum, the Chief Justice, writing for a majority that includes Justice Deschamps (Justice Charron did not sit), and Justice Abella agree about reshaping of the fourth prong of the proportionality test. Two major consequences follow. One is that these Justices reject outright Professor Hogg's redundancy approach to this prong, preferring the approach of former Chief Justice Dickson. More important, albeit implicitly, they disavow reliance on the reasonableness or deference approach that had previously dominated the first three prongs of the proportionality test. That is, even if the state meets the first three prongs of the test such that reasonableness or deference seems appropriate, the state must also meet the fourth prong – proportionality or balancing of effects – to save the impugned legislation.

These Justices are not inventing a new approach. They are reshaping the prevailing approach by rereading and reapplying former Chief Justice Dickson's opinion in *Oakes*. However, their arguments highlight the existence of a controversy among the Justices about the meaning of proportionality in the context of competing rights cases. Should proportionality mandate deference, or must it include a balancing exercise? This controversy may actually be longstanding, only becoming transparent in the *Hutterian Brethren* case with the juxtaposition of the opinions of Chief Justice McLachlin and Justice Abella on one side and those of Justices LeBel and Fish on the other. The latter, dissenting, continue to support Professor Hogg's redundancy approach that mandates deference.⁹³

To return to the women's proportionality strategy, therefore, constitutionalists will support any approach including this one that displaces the reign of deference. They recognize that a reshaped proportionality approach may not guarantee limits on state action but it will give those who seek limits more opportunity to make persuasive arguments than does the deference approach. But the reasons that endear the women Justices' reshaped proportionality test to constitutionalists are likely to be precisely the ones that turn away feminists who support criminalization. The only way for

---

⁹⁰ *Id.* at ¶ 77 (McLachlin CJC, continuing by citing in support Bastarache J in *Thomson Newspapers Co. v. Canada* [1998] 1 S.C.R. 877 at ¶ 125).
⁹¹ *Id.* at ¶ 78 (McLachlin CJC).
⁹² *Id.* at ¶ 78 (McLachlin CJC).
⁹³ *Id.* at ¶ 191 (LeBel J stating: "Indeed I believe that the proportionality analysis depends on a close connection between the final two stages of the Oakes test. The court's goal is essentially the same at both stages"; and at ¶ 192 "It may be tempting to draw sharp analytical distinctions between the minimal impairment and balancing of effects parts of the Oakes test"); and ¶ 203 (Fish J stating that he agrees with Justice LeBel and for the reasons he has given).

constitutionalists to bridge the gap is to try to convince these feminists that the reshaped proportionality or balancing test is here to stay. As a bridging exercise, this is unlikely to yield more support for the relationship between feminism and constitutionalism.

Polygamous Wives' Strategy

This strategy is speculative, albeit grounded pragmatically and legally. It requires inclusion in the courtroom of the voices of women living in polygamous relationships. If asked, will they speak? What will they say? In her study of polygamous women living in Bountiful, Professor Campbell reports their stories as being "rich, complex, sophisticated, and diverse."[94] In fact, they "belie the caricature of them as benighted, hidden, and subverted."[95] The women's power dynamics are complex, involving relationships with sister wives, husbands, and children. They manage normal household tasks and family planning, as well as (for some) attending college or working in shops in neighboring towns. They do not deny "there may be vulnerability, exploitation, and cases of abuse in Bountiful."[96] However, "they reject the assumption that these ills are inherent to polygamous life."[97] Because criminalization exposes them to "the risk of up to five years imprisonment," Campbell concludes that hearing their stories "is essential" to assessing "the propriety of the criminal law's current approach to polygamy."[98]

But would they speak, not just in interviews with academic researchers but also in a courtroom? Some historical and contemporary evidence of FLDS women's activism exists. In the late nineteenth century, Zina Card, one of Utah Mormon leader Brigham Young's daughters and the third wife of Charles Ora Card (founder of Cardston), was an outspoken supporter of plural marriage both in the United States and after she moved to Alberta.[99] Addressing the U.S. Senate and House Judiciary Committee in 1879, she said that "polygamy 'seemed far more holy and upright and just to womankind than any other order of marriage.'"[100] More recently, American Mormon polygamist Mary Batchelor published *Voices in Harmony: Contemporary Women Celebrate Plural Marriage*[101] in 2000, a book containing "a hundred positive accounts of polygamy – all recounted by women."[102]

---

[94] Angela Campbell, *In the Name of the Mothers*, GLOBE AND MAIL, January 10, 2009, A 17. For more detail, *see* Angela Campbell, *Bountiful Voices, supra* note 68.

[95] *Id.*

[96] *Id.*

[97] *Id.*

[98] *Id.*

[99] Carter, *supra* note 3, at 46–49.

[100] *Id.* at 48.

[101] Mary Batchelor, Marianne Watson, and Anne Wilde, VOICES IN HARMONY: CONTEMPORARY WOMEN CELEBRATE PLURAL MARRIAGE (2000).

[102] Jeffrey Michael Hayes, *Polygamy Comes Out of the Closet: The New Strategy of Polygamy Activists*, 3 STANFORD JOURNAL OF CIVIL RIGHTS AND CIVIL LIBERTIES 99 at 109 (2007).

As a result of this publication, "once silent Fundamentalist Mormon polygamists...[spoke] publicly for the first time in generations."[103] This book also
led to "the creation of the nascent polygamy advocacy movement – particularly one group, Principle Voices."[104] A leading pro-polygamy American advocacy group, Principle Voices "has consciously presented to the world polygamy's
female face, to provide a powerful visual suggestion that many polygamist wives
are, indeed, happy to consent to such relationships."[105] Canadian counterparts
have followed suit, establishing the Bountiful Women's Society, which held a
press conference in 2005 to discuss the various benefits of plural marriages, "such
as pooling resources and talent, and higher household incomes."[106] As well, the
Canadians produced their own monograph entitled *Bountiful: As We Love It and
Live It.*[107]

Feminists fear this activism is the product of false consciousness. They assume "a
woman who claims to have made an autonomous and free choice about polygamous
marriage has no sense of the truth"; "she has been 'co-opted' by her culture";
and/or she is "controlled (maybe even brainwashed) by her environment."[108] Before
interviewing women in Bountiful, Professor Campbell addressed this assumption.
She referred to Nancy Kim who "points out that, if false consciousness exists, then
all women are subject to overriding patriarchal influences that prevent any of us
from knowing or seeing 'the truth.'"[109] Rather than attribute false consciousness to
women who "retain their cultural membership in settings that, at least from the
outsider's perspective, fail to privilege gender equality,"[110] Professor Campbell chose
to assume "the authenticity, 'truth,' and legitimacy of the stories [Bountiful] women
tell."[111] She would question these accounts but only after critical self-reflection about
her "own cultural and normative starting points."[112]

When it comes to perspectives on polygamy, scholars are not the only feminists
who should practice critical self-reflection. When retired Canadian Supreme Court
Justice Claire L'Heureux-Dubé recently spoke out against polygamy, she stated that
she regards it as "contrary to the equality of the sexes."[113] Her self-reflection consisted

---

[103] *Id.* at 100–101.

[104] *Id.* at 100–101.

[105] *Id.* at 108.

[106] Meghan Wood, *Bountiful Polygamists Speak Up, available at* www.canadianchristianity.com/cgi-bin/
na.cgi?nationalupdates/050428bountiful.

[107] Bramham, *supra* note 18 at 246.

[108] Campbell, *Wives' Tales, supra* note 68 at 129.

[109] *Id.* (emphasis in original), citing Nancy Kim, *Toward a Feminist Theory of Human Rights: Straddling
the Fence Between Western Imperialism and Uncritical Absolutism*, 25 COLUMBIA HUMAN RIGHTS LAW
REVIEW 49 at 99 (1993–1994).

[110] *Id.*

[111] *Id.* at 130.

[112] *Id.* at 140.

[113] Kevin Dougherty, *Polygamy 'Contrary to the Equality of the Sexes': Retired Justice*, NATIONAL POST,
26 March 2009, *available at* www.nationalpost.com/story-printer.html?id=1430857.

of translating her ideological commitment to monogamy – "Marriage is a union of two people, period"[114] – into the discourse of sex equality. Moreover, her views may give substance to those of Justices Michel Bastarache and Louis LeBel dissenting in *R. v. Labaye*,[115] which contains the only reference to polygamy in the court's Charter-era jurisprudence. In an obiter, these Justices compared the crime of polygamy to the crimes of child pornography, incest, and bestiality, stating "contemporary Canadian social morality" considers them unacceptable acts "regardless of whether or not they cause social harm."[116] Although *Labaye* is a case about group sex in a private club, not the constitutionality of the polygamy prohibition, this view is troubling.

What eulogizing monogamy, social morality, and public policy have in common is avoidance, denial, and/or rejection of harm. More specifically, eulogizing monogamy avoids the necessity of acknowledging the perils it holds for women, ranging from spousal assault and murder to the many ways of subordinating individual wives within privacy of households where one-on-one domestic relationships are hidden from view. Eulogizing social morality denies the inappropriateness of resorting to the criminal law to penalize conjugal relationships voluntarily entered into by adults. Eulogizing public policy, assuming it is enacted into legislation and not simply declared, is another form of sanctioning majoritarianism, *viz.* majority domination of minorities. Thus, feminists who rely on monogamy, social morality, and public policy to justify criminalizing polygamy should reflect on their own lived experiences. That is, they should consider whether their experiences lead them to perceive polygamous wives from the perspective of what social scientists criticize as "othering."

According to Professor Susan Stabile, "othering" is "a process by which individuals and groups view and label people who are different from them in a way that devalues and dehumanizes them."[117] Scholars (and justices) might assess public policies differently "if, instead of proceeding from a view of others as fundamentally 'not us,' we possessed an attitude of valuing others and seeing them as not separate or other."[118] Professor Stabile's rejection of "othering" is reminiscent of the late Justice Bertha Wilson's advice to judges, namely that they should "enter into the skin of the litigant and make his or her experience part of your experience and only when you have done that, to judge."[119] Her anti-bias advice may be particularly apposite to the

[114] *Id.*

[115] *R. v. Labaye* 2005 SCC 80.

[116] *Id.* at ¶109 (Bastarache and LeBel JJ).

[117] Susan J. Stabile, *The Effect of "Othering" on Public Policy Debates* (2009) at 2, n. 2, *available at* http://works.bepress.com/susan_stabile/1.

[118] *Id.*

[119] Madame Justice Bertha Wilson, *Will Women Judges Really Make a Difference?* 28 Osgoode Hall Law Journal 508 at 521 (1990).

Justices currently sitting on Supreme Court of Canada because, according to their short biographies on the court's website,[120] all are monogamously married.

It remains to be seen whether Mormon and Muslim women living in polygamy will speak in court and if so how they will address questions about harm, whether of polygamy or monogamy. Moreover, in the absence of any significant body of Canadian research about their lived experiences, we do not know how polygamous wives would respond to questions about the equality of the sexes in polygamous relationships. Would they counter former Justice L'Heureux-Dubé's opinion that the equality of the sexes can be found only in monogamous marriages?

Taking the issue of the relationship between sex equality and polygamy one step further, we do not know whether Mormon and Muslim polygamous wives would share the same perspective. Perhaps Muslim polygamous wives would claim polygamy is no more contrary to the equality of the sexes than is Christian monogamy. Perhaps FLDS polygamous wives would join their Muslim counterparts, claiming equality in their relationships as well. Although such claims might seem counterintuitive, perhaps they are only counterintuitive in a world dominated by the concept of formal equality. Further research might show polygamy to be as conducive to substantive equality as monogamy. It certainly should lead to questions about relying on monogamy as the standard-bearer for substantive equality.

Moreover, speculation about the relationship between polygamy and sex equality would give constitutionalists cause to reassess the state's Section 1 justification. Because one scenario could have Mormon and Muslim women claiming polygamous relationships protect their substantive sex equality, their claim would challenge and subvert the state's Section 1 justification. In other words, religious freedom and the right to sex equality would both be ranged against whatever justification the state might be forced to cobble together. Because the issue would no longer be one of "competing rights," any balancing of deleterious and salutary effects should weigh more heavily on the deleterious side. Thus, a finding favoring decriminalization would follow.

Would the foregoing, highly speculative, polygamous wives' strategy bring feminism and constitutionalism together? If polygamous wives could persuasively attribute sex equality to their relationships, feminists would have no further basis for objecting to decriminalization. Constitutionalists who might be hard pressed to understand how polygamy could be consistent with sex equality nevertheless could not object because they favored decriminalization all along. Feminists and constitutionalists would, in short, be on the same page.

---

[120] Supreme Court of Canada, Current Judges, *available at* www.scc-csc.gc.ca/court-cour/ju/cju-jua-eng. asp. Interestingly, only the Chief Justice's marital status is not mentioned on this website; it can be found at http://wapedia.mobi/en/Beverley_McLachlin#1.

Conclusion

If nothing else, conclusions should introduce a note of reality. In this study of polygamy and feminist constitutionalism, two such notes are necessary. First, there is as of yet no evidence connecting polygamy and sex equality. Western feminists and liberal constitutionalists would have to engage in a major overhaul of their mindsets to accommodate the idea of such a relationship. I argue this has to begin with the voices of Mormon and Muslim women living in polygamous relationships. If and when they speak, feminists and constitutionalists will have to strain to hear, and after self-reflection, question them. The reality is, however, that we desperately need to listen to them. The constitutional reference presents an opportunity for this to happen but the bottom line may be the requirement to fund their participation.

The second note of reality involves addressing the competing rights approach. On the one hand, it is a healthy development in Charter law because it forces parties, litigators, judges, and scholars to acknowledge that Charter conflicts are rights contests. Section 1 claims should be founded on rights, not values or policies.[121] Applied to the polygamy reference, this approach means asking if the conflict is really about religious freedom versus sex equality. If it is, it poses a dilemma for the concept of feminist constitutionalism. On the other hand, if strategies such as the polygamous wives' strategy challenge the competing rights approach, they may nevertheless portend a future for feminist constitutionalism. For feminist constitutionalism to become a reality, in other words, neither feminists nor constitutionalists can afford to rely on stereotypes, allegations of false consciousness, or "othering" of women living in polygamous relationships. They must, in short, ensure the lived experiences of polygamous wives are self-reported.

---

[121] Contrast: Janet L. Hiebert, Limiting Rights: The Dilemma of Judicial Review (1998).

Index

Muslim women
  Canada, 380–383, 458, 472–473
  generally, 381–384, 391–392, 410
  India, 378–383, 386–387, 390, 409. *See also*
    divorce law; headscarf; *Mahr*; polygamy

parenthood (right to choose)
  abortion, 79, 276
  surrogacy, 91–92, 269–271
  unwed fathers, 265–268, 279. *See also* children
parity. *See* election law
primogeniture. *See* estate law
polygamy
  feminist, perspectives on, 389, 463–473
  legal status
    Canada, 454–463
    South Africa, 319–320, 326, 363
    Tunisia, 438
  Mormon women, 458, 469–470, 472–473
  Muslim women, 458, 472–473
pornography, 89, 93–94, 471
privacy (right to). *See* abortion; constitutions
public-private distinction, 43, 121–122, 177–178,
  199, 217, 220, 253, 379–380, 382, 384,
  387–390

religion
  abortion, 210, 218, 289, 301, 313
  freedom of, 92–93, 210, 246–247, 378–381,
    386–387, 389, 418, 421, 423–432, 459–461,
    466
  patriarchy, 216, 346, 352–353, 383, 417. *See also*
    divorce law; headscarf; *Mahr*; marriage
    law; Muslim women; polygamy

secularism, 379, 382–383, 389–391, 414–422,
  423–428, 430–432, 443–446, 451, 460.
  See also headscarf
sexual offenses, 89–90, 137, 145, 218, 233, 236–238,
  344, 352. *See also* violence against
  women
sexual orientation (same-sex couples), 53–60,
  104–107, 108–110, 246–247
social rights, 88–89, 96
surrogacy, 91–92. *See also* parenthood

violence against women, 96, 205–207, 218, 221,
  229–231, 336–356, 389, 407, 447, 450,
  471. *See also* immigration; sexual
  offenses
voting. *See* election law

For EU product safety concerns, contact us at Calle de José Abascal, 56–1°,
28003 Madrid, Spain or eugpsr@cambridge.org.

www.ingramcontent.com/pod-product-compliance
Ingram Content Group UK Ltd.
Pitfield, Milton Keynes, MK11 3LW, UK
UKHW020345140625
459647UK00019B/2313